D0935892

STUDIES IN THE SEPTUAGINT: ORIGINS, RECENSIONS, AND INTERPRETATIONS

LIBRARY OF
BIBLICAL STUDIES

edited by

HARRY M. ORLINSKY

Professor of Bible

Hebrew Union College - Jewish Institute of Religion

New York City

STUDIES IN THE SEPTUAGINT: ORIGINS, RECENSIONS, AND INTERPRETATIONS

Selected Essays with a Prolegomenon by

Sidney Jellicoe

KTAV PUBLISHING HOUSE, INC.
NEW YORK

NEW MATTER
© COPYRIGHT 1974
KTAV PUBLISHING HOUSE, INC.

SBN 87068-219- 9

LIBRARY OF CONGRESS CATALOG CARD NUMBER: 73-1344
MANUFACTURED IN THE UNITED STATES OF AMERICA

221.48
J48s

TABLE OF CONTENTS

ACKNOWLEDGMENTS

On his own behalf, and on behalf of the General Editor of *The Library of Biblical Studies* and the Publisher, the Editor of the present volume has the greatest pleasure in expressing thanks to the authors (or their representatives) of the articles which follow, to the Editors of the respective journals or composite works in which articles or essays originally appeared, and to the Publishers who have kindly permitted the reproduction of copyright material. Original sources are indicated at the bottom of the first page of each article.

Chapter 1 appears by permission of the University of Chicago Press; chapters 2, 6, and 30 by permission of the Cambridge University Press; chapters 4, 18, and 31 by courtesy of the Akademie Verlag, Berlin. Chapter 7 is reproduced by permission of the University of Toronto Press and the Oriental Club of Toronto; chapters 8 and 14 by courtesy of Messrs. E. J. Brill of Leiden, and chapters 15, 24, and 26 by consent of the Akademie der Wissenschaften in Göttingen. Chapters 19, 27, and 29 are reprinted by permission of the Clarendon Press, Oxford; chapter 28 by that of La Biblioteca Apostolica Vaticana; and chapter 35 by courtesy of the Chr. Kaiser Verlag, München.

ABBREVIATIONS

AJSL: American Journal of Semitic Languages and Literatures.

BA: The Biblical Archaeologist.

BASOR: Bulletin of the American Schools of Oriental Research.

BDB: F. Brown, S. R. Driver, C. A. Briggs: *A Hebrew and English Lexicon of the Old Testament* (Oxford, 1906).

BJRL: Bulletin of the John Rylands Library.

CBQ: Catholic Biblical Quarterly. Ency. Brit.: The Encyclopaedia Britannica.

HDB: A Dictionary of the Bible, ed. James Hastings (Edinburgh and New York, 5 vols., 1898-1904).

HTR: Harvard Theological Review.

ICC: International Critical Commentary (Edinburgh and New York).

IEJ: Israel Exploration Journal.

IOSCS: International Organization for Septuagint and Cognate Studies.

JAOS: Journal of the American Oriental Society.

JQR: Jewish Quarterly Review.

KB: L. Koehler and W. Baumgartner, *Lexicon in Veteris Testamenti Libros* (Leiden, 1953).

MSU: Mitteilungen des Septuaginta-Unternehmens (I-V, Berlin; VI ff., Göttingen).

NTS: New Testament Studies.

O'. The (Hexaplaric) Recension of Origen. *Pars Prior:* P.A. de Lagarde, *Librorum Veteris Testamenti Canonicorum Pars Prior Graece* (Göttingen, 1883).

RB: Revue Biblique. Schleusner, *Lex.:* J. F. Schleusner, *Novus Thesaurus philologico-criticus, sive Lexicon in LXX* . . . 3 vols. (Leipzig, 1820-21 Glasgow, 1822; London, 1829).

Schürer, *Geschichte:* Emil Schürer, *Geschichte des Jüdischen Volkes im Zeitalter Jesu Christi.* 3rd-4th edn., 3 vols. (Leipzig, 1901-11; repr. Georg Olms, Hildesheim, 1964).

SMS: S. Jellicoe, *The Septuagint and Modern Study* (Oxford, 1968). Swete, *Introd.:* H. B. Swete, *An Introduction to the Old Testament in Greek,* revised by R. R. Ottley (Cambridge, 1914; repr. KTAV, New York, 1968).

TU: Texte und Untersuchungen zur Geschichte der altchristlichen Literatur (Leipzig; Berlin). *VT: Vetus Testamentum.*

ZAW: Zeitschrift für die alttestamentliche Wissenschaft.

PROLEGOMENON

When the present writer agreed—as he did with enthusiasm—to compile from the writings of others a volume of essays and articles bearing directly on the Septuagint, he soon found, on embarking on the enterprise, that he had undertaken a much more difficult task than he had initially envisaged. In framing a volume of this nature, an editor's function is virtually that of anthologist, whose task, as Ivor Brown has so pointedly observed, "is a vexing one because there is so much that he has to leave out."[1] Herein lay the basic problem, that of selection from a plenitude of material, extensive both in nature and scope. For, contrary to the by no means uncommon but uninformed opinion, the Septuagint is far from a "deserted village" or at best a poor relation of the more prosperous families in the wide world of biblical studies. It is certainly true that in comparison with many, though not all, of the various theological disciplines the laborers are few, but there has never been lacking a succession of scholars of insight and competence whose energies have been directed to the study of the Old Testament in Greek.

The object of the present volume was envisaged as twofold: first, to bring together a selection of original articles and essays covering the more important aspects of the field, such as might serve the convenience of those already engaged in Septuagint and cognate studies, and secondly to present to the more general reader a conspectus of a specialized branch of biblical studies—its content and scope—not without the hope that he might thereby be stimulated to further study in a rich and rewarding field and perhaps ultimately make his own contribution to the elucidation of problems as yet unresolved. Accordingly the compiler's chief endeavor was to make a selection of items which would be both comprehensive and representative, embracing the essential elements of the discipline, and illustrating the procedure by representative studies.

As an aid to clarification, the constituent elements appear as sectional headings, under each of which follow representative contributions to that particular division of the wider field of study. As with all attempts at classification, the subject-matter in many cases embraces a wider horizon and may well be found, in certain aspects, to fall within other categories. Division at best can be no more than a convenience, since the study of the Septuagint, involving as will be plain from the contents of this volume very varied elements, nevertheless with all its ramifications constitutes an integrated whole. It is a matter of regret that limitations of space—and these alone—have precluded direct representation of numerous articles that have appeared on the versions (other than Greek). The significance of these studies, however, will be readily apparent from the references to them throughout the present volume, and later in this Prolegomenon we shall survey some of the recent work in this connection.

Why study the Septuagint? It is surprising that the intrinsic importance of this version should have failed, on the whole, to receive due recognition. Quite apart from its claim to attention as a literature in its own right,[2] the Septuagint holds a place in history, the significance of which deserves a wider understanding and appreciation. It first came into being as a pure matter of necessity: to provide the People of God dispersed throughout a Greek-speaking world with a medium through which the sacred writings could be read and understood. Accordingly, the Greek version came to constitute "the Scriptures" for by far the greater part of Jewry. With the rise of the Christian Church, and its claim to continuity with the Israel of old, it was but natural that, as with the liturgical pattern of the worship of the synagogue, it should make the Jewish scriptures its own, an action that has been aptly described by Professor Moule as "one of the most remarkable take-over bids in history."[3] In other words, it was the Old Testament *in Greek*—the Septuagint—that, in turn, constituted the Scriptures, and initially the only Scriptures, of the infant Christian Church. In course of time, and side by side with the writings of the Old Covenant, those of the New came into being and acquired canonical recognition as the fulfilment of the Old, which was the keynote of the primitive Apostolic Preaching[4]; hence the abundance of citations from the Greek version of the Old Testament in the New.

It was not long before the same necessity that brought the Septuagint into existence arose in the Christian Church. From its far-flung outposts came the demand for the Scriptures in the vernacular, a need that was satisfied, almost entirely as far as the Old Testament was concerned, by the Septuagint as exemplar. Accordingly the version is of prime concern for the patristic scholar, since it was upon the Septuagint and its offspring the Old Latin that the writings of the early Fathers, both in East and West, were dependent for their Scriptural authority.

We place these matters at the forefront of our introduction as setting the subject of the essays which follow in what we believe to be its proper perspective. In so doing we would not overlook another of the version's claims to attention, for it is one that with a number of scholars has been the principal, if not the sole, focus of attraction. Being by far the earliest of the translations, the Septuagint in its original state holds the unique position of reflecting a very early form of its archetype, the Hebrew text. This text, with its changes acquired in the course of transmission, underwent standardization toward the close of the first century of the Christian era and in a number of instances—at times markedly—the revision differed from the text that underlay the Greek. This had long been apparent to the textual scholar, but only with the discovery of the Qumran documents has documentary evidence become available. But extreme caution is necessary in this delicate matter. For example, the Qumran text of the Books of Samuel, which have traditionally been regarded as an outstanding example of textual divergence, is very fragmentary, rendering it precarious to draw anything but tentative conclusions on the nature of the Hebrew *Vorlage*. That there are differences—and these are not confined to Samuel—between the Hebrew as used by the Greek translators and as known to us today is not in doubt, but the supposed extent of these differences must be considerably modified in the light of a more careful and judicial analysis on the part of those who have made first-hand acquaintance with the actual text their fundamental concern, foremost among whom stand the Göttingen editors and their collaborators, along with the late Dr. Walters (Peter Katz) on the one side of the Atlantic, and on the other Professors Orlinsky and the late Max L. Margolis. Among the supposed variants some have been shown to be inner-Greek corruptions; others are explicable by "hibernation," that is, equivalents of Hebrew words which were in current usage, and were rendered accordingly by the Greek translators but which later fell into desuetude, have tended to be construed either as mistranslations or as indicative of a different Hebrew term. The recovery of these earlier meanings by recourse to the cognate languages has been one of the services rendered by comparative Semitic philology with its resources enriched from Akkadian and, more recently, Ugaritic.[5] But here again caution is necessary in the determination of linguistic equivalents: enthusiasm can too easily promote subjectivism, with attendant imbalance in the conclusions offered.

In passing, the question might be raised of possible "hibernations" in the Greek language itself, a matter which would appear to merit further investigation. An example must here suffice. In Psalm 77:36a LXX reads καὶ ἠγάπησαν αὐτὸν ἐν τῷ στόματι αὐτῶν = Hebrew (78:36a) וַיְפַתּוּהוּ בְּפִיהֶם (Piel פתה , BDB, KB, s.v., "deceive"; in other contexts "persuade, seduce, fool, entice"). Grabe, in his famous edition of Alexandrinus, emended to ἠπάτησαν , the reading adopted by Rahlfs in the text of his Göttingen edition (*Psalmi cum Odis,* 1931, repr. 1967, p. 125) and his manual edition of 1935 (vol. II, p. 84). Were this an isolated instance, emendation might well pass without comment; but the recurrence of ἀγαπάω in a similar context (II Chron. 18:2, R.S.V. "Ahab . . . induced him" [סות Hiph.] better, "enticed, allured") suggests that the Greek translators may have been familiar with an unpropitious sense of ἀγαπάω in current usage, i.e. "to simulate friendship with intent to deceive".[6] This sense of ἀγαπάω may, in fact, explain the usage of the verb in contrast with φιλέω in St. John 21:15-17, a problem which has perplexed the commentators and has never been satisfactorily resolved.

Attention should be directed to what is written below in Essays 1, 2, and 12 on the use and misuse of the "Septuagint" in textual criticism and the hazards of reliance upon an unverified critical apparatus. Akin to this, and due largely to the lack of a complete critical edition of the Old Testament in Greek, is the common error of taking the manual edition of Swete or Rahlfs as "the Septuagint", a practice which has been well nigh universal with commentators. Regarding critical editions, it should be mentioned that of the two enterprises initiated early in the current century that of Cambridge ceased publication with Esther, Judith, and Tobit (Vol. III, part I) in 1940 and continuation with the series is not contemplated. The Göttingen Septuaginta-Unternehmen, on the other hand goes apace under the Directorship of Dr. Robert Hanhart. The origins, history, and methodology of this enterprise are recounted in Dr. Walters' essay (Chapter 2). Since he wrote, the Books of Maccabees (I-III), begun by Werner Kappler in 1936, have been completed by Dr. Hanhart (1959-60); Wisdom of Solomon (1962) and Sirach (1965) by Dr. Joseph Ziegler of Würzburg, who had already edited the Major and Minor Prophets; Esther (1966) by Dr. Hanhart, who is currently preparing I Esdras. Genesis (replacing Rahlfs's edition of 1926) by Dr. J. W. Wevers of Toronto is due for publication early in 1973, and will be followed by Deuteronomy under the same editor. The valuable *Mitteilungen,* issued by the Unternehmen, were revived in 1958 with the publication of volume VI, Ziegler's *Beiträge zur Ieremias-*

Septuaginta. Four further volumes have appeared to date.[7]

From the range of material in the body of the work the reader will be made aware both of the wide nature of the subject matter embraced in LXX studies and the magnitude of the field. Despite intensive investigation over the years many of the basic problems are still far from solution. Fresh source materials come steadily to hand, such as papyri from Egypt and the copious yields of the Judaean desert. With all these acquisitions, laborious and exacting tasks of assembling, transcription, and editing, are involved, and these, together with further delays which are often experienced at pre-publication stage, mean that a considerable time must elapse before the fruits of modern discoveries are available for the use of scholars. Not infrequently however, fresh materials which might be expected to contribute to the solution of problems serve only to intensify the quest. This is certainly so with some of the materials that have come to be known conveniently, though incorrectly since the location is wider, as "Qumran." To the particular problems occasioned by some of these documents we shall return in due course.

The Modern Approach: Antecedents and Progress. Modern critical study of the Septuagint, in common with its counterpart the New Testament, has its point of departure in a break with the *textus receptus.* Apart from Grabe's monumental edition of Codex Alexandrinus (Oxford, 1707-20), the various printed editions were based, almost exclusively, on the Sixtine (Rome, 1587).[8] The advent of the "historical method," which arose in reaction to the artificial historiography of the eighteenth century, occasioned the demand for reliable texts as fundamental to scientific investigation. Concomitant with the extension of the method (first applied to the classical literature) into the domain of biblical studies, came Tischendorf's discovery of the Sinaitic codex in 1844 and the publication of a facsimile edition of the Vatican codex (B) by Vercellone and Cozza of which the Old Testament books were issued in four volumes between 1869 and 1872. Despite its defects this edition, completed in 1881, made the entire codex available to scholarship for the first time, and served until the publication of the photographic edition in five volumes (1889-90) under the auspices of Pope Leo XIII. With these great uncials to hand (though neither is complete), and other manuscript materials which were coming to light, many only fragmentary, together with editions of codices resting in the libraries of Europe, only the initiative was necessary for embarkation on the quest for the true text of the Septuagint. The twin enterprises already mentioned were the outcome. Göttingen's aim—reconstruction—was the more ambitious; Cambridge was content "to present as clearly and fully as is possible within reasonable limits of space the evidence available for the reconstruction of the text or texts of the LXX,"[9] with B as basic text as far as extant. A trail had already been blazed in this direction in the sister University in the pioneer work of Holmes and Parsons (5 vols., Oxford, 1798-1827). Though lacking, perforce, in source materials that were available a century later to the Cambridge editors, the apparatus nevertheless embodies the most extensive collation of readings published to date.

The opening section of the present volume comprises three essays which set the stage, embracing as they do the course and development of Septuagint studies over the last century. The earliest of these, by Professor Orlinsky, centers upon the ultimate objective—the recovery of the Greek text as it left the hand of the original translator. Primary emphasis is laid on sound methodology, with the principles that must govern all research in the field if fruitful results are to be attained. Examples are cited from the work of leading exponents; to these there might well be added the application of these principles to the text of Job by the author of the article himself.[10]

Links with the past and contemporary issues form the subject-matter of the study by the late Dr. Walters, better known to scholarship as Peter Katz. Methodology is again emphasized and the perils of aberration are illustrated by examples. As mentioned above, the origins and history of the Cambridge and Göttingen editions are outlined, the latter with some intimate sidelights, and the respective procedure ably analysed and compared. The reader is introduced to points of grammar and morphology and, as in the preceding article, independent studies are evaluated. Apart from his wide range of contributions to the learned journals, an extended example of Walters' methodology is to be found in his *Philo's Bible* (Cambridge, 1950). His posthumous volume, *The Text of the Septuagint: its Corruptions and their Emendation,* edited by his pupil, Dr. D. W. Gooding, has recently been published by the Cambridge University Press (1973).

The last, and most recent, of our representative survey articles is the work of one of a younger generation of scholars who are making the Septuagint a specialized field of study. He brings the survey up to date by delineating current problems and points out the much closer liaison prevalent today between Old and New Testament scholars in the field of textual criticism. In biblical exegesis the genetic connection between the two Testaments has been recognized from earliest times often through the centuries to the detriment of the Old when its *Sitz in Leben* has been obscured in the interests of typological and mystical interpretation. Text-critical studies, on the other hand, have not enjoyed a like unification. With few exceptions, textual scholars have tended to confine their energies, well nigh exclusively, either to the New Testament or to the Old in Greek, a situation inimical to the interests of both. The change in climate, and its effects in practice, are exemplified in the course of Dr. Howard's article.

An avenue for further implementation and co-ordination on an international scale has been afforded by the New Testament Society (Studiorum Novi Testamenti Societas) in the inauguration in 1969 of a continuing seminar on "The Greek New Testament and the Septuagint" which meets annually and is at present concerned with lexicography. Accounts of its proceedings by the Recording Secretary, Dr. Robert A. Kraft of the University of Pennsylvania, appear regularly in the Society's journal, *New Testament Studies.*

The first of these reports[11] includes an account of a landmark in the terrain of the Old Testament in Greek—the founding of the International Organization for Septuagint and Cognate Studies at Berkeley, California, in December 1968, under the presidency of Professor Orlinsky. The purpose of the Organization, as its title implies, is the co-ordination of research in its own and in kindred fields, and the further promotion of these studies by holding regular sessions for the presentation of papers and discussion; by co-operation and joint meetings with related organizations, societies, and undertakings; by the publication of a Bulletin recording its own proceedings, together with work recently completed, currently in progress, or projected, on the part of individual scholars or in conjunction with others; by encouraging, sponsoring, or by active participation in, the preparation for publication of works for the furtherance of Septuagint and related studies. A comprehensive bibliography of the Septuagint is in the press,[12] and it is hoped that work will begin in the near future on an up-to-date lexicon under the joint auspices of the Research Committee of the Lutheran Missouri Synod (sponsors of the Bauer-Arndt-Gingrich New Testament Lexicon) and the International Organization for Septuagint and Cognate Studies.

Septuagint origins. The central question of the Old Testament in Greek remains that of the *Vorlage:* was there one, original "official" version, of which the various extent manuscripts represent, in larger or smaller respects, deviations? Or, on the analogy of the Aramaic Targums, did each one translate, in a phrase of Justin Martyr's in another connection, "as he was able"? For former generations no such problem existed: that an official or semi-official version was made for the Diaspora, beginning with the Pentateuch, was axiomatic. The problem belongs to the current century, and each side has had vigorous proponents. On the one hand the traditional view formed the keystone of the work of Paul Anton de Lagarde, whose methodology was founded on the hypothesis that, working backwards from the three recensions current in the time of St.

Jerome, the text of the Greek version as it left the translators' hands would be ascertainable and, ideally, capable of reconstruction. This "Lagardian hypothesis," as it has come to be known, was challenged by Paul Kahle in an article which appeared in *Theologische Studien und Kritiken* in 1915, and his "Targum theory," although the subject of severe criticism on the part of others who had worked independently and at first hand on the text of the Septuagint, was maintained vigorously by the Bonn scholar to the end of his days. His own views are represented in section II of the present volume by one of his later contributions, while the whole matter of Septuagint origins, in its wider horizon, forms the subject of the penetrating essays in the same section by Professors Orlinsky and Wevers, both of whom find the evidence in relation to the *Vorlage* to point strongly to the one rather than the many. Among others whose direct acquaintance with recently discovered source materials has led to alignment with the Lagardian position are Frank M. Cross, Jr., of Harvard and Père Dominique Barthélemy of Fribourg. A mediating suggestion has been advanced by George Howard, who sees "a third possibility" in the LXX as a revision of one text among many which ultimately eclipsed all others,[13] but how this differs essentially from Kahle's "Christian Septuagint" is not easy to discern.

Kahle's line of approach has been followed in the writings of his pupil Alexander Sperber, whose views on LXX origins, as presented in a series of articles published from 1935 onwards, are crystallized in his recent contribution to the *H. A. Wolfson Jubilee Volume* (Jerusalem, 1965), published shortly after Professor Wevers wrote. He holds that of Jerome's *trifaria varietas* (i.e. Hesychius, Lucian, and the text of Origen's fifth column of the Hexapla), those of Hesychius and Lucian represent not recensions but two individual translations, Origen's text being in fact not a recension but a combination of these two and indicating, by the use of the Aristarchian symbols, "the respective source and extent of those readings which are peculiar to only one of these translators."

Each of these, Sperber maintains, was subsequently translated into Latin, hence the procedure advocated in the essay "How to edit the Septuagint" (op.cit., pp. 751-73) has as its aim, in his own words, "the publication of the Greek *Vorlage* or *Vorlagen* (plural!)[14] of the *Vetus Latina,*" or as Sperber would prefer to call it, "the Church Fathers' Greek Bible" (p. 770), for which the criterion of this "entirely new procedure, representing a complete break with the past" would be "NO Septuagint manuscript at all to serve as basic text."[15] What is here advocated is essentially the Beuron procedure with the Old Latin, itself affording valuable early testimony to the LXX text though fraught with problems peculiar to itself. With the Septuagint the procedure would add nothing apart from increasing the bulk of the volume, since relevant information on readings can be systematized and clearly presented within the compass of a single apparatus. The "basic text," whether a reconstruction, a resultant, or the text of a single manuscript, serves only in a critical edition as a framework for the apparatus. We need not dwell upon the hypothesis which underlies the proposed new departure, as this is subjected to searching examination in the course of chapters 2 and 5 below.

Professor Schwarz's essay is of particular interest as the work of one whose direct field of specialization lies outside the Septuagint, but who nevertheless, for the purpose of his volume—"a learned work of freshness and merit, by an expert philologist with capacity for historical writing"[16]—has made himself thoroughly at home in the milieu of the version, and for that matter the Vulgate. Much ground is covered within the brief compass of the chapter which is highly pertinent to an age in which Scriptural translations are pouring out with bewildering frequency accompanied by manuals offering guidance to the translator, whose task, in the words of C. H. Dodd, a veteran in the arena, "is an impossible art, for the words of one language seldom or never convey precisely the same ideas as the corresponding words of another language."[17] Yet an ever increasing demand, with its burden of responsibility, falls upon the shoulders of a translator. Fewer and fewer are able to read the classical authors in the original; hence students in ancient history, philosophy, and Roman law are entirely in the hands of the translator for their sources, a situation paralleled, though still to a lesser degree, by the theological student incapable of reading the Scriptures, which it will be his business to expound, in their native Hebrew and Greek. Never was there more "education" and, proportionately, fewer educated people!

The Letter of Aristeas. One of the early writings falling within Dr. Schwarz's discussion is the so-called *Letter of Aristeas.* Confining itself to the Torah, it purports to give an eye-witness account of the translation of these five books into Greek at Alexandria by six translators from each of the twelve tribes, sent down from Jerusalem at the request of Ptolemy II. By a popular fiction the entire version was in due course embraced, and went down to posterity as the rendering of the Seventy (-two). In earlier days the prestige enjoyed by the *Letter* lay in its supposed historicity, and it has survived in no fewer than twenty-three manuscripts, not all complete. Removed from the microscope of the historical critic (though a historical kernel is generally conceded as discernible),[18] the document in modern times has found its proper *mise-en-scène* in the wider corpus of Jewish-Hellenistic literature, and concern has centered upon such questions as its nature and purpose, its intended audience, and its ideology. A critical conspectus of recent studies from the pen of Dr. Gooding, together with the articles of Dr. Zuntz of the University of Manchester and the late Dr. Tcherikover of the Hebrew University, Jerusalem, will serve the reader as indicative of the modern approach. Various aspects of the *Letter* have received attention more recently: the ethico-didactic element in J. J. Lewis, "The Table-talk Section in the Letter of Aristeas" (*NTS* 13 [1966-7], 53-56), and the kingship *motif* in Oswyn Murray, "Aristeas and Ptolemaic Kingship" (*JTS* N.S. 18 [1967], 337-71).[19] The particular translation that may have occasioned the *Letter* is discussed by A. F. J. Klijn in *NTS* 11 (1964-5), 154-8, and by the present writer in *NTS* 12 (1965-6), 144-50; the politico-legal situation of the Jewish community in Egypt as its milieu by Leonhard Rost in the Eichrodt *Festschrift*[20] and its meaning, purpose, and literary *genre* by George Howard in *JTS* N.S. 22 (1971), 337-48.

Such lines of investigation promise to be much more fruitful than the historico-critical approach, since no more than Virgil or the author of Daniel or Esther would pseudo-Aristeas claim to be writing history: these works must be evaluated on other criteria. Certainly the present-day student of the *Letter* is in the fortunate position of being well equipped for his task. He has good texts with *apparatus critici* enabling him to form his own judgment on the reading to be preferred, *stemmata* tracing out the manuscript tradition, translations should he feel the need of recourse to them, linguistic and stylistic studies, complete *indices verborum* and *nominum,* comprehensive introductions, as well as the goodly array of sidelights from the articles in the learned journals.[21]

Transmission history. What may be termed the "traditional" view of the transmission history of the Old Testament in Greek presented a neat, straightforward pattern. It underlay the Lagardian method and is set out in detail in Swete (*Introd.* chaps. 1-3), in outline in Rahlfs's manual edition ("History of the Septuagint Text," *Septuaginta,* vol. I, pp. XXII-XXXI), and summarily in the first of Thackeray's Schweich Lectures (op. cit., pp. 12-15). Briefly stated, the second century A.D. was held to have produced the Jewish revisions of Aquila, Theodotion, and Symmachus, and the following century or so the recensions of Origen, Hesychius, and Lucian of Antioch. Although as early as Karl Credner's *Einleitung*[22] the presence of readings attribued to one or other of these revisers prior to his *floruit* had been discerned, aside from some attention on the part of a few individual scholars[23] the matter has become a live issue only in our own times, yet one destined to demand a radical re-orientation.

Following upon these overtures the curtain was raised in

Père Barthélemy's article of 1963, reprinted below, which arose from the discovery of the now famous Greek Scroll of the Minor Prophets. Further fragments of the same scroll were published by B. Lifschitz in the *Israel Exploration Journal* 12 (1962), pp. 201-7. Pending the publication of the definitive edition of these fragments by the Clarendon Press, Barthélemy has amplified his *avant-courier* in his challenging volume *Les devanciers d'Aquila* (*Supplements to Vetus Testamentum,* vol. X; Leiden, 1963). In an extended appraisal of the work a reviewer aptly anticipated the consensus of scholarly reaction to the work: "It will require several years (if not decades) and a wealth of detailed investigation to provide the kind of thorough critical evaluation that this important contribution warrants."[24] Among the positions advanced (though not all are new) are the identification of the LXX Ecclesiastes with Aquila, the identification of Aquila and Theodotion respectively with Onqelos and Jonathan who were the producers of Greek rather than Aramaic versions, and the attribution of the Quinta column of the Minor Prophets to Theodotion,[25] which column in the Hexapla is "a recension, late, eclectic, and pseudepigraphic" (op. cit., p. 269). The features that have attracted most attention are the removal of the so-called Lucianic recension from its traditional historical setting (to which we shall return later) and the identification of an "R" (*kaige*) recension which represents a stage in revisional activity that culminated in the work of Aquila. Theodotion, with whom the recension is identified, was thus a predecessor of Aquila and flourished in the mid-first century A.D., having as his object the bringing of the old Greek translation (LXX) into closer conformity with the Hebrew of his day. Not only was Aquila influenced by this recension—according to Barthélemy it was this revision, not LXX, that underlay his version of the Minor Prophets—but also Symmachus who appears to ignore LXX and Aquila in favor of R, with which he shows a direct acquaintance. Justin Martyr (whom the present writer's independent researches have found to exhibit an exceedingly mixed text) embodies a number of its readings,[26] as does

Jerome in his commentaries on the Minor Prophets, and its influence is also to be seen in the Coptic versions and in the Hebraisms of the first and second hands of the Freer Codex of the Minor Prophets (W) in the Smithsonian Institution, Washington.

"The Three". A few observations may be interposed on the translators Aquila, Theodotion, and Symmachus who come to the fore in Barthélemy's work, the two first named prominently. The origin, date, and authorship of the last named still remain enigmatical, and to the knowledge of the present writer nothing of importance on the version has appeared since the studies of H. J. Schoeps (1942-9) apart from its adduction by Barthélemy and in the editions and ancillary publications of the Göttingen Unternehmen.

The identification of Aquila with Onqelos and Theodotion with Jonathan ben 'Uzziel seems steadily to be gaining ground. Kahle asserts it categorically in his Schweich Lectures,[27] although he denies the association of either with the Targumim. Both of these equations go back well beyond our times—Aquila-Onqelos to the Middle Ages, when it was claimed to have been refuted by Azariah de Rossi,[28] and Jonathan-Theodotion to Samuel David Luzzatto in 1844.[29]

One of the questions arising from Barthélemy's study is how, in any manner other than purely temporal, Theodotion may be regarded as a "predecessor" of Aquila. The translation-technique is entirely different, that of Aquila being so distinctive as to render the version *sui generis*. The characteristics are too well known to need repetition; the question at issue is the purpose: why was such a translation ever made? What need was it intended to satisfy? Its marked peculiarities suggest the unlikelihood of its ever having been intended for reading in public: its infelicitousness as a literary production could hardly fail to have a jarring effect upon the ears of a congregation and produce a reaction comparable to the reading of the lessons today in a word-for-word translation designed for the elementary student of the original. At the most,

Justinian (Novella 146; A.D. 553)[30] permitted such use of Aquila, though grudgingly.

The analogy of the modern interlinear translation, taken in conjunction with Origen's assertion that Aquila's version "is most commonly used by those who do not know Hebrew" (*ad Africanum,* 2) and Jerome's reference to "Aquilae . . . secunda editio" (*Commentary on Ezekiel* 3:15) may serve to throw light on the purpose of the version and elucidate the problem of the two Aquilas.

In the early days of the currency of the Old Testament Scriptures in Greek it is not unlikely that an official, or quasi-official, version was prepared to give a literal *seriatim* rendering of the Hebrew text in Greek—not itself a rival to the LXX any more than the student's interlinear version is intended to displace a standard translation. First, it would provide a check to the over zealous copyist who might be inclined to "improve" on his Greek exemplar[31]; secondly, it would constitute an authoritative guide in matters of exegesis to a teacher who was dependent entirely on the Greek version; and thirdly, it would serve the Greek-speaking student, desirous of mastering Hebrew, with what Burkitt has called "a learned crib." Accordingly it might be suggested that it was a work of this nature, revised in conformity with the Hebrew text of the Aqiba movement, that underlay the version of Aquila and accounts for its purpose and unique translation-technique.

The claim for the admission of an Ur-Theodotion into the translational chain, which may now be taken as reasonably well founded, must be regarded as an additional link rather than a substitution for the traditional Theodotion of the latter half of the second century A.D. Elsewhere the present writer has endeavored to show that Theodotion of Ephesus must still, as a reviser, have a place in history, while the activity of his predecessor Ur-Theodotion, also of Ephesus, which was supplemental and revisional, must be placed a century or so earlier than the date suggested by Père Barthélemy.[32] It might be added that there is every reason for identifying Ur-

Theodotion with the *kaige* recension rather than, as some have seemed disposed, to regard the latter as independent.[33]

By far the most revolutionary of recent Theodotionic studies is Armin Schmitt's monograph, *"Stammt der sogenannte 'θ -' Text bei Daniel wirklich von Theodotion?"* (*MSU* IX, 1966), in which the author, a pupil of Dr. Ziegler's, subjects the "Theodotion" version of Daniel (which at an early date almost entirely eclipsed the "LXX") to critical examination in the light of the biblical material preserved elsewhere as Theodotionic. It is surprising, in view of the author's conclusion that the answer to his question must be "a clear No," that the monograph has not received more attention. While it is certainly a careful and penetrating study, it raises in the mind of the present writer the whole question of the reliability of the marginal sigla and in some cases their interpretation. *Theta* is not always Theodotion as *lambda* is not always Lucian, and in the absence of a thoroughgoing investigation of the sigla in the manuscripts and attributions in patristic writers, an urgent though difficult task, one would reserve judgment in a matter upon which, at the present state of our knowledge, certitude would be misplaced. Whatever be the final verdict, Dr. Schmitt's work brings to notice once again the question of additional versions or recensions. Examples of other possibilities are to be seen in the essay by Professor Krauss, while the problems of identification attaching to translators mentioned by ancient writers form the subject of Rahlfs's article on "The Syrian," in which earlier attempts at isolating this translator are taken into account.

The Hexapla. One of the monumental undertakings of biblical scholarship—a model of precision, industry, and patient endurance—is the Hexapla of Origen, compiled over a period of years and completed *c.* A.D. 243. The text of its fifth column—the LXX as reconstructed by the compiler—has given its name to the group of manuscripts in which it is subsequently reflected (Hexaplaric), but the determination of this text is one of the problems of critical scholarship owing to omission or imprecision on the part of copyists in recording the Aristarchian symbols. But this is only one of the problems. Under the microscope of modern research the traditional assignation of columns 3, 4, and 6 respectively to Aquila, Symmachus, and Theodotion has become *per se* no longer tenable, while the extent and content of the additional Greek columns, known as Quinta, Sexta, and Septima, has always been indeterminate. The columnar order, its chronology and signification, together with the question of the Tetrapla (commonly regarded as an abridged version of the Hexapla) are discussed by Professor Orlinsky in chapters 21 and 22, while a re-examination of Origen's purpose in compiling such a colossal work (estimated by Swete, exclusive of Quinta and Sexta, to have extended at least to 3250 leaves or 6500 pages) forms the subject of Dr. Brock's paper on the compiler's aims as textual critic.

No copy of the Hexapla is extant. The original is thought to have perished when Caesarea fell to the Saracens in 638, and we are dependent for first-hand testimony regarding its format and method on what Eusebius tells us in his *Ecclesiastical History* (VI, 16) and the brief references of Origen himself in his Letter to Africanus and his Commentary on St. Matthew (15:14). There are, however, sidelights. The format as reconstructed from Eusebius' description has been confirmed by Mercati's discovery of Psalms fragments in the Ambrosian Library (though the Hebrew is lacking), now published in full (see n.25), and the Syro-Hexaplar, the subject of Professor Fritsch's study, is valuable for its reproduction of the Aristarchian symbols.

Among the outstanding problems of the Hexapla is the purpose underlying the second column, a transcription of column I (the Hebrew text) in Greek characters. Professor Emerton takes up the question in his article reproduced below. Since the appearance of this article Professor Emerton has pursued the matter further, and the fruits of his researches are presented in two subsequent articles in the *Journal of Theological Studies*. In the former of these, "Were Greek

Transliterations of the Hebrew Old Testament used by Jews before the Time of Origen?" (*JTS*, N.S.21 [1970], 17-31), he examines the evidence advanced by certain scholars (J. Halévy, Ludwig Blau, M. Schwab, and J. Levy) for the use of transliterated texts in rabbinical writings. He leaves open the possibility that such texts were in use by Jews, but holds that attempts to establish it on documentary evidence from the sayings of the rabbis have failed upon examination. In the second of these articles, "A Further Consideration of the Purpose of the Second Column of the Hexapla" (*JTS*, N.S. 22 [1971], 15-28), he adduces further evidence in support of his theory and replies, with his customary courtesy, and be it added convincingly, to the criticisms of the present writer (*SMS*, pp. 110 f.)

In the prevailing climate of uncertainty it may be temerarious to attempt a re-assessment of the Hexapla, or to suggest lines on which further investigation might profitably proceed. None the less, the following reflections may be offered for consideration as a fresh approach to the Hexapla and its problems.

As LXX is a translation from the Hebrew, columns I and II are in their logical position. Pride of place among the Greek versions is naturally assigned to Aquila, taking its place as Column III on the grounds of its being the most verbally exact. Symmachus follows, it may be suggested, not as being a revision of Aquila or as furnishing intelligibility in terms of literary Greek—features which have no bearing on Origen's function as textual critic—but because, apart from Aquila and the text underlying Origen's own column which was basically the standard "LXX" of his day, it was the only other complete translation of the Hebrew currently in circulation. To the immediate right of Origen's column (the fifth) came the so-called "Theodotion" column, followed as necessary by such further columns as might be required to accommodate other translations to which the compiler had access, hence the uncertainty prevailing on the extent of the material in these columns. Field, for example, expressed doubts on the existence of Septima (*Origenis Hexaplorum* . . . I, p. xlvi). In the midst of these Greek columns stood the famous fifth column, occupying that place on no grounds other than those of convenience. To the left stood the Hebrew with the Greek versions attesting it in its entirety; to the right those translations representative of the Hebrew Old Testament in part only and furnishing material on which the editor could draw as required. The sixth column, the so-called Theodotionic, would be reasonably full. In this, Origen seems to have placed the more extensive of the materials to hand, including what he believed to be Theodotion, while the remaining columns, partial and added as necessary, served as a repository for other material.

That Origen did not always know the identity of his sources is an inference that might reasonably be drawn from modern study. Toward the end of the last century Freudenthal conjectured that the LXX of Ecclesiastes and Cantica was in fact Aquila[34]; Swete is content to remark that the former "savours of the school of Aquila[35]; McNeile takes it as an earlier edition of Aquila[36]; Barthélemy attributes it unequivocally to Aquila and its being placed in the fifth column to Origen's not knowing this[37]; Torrey assigned the canonical Chronicles-Ezra-Nehemiah to Theodotion[38], and we have already noted the denial of the sixth column of the Hexapla in the Psalms and Minor Prophets to its traditional author.

Dr. Brock has pointed out (chapter 18) that Origen's purpose in compiling the Hexapla was primarily apologetic, and cites examples from the compiler's own writings to this effect. That the respective columns were intended to embody *seriatim* the versions of "The Three" is a pure inference from the descriptive passage in Eusebius referred to above. If this, in fact, were not Origen's intention it would absolve him from ignorance of the nature of his major sources and would also lend point to Barthélemy's conjecture that for Ecclesiastes in the "Aquila" column he placed "another version," which, he continues, "all users of the Hexapla, accustomed to finding Aquila in the third column, have taken for the version of Aquila" (op. cit., p. 30).

It may well be questioned at this point whether at all, in the putative Aquilanic, Symmachian, and Theodotionic columns, Origen had any intention of presenting these versions in unitary form. Rather, it would seem, the Hexapla was his "workbook" in which he was concerned to produce in column V, from the chaos of versions in current circulation and on the basis of the Hebrew text of his day, a reconstructed text. As basis he used the "standard" LXX—the Old Greek of the Seventy—but avoided following it slavishly. For example, he replaced the "LXX" of Daniel with "Theodotion" and embodied the longer recension of Ezra-Nehemiah and the "Aquila" of Ecclesiastes and Cantica. In sum, Origen's object in compiling the Hexapla would appear to have been not the reproduction of current versions, or partial versions, as they stood, but rather comprehensiveness: to have before him, in conspectus, *all* available sources from which to compile in the fifth column what he believed, with reference to the Hebrew, to have constituted the true Septuagint. This comprehensiveness, and Origen's diligent self-application to the achievement of that end, comes out clearly in Eusebius's account. After describing the "editions of the other translators of the sacred writings besides the seventy," and their origins as far as known to him, he continues: "all these he brought together, dividing them πρὸς κῶλον , and placing them one against the other with the actual Hebrew text" (*H.E. VI.* 16.4). One would only with the greatest reluctance charge Origen with ignorance of his sources. If, however, his Hexapla be of the nature suggested—a critically reconstructed text flanked by an undefined *apparatus criticus*—he has bequeathed to posterity a confusion extending beyond the so-called Hexaplaric text of the fifth column, and far exceeding the imagination of the scholars of the late nineteenth and early twentieth centuries who have worked on this monument of industry. Père Barthélemy has informed the present writer that he is assembling materials for a new edition of the remains of the Hexapla, but conceives of this as a long term project.

The "trifaria varietas." The whole world, Jerome tells us in his Preface to Chronicles, was in conflict over the threefold variety of texts in circulation in his day—the Hesychian in Alexandria and Egypt, that of Lucian the Martyr from Constantinople to Antioch, and that of Origen in Palestine. Of the last-named, notice has already been taken; the quest for Hesychius has suffered, unhappily, increasing neglect, in mitigation of which we have included in this volume an article by the late Father Vaccari, among the last of a long sucession of textual studies to appear before his death in December, 1965, in his ninety-first year. In contradistinction to Hesychius, Lucian has stood out prominently in the effulgence of the Septuagintal floodlights.

There could hardly be a better introduction to the Lucianic recension than that of Professor Bruce Metzger in his *Chapters in the History of New Testament Textual Criticism,* which in its complete form of forty-one pages furnishes a model of an integrated study of the Greek Old Testament and the New. Below we reproduce only those sections relating specifically to the Old, but the whole, which places Lucian in his *mise-en-scène* with ancient testimonies to his person and work, including of course his work on the New Testament, is to be commended as preliminary to a serious study of the recension that bears his name.

The same year in which Professor Metzger's volume appeared, saw the publication of Père Barthélemy's *Devanciers* which, as already mentioned, denies the recension to the presbyter of Antioch—his term is "la prétendue 'recension Lucianique'"—and regards it as "essentially the ancient LXX, more or less debased and corrupted" (op. cit., p. 127). As Aquila had his predecessor in Theodotion, so Barthélemy had his predecessor in Thackeray (an example of whose methodology appears in chapter 27 below), who held that the earliest Greek version of Samuel-Kings ("Reigns," as he terms it) was an expurgated version which omitted all that was derogatory to David together with the narrative of the growing degeneracy of the divided monarchy which led to the double captivity. These lacunae were supplied later by an Asiatic translator, a "proto-Theodotion." In his Schweich Lectures[39] Thackeray distinguished three main text types in Samuel-Kings: (1) Vaticanus (B) and its congeners; (2) Alexandrinus (A); and (3) the Lucianic. The second of these, a mosaic and a recension of the shorter B text, he regarded as negligible, and based his hypothesis substantially on B, to which the Lucianic was the only serious rival. In the last named, represented by the cursives b o c_2 e_2, he recognized an ancient element discernible in the text used by Josephus, a point developed in his Hilda Stich Stroock Lectures (*Josephus the Man and the Historian* [New York, 1929], pp. 83-9), where he postulates an "Ur-Lucian" as text source. It is here that Barthélemy takes up the matter. From a wealth of detail emerge the conclusions that Thackeray's B-text represents a revision of the Old Greek (the *kaige* recension), whereas the Lucianic represents not an autonomous recension but the Old Greek (LXX) corrupted in the course of transmission. The *kaige* recension is not however confined to Thackeray's Asiatic supplementer: it extends not only to the Greek Scroll of the Minor Prophets, but also to Lamentations, certain manuscripts of Judges, the Theodotion of Daniel and the Theodotionic additions to the LXX of Job, the anonymous additions to the LXX of Jeremiah, in general only to the sixth column of the Hexapla, the Quinta of the Psalter, and probably Cantica and Ruth. Following upon Barthélemy's lead, other scholars have discerned what they believe to be further characteristics of this translator, for example, J. D. Shenkel in an appendix to his *Chronology and Recensional Development in the Greek Text of Kings* (Cambridge, Mass., 1968, pp. 113-6), Michael Smith in *Biblica* 48 (1967), pp. 443-5, and John A. Grindel in the *Catholic Biblical Quarterly* 31 (1969), pp. 499-513.[40]

Three studies on the Lucianic recension have recently appeared. In the first of these S. P. Brock adduces evidence indicating that the "Antiochene" text (Barthélemy's term for the so-called Lucianic) received its final formulation at a time close to Lucian (*ob.* 312). Although it escaped the Hebraising revision that produced *kaige,* it nevertheless remains a recensional text.[41]

George Howard[42] presents a comparative table of readings as found in the Greek Scroll of the Minor Prophets (R), Ziegler's Lucianic *Hauptgruppe* (*L*), the Freer Codex (W), and Vaticanus (B), in the light of which he questions Hexaplaric influence on the Lucianic recension as conjectured by Ziegler. He stresses the affinity of Lucianic readings with R, a line of investigation that might well be pursued on a wider scale. The basis here is, of course, the Minor Prophets, but in this connection one might recall the oblique statement of Thackeray on the text of Samuel-Kings to the effect that although he follows the B text, i.e. Barthélemy's R, his theory rests largely on readings in which all manuscripts are agreed. R, moreover, according to Howard, is a source for Hebraistic tendencies preserved in Lucian and in W, and by way of these in B: accordingly it is itself "the ultimate basis for many readings customarily called Hexaplaric." The present writer has always regarded as unsatisfactory any theory of the Lucianic recension which presupposes recourse to a Hebrew text since no tangible evidence in its support is adducible. The purpose of the recension was to discover and incorporate, from current Greek manuscripts, the most ancient and best attested readings, for the presentation of which the recensionist had no hesitation in resorting to conflation. Purity of orthography and literary style governed the manner of presentation.[43] Howard finds that "Lucian never revised LXX toward MT at all. The Lucianic recension represents *a drifting away from* MT . . . and the readings of Lucian which agree with R are simply *remnants* of the R-type text left intact." (Italics Howard's, loc. cit., pp. 58 f.).

The third study is by Emanuel Tov of the Hebrew University, Jerusalem: "Lucian and Proto-Lucian: toward a new Solution of the Problem" (*Revue Biblique* 79 [1972], 101-13). The author considers that while previous studies have marked out the lines on which this recension should be investigated, they leave room for a new working hypothesis directed to the contents of the manuscripts b o c_2 e_2 with special reference to the proto-Lucianic sources. Rahlfs, who distinguished the constituent elements of the Lucianic recension in his *Septuaginta-Studien* III (1911)[44], underestimated the importance of this earliest layer, while F. M. Cross[45] understood it as a proto-Lucianic revision. Tov suggests that the existence of such a revision has not been established, hence this substratum should be approached as either "*the* Old Greek or any single Old Greek translation." The second layer consists of Lucian's borrowings from "the Three" and the fifth column of the Hexapla, and the third and final layer embodies Lucian's own corrections. Criteria are offered for distinguishing the three layers (e.g. the use of the Old Latin for the substratum) and a pilot study of readings in Samuel-Kings is appended. The author is fully conscious of the difficulties attending an investigation of this nature and claims no more for his approach than "programmatic and tentative," but it is in studies of this nature, actuated by an informed appreciation of the problems and controlled by sound methodology, that the ultimate goal of all LXX studies—the establishing of the *Vorlage*—will be reached. A noticeable feature of these three articles on the Antiochian recension is that each reserves to St. Jerome's Lucian the Martyr his place in history.

Manuscripts. To the early witnesses to the Lucianic text mentioned by Professor Metzger (chap. 14) there must now be added Papyrus Fouad Inv. 266 of the first century B.C., consisting of three fragments of Genesis (7:17-20 and 38:10-12) and 113 of Deut. 17:14 to 33:29. The papyrus first came to notice when a fragment of the Greek text of Deut. 31:28-32:7 was published by the late W. G. Waddell in 1944 (*JTS* 45, pp. 158-61) who would have completed publication of the whole had not death intervened. A few more fragments were published in the Foreword to the *New World Translation of the Greek Scriptures* (Brooklyn, N.Y., 1950, pp. 11-14) and were evaluated by Fr. Vaccari at the request of Professor Kahle[46] (*Studia Patristica I = TU* 63, [Berlin, 1957], 339-42), but it was not until 1966 that the definitive edition appeared.[47] This was published in advance of the complete *tome neuvième* (1971) of which it forms a substantial part. Meanwhile some fifty-four fragments, deposited in the archives of the Egyptian Society of Papyrology in Cairo, have proved to be fragments of the same papyrus. These are now being studied by Dr. Zaki Aly, President of the Society, in collaboration with Professor G. D. Kilpatrick, and publication may be expected in due course.[48] While this papyrus is later than Rylands Greek 458 (which still remains the oldest known example of the Old Testament in Greek), it is more extensive, and its prime value consists in its presentation of a text antedating the changes and revisions of the early centuries of the Christian era. It has its own stylistic and grammatical peculiarities and distinctive readings and, as might be expected, is referable to no particular text type. In comparison with the major uncials (*Sinaiticus* is lacking in Deuteronomy) its alignment in general is with B, though it sometimes supports A in divergences from that manuscript. Its publication at this time, when work on the Göttingen edition of Deuteronomy is about to begin, is most opportune.

Included in Mlle. Dunand's introduction to the Fouad Papyrus is a table of divergences from Chester Beatty Papyrus VI (963) which dates from the mid-second century A.D. It is well known that not all the leaves of this codex were acquired by the veteran collector.[49] In addition to the Scheide leaves at Princeton[50] parts of the same manuscript found their way to Cologne[51], Madrid, and Barcelona. The text of the Madrid leaves has been published by Professor M. Fernandez-Galiano,[52] who has also collated them with the Antinoopolis Ezekiel Papyrus[53] published by C. H. Roberts of Oxford in 1950. A revision of Sir Frederic Kenyon's edition of the Genesis of Chester Beatty Papyri IV and V (961, 962) with up-to-date collations by Dr. A. Pietersma of Toronto is to be published shortly by the American Society of Papyrologists.

Some second thoughts on the Giessen Papyri are invited in a reexamination of these Deuteronomy fragments by Emanuel Tov (*RB* 78[1971] 357-83). Emanating from Antinoopolis, these fragments were published by Paul Glaue and Alfred Rahlfs, who regarded them as representative of a Greek version of the Samaritan Pentateuch (*MSU* 1:2, 1911). While not ruling out this identification, Tov advances data in support of a "simpler view," namely that they reflect rather an anonymous revision of LXX at an early, but indeterminate, date.

Before leaving the manuscripts, mention should be made of two papyri of special interest to the Septuagintalist which were published, along with others in the Rylands Library, Manchester, by R. A. Kraft and Antonia Tripolitis in 1968.[54] The one contains a fragment of Psalm 19 (LXX); the other, thought to be from a prayer amulet of the sixth century A.D., incorporates, according to Kraft's reconstruction, an early gloss on Psalm 50:9 (LXX) for which there is other evidence (e.g. Leipzig Papyrus 39), and recalls the well-known gloss on Psalm 95:10, "the Lord reigned *from the tree*" (ἀπὸ τοῦ ξύλου) as found in Justin Martyr (*Apology* 1, 41; *Dialogue with Trypho* 73:4). The Rylands reading, as reconstructed, would run: "Thou shalt purge me with hyssop *from the blood of the cross* (ἀπὸ τοῦ ἅιματος τοῦ ξύλου) and I shall be clean."

While papyri, as they have come to light, have played an important part in textual criticism, there has also been a concomitant increase in the status accorded to the cursives. Their value was, indeed, recognized as early as the era of Holmes-Parsons, whose list as subsequently corrected by Rahlfs[55] stands at 280 in number. Later in the nineteenth century their standing declined in favor of the uncials, due, one may conjecture, to the romantic discovery of the Sinaitic Codex together with the publication of the hitherto closely guarded Codex Vaticanus which served as the basic text of both of the Cambridge editions. Where both B and A failed, the uncial "which occupies the next place in point of age or importance"[56] supplied the defect, an error of judgment the consequences of which were pointed out by George Foot Moore (*AJSL* 29 [1912-13], p. 54, n.39). This "superstition," as Moore called it, no longer prevails.

The Versions. That the early versions, together with biblical citations in the Church Fathers, are of prime importance for the text of the LXX is universally recognized, and it is an encouraging feature of modern textual scholarship that increasing attention, especially in the way of critical editions, is being given to this constitutive aspect of LXX textual investigation. This is not to say, however, that such attention is entirely new. Collations were made on an extensive scale for the edition of Holmes-Parsons, but their uneven quality, together with the abundant material that has since become accessible, renders revision imperative, and pending this, caution in the use of the apparatus. The versions, too, were much to the fore in the work of Lagarde who devised his own sigla for their notation. Here we must necessarily confine ourselves to recent work, and for further information refer the reader to the standard introductions and to the articles on the early versions in the various dictionaries and encyclopaedias.

(1) *The Latin Versions.* Unfortunately for the Septuagintalist, but happily for his New Testament colleagues, the Beuron revision of Sabatier's edition of the Old Latin—apart from Genesis which was completed in 1954—has concentrated on the New Testament Epistles. There has, however, been a continuous flow of studies on the version in respect of text and origin, for which reference may be made to section 40g of the forthcoming *Classified Bibliography of the Septuagint.* This is the case also with the Vulgate, but here work on the revised critical edition has continued, volume XIII (Isaiah) having been published by the Vatican Press in 1969.[57] Apart from the text with critical apparatus, each volume includes a valuable introduction (particularly extensive in Isaiah) together with a critical edition of Jerome's prefaces. Mention should also be made of the most serviceable manual edition of

the Vulgate (*Biblia Sacra iuxta Vulgatam Versionem*), in two volumes, with brief apparatus, published in 1969 at Stuttgart by the Württemberg Bible Society.

(2) *The Armenian.* Bo Johnson of Lund has followed up his work on the hexaplaric recension of I Samuel with an examination of the Armenian version of this Book (*Die armenische Bibelübersetzung als hexaplarische Zeuge im I. Samuelbuch,* Lund, 1968). In common with the versions in general, there is no up-to-date critical edition of the Armenian, the standard edition being that of H. Y. Zohrab, published in Venice in 1805, which furnishes the readings in the apparatus of the Larger Cambridge Septuagint. For the purposes of his study Johnson examined twenty-seven of the extant manuscripts, and his comparison of these with Zohrab's edition showed the variants to be of minor moment. In the transmission-history of the version three stages are distinguished: an original translation from a Syriac *Vorlage,* followed by a revision reflecting affinities with the Lucianic; the Ethiopic; and the Coptic version as witnessed by the Pierpont Morgan MS. M 567 (containing I & II Samuel complete, with the exception of II 15:20-30). The final product was the outcome of a complete revision on the basis of a Hexaplaric text, and acordingly is of exceptional value as an early witness to this recension, which it follows, in Johnson's words, "very slavishly, and generally word for word" (p. 50). Apart from the common text form reflected by the manuscripts (p. 62), the version is valuable text-critically for the plenitude of Hexaplaric signs. Vulgate influence, as far as I Samuel is concerned, is held to be negligible.

Some further observations on the Armenian version were offered by Dr. Johnson in a paper presented at one of the sessions of the International Organization for LXX and Cognate Studies at Uppsala in August, 1971. While emphasizing the Hexaplaric nature of the text, the paper concerned itself more especially with apparent traces of the Peshitta and a non-Hexapla Greek text form, the latter being identified as Lucianic. Prior to the Hexaplaric revision, the greatest degree of the affinity of the Armenian version was with the Lucianic, next to which comes agreement with the Ethiopic, and then with the Coptic versions. Extending the comparison to the other versions, based on LXX, it is suggested—tentatively since Johnson points out that his findings are based on I Samuel alone—that almost all these versions demonstrate in their present form, or in earlier strata, affinities with the Lucianic which, as we have already had occasion to note, embodies some very ancient readings.

(3) *The Coptic.* This, to some extent, is a misleading term, as it embraces the Scriptures circulating in the several dialects of Egypt, foremost among which are the Sahidic version of Upper (i.e. Southern) Egypt and the Bohairic of the Nile delta and its approaches (Lower Egypt). Offshoots of these are the Fayyumic, the Akhmimic, and the Memphitic. The two principal versions, of which the Sahidic is the older, have fared remarkably well in the attention they have received from text-critical scholarship. Investigation has been facilitated by the extent of the manuscript evidence available, while Coptic studies as a whole have received fresh impetus from the discoveries at Nag Hammadi, first announced in 1948, which are to be published on a systematic basis in a facsimile edition by an international board of editors under the auspices of the Department of Antiquities of the Arab Republic of Egypt in conjunction with UNESCO. These codices, however, are of only indirect interest to the Septuagintalist, whose concern with the Coptic versions is their Greek *Vorlage*.

The Bodmer Papyri, the most important of recent source acquisitions, have been in course of publication from 1958. Coptic fragments from the Chester Beatty Library in Dublin, hitherto unpublished, are to be edited by Dr. Pietersma and Miss S. Turner, and the Isaiah text of the Coptic MS. M 568 in the Pierpont Morgan Library, New York, by Dr. Drescher who has already published the text of the Coptic (Sahidic) manuscript M 567 of I-II Kingdoms (I-II Samuel) housed in the same Library.[58] The closest agreement of the latter is found by its editor to be with the B text, though Lucianic and Hexaplaric readings often occur. In Isaiah, however, the manuscript accords more closely with Ziegler's "Alexandrian" group (A Q 26 86 106 710) than with B-V, which in this book exhibit a Hexaplaric text.

(4) *The Ethiopic.* The origin of this version still remains much an open question. A study of the text of Micah by H. F. Fuchs was published in 1968.[59] The author concludes that the textual history of the version originates in a Greek *Vorlage* which was revised, on the evidence of some of the MSS, on the basis of the Hebrew, and according to others from the Syriac, thus ruling out Lagarde's theory of the version as a fourteenth century production based on the Coptic or Arabic. The latter as origin was originally entertained by Ludolf but later retracted in favor of Greek. The earliest Ethiopic MSS reflect, according to Fuchs, the Greek *Vorlage,* the text-type of which, in our own times, has been much in dispute. Fuchs finds its closest affinities to be with 26, 91, and 239. The first-named (Vatican Greek 556, 10th century) is one of Ziegler's principal witnesses to the Alexandrian text in the Minor Prophets, and *à priori,* on grounds of contiguity alone, one would expect an "Alexandrian" text form as the exemplar of the Ethiopic. But the term "Alexandrian" is still too wide to satisfy the ultimate quest for the exact *type* of text, failing as it does to take account of, for example, the textual differences between B and A, which in Micah alone are in the neighbourhood of 150, though some are morphological and others of a minor nature.

Dr. J. W. Clear of Seattle is working on the Ethiopic text of Chronicles, and mention should be made of the important work of H. C. Gleave, *The Ethiopic Version of the Song of Songs* (London, 1951). While over the years there has been a succession of studies on the version and its constituent books, the necessity of a full critical edition, such as would determine its contribution to the transmission-history of LXX, was emphasized as recently as 1966 by Oscar Lofgren at the International Conference on Ethiopic Studies at Addis Ababa. One might venture to hope that not the least important outcome of the study of those versions deriving from an Alexandrian text might be the isolation of the so far elusive Hesychian recension.

A valuable contribution to the study of the origin of the Ethiopic version will be found in chapter I of Edward Ullendorff's Schweich Lectures for 1967 (*Ethiopia and the Bible* [London, 1968], pp. 31-62).

(5) *The Georgian.* Studies on this version, which a generation ago received considerable attention from R. P. Blake of Harvard (who demonstrated that by the end of the sixth century A.D. a complete translation of the Bible into Georgian has been made), are being actively pursued by Dr. J. Neville Birdsall of the University of Birmingham, England, who, in the earlier part of 1968 examined a collection of manuscripts in Vienna. These manuscripts, mostly palimpsest, reflect the earliest period of Georgian literature, going back in some instances as witnessed by the "Khanmeti"—the oldest known form of the script—to the late sixth or early seventh century. Of special interest to the Septuagintalist are the Old Testament fragments in this collection. Along with fragments of the Synoptic Gospels and early Christian apocryphal literature, parts of Exodus, Deuteronomy, Judges, I Chronicles, Isaiah, and I Esdras have been identified and are in course of publication by Dr. Birdsall.

(6) *The Arabic.* In a progress report on his Gottingen edition of the Book of Genesis, presented to the meeting of IOSCS at Toronto in November, 1969, Professor Wevers dealt with the Arabic versions of this book and their bearing on the LXX.[60] His findings confirm J. F. Rhodes's conclusion (*The Arabic Versions of the Pentateuch in the Church of Egypt,* Diss., Washington, D.C., 1921) that two distinct versions of the Pentateuch were current in Egypt. The one was translated from the Bohairic for the use of the Coptic (Jacobite) Church; the other, in use by the smaller Melchite group, was made direct from the Greek. Not a little intriguing are the affinities of the latter with Chrysostom and Theodoret, who are prime witnesses to the Lucianic text. The principal manuscript

(Paris, Bibliothèque Nationale 9) attesting the Melchite version, together with its congeners, stem presumably from Alexandria, which would seem to give added point to one's suggestion elsewhere (*SMS*, pp. 346 f.) that readings commonly designated Lucianic may have their *textual* origin in Lower Egypt. This by no means implies an Alexandrian provenance for the Lucianic *recension* as commonly understood, which, with Jerome and most moderns, one takes as Syrian (Antiochian).

Having reviewed, though perforce in outline and with a certain measure of selectivity, the recent trends in LXX studies, we may now revert, in the light of our survey, to the transmission history of the version which has occupied a foremost place in the last decade or so, consequent largely upon the discoveries in the region of the Dead Sea. Our particular concern is an attempted reconstruction of the early history of the text which allegedly has been facilitated by these discoveries.

It is not alone the Greek texts (which proportionately are few in number) that constitute the main contribution of Qumrân to LXX origins and transmission-history. Of not less interest to the Septuagintalist are the Hebrew manuscripts, some of which bear tangible witness, for the first time, to the Hebrew text used by the LXX translators when their archetype differed from the Hebrew as transmitted to us today. This is particularly the case in the Books of Samuel, where it had long been suspected, though hitherto incapable of demonstration, that the *Vorlage* of the LXX translators differed considerably from MT.[61] These newly-discovered Hebrew MSS have already gone far in clarifying an issue on which Old Testament commentators were sharply divided. There were those who, assuming that where LXX appeared to differ from MT it represented an earlier and superior Hebrew *Vorlage*, gave preference to "LXX"; on the other side were the staunch defenders of MT, who saw LXX renderings as corruptions, misunderstandings, paraphrases, or even as deliberate alterations on the part of the translators arising from theological predilections. A representative example is the supposed aversion of the Greek translators to the use of anthropomorphic terminology in relation to the Deity, a theory which is the subject of examination, with reference to a specific book, in Chapter 23 of the present volume. The mean between the extremes was the endeavour—and to this comparative philology, as already noted, has made a noteworthy contribution—to show that the *Vorlage* was, in fact, identical with, or approximated closely to, MT. Indeed, over the last generation, a growing respect for MT has been evident in Old Testament scholarship, but it is only to a limited extent that this finds support from Qumrân. LXX has been no less clearly vindicated: the faithfulness of the translators to their Hebrew exemplar at every stage has been well attested.

Long before the era of the Scrolls it had become evident that the accepted transmission-history of the Greek Old Testament stood in need of modification. What formerly could have been but speculative, Qumrân has rendered at least more tangible, and has, in fact, evoked an attempted reconstruction of the history of both the Hebrew text and the Septuagint. Although it is associated with the name of Frank Moore Cross of Harvard, it was first advanced in systematic form over a decade and a half ago by W. F. Albright.[62] He put it forward as "programmatic" and with no claim to its being more than a "pioneer attempt," but as arising from the conviction that "the publication of the Dead Sea Scrolls, though still in an early stage, has now reached a point where we can begin to discuss recensional problems in the early Hebrew text of many books of the Bible."

In the light of the Qumrân materials that were coming increasingly to hand the hypothesis of Albright was developed by Cross, whose exposition is best known from his Haskell Lectures of 1956-7, published in 1958 under the title *The Ancient Library of Qumrân and Modern Biblical Studies,* (Garden City, N.Y., and Duckworth, London, 1958) and virtually identical in the revised edition of 1961. Cross's approach is based upon first-hand acquaintance not only with the manuscripts, but also with the relevant literature, which has given him a firm grasp of the problems both of LXX origins and transmission-history. Avoiding the error of assuming the uniformity of LXX he reviews systematically the books of the Old Testament in so far as they are represented at Qumrân. Various points are amplified in two subsequent articles, the one in the *Harvard Theological Review* (1964)[63] and the other in the *Israel Exploration Journal*[64] (1966), the former taking especially into account the *kaige* recension of Barthélemy. Having noted the situation in the Books of Samuel, which Shenkel in his recent monograph extends to the Books of Kings,[65] we may consider some of the implications of the Qumrân material for the transmission-history of the Hebrew text and the Greek. If Thackeray was correct in supposing that the Latter Prophets, beginning with Isaiah, and the Former (in part) were translated into Greek shortly after the Pentateuch,[66] it would appear that in the 3rd-2nd centuries B.C. there were in circulation in Egypt two distinct Hebrew text forms, the one represented by the LXX of Kingdoms (in which Cross would include Joshua) and the other by Isaiah, which is close to MT. Some confirmation of this is adduced from the longer or shorter texts of Jeremiah (4Q Jer.[a] *c.*200 B.C.) and 4QJer.[b] (Hasmonean).

Less clearly defined are the other books of the Old Testament. For the Pentateuch, as might be expected, the proto-Massoretic is predominant, though the Song of Moses fragment and 4QEx.[a] are Septuagintal, and others are redolent of the Samaritan. Like Isaiah, Ezekiel and the Twelve reflect proto-MT.

The Chronicler, formerly much maligned but now acquiring an increasing respectability, constitutes an interesting case. Direct textual evidence from Qumrân is negligible, but a comparison of the MT of the Books of Chronicles and Samuel reveals that when the Chronicler is using Samuel as a source his exemplar was much closer to that of the Cave IV fragments than the current Hebrew text of that book. The situation has been pointed up sharply in the recent Klein-Allen controversy in the *Harvard Theological Review*.[67] Both agree basically on the textual problem, but are divided on whether the additions in Chronicles were made in Hebrew or in Greek.

In illustration of divergent texts within the LXX itself we may take the Book of Esther. Lagarde, it will be recalled, in his *Pars Prior* reconstructed what he believed to be the "Lucianic" text on the basis of the MSS 19, 93, 108.[68] This is not only shorter than the LXX text (B-text = *O′*-text [Göttingen], represented by the uncials B, A, S, N, Chester Beatty, and most cursives) by about a sixth, but differs so much from it that both Cambridge and Göttingen print the texts separately. Hanhart regards it not as Lucianic, nor a recension of the *O′* (i.e. LXX), but as "a new edition" *(Neugestaltung)* of the traditional Greek version, dependent in large measure on the *O′*-Text.[69] Carey Moore of Gettysburg, Pa., working independently, concludes that the Lucianic ("A"-text) is not a recension of LXX, but a translation of a Hebrew *Vorlage* differing at certain points from both MT and that presupposed by LXX. He regards its significance less as indirectly contributing to final reconstruction of the Proto-LXX (which was the objective of Lagarde) than as witnessing directly to the history and content of the Hebrew text by attesting one differing radically at places both from MT and the LXX Hebrew *Vorlage*. "The Greek texts of Esther", he asserts, "must also be resurrected as a primary tool for the Hebrew text of Esther."[70]

We now return to the reconstruction of the textual history as formulated by F. M. Cross on the basis of the data at his disposal, the main points of which are the following:

(1) the plurality of textual families, known (or postulated) before Qumran from MT, LXX and its recensions, the Samaritan Pentateuch, apocryphal works, New Testament citations, and the biblical text of Josephus, was not immediately apparent, since Isaiah was the first of the Qumrân materials to receive attention. Non-traditional text types were first recognized in the Cave IV yields, which came to light only in the summer of 1952.

(2) The history of the recensions is reconstructed as follows, the successive stages being

1. The Old Greek, popularly known as "LXX".
2. Revision of the Old Greek in the light of the current Hebrew text=proto-Lucian, the text used by Josephus, 2nd-1st century B.C.
3. Further revision, using proto-MT as Hebrew base (*kaige*). Mid-first century A.D.
4. Final revision of the *kaige,* resulting in the version of Aquila.

The strengths and weaknesses of the hypothesis must now be examined. On the positive side its merits lie in the points which follow.

(1) It presents, on the whole, a coherent picture of the transmission-history both of the LXX and the Hebrew text, in that it views their respective development and mutual relations as a concurrent process. It is now clear that up to the time of its fixation under Aqiba there was development within the Hebrew text. Mgr. Skehan has consistently drawn attention to what he calls "an exegetical process at work within the transmission of the text itself, in Hebrew." [71] Ziegler, more than a generation ago, illustrated this from Isaiah,[72] demonstrating that the Greek translators had faithfully reflected the expansionist, harmonizing, and exegetical technique of their Hebrew *Vorlage.* Ezekiel is another case in point, and the same process would appear to account for the longer text of Jeremiah and possibly the Book of Job. Orlinsky's "new approach" to the Kethib-Qere system is of direct relevance in this connection as pointing to the numerous variants obtaining in the Hebrew manuscripts.[73]

(2) It demonstrates the fact, widely overlooked, that LXX is not a uniform translation. No manuscript is self-consistent in witnessing throughout to a single text type. Each group of books (e.g. the Octateuch, Minor Prophets, etc.), and even single books in whole or in

part, are independent translational units and must be studied as such.

(3) The hypothesis attempts to account for the presence of early readings (proto-Theodotion and proto-Lucian) formerly attributed to later recensionists.

(4) It is provocative of further investigation into, and a reassessment of, the respective columns of the Hexapla, not least the nature and purpose of the fifth column.

(5) It aims at comprehension in that it endeavours to take into account, with palaeographical and text-critical evaluation, the material identified and assembled to date from the Dead Sea area.

On the negative side the following should be considered:

(1) In the absence of full or reasonably full texts, conclusions are drawn from fragments.[74] Some are presented on the basis of unpublished material, hence precluding independent judgment on the part of others in evaluating both the data and inferences drawn.

(2) The structure, with the clear and attractive manner of presentation, lend themselves to the supposition that the reconstruction is more than hypothetical. This is apparent in the publications of scholars who have tended to assume its validity as a basis for their own work.

(3) The theory takes no account of any light that might be thrown by creditable elements in the *Letter of Aristeas,* nor of the effect that Philo's recognition of LXX as of equal inspiration with the Hebrew (a recognition perpetuated in the early Christian Church) might have had in stabilizing the transmission of the Greek text.

(4) Another weakness is the lack of evidence for a "Babylonian" text introduced into Palestine in the Hasmonaean or Herodian era,[75] together with the

lack of proper attention to the "Egyptian" text which would have an important bearing on LXX as the rock whence the latter was hewn.

(5) While a place is reserved for Lucian of Antioch, no place appears to be found for the well attested activity of the traditional Theodotion of the second century A.D. Kahle's remark is well founded: "It is very likely that in the version ascribed to Theodotion we have to see in reality Theodotion's edition of a Greek Bible used in Ephesus and in the synagogues of Asia." [76]

(6) The reconstruction uses Thackeray, but takes no account of his strong linguistic argument for an Asiatic translator. Following from this, no explanation is offered for the *partial* nature of *kaige*[77] for which Thackeray's theory accounts satisfactorily, nor is any light thrown upon the peculiar nature of the version of Aquila.

The foregoing reflect some of one's own reflections on the hypothesis and should be considered along with those of H. M. Orlinsky and G. Howard.[78]

The Future. "What", many will ask, "of the future?" To this we can only answer: none can predict. While some, including the present writer, have attempted to indicate the lines along which fruitful study might profitably proceed, the future is very much a wide and open field. Who would have thought a generation ago that so much of the then apparently solid framework would have been thrown into the melting pot by the Qumrân discoveries alone? And these, as already mentioned, are not the only factor responsible for the present change in climate. We are, in fact, still very much in the process of acquiring the "tools for the job"—a term savouring of utility rather than elegance! We are still without complete critical editions of the LXX itself, not to mention the versions and that extensive body of literature that has such a considerable bearing on our field—the Apocryphal and Pseudepigraphical writings, the Judaeo-hellenistic literature, and Patristica, to give but some examples. But in all these disciplines—to the Septuagintalist "cognate studies"—the future is bright though the burdens are heavy, but should be eased by the growing regard for, and movement in the direction of, co-ordination and collaboration. The Centre d'Analyse et de Documentation at Strasbourg, for example, which is compiling an inventory of citations from the Old and New Testaments in the Christian Greek writers up to the time of Photius (9th century), is working in close association with the Institut für Neutestamentliche Textforschung at Münster, a combination that will be further enriched by the prospective collaboration of the Septuaginta-Unternehmen at Göttingen.

The pioneer work of the two outstanding scholars of a former generation, R. H. Charles and Emil Kautzsch, in the realm of the Pseudepigrapha, is being diligently pursued and extended in our own times. The Leiden-Louvain Pseudepigrapha Project (Comité de Direction pour littérature pseudepigraphique grecque d'Ancien Testament), under the editorship of Père A.-M. Denis of Louvain and Professor M. de Jonge of Leiden, has already published three volumes of texts (with introduction and apparatus criticus) together with an introductory volume to the literature as a whole and a Concordance to the Greek Apocalypse of Baruch, and further volumes are in active preparation.[79] A kindred enterprise, the recently inaugurated Pseudepigrapha Seminar of the Society of Biblical Literature under the presidency of Professor Walter Harrelson of Vanderbilt University, working in close co-operation with the foregoing, has as its primary objective the production of inexpensive editions (text and translation) of apocryphal works otherwise difficult of access.[80] The Dropsie College (now University) series of Jewish Apocryphal Literature, begun in 1950 with I Maccabees, resumed publication in 1972 after a lapse of fourteen years, with the Book of Judith. Volume VIII (Ben Sira) is in preparation. The Institutum Delitzschianum at Münster has recently published, in its *Arbeiten zur Literatur und Geschichte des hellenistischen Judentums* series (ed. K. H. Rengstorf), a Josephus bibliography and four volumes on Philo, and the first volume of a complete concordance to the works of Josephus is about to appear. The Philo Institute at Chicago is likely in due course to have its near Eastern counterpart in Israel, where plans are in hand for a project directed specifically to Philonic and Josephan studies. In the area of individual studies Pseudo-Philo's biblical text and the original language of his *Liber Antiquitatum Biblicarum* have claimed the attention of Daniel J. Harrington of Cambridge, Mass., who, on the sources of the biblical text, finds the evidence for the Pentateuch inconclusive, but for Joshua-Judges-I Samuel a relation to Lucian or proto-Lucian.[81] Another recent study, this time on Josephus by Louis H. Feldman, is concerned with Hellenizations in that historian's retelling of the story of Esther,[82] while in the realm of onomastica R.J.H. Shutt has made a morphologico-hermeneutical study of the biblical names in Books I and II of the *Antiquities*.[83] The foregoing, which extends no farther than representative examples, will give some indication of the vastnesses embraced in "cognate studies", all of which must be taken into account by the serious student of the Old Testament in Greek.

We have already mentioned the lexicon as an urgent desideratum. A revised concordance, with especial attention to Hebrew-Aramaic-Greek equivalents, would prove a most serviceable, though necessarily long-term, undertaking.[84] Some have advocated embarkation on a grammar of LXX Greek, a venture begun but never completed by H. St. J. Thackeray,[85] "the grammarian of the [Cambridge] school" as Walters describes him.[86] One would hesitate to concede this high priority. The Septuagintalist, for the present, is reasonably well equipped in this respect,[87] and were a fresh undertaking contemplated it should be a grammar of *biblical* Greek embracing both Testaments with their common grammatical features.[88]

All in all, though the path be long, and may appear at times unclear or uncertain, it may be said that today, as at no time before, there is a growing consciousness of, and an increasing readiness to apply, the sound methodological principles that have been formulated and proved in their own practice by the masters in the field.

February 1973

SIDNEY JELLICOE
Bishop's University
Lennoxville, Que.

ADDENDA ET CORRIGENDA

(as submitted by the respective authors)

CHAPTER 3 (G. Howard)

Page 59, line 13. For "B O C_2 E_2" read "b o c_2 e_2."
Page 62, line 14. For "This revision influenced the development of the LXX text . . ." read "The latter influenced the development of the Greek Bible . . ."

CHAPTER 6 (W. Schwarz)

Extract from Preface: "I have always referred to the pages of Migne, *Patrologia Graeca* and *Patrologia Latina,* since they are easily accessible, although modern editions have been used throughout."

CHAPTER 24 (G. D. Kilpatrick)

Addendum.

CHAPTER 32 (S. P. Brock)

See further, on the subject of this Chapter (with documentation), the same author, "The Phenomenon of the Septuagint," *Oudtestamentische Studiën XVII* (Leiden, 1972), pp. 11-36.

IN MEMORIAM

It is our sad duty to record the passing of Dr. Sidney Jellicoe (Aug. 25, 1906—Nov. 24, 1973), editor of this volume. He had responded enthusiastically to our cordial invitation to work up for our *Library of Biblical Studies* a volume of essays in the field of Septuagint that would reflect the variety and character of research in the field, both in the more recent past and currently. Widely acquainted with the subject at large—as witness his volume on *The Septuagint and Modern Study* (Oxford University Press, 1968)—Dr. Jellicoe succeeded in making a selection of articles that reflected unusually well the present state of research in matters septuagintal. Had Dr. Jellicoe lived to see the page proofs, he'd have proceeded with the plan to work up the Indices for this volume. His Prolegomenon has put the entire subject in proper perspective,

A founding member of the International Organization for Septuagint and Cognate Studies (IOSCS) since 1968 and the Editor of the first five issues of its *Bulletin,* Dr. Jellicoe played a significant role in the current upsurge of interest in Septuagint study, a recognition of which may be seen in his appointment as Grinfield Lecturer on the Septuagint at Oxford University for the two terms, 1970-71 and 1972-73.

But recently retired as Dean of Divinity and Theology of Bishop's University, Lennoxville, Quebec—an institution that he served with distinction for two decades—it is hoped that the manuscript of the Grinfield Lectures on which Dr. Jellicoe had been working will yet see the light of day.

Dr. Jellicoe's colleagues in scholarship join his family and friends in mourning his passing.

HARRY M. ORLINSKY
Editor, Library of
Biblical Studies

NOTES

1. Ivor Brown (ed.), *A Book of London* (London and Glasgow, 1961), p. 16.
2. See further, H. M. Orlinsky, infra.
3. C. F. D. Moule, *Faith, Fact and Fantasy* (London, 1964), p. 106.
4. See further, C. H. Dodd, The *Apostolic Preaching and its Developments,* new edn. (London, 1944), Lecture I.
5. See further, for examples and references, the present writer in *SMS,* chap. X, esp. pp. 324-9.
6. Cf. Schleusner, *Lex.,* s.v. ἀγαπάω , pp. 10 f. That the accuracy of what is unquestionably the true LXX reading in II Chron. 18:2 was a cause of difficulty to some copyists is evident from the variant readings: fj, ἠπάτα (followed by Rahlfs, *Septuaginta,* manual edn., vol. I, p. 836); be$_2$, ἔπεισε . Patristic testimony to the reading ἠγάπησαν in Psalm 77:36 (LXX) is as early as Clement of Rome (*Ep. ad Cor.* 15:4), *ca.* A.D. 96.
7. VII: R. Hanhart, *Zum Text des 2. und 3. Makkabäerbuches. Probleme der Überlieferung der Auslegung und der Ausgabe* (1961); VIII: Kurt Treu, *Majuskelbruchstücke der Septuaginta aus Damaskus* (1966); IX: Armin Schmitt, *Stammt der sogenannte "O'"-Text bei Daniel wirklich von Theodotion?* (1966); X: J. Ziegler, *Sylloge. Gesammelte Aufsätze zur Septuaginta* (1971).
8. For details of these editions see Eberhard Nestle, *Urtext und Übersetzungen der Bibel in übersichtlicher Darstellung* (Leipzig, 1897), pp. 65 ff.; idem in *HDB,* vol. IV, p. 440; Swete, *Introd.*, pp. 180-82.
9. Larger Cambridge edn., vol. I, pt. 1 (1906), p. i.

10. H. M. Orlinsky, "Studies in the Septuagint of the Book of Job," *Hebrew Union College Annual* 28 (1957), 53-74; 29 (1958), 229-71; 30 (1959), 153-67; 32 (1961), 239-68; 33 (1962), 119-51; 35 (1964), 57-78; 36 (1965), 37-47. See also the same writer, "The Hebrew *Vorlage* of the Septuagint of the Book of Joshua," Congress Vol., Rome 1968 (*Suppts. to Vetus Testamentum* XVII, 1969), 187-95, and articles listed in *SMS,* p. 396.
11. R. A. Kraft, "Jewish Greek Scriptures and Related Topics: Reports on Recent Discussions," *NTS* 16 (1969-70), 384-96.
12. S. P. Brock, C. T. Fritsch, S. Jellicoe, *A Classified Bibliography of the Septuagint* (*Arbeiten zur Literatur und Geschichte des Hellenistischen Judentums,* ed. K. H. Rengstorf, vol. VI), Leiden: E. J. Brill, 1972.
13. *Restoration Quarterly* 13:3 (1970), p. 162. In an earlier article (*Rest. Qtly.* 7:3 (1963), p. 142) Howard writes: "Kahle's position appears to be the right one."
14. Parentheses and enclosure are Sperber's.
15. Op. cit., p. 768.
16. Gordon Rupp in *JTS,* N.S. 8 (1957), p. 203.
17. *The Bible and the Greeks* (London, 1935), p. xi.
18. Cf. Swete, *Introd.,* pp. 11-22; H. St. J. Thackeray, *The Septuagint and Jewish Worship* (Schweich Lectures, 1920), 2nd edn. (London, 1923), pp. 11 f.
19. For the *motif* in the Book of Wisdom, with references to other examples, see James M. Reese, *Hellenistic Influence on the Book of Wisdom and its Consequences* (Analecta Biblica 41; Rome, 1970), 71-87.
20. "Vermutungen über den Anlass zur Griechischen Übersetzung der Tora", *Wort-Gebot-Glaube* (Zürich, 1970), 39-44. Cf. for this view B. H. Stricker's work of 1956. Full title in n.2 of Gooding's survey article, chap. 8 infra.
21. For critical editions, translations, studies, and bibliography see the present writer, *SMS,* chap. II, and pp. 377-9.
22. *Beiträge zur Einleitung in die biblischen Schriften,* 2 vols. (Halle, 1832-38).
23. E.g., G. Salmon, *A Historical Introduction to the . . . New Testament,* 8th edn. (London, 1897), pp. 538-51; E. Schürer, *Geschichte . . . ,* 3rd edn. (Leipzig, 1898-1901), vol. III, p. 324; J. A. Montgomery, *Daniel* (1CC) (1927), pp. 46-50;

H. St. J. Thackeray, *Josephus, the Man and the Historian* (New York, 1929), pp. 83-89; H. M. Orlinsky, *The Columnar Order* .

24. R. A. Kraft in *Gnomon* 37 (Munich, 1965), 474-83. For the present writer's review see *JAOS* 84 (1964), 178-82.
25. For the "Theodotion" of the Psalter cf. G. Mercati, *Psalterii Hexapli Reliquiae,* Pars Prima (Vatican City, 1958), pp. XIX-XXXV. (This handsome volume contains the plates and transcription of the Ambrosian Hexapla fragments with Introduction and text-critical notes. Volume II (Commentary) was published in 1965).
26. See further on Justin and the Scroll of the Minor Prophets, chapter 31 below.
27. *The Cairo Geniza* (London, 1947), p. 117 f; 2nd edn. (Oxford, 1959), pp. 191, 195 f.
28. *Ency. Brit.,* 9th edn., vol. 23 (1888), p. 63. For a full discussion see A. E. Silverstone, *Aquila and Onkelos* (Manchester, 1931).
29. Kahle, op. cit., 1st edn., p. 118, n.3, with refs. Not in 2nd edn.
30. Text in *Corpus Juris Civilis,* vol. 3: *Novellae,* ed. R. Schoell and W. Kroll (Berlin, 1895), pp. 714-8. Transl. in Kahle, op. cit., 2nd edn., pp. 315-7.
31. Cf. the imprecation in *Aristeas,* para. 310 f.
32. *SMS,* pp. 83-94.
33. For an examination see the writer's article "Some Reflections on the *Kaige* Recension" in VT 23 (1973), 15-24, an expansion of a paper delivered at the Atlanta meeting of IOSCS, October, 1971.
34. *Hellenistische Studien* I (Breslau, 1875), p. 65 n.
35. *Introd.,* p. 316.
36. *An Introduction to Ecclesiastes* (Cambridge, 1904), pp. 115-68.
37. *Les devanciers d'Aquila,* p. 30.
38. *Ezra Studies* (Chicago, 1910; repr. KTAV, New York, 1970), Chap. II et passim.
39. See n. 18 above.
40. For *eis nikos* (Grindel) in New Testament usage, cf. R. A. Kraft, *Septuagintal Lexicography,* (Septuagint and Cognate Studies, I (Missoula, Montana, 1972)), pp. 153-6.

41. "Lucian redivivus . . .," *Studia Evangelica* V (= *TU* 103, Berlin, 1968), 176-81.
42. "Lucianic Readings in a Greek Twelve Prophets Scroll from the Judaean Desert," *JQR* N.S. 62 (1971-2), 51-60. Cf. for the Samuel text the same writer's "Frank Cross and Recensional Criticism" in *VT* 21 (1971), 440-50.
43. See fully *SMS,* pp. 160-169.
44. *Lucians Rezension der Königbücher.* Rahlfs's three *Septuaginta-Studien* are now available in a one-volume reprint which also contains an appreciation by Walter Bauer, a posthumous study of the Ethiopic version, and a bibliography of Rahlfs's writings (Göttingen, 1965).
45. "The History of the Biblical Text in the Light of Discoveries in the Judean Desert," *HTR* 57 (1964), 281-99.
46. See *The Cairo Geniza,* 2nd edn. (1959), pp. 218-20.
47. Text and plates: *Papyrus grecs bibliques (Papyrus F. Inv. 266). Volumina de la Genèse et du Deutéronome* par Françoise Dunand. Extrait des *Études de Papyrologie,* Tome IX (= pp. 81-150 + XV plates). The Introduction is published separately (same title and authoress) as *Recherches d'Archéologie, de Philologie et d'Histoire,* Tome XXVII. Both publ. Cairo, 1966.
48. A specimen of these additional fragments, with plate, is published in *Études de Papyrologie,* Tome IX (1971), pp. 227 f., with an evaluation of Mlle. Dunand's edition of Pap. Fouad 266 by Professor Kilpatrick (pp. 221-6; see also Preface, p. vii). The present writer is indebted to Dr. Zaki Aly for kindly sending him a copy of the volume.
49. Sir Alfred Chester Beatty, died 19 January, 1968, in his 93rd year. It should be noted that the present home (since 1950) of his collection of manuscripts and works of art is the Chester Beatty Museum and Library, Dublin, not the British Museum as is sometimes erroneously stated.
50. See *SMS,* pp. 229-32.
51. The Esther fragments were collated by R. Hanhart in his Göttingen edition (Vol. VIII:3 [1966], q.v., p. 12). Professor Kilpatrick informs the writer that the Ezekiel fragments are about to be published by the Institut für Altertumskunde of the University of Cologne.

52. *Nuevas Páginas del Códice 967 del A. T. Griego (Ez. 28, 19-43, 9) = Studia Papyrologica* X:1 (Barcelona, 1971). See also M. F. Galiano, "Notes on the Madrid Ezekiel Papyrus," *American Studies in Papyrology, VII* (Toronto, 1970), 133-8.
53. *Emerita* 39 (Madrid, 1971), 51-61.
54. "Some Uncatalogued Papyri of Theological and other Interest in the John Rylands Library," *BJRL* 51 (1968-9), 137-63.
55. *Verzeichnis der griechischen Handschriften des Alten Testaments* (*MSU* II, 1914), 335-7.
56. H. B. Swete, Manual edn., Preface to Vol. I, p. xii; Larger edn., ed. A. E. Brooke and N. McLean, Prefatory note to Genesis, Vol. I:1 (1906), p. i.
57. For the foundation and progress of this undertaking, and also for the Beuron revision of the Old Latin, see *SMS,* pp. 249-56.
58. *Corpus Scriptorum Christianorum Orientalium,* 313-4 (Louvain, 1970).
59. *Die äthiopische Übersetzung des Propheten Micha.* (*Bonner Biblische Beiträge,* 28 [Bonn, 1968]).
60. The report is published in full in *IOSCS Bulletin* No. 3 (October, 1970), pp. 8-11. Copies of the Bulletins published to date (Nos. 1/2-5) are available.
61. The term MT (Mas(s)oretic Text) is here used purely for convenience and, to adopt the legal terminology, "without prejudice." For the chimera of "*the* Masoretic Text" see H. M. Orlinsky, "The Masoretic Text: a Critical Evaluation," Prolegomenon to C. D. Ginsburg, *Introduction to the Massoretico-critical Edition of the Hebrew Bible* (1897), repr. Ktav Publishing House Inc., New York, 1966, pp. I-XLV; also the same writer, "The Origin of the Kethib-Qere System: a New Approach," *Supplements to VT,* 7 (1960), 184-92.
62. "New Light on Early Recensions of the Hebrew Bible," *BASOR* 140 (1955), 27-33.
63. See n. 45 above.
64. "The Contribution of the Qumran Discoveries to the Study of the Biblical Text," *IEJ* 16 (1966), 81-95.
65. Op. cit., p. 3 et passim.
66. Op. cit., p. 28.

67. R. W. Klein, "New Evidence for an Old Recension of Reigns," *HTR* 60 (1967), 93-105; "Supplements in the Paralipomena: a Rejoinder (to L. C. Allen)," id. 61 (1968), 492-5. L. C. Allen, "Further Thoughts on an Old Recension of Reigns in Paralipomena," *HTR* 61 (1968), 483-91.
68. b′ e_2, *b* respectively in the Cambridge notation; Lagarde $= \alpha$; Göttingen $= L$.
69. *Esther (Septuaginta* VIII: 3, Göttingen, 1966), pp. 15, 87-96.
70. "A Greek Witness to a Different Hebrew Text of Esther," *ZAW* 79 (1967), 351-8. See also H. J. Cook, "The *A* Text of the Greek Versions of the Book of Esther," id. 82 (1970), 369-76.
71. "The Qumran Manuscripts and Textual Criticism." *Supplements to VT,* IV (Congress Volume, Strasbourg, 1956) (Leiden, 1957), p. 151. Whole article = pp. 148-60; cf. also the same writer in *BA* 28 (1965), p. 99, and the *McCormick Quarterly* 21 (1968), pp. 277 f.
72. *Untersuchungen zur Septuaginta des Buches Isaias* (Münster, 1934), chaps. VI, VII, and pp. 44-7.
73. See n. 61 above, last item.
74. Cf. H. M. Orlinsky, infra .
75. Cf. M. H. Goshen-Gottstein, *The Book of Isaiah: Sample Edition with Introduction* (Jerusalem, 1965), p. 14, n. 15.
76. "Problems of the Septuagint", infra. p.
77. Cf. J. D. Shenkel, *CBQ* 31 (1969), p. 259.
78. "Frank Cross and Recensional Criticism", *VT* 21 (1971), 440-50.
79. See report in *IOSCS Bulletin,* No. 5 (1972), pp. 11-13.
80. See further, James H. Charlesworth "De Pseudepigraphorum Studio" in *Septuagint and Cognate Studies,* ed. R. A. Kraft, Vol. 2 (Missoula, Montana, 1972), Part II, pp. 129-33, where details are given of works published and projected on both sides of the Atlantic.
81. "The Biblical Text of Pseudo-Philo's Liber Antiquitatum Biblicarum". *CBQ* 33 (1971), 1-17, also id., "The Original Language of Pseudo-Philo's *Liber Antiquitatum Biblicarum*". *HTR* 63 (1970), 503-14; *IOSCS Bulletin* No. 4 (1971), p. 8, for abstract of paper at New York meeting, 1970.

82. Hellenizations in Josephus' Version of Esther". *Transactions and Proceedings of the American Philological Association,* 101 (1970), 143-70.
83. "Biblical Names and their Meanings in Josephus Jewish Antiquities, Books I and II, 1-200." *Journal for the Study of Judaism,* 2 (Leiden, 1971), 167-82.
84. For Margolis' pioneer work in this connection (with references) see H. M. Orlinsky in *Max Leopold Margolis, Scholar and Teacher* (Philadelphia, Pa., 1952), pp. 36 f., and the present writer in *SMS,* pp. 335-7.
85. *A Grammar of the Old Testament in Greek according to the Septuagint.* I: Introduction, Orthography and Accidence (Cambridge, 1909).
86. Infra.
87. See further, *SMS,* pp. 332-4.
88. Cf. C. F. D. Moule, *An Idiom-Book of New Testament Greek,* 2nd edn. (Cambridge, 1959), pp. 3f.

I. SURVEYS OF SEPTUAGINT STUDIES

CHAPTER EIGHT

Current Progress and Problems in Septuagint Research

HARRY M. ORLINSKY
Jewish Institute of Religion, New York City

THE main purpose of this essay is to describe and analyze wha has been done in Septuagint research in the past few decades and to outline the more important aspects of this discipline which demand attention in our own time.

THE RECOVERY OF THE ORIGINAL SEPTUAGINT TEXT

1. Far and away the greatest value of the Septuagint (LXX) is to be found in the data offered by this version for the Hebrew text with which the "Seventy-two" translators operated. However, before this Hebrew *Vorlage* can be recovered, it is first necessary to determine the original text of the LXX, the text which the translators brought into being (Proto-LXX). No one saw better than did Paul de Lagarde (1827–91) in the latter half of the nineteenth century the special problems and correct methodology pertaining to the recovery of the text of the Proto-LXX.[1] The work of Alfred Rahlfs (1866–1935), Lagarde's successor at Göttingen and for over a quarter of a century director of studies in the Septuagint at the Gesellschaft der Wissenschaften at Göttingen,[2] and that of James Alan Montgomery (1866——), of the

1. Cf. A. Rahlfs's appraisal of *Paul de Lagardes wissenschaftliches Lebenswerk im Rahmen einer Geschichte seines Lebens dargestellt* ("Mitteilungen des Septuaginta Unternehmens," Vol. IV, No. 1 [Berlin, 1928]); G. Bertram, "Theologische Kritik und Textkritik bei Paul Anton de Lagarde," *Kirche im Angriff*, XIII (1937), 370–81. The new interest in Lagarde's religious *Anschauung* (the principles of German fascism were largely anticipated by Lagarde, and loved by him!) is indicated also by such an article as "Paul de Lagardes religiöse Entwicklung," by W. Hartmann, in *Theologische Blätter*, XX (1941), 334–41.

2. Someone should appraise the important studies of Rahlfs in some detail. In the meantime see "Alfred Rahlfs," by Walter Bauer, in *Nachrichten von der Gesellschaft der Wissen-*

Reprinted from *The Study of the Bible Today and Tomorrow*, ed. H. R. Willoughby. Chicago Univ. Press, 1947.

University of Pennsylvania, advanced the problem nearer to solution.[3] The solution itself, in the most concrete manner, was offered by Max Leopold Margolis (1866–1932) of the Dropsie College.[4]

It may be worth while to describe here briefly the nature both of the problem and of the solution.

2. The textual critic finds himself in possession not of any one manuscript containing the original LXX translation of the Hebrew Bible, but of many Greek manuscripts, uncials and cursives, each one containing a text differing from the others to a greater or lesser extent. Furthermore, there are available to him scores of manuscripts of translations from the LXX into Latin (second century), Sahidic-Bohairic (second–third centuries), Armenian (fourth century), Gothic (*ca.* A.D. 350), Ethiopic (fourth–fifth centuries), Georgian (fourth?–fifth centuries), Arabic (seventh?–eighth centuries), and Slavonic (ninth–tenth centuries).[5] The critic thus finds himself confronted at once by the task of determining which manuscript or group of manuscripts, whether in Greek or in any of the languages enumerated just above, has preserved the original, or the nearest to the original, text of the LXX.

3. Margolis compared these secondary versions of the LXX with the many Greek manuscripts representing the LXX, and

---

schaften zu Göttingen, 1935, pp. 60–65; J. L. Seeligmann, "Problemen en Perspectieven in het moderne Septuaginta-Onderzoek," *Jaarbericht No. 7 van het Vooraziatisch-Egyptisch Gezelschap, Ex Oriente Lux*, 1940, pp. 359–90*e passim*.

3. See especially Sec. III ("Ancient Versions," pp. 24–57) of the Introduction in Montgomery's *International Critical Commentary on Daniel* (New York, 1927), and the corresponding section in his forthcoming *Kings* in the same series.

4. *The Book of Joshua in Greek* (Paris, 1931——) (Parts I–IV cover 1:1—19:38), with which should be studied his "Specimen of a New Edition of the Greek Joshua," in *Jewish Studies in Memory of Israel Abrahams* (New York, 1927), pp. 307–23. For an analysis of the problem as a whole, cf. Orlinsky, *On the Present State of Proto-LXX Studies* ("American Oriental Society Offprint Series," No. 13 [New Haven, 1941]). An interesting sketch of Margolis' life and works was written by Alexander Marx for the *Proceedings of the Rabbinical Assembly of America*, IV (1933), 368–80 (reprinted in Alexander Marx, *Studies in Jewish History and Booklore* [New York, 1944], pp. 418–30).

5. For a graphic representation of these data see the chart in the *Biblical Archaeologist*, Vol. IX, No. 2 (May, 1946).

these same Greek manuscripts one with another and with the citations from these manuscripts and other pertinent material in the various editions of the *Onomasticon* of Eusebius and in the writings of such early authorities in the church as Justin, Origen, Eusebius, and Theodoret. Margolis chose the Book of Joshua of all the books in the Bible because it lent itself admirably to textual and exegetical analysis and—what is of supreme importance—because it contained hundreds of proper names whose *Überlieferungsgeschichte*, in context, could readily be traced. Margolis found:

> The sum of the witnesses yields four principal recensions, PCSE, and in addition a number of MSS. variously mixed which I name M. At the outset it must be remarked that all of our witnesses are more or less mixed; the classification has in mind the basic character of a text, which alone is the determinant. P is the Palestinian recension spoken of by Jerome, that is the Eusebian edition of the Septuagint column in Origen's Hexapla-Tetrapla [then, as in the case of CSEM below, follows a sketch of the more important manuscripts which belong to this recension]. . . . . C is a recension which was at home in Constantinople and Asia Minor. We are helped in localizing the recension by the aid of the Armenian version. . . . . Whether the recension had any relationship to the fifty copies ordered by Constantine from Eusebius, as CONYBEARE suspects, must remain a matter of conjecture. Jerome says nothing of a fourth recension; but then he is by no means exact, or the recension was at his time just in the process of formation. . . . . S is the Syrian (Antiochan) recension. . . . . An outstanding characteristic of the S recension is the correction of the Greek style, as shown by the substitution of Attic grammatical forms for Hellenistic. . . . . The Egyptian recension, E, is preserved with relative purity in B [Codex Vaticanus]. . . . . The Coptic and Ethiopic versions unmistakably point to the Egyptian provenance of their text. Hence the designation of the recension [as Egyptian]. There remain a number of MSS. which may be classed together as M, i.e. mixed texts. Mixture is the general characteristic, the elements coming from the four principal recensions in diverse processes of contamination. . . . . The road to the original text of G [the LXX] leads across the common, unrevised text. In order to get at the latter, we must abstract from the recensional manipulations. . . . . A study of the translator's mannerism of rendition becomes imperative. . . . . The scope of my edition is to restore critically the original form of the version. I print the critically restored text at the top of the page. Below follow the forms assumed in the four classes, E, S, P, CM. Omis-

sions and contractions of the text, by which certain witnesses or groups of witnesses step out as silent on the textual form, receive a rubric of their own. Then follow individual variations of class members, such as leave the characteristic class reading undisturbed in its main features. Lastly marginal readings in so far as they have not been embodied above. . . . .[6]

4. What Margolis has done for Joshua needs to be done also for the other books of the Old Testament. Yet it is very doubtful that there will arise in the future other scholars of the quality of Margolis to perform this task. Consequently, our hopes and plans for the coming several decades must be modest.

a) There is a considerable amount of preliminary work to be done in the recovery of the Proto-LXX. This work revolves about the determination of the family relationship of the manuscripts containing the text of the LXX and of the secondary versions. It seems to the writer that a very acceptable sort of subject for a doctoral dissertation would be the analysis of, say, the Ethiopic or Arabic or Old Latin, etc., in relation to the manuscripts containing the LXX text, with a view to determining the recensional affinity of these data, viz., whether the recension be Syrian (Lucianic) or Palestinian (Origenian) or Egyptian (Hesychian) or Constantinopolitan. Thus a number of students of Montgomery's wrote such theses (Benjamin, Gehman, Haupert, Wyngaarden, Yerkes); and Gehman, in turn, has some of his students working on such topics.

b) In this connection it is important to make readily available

6. "Specimen of a New Edition of the Greek Joshua," pp. 308–16. It is of the greatest significance that Montgomery, working independently and on another book altogether, found the facts and interpretation in Joshua to hold true essentially also for Daniel (for the references, not only to Montgomery's work but also to the important work done by Henry S. Gehman, see n. 9 of the writer's work cited in n. 4 above). It should not go unnoted that, working on Joshua independently of Margolis, Otto Pretzl (1893–1941) came to the same conclusions with regard to the LXX manuscripts as Margolis did ("Die griechischen Handschriftengruppen im Buche Josue untersucht nach ihrer Eigenart und ihrem Verhältnis zueinander," *Biblica*, IX [1928], 377–427); for a sketch of Otto Pretzl, see A. Spitaler, *Zeitschrift der Deutschen morgenländischen Gesellschaft*, XCVI (1942), 161–70. "The List of Levitic Cities," by W. F. Albright (*Louis Ginzberg Jubilee Volume* [New York, 1945], English section, pp. 49–73; see esp. pp. 50–51 and n. 4), goes a very long way in demonstrating the correctness of Margolis' method. Cf. R. Marcus, "Jewish and Greek Elements in the Septuagint," *Louis Ginzberg Jubilee Volume*, English section, p. 227, n. 2; and Giovanni Cardinal Mercati, *Nuove note di letteratura biblica e cristiana antica* (Vatican City, 1946), chap. v.

both for the student who is working on such a project and for the general biblical scholar two kinds of data: (i) critical editions of the secondary versions, utilizing all the manuscripts still available even after the destruction wrought during World War II (this is an urgent desideratum for all the secondary versions of nearly every book in the Old Testament);[7] (ii) a critical apparatus containing the variants of all the LXX manuscripts of the Old Testament. From 1798 to 1827 the Oxford Press published, for the scholarly world, Holmes and Parsons' *Vetus Testamentum Graecum cum variis lectionibus*, still the greatest and, generally speaking, a reliable enough collection of variant readings of no less than three hundred and eleven LXX manuscripts and, in Latin dress, of some secondary versions: Old Latin, Coptic (Memphitic and Sahidic), Arabic, Slavonic, Armenian, and Georgian; and since 1906 the Cambridge Press has been making available Brooke and McLean's (and Thackeray's) *The Old Testament in Greek* with its more select and reliable collection of variants.[8] In view of the fact that quite a bit of Holmes and Parsons' material has not been duplicated in the work of Brooke and McLean and is not readily accessible anywhere else, it becomes obvious at once how much indebted biblical scholarship would be to the Oxford Press if this great institution were to reproduce Holmes and Parsons' critical apparatus.[9]

7. Oscar Löfgren has published *Die äthiopische Übersetzung des Propheten Daniel nach Handschriften* . . . . (Paris, 1927) and *Jona, Nahum, Habakuk, Zephanja, Haggai, Sacharja and Maleachi äthiopisch* . . . . (Uppsala, 1930). Heinrich Dörrie published in 1938 a very fine critical edition of the Old Latin of IV Maccabees (*Passio SS. Machabaeorum, die antike lateinische Übersetzung des IV. Makkabäerbuches* [Göttingen]); there has now come to hand the same scholar's useful article "Zur Geschichte der LXX im Jahrhundert Konstantins," *Zeitschrift für die neutestamentliche Wissenschaft*, XXXIX (1940), 57-110 (on which see G. Mercati, "Di alcune testimonianze antiche sulle cũre bibliche di San Luciano," *Biblica*, XXIV [1943], 1-17). In 1923, A. Dold made available *Konstanzer altlateinische Propheten- und Evangelienbruchstücke* . . . . (Leipzig); cf. its enthusiastic reception in Montgomery, *Daniel*, p. 30).

8. Yet note even here the extent to which Margolis was able to make "Corrections in the Apparatus of the Book of Joshua in the Larger Cambridge Septuagint," *Journal of Biblical Literature*, XLIX (1930), 234-64.

9. The writer is aware of the criticism leveled at the *apparatus criticus* of Holmes and Parsons who "entrusted no small part of the task of collation to careless or incompetent hands"; cf. Edwin Hatch, *Essays in Biblical Greek* (Oxford, 1889), pp. v-vi and 131-33; and now J. Ziegler, *Zeitschrift für die alttestamentliche Wissenschaft*, LX (1944), 121-23.

THE USE OF THE LXX AND ITS DAUGHTER-VERSIONS IN THE TEXTUAL CRITICISM OF THE HEBREW BIBLE

Whether or not the (nearest to the) original Septuagint text of any book in the Old Testament has been recovered, there still remains the task of using the primary and secondary versions properly in order to determine their Hebrew *Vorlagen* for comparison with the Textus Receptus of the Hebrew Bible, the Masoretic text.

5. There can be little doubt that the field of Old Testament textual criticism has not been worked since the end of World War I by as many and as skilful workers as in the epoch preceding. First, it was the disciplines of Egyptology, cuneiform studies, and comparative Semitic linguistics and, later on, archeology and northwestern Semitic which drew away many thoroughly competent scholars who would have advanced materially the discipline in which we are here interested. But another, no less important, factor in the general decline of the textual criticism of the Hebrew Bible has been, strange as it may strike the reader, the publication of Swete's edition of the LXX (also Rahlfs's edition in 1935) and Kittel's *Biblia Hebraica*.

a) Ever since the appearance of Swete's Smaller Cambridge Septuagint (1894; 2d ed., 1899), it has become increasingly customary for the average biblical critic, when turning to the Septuagint translation of whatever word or passage in the Hebrew Bible he wishes elucidated, to consult this convenient handbook. But whether the critic is aware of it or not, the "Septuagint" in the edition of Swete (as of Rahlfs) was never meant to be more than "a portable text . . . . taken from the Vatican MS., where this MS. is not defective, with the variations of two or three other early uncial MSS." (Swete, *Introduction to the Old Testament in Greek*, p. 189).[10] The average critic has come to look upon the

10. Margolis had this to say about Swete's edition: "For the uncials [of Joshua] I have used the phototypic editions. . . . . I say this because I have discovered numerous inaccuracies in Swete's edition" (*American Journal of Semitic Languages*, XXVIII [1911–12], 3). And Ziegler ("Bei der Ausarbeitung des Dodekapropheton für die grosse Göttinger Septuaginta-Ausgabe," *Zeitschrift für die alttestamentliche Wissenschaft*, LX [1944]) has this to say after a study of Swete: "Diese Nachkollation von Amos zeigt zur Genüge, dass die Handausgabe von SWETE für die wissenschaftliche Erforschung der Textkritik, die sauberste Arbeit ver-

impressive fourth-century uncial, Codex Vaticanus, as *the* "Septuagint" and has almost completely lost the habit of consulting the variants in the critical apparatuses of Holmes and Parsons and Brooke and McLean. Professor Montgomery has put it this way:

> . . . . Scholars have perpetrated the mistake of baldly citing B as though it were ultimate, with no attempt to criticise it apart from its group and to recover the original text . . . . [*Daniel*, p. 40]. In many cases they (Sahidic-Coptic) help to correct B where it can otherwise be proved to be untrue to its group . . . . [p. 42]. [The Old Latin] is of great value in showing the antiquity of errors, glosses, etc., in B . . . . [p. 43]. Codex A must be extremely discounted as a witness; an early listing has disclosed more than 175 errors, some of them most glaring. . . . . Its colleague [the Arabic translation] . . . . is infinitely superior in the text it represents to A . . . . it must have been made of an early authoritative codex of which A is a base offspring . . . . [p. 52].

Nine years later (*Journal of Biblical Literature*, LV [1936], 309–11), Professor Montgomery criticized Sir Frederic Kenyon (who edited the Chester Beatty papyri) and C. H. Roberts (who edited the Rylands papyri) and, three years after that (*Journal of the American Oriental Society*, LIX [1939], 262–65), some of the editors of the Scheide papyri, because they compared their newly discovered material with only two or three uncial manuscripts. At best such an "analysis" can be but inconclusive; at worst, it can be, and too often has been, utterly misleading.

b) In 1900 the Dutch scholar, Henricus Oort (1835–1927), conceived the excellent idea of putting within the confines of one book some of the results of the textual criticism of the Hebrew Bible (*Textus Hebraici emendationes quibus in Vetere Testamento Neerlandice vertendo*, usi sunt A. Kuenen, I. Hooykaas, W. H. Kosters, H. Oort). In 1905–6 there appeared the much more elaborate project of Rudolf Kittel (1853–1929), *Biblia Hebraica*[2] (3d ed., 1929), which was composed of the Hebrew text of the second edition of the Bomberg Bible, edited by Jacob ben Chayyim (Venice, 1524–25), and a critical apparatus, consisting essen-

langt, ungenügend ist . . . . " (p. 128). Rahlfs's edition, on the other hand, he says: ". . . . in dieser Hinsicht Lob verdient. Gewiss finden sich auch verschiedene Mängel und Versehen; aber im Vergleich zu den oben besprochenen Werken sind sie verschwindend gering . . . . " (pp. 128–29).

tially of various readings from Hebrew manuscripts, the versions, and conjecture. It is a pity that one usually remembers this statement by S. R. Driver, the master-critic: "The best collection both of variants from the versions and of conjectural emendations is that contained in Kittel's *Biblia Hebraica*" (*Notes on .... Samuel*[2], p. xxxv, n. 6), whereas it has become all but forgotten that Driver followed up with the following strong *caveat:* "But in the acceptance of both variants and emendations, considerable discrimination must be exercised."[11]

(1) It is no exaggeration to assert that the critical apparatus in this edition of the Hebrew Bible has become to many scholars more sacred and authoritative than the Hebrew text itself. The average critical student of the Bible only too infrequently goes beyond the convenient collection of footnotes in *Biblia Hebraica*[2,3], unless it is to look at Swete's or Rahlfs's edition of Codex Vaticanus and their all too meager apparatus.

(2) Were the critical notes in *Biblia Hebraica*[2,3] generally reliable, there might be some justification for the nonspecialist in not going beyond them. It so happens, however, that the overwhelming majority of the twenty-four books in the Hebrew Bible were done by scholars whose *forte* was not textual criticism (notable exceptions were Driver in *Biblia Hebraica*[2] and Bewer in *Biblia Hebraica*[3]). The writer does not consider it an exaggeration to assert that nearly every line of their footnotes swarms with errors of commission and omission, as regards both the primary and the secondary versions.[12]

11. A posteriori, no one should really be surprised that the textual criticism of the Hebrew Bible, involving the correct use of the LXX and other primary, as well as secondary, versions, is so poorly done in Kittel's *Biblia Hebraica*. A perusal of Kittel's useful study, *Über die Notwendigkeit und Möglichkeit einer neuen Ausgabe der hebräischen Bibel* (Leipzig, 1901) ("Zur Feier des Reformationsfestes und des Übergangs des Rektorats [of the University of Leipzig] auf Dr. Eduard Sievers .... ") will show that in the chapter (iii) devoted to "Das erreichbare Ziel" (pp. 32–47) the author failed to grasp the character and problems of the textual criticism of the Hebrew Bible.

12. For some years the writer has been waging virtually a one-man battle against the footnotes in Kittel's *Biblia Hebraica* (cf. the remarks in the *Journal of Biblical Literature*, LXIII [1944], 33, and in n. 18, the references to the specific instances which are discussed in detail elsewhere). He is now happy to welcome into the fold a ranking textual critic, Joseph Ziegler, whose extremely valuable "Studien zur Verwertung der Septuaginta im Zwölfprophetenbuch" have just come to hand (*Zeitschrift für die alttestamentliche Wissen-*

(*a*) It is too often forgotten that the Septuagint translation of the Hebrew Bible is not only a thoroughly Jewish work but also that it was popular among the Jews until after they lost their sovereign state in A.D. 70–135 and (Judeo-)Christianity, with the LXX rather than the Hebrew original as its Bible, had become a distinct and increasingly powerful group. The unique Greek translation by Aquila, in keeping with the Jewish exegesis current in the first and second centuries, replaced the LXX, until its use in the Synagogue was forbidden by the Code of Justinian (A.D. 555).[13] The failure to bear the LXX in mind as a Jewish work and to treat it as such in the textual criticism of the Hebrew Bible, far from being purely an academic problem, has resulted in an enormous waste of talent, time, and paper in the unscientific use of the LXX for the "elucidation" and "restoration" of the text of the Hebrew Bible.

(*b*) The Hebrew Bible was read, studied, and interpreted by the Jews during the Maccabean, Mishnaic, and Talmudic periods, no less than it was before the second century B.C. and after the sixth century A.D. It is only reasonable to assume that where the LXX points, or appears to point, to a Hebrew reading which differs from the reading preserved in the Hebrew text currently in use, there may be involved not two variants, of which only one can be original, but only one reading, of which the LXX is simply an interpretation. This interpretation, of identical or similar character, should be sought in the vast literature which the Jews produced from the Maccabean through the Talmudic periods, a literature which is a mine of information for the discerning biblical scholar. It was the great contribution of Rabbi Zecharias

---

schaft, LX [1944], 107–31). At the end of his "Kritische Bemerkungen zur Verwendung der Septuaginta im Zwölfprophetenbuch der Biblia Hebraica von Kittel [3d ed., 1937]," pp. 107–20, we read: "Bei einer Neuausgabe der Biblia Hebraica des Dodekapropheton muss das gesamte G-Material, wie es die eben erschienene Göttinger Septuaginta-Ausgabe vorlegt, neu bearbeitet werden."

13. The earlier attitude of the Jews toward the LXX is found in the Letter of Aristeas and in the works of Philo and Josephus; the later attitude is expressed, e.g., in the tractates, Megillat Taᶜanit and Masseket Soferim. English translations of these and other materials are conveniently available in Thackeray, *The Letter of Aristeas* (London and New York, 1918), Appendix.

Frankel, of Dresden (1801–75), to one phase of correct LXX and Bible study that he collected and classified material of this kind in such works as *Vorstudien zu der Septuaginta* (1841), *Über den Einfluss der palästinischen Exegese auf die alexandrinische Hermeneutik* (1851), and *Zu dem Targum der Propheten* (1872), demonstrating the manner in which the LXX exhibits the kind of exegesis (and sometimes the *eis*egesis, too) found in the Targumim, Mishnah, Tosefta, Midrashim, and Gemara. Had they kept this important approach in mind, would such better-known critics as Briggs, Duhm, Ehrlich, Gunkel, and Marti—not to list dozens of others equally or less known—have so recklessly and indiscriminately emended the preserved Hebrew text in accordance with what they supposed must have been the reading in the Hebrew manuscripts used by the LXX translators?[14]

(*c*) The Hebrew Bible was to the Jews a collection of sacred books. They turned the Bible from Hebrew into Greek precisely because their Sacred Scriptures had to be made accessible to those Jews who no longer knew enough Hebrew to read the original (cf., e.g., the *raison d'être* of the Aramaic Targumim, Saadia's Arabic translation, and the English version published by the Jewish Publication Society of America). Is it reasonable to sup-

14. To cite but one, hitherto unnoted, case in point: nearly all critics have emended drastically either the LXX or the Massoretic text (or both) in Job 3:10, where the latter's "(And the servant) is free (from his master)" is reproduced in the former by "does not fear." Yet all that we have here, as so often in the LXX of this book, is a nice interpretation of the Hebrew; and it is interesting that a medieval Jewish commentator, Zerahiah ben Isaac ben Shealtiel, of Barcelona (quite independently of the LXX!), has precisely the same exegesis, viz., What does *hofshī* "free" mean here? *lōʾ yifhád* "he does not fear." The reader will find it to his advantage to pore over and apply the sober statements to be found, e.g., in Driver's *Notes on . . . . Samuel*[2] (pp. lv–lxix) and Montgomery's *Daniel* (pp. 35–38).

It should be observed here that only infrequently will the critic meet an anomalous LXX rendering of the Hebrew also in rabbinic literature. It is primarily the critic's knowledge and "feel" of early Jewish exegesis which will help him comprehend the true character of the Jewish exegesis, which constitutes the LXX. Among the recent attempts in this direction may be cited: A. Kaminka, "Septuaginta und Targum zu Proverbia," *Hebrew Union College Annual*, VIII–IX (1931–32), 169–91; Ch. Heller, *Die Tychen-Wutzsche Transskriptionstheorie* (Berlin, 1932) and *The Septuagint References in Mandelkern's Concordance* ([in Hebrew] New York, 1943); S. Lieberman, *Greek in Jewish Palestine* (New York, 1942), chaps. i and ii, and "Two Lexicographical Notes," *Journal of Biblical Literature*, LXV (1946), 67–72; D. Daube, "κερδαίνω as a Missionary Term," *Harvard Theological Review*, XL (1947), 109–20.

pose that these same Jews wilfully and/or negligently altered and corrupted their Hebrew Bible between the time the LXX was made (third–first centuries B.C.) and the *floruit* of Theodotion and Aquila (second century A.D.) to the extent that the footnotes in *Biblia Hebraica*[2, 3], would indicate? Is it not so much more reasonable for scholars first to have made an independent and thorough study not only of the preserved Hebrew text of whatever book in the Bible they were commenting on, but also of the LXX? Had they done so—and not one of the better-known critics mentioned above, or most of their fellow textual critics, ever did so—they would not have abused the LXX so frequently and unjustifiably as to create from it a Hebrew *Vorlage* which never existed outside their own imagination. They should have realized that there must be something fundamentally wrong with an approach to the LXX such as theirs which resulted in such a far-reaching divergence between the preserved Hebrew text, on the one hand, and, on the other, the Hebrew text which they derived from the LXX.

6. From the foregoing it will have become clear why the writer believes that a real and urgent need for the textual criticism of the Hebrew Bible is the proper analysis of the LXX and of its daughter-versions in relation to it. Very much has already been accomplished in such works as Wellhausen's *Der Text der Bücher Samuelis* (1871); S. R. Driver's unexcelled *Notes on . . . . Samuel*[2] (1913) and footnotes to Deuteronomy, Joshua, and Ecclesiastes in *Biblia Hebraica*[2]; Rahlfs's *Septuaginta-Studien* (1904–11)—studies in the books of Kings and Psalms—and *Studie über den griechischen Text des Buches Ruth* (1922); Dhorme's *Le Livre de Job* (1926); Montgomery's *International Critical Commentary on Daniel* (1927) and forthcoming commentary on *Kings* in the same series; Margolis' *The Book of Joshua in Greek* (1931——); Ziegler's excellent *Untersuchungen zur Septuaginta des Buches Isaias* (1934); and Bewer's footnotes to Ezekiel in *Biblia Hebraica*[3].[14a]

14a. The work of Peter Katz should not go unnoted here. Cf. such articles of his as in the *Theologische Literaturzeitung*, LXI (1936), 265–87; *ibid.*, LXIII (1938), 32–34; *Journal of Theological Studies*, XLVII (1946), 30–33, 166–69; "Eyes to the Blind, Feet to the Lame," in the German Refugee Pastors' Volume in honor of the Bishop of Chichester (Cambridge, 1942); *Journal of Biblical Literature*, LXV (1946), 319–24; and an unpublished book on the text of the Septuagint.

When biblical scholarship comes to realize the many and serious shortcomings in Kittel's *Biblia Hebraica*, a grand opportunity will arise for biblical societies in the United States and Canada to organize and sponsor the sort of major project which should replace it. Time alone will tell whether or not we shall successfully meet the challenge.

THE RISE AND FALL OF THE (TYCHSEN-)WUTZ TRANSCRIPTION THEORY

7. The two decades between the end of World War I and the beginning of World War II saw both the resurrection of an interesting theory and its demise. It was in 1772 that the learned and eccentric Olaus Gerhard Tychsen (1734–1815) first advanced the rather novel theory that the LXX translation of the Hebrew Bible (as also the versions of Aquila, Theodotion, and Symmachus) was made from a text written not in Hebrew but in Greek characters (see his *Tentamen de variis codicum Hebraicorum Vet. Test. MSS. generibus* [Rostochii], Sec. I, pp. 59–134). Tychsen based his theory on a fair amount of inductive material and theoretical reasoning, but no one else followed it up in any detail. Passing reference to Tychsen's *Tentamen* is about all one finds in the nineteenth century, and that in few works (cf., e.g., Eichhorn, *Einleitung in das Alte Testament*[3] [Leipzig, 1803], I, 249–50; König, *Einleitung in das Alte Testament* [Bonn, 1893] p. 92, n. 1; Frankel, *Vorstudien*, pp. 31–32, n. *r*, 183, n. *j*, 204–5, n. *c;* Blau, *Zur Einleitung in die heilige Schrift* [Budapest, 1894], pp. 80 ff.).

8. In 1925 (Part II was published in 1933) there appeared the entirely independent work by Franz Xavier Wutz (1883–1938) of the Catholic Philosophico-theological Institute in Eichstätt, *Die Transkriptionen von der Septuaginta bis zu Hieronymus*, advancing essentially the same theory but basing it on a mass of evidence and drawing many far-reaching conclusions. Rudolf Kittel, editor of *Biblia Hebraica*[2], greeted the work in the following words (*Deutsche Literaturzeitung*, Vol. XLVI [1925], cols. 657–64): ". . . . *amicus Plato*, *amica 'Biblia Hebraica,' magis amica veritas* [col. 659]. . . . . Meine Absicht ist nicht, zu zensieren, sondern die Leser auf eine grosse weittragende Entdeckung hinzuweisen,

die vielleicht bestimmt ist, eine gewaltige Revolution in unserer ganzen Bibelforschung, der griechischen wie der hebräischen, hervorzurufen [col. 664].''[15] More skeptical were the comments, e.g., of Margolis (*Jewish Quarterly Review*, XVI [1925–26], 117–25) and Montgomery (*Daniel*, p. 27, n. 2). Since most of the important literature on the subject has been cited on pages 378–79 of J. L. Seeligmann's excellent review article cited in note 2, the writer will limit himself here to but a few observations.

a) In his very stimulating work, *Zur Einleitung in die heilige Schrift* (pp. 89–90), Ludwig Blau demonstrated the use of transliterations into Greek of the Hebrew text of the Pentateuch and of those portions of the Prophets and the Hagiographa that were read in the Synagogue as Haftarot and Megillot. And both Epiphanius (in the so-called "essay" *De mensuris et ponderibus*, sec. 7) and a Latin scholium found in an Arabic manuscript of the Pentateuch (Hody, *De Bibliorum textibus originalibus* [1705], p. 597) attest to the use of the second column of the many-columned Bible of Origen (viz., the vocalization in Greek characters of the consonantal Hebrew text of the first column) by Christians who could not read the first column.[16] A priori, therefore, Wutz's theory is reasonable enough.

b) Certainly, in this case "the proof of the pudding is in the eating." In the decade and a half following the appearance of Wutz's work, so many scholars published detailed, critical studies of various words and passages discussed by Wutz that his transcription theory has already become nothing more than a curiosity. P. A. H. de Boer (*Research into the Text of I Samuel I–XVI* [Amsterdam, 1938], p. 86) has put it into classical form: ". . . . he [viz., Wutz] is caught in a vicious circle, when he . . . . speaks in his final conclusion, which gives a remarkable agreement of G [= the LXX] and M [= the Massoretic Hebrew text], of: 'Be-

15. It will be seen even from this brief excerpt that the *Philadelphia Ledger* of April 25, 1925, was not justified in paraphrasing Kittel's review of Wutz to the effect that "his own life's work of research [in biblical research] had been rendered worthless."

16. On the proposition that the columnar order of Origen's many-columned Bible was determined by pedagogic considerations, see the *Jewish Quarterly Review*, XXVII (1936–37), 137–49, to which the writer can now add considerably more data. This view has been accepted most recently by Giovanni Cardinal Mercati, *Biblica*, XXVIII (1947), notes on pp. 6 f.; cf. also his *Nuove note di lett ratura biblica e cristiana antica*, p. 145, n. 3.

stätigung der Richtigkeit der Methode.' This agreement is no more than an agreement of G, revised by Wutz, with M, revised by Wutz!"[17]

c) It has not generally been noted, however, that Wutz himself gave up his transcription theory. It is true that Wutz did not admit this openly, but on pages 15–16 of his commentary on *Das Buch Job* (1939), where "Septuaginta und Urtext" are discussed, the reader will learn that the LXX of Job, along with Psalms—the key book in the Bible for Wutz's theory—was made directly from a Hebrew text, no mention being made at all of any transcription text (cf. *Journal of Biblical Literature*, LIX [1940], 529–31).

THE LXX AS A SOURCE FOR THE SEMANTICS AND LINGUISTICS OF BIBLICAL HEBREW

9. It has long been known that any ancient primary translation of the Hebrew Bible constitutes an important source for the determination of the meaning and grammatical form and function of words and combinations of words in biblical Hebrew; those rabbis of the Talmudic period who were interested in determining the form and meaning of some biblical word must have turned to the Greek and Aramaic translations for aid. The Jewish biblical philologians of the Golden Era in Spain and other countries under Moslem influence, who knew little or no Greek, made extensive and systematic use of the Targumim (as of Arabic) with that end in view. In recent times much work has been done by commentators in the use of the LXX and Targumim for the grammar of biblical Hebrew, usually in complete ignorance of the work already accomplished almost a millennium earlier by such lexicographers, grammarians, and exegetes as Saadia, David ben Abraham, Yefet ben ᶜAlī, Judah ben David Hayyūj, Abulwalīd Merwān ibn Janāḥ, and many others, not to mention the "Big Three"—Rashi, Abraham ibn Ezra, and David Qimḥi.[18]

17. W. F. Albright's study of "The List of Levitic Cities" in Joshua, chap. 21 and I Chronicles, chap 6 (see end of n. 6 above) has convinced him that it is impossible to operate with Wutz's transcription theory (cf. pp. 50–51 and nn. 4 and 6).

18. It is a pity that one is justified in adding the words "and their modern successors" to this statement by A. Eustace Haydon: "Unfortunately, the immense library of linguistic knowledge, the brilliant achievements of the Jews in biblical scholarship, were ignored by the medieval Schoolmen" (pp. 240–41 of his chapter on "The Influence of Medieval Ju-

As in medieval, so also in modern, times the biblical scholar is not infrequently a commentator, lexicographer, and grammarian rolled into one (cf., e.g., the scholars mentioned just above and, in modern times, Gesenius, Böttcher, Stade, König, S. R. Driver, Briggs). Withal, there is very much more work which remains to be done.

10. Of course, the cognate languages are a primary source for the etymology and semantic history of biblical Hebrew. Yet by themselves they are not sufficient; the usage of the word(s) involved, within the Bible itself, is paramount (cf., e.g., the pertinent remarks of Professor Meek, *Journal of Religion*, XXI [1941], 408–9). For this usage such early Jewish primary versions of the Hebrew Bible as the LXX and Targumim constitute a source no less primary than the cognate languages and should be used together with them. As cases in point, cf. Otto Eissfeldt, "Der Maschal im Alten Testament" Beihefte zur *Zeitschrift für die alttestamentliche Wissenschaft*, XXIV (1913), 21–25; Robert Stieb, "Die Versdubletten des Psalters," *Zeitschrift für die alttestamentliche Wissenschaft*, LVII (1939), 102–10 (biblical *sělāḥ̥* according to the LXX); Orlinsky on *tpś*, "lay hold of," in *Jewish Quarterly Review*, XXXIV (1943–44), 281 ff., and XXXV (1944–45), 351–54; Israel Lévi, "La Racine *ᶜyp-yᶜp* et sa traduction dans la Septante," *Revue des études juives*, LXIV (1912), 142–45; S. H. Blank, "The Septuagint Renderings of Old Testament Terms for Law," *Hebrew Union College Annual*, VII (1930), 259–83; C. H. Dodd, *The Bible and the Greeks* (London, 1935), Part I, pp. 3–95, "The Religious Vocabulary of Hellenistic Judaism," *passim;* Georg Bertram, "Der Sprachschatz der Septuaginta und der des hebräischen Alten Testaments," *Zeitschrift für die alttestamentliche Wissenschaft*, LVII (1939), 85–101; N. H. Snaith, *The Distinctive Ideas of the Old Testament* (Philadelphia, 1946), chap. viii.

11. Everyone knows that the phonology and morphology of biblical Hebrew are much better analyzed than is the syntax.[19]

---

daism on Christianity," in *Environmental Factors in Christian History*, ed. McNeill, Spinka, and Willoughby [Chicago, 1939]).

19. See most recently Professor Meek's presidential address, *Journal of Biblical Literature*, LXIV (1945), 1–13.

Our knowledge of this phase of biblical Hebrew would be considerably increased if the LXX and Targumim were studied more carefully from the point of view of grammar. In a forthcoming article in the *Journal of the American Oriental Society* (Vol. LXVII, No. 2 [April–June, 1947]) the writer has made extensive use of these primary versions to help determine the presence and widespread use in biblical Hebrew of the verbal noun.

12. This continent could have been foremost in the study of the Greek and Latin transcriptions of the Hebrew Bible in the intertestamental period; the writer has in mind the studies of Margolis, Speiser, Sperber, and Staples. The Old World, between the two world wars, contributed to this aspect of Greek and Hebrew through the writings of Pretzl and Wutz, and now there has come to hand the most detailed *Studien über hebräische Morphologie und Vokalismus auf Grundlage . . . . der zweiten Kolumne der Hexapla* . . . . (Leipzig, 1943), by Einar Brønno, with full discussion both of the hexaplaric material and of the treatment of this material at the hands of the aforementioned scholars.[19a]

THE LXX AS A LANGUAGE IN ITS OWN RIGHT

13. It is only since the turn of the century that the LXX has come to be regarded as a language which really lived in the mouths of people. It is no longer considered to be an artificially contrived vehicle for expressing the Hebrew Bible in Greek form. As is well known, it is essentially the discovery of so many Greek papyri deriving from the Mediterranean world of the intertestamental period which has given us the correct perspective, as the generation preceding ours was thrilled to discover in Adolf Deissmann's *Licht vom Osten* (as also in his [*Neue*] *Bibelstudien*).[20]

19a. See also Giovanni Cardinal Mercati, *Nuove note di letteratura biblica e cristiana antica*, chap. i; *Il problema della colonna II dell' Esaplo* (Vatican City, 1947; reprinted from *Biblica*, XXVIII [1947], 1–30, 173–215), with reference in the Post Scriptum on p. 75 to a work I have not yet seen, G. Lisowsky, *Die Transskriptionen der hebräischen Eigennamen des Pentateuchs in der Septuaginta* (Basel, 1940).

20. One should be careful to distinguish between the form and the substance of the LXX. This is brought out clearly by placing side by side these two statements from "Jewish and Greek Elements" by Ralph Marcus (*Louis Ginzberg Jubilee Volume*, English section [New York, 1945]), pp. 233 and 244: ". . . . the language of the LXX is part of the Egyptian Koiné and differs from contemporary pagan Greek only because it is translation-Greek

14. The Greek of the New Testament has been rather well studied in the light of the Greek of the classical, Hellenistic, Roman, and Byzantine periods; this is, however, not true at all of the Greek of the Old Testament. An excellent beginning in this direction was made by that careful scholar, Edwin Hatch, in his *Essays in Biblical Greek;*[21] of especial interest are his Essays II ("Short Studies of the Meanings of Words in Biblical Greek" [pp. 36–93]) and III ("On Psychological Terms in Biblical Greek" [pp. 94–130]). In 1916 there appeared Karl Huber's very useful *Untersuchungen über den Sprachcharakter des griechischen Leviticus* (Giessen), following upon Martin Flashar's very fine "Exegetische Studien zum Septuagintapsalter" in 1912 (*Zeitschrift für die alttestamentliche Wissenschaft*, Vol. XXXII). In 1926 Martin Johannessohn published (in *Zeitschrift für vergleichende Sprachforschung*, LIII, 161–212) a detailed study of "Das biblische *καὶ ἐγένετο* und seine Geschichte"; and in 1942–43 (*Zeitschrift für die alttestamentliche Wissenschaft*, LIX, 129–84) he supplied the corollary, "Die biblische Einführungsformel *καὶ ἔσται*"; these studies must be consulted by anyone who wants to study the syntax of biblical Hebrew. Worthy of note is *προφήτης*, *Eine sprach- und religionsgeschichtliche Untersuchung* (Giessen, 1927) by Erich Fascher, especially chapter iii (pp. 102–65). Easily the finest study of the LXX per se of any book in the Bible is Joseph Ziegler's *Untersuchungen zur Septuaginta des Buches Isaias* (1934).[22]

---

and not because the Jewish translators spoke a peculiar Jewish Greek jargon" and ". . . . the Greek elements of the LXX are merely superficial and decorative while the Jewish elements are deep-lying, central and dominant." There has just come to hand F. Büchsel's "Die griechische Sprache der Juden in der Zeit der Septuaginta und des Neuen Testaments," *Zeitschrift für die alttestamentliche Wissenschaft*, LX (1944), 132–49. Cf. also S. E. Johnson, *Journal of Biblical Literature*, LVI (1937), 331–45

21. Not to be overlooked even now are the labors of Schleusner, *Novus thesaurus philologico-criticus sive lexicon in LXX et reliquos interpretes Graecos . . . . Veteris Testamenti* (5 vols.; Leipzig, 1820-21).

22. Also to be consulted are the works of Dodd and Bertram, cited at the end of sec. 10 above. It will readily be seen that no attempt has been made here to catalogue everything that has been done in recent decades on this aspect of the LXX, e.g., E. Schwyzer, "Altes und Neues zu (hebr.-)griech. *σάββατα* (griech.-)lat. sabbata usw.," *Zeitschrift für vergleichende Sprachforschung*, LXII (1934), 1–16; A. Fridrichsen, "*ἰσόψυχος* [Ps. 55(54):14]," *Symbolae Osloenses*, XVIII (1938), 42–49; W S. van Leeuwen, *Eirene in het Nieuwe Testament:*

15. What H. G. Meecham has done for the Greek of *The Letter of Aristeas* (Manchester, 1935) and what Ziegler has done for the LXX of Isaiah, it is important that scholars do for the LXX throughout. And it should be noted that it must be primarily the Old Testament scholar who must perform this task; unfortunately, the scholar who comes to this task from the classical side lacks the specialized training which is so necessary for the proper treatment of the Greek-Hebrew of the Bible.

Limitation of space prevents the writer from touching on other aspects of the LXX, e.g., the *alleged* tendency on the part of the LXX translators to avoid the anthropomorphisms and anthropopathisms in their Hebrew original (cf. the *Crozer Quarterly*, XXI [1944], 156–60); the width of the columns in the earliest manuscripts of the LXX; the kind of alphabet used in the Hebrew *Vorlage* of the LXX (cf. the *Biblical Archaeologist*, IX [1946], 31–33). However, the interested reader will find abundant food for thoughtful digestion in the splendid review article by J. L. Seeligmann (cited at the end of n. 2 above).[23]

Een semasiologische, exegetische Bijdrage op grond van de Septuaginta en de joodsche Literatuur (Wageningen, 1940); cited from *Zeitschrift für die alttestamentliche Wissenschaft*, LVIII (1940–41), 153.

23. The writer has refrained from citing anywhere Otto Stählin's detailed contribution to Wilhelm von Christ's *Geschichte der griechischen Litteratur*, ed. Wilhelm Schmid [6th ed.; München, 1920]), II, 1 [= Vol. VII of Iwan von Müller's *Handbuch der klassischen Altertums-Wissenschaft*), for the simple reason that in no one section of this reference monograph (pp. 535–656, "Die hellenistisch-jüdische Litteratur") is there any indication that the vast range of the fundamentally important literature produced by the Jews in Hebrew and Aramaic in the postbiblical period has been worked. The primary source, which is the rabbinic literature, has remained a closed book to Stählin. Such a procedure is tantamount to utilizing only the rabbinic sources for a study of the New Testament period in the Greco-Roman world! Nor is it only this procedure of "omission" which vitiates so much in the monograph under discussion; there is also the no less grave error of "commission," viz., the prejudice against the idea that the Jews in the intertestamental period could and did write reliable history. It is the direct continuation of the work and spirit of Schürer (himself an able scholar who, however, was devoid of any direct knowledge and use of the all-important rabbinic literature), who branded so much of the literature which he did not know directly as "Jewish Propaganda under a Heathen Mask" when, in reality, Schürer, himself was guilty of "anti-Jewish propaganda under a scholarly mask." American scholarship has before itself the important and urgent task of re-writing and understanding correctly the history and literature of the intertestamental period, of which the LXX is a part.

SEPTUAGINTAL STUDIES IN THE MID-CENTURY

THEIR LINKS WITH THE PAST AND THEIR PRESENT TENDENCIES

P. KATZ

ONE HUNDRED AND THIRTY YEARS ago J. F. Schleusner was able to produce extensive Lexica both of the Septuagint (LXX) and the New Testament. Today such a feat seems almost to belong to the realm of fairy tales. No N.T. student is now prepared to follow his example. In this age of specialization both O.T. and N.T. studies have been branching out widely, without much regard for the LXX, though the LXX is by nature a connecting link between them both.

The contributors to this symposium, however special their chosen subjects may be, all enjoy a common privilege: they are addressing a body of fellow-students who are familiar with their problems and know how to assess the possible value of forthcoming solutions. The field of N.T. studies is well circumscribed. Its map therefore is always before the eyes of the writers, to whatever great lengths their special subject may carry them. They are geared to a common task of teaching, which links them both to the past and future. There is continuity, due to a large extent to the necessity of elementary instruction and its requirement for handbooks at all stages. There are examinations and there are chairs.

This is not so, however, in the field of Septuagintal studies. The absence of professorships limits regular teaching and deprives Biblical scholars of useful neighbourly consultation. Hence a note of uncertainty is sounded whenever the LXX is touched upon. Even when problems are rightly seen and fully treated, it is often forgotten that, seen primarily from the point of view of the LXX, these problems may present very different aspects. The learned literature provides,

Reprinted from *The Background of the New Testament and its Eschatology* [Festschrift C. H. Dodd], ed. W. D. Davies and D. Daube. Cambridge Univ. Press, 1956.

alas, little guidance. It is significant that Swete's *Introduction* was never brought up to date nor replaced.[1] No wonder that studies published in monographs are frequently erratic, a fact that can make reviewing an invidious task. This fact points to an absence of co-ordination and common understanding, and much of real promise fails to find a ready response in the wider circles of Biblical scholarship. There will certainly be a change for the better as soon as the basic principles which have led to recent progress have been stated in an up-to-date introduction to the study of the LXX.

It would be to no purpose merely to pass in review a number of important publications and attempt to assess what is new and useful in them. Rather we should try to fix some point from which a new departure will be readily understood by the N.T. student. If that point is well chosen, juxtaposition of past and present methods will expose their differences in full relief.

There is a period that will serve us well in this respect. In the 1880's there was a definite break both in the study of the N.T. and that of the LXX. Those years saw the conclusion of Westcott and Hort's N.T. Text and Introduction, the first critically established and carefully substantiated edition, which brought to an end the domination of the Received Text. Text and grammar had been examined with great circumspection, their rules being laid down in a masterly poised code of law, as it were. This work left its impression on all subsequent study, for it was the first to offer definite standards with which to contend. What has been done textually since then is adjustment rather than refutation. It has been different with the grammatical factors. Here the reaction was bound to be more violent.

The same 1880's witnessed a break in Septuagintal work. Again it was Hort who gave the first impulse. As soon as his mind was set free from the 'many long years' preparation of the N.T., he turned to the LXX and eventually drew up a scheme which resulted in the Cambridge editions of Swete and of Brooke and McLean. There was, however, a great difference in method. While the N.T. was

[1] A promising first step has been taken in Part II of B. J. Roberts' book, *The Old Testament Text and Versions* (Cardiff, 1951), pp. 101–87. Cf. E. Vogt's review in *Biblica*, vol. XXXII (1951), pp. 441 ff., and mine, in *T.L.Z.* vol. LXXVI (1951), cols. 535 ff.

issued in a critical edition, the LXX, a long neglected text, was to be edited in the provisional form of a reliable collection of the evidence, leaving the reconstruction of a critical text to subsequent endeavours. Caution was certainly well advised, and the edition was timely, as it involved a break with the Received Text of the Sixtine, the place of which was to be taken by the true text of Vat. B,[1] or its next best substitute. It was Hort's hope that each of the four volumes of the larger edition might take no more than five years' preparation, and if this edition could have been completed in this time, a solid basis for work on a critical text would have been created. Hort's assumption, however, that the collations of minuscules in the Holmes and Parsons edition, together with those done by Lagarde, might suffice, proved mistaken, and the necessary search for MSS. and their collation took much more time, so that by 1940 the edition was only half finished.

Nevertheless, Hort's feeling that there was need for an edition to be completed within a short space of time was correct; for there were early forebodings of a development in the direction of a definitively constituted text in the same 1880's. In 1883 Lagarde's first and only volume of Lucian's recension was published.[2] As we can see now, its shortcomings vindicated Hort's more cautious plan. It was, however, the first sign of a development which, as soon as it achieved maturity, was bound to make mere collections of evidence obsolete.

Thus the common denominator of both N.T. and LXX studies was their interest in establishing the text. As this interest receded in N.T. studies, concern for the problems of the LXX correspondingly waned. Texts are, however, tools of primary importance. It is therefore worth while devoting more space to these two types of LXX editions, for they point to different lines of procedure, neither of which can be said wholly to belong to the past.

[1] The Sixtine was printed from a still existing copy of the Aldine with superficial corrections from Vat. B and other MSS. (A. Rahlfs, *Z.A.W.* vol. XXXIII (1913), pp. 30–46; M. L. Margolis, *J.B.L.* vol. XXXVIII (1919), pp. 51 f.; J. Ziegler, *Biblica*, vol. XXVI (1945), pp. 49 ff.).

[2] *Librorum Veteris Testamenti Canonicorum Pars Prior Graece* (Göttingen, 1883).

Septuagintal studies in the mid-century

I. THE FIRST GENERATION

(*a*) *The Cambridge Procedure*

Hort's scheme provided for two editions, each to be done by a distinguished Cambridge N.T. scholar, H. B. Swete. The first was to be 'portable'. It was to give to the ordinary reader for the first time a text based on the MSS. and, at the same time, to serve as an instrument for collation. The second 'larger' edition was to present the same text but, in addition, 'to give the variations of all the Greek uncial MSS., of select Greek cursives, of the more important Ancient Versions, and of the quotations made by Philo and the earlier and more important ecclesiastical writers'. The text was to attempt no approach to an hypothetical original text behind the evidence. Whenever it departs from the leading MS. where this is corrupt, this is done merely to shorten the annotation. Brooke and McLean (BM), who were entrusted with the task after Swete had felt unable to do also the larger edition, gradually introduced more departures from the MS. than Swete had done; but they stopped half-way. What has been shown for I Esdra[1] applies to all books: in many passages they retain individual corruptions of B* in close proximity to other similar corruptions which they correct, though all equally demanded correction. It is, however, intelligible why the editors refrained from broadening their approach. They avoided the temptation of emendation. The result is an uneven compromise between diplomatic reproduction and the exclusion of the most obviously intolerable readings. In rare instances Swete and after him BM took the desperate step of 'emending' singular readings of B* without regard for the correct reading of the other MSS.[2]

The true test of diplomatic reproductions is reliability. Swete's second and third editions were much improved by fresh collations by E. Nestle; yet M. L. Margolis in preparing his edition of the Greek Joshua considered it 'desirable, in view of the inaccuracies in Swete's apparatus', to base his work on entirely fresh collations.[3] Rahlfs found Swete's collations of the Psalms 'fairly reliable', but inferior

[1] *T.L.Z.* vol. LXII (1937), cols. 341 ff.

[2] *Ibid.* col. 343. In I Esdr. viii. 67 (71) B reads τας, an obvious corruption of γάρ. Both editions insert an unwarranted †τινας† into the text.

[3] *J.A.O.S.* vol. XXXI (1911), p. 366.

to those of Lagarde's *Psalterii Graeci Quinquagena Prima.*[1] J. Ziegler expresses his disappointment that Swete's edition, so beautiful in appearance and so full of the most detailed information, should be marred by many mistakes.[2] Nevertheless, it represented real progress at its time. The remarkable thing is that the criticisms quoted above all came from editors of critical texts. Their evaluation of individual MSS. was based on first-hand study and their work on MSS. groups accustomed them to recheck all strange readings in the collation of individual MSS. Even a diplomatic edition can be done to perfection only by those whose work enables them to look behind the façade.

Brooke and McLean based their edition on fresh collations (many provided by Rahlfs' Göttingen LXX Bureau which they checked), attaining a much higher standard of accuracy. Nevertheless, Margolis published thirty pages of 'Corrections in the Apparatus of the Book of Joshua' alone.[3] At times their demarcation of the lemmata in the apparatus could have been improved by a knowledge of the recensional problems. In spite of these defects their presentation of the evidence is a solid piece of work, and many students have gratefully profited by its merits.

There are, however, some points in which the methods chosen

[1] *Sept.-Stud.* vol. II, p. 4.

[2] 'The text is tolerably well reproduced; among the MSS. the collations of B and S (after Tischendorf) are the best; A is frequently recorded inexactly. The collation of Q is completely insufficient, in spite of its great importance for the prophetical books; for it offers a good text of Isaiah, Jeremiah and the Minor Prophets, and subsequently was worked over after a hexaplaric MS. by a corrector, who has marked the hexaplaric additions and omissions by asterisks and obeli and himself has added plenty of hexaplaric readings and, more especially, those of the more recent translators. Swete certainly has many notes about Q^{a} and Q^{mg} (=corrector of Q), but many are omitted or wrongly recorded; frequently the hexaplaric notes are not given, and the signs for transposition are not even recognized. In Jon. ii. 3 ειπεν] + ως Q^{mg} should read ειπεν] + ωδη ϛ′ Q^{mg}: it is the superscription of the sixth Ode, =Jon. ii. 3–10.' After giving his re-collation of Amos, he comes to the conclusion that 'Swete's edition is insufficient a basis for scholarly investigation, since textual criticism calls for the most extreme accuracy.... If only he had checked his collations with the edition of Cozza-Luzi these mistakes could have been avoided from the very first, and much additional material added. Unfortunately, reviewers did not consult the MSS. either and consequently the new editions and reprints have been published in this deficient form to this very day' (*Z.A.W.* vol. LX (1944), pp. 126ff.).

[3] *J.B.L.* vol. XLIX (1930), pp. 234–64.

were regrettable. One was taken over from Swete. Both Cambridge editions professedly based their text on B. But the evidence of B is often distorted by the inclusion and treatment on an almost equal footing of its correctors, the latest of whom may be dated in the fourteenth century. When the readings of B* appear implausible, three of his correctors are cited as substitutes. Often the work of a corrector cannot be dated, but it is of a much more recent date than other MSS. which, according to the principle underlying the editions, should be preferred to B*. More particularly, there are sets of corrections which, far from merely restoring a blunder of the first hand, replace its text by that of a different recension. In such instances the corrector's reading merely attests a recension for which there are earlier and more reputable witnesses. This has been overlooked by the editors who have neglected the truly editorial problems. Once the strict reproduction of evidence was abandoned, the Cambridge editions became involved in the meshes of the LXX recensions and the editors were caught unawares. But how could they be aware? Unless the basic problems posed by a text are constantly in the mind of an editor, not even a pre-critical edition can be done to perfection.

If subjectivity enters the field here where one would least expect it, in the treatment of the secondary versions of the LXX objectivity goes much too far. The reason for their use is to make available to the critic forms of the Greek text which have survived only in translations. All we want to know is what Greek underlay them. All the secondary versions are at points corrupt and remote from the original Greek. Here the student requires critical conjectures about the underlying variants. It is unfortunate that BM cite only the corrupt texts, even when the original editors have intimated solutions which might appear quite natural to those familiar with the language in question.

I give an example from the Old Latin. For II Reg. vii. 14 BM record 'αφαις] *actibus* Tyc-codd'. Here 'codd' points to a different reading in the edition. Burkitt has suggested the obvious emendation *tactibus* = ἁφαῖς. No reference therefore to Tyconius is required, for an edition of the LXX is not concerned with the incidental corruptions of the versions, but only with evidence for Greek variants. The Lyons Old Latin abounds with similar corruptions, most of which have been corrected by U. Robert. BM ignore this and inflate their apparatus with superfluous 'variants'.[1] The student who knows Latin finds an easy solution but Latin renderings of readings from the Oriental versions pose a different problem. Are they errors or variants? The editor, not the unfortunate student should give the answer. In an edition done on recensional lines it would be indicated whether the Oriental witness be supported by some Greek evidence. This should have been indicated in BM too.

In spite of Nestle's warning, Swete's edition was taken by many readers to be *the* Septuagint and gave the impression that in fact there are two rival texts, those of B and of A. These MSS. came to be considered as individual quantities, homogeneous throughout the LXX and consequently offering a clear-cut choice to the 'critical' reader. N.T. students will be reminded here of attempts to define the characteristics of MSS. which in fact reflect the work of generations of copyists with their varying whims and idiosyncrasies. The same conception underlies Procksch's strange imagery about the path to the source of the LXX leading through a porch, the two pillars of which are B and A.[2] When the early Chester Beatty papyri of the LXX were first discussed scholars asked: 'Do they give a B-text or an A-text?' *Tertium non datur.* This fallacy sprang from a misunderstanding of Swete's purpose in selecting only a few MSS. for his text. Much of this misunderstanding survives in the apparatus of *Biblia Hebraica* (*BH*3). BM's presentation of an abundance of deliberately unanalysed information had the opposite effect. L. Koehler described it as 'but a roaring sea of variants', in which cabin boy and master mariner alike perish; for the number of seamen able to navigate through this material is small. Swete's Introduction indicates that a reliable chart was not yet available in spite of the wide range of information at hand, which was a kind of antiquarian stocktaking. The student of the O.T. or N.T. cannot, however, dispense with critical guidance which must necessarily come from quarters

[1] In using Field's Hexapla, they draw on his text only and neglect the rich notes in which he offers his observations and emendations. This shortcoming was anticipated by the Concordance.

[2] Elsewhere he alleges many more supports. In his attempt to restore a metrical text of almost the whole of Genesis he selects any group of LXX MSS. which yields what he requires, retranslates their readings into Hebrew and presents them as the original Hebrew text!

the learned editors were bound to shun, by virtue of the very principles which they chose to adopt.

The Cambridge editions of the LXX are younger sisters of Westcott and Hort's N.T. They are the Cinderellas of the family. In the N.T. choices of readings were based on firmly established principles. Each decision rested on appropriate references to the introductory volume. The editors of the LXX had nothing of the kind to rely on and trusted vague analogies applied to a text centuries older and of a very different character. This is most noticeable when we now consider the grammatical aspect of both editions.

Grammar

Hort's Introduction devotes as much attention to matters of spelling as to recensional problems, for he regards them both as connected in a peculiar way. In his study of the N.T. recensions he had come to the conclusion that the group headed by BS (א) was far superior to the rest. In it he saw the pre-recensional, 'neutral' text. In matters of orthography he made some reservations,[1] but these do not prevent him from dealing with matters of spelling in close connection with the problems of textual criticism. To him spellings form as much a part of the evidence as variants in readings, so that he placed a high estimation on the spelling of MSS. which he regarded as textually superior. It never occurred to him that he was moving in a vicious circle when he believed his grammatical standards confirmed by the 'neutral' text from which they were taken. Text and editor had much in common; both deliberately refrained from extremes (which, in a text, is the unmistakable mark of *recension*). In fact spelling, except for the deliberate Atticizers of a later period, was obviously a matter of minor concern to ancient authors and copyists, and no one can distinguish spellings of copyists from those transmitted from the archetype.

In practice Hort's attitude was an uneasy compromise between his knowledge of Attic spelling and the evidence of MSS. which for other reasons had a just claim on his favour.[2] This uneasiness, which

[1] § 403; § 399 about B and S.

[2] He justified his own inconsistencies by the maxim: 'absolute uniformity belongs only to artificial times' (Intr. p. 308). Editing, however, involves a certain amount of standardizing, especially when it is claimed that itacisms have been corrected.

does him credit, has a curious way of upholding forlorn causes: 'Tabulation renders it morally certain that ἱστήκειν is nowhere a mere itacism.'[1] Here, if anywhere, we have 'the mistake of assuming the identity of the morally-acceptable with the historically-true.'[2] J. H. Moulton long ago gave the right answer: 'It is perfectly futile to follow our best uncials in printing abnormal forms like ἴδον for εἶδον and ἱστήκειν for εἱστήκειν.... The MS. evidence is not adequate proof that such forms really existed.'[3]

It is useful here to glance at the work of H. St J. Thackeray, the grammarian of the school. In fact he was much more than that: he was a co-editor with Brooke and McLean and a loving connoisseur of the whole range of Jewish Hellenists, was versed in Josephus and familiar with the papyri as well as with the grammars of Blass, Mayser, and J. H. Moulton but a thorough Hortian. Though he disposes of Hort's ἱστήκειν, yet on the same page (201) he tries to justify ἴδον and even offers alternative explanations for it. He considers the itacistic participle ἰδώς acceptable,[4] and is able to explain the slip ΑΝΟΡΑΣ (I Reg. viii. 22*a*) as 'a relic of the Epic ΑΝΕΡΑΣ'.[5] It was not by chance that he chose to postpone writing his chapter on word formation. Had he considered its problems in time, much of his chapters on phonetics and accidence would have read very differently. He made some attractive suggestions; for example, that for the translation some books were divided among two translators. Some of his observations, however, are based on Swete's edition, and earlier papyri which have since come to light change the picture. We now see that phenomena which Thackeray attributed to translators arose at a later stage of transmission and the same holds good of some of his grammatical points; for he regarded the Cambridge LXX as representative of primitive usage. For this reason also a new edition of his grammar would have to undergo far-reaching alterations.

Swete's few introductory remarks about spelling should be read in the light of Hort's principles. Brooke and McLean do not touch this point, for their text is usually Swete's. Swete's spelling and accentuation reveal much care and erudition. He candidly states,

[1] Appendix, p. 162b.

[2] C. J. Cadoux, *The Historic Mission of Jesus*, p. 3.

[3] *Grammar*, vol. II, p. 77.   [4] *Ibid.* p. 278 n. 2.   [5] *Ibid.* p. 150.

'It is premature to enter upon a detailed examination of the principles which direct the judgement in the acceptance or rejection of particular forms; and it is possible that not a few of the results to which the Editor has been led may be modified by further consideration'.[1] But when he further assures us that itacisms have been corrected, he is obviously unaware that numbers of sheer mistakes are left untouched. In fact, a list of them would amount to a fairly complete treatise on phonology. The rules underlying word formation are likewise ignored, in favour of traditional spellings, especially if those spellings are found in B*. This is a survival of another Hortian peculiarity: an exaggerated confidence in the first hand of B in matters of spelling, for in the last analysis their idea about what is correct derives from B*. Actually B* ought to be abandoned much more frequently. For example ἑώρων<ἠϝόρων and ἑόρακα<ϝεϝόρακα, though different, are the correct forms. Thackeray, relying on W. Veitch's rich and useful but philologically uncritical compilation,[2] considered ἑώρακα the 'older Attic form' and admitted both. He maintained that ἑώρακα is 'universal in the Pentateuch', but this can no longer be maintained in view of the Chester Beatty papyri. Here instances of the correct spelling have survived, and Sir Frederic Kenyon accordingly should not have supplied the lacunae from Swete. Our texts betray Hort's dislike of uniformity, III Reg. xx. 29 ἑώρακας; xxi. 13 ἑόρακας, both with B*. The rejected correct form of xx. 29 is duly recorded in BM's first apparatus of 'mistaken' spellings. Unfortunately, this edition never indicates what other MSS. share the mis-spellings noted in the first apparatus. Hence this edition, which purposely confines itself to a reliable record of all the details, nowhere enables the student of grammar to make sure how widely this kind of mistake is spread. The irony of it all is that there are all sorts of correct forms listed as mistaken spellings in the first apparatus.

The two determinants of Swete's orthographical presentation, grammar and his preference for the first hand of B, conflict. This was perhaps excusable in his first edition but with the rapid increase in knowledge it is hard to understand what purpose is served by perpetuating error in edition after edition. Such as it is, the larger

[1] *The Old Testament in Greek*, vol. I, p. xii.
[2] *Greek Verbs Irregular and Defective.*

edition would also have been a real boon if it had been completed before the First World War. If it is ever resumed the least to be hoped for is a thorough revision of these blemishes.

(*b*) *The Göttingen Procedure*

This all began with one man and one book, Lagarde's *Lucian.* His faithful pupil, who carried on the master's work after his premature death, judges that it was Lagarde's biggest failure. Rahlfs bases his judgment both on its leading principles and on the way in which it was produced.

Over a period of many years Lagarde was again and again attracted to the study of the LXX, but his approach to its problems underwent several radical changes. What is generally considered 'Lagarde's method' was only the last phase. The earlier ones became better known when, a hundred years after his birth, his personal papers and correspondence were opened.[1] As a young student he used to correct the Greek by the Hebrew which, he thought, had never undergone change. His *Anmerkungen zur griechischen Uebersetzung der Proverbien* (1863) started with his renowned axioms[2] and was a sober and penetrating critical work. In 1868, when editing *Hieronymi quaestiones hebraicae in libro Geneseos* and *Genesis graece*, he developed a plan for an edition of the LXX, worthy of an admirer of K. Lachmann whose edition of the N.T. was the first to ignore the Received Text and to substitute for it a fourth-century text. The plan was as follows. Because of the scarcity of uncials, full use was to be made of the early versions, but only after a thorough study of their methods of translation, as otherwise inferences about their originals would be rash. Related minuscules were to be grouped with a view to tracing the ancient uncials which were their direct or indirect parents.[3] All this sounds very familiar to the N.T. student of our

[1] A. Rahlfs, *Paul de Lagardes wissenschaftliches Lebenswerk, im Rahmen einer Geschichte seines Lebens dargestellt, Mitteil. d. Sept.-Unternehmens* (Berlin, 1928), Band 4, Heft 1.

[2] Quoted in Swete's *Introduction*, pp. 484 ff.

[3] There were to be three editions: (1) the pre-hexaplaric text of the LXX, without apparatus; (2) the hexaplaric text together with the remains of the more recent translations, fresh collations of which were to yield a rich harvest; and (3) a complete edition of the pre-hexaplaric text, giving the readings of the small or larger groups, with the mistakes of individual MSS. forming a second apparatus in smaller print.

day, whose work is done on identical lines. He cannot but be struck by this anticipation of modern principles and by the fact that they were boldly applied to the much neglected LXX.

The fresh material to which Rahlfs gives us access reveals the sad story how this plan came to be abandoned. Lagarde's ideas appealed to the great O.T. scholar Justus Olshausen who, in his capacity as a civil servant, recommended them to his chief, and the Minister offered Lagarde money to employ an assistant. During and immediately after the war of 1870, however, Lagarde could find no one to train and, being both impatient and impetuous, declined the offer which was never renewed. Similarly he declined repeatedly offers by British scholars, made at the suggestion of William Wright, to provide a yearly sum towards the formation of a bureau. He may have felt that his plans and ideas were far from final and, in fact, they were constantly changing.

In 1870 he advanced the novel idea of local, provincial texts but emphasized that this did not imply a preference for one recension to the exclusion of others, since each province merely perpetuated the text with which it was familiar. A few years later, however, he suggested printing the recensions of Lucian and Hesychius in parallel columns and referred to Jerome's statement in the *prologus galeatus* that about A.D. 400 there were 'three editions' or, as we would say, 'recensions' of the LXX: those of Hesychius in Alexandria and Egypt, of Lucian in Constantinople 'usque Antiochiam', and of Origen in Palestine. He not only abandoned his earlier view that this differentiation occurred spontaneously through force of circumstances, but, contrary to the historical evidence, he gave Jerome's words a meaning which Jerome never intended; he claimed that the provincial churches had official texts, imposed upon them 'under the control of the bishops'.

Lagarde's *Lucian* remained a torso. There never was a second volume nor an edition of the remaining recensions. The preparation of this volume was involved in awkward changes of plan, characteristic of Lagarde. He lived in deliberate isolation, yet longed for agreement and appreciation. He consulted no one but himself—worked hard and at an astounding pace, but was given to moods. His first plans were frequently too ambitious and required modification. The swing of the pendulum could be amazingly broad.

While doing the collations for his *Lucian* he became so satisfied that he had found the solution that he failed to sort his material and rushed prematurely into print. He began with an enormously inflated apparatus and when he saw its impracticability—he was his own publisher—he first reduced the annotation and finally abandoned it.[1] Thus his text 'could not be checked' (E. Nestle). As printer's copy he used one of his MS. transcriptions. The printing was done quickly and, as Rahlfs points out, the spacing still indicates the many changes which were introduced in the course of printing. He was half submerged in his material and in the end some of it was not used at all and instead of checking it carefully, he disfigured his text by many mistaken conjectures. He had fits of weariness with his work and disposed of it with undue haste.

The published text was welcomed by some as the true LXX, by others as the true Lucianic, but sober students sensed that it had something erratic about it. This was the root of the repeated assertion, even in our day, that 'Lagarde's method' has failed. In fact the edition was a distortion of the best that Lagarde had to teach. He never returned to these problems but went on publishing most useful detailed information. He complained himself that his 'Septuagint Studies have eaten up the Septuagint'.

So much for the story of the 1880's and it is amazing how remote it sounds. There were, however, things in common between the Cambridge and the Göttingen efforts. Nowhere was it recognized that MSS. are far from homogeneous throughout. Hence the reliance on B in Cambridge[2] and that on the Lucianic MSS. in Göttingen.[3] In both distinguished scholars worked tirelessly in isolation, without dividing work which even now that photographs of MSS. are readily available, seems to us indispensable.

[1] Lagarde tells the full story himself in *Ankündigung einer neuen Ausgabe...* (Göttingen, 1882).

[2] B is hexaplaric in Isaiah. Its text of Judges is unknown to Origen and may not have been in existence when he composed the Hexapla.

[3] Lagarde's *Lucian* becomes Lucianic first on p. 259, where there is a change in text between Ruth iv. 10 and iv. 11 (Rahlfs, *P. de Lagardes wiss. Lebenswerk*, p. 77).

2. THE SECOND GENERATION

Compared with the zeal with which N.T. students set to work to check, refine, or undo the results achieved by Westcott and Hort's N.T., there has been nothing in the field of the LXX except the painfully slow progress of BM. The amazing thing, however, is that after the apparent failure of Lagarde's long sustained efforts and extravagant claims, work along his lines was in fact not at its end. There was at first a period of apparent unresponsiveness but actually of serious preparation. Rahlfs tells the moving story of how Lagarde, immediately before his fatal operation, showed him all his unfinished work and developed his ideas as to how it should be continued. Rahlfs did not fully understand but learned soon afterwards that he was given the task of completing and editing Lagarde's last works.

It took the young Göttingen lecturer years before he got a firm hold of this vast field. It was not until the end of the century that his first two short articles appeared in the Göttingen *Nachrichten*.[1] In the second[2] he proved that the date of B must be later than 367 by observing that its content followed the Bible canon of Athanasius' 39th Festal Epistle. In 1901 he edited the Berlin MS. of the Sahidic Psalter with an extensive commentary. In 1904 he began his series of *Septuaginta-Studien*, 'dedicated to the memory of Paul de Lagarde'. Here he came to grips with Lagarde's unsolved problems. The first essay showed that min. 82 (= o BM) displays a text that is a mixture of Lucian (*L*) and the real LXX (𝔊), and that the 𝔊 readings are confined to one or more double pages each. The parent MS. had been a defective *L* MS., supplied from a 𝔊 MS. The second volume analysed the different recensions of the Greek Psalter, the third was a study of the Lucianic text of Kings. In both volumes the versions, especially the Old Latin, and the patristic quotations were treated with exemplary lucidity. Meanwhile the Septuaginta-Unternehmen of the Göttingen Academy had been founded on the initiative of R. Smend and J. Wellhausen, and the *Mitteilungen des Septuaginta-Unternehmens* took the place of Rahlfs' *Septuaginta-Studien*. Its

[1] Cf. Walter Bauer's obituary in *N.G.W.*, Jahresbericht 1935, pp. 60ff.

[2] 'Alter und Heimat der vaticanischen Bibelhandschrift', *N.G.W.*, Philos.-hist. Klasse (1899), pp. 72–9.

volumes reveal Rahlfs' skill as a teacher and director of research. Half of the contributions are by his pupils and none of them immature. The second volume gives a full account of the extant LXX MSS. with most useful additional lists.[1] In the first, which was published in the years 1909–15, Rahlfs' 120 pages on *The O.T. Lessons of the Greek Church* provide much more than its title would suggest (Ch. v, 'Contributions to an understanding of the Greek lectionary system'). Further, there are several editions of newly found MSS., all with full comment, including the edition of the hexaplaric marginal notes to Isa. i–xvi from min. 710. Its 582 footnotes form an incomparable introduction to the study of the more recent translators. The third volume offers Rahlfs' model of an analysis of all extant forms of the text of a single book and contains the important discovery of an hitherto unknown recension *R*, a source of the Catenae-recension *C*. To cover all the details Rahlfs chose the Book of Ruth which contains eighty-five verses only. There is no better introduction to the recensional problems of the LXX than this painstaking and unassuming study.

All this was done with a critical edition in mind. Its fate was more than once in the balance, owing to war and post-war conditions.[2] Rahlfs therefore had to do his editions of Ruth and Genesis on a reduced scale,[3] and it is evident that even the fuller edition of the Psalms[4] was originally planned as an *editio minor*. After the First World War he began an edition of the whole LXX on a much smaller scale, a 'German Swete', which was published immediately before his death in 1935. The plan was to base the text on the uncials BSA, but increasingly Rahlfs used additional sources, including the versions, all of which were at his command, and he set out to give the nearest possible approximation to the original at all points. In contrast to his master Lagarde he had no illusions, was an exact analyst and governed by a sure sense of what was possible. He never lost himself in speculation and knew how to get things done in time.

[1] *Verzeichnis der griechischen Handschriften des Alten Testaments*, Beiheft zu *N.G.W.*, Philos.-hist. Klasse (1914). The first volumes contain matter that can be found in *N.G.W.* too. From vol. IV onward there is only the separate edition, in *Mitteil. d. Sept.-Unternehmens*, which perished in the war.

[2] Cf. Rahlfs' Preface in the Stuttgart edition.

[3] *Das Buch Ruth griechisch*... (Stuttgart, 1922); *Genesis* (Stuttgart, 1926).

[4] *Psalmi cum Odis* (Göttingen, 1931).

He therefore did his work on the Psalms without first collating afresh the mass of late MSS., and his Stuttgart edition, though marking enormous progress in grammar and the constitution of a critical text, left much for his successors to do.[1] The wisdom of his policy was realized after his sudden death. L. Koehler, commenting on his Stuttgart edition, says: 'There are pieces of work in which all labour is lost, unless the author himself is able to complete them.'[2] Rahlfs left a complete edition. Its basic foundations are thoroughly sound, others can build on it. He was furthermore the only one among the specialists of the LXX who left behind him a school to continue his work.

There was a second editor who followed Lagarde's lead but quite independently of Rahlfs, his contemporary M. L. Margolis. His early publications were in German, but his main work was done in America where he taught at Dropsie College. His erudition was exceptionally wide, for he combined a first-hand knowledge of rabbinic exegesis with an expert's handling of classical philology, and could read the Oriental versions in their originals. He was almost forty when he began a series of brief studies on the LXX and its relation to the Hebrew text.[3] They are models of an intelligent use of the Concordance for the study of the Greek and Hebrew Bibles. For him the pursuit of single Greek words throughout the LXX and the comparative treatment of Greek and Hebrew idioms was the way to look over the translators' shoulders and become familiar with their difficulties and techniques. He felt strongly about the shortcomings of the big Concordance in the imprecise indication of Hebrew and Aramaic equivalents, the false economy of space in the Hebrew Index which gives hopelessly long arrays of sheer numbers instead of the Greek equivalents themselves, and the niggardly presentation of the hexaplaric material. This last item he planned to

[1] *T.L.Z.* vol. LXI (1936), cols. 265–87.

[2] *Neue Zürcher Zeitung*, 14 April 1935, no. 656.

[3] For the titles and much more detail I refer to H. M. Orlinsky, 'Margolis' Work in the Septuagint' (in *Max Leopold Margolis—Scholar and Teacher* (Philadelphia, 1952), pp. 35–44); to his monograph 'On the Present State of Proto-Septuagint Studies', *J.A.O.S.* vol. LXI (1941), pp. 81–91, also separate; and to his 'Current Progress and Problems in Septuagint Research' in *The Study of the Bible Today and Tomorrow* (Chicago, 1947), pp. 144–61, a survey not superseded by the present essay.

have redone on new lines by his students. Only Joseph Reider's Aquila Lexicon was completed and its manuscript was stored until the other portions of the work should be completed. We have therefore nothing but Reider's excellent thesis[1] and can only regret that Margolis' example has not encouraged other students to bring his original plan to completion.

He next turned to the study of the transliterations found in the LXX. From them, especially from the place-names of which there is an accumulation in Joshua xv and xvi, he discovered definite groups within the LXX MSS. and collected evidence for the pronunciation of the Hebrew.[2] He then decided to do a critical edition of the Greek Joshua, and thus became the first in the field to check Lagarde's brilliant surmises by a careful inductive procedure. A report of his first results dates from 1910;[3] another in 1927 is more detailed.[4] In the meantime he transcribed the elaborate edition, which was complete at his death in 1931. Four parts were published posthumously, in an autograph edition,[5] but the fifth, including his Introduction, appears unhappily to have been lost, as was a monograph on Masius' excerpts from the lost Syro-Hexaplar which Margolis' edition frequently quotes. Once again we must deplore the absence of any organization which could have spared this brilliant scholar many years of purely mechanical labour and enabled him to carry on his work. Posterity has been thus deprived of much that he could otherwise have achieved.

It is useful to compare Margolis' grouping with Rahlfs' in Ruth (1922), a work of which he betrays no knowledge.[6] The *BOL* groups are the same but the others differ and Margolis would have

[1] *Prolegomena to a Greek-Hebrew and Hebrew-Greek Index to Aquila* (Philadelphia, 1916).

[2] His pupil E. A. Speiser wrote an early thesis on 'The Pronounciation of Hebrew based chiefly on the Transliterations in the Hexapla', *J.Q.R.* 1925–6 ff.

[3] 'The Grouping of the Codices in the Greek Joshua', *J.Q.R.* vol. 1 (1910), pp. 259–63.

[4] 'Specimen of a new Edition of the Greek Joshua', in *Jewish Studies in Memory of Israel Abrahams* (New York, 1927), pp. 307–23.

[5] Paris, 1931–8.

[6] Margolis' E(gyptian) group is the pre-hexaplaric B q r (h o) 𝔈𝔅ℭ; his S(yrian) the Lucianic recension including 𝔏; his P(alestinian) Origen's recension which he divides into hexaplaric (G b c) and tetraplaric (x 𝔖 Onom.(d_2)). He adds a C(onstantinopolitan) group (A M N W l y b_2 122 68 71 (h o u) 𝔄, and a M(ixed) group, comprising F a i k m 64 18 128 461, the Catenae-MSS. e f j s v z 343 730 (= C), and u 509 (= E/a_2) 661 (= Δ_8). For the benefit of the reader I have transferred his

greatly profited by Rahlfs' analysis of Ruth,[1] and the apparatus criticus in his edition of Ruth (1922). Apparently there was no contact between the two scholars whose methods and aims had so much in common. Margolis devised a needlessly complicated presentation of the evidence, an elaboration of Lagarde's idea of printing the several recensions in parallel columns.[2] Its nine separate sets of annotation can be reduced to three without loss.[3] Rahlfs had demonstrated that the single apparatus used by classical students is able with careful arrangement to indicate at a glance even the most minute sporadic variants. His example would have greatly simplified Margolis' presentation.

Some of the finest American scholars adopted his method, foremost among them J. A. Montgomery, whose commentary on Daniel has an excellent chapter on the versions.

notation, which is on a par with von Soden's in the N.T., into that of BM and those MSS. not in BM into Rahlfs' symbols. *OLC* are the recensions as in Rahlfs, 𝔏 is the Old Latin, 𝔅 the Bohairic, ℭ the Coptic, 𝔈 the Ethiopian, 𝔖 the Syriac version.

[1] In Ruth, together with other MSS., M N y b_2 71 h u 𝔄, the majority of Margolis' Const. group, form a definite recension *R* which Rahlfs proved to be the source of the *C*(atenae) recension (cf. p. 190). Rahlfs further traced this recension *R* in Judges and Reg. In my *Philo's Bible* an effort has been made to show that the aberrant set of Pentateuchal quotations in Philo is identical in method with *R*. The fact that Margolis singled it out for Joshua was concealed by his unconventional notation. It provides, however, valuable addition to our knowledge and encourages us to study his edition. That Alex. A should form part of this group is astonishing and should be checked. It would also seem advisable to find out whether the Catenae-MSS., instead of being relegated to the limbo of 'Mixed' texts, do not rather represent a recension of their own, as they do elsewhere. It is generally 'mixed', but distinctive. Commenting upon his Const. group Margolis surmised that it may have 'made use of the common text prevalent in Palestine. This Pal. *koine* was only slightly touched upon by Theodotion—*Urtheodotion* would accordingly be nothing but the Palestinian *koine*'. This argument is particularly infelicitous. Theodotion lived no later than the end of the second century and it is advisable not to speculate about his archetype in terms of a serious hypothesis. The *R* recension is unmistakably post-Origenic, for it is based on a late and independent approach to the Hexapla as a whole. As Rahlfs has seen, the use made of it in Ruth by the Latin and Armenian suggests a date not later than the second half of the fourth century, i.e. two centuries after Theodotion! Since it is certainly much later than the Caesarean edition of Origen's hexaplaric LXX-column, it can hardly be as early as the third century.

[2] Cf. p. 187.

[3] Only the last two must remain separate, for they contain the remains of the late translators (8) and Margolis' comments on the relation of the Greek to the Hebrew (9). But the first seven ought to be one only.

He follows Margolis even where the latter is mistaken. In section 14 of his Introduction he discusses the relative value of the two branches constituting the hexaplaric recension. Montgomery distinguishes two Origenic groups, a Palestinian O^P (V 62 147) and a Constantinopolitan O^C (A-group, Arab., Bohair.). His conclusion is that O^P represents the earlier form of Origen's revision of Theodotion's version which was subjected to a subsequent revision as extant in O^C—'critically retrograde in its approximation toward the elder Textus Receptus'. This retrograde development is in itself most implausible and the designation 'Const.' rests merely on the precarious assumption that descendents of the fifty copies of the Bible ordered by Constantine for the metropolitan churches must have survived. Montgomery himself realizes that 62 147 are 'degraded and contaminated types' and that 'the group is Aquilanic in the secondary sense that it presents Origen's work in its closest approximation to his Jewish master'.[1] Now 62–147(–407) form a distinct group within the Origenic recension of the preceding book of Ezekiel[2] which here also draws largely on Aquila in about 800 individual readings. Ziegler considers them a sub-group *o* beside O (=Q-88-$\mathfrak{S}^h$). There are, indeed, instances in which the genuine O follows Theodotion, but *o* Aquila: so xiii. 4 Ισραηλ] + ⁎ησαν 88-𝔖 = θ'; +εγενοντο 62 = α' σ'. So extensive a transformation is, however, inconceivable. My inference therefore is that the latter is neither *O* nor *o*, but *R* whose preference for Aquila we have come to know. In my opinion the same applies to Montgomery's O^P in Daniel: it is not Origen's revision and certainly not its earliest form. It was done independently of him, at least a century later. Only O^P can properly be styled Constantinopolitan, as Margolis understands it. Montgomery's O^C, though not uniform as a group, is more in the nature of O (or P after Margolis), but certainly does not reflect it faithfully. In his edition of the Greek Daniel Ziegler too reverses Montgomery's grouping; but his argument is different.

Thanks to Montgomery a succession of students have been working on Margolis' line, H. S. Gehman in the second generation, and J. W. Wevers, now in Toronto,[3] in the third.

[1] Pp. 51f. [2] Ziegler, *Ezechiel*, pp. 34ff.

[3] Cf. Wevers' bibliographical notes in the *Catholic Biblical Quarterly*, vol. XIV (1952), p. 40, and vol. XV (1953), p. 30. Here he refers to 'a Gehman School of

By this time the climate had completely changed. It was no longer a question of doing merely preparatory work. The reconstruction of a critical text which had been considered rash only a few years earlier was confidently and methodically undertaken. Once again after K. Lachmann, the dividing walls between theological and classical texts and methods were broken down. As more reliable texts were established theology gained a much firmer foothold for exegesis, for as long as it had to rely on a pre-critical text its results were inevitably haphazard.

I give an example to show that the textual basis of some of today's typological work must be more critically examined before the far-reaching inferences now drawn from it can be justified.

In a note on 'The Choice of Matthias',[1] Dr L. S. Thornton considers ἔλαχεν, Acts i. 17 (Luke i. 9), and observes, 'The solitary analogy for this use of λαγχάνω in the LXX is I Sam. xiv. 47, which states that Saul obtained the kingdom by lot. The reference is to the incident already described in x. 21' (p. 52). And 'Like Saul, Judas, as one of the twelve princes of the new Israel (Luke xxii. 30), obtained a "kingdom" by lot. But in I Sam. xiv. 47 ἔλαχεν renders לָכַד which appears to mean that Saul "took" the kingdom by force of arms' (p. 54). It is useless to try to reconcile these two interpretations. λαγχάνω would be unique in the LXX proper and is, indeed, not 'LXX' at all, except in Swete's text. It is the reading of B* and derives from a hexaplaric insertion by which the misreading מְלָאכָה for מְלֻכָה was corrected. If Origen took it from one of the more recent translators its choice might be due to similarity in sound, without regard to the meaning. If, however, the insertion is Origen's own, he can very well have chosen the word with the same N.T. passages in mind which Dr Thornton would like to explain by it. Origen is not averse to typology either. Rahlfs' apparatus precludes any mistakes: κατακληρ. (+το *L*†) εργον B*L* (†)] +του βασιλευειν *L*†, ελαχεν του βασιλευειν *O*, pr. ελαχεν του βασιλευειν B†. His edition abounds with such unobtrusive helps. Accordingly, W. Bauer,[2] who uses Rahlfs' text, avoids this pitfall.

LXX studies'. The leading authority on the LXX in America, H. M. Orlinsky, owed his original inspiration to Margolis but has long outgrown the limits of any school. His book on the Greek Job is still under revision, but the specimens published raise high hopes.

[1] *J.T.S.* vol. XLVI (1945), pp. 51 ff.

[2] *Wörterbuch*[4], 1952, col. 837.

3. THE PRESENT GENERATION

Here again the most significant achievement is in an edition, J. Ziegler's Göttingen edition of the Prophets.[1] Each volume has a full Introduction which presents and discusses the evidence and then proceeds to its analysis. He gives a sober account of the groups and their nature and is equally candid about any residual difficulties. Good use is made of the patristic evidence and each volume has full lists of the abundant variants in spelling which would have unduly enlarged the apparatus and are therefore put in the Introduction, following Thackeray's paragraphs. Ziegler's methods have been refined in each succeeding volume so that increasingly everything noteworthy is recorded. The list of grammatical variants includes even those of late minuscules. The remains of the hexaplaric translations are edited afresh from the MSS. with much new material added and not from old collations as in Field. There is some emendation, which increases with each volume but is never extravagant.[2] The extreme usefulness of his edition is everywhere recognized, even among those who do not approve of the Göttingen method.

Ziegler is publishing a number of small monographs on special points which cannot be included in his introductions and these cover a very wide range.[3] He has developed a master method of deter-

[1] *Isaias* (1939); *Duodecim Prophetae* (1943); *Ezechiel* (1952); *Daniel* (1954), all published in Göttingen. *Jeremias* is under preparation.

[2] At times Ziegler's judgments are perhaps unduly influenced by the impressive strength of the evidence. This evidence may, however, prove misleading if we clearly distinguish two stages, that of the translator, however mistaken, with the Hebrew before him, and that of later copyists who had only the Greek to rely upon. An obvious example which, of course, does not deceive Ziegler, viz. the frequent confusion of ἡμ- and ὑμ-, is secondary; for ־ֵנוּ and ־ֶכֶם could not be confused by any translator but ἡμ- and ὑμ- were both pronounced *im-* at a later date. Grabe had corrected them throughout but Rahlfs overlooked a number of his corrections. We may compare the impossible dialectal changes in the entire evidence and the editions of Herodotus (F. Bechtel, *Die griech. Dialekte*, III, 1924, pp. 10–20). I refer to the discussion 'Zur Textgestaltung der Ezechiel-Septuaginta' in *Biblica*, vol. XXXIV (1953), pp. 435 ff. (Ziegler); vol. XXXV (1954), pp. 29 ff. (Katz).

[3] 'Textkrit. Notizen zu den jüng. griech. Uebersetzungen des Buches Isaias', *N.G.W.* (1939), pp. 75–102; 'Beiträge zum griech. Dodekapropheton', *N.G.W.* (1943), pp. 345–412; *Die jüng. griech. Uebersetzungen als Vorlagen der Vulgata in den prophet. Schriften* (Progr. Braunsberg, 1943); 'Beiträge zur kopt. Dodek.-Ueber-

mining whether more than one translator worked on a single book.[1] In his monograph on Isaiah he was the first to study the general attitude of translators toward the original and their degrees of competence. Since it is not sufficient to deal with isolated words, he always considers contexts and assesses Greek words representing several Hebrew words or Hebrew words translated in various ways. By widening the range of observation he has demonstrated that even in the Minor Prophets the apparent existence of more than one translator is illusory. His remarks about the translators' range of vocabulary are illuminating. It must be earnestly hoped that collaborators will be found to complete the Göttingen edition.

4. PROBLEMS

So far we have mainly emphasized editions, for they are tools with which the student of the Bible must be familiar. Their planning is based on definite principles, some of which we shall now consider.

First comes the Greek text, the presentation of which has been so improved by Rahlfs and Ziegler that only isolated points remain to be cleared up. This is an important, if unsensational task. Once Atticism had consigned Hellenistic literature to oblivion and post-Aqiban Judaism had done the same to its own Hellenistic literature, the LXX as adopted by the Church remained the most comprehensive body of Hellenistic writing to survive. Neither its contribution to our knowledge of Hellenistic speech in general nor its peculiar reflection of Hebrew idioms have been fully explored.[2]

Then comes the question of the critical value of the LXX for emending the Hebrew text. For well-known reasons the Hebrew

setzung', *Biblica*, vol. XXV (1944), pp. 105–42; 'Der griech. Dodek.-Text der Complutenser Polyglotte', *ibid.* pp. 297–310; 'Der Text der Aldina im Dodek.', *ibid.* vol. XXVI (1945), pp. 37–51; 'Die Bedeutung des Chester Beatty-Scheide Papyrus 967 für die Textüberlieferung der Ezechiel-Septuaginta', *Z.A.W.* vol. LXI (1945/8), pp. 76–94; 'Der Bibeltext im Daniel-Kommentar des Hippolyt von Rom', *N.G.W.* (1952), pp. 165–99; 'Die Septuaginta Hieronymi im Buch des Propheten Jeremias' in *Festschrift Alban Dold* (1952), pp. 13–24.

[1] 'Der textkrit. Wert der Septuaginta des Buches Job', *Miscellanea Biblica*, vol. II, pp. 277–96; *Die Einheit der Septuaginta zum Zwölfprophetenbuch* (Progr. Braunsberg, 1934); *Untersuchungen zur Septuaginta des Buches Isaias*, 1934.

[2] My forthcoming *The Text of the Septuagint* will contribute to the elucidation of this subject.

Bible is almost without variants but to what extent can we recover variants from the LXX and how should we decide which is right in places where the original and the versions differ? If we neglect, as well we may, Philo and St Augustine, to whom the LXX was an inspired text, there seem at first sight to be two alternatives.

The first accepts nothing but the *Hebraica veritas*. Origen, Jerome, Grabe, and Z. Frankel, to mention only a few examples, ignore the fact that the Hebrew underwent development, and therefore underestimate the LXX when it derives from a variant Hebrew text. Grabe demonstrated that in many instances the Greek variants are due to corruption.[1] In many more passages emendation of the Greek merely restores its original identity with the Hebrew.[2]

The opposite idea that 𝔐 might be emended from 𝔊 is relatively new. Bishop Lowth was the first to make wide use of this for the text of Isaiah. In his later years Lagarde became convinced that 𝔐 was so corrupt that it could not be used with a good conscience until an emended text of 𝔊 was forthcoming. I mention this gross exaggeration only because it strongly influenced Duhm and his school. Contrary to Lagarde's intentions they confined their interest in the LXX to those passages which seemed hopeless in the Hebrew. One may say with truth: Never was the LXX more used and less studied! Unfortunately much of this misuse survives in BH3. I have long given up collecting instances. Ziegler, after ten pages of corrections from the Minor Prophets alone, rightly states that all the references to 𝔊 must be rechecked.[3] H. M. Orlinsky who comes back to this point time and again is not very far from the truth when he says that not a single line in the apparatus of BH3 is free from mistakes regarding 𝔊.

However, the alternative '𝔐 or 𝔊' is not the whole problem, as Wellhausen realized better than any one. He attempted an answer

[1] In others he unduly approximates 𝔊 to 𝔐.

[2] I refer to ⟨στ⟩ε⟨ι⟩ρωσ⟨ις⟩ Prov. xxiv. 51 (xxx. 16), as mentioned on p. 204 n. 3, further to Prov. xxvi. 7, where the nonsense ΑΦΕλου ΠΟρεΙΑΝ σκελων και παρανομιαν must be read ΧΩλου ΠΑρεΣΙΣ σκελων και παροιμια in complete agreement with 𝔐, and to Num. x. 31 in which the confusion of οἶσθα and ᾔσθα (which is found also in Deut. ix. 2 ΑΘ ... and in the Menander Papyrus) led to the corruption of the whole verse, worst of all in the last word ΠΡΕΣΒΥΤΗΣ which, through a frequent corruption, due to popular etymology, into ΠΡΟΣΒΥΤΗΣ, is a distortion of ΠΡΟΣ ΟΨΕΙΣ = לְעֵינַיִם.

[3] *Z.A.W.* vol. LX (1944), pp. 107–20.

by telescoping 𝔐 and 𝔊 into one. They have many aspects in common. Both are in a state of flux, and it is hard to tell when this ended.[1] Where there are quantitative differences nothing that is in the Hebrew alone should for that reason be given preference; conversely nothing that is in the Greek alone should be condemned on that account. Both indulge occasionally in additions and embellishments and the choice between them does not lie in a simple preference for the 'original' against the 'translation', but must be governed by a strict interpretation of the context. For example, Wellhausen observes that subjects and objects are frequently implicit. If 𝔐 and 𝔊 have different *explicita* both are likely to be later additions.[2] This observation lends itself to fruitful application.[3]

Only after careful consideration of all the possibilities are we in a position to decide whether the Greek actually supplies a variant of the Hebrew. Influence from parallel passages or a translator's mannerism may produce divergences that are not 'variants'.

Even before BH³ was complete H. S. Nyberg strongly objected to unjustified confidence in the Greek and Syriac versions.[4] He emphasized that their *Vorlage* was greatly inferior to 𝔐 and that the translations abound with facile misunderstandings. Such blunders do not become emendations through being reiterated by modern scholars, who succumb to the same temptations as the ancient translators. Agreement in misunderstanding is suspect However timely, Nyberg's defence of 𝔐 is on occasion a *tour de force* and cannot therefore obviate the need for emendation, even if the emendations have no support from the translations. The translation of the Minor Prophets from which Nyberg derives his results is among the most incompetent. I doubt whether he could have attained the same results from the Books of Samuel. We should beware of generalizing.

[1] *Der Text der Bücher Samuelis* (Göttingen, 1871). Wellhausen's conclusions, which he never applied to other books than those of Samuel, have been brilliantly vindicated by the discovery of fragments of a pre-Christian Hebrew text of I Samuel (Frank M. Cross, Jr. in *B.A.S.O.R.* vol. CXXXII (Dec. 1953), pp. 15–25).

[2] Accordingly not even such *explicita* as fit the context are above suspicion.

[3] Even passages in which 𝔐 and 𝔊 are corrupt in divergent directions permit emendation in an analogous way. After Galling had restored Isa. viii. 1 by changing גִּלָּיוֹן גָּדוֹל to גִּלָּיוֹן גּוֹרָל, it was easy to see that in καινου μεγαλου the former must be κλήρου and the latter cancelled as deriving from the corruption of 𝔐 (*J.T.S.* vol. XLVII (1946), pp. 130f.).

[4] *Z.A.W.* (1934), pp. 241–54; *Studien zum Hoseabuche* (Uppsala, 1936).

More recently doubts have been raised as to the extent to which 𝔊 is strictly a translation. Translation always involves transposition to a new period and *milieu*. There are always two voices speaking and the minds behind them may clash every now and then. The translator may do his work conscientiously and yet never be aware that he is really interpreting.[1] All this, however, matters practically very little when we are given in the main a true reproduction of the original, as in most books of the LXX. The books, however, vary in their reliability. The translators of the Pentateuch sometimes call to mind the Bible histories for children done by men of the period of eighteenth-century Rationalism. God and his Word meant everything to them, but they had their peculiar ideas about what was suitable and seemly for God's Word. They deleted everything they considered crude or unworthy and replaced it by something 'better'. The LXX was, however, not as consistent in this respect as were the Targums. At times the Greek has crude, 'anthropopathic' modes of speech even when they are not in the Hebrew.[2] Orlinsky is therefore right in flatly denying that any 'antianthropomorphism' is characteristic of the LXX.[3]

Elsewhere the difference between 𝔐 and 𝔊 which is sometimes considerable is due to mere incompetence on the part of the translator. As was shown by Thackeray,[4] Ottley, and Ziegler, the translator of Isaiah who worked at an early date was completely unequal to his task. Many Hebrew words were unknown to him and 'often we can see him reduced to guessing or a stop-gap

[1] I. L. Seeligmann, *The Septuagint Version of Isaiah. A discussion of its problems* (Leiden, 1948), cites instances in which the translators, when faced with prophecies, had in mind events of their own time, an association of ideas that led to subtle modifications. This is an excellent suggestion, but convincing demonstration is difficult owing to the evasiveness of the allusions. Seeligmann's first contribution to LXX studies is the illuminating survey 'Problemen en Perspectieven in het moderne Septuaginta-Onderzoek', *Jaarbericht No. 7 van het Vooraziatisch-Egyptisch Gezelschap, Ex Oriente Lux*, 1940, pp. 359ff.

[2] This confirms Wellhausen's assertion that 𝔐 and 𝔊 were under identical influences, but at times in different places.

[3] Review of *The Anti-Anthropomorphisms of the Greek Pentateuch* by Ch. T. Fritsch, in *The Crozer Quarterly*, vol. XXI (1944), pp. 156–60; of Gerleman, *Book of Job* in *J.B.L.* vol. LXVII (1948), p. 385; and 'The Treatment of Anthropomorphisms and Anthropopathisms in the LXX of Isaiah' (*Eretz Israel III*, Casuto memorial volume).

[4] *J.T.S.* vol. IV (1903), p. 583.

rendering,... falling back on certain favourite words and using them almost at random'.[1] One of his favourites is παραδιδόναι. It is therefore bad method to change παραδῶ, Isa. xlvii. 3, to παρίδω (BH³) in order to make sense where the translator was unable to do so. Instances occur in which the translator proceeded in happy ignorance that an initial misunderstanding had led him completely astray.

In some books the emphasis shifts markedly from translation to interpretation, as has been demonstrated by Gerleman for Job and Proverbs.[2] The original Greek Job is shorter than the Hebrew by a sixth. Gerleman has shown that this is not merely a question of omission. The translator frequently contracts his text. A line or two may stand for a longer text in 𝔐, and here the Greek is of no use for the reconstruction of the Hebrew. This shortening is due neither to incompetence nor to any exception taken to the content. It is rather a matter of style and taste. As L. Koehler has seen,[3] the Book of Job is not a Platonic symposium, but a forensic exchange of pleas, hence its redundancies and repetitions. The translator disliked these and so weeded out parallels and synonyms not without discrimination. Elihu's speeches are the most ruthlessly curtailed; God's are treated with more respect. Metaphors are frequently transformed into non-figurative language. In ch. xxviii, which concerns divine wisdom, the description of mining is replaced by moralistic platitudes. In ch. xxiv the original pictures the poor man's lot out of pure delight in portrayal, but the Greek produces accusations against oppressors, interlaced with sentences about the ways of divine justice. Gerleman is not always right, e.g. when he states that the doctrine of strict retaliation as taught by Job's friends is toned down by the translator. Gerleman's only proof is the use of the optative aorist for a Hebrew future, but in this he is mistaken. Job reproduces in an idiomatic rendering the Hebrew jussive by an optative aorist, which is impossible in Greek. It has recently been demonstrated that there is Jewish

[1] R. R. Ottley, *Isaiah according to the Septuagint*, vol. I, p. 50.

[2] G. Gerleman, *Studies in the Septuagint, I. Book of Job* (Lund, 1946). 'The Septuagint Proverbs as a Hellenistic Document', *Oudtestamentische Studiën*, vol. VIII (1950), pp. 14–27. As to Proverbs some of his observations were anticipated by G. Bertram, *Z.A.W.* N.F. 13 (1936), pp. 153 ff.

[3] *Die hebräische Rechtsgemeinde* (Zürich, 1931), reprinted in *Der hebräische Mensch* (Tübingen, 1953).

evidence for this outside the Bible.[1] There are other fine observations in Gerleman's essay. The picture of Job in the N.T., the Fathers, and the arts, not as the Promethean rebel, but as the martyr hero, derives from the LXX, not from the Hebrew.

The translator of Proverbs also adapts much of the Hebrew to Greek standards of style. Where the Hebrew employs parallelism, the translator prefers antithesis and this involves him in more alteration. He obviously shuns tautology and reads his text with a townsman's eyes. Thus x. 5, 'He that gathereth in summer is a wise son' becomes: 'A wise son is protected from the heat'; xxiv. 30ff. which describes the dismal appearance of 'the field of the slothful', is transformed into a lame parable: 'A fool is like a field.'

Where this kind of translation prevails not much can be hoped for in emending the Hebrew. In Proverbs the quotations found in Clement of Alexandria indicate that the Greek text long remained fluid. The text of the Greek Job, however, is attested by an author of the second century B.C.[2] We should not forget that we are moving here on the fringes of the canonical literature.

As early as 1912 a promising student soon to become a victim of the First World War, M. Flashar,[3] observed extensive rephrasing caused by an 'advanced' theology in the Greek Psalter. Among many good things in his essay, the most important is perhaps the observation that wherever the translator could see his way clearly he advanced securely, but when baffled he was like a schoolboy following literally his original. Each Greek word equates the Hebrew, but the total result makes no sense. There are parallels in other books.[4] Hence we should take the warning: where betrayed to bungling literalness, a translation is no guide, however desperately it be needed for understanding the Hebrew.

It might appear that the translation of the Deutero-canonical *ketubim* offered a wider scope for the idiosyncrasies of unofficial translators. Similar claims, however, are made for Samuel and

[1] P. Katz, 'Papyrus Fuad 203 und die Septuaginta', *T.Z.* vol. IX (1953), pp. 228–31.

[2] Schürer III[4], p. 480. Gerleman, *Book of Job*, pp. 73f.

[3] 'Exegetische Studien zum Septuagintapsalter', *Z.A.W.* vol. XXXII (1921), pp. 81–116, 161–89, 241–68.

[4] Ziegler observes the same for the Minor Prophets in *Z.A.W.* vol. LX (1944), pp. 107f.

Kings.[1] I cannot here go into the detail, however interesting. A number of conclusions have been based on pre-critical texts and can be eliminated by emendation.[2] Others, however, stand the test better. Here I confine myself to P. A. H. de Boer's painstaking *Research into the Text of I Samuel*.[3] The first part has a useful Historical Introduction in which the value of Wellhausen's contribution is freely acknowledged but the notions that the 'history of the text' can be established only by a quantitative comparison of the versions with the Hebrew and that, only when this has been done, 'the actual criticism of the text can be embarked on' preclude the author's use of his predecessors' valuable results in the first stage of his work, the comparison of the text and versions.[4] It would be a pity to under-

[1] H. S. Gehman, 'Exegetical Methods employed by the Greek Translators of I Samuel', *J.A.O.S.* vol. LXX (1950), pp. 292ff.; J. W. Wevers, 'Exegetical Principles underlying the Septuagint Text of I Kings ii. 12 – xxi. 43', *Oudtest. Stud.* vol. VIII, pp. 300ff.; 'Principles of Interpretation guiding the Fourth Translator of the Book of the Kingdoms', *Cath. Bibl. Quart.* vol. XIV (1952), pp. 40ff.; 'A Study in the Exegetical Principles underlying the Greek Text of II Sam. xi. 2 – I Kings ii. 11', *C.B.Q.* vol. XV (1953), pp. 30ff.

[2] In III Reg. viii. 46 ἐπάξεις αὐτούς does not 'avoid attributing anger to God' (*Oudtest. Stud.* vol. VIII, p. 318), as it cannot be translated *thou shalt lead them on.* Rahlfs rightly reads ⟨ἐπ'⟩ αὐτούς, against Bq. This intransitive use *to fall upon somebody as an enemy* occurs in I Reg. v. 6 (=שמם Hiphil) and in Polyb. II, 29, 2 τῶν πολεμίων ἐπαγόντων αὐτοῖς, X, 21, 7 αἱ ἐπαγωγαὶ αἱ ἐπὶ τοὺς ἐναντίους and is an appropriate translation of אָנַפְתָּ *art angry with them.* πατάξεις, the reading of the parallel text II Par. vi. 36 and of a_2 in our passage, looks like a corruption of ἐπάξεις for which there are parallels elsewhere.

[3] *Research into the Text of I Samuel i–xvi* (Amsterdam, 1939). Continued in *Oudtest. Stud.* vol. I, pp. 79–103 (ch. XVII) and vol. VI, pp. 1–100 (chs. XVIII–XXXI).

[4] I give a few examples. In I Reg. xi. 7 ἐβόησαν is not an 'exaggeration' of יֵצְאוּ, but stands for יִצְעֲקוּ which is required by the context. In xv. 29 διαιρεθήσεται εἰς δύο certainly 'anticipates the history', but it does so only because the translator did not understand the unique נֵצַח יִשְׂרָאֵל and ventured—or repeated from a source—a guess נֶחֱצָה. It reveals an embarrassment which is shared by modern expositors but is not 'an exegetical enlargement'. The mistranslation ἐν ἐμοί for בִּי i. 26 betrays sheer ignorance; too much honour is done to the translator by rendering his nonsense by 'the responsibility of the following rests with me'. Accordingly one should not speak of a 'difference' between 𝔐 and the *Vorlage* of 𝔊. Unfortunately de Boer scatters his observations by grouping them under the headings 'Minus', 'Plus', 'Difference'. To get at his interpretation of a verse one has to piece them together from many places. Thus it remains obscure whether he intends to suggest a solution of the difficulties offered by iv. 14f. other than those of Wellhausen and A. Klostermann. On xv. 23 he

estimate his careful observations, but this preliminary part of his investigation, which postpones evaluation of the variants, implies a finality impossible without such evaluation. The translator, he claims, is an independent story-teller, his Hebrew text identical with 𝔐, and his translation is 'of little value for the determination of the "original" Hebrew text'.[1] These sweeping statements and the way in which they are obtained are remote from Wellhausen's '*discriminating* use of the ancient versions for purposes of textual criticism',[2] but I am unable to see how they could ever supersede it. Especially in II Samuel there are a number of passages in which Wellhausen, with his fine flair for emendation, found that a special group of LXX MSS. (the Lucianic, as he realized later) reflected a Hebrew better than ours. In I Samuel the *L* group offers at least one unexceptionable reading which the others have mutilated: xx. 11 נֵצֵא ἐξέλθωμεν *L*] μενε rell.[3]

In conclusion, signs of incompetence are found in many books, least in the Pentateuch, and translation is more interpretative in some of the 'Writings'. None of the latter, however, forfeit their value as evidence for the Hebrew even in passages where they transform it in accordance with their own bias. The problem is not the absence of individual traits, but their preponderance. This is, however, contested by those scholars who deny that the LXX is a translation

has comments under each of his three headings: 'gives a free translation' ('Minus', p. 54); 'πόνους and θεραφιν probably explanation' ('Plus', p. 56); '23ª is a paraphrase of the pregnant mašal-text' ('Difference', p. 67). Everything essential is, however, contained in Wellhausen's short sentence (p. 100): 'The divergences of the versions rest on misunderstanding of הַמִּצְר.' Moreover the Old Latin and the 𝔊 half of Lucian's doublet (the other half is Theodotion) indicate that neither θεραφιν nor even its late Grecizing θεραπειαν (Bvy) was in the original Greek.

[1] P. 69.

[2] Quoted from S. R. Driver's *Notes on...Samuel*², p. vii. The whole page seems to me as true as ever.

[3] *T.L.Z.* vol. lxi (1936), col. 276. Wellhausen's ἴωμεν is not LXX Greek. This μενε, with which we may compare other mutilations such as ερως for στείρωσις = עֹצֶר *barrenness* Prov. xxiv. 51 (xxx. 16) (*T.L.Z.* vol. lxiii (1938), col. 34), was one of the ever repeated arguments for the mistaken theory of F. Wutz according to which the LXX was translated from a Hebrew text written in Greek characters (MENE < NEΣE !). In the end this theory was tacitly given up by its author and is now duly forgotten. Its obituary was written by P. Kahle who had favoured it for many years (*Z.D.M.G.* vol. xcii (1938), pp. 276ff.) and by H. M. Orlinsky, 'Current Progress and Problems in Septuagint Research' in *The Study of the Bible Today and Tomorrow* (Chicago, 1947), pp. 155ff.

in the strict sense of the word and insist that it is merely a Greek Targum.

P. Kahle is the champion of this theory which he has propounded many times since 1915.[1] He argues that the LXX was formed in the same way as the Aramaic Targums, and that uniformity was attained only at the end of a long process of assimilating isolated fragments of translation.[2] Consequently any search for the 'original' behind the variants, following the methods developed by classical students, is useless.[3] Instead we must tackle in earnest the wealth of variants, including those found in the indirect evidence of later quotations, with a view to unearthing any survivals of hypothetical early rival translations which merged in the 'LXX'. The pursuit of remnants of this kind was begun,[4] often in complete neglect of the results established by solid investigation of recensional problems which this school of thought considered superfluous. Struck by the obvious irrelevance of this new branch of study as presented in *The Cairo Geniza*,[5] I subjected it to a searching study,[6] only to find out that it involved no cogent argument,[7] but merely a mass of uncoordinated information. The chapter on the LXX is an impassioned plea for an arbitrary choice of authorities, omitting anything that might prejudice the author's case. In reply I undertook to demonstrate that the comparison with the Targums rested on loose analogies, that the several books of the LXX at their first stage disclose the individual traits of their authors, that the wealth of variants is perplexing only as long as they are neither grouped nor analysed, and that most of them, including the indirect quotations, derive from well-known secondary recensions and are neither LXX nor early. For example the quotations found in the branch of Philonic evidence, from which Kahle's repeated argument is taken,

[1] 'Untersuchungen zur Geschichte des Pentateuchtextes', *Theol. Stud. u. Krit.* vol. LXXXVIII (1915), pp. 399ff.

[2] It is not clear whether Kahle realizes that this would also imply that the LXX, owing to its composite nature and the late date of its final formation, would be almost valueless as a witness for the early Hebrew text.

[3] 'A wild-goose chase' (T. W. Manson in *Dominican Studies*, April 1949).

[4] 'A wild-goose chase' (H. M. Orlinsky in *J.A.O.S.* vol. LXIX (1949), p. 165).

[5] *The Schweich Lectures for 1941* (London, 1947).

[6] For the titles see below, p. 207 n. 2.

[7] This confirms Orlinsky's statement in 'On the State...', pp. 86, 91.

are confined to the *lemmata* unconfirmed by Philo's own comments.[1] Actually they draw freely on Aquila.[2]

These secondary Philonic quotations and others claimed by Kahle as pre-LXX translations are all closer to the Hebrew than is the LXX. It has been demonstrated that they possess characteristics of very late recensions of the LXX, but the fact remains, texts exist which reveal early, pre-hexaplaric approximations to the Hebrew, among them Upper Egyptian translations and the Greek Washington papyrus of the Minor Prophets (third century A.D.). This raises the question whether there were not repeated consultations of the Hebrew, before and after Origen,[3] and if there were, to what extent they can be distinguished. A recent discovery may assist us to a solution but since it has not yet been published in full we can only estimate it provisionally.[4]

Fragments of a Greek Dodekapropheton, said to be buried in a cave during the reign of Bar Kochba, have a LXX text approximated to the Hebrew, and this text has very much in common with Justin's quotations[5] (though it does not contain any of those few which

[1] This observation has been accepted by G. D. Kilpatrick, who in other respects is close to Kahle's theory (*J.T.S.*, n.s. II (1951), p. 88).

[2] Patrick W. Skehan, reviewing Kahle's *Die Handschriften aus der Höhle* in *J.B.L.* vol. LXXI (1952), remarks on p. 121: 'The observations on P. Katz' *Philo's Bible* which this section contains prescind from the point made by the latter, that the variant tradition of text in some of the MS. evidence for Philo shows a dependence on Aquila.' Thus Kahle's only answer to my list of his misquotations is a fresh example of the same. His latest contribution (*T.L.Z.* vol. LXXIX (1954), col. 91) dates the Aquila readings back to Philo's lifetime. If only he could bring himself to check Philo's expositions as to the underlying form of quotations he would soon realize that they do not support his theories.

[3] *T.Z.* vol. V (1949), p. 22; *Actes*...(cf. p. 207 n. 2), p. 181; W. G. Lambert in *Vet. Test.* vol. II (1952), p. 185.

[4] D. Barthélemy, 'Redécouverte d'un chaînon manquant de l'histoire de la Septante', *Revue Biblique*, vol. LX (1953), pp. 18–29. Of this E. Vogt has given a full abstract in *Biblica*, vol. XXXIV (1953), pp. 423–6.

[5] A distinctive set of O.T. quotations in Justin, however, is not affected by this new perspective. There are numerous passages in which Justin takes a stand against 'Jewish falsifications of the Bible', passionately defending readings which are, in fact, early Christian interpolations. As was seen by Hilgenfeld, *Theol. Jahrb.* vol. IX (1850), pp. 394 f., 398 ff.; Hatch, *Essays in Biblical Greek* (Oxford, 1889), pp. 188 ff.; Bousset, *Die Evangelienzitate Justins des Märtyrers* (Göttingen, 1891), pp. 18–35; Rahlfs, *Sept.-Stud.* II (Göttingen, 1907), pp. 203–6, 223 f., but ignored in Swete's *Introduction*, pp. 417 ff., and in B. J. Roberts' *The Old Testament Text and Versions*, p. 118, these interpolations have disappeared from the long quotations

Justin professes to borrow from the Jews' own version), with the Upper Egyptian translations of the Minor Prophets,[1] and also with Aquila and Symmachus and still more with the Quinta. If this text could be demonstrated to be as early as its editor suggests it would prove the existence of a first-century revision of the LXX though not a rival translation, as rightly emphasized by the editor. The basis of this revision would be the Quinta, and Aquila and Symmachus could be seen as the final stages of a development rather than its inception. This would confirm the impression that quotations with a text closer to 𝔐 than the unaltered LXX are earlier than the hexaplaric recension but they would still be secondary to the LXX text into which they came as sporadic corrections by Jewish revisers. This would raise the question whether post-hexaplaric recensions such as *RC*, have an early basis.[2] Although nothing would be gained for the theory of early independent and rival translations, many of its defenders would be satisfied that their claim for the existence of a modified form of text, a 'revised version' of the first century A.D., was justified.

Barthélemy's dating, 'iowever, rests on the assumption that none of the MSS., coins, etc., were deposited later than *c.* 130. If, however, this cave, like others, served as a depository down to the period of the Arab conquest, the assumption of the early date of the Dodekapropheton papyrus and its text would require close scrutiny and the burden of proof would rest on those who made this claim. In this

heading Justin's expositions. Their place is taken by the ordinary text of the LXX as we read it now, and consequently the peculiar points which were closest to Justin's heart are no longer found in the *lemmata* to which he refers. The same applies to those long passages of which our single MS. gives only the first and last verses connected by καὶ τὰ ἑξῆς.

[1] And the Washington papyrus W!

[2] Ziegler, *Theol. Revue*, vol. XLVII (1951), pp. 202f. Similarly Kilpatrick, *J.T.S.* (1951), pp. 88f. and W. D. Davies in *Theology* (August 1950), all in reviews of *Philo's Bible*. With the final publication of the Greek Dodekapropheton fragments we shall be in a better position to investigate this problem, and it is therefore wiser to wait until then. For this reason I have concentrated in this paper on the texts and editions; but for what may be said at the present juncture on the question of recensions I would refer to earlier publications, copies of which are available to those interested: 'Das Problem des Urtextes der Septuaginta' (*T.Z.* vol. v (1949), pp. 1–24) and 'The Recovery of the Original Septuagint. A Study in the History of Transmission and textual Criticism', *Actes du 1er Congrès de la Fédération Internationale des Associations d'Etudes Classiques* (Paris, 1951), pp. 165–82.

case Justin's quotations could not by themselves prove an early date of the new MS. They would be another example of what has been shown for the inferior Philonic quotations. Nevertheless, if the text could be proved to be early we should welcome this fresh light on the century beginning with A.D. 30 which is so much in need of illumination.

The sequence of LXX recensions as worked out in accordance with Lagarde's suggestions will stand any fresh examination, for it is both solid and elastic. The preliminary investigations by which it was established should be much more carefully studied by the student of the N.T., for the problems of the two Greek Testaments are similar and frequently correlated. The seventy years since 1883 have seen as much progress in the field of the LXX as in that of the N.T., if we take into account their difference in scale. It will perhaps one day be recognized that work on the O.T. in Greek requires, and deserves, the same measure of security as has been allowed N.T. research.

The Septuagint: A Review of Recent Studies

GEORGE HOWARD
University of Georgia

INTEREST in Septuagintal studies has reached an all-time high in the course of the present century. The recent establishment of the International Organization for LXX and Cognate Studies and the publication of the *Septuagint and Modern Study* by S. Jellicoe (1968) have placed the crowning touches on seven decades of hard labor. Before these two events scholars worked mainly in isolation and were often ignored by students of both Testaments. The latter were not always to blame for their lack of attention to Septuagint research, since the results of many a scholarly work were buried in the most obscure places. Two important surveys of developments in the field were among these buried treasures.[1] It is gratifying that such surveys have appeared lately in more accessible publications.[2]

This century has seen the emergence of two major critical editions of the Septuagint. The larger Cambridge Septuagint in 1906 began with Genesis and has since then covered the text through Esther-Judith-Tobit.[3] Nothing has appeared since 1940. The Göttingen edition of the Septuagint, also still incomplete, now covers Esther, I-II-III Maccabees, Psalms with Odes, Isaiah, Jeremiah, Baruch, Threni, Epistle of Jeremiah, Ezekiel, Susanna, Daniel, Bel and the Dragon, Twelve Prophets, Wisdom of Solomon, and Sirach. In active preparation are Genesis, Numbers-Deuteron-

1. H. M. Orlinsky, "Current Progress and Problems in Septuagint Research," *The Study of the Bible Today and Tomorrow*, ed. by H. R. Willoughby, 1947; P. Katz, "Septuagintal Studies in the Mid-Century," *The Background of the New Testament and its Eschatology*, eds. W. D. Davies and D. Daube, 1956.

2. S. Jellicoe, "The Septuagint To-Day," *Expository Times*, 77 (1956–1957), 68–74; "Septuagint Studies in the Current Century," *JBL*, 88 (1969), 191–199; especially J. W. Wevers, "Septuaginta Forschungen seit 1954," *Theologische Rundschau* (N.S.), 33 (1938), 18–76.

3. Edited by A. E. Brooke, N. Mclean, and later by H. St. John Thackeray.

Reprinted from *Restoration Quarterly*, Vol. 13, No. 3, 1970.

omy, Esdras, and IV Maccabees.[4] The recently increased pace of publication in the series promises completion of the work, hopefully, within the foreseeable future.

These editions represent two approaches to the text of the Septuagint. The Cambridge edition published Codex B, or where it fails, the next best MS, while placing the variants of other MSS in a large apparatus at the bottom of the page. The Göttingen edition presents an eclectically reconstructed text, also with a large apparatus at the bottom.

Debate over the origin of the Septuagint has disrupted progress in Septuagint studies in the past several decades. The century began with scholars still under the influence of P. Lagarde, who believed that the Septuagint could be traced back to one prototype. In the latter part of the last century he set out to recover the original Septuagint by grouping the MSS into recensions. He followed closely the statement of Jerome that in his day three editions of the Greek Bible were available, that of Origen (Palestine), Hesychius (Egypt), and Lucian (Syria).[5]

Early in the present century P. Kahle challenged this thesis and continued to do so throughout his career.[6] According to Kahle, the text which later generations came to call the "Septuagint" was the result of a standardizing process which attempted to form an authoritative Greek version from a mixture of many different Greek translations or Targums.[7] Kahle's theory has been rejected by most Septuagintal scholars,[8] though he has found support from some.[9]

4. The editors to date are J. Ziegler, W. Kappler, R. Hanhart, A. Rahlfs, J. W. Wevers, D. W. Gooding, and H. Dörrie.

5. Jerome, *Praef. in Lib. Paralip.*; Migne, Pl. xxviii, 1324–1325; Lagarde, *Anmerkungen zur griechischen Übersetzung der Proverbien* (1863); *Septuaginta Studien* (1891).

6. "Untersuchungen zur Geschichte des Pentateuch Textes," *TSK*, 88 (1915), 399–439.

7. See especially his *The Cairo Geniza*, 2nd ed. (1959), pp. 209–264.

8. See, for example, H. M. Orlinsky, "On the Present State of Proto-Septuagint Studies," *JAOS*, 61 (1941), 81–91. J. W. Wevers, "Proto-Septuagint Studies," in *The Seed of Wisdom Essays in Honour of J. T. Meek*, ed. W. S. McCullough (1964), 58–77.

9. Especially from A. Sperber, *Septuaginta Probleme* (1929); "The Problem of the Septuagint Recensions," *JBL*, 54 (1935), 73–92.

By far the most significant single advancement in the quest for the original Septuagint has been the discovery (from somewhere in the Judaean desert) of a leather Greek scroll of the Minor Prophets which dates to the first century A.D. D. Barthélemy drew attention to the scroll in 1953[10] and published it in full in 1963 along with his analysis of the position it holds within the transmission-history of the Septuagint.[11] The scroll presents a form of the LXX text which seems to have been revised toward the emerging *textus receptus*. Some of the best Old Testament textual critics, such as F. M. Cross, Jr., have given a qualified victory to Lagarde on the basis of the scroll.[12] The scroll has also given impetus to the theory of local texts of the Hebrew Bible.[13]

A number of excellent studies limited to the text of one LXX book have appeared in this century. The most notable, perhaps, is the work of Max Margolis on Joshua.[14] There have been many others, however, which deserve credit for pushing forward the establishment of a sound text.[15]

Of particular significance has been the publication of several fragments of MSS of the Greek Bible which date to a pre-Christian period. The Twelve Prophets scroll published by Barthélemy has already been mentioned. In 1936 C. H. Roberts published Rylands' Greek 458, which consists of fragments of a papyrus scroll, found in a mummy, containing Deuteronomy 23:24–24:3; 25:1–3; 26:12, 17–19; 28:31–33. It dates to the second century B.C.[16] Part of another ancient papyrus roll, Fouad 266, was published by W.

10. "Redécouverte d'un chainon manquant de l'histoire de la Septana," *RB*, 60 (1953), 18–29.

11. *Les devanciers d'Aquila* (1963).

12. *The Ancient Library of Qumran and Modern Biblical Studies*, 1st ed. (1958), pp. 120–145; 2nd ed. (1961), pp. 163–194.

13. Beginning with W. F. Albright, "New Light on Early Recensions of the Hebrew Bible," *BASOR*, 140 (1955), 27–33, this line of reasoning continues through two successive generations in F. M. Cross, Jr., "The History of the Biblical Text in the Light of Discoveries in the Judaean Desert," *HTR*, 57 (1964), 281–299; R. W. Klein, "New Evidence for an Old Recension of Reigns," *HTR*, 60 (1967), 93–105.

14. *The Book of Joshua in Greek* (1931–1938).

15. See S. Jellicoe, "Septuagint Studies in the Current Century," p. 197.

16. *Two Biblical Papyri in the John Rylands Library* (Manchester, 1936).

G. Waddell in 1944.[17] The part published covers Deuteronomy 31:28–32:7. The date of the document is late second or early first century B.C. P. W. Skehan partially published Greek fragments of scrolls found at Qumran.[18] One group of fragments (4 Q LXX Numbers) comes from a leather manuscript which includes Numbers 3:30–4:14 and dates to the first century B.C. A second group (4 Q LXX Lev.[b]) also from the first century B.C., covers parts of Leviticus chapters 2–5. A third set (4 Q LXX Lev.[a]) covers Leviticus 26:2–16. It dates to the first century A.D. Another fragment of the Greek Bible was published in 1962, [19] covering Exodus 28:4–7. About 100 B.C. is the date given.

The significance of these finds lies in the age of the fragments and the fact that the texts presented by them often vary from our so-called Septuagint. Future debates over the origin of the LXX will have to take into account their testimony.

The *Letter of Aristeas* has again drawn attention to itself in this century. From the earliest of times the *Letter* was held as an authoritative account of the origin of the LXX. This view was challenged in 1522 by Luis Vives,[20] in 1606 by the younger Scaliger,[21] and finally eclipsed in 1684 by Hody.[22] The revival of interest in *Aristeas* has produced three critical editions of the text by Wendland,[23] Thackeray,[24] and now more recently by A. Pelletier.[25]

17. "The Tetragrammaton in the LXX," *JTS* (o.s.), 45 (1944), 158–161. Kahle, *Cairo Geniza*, pp. 218f., reports that a few more fragments of the papyrus were reproduced in America in the *New World Translation of the Christian Greek Scriptures* (Brooklyn: Watchtower Bible and Tract Society, Inc., 1950), pp. 13, 14.

18. "The Qumran Manuscripts and Textual Criticism" in *Supplements to Vetus Testamentum*, IV, 148–160.

19. M. Baillet, J. T. Milik, R. de Vaux, *Discoveries in the Judaean Desert of Jordan III: Les 'Petites Grottes' de Qumran* (1962), pp. 142f.

20. In his commentary on St. Augustine, *De Civitate Dei*, pp. xviii, 42.

21. "Animadversiones in Chronological Eusebii," para. 1734, in *Thesaurus Temporum Ensebii Pamphili* (Leiden, 1606).

22. *Contra Historian LXX Interpretum Aristeae nomine inscriptam Dissertatio*. This was reprinted in his *De Bibliorum Textibus Originalibus* (Oxford, 1705).

23. *Aristeae ad Philocratem Epistula* (Leipzig, 1900).

24. Cf. Appendix in H. B. Swete, *Introduction to the Old Testament in Greek* (1902).

25. *Lettre d'Aristee a Philocrate* (Sources Chretiennes, 89) (1962).

The last of these takes into account all the known MSS of the *Letter*.

Scholars have shown special interest in *Aristeas* paragraph 30 which has relevance for the debate over the origin of the Septuagint. Kahle, followed by others, believed that the paragraph refers to earlier carelessly made translations of the Greek Torah.[26] A host of scholars reject this view and believe that paragraph 30 refers to carelessly prepared Hebrew MSS.[27] There have also been attempts at explaining the meaning and purpose of the *Letter* as a whole.[28] This has been sorely neglected in the past and will demand more attention from exegetes and historians of the Intertestamental period in the future. Hopefully, now that the importance of the *Letter* has come to light, its significance as a witness to the nature of Diaspora Judaism will be explored.

Much has been done in this century on the various recensions of the Greek Bible, both Jewish and Christian. As to the former of these the reprinting of F. Field's classic work[29] by Georg Olms of Hildesheim in 1964 has been a welcome sight to scholars, who previously had little or no accessibility to this useful collection of the remains of Origen's Hexapla. The publication in 1915 by L. Lütkemann and A. Rahlfs of the *Hexaplarische Randnoten zu Isaias 1–16* in the tenth-century Sinai Codex Greek 5 (710 Göttingen) is a useful addition to Field.[30] The most fascinating advancement in Hexaplaric studies in this century, however, is the publication of Mercati's Milan fragments of the Hexapla Psalms.[31]

Concerning the Christian recensions perhaps a word about

26. *Cairo Geniza*, pp. 212–214. See also H. St. John Thackeray, "Translation of the Letter of Aristeas," *JQR* (o.s.), 15 (1903), 347; M. Hadas, *Aristeas to Philocrates* (1951), pp. 110f.

27. E. J. Bickermann, "The Colophon of the Greek Book of Esther," *JBL*, 63 (1944), 343; G. Zuntz, "Aristeas Studies II: Aristeas on the Translation of the Torah," *JSS*, 4 (1959), 117; D. W. Gooding, "Aristeas and Septuagint Origins: A Review of Recent Studies," *VT*, 13 (1963), 361f.

28. G. Zuntz, "Aristeas Studies I: 'The Seven Banquets,'" *JSS*, 4 (1959), 32f.

29. *Origenis Hexaplorum Quae Supersunt: Sive Veterum Interpretum Graecorum in Totum Vetus Testamentum Fragmenta* (1875).

30. *Mitteilungen des Septuaginta-Unternehmens der Akademie der Wissenschaften in Göttingen*, i, 6, pp. 345–385.

31. G. Mercati, *Psalterii Hexapli Reliquiae*, Vol. I (1958); Vol. II (1965).

Proto-Lucian will suffice as an example of interest that has been shown in this area. According to tradition Lucian, the Antiochian Presbyter and martyr, prepared a recension of the Greek Bible in the third century A.D. Scholars had observed already in the nineteenth century that the so-called Lucianic text was quoted by Justin Martyr, a second century writer.[32] It is now known that the recension of Lucian was used by Josephus in the first century[33] and appears in John Rylands' Greek Papyrus 458, which dates in the second century B.C.[34] The *Vorlage* of this recension apparently goes back to 400 B.C., when the Chronicler wrote. At times he agrees with LXX^L and 4Q Sam.[a] (a Qumran MS of the first century B.C. which coincides on occasion with the Lucianic Greek minuscles BOC_2E_2) against LXX^B.

The possibilities of these new discoveries have been fascinating to scholars. Barthélemy concludes that MSS BOC_2E_2 of the so-called *Beta-Gamma*, *Gamma-Delta* sections of Reigns are actually witnesses to the ancient Septuagint while the *Kaige* group (including Codex B) is a later recension.[35] Cross, on the other hand, thinks that the Proto-Lucianic texts of Samuel-Kings is a revision of the Ancient Septuagint, which is now lost, toward a Hebrew *Vorlage* similar to that of the Chronicler and the scrolls found at Qumran.[36] Whatever the case might be, it is becoming increasingly clear that the nature of Septuagint recensions is more elusive than formerly thought.

Another sphere of research which is drawing attention today is the significance LXX has for NT studies. Much in particular has appeared on the NT quotations of the OT.[37] These studies focus on

32. Wilhelm Bousset, *Die Evangeliencitate Justins des Märtyrers in ihrem Wert für die Evangelienkritik* (1891), 20.

33. Cf. H. St. J. Thackeray, *Josephus, The Man and the Historian* (1929), 83.

34. Cf. B. Metzger, "The Lucianic Recension of the Greek Bible," in *Chapters in the History of New Testament Textual Criticism* (1963), p. 35.

35. *Les devanciers d'Aquila*, p. 91.

36. "The History of the Biblical Text . . . ," p. 295.

37. The literature is so vast here that I list only sample works. K. Stendahl, *The School of St. Matthew* (1954); C. H. Dodd, *According to the Scriptures* (1952); E. E. Ellis, *Paul's Use of the Old Testament* (1957); E. D. Freed, *Old Testament Quotations in the Gospel of John* (1965); J. De Waard, *A Comparative Study of the Old Testament*

various problems ranging all the way from textual criticism of either the OT or NT to the theological bent of the authors who employ the quotes.[38]

The Septuagint has also come to be recognized for its importance for NT philology, both in lexicography and grammar. In the last century the language of the NT was considered as a "language of the Holy Ghost."[39] Around the turn of the century papyri discoveries in Egypt came to light and, in the minds of many, showed that the Greek of the NT was nothing more than the common Greek of the day.[40] It appeared to be the language of the papyri which contained receipts, everyday notes, etc., to be read once and thrown away.[41]

However, this emphasis on the Koine element in NT Greek has abated today. It did not take long for scholars to realize that the letters of the NT were not written to be read once and thrown away. As early as 1908 H. B. Swete challenged the idea.[42] If the writers of the NT were influenced by secular Greek they were influenced more by LXX. Separated from LXX the NT would have been almost unintelligible to the contemporary reader, according to B. Atkinson.[43] Scholarship today, with some reservation, would agree with A. D. Nock when he said, "Nothing could be less like the Pauline letters than the majority of the documents in Deissmann's *Light from the Ancient East.* Paul is not writing peasant

---

Text in the Dead Sea Scrolls and in the New Testament (1966); A. Sperber, "Ha-Evangelion Ve-Targum Ha-Shevim Le-Tanach," *Tarbiz*, 6 (1934), 1–29; "New Testament and the Septuagint," *JBL*, 59 (1940), 193–293.

38. For example see "Hebrews and the Old Testament Quotations," *NT*, 10 (1968), 208–216.

39. H. Cremer, *Biblico-Theological Lexicon of New Testament Greek*, 1872, p. v.

40. Cf. A. Deissmann, *Bibelstudien*, (1895); *Neue Biblstudien* (1897); J. H. Moulton, *A Grammar of New Testament Greek, Prolegomena* (1908).

41. E. J. Goodspeed, "The Making of the New Testament: Greek and Roman Factors," *An Introduction to the Revised Standard Version of the New Testament* (1946), p. 32.

42. *The Apocalypse of St. John* (1909), p. cxxv, n. 1. Cf. also the cautious statement in F. Blass and A. Debrunner, *Grammatik des neutestamentlichen Griechisch* (10th ed., 1959), p. 3.

43. *The Greek Language* (2nd ed.; 1933), p. 286.

Greek or soldier Greek; he is writing the Greek of a man who has the LXX in his blood."[44]

At any rate, in the past decades there has developed an appreciation for the influence which LXX vocabulary had on NT thought and the contributions in this area of Septuagintal research are still coming.[45] Consequently, the debate over which source is more important for NT lexicography, Greek or Hebrew, will probably be resolved in terms of LXX.[46]

It is also becoming clear that LXX has significance for NT textual criticism especially in regard to the recensions of the Greek Bible. Apparently Hort recognized some relationship between LXX and NT textual problems since he turned his attention to LXX text as soon as he finished his monumental work, with Westcott, on the NT.[47] By and large, however, his attitude was one of turning from one discipline to another remotely related. Metzger shows a deeper insight into the relationship of the two in his work on the Lucianic recension of the Greek Bible. He expresses the relationship in the following way. "Just as the grammarian and the lexicographer of the New Testament can learn much from an examination of the language of the Septuagint, so too the textual critic of the New Testament will profit from considering the problems and tasks of Septuagint-Forschung."[48]

THE FUTURE

What course will Septuagintal studies follow in the remaining decades of this century? It seems to me that there remain a number

44. "The Vocabulary of the New Testament," *JBL*, 52 (1933), 138.

45. G. Kittel, *Theologisches Wörterbuch zum Neuen Testament* (1933–64); C. H. Dodd, *The Bible and the Greeks* (1935); J. Barr, *The Semantics of Biblical Language* (1961); *Biblical Words for Time* (1962); T. Boman, *Hebrew Thought Compared with Greek* (1960); C. B. Caird, "Towards a Lexicon of the Septuagint I," *JTS* (NS), 19 (1968), 453–475; "Towards a Lexicon of the Septuagint II," *JTS* (NS), 20 (1969), 21–40.

46. Cf. D. Y. Hadidian, "The Septuagint and its Place in Theological Education," *ET*, 76 (1964), 102–103.

47. G. Howard, "Introduction to Septuagintal Studies," *Rest. Q.*, 7 (1963), 133.

48. "The Lucianic Recension of the Greek Bible" in *Chapters in the History of New Testament Textual Criticism* (1963), pp. 2–3.

of problems which will demand solution. In the first place, the origin and nature of the Septuagint text is still a question. At the present time most scholars have concluded that Kahle is wrong and Lagarde is right. A priori, however, it does not necessarily follow that Lagarde is right if Kahle is wrong. There are alternatives which may eventually lay claim to the truth. In fact, it is surprising that scholars have limited themselves to these two alone.[49]

It has already been noted that Lagarde believed that LXX MSS evolved from a single prototype or ur-text, while Kahle believed that LXX was the culmination of a process of standardization. A third possibility, unstated up to this time, is that LXX is a revision of one text among many. This text in early times became accepted by the popular majority and eventually eclipsed all other versions. This revision influenced the development of the LXX text but only in a minor way. This position is halfway between Lagarde and Kahle and agrees with both where they are strongest, i.e., the archetypal origin of LXX and the evidence for a multiplicity of versions in pre-Christian times.

Another issue which will demand solution in the future is the use textual critics should make of LXX in their attempt to restore the original Hebrew Bible. Since the discovery of the DSS there has developed a tendency to accept at face value the LXX as representative of a Hebrew *Vorlage* when it varies from MT.[50] Those who have worked directly with the LXX text itself, however, without confining themselves to comparing it with fragments from the Dead Sea area are convinced that the LXX often varies from the MT and all other Hebrew texts because of the idiosyncrasies of its translators. A median course between the two will no doubt win out in the end.

The recensions of the Greek Bible will demand continued attention. Any scholar who works under the assumption that there was at one time an original LXX will find this ur-text only after he has

49. Jellicoe has attempted a type of reconciliation between Lagarde and Kahle but finally concludes that the only benefit of Kahle's position is to warn the Lagardian school against a "too ready optimism," "Aristeas, Philo, and the Septuagint *Vorlage*," *JTS* (N.S.), 12 (1961), 271.

50. Cross, *Ancient Library of Qumran*, 2nd ed., p. 180.

properly separated the existing MSS into recensions and has evaluated each for its merit. Traditionally, the Lagardian school explains variant readings in LXX MSS as due to early scribal activity designed to bring the existing Greek text in line with the emerging *textus receptus*.[51] Now that we have Hebrew texts from Qumran that agree with the LXX against the MT this theory needs revision. Whenever one Greek MS lies closer to MT than another, one cannot be absolutely sure that the former is a revision of the latter. In other words, proximity to MT is not a definite sign of revision. It is possible that the MS which lies farther from MT is the revision made in favor of a *Vorlage* like the Qumran Scrolls.

This type of reasoning will, of course, slow down the rapid pace theories in LXX recensional criticism have recently taken. For example, both Cross and Barthélemy have concluded that the Proto-Lucianic text of Reigns is earlier than the *Kaige* recension.[52] Since it is farther from MT than *Kaige* it appears that *Kaige* has revised it toward MT. It is possible, however, that just the opposite is true. Proto-Lucian might be a revision of *Kaige* in favor of a Hebrew *Vorlage* like the texts presented by the Qumran Scrolls. That this possibility is not farfetched can be seen in the way the Deuteronomy MS from Cave 5 of Qumran, which dates to the early second century B.C., is corrected by a MS of the Septuagintal type against the Proto-Massoretic tradition.[53]

Use of the LXX in determining recensions of the Hebrew Bible will also demand careful watch. Cross, who has taken the lead in identifying local texts, suggests that there were three localities where early recensions of the Hebrew Bible developed: Egypt, Palestine, and Babylon.[54] He equates the Palestinian with the

51. See, for example, P. Katz, "Justin's Old Testament Quotations and the Greek Dodekapropheton Scroll," *Studia Patristica*, K. Aland and F. L. Cross, eds. (1957), I, 349; H. M. Orlinsky, "Studies in the Septuagint of the Book of Job; Chapter IV The Present State of the Greek Text of Job," *HUCA*, 33 (1962), 121.

52. Cross, "History of the Biblical Text," pp. 295f.; Barthélemy, *Les devanciers d'Aquila*, p. 91.

53. *Discoveries in the Judaean Desert*, III, 169–171, pl. xxxvi. Notice the remarks of S. Talmon, "Aspects of the Textual Transmission of the Bible in the Light of Qumran Manuscripts," *Textus*, IV (1964), p. 97.

54. "History of the Biblical Text . . . ," pp. 297–299.

Proto-Samaritan text present at Qumran. The Egyptian text he identifies with the *Vorlage* of LXX. And finally, for want of a better place, he locates the Proto-Massoretic text in Babylon. Since all text-types are found at Qumran, however, a great deal depends on the identification of the LXX *Vorlage* as Egyptian. It must be remembered that the actual text of the original LXX has not yet been established. Furthermore, it is becoming increasingly clear that the LXX which appears in the Codices of the Christian Church is a mixture of texts of all types including the Egyptian, Lucianic, *Kaige*, Theodotianic, and many others. Since each of these is related in some way to the Qumran Scrolls, one must show caution in identifying too closely any element with the Egyptian text. In almost any given instance the LXX, as we have it today, can be equated with one of the Palestinian recensions which have turned up at Qumran.

Much more could be said about problems which await solution, but perhaps these few are enough to illustrate the path Septuagint research will probably take in the future.

II. SEPTUAGINT ORIGINS

(i) *Studies*

Problems of the Septuagint

P. KAHLE, Oxford
(Appendix by A. Vaccari S. J., Roma)

Paul de Lagarde, who devoted to problems of the Septuagint a great deal of his life-work, published two years before his death a statement on the condition of the manuscripts of the Septuagint in which he declared[1]:

> The various readings in the Christian manuscripts of the Septuagint have their special characteristics. Nine-tenths of them are not disfigurations of the original words, due to the carelessness and stupidity of copyists. They are intentional adaptations to a form of the Hebrew text which was closely connected with our Masoretic text. It is very likely that they originated from the later Greek translations of the Old Testament, which unfortunately are preserved to us in a fragmentary form only.

Lagarde understands by these later translations the texts used by Origen in his Hexapla. He was convinced that the Christian manuscripts might enable us to find a text of the Septuagint which was used in the time of the Apostles, and he thought that quotations by Jewish Hellenistic authors like Philo and Josephus might help us to find a text which may have been used 50 years earlier.

Lagarde speaks of Christian manuscripts only, he was certainly aware that Jewish manuscripts preceded the Christian ones, but of such Jewish manuscripts nothing was known in his time. He scarcely doubted, however, that it was a uniform text which was handed over to the Christians by the Jews.

Conditions have changed since Lagarde's time. To-day we know of several specimens of the Greek Bible which were written

[1] Mittheilungen von Paul de Lagarde. III, Göttingen 1889, S. 230—234.

Reprinted from *Studia Patristica,* Vol. 1, Part 1. Berlin, 1945.

by Jews for Jews. They must be consulted when we desire to know the kind of texts of the Greek Bible used by the Jews.

The first of these specimens consists of remnants of a Papyrus Scroll bearing verses from Deuteronomy chapters 23—28, discovered in a mummy sarcophagus from which they had to be carefully freed. The fragments are preserved as Papyrus Greek 458 in the John Rylands Library at Manchester. They were published by C. H. Roberts[1]. The Papyrus seems to have been written in the middle of the second Century BC. It is the oldest remnant of the Greek Bible known to us. The text has been compared with the chief Uncial manuscripts of the Septuagint, but without real success[2]. Finally Pater Alberto Vaccari, of the Pontifical Bible Institute in Rome, pointed out that the text of the Papyrus stands in closest relation to the Lucianic text of the Bible, a text attributed to the martyr Lucian of Samosata (died 7th January 312 AD), who is said to have revised the text of the Greek Bible used in his time[3]. In the Papyrus fragments we have parts of this text which were written about 500 years before Lucian. It is well known that Paul de Lagarde was especially interested in this text and published the first half of it in 1883[4].

Unfortunately the divine name is not preserved in these fragments. In Dt 26. 17, however, line 27 of Roberts' edition, the text breaks off just before the name of God. Roberts supposed that the name *kyrios* usually found as *nomen sacrum* written in an abbreviated form in the manuscripts of the Greek Bible, must have been written here in full, as the space in the line requires it. But from fragments of the Greek Bible discovered recently we know that in manuscripts written by Jews the divine name was not translated, but was always

---

[1] Two Biblical Papyri in the John Rylands Library, Manchester, by C. H. Roberts. Manchester 1936.

[2] See, for instance, H. G. Opitz und H. H. Schaeder, Zum Septuaginta-Papyrus Rylands Greek 458. ZNW 35, 1936, S. 115—117.

[3] P. A. Vaccari S.J., Fragmentum Biblicum Saeculi II ante Christum. Biblica 17, 1936, p. 501—504.

[4] Librorum Veteris Testamenti Canonicorum Pars Prior Graece Pauli de Lagarde studio et sumptibus edita. Gottingae, 1883.

indicated by the Tetragrammaton written in Hebrew letters. There can be no doubt that here in line 27 the divine name was written as Tetragrammaton with Hebrew letters and in this way completed the line. C. H. Roberts agreed with me when I pointed this out. We only do not know whether the Tetragrammaton was written here in ancient Hebrew letters as in the third specimen discussed below and in the Aquila fragment from the Genizah, published by Burkitt[1], or in Hebrew square letters as in the second specimen.

This second specimen is the Cairo Papyrus Scroll Fouad 266, of which a few verses from Deuteronomy, Chapters 31 and 32, were published by W. C. Waddell[2] in order to show that the divine name was written here as the Tetragrammaton with Hebrew square letters. Professor G. D. Kilpatrick drew my attention to the fact that some further parts of the Papyrus had been reproduced in America, not well, but recognizably[3], in all of which the Tetragrammaton was to be seen. I asked Pater A. Vaccari in Rome to give me an estimate of the Textcharacter of the Papyrus. He has come to the following conclusions:

> The Papyrus has definitely to be grouped with the Uncials B A F against the Hexaplaric or Lucianic recensions or groups of later Minuscules. Not so clear is its position between the groups of B A F and the related Minuscules, between which it seems to vaccillate. But when we take into account that the Papyrus deviates from the Codex Vaticanus (B) where this manuscript stands alone, that is to say, has individual readings, not those of a family, and when we take into account again the important agreements with B and the Minuscule a_2 in some places, I should think that one must

[1] Fragments of the Books of Kings, according to the Translation of Aquila, by F. Crawdorf Burkitt. Cambridge 1898.

[2] The Tetragrammaton in the LXX. JThSt 45, 1944, pp. 157—161.

[3] New World Translation of the Christian Greek Scriptures. Rendered from the Original Language by the New World Bible Translation Committee — AD. 1950. Publishers: Watchtower Bible and Tract Society, Inc. International Bible Students Associon. Brooklyn, New York, USA Foreword. p. 13 and 14. Dr. Abram Spiro was kind enough to procure me a copy of this book.

include the Papyrus in the group B and the Minuscule a_2, that it should be regarded as better than these two manuscripts, as it does not share in their deteriorations which were in B individual errors, in the Minuscule influences of classes. The text of the Papyrus contains ancient elements which later disappeared from the tradition.

Thus far the results of P. Vaccari's investigation. His account may be read in the Appendix to my paper. What Vaccari has shown is, that we have here in a papyrus scroll a Greek text which represents the text of the Septuagint in a more reliable form than Codex Vaticanus and was written more than 400 years before this Codex.

Unfortunately we cannot compare the readings of the Cairo Papyrus Scroll with the text of the Chester Beatty Papyrus Codex of Numbers and Deuteronomy, written in the first half of the Second Century AD, ed. by Sir Frederic Kenyon, The Chester Beatty Biblical Papyri, Fasc. V, London 1935, Kenyon has shown that the text of Numbers in this Codex has the closest affinities with Codex B and a_2 of the Septuagint, the text of Deuteronomy with Codex A and a_2 of the Septuagint. The Chester Beatty Codex is written just in the middle of the period between the Cairo Papyrus Scroll and the Codex Vaticanus (B). The text so far known of the Cairo Scroll is not preserved in the Chester Beatty Codex. Perhaps the publication of the whole Scroll from Cairo may give us the opportunity to make a comparison.

The third specimen consists of fragments of a leather Scroll with the Greek text of the Minor Prophets, discovered in 1952 by Bedouin, probably in one of the Murabbaʿa caves. It is now in the Palestine Archaeological Museum in Jerusalem. A few indications concerning the scroll were given by P. Barthélemy in 1953[1], I myself dealt with the Scroll in 1954[2].

[1] Redecouverte d'un Chaînon manquant de l'histoire de la Septante, Revue Biblique LX, 1953, pp. 18—29.

[2] Die im August 1952 entdeckte Lederrolle mit dem griechischen Text der kleinen Propheten und das Problem der Septuaginta. ThLZ 1954, Sp. 81—94 = A Leather Scroll of the Greek Minor Prophets and the Problem of the Septuagint, in: *Opera Minora*, Leiden 1956, p. 113—127.

I hear from Pater G. Vermès, Paris, that the Jerusalem Museum has recently acquired some more fragments of the same scroll from the Bedouin. There is no doubt that the scroll was written by a Jew, and in the opinion of C. H. Roberts, whom I consulted[1], it is very likely that the Scroll was written in the closing decades of the pre-Christian era, certainly not later than 50 AD.

It is of special interest that the text of the Scroll is in the main identical with the text given in the quotations from the Old Testament by Justin the Martyr. Justin's quotation of Micah 4. 1—7, of which 5 verses are preserved in the Scroll, was discussed by Credner, more than a hundred years ago, in the following terms[2]:

> The basic text of Justin is the Septuagint, altered, however, in special directions. In several places it agrees with Aquila, but the text is not Aquila . . . there are remarkable deviations from Aquila. In Micah 4. 4 we find readings of Symmachus and Theodotion . . . Apart from a clear anxious exactness in adapting the text to the Hebrew original we see negligencies which cannot be expected from Aquila.

Further, Credner has shown that the Septuagint text quoted by Justin has a Lucianic character and deviates definitely from the text of Codex Vaticanus (B).

Some 60 years ago, Wilhelm Bousset tried to explain the Lucianic readings in Justin's quotations by supposing that the text of Justin must have been copied in a province of the Church in which the Lucianic text had become the approved text. There the quotations of Justin must have been thoroughly corrected in accordance with that text[3].

We find now the same text of the Greek Bible together with readings known to us from the so-called later Greek trans-

---

[1] See ThLZ 1954, Sp. 81.

[2] Karl August Credner, Beiträge zur Einführung in die biblischen Schriften, vol. II, Halle 1838. S. 282.

[3] Wilh. Bousset, Die Evangeliencitate Justins des Märtyrers in ihrem Werte für die Evangelienkritik von neuem untersucht. Göttingen 1891, see § 4, Die alttestamentlichen Citate J.'s, S. 18—32, especially S. 31.

lations, which had been used by Origen in his Hexapla, in a Codex written by a Jew about 300 years before Origen. The Greek Bible used by the Jews at the time of the beginning of Christianity was not at all a uniform text as supposed by Lagarde. The ancient Christians used texts of the Greek Bible which had already been adapted to the Hebrew original by the Jews in pre-Christian times.

For the history of the standard text of the Greek Torah called Septuagint we find in the letter of Aristeas valuable information which has been mistakenly disregarded in the history of the Greek Bible. In order to understand the latter correctly we have to realise that the letter was written as propaganda for a standard translation of the Greek Torah. Propaganda is always made for something contemporary, some pressing need at the time when the propaganda is made. The letter of Aristeas must have been written when the text with which it was concerned was just finished. When we know the date of the letter, we know at what time the standard text of the Greek Torah was made.

For dating the letter of Aristeas E. Bickermann has provided an argument by showing that certain formulas occurring in documents contained in the letter cannot be expected before 145 BC and not after 127 BC[1]. 'His argument seems to me most convincing, for it is on such minutiae too unimportant to be thought of by the average man that a forger most often trips up', declared an authority like Sir Idris Bell (see my Cairo Geniza, p. 135). If the letter was written in about 130 BC, the Greek Torah for which it is propaganda must only just have been made. At that time the influence of Greek Philology seems to have given rise to a desire for authentic texts among the Jews[2]. We must suppose that official circles in Alexandria were anxious to overcome inconveniences created by Greek texts of the Jewish Law circulating previously. They needed

---

1 E. Bickermann, Zur Datierung des Pseudo-Aristeas, ZNW 29, 1930, pp. 280—294.

2 Elias J. Bickermann, The Colophon of the Greek Book of Esther, JBL 63, 1944, p. 343.

a standard text, and such a text was made and approved by the community of Alexandria.

That this text was highly appreciated by the Jews we see from Philo's report of an annual festival held on the Island of Pharos

> to pay reverence to the spot on which the translation first shed its light and to render God thanks for a benefit ancient yet ever new . . .

It is hard to believe that such a festival was instituted and kept alive for 150 years without any justification. But the commission entrusted with the work of translation was selected by the community of Alexandria which accepted the text as the standard one, and the commission had to work like a modern commission entrusted with a revision of the text of the Bible: It had to work until all members of the commission agreed on every word of the text.

That the text was the first translation ever made, that it was made on the orders of a king, from a parchment scroll written with golden letters, by a commission of 72 members, six of each of the twelve tribes of Israel, selected by the high-priest of Jerusalem, that they made the work independently of one another, and in a period of 72 days agreed on every word of the translation, belongs like other features to the embellishment of Aristeas' letter intended to help the propaganda. Philo describes the way in which the work was done with the words:

> Sitting here in seclusion . . . they became as it were possessed, and under inspiration wrote not each several scribe something different, but the same word for word as though dictated to each by an invisible prompter . . . they worked not as translators, but as prophets and priests of God's mysteries. . . .

and for Philo it is completely the same whether the Hebrew or the Greek text was used.

Philo has little understanding for problems of philology. He speaks as an ecstatic theologian with special philosophical interests, without being aware that his own quotations from the Greek Torah differ widely from the standard text approved by the Alexandrian Jews. A professional expert who was contemporary with the letter of Aristeas and the standard translation to which it refers comes to a quite different judgement of the translation. Such an expert was the grandson of Ben Sira who translated the proverbs composed in Hebrew by his grandfather into Greek. In the Prologue he tells us that he came to Egypt in the 38th year of King Euergetes, i. e. 132 BC, and Ulrich Wilken has made it very likely[1] that the translation was made after the death of the king (117 BC), according to Bickermann in about 110 BC[2]. During his sojurn in Egypt he had learned not only the Egyptian Koine, in which the Prologue was written, but also the much more difficult translation-Greek into which he translated the book of his grandfather. He was aware of the imperfections of his own translation for which he excuses himself with the words — I quote the translation in Charles' Apocrypha:

> Ye are entreated, therefore, to make your perusal with favour and attention, and to be indulgent if in any parts of what we have laboured to interpret we may seem to fail in some of the phrases, for things originally spoken in Hebrew have not the same force in them when they are translated into another tongue.

But he is aware that the translations of the Bible which had been the model for his own work had suffered under the same difficulties:

> and not only these, but the Law itself, and the Prophets and the rest of the books have no small difference when they are spoken in their original form.

Here speaks someone who knows from his own experience the difficulties involved in translating a Hebrew text into the Greek language. The same imperfections which he attributes to his own work are to be found in the translations of his predecessors

---

[1] Archiv für Papyrusforschung, III, 1906, S. 451.
[2] Journal of Biblical Literature LXIII, 1944, p. 343.

also. When he mentions here the translation of the Law itself, he certainly refers to the standard edition of the Greek Torah, to which the letter of Aristeas refers. We have seen that this standard edition was made only a short time earlier. That in the Prologue the Prophets and the rest of the books are mentioned also, shows that the translation of these books must soon have followed the translation of the Law, and that Ben Sira was convinced that they had been made under similar circumstances. The grandson of Ben Sira considers himself as an immediate successor in the work of translation of the Bible and we may suppose that he was really contemporary with the work of the Alexandrian Committee.

I make the last statements with a caveat! Professor Kilpatrick has drawn my attention to the fact that there are reasons for taking the Prologue to Ben Sira at less than its face value. It is true that the Prologue does not occur in the oldest form of the Old Latin, and that it is absent from some Greek cursives, and other manuscripts have another Prologue which is, however, certainly later. Unfortunately the editions of the Greek Ben Sira are very inadequate. A real critical edition is not easy as the text of the Wisdom of Ben Sira, the Hebrew text as well as the Greek one, has undergone major revisions. The Cambridge scholar J. H. A. Hart speaks of a Pharisaic revision of the text — I think, rightly — and he discusses the many problems raised by the quotations of Clement Alexandrinus[1]. As far as I can see, it is in the main the revised texts which contain the differences in the Prologue.

It is further true that the Prologue is the only document before 70 AD which shows knowledge of the threefold Canon, the Law, the Prophets and the Scriptures. But the few lists of the Old Testament books preserved are of Palestinian origin, as also what is perhaps the oldest of these lists, a Hebrew-Aramaic list recently discovered by Jean-Paul Audet in the Jerusalem MS 54 in the Library of the Greek Patriarchate dated AD 1056 from which Philotheos Bryennios published the

[1] See his book: Ecclesiasticus, the Greek Text of Codex 248. Edited with a textual Commentary and Prolegomena. Cambridge 1909.

text of the Didache in Constantinople 1883. The list was known to Epiphanius also, and Audet has shown that it must be very old and that it refers to books partly written in Hebrew, partly in Aramaic[1]. The Prologue of Ben Sira was written in Egypt, just at the time when the great revision of the Greek Bible had been finished there. It is very likely that the tripartite Canon was known in Egypt long before it was known in Palestine. To me the chief reason for accepting the authenticity of the Prologue is to be found in the fact that it is hardly possible to discover any tendency which could explain its later insertion in view of its unusual nature. Besides it is clear that the critical way in which Ben Sira speaks of the Greek translation of the Law is to be understood far better if it is dated shortly after the translation had been finished than later when the propaganda of the letter of Aristeas had become effective.

What have we to say of these three texts of the Greek Bible written by Jews for Jews? In the first instance we have a Lucianic text written in about 150 BC. I think we must suggest with T. W. Manson that from a very early date Greek versions of the Bible were in use in places besides Alexandria and that such versions survived in whole or in parts[2]. One of such early Greek translations seems to have been the Greek Bible which was in use in Antioch and the province of Syria. This Greek Bible seems to lie behind the editorial work done by the martyr Lucian (d. 312 AD). In the Manchester fragment we have an interesting specimen of this text written about 500 years before Lucian, a text which must have existed long before the standard translation of the Torah was made in Alexandria which we are accustomed to call Septuagint. Another form of early translation was the Greek Bible which was used at Ephesus and Asia Minor, and which must have been the basis of the text

[1] The Biblical books are mentioned in the list in the following order: Gn Ex Lv Jos Dt Nu Ru Hi Jdc Ps 1S 2S 1R 2R 1Ch 2Ch Prv Qoh Cant Jer XII Proph Jes Ez Da 1Esr 2Esr Est. The list is published and all problems discussed by Audet in JThSt 1950, 135—154.

[2] I may refer here to T. W. Manson's review of my book The Cairo Geniza, in Dominican Studies II, April 1949, p. 183—194.

called in later times the text of Theodotion. No specimen of this text from pre-Christian times has so far been found. But St. Paul, writing in Ephesus, at 1 Cor 15. 54 quotes Is 25. 8 in a form verbally identical with the Theodotion text and with the Peshitta, against the Masoretic text and the Septuagint, and in the Gospel of St. John 19. 37 is quoted Zech 12. 10 according to Theodotion. It is very likely that in the version ascribed to Theodotion we have to see in reality Theodotion's edition of a Greek Bible used in Ephesus and in the synagogues of Asia.

In the second instance we have fragments of a Greek Bible written in about 100 BC, shortly after the standard Text of the Torah had been finished, a text closely related to Codex Vaticanus (B) of the Septuagint and in some ways superior to it, a text written 400 years or more before the Codex Vaticanus. Let us hope that an edition of all remnants of this important Papyrus Scroll will soon be published.

In the third instance we have a specimen of the Greek Bible as it was used by Jews at the time of the beginning of Christianity. The text has a Lucianic character, and besides has largely been approximated to the Hebrew original by readings known to us as such of the so-called Later Greek Translations like Aquila and Theodotion of which the beginnings must have existed in pre-Christian times. It is of especial interest that a text like this, written by a Jew for Jews in pre-Christian times, was quoted as his Septuagint by a Christian author like Justin the Martyr. We urgently need an edition of this important leather Scroll of which there is now more material in the Jerusalem Museum than was seen by Barthélemy. To explain some features of the Scroll, Barthélemy has referred to Willem Grossouw's book *The Coptic Versions of the Minor Prophets. A contribution to the study of the Septuagint.* Rome 1938 (Monumenta biblica et ecclesiastica 3). I discussed the matter with my son, the late Dr. Paul Eric Kahle, and have published the result of our discussions in ThLZ 1954, Sp. 92—94.

ON THE PRESENT STATE OF PROTO-SEPTUAGINT STUDIES

HARRY M. ORLINSKY
BALTIMORE HEBREW COLLEGE

DEDICATED TO THE MEMORY OF MAX LEOPOLD MARGOLIS (OCTOBER 1866–APRIL 1932)*

FOR THE past four-five years I have been working, *tempore volente,* on what amounts to a revised edition of some of the more important and controversial chapters in Swete(-Ottley)'s *Introduction to the Old Testament in Greek*[2] (1914). It has become increasingly clear to me that it may be several years more before I shall have all the material ready for publication. I have decided, therefore, to present at intervals a discussion of some specific phase of the field at large. Here I present, with some alterations and additions, the paper read two years ago (April, 1939) at the Baltimore meeting of the Society.[1]

The problem of the Proto-Septuagint, at no time since the days of Lagarde far from the background of Old Testament research, has come very much to the fore in the past decade, owing largely to the appearance of Montgomery's *Daniel,* Margolis' Greek Joshua, the publication of the Chester Beatty, Rylands, and Scheide papyri, and the writings of A. Sperber. I have discussed briefly the value of these groups of manuscripts in relation to our own specific problem in the course of a

Reprinted from *Journal of the American Oriental Society,* Vol. 61, 1941.

rather detailed review of Allgeier's *Die Chester Beatty-Papyri* in *JQR* 32 (1941-42). It is my purpose here to sketch summarily the recent history and nature of the problem, the decisive importance of the contributions of Montgomery and especially Margolis, and the character and value of Sperber's criticisms.

The basic result of Septuaginst studies down to the last quarter of the nineteenth century amounted essentially to this: there was one original, more or less official Greek translation of the Hebrew Bible, known to us through the Letter of Aristeas as the Septuagint. The best representative of this version is the rather imposing fourth-century uncial, Codex Vaticanus. To find it, one has but to consult any edition of the Septuagint that has appeared since the days of the Renaissance and the invention of printing. This view is still held today by many students of the Bible, so that the texts edited, e. g., by Tischendorf (-Nestle), Swete, and now Rahlfs, have become for them the Septuagint itself.

A great step forward in Septuagint studies was made in our own time when Brooke-McLean, following up the great, and still quite indispensable *Vetus Testamentum Graecum cum variis lectionibus* of Holmes-Parsons, began to make available in the Larger Cambridge Septuagint a mass of reliable evidence bearing on the history and text of the Septuagint. In the critical apparatus of these two works are to be found variants from practically all extant Greek manuscripts of the Old Testament, from the daughter and minor versions, and from the earlier patristic writings.

It is the great merit of that versatile mind, Paul de Lagarde, to have presented, beginning with 1880, the first really scientific analysis of the problem of the Proto-Septuagint.[2] He argued that all the preserved manuscripts of the Old Greek translation of the Bible (as distinct from the Minor Versions, etc.), as well as all the manuscripts of the translations made directly or indirectly from the Septuagint, such as the Old Latin, Ethiopic, Coptic, go back to the *trifaria varietas* of the Septuagint which, according to St. Jerome, was made in the third-fourth centuries A. D. in Egypt, Palestine, and Syria by Hesychius, Origen, and Lucian respectively. These three varieties, or recensions, in turn go back to the original Septuagint translation. Furthermore, it is possible to identify the Septuagint manuscripts as belonging to the one or the other recension with the aid of patristic citations and some of the daughter versions. When the Greek text used, e. g., by Cyril of Alexandria (fifth century), and when the Greek text underlying the Old Latin [3] and Ethiopic translations made for Africa, coincide substantially with the text found in one or more Greek manuscripts, then those manuscripts may safely be assigned to the Egyptian (Hesychian) recension. Again, when the text of a group of Greek manuscripts coincides overwhelmingly with the Greek text underlying the commentary of Theodoret of Antioch (fifth century), then that group of manuscripts may be designated as belonging to the Syrian (Lucianic) recension. The same applies to the Palestinian recension of Origen. Once the basic text within each recension has been attained, with the proper use of textual criticism, then the three texts of the three recensions, again with the application of the principles of the textual criticism peculiar to the Hebrew-Greek, are reduced to a basic text which is, in the words of Margolis, "the nearest approach to the Greek original as it left the hands of the translator(s)."

Cut short by death in 1891, Lagarde's work was assigned later on, in 1907, to Alfred Rahlfs, who himself passed away just a few years ago (April, 1935). The ideas of Lagarde found notable expression in such standard commentaries as Cornill's *Ezechiel* (1886), Moore's *Judges* (1895, cf. his discussion of the Antiochian recension, *AJSL* 29 (1912) 37-62), Driver's *Notes on . . . Samuel* (1899; 2nd ed. 1913), but above all and with the greatest acumen in Montgomery's *Daniel* (1927).[4]

It was, however, the late Prof. Margolis who carried out the Lagardian idea most completely and successfully to its logical conclusion. For two decades he devoted himself to the problem of reconstructing the text of the Septuagint translation of the book of Joshua, providing us with the most exhaustive investigation ever made by any one man or group of men of the entire textual history of any one Book in the Old Testament. From his all too few publications on the problem,[5] and from what can be learned from the four fascicles of his Greek Joshua that have appeared to date,[6] we can see that Margolis worked out the problem in the following manner, guided it is true by Lagarde's hypothesis, but basically, like the careful and methodical scholar that he was, following the road indicated by the material itself, using the inductive method throughout.[7] Whenever possible, he gathered from all corners of the earth photographic reproductions of every uncial and cursive Greek manuscript, catena, lectionary, and the like, containing all or part of Joshua. In addition he had before him the various editions of the Onomasticon and of all the secondary versions, such as the Old Latin, Syriac, Sahidic, Bohairic, Ethiopic, Arabic, Armenian, and of all the earlier patristic writers, such as Justin, Origen, Eusebius, and Theodoret. He chose Joshua of all the books in the Bible because it lent itself admirably to textual and exegetical analysis and, what is of supreme importance, because it contained hundreds of proper names in the text.[8]

The conclusions reached by Margolis I quote from his last pertinent article, brief but comprehensive, " Specimen of a New Edition of the Greek Joshua " (in *Jewish Studies in Memory of Israel Abrahams,* New York, 1927, 307-23) : " The sum of the witnesses yields four principal recensions, PCSE, and in addition a number of MSS. variously mixed which I name M. At the outset it must be remarked that all of our witnesses are more or less mixed; the classification has in mind the basic character of a text, which alone is the determinant. P is the Palestinian recension spoken of by Jerome, that is the Eusebian edition of the Septuagint column in Origen's Hexapla-Tetrapla [then as in the case of CSEM below, follows a sketch of some of the more important manuscripts that belong to this recension] . . . C is a recension which was at home in Constantinople and Asia Minor. We are helped in localizing the recension by the aid of the Armension version . . . Whether the recension had any relationship to the fifty copies ordered by Constantine from Eusebius, . . . as CONYBEARE suspects, must remain a matter of conjecture. Jerome says nothing of a fourth recension; but then he is by no means exact, or the recension was at his time just in the process of formation . . . Perhaps we may suppose that C made use of the common text prevalent in Palestine, which naturally remained freer from corruptions in the geographical names. This Palestinian *koine* was only slightly touched up by Theodotion—*Urtheodotion* would according be nothing but this Palestinian *koine* . . . S is the Syrian (Antiochian) recension . . . An outstanding characteristic of the S recension is the correction of the Greek style, as shown by the substitution of Attic grammatical forms for Hellenistic. Otherwise Jerome's description of Lucian as but a form of the common text holds good. But it is a distinct form, as the proper names show with all the desired evidence. The Egyptian recension, E, is preserved with relative purity in B . . . The Coptic and Ethiopic versions unmistakably point to the Egyptian provenance of their text. Hence the designation of the recension. There remain a number of MSS. which may be classed together as M, i. e. mixed texts. Mixture is the general characteristic, the elements coming from the four principal recensions in diverse processes of contamination. Perhaps it may be said that the ground work is the C type, but not quite wholly so. Certain groups emerge . . . The road to the original text of G leads across the common, unrevised text. In order to get at the latter, we must abstract from the recensional manipulations . . . A study of the translator's mannerism of rendition becomes imperative . . . The scope of my edition is to restore critically the original form of the version. I print the critically restored text at the top of the page. Below follow the forms assumed in the four classes, E, S, P, CM. Omissions and contractions of the text, by which certain witnesses or groups of witnesses step out as silent on the textual form, receive a rubric of their own. Then follow individual variations of class members, such as leave the characteristic class reading undisturbed in its main features. Lastly marginal readings in so far as they have not been embodied above. The subjoined Specimen illustrates the arrangement."

This lengthy quotation from Margolis speaks for itself. I accept his argument and method as correct. Moreover, and this is of decisive importance in view of the nature of the problem, Prof. Montgomery, working quite independently and on another type of book altogether, found the facts and interpretation in Joshua to hold true by and large in the case of the text of Daniel also.[9]

In the second third of the nineteenth century, Rosenmüller, Olshausen, and Lagarde, especially the last-named, advanced the view, which is held by practically all competent scholars today, that all preserved manuscripts of the Hebrew text of the Old Testament go back to the one recension, which came to dominate in the first-second century A. D. at the latest.[10] In this I concur. One has merely to consult Kennicott's *Vetus Testamentum Hebraicum cum variis lectionibus,* De Rossi's *Variae Lectiones Veteris Testamenti,* the critical apparatus in the Baer and Ginsburg editions of the "masoretic" text, the scores of Babylonian and other biblical fragments discovered and studied by Kahle,[11] to realize that outside of Kethib-Qere variants, innumerable cases of *scriptio plena* and *defectiva,* scribal errors of the usual kind ([pseudo-] dittography, [pseudo-] haplography, homoioteleuton, homoioarcton, confusion of letters, and the like), glosses, etc., the manuscripts collated do not offer such deviations in text (I do not, of course, refer to order of books, section, chapter, and verse arrangements, and the like) as to indicate recensional differences.[12] There can be no serious doubt that once each of the three sections of the Hebrew Bible were canonized[13] and the consonantal text fixed practically no changes, if any at all, were made.

Up to the end of the nineteenth century Strack stood practically alone among competent scholars in denying "that all Hebrew MSS go back to a single standard copy."[14] However, from the beginning of this century he has been joined by Paul Kahle, who has contended that there were originally many Hebrew manuscripts differing one from the other. In the course of time variants and other differences were eliminated, so that what resulted was the "masoretic" text with which we operate today. From this, essentially *a priori,* reasoning Kahle deduced that Lagarde's thesis was erroneous, and that it was methodologically impermissible to attempt to trace back all current manuscripts of the Hebrew Bible to one text-tradition.[15]

I can see no basis for this sort of hypothetical argument, even apart from the pertinent factual evidence available. Of course there was at one time more than one text-tradition of the Hebrew Bible. The Hebrew manuscripts used by the several Septuagint translators of the various books in the Old Testament differ at times not in minor details alone, but, as is the case in such books as Jeremiah, Job, Esther, *recensionally* from the masoretic text-tradition. But those text-traditions have long perished, driven out by the Hebrew text that was used by the Mishnah and Talmud,[16] by Theodotion,[17] Aquila,[18] Symmachus,[19] Origen,[20] Jerome,[21] from the first-second to the fifth centuries A. D. Lagarde is therefore right, and Kahle is wrong, when the latter objects to the former's judgment that all *extant* Hebrew manuscripts of the Bible go back to one text-tradition.

In 1915 [22] Kahle applied the same purely *a priori* reasoning to the field of the Septuagint. He disagreed with Lagarde that all Greek manuscripts go back to one text-tradition or recension; they go back to a number of totally independent and original Greek translations. Kahle presented no specific evidence to prove his hypothesis with regard to the Septuagint, any more than he did with regard to the Masorah. Excellent organizer that he is (cf. my remarks in *JQR* 31 (1940-41) 63 n. 7), Kahle later entrusted the task of refuting the Lagardian theory, with facts, to his pupil, Alexander Sperber, who is really the only one to have written in defense of Kahle's position against that of Lagarde and Rahlfs. I propose now to analyze Sperber's arguments.

In his monograph, *Septuagintaprobleme* (1929),[23] Sperber declared that all attempts to identify individual Septuagint manuscripts according to families were methodologically unsound, since they were based on ordinary text open to all kinds of interpretation. The only decisive criterion was proper names, since, among other things, with the minimum of room for exegesis it was possible to determine the genetic relationship of manuscripts by the forms of the names preserved in these manuscripts. Although this argument is one of technique rather than of principle, the important point for us here, as emphasized so fully above, is that Margolis chose Joshua and worked twenty years over it for precisely that reason!—its preponderance of names. Sperber knew this to be so, since he reviewed the Israel Abrahams Memorial Volume in the *OLZ* 32 (1929) 361 f., and makes specific reference to Margolis' "Specimen."[24] In short, knowing that Margolis chose Joshua because of its multitude of proper names, Sperber nevertheless proceeds to ignore completely all of Margolis' work, as he does likewise the work of Montgomery, Gehman, Allgeier, and others,[25] and to devote himself to attacking the Lagardian theory and practise because proper names were not being utilized! The very obvious and just question immediately presents itself: since Margolis' method and perspective, i. e., the use of proper names inductively, are exactly what Sperber advocates in any analysis of the Proto-Septuagint, precisely with what in Margolis' analysis and conclusions, as expressed in his "Specimen" and Greek Joshua, does he disagree? And quite apart from his negative attitude, there is this to be said about Sperber's positive treatment of proper names in *Septuagintaprobleme*: since he limited himself to an analysis of proper names in various chapters of the Hexateuch, *removed from their context*, his study could at best be stimulating and tentative, but never decisive. Margolis' study, on the other hand, was based on names and text, all in context, of an entire book, the work of a single translator, and hence possesses decisive character. Finally it should be noted that Montgomery's independent inductive study of a text like Daniel, so lacking in proper names and so flexible at times in exegesis, led him to the same conclusions that Margolis had reached.

In 1934 there appeared an article by Sperber in the Hebrew University quarterly, *Tarbiz*,[26] in which readings in the New Testament were compared with their correspondents in the Old Testament, to prove, since the two differ occasionally, that there had not yet sprung up in New Testament days a fixed text of the Greek Old Testament. This conclusion, of course, has long been well known,[27] but the method employed by Sperber in this study, it seems to me, is too full of fundamental errors to be of any value for our problem. Thus, e. g., since practically all printed editions of the Septuagint use Codex Alexandrinus for the first forty-six chapters of Genesis, for which Codex Vaticanus is lacking, Sperber takes the reading of Alexandrinus as the Septuagint. All the variants in all the other individual manuscripts, not to mention families of manuscripts, are ignored.[28] From the New Testament, which has very complex textual problems of its own, he takes the reading in Vaticanus; once again all other variants and recensions and daughter versions are ignored. In Gen. 2:24 the masoretic text reads אֶת־אָבִיו "his father." Alexandrinus in the Old Testament renders literally, τὸν πατέρα αὐτοῦ "his father." Vaticanus in the New Testament, Math. 19:5, reads simply τὸν πατέρα, to be rendered *per se* "the father," but in context "his father." Therefore, argues Sperber, the Greek New Testament differs from the Greek Old Testament because the former was based on a Greek translation of the Old Testament entirely independent of the latter. To reduce the two independent translations to the one text-tradition is impossible.

But one has merely to study these passages and words properly to realize the error in Sperber's reasoning. There are many manuscripts in Genesis that read simply τὸν πατέρα, and many manuscripts in the New Testament that read τὸν πατέρα αὐτοῦ. How much more logical and straightforward to see the problem not as a Vaticanus New Testament vs. Alexandrinus Old Testament one, but as an inner Greek Genesis one. And what is decisive here is the fact that those manuscripts in Genesis that read τὸν πατέρα αὐτοῦ have a text that is basically and overwhelmingly identical with the text of those manuscripts in Genesis that read simply τὸν πατέρα (cf. Brooke-McLean for the textual evidence; unfortunately the Chester Beatty papyri do not cover this passage). All talk of independent and equally original Greek translations is without foundation.[29]

For essentially the same reasons I am unable to accept Sperber's arguments advanced in "The Problems of the Septuagint Recensions" (*JBL* 54 (1935) 73-92). The Greek text underlying the commentary on the Minor Prophets by Theodoret of Antioch (fifth century) is doubtless of the Syrian (Lucianic) recension. The Greek text underlying the commentary on the same Books by the contemporary Cyril of Alexandria is doubtless of the Egyptian (Hesychian) recension. Sperber emphasizes three words in the masoretic text that are rendered in Theodoret's text differently from Cyril's text: Hebrew חסד "loving-kindness" is τὸ ἔλεον in Theodoret, τὸ ἔλεος in Cyril; [30] חרב "sword" is μάχαιρα in Theodoret, ῥομφαία in Cyril; and על "on" is ἐν in Theodoret, ἐπὶ in Cyril. From this Sperber deduces that the Greek text underlying Theodoret is totally independent of the Greek *Vorlage* of Cyril, and that both texts go back to different original translations.

We must bear in mind, however, that Lucian frequently transforms *koine* Greek forms into the corresponding Attic; that he alters prepositions and the like so that the context results in smoother Greek; that he replaces a word or phrase by a synonym, sometimes both the original and the gloss remaining in the texts side by side, giving rise to doublets.[30a] In our own problem, τὸ ἔλεον of Theodoret is nothing more than the Attic form of Cyril's τὸ ἔλεος; μάχαιρα is Theodoret's synonym of Cyril's ῥομφαία; Theodoret's ἐν for Cyril's ἐπὶ was to Lucian smoother Greek. In fine, Theodoret's text is different from Cyril's only recensionally; basically they come from the same ancestor.[31]

As pointed out above in the long quotation from Margolis, and this has long been the dictum of all textual analysis in all fields, " the classification [of manuscripts into recensions] has in mind the basic character of a text, which alone is the determinant." To bring this out more strikingly, it would be of interest for one to record not merely the differences between Theodoret and Cyril, but also where they agree, and what is more important, an analysis of the disagreements in light of the accepted laws of textual criticism, bearing in mind the fact that *variae lectiones non sunt numerandae, sed pensandae.* Finally, for a most instructive methodological analysis of precisely this kind of problem, I can refer to nothing better than Rahlfs' " Theodorets Zitate aus den Königsbüchern und dem 2. Buche der Chronik " (pp. 16-46 of *Septuaginta-Studien* I 1904), from which I may cite the following: " Theodoret hat durchweg nicht nur die lucianischen Lesarten, sondern auch die lucianische Anordnuug des Textes [p. 17] . . . Als Resultat unserer Untersuchung ergibt sich, dass Theodorets Zitate . . . sind sehr wertvoll für die Nachweisung der lucianischen Rezension in unsern Bibelhandschriften [p. 43]. Cf. also, e. g., his " Der Text des Septuaginta-Psalters " (= *Septuaginta-Studien* II, 1907), § 39, p. 171, " Von Theodoret, dem bekannten Exegeten der von Lucian gegründeten antiochischen Schule . . ."

It is really in his "Wiederherstellung einer griechischen Textgestalt des Buches Ruth" (*Monatss. f. Gesch. u. Wiss. d. Jud.*, 81 (1937) 55-65) that the character of Sperber's criticism of the Lagardian theory reveals itself as so obviously without foundation that I devote a few sentences to it here only to complete the discussion of all his pertinent works.[32] The essence of the article is as follows. In his detailed study of the Septuagint and other versions of Ruth (cf. n. 37 below), Rahlfs dealt with an Old Latin manuscript that he found to belong essentially to the same family of which Vaticanus was a member. Sperber denied any basic relationship whatever between the two. To prove his contention, Sperber turned the Old Latin translation back into Greek, obtaining a Greek text that differed considerably from anything known to us hitherto. This new Greek text, he concluded, proved that this Old Latin manuscript had nothing to do with Vaticanus or any other Greek manuscript extant, and was actually descended from a lost Greek translation which has left no trace of itself and which was completely independent of the Septuagint text-tradition.

One can but agree that this new translation is different from any devised heretofore. It is characterized by its artificial Latin-into-Greek dictionary and concordance translation. Witness, e. g., the omission at times of the definite article in this new Greek version simply because the Old Latin lacked one, ignoring the fact that Latin did not operate with the definite article![33] As a matter of fact, all four of the key passages in the Old

Latin-Greek that Sperber himself emphasizes as being altogether new and different from all other manuscripts and providing evidence for an independent and original translation, find rather obvious solutions and certainly legitimate ancestors in Greek manuscripts collated in the Larger Cambridge Septuagint. Thus the OL reading in 1: 1, *in diebus iudicis iudicum* indicates to Sperber a Greek *Vorlage* ἐν ἡμέραις τοῦ κριτοῦ τῶν κριτῶν, and a Hebrew text-tradition בִּימֵי שְׁפֹט הַשֹּׁפְטִים (pp. 58 [ad loc.], 63 f.),[34] as opposed to masoretic . . . בימי שְׁפֹט. As a matter of fact a good Greek *Vorlage* of the OL may be found, e. g., in ἐν ταῖς ἡμέραις τοῦ κρίνοντος τοὺς κριτάς, and this is precisely the reading preserved in N. And as for *iudicis,* Rahlfs has noted the reading in the Vulgate, *in diebus unius iudicis* (p. 130), and the general influence of the Vulgate on this eleventh century OL manuscript (129 f., § 7).[35] The OL reading at 2: 23, *et adiunxisti te,* according to Sperber, points to an underlying καὶ προσκολλήθητι and an original וְתִדְבְּקִי, as opposed to " MT: וַתִּדְבַּק : LXX: καὶ προσεκολλήθη." But the Septuagint does not read simply καὶ προσεκ.; all extant Greek manuscripts and daughter versions read καὶ προσεκ. Ῥούθ, " and Ruth clave unto." The ρουθ element precludes Sperber's assumed προσκολληθητι. If the problem be inner-Greek then one may perhaps guess that an original (προσεκολληθ)η ρουθ became either by dittography or because of the proper name following (προσεκολληθ)η η Ρουθ (note that *m* in Brooke-McLean [= Rahlfs 72, d_2 in Margolis' Greek Joshua] is described as " ρουθ] pr η " !) ; the newcomer η was misread τι (H > TI in uncial form),[36] whence και προσ(ε)κολληθητι gave rise to *et adiunxisti te,* and ρουθ, now quite impossible in the context ("and you shall attach yourself to, Ruth . . .") was dropped altogether. In any case, to ignore any possible inner-Greek or inner-Old Latin solution, and to assume an entirely different Hebrew text-tradition because of "das lateinische Original, dessen Wert als Textzeuge doch nicht angezweifelt werden kann" (p. 63), is contrary to all accepted rules of textual criticism involving a secondary version, in this case of the eleventh century, particularly when we cannot at all be sure that it has come down to us in its original textual form; cf. above, n. 31, for the many textual corruptions preserved in this OL manuscript, and the possibility of an additional one.

In the third instance, involving the syntax of the definite article in הַלַּיְלָה (3:13), Sperber rejects the unanimous Septuagint τὴν νύκτα, and assumes ταύτῃ τῇ νυκτί as the Greek reading responsible for the OL *hac nocte.* As I have pointed out elsewhere (*JQR* 30 (1939-40) 43 n. 25), what is involved is not the Hebrew, but the character of the translation-Greek. The final case in point, *ut inires* (3:10), is most instructive. Sperber assumes an underlying corrupted Greek text, τοῦ πορευθῆναί σε (as opposed to received τοῦ μὴ πορευθηναί σε for masoretic לְבִלְתִּי לֶכֶת), which he declares to have been lost until rediscovered by himself in his retroversion. He might have spared himself the entire discussion had he but utilized the apparatus in Brooke-McLean—two cursives, b′ q, read precisely τοῦ πορευθῆναι!

Finally, quite apart from the above criticism of detail (cf. also n. 32, on Ruth 1: 11), there are two important principles involved: (1) as emphasized repeatedly, e. g., by Montgomery, "The only method for the study of the VSS lies in the way of their genetic relationships, their language is a very secondary item" (*Daniel,* p. 24) . . . The sub-versions have to be handled with care. They may not be treated as though they were prime versions, but only as representatives of their groups. So treated they are invaluable, but without laying down their genetic history such comparison is most fallacious" (p. 57); "Again, it is not a dispute among codices but among manuscript groups (e. g., Ethiopic and Old Latin are often closest to B), as so to say, not a personal but a family affair, a fact that much current criticism tends to ignore" (*JBL* 55 (1936) 310); (2) instead of basing conclusions on scribal errors and the like in this secondary version it would have been more reasonable and profitable to have made note of the overwhelming extent to which this OL manuscript agreed with other primary and secondary versions, and thus to determine its basic text and affinity.[37]

This entire discussion may now conveniently be summed up as follows:

I. Lagarde's principles, plausible enough *a priori,* have been found to be essentially sound in the inductive works of men like Rahlfs, Montgomery, and Margolis.

II. The new pertinent manuscript data, such as the Chester Beatty, Rylands, and Scheide papyri, serve to push back the problem of recension and of the Proto-Septuagint chronologically nearer to its date of composition; they do not alter the problem.

III. The criticism levelled against the Lagardian theory by Kahle-Sperber have neither refuted anything nor do they have any positive basis whatever in themselves.

On another occasion I hope to deal with other aspects of the Lagardian theory and the problem of the Proto-Septuagint, e. g., on how to use the numerous Greek manuscripts and editions that go to make up the "Septuagint," especially in the textual criticism of those books in the Old Testament for which works like Rahlfs' Ruth, Montgomery's Daniel, and Margolis' Joshua are lacking.

* It is now nine years since this great teacher and scholar passed away. His contributions to biblical philology, especially to the Septuagint, are not as well known as they deserve to be; his *magnus opus*, the Greek Joshua, has not received even a fraction of the attention it merits. Perhaps this brief sketch of the Proto-Septuagint, which touches on the character and value of his work, may in some measure help to right this wrong.

I may note here in passing that I entered the Dropsie College in October 1931 in order to specialize in biblical studies under Margolis. He was then already a very sick man. In November he was stricken and I never saw him again. Nevertheless, the influence of Margolis was felt in the College and it led me to become interested in the rather complex field of the Septuagint.

This article has been made much clearer and more presentable by the many helpful suggestions of Prof. Albright and Dr. Louis L. Kaplan. Prof. Speiser's editorial hand is likewise in evidence. It is interesting that both Kaplan and Speiser studied under Margolis at the Dropsie College, and Albright has more than once alluded to his "privilege of attending a course in the Greek of Joshua given by Margolis in the year 1924-5, while the latter was Annual Professor at the School in Jerusalem" (*JBL* 56 (1937) 173; cf. also *ZAW* 3 (1926) 225 f. and n. 1).

[1] See the abstract in *JAOS* 59 (1939), 401. The paper read at the Society's meeting in Ann Arbor (April, 1935) on another phase, "The Columnar Order of the Hexapla," appeared in *JQR* 27 (1936-7) 137-49. My paper on "The Priority of the Tetrapla to the Hexapla," read before the Society of Biblical Literature, Dec. 1936 (cf. *JBL* 56 (1937) p. x), is part of a much larger discussion, and has not been prepared as yet for publication.

[2] Cf. *Symmicta*, II, 1880, 137 ff.; *Ankündigung einer neuen Ausgabe der griechischen Übersetzung des A. T.* (1882).

[3] On the basis of a possible interpretation of a formula in Latin inscribed on a column recently uncovered in Pompeii, F. V. Filson has asked "whether the earliest Latin translations of the New Testament may have been made, not in Africa as usually held, but in Italy" (*Biblical Archaeologist* 2 (1939) 13-16). The most recent lucid discussions of the Old Latin and the problem of its sources, together with references to the earlier literature, may perhaps be found in Driver, *Notes on . . . Samuel*[2], Introd., lxxvi ff.; Montgomery, ICC on *Daniel*, Introd., 29 ff., 43 ff. Cf. also Haupert's doctoral dissertation on *The Relation of Codex Vaticanus and the Lucianic Text in the Books of the Kings from the Viewpoint of the Old Latin and the Ethiopic Versions* (Phila., 1930).

[4] On pp. 138 f. of his *Canon and Text of the O. T.* (1892), Buhl notes that "before him [viz., Lagarde] the Danish bishop Fr. Münter conjectured that the Recension [of Hesychius] might be found in some one of the Coptic translations." Münter's work, *Specimen versionum Danielis coptiarum* (Rome 1786), cited by Buhl on p. 141 (§ 3), is not accessible to me.

[5] Among the most pertinent may be cited: "The Grouping of the Codices in the Greek Joshua, a Preliminary Notice," *JQR* 1 (1910) 259-63; "The K Text of Joshua," *AJSL* 28 (1911) 1-55; "The Washington MS. of Joshua," *JAOS* 31 (1911) 365-7; "Corrections in the Apparatus of the Book of Joshua in the Larger Cambridge Septuagint," *JBL* 49 (1930) 234-64; and especially "Specimen of a New Edition of the Greek Joshua," in *Jewish Studies in Memory of Israel Abrahams* (New York 1927) 307-23. It is extremely to be regretted that Margolis' important monograph on the three forms of the Syriac version and on the character of the Palestinian recension (Hexapla-Tetrapla) of the Greek Joshua, which was stated in the "Specimen" (p. 308) "to appear in the Harvard Theological Series," has not seen the light of day.

Time and again sweeping reference is made in the "Specimen" to "my monograph on Masius." In view of the fact that war conditions will long make impossible Geuthner's publication of Margolis' Introduction to the Greek Joshua (and perhaps also of the concluding part V of the text), if the manuscript is not already destroyed, the significance of this monograph becomes only too evident. Biblical scholarship will indeed be grateful to the Editors of the Harvard Theological Series if they will spare no effort to locate and publish it.

[6] *The Book of Joshua in Greek*, Parts I-IV (covering 19: 37 f.) have appeared from 1931 to 1938. See Montgomery's review of Part I in *JQR* 23 (1932-3) 293-5.

[7] In view of a prevalent idea that Margolis was simply carrying out Lagarde's *a priori* reasoning, and because I shall have to refer to this again below, it may be well worthwhile citing a few pertinent passages to dispel this notion: "While engaged in a study of the transliterations occurring in the Greek Old Testament . . . I I deemed it advisable to include geographical terms . . . and names of places. . . . This additional material being particularly abundant in the Book of Joshua, my attention was caught by the frequently recurring collocation of certain sigla in the apparatus of Holmes-Parsons. In one instance where an entire verse had to be investigated, the grouping was unmistakable. With the key found, I set about working up chapters 15 and 19 which are replete with place-names, but also other passages, covering in all one-half of the book. My key proved to work; of course, as my range of observation widened, slight rearrangements in detail ensued which, however, left the general grouping intact. . . . My results, while at present naturally only tentative (especially with regard to the sub-groups), go to reveal the following six groups. . . . I intend to follow up the present preliminary notice. . . . Naturally the determination of the sub-groups and of much else besides will become more accurate as the complete induction becomes ready for tabulation. . . ." (from "The Grouping of the Codices . . .," listed in n. 5 above); "I am preparing for publication an edition

of the Greek Joshua according to the text of the cursives with which Tischendorf's uncial [viz., K] stands in affinity. . . . In presenting on this occasion an edition of K ahead of my forthcoming edition of the entire text . . . I am guided by the desire to take my bearings for the latter . . ." (from "The K Text of Joshua"); "An accurate estimate of the place of θ [= Washington ms. in Freer Collection] and A in the narrower group to which they belong is impossible without a fresh collation of its constituent codices, both uncial and cursive. In view of the inaccuracies in Swete's apparatus . . . an edition of . . . θ with . . . A is deemed desirable . . . to serve as a basis for a collation of the other group-members, like M and N and the rest . . ." (from "The Washington MS. of Joshua"); and finally, "My own work on the Greek Joshua was begun in 1910. . . . The preliminary notice then published on the grouping of the codices . . . was based practically on HOLMES-PARSONS and lacks, of course, the precision which I have now arrived at after sixteen years of labor. The sum of the witnesses yields four principal recensions . . . and . . . a number of MSS. variously mixed . . ." (from "Specimen . . .," 308).

[8] As is evident already from "The Grouping of the Codices . . ." cited in the preceding note, Margolis first came to recognize in "geographical terms . . . and names of places . . . [the key to the] collocation of certain sigla in the apparatus of HOLMES-PARSONS," noting "that Hollenberg was once engaged in a similar occupation (for Joshua and Judges); his one short article in the *ZAW*. I (1881) 97-105, deals with the matter only casually." Or again, a year later, in the "Washington Ms. of Joshua," "The disagreements between Θ and A in the proper names are, generally speaking, of a nature to substantiate rather than to invalidate the affinity of the two uncials, the divergence between them being trifling, when their common deviation from B is compared. . . . On our steep road to the earliest form of the Septuagint, we need resting places, points of vantage; such are the groups, narrower and wider, into which the extant texts may be divided. The proper names in the

Book of Joshua are the milestones which guide the investigator in finding his way to texts held together by group affinity."

This is an extremely important fact to be kept in mind, and I shall return to it below, in connection with A. Sperber's criticisms.

[9] Cf. "The Hexaplaric Strata in the Greek Texts of Daniel," *JBL* 44 (1925) 289-302 (with reference to the related studies by Ch. D. Benjamin and Gehman that follow immediately, pp. 303-326 and 327-52 respectively); ICC on *Daniel* (1927), Introd., § III "Ancient Versions," pp. 24-57 (verily *multum in parvo*!); also his reviews of the *editiones principes* of the Rylands and Scheide papyri (respectively, *JBL* 55 (1936) 309-11 and *JAOS* 59 (1939) 262-5). In recent years Gehman has done much important work on recensional groupings of versions and sub-versions in various Books of the Old Testament (cf. *JAOS* 54 (1934) 53 ff. and n. 1; also the references to Gehman in my review of Allgeier).

[10] For the literature on the subject cf. Buhl's *Canon and Text* . . . , 258; Reider, *Prolegomena to ι[n]* . . . *Index to Aquila*, Chap. IV, § 33 and the notes *ibid.*

[11] Cf. Kahle, § III of the Prolegomena in Kittel's BH^3 (pp. vi-xv), and the Index Codicum Veteris Testamenti Babylonicum (*ibid.*, pp. xxx-xxxiii).

[12] It is not very often that a Hebrew manuscript of the Bible will differ from the received text to the extent that Kenn 223 does in Job 5:8, where it reads שַׁדַּי in place of the reading preserved in hundreds of other manuscripts and in our own "masoretic" texts, אֱלֹהִים. There can be no doubt that שׁדי is the original reading (cf. my "Job 5:8, a Problem in Greek-Hebrew Methodology," *JQR* 25 (1934-5) 271-8. To the three arguments listed on p. 278 may now be added a fourth, viz., the parallel passage, 13:3, which likewise reads שׁדי [// אֵל]). But does that make Kenn 223 a member of another text-tradition or recension? A careful collation of this manuscript dispels any such notion completely. The same is true, e. g., of Kenn 248 at 32:1 (where we

read בְּעֵינֵיהֶם for masoretic בְּעֵינָיו; cf. idem, n. 19), of the variant לבתים for masoretic לַגְּבָרִים at Josh. 7: 17 (cf. Margolis' thorough study, *JQR* 3 (1912-3) 319-336, overlooked, e. g., in Noth's *Das Buch Josua* [1938]), and of all other extant manuscripts with unique readings. Cf. Montgomery, *Daniel*, pp. 11 ff. The Hebrew manuscripts discussed recently by Blank (*HUCA* 8-9 (1931-2) 229-55), Hempel (*Nachrichten v. d. Gesell. d. Wiss. zu Göttingen* [Philolog.-Hist. Klasse, N. F. Band I Nr. 7], 1937, 227-37), and Bewer (*Jewish Studies in Memory of George A. Kohut*, New York, 1935, 86-8), e. g., likewise bear this out fully enough. It is unfortunate that the Nash papyrus, recently demonstrated by Prof. Albright to be of Maccabean age ("roughly . . . 165-37 B. C."; cf. the exhaustive paleographic discussion in *JBL* 56 (1937) 145-76), cannot be used with confidence for our purposes, since it is a lectionary or the like, quite fragmentary (containing the Decalogue and the Shema), and probably copied *memoriter*.

[13] On the most recent "Historical Study of the Canonization of the Hebrew Scriptures," by S. Zeitlin, see *Proc. of the Amer. Acad. for Jew. Res.* 3 (for 1931-2) 121-58.

[14] See his article, "Text of the Old Testament," in Hastings' DB, IV (1902) 727 f.; and his earlier paper, "Ueber verloren gegangene Handschriften des Alten Testaments," in *Semitic Studies in Memory of . . . Alexander Kohut* (1897), 560-72. Cf. also, e. g., Driver, *Notes on . . . Samuel*[2], Introd., p. xxxiv, n. 6.

[15] Kahle's general remarks may be found, e. g., in *Masoreten des Ostens* (1913), "Der masoretische Text des Alten Testaments" (*Einleitung*, pp. vii-xx; Kahle's use of the term "Renzension" with regard to Jacob ben Hayyim, Ben Asher, etc., is to be understood, of course, in relation to the use of the metheg, hateph, maqqeph, some Kethib-Qere, and the like. So far as the consonantal text-tradition is concerned, no separate recension is involved—one has but to compare any edition of the "masoretic" text, such as those by Baer, Ginsburg, and the rabbinic Bible known as *Miqra'ot Gedolot*, with that of Jacob ben Hayyim [16th cent.; = essentially

Kittel's BH[2]] and Ben Asher [10th cent.; = essentially BH[3]] to realize this. Cf. my remarks in *JQR* 31 [1940-1] 62 f.); *Theologische Studien und Kritiken*, 88 (1915) 426 ff.; "Die Punktation der Masoreten," pp. 167-72 of the Marti number of the *Beihefte zur ZAW* 41 (1925); *Masoreten des Westens* (1927), "Der masoretische Textus receptus des Alten Testaments und der Text der Ben Ašer," pp. 1-23.

As indicated above, it is to be regretted that Kahle has not attempted publicly to demonstrate his hypothesis inductively (and no one in the scholarly world had more ready access to biblical manuscripts, and well-trained students to work under him), for then this baseless proposition would be withdrawn from circulation once and for all.

[16] Cf., e. g., V. Aptowitzer, *Das Schriftwort in der Rabbinischen Literatur* (1906-15).

[17] To appreciate the inclusion here of Theodotion (2nd cent. On his priority to Aquila, see my references to Schürer and Montgomery, *JQR* 27 [1936-7] 143, n. 14) it is sufficient to list the following facts: (1) ". . . the common text prevalent in Palestine . . . naturally remained freer from corruptions in the geographical names. This Palestinian *koine* was only slightly touched up by Theodotion—*Urtheodotion* would accordingly be nothing but this Palestinian *koine*" (from Margolis' "Specimen . . .," 311); (2) the Hebrew text of the Bible current in the days of Origen (late 2nd-first half of the 3rd cent.) was so identical with Theodotion's Greek version and Hebrew text-tradition that Origen invariably resorted to this version when squaring the *textus receptus* of the Septuagint with the *textus receptus* of the Hebrew in his Hexapla. One has but to glance through Field's edition of *Origenis Hexaplorum quae supersunt* to convince himself of this.

[18] Cf. Reider's authoritative *Prolegomena . . .*, Chap. IV, § 34, "There is just as little doubt in turn that in the times of Akiba, when Aquila and his cogeners lived and laboured, the Hebrew text had, roughly speaking, assumed the form of our Masoretic text." See also the following sections in this chapter.

[19] St. Jerome (4th-5th cent.), in composing the Vulgate, made frequent use of Symmachus (cf. the instructive discussion and examples in Driver, *Notes on . . . Samuel*[2], pp. liii f. and lxxx ff., and the references there to other works, especially to Nowack's standard work, *Die Bedeutung des Hieronymus . . .*). That this Greek version sacrificed literalness for the sake of Greek idiom should not blind us to the important fact that its Hebrew *Vorlage* belonged to the same recension that gave rise to the masoretic text-tradition. It cannot be emphasized too strongly that it is the character not merely of the overwhelming agreement but even of the disagreements that indicates the close affinity between the masoretic and these other text-traditions.

[20] The textual results of Origen's Fifth Column activities in his Hexapla are proof enough of this.

[21] See n. 19 above.

[22] *Theologische Studien und Kritiken* (vol. 88, 410-26). All of Kahle's "Untersuchungen zur Geschichte des Pentateuchtextes" (pp. 399-439), which begins with and flows essentially from "Der Pentateuch der Samaritaner" (402-10), is most stimulating, even though I cannot always follow him in his reasoning.

[23] In series *Beitr. zur Wissen. v. A. und N. T.*, Heft 49. See the excellent reviews by such competent critics like Rahlfs (*TLZ* 55 (1930) cols. 104-6) and Bertram (*OLZ* 33 (1930) cols. 890-2). Actually, it would appear to me, there is a fundamental contradiction in Sperber's monograph between his Chap. A on the one hand and his Chaps. B and C on the other. In A he argues that only a fallacious criterion has prevented Lagardians from getting back to Jerome's three recensions (exactly three, not more and not less). He claims to have discovered the true criterion, viz., proper names (on how Sperber's own treatment of his own criterion ends up in a hopeless jumble, see Rahlfs' review). In B and C, on the other hand, he tries to prove that it is utterly impossible to get back to Jerome's three recensions, and behind them to the Proto-Septuagint, because the Greek manuscripts go back to independent and original Greek translations.

How, then, can he claim to demonstrate in A what he states in B and C to be impossible?

[24] All of Margolis' work, both published (e.g., the "Specimen") and unpublished (the Greek Joshua), is dismissed in the following paragraph, with no more reference to these works since: "Jos. 6_{1-12} wird probeweise hier editiert; da Margolis seine Ausgabe der Septuaginta zu Josua bereits in Druck hat, behält sich Ref. eine ganz eingehende Auseinandersetzung bezüglich der Prinzipien einer solchen Editionsarbeit für einen späteren Zeitpunkt vor, wenn M.'s Josua ganz vorliegen wird. Doch sei schon jetzt auf Grund dieses Specimen bemerkt, dass Ref. die ganze Anlage der Edition für verfehlt hält und dass auch demgemäss unsere Erkenntnis der Probleme der Septuaginta dadurch keineswegs gefördert wird" (col. 362).

[25] For some of the pertinent literature, see my review of Allgeier referred to at the beginning of this article.

[26] Vol. VI, האוונגליון ותרגום השבעים לתנ"ך ("The New Testament and the Septuagint Translation of the Old Testament"), pp. 1-29.

[27] See, e.g., Swete, *Introduction*, Part II, Chap. II, "Quotations from the LXX. in the New Testament" (pp. 381-405, where due reference is made to the "exhaustive list . . . at the end of Westcott and Hort's *New Testament in Greek*," and other works), especially § 3 (pp. 392-403). As I have stated elsewhere (*JQR* 31 (1940-41) 60 f., n. 4) in the case of his "Hebrew Based upon Greek and Latin Translations" (*HUCA* 12-13 (1937-8) 103-274) and "Hebrew Based upon Biblical Passages in Parallel Transmission" (*HUCA* 14 (1939) 153-249), "the material collected by Sperber . . . [is] so listed as to give a misleading conception of its historical origin and value . . ."

[28] See further below on the discussion of Sperber's "Wiederherstellung . . ." and Montgomery's pertinent remarks cited there.

[29] This is likewise the considered judgment of Allgeier as a result of his thorough study of the Rylands frag-

ments of Genesis (see my review mentioned above). It is not difficult to imagine the reaction among scholars in the field of textual criticism, whether it be in the New Testament, classical Greek and Latin texts, related Sumerian, Accadian, and Hittite texts, etc., if trifling and sporadic differences were made the basis for entirely independent translations or sources. As a fairly good illustration of what Sperber does inadmissibly with our own problem, and Kahle with the problem of the masoretic text, but which is methodologically quite in order in the case of "The myth currently known as 'Ishtar's Descent to the Nether World' [which] has come down to us in two versions, the Semitic and the Sumerian," reference may be made to Kramer's interesting article in *BASOR* 79 (Oct. 1940) 18-27, especially pp. 19 f. As is well known, "The Sumerian version of the Myth is inscribed in the Sumerian language on tablets dated approximately 2000 B. C.; they precede by more than a millennium the tablets containing the Semitic version . . . As a comparison of the two versions clearly shows, the Sumerian account differs radically from that developed by the Semites. Only in the most general outlines of the story do the two agree . . . But few of the details that go to fill in these skeleton lines of the myth are alike in the two versions. What is even more interesting is the palpable difference in style and tone . . . There is little doubt that the Sumerian version is the more original; the Semitic account developed from it in the course of the centuries as a result of modifications made by the Babylonians in accordance with their own temper and genius" (pp. 19 f.). But a problem of this kind has nothing to do, e. g., with the problem of the relationship between Lucian and Origen, or between any two or more 4th-6th century uncials of the Septuagint, and the like. See further below, n. 31.

[30] Cf. Montgomery's recent note on "Hebrew *Hesed* and Greek *Charis*" in *HTR*, 32 (1939) 97-102.

[30a] Note, however, Margolis' caveat ("Specimen," 312), "The supposition that Lucian indulged in doublets will, I believe, not be substantiated as a general practice."

[31] It would be very instructive to place in parallel columns *in context*, the differences, e. g., between Theodoret and Cyril on the one hand, and the differences between any of the Septuagint manuscripts of any book of the Bible and each of the Minor Versions (Theodotion, Aquila, Symmachus, etc.) on the other. Then one will see how independent translations really look and read. Or again, one may compare the Greek translation of any one book of the Old Testament with that of any other book (cf., e. g., Swete, *Introduction* . . . , 315 ff.; Thackeray, *Grammar of the Old Testament in Greek* (1909), Chap. I), or even that of two or more translators within the one book (and there is now a respectable bibliography on this phase), to realize how different the character of an independent translation is from that of a different recension. Nor is the result any different when one compares, e. g., the *Graecus Venetus* (see Swete, *Introduction* . . . , 56 ff.) with any other Greek translation of the corresponding books of the Bible—here is no mere recensional disagreement! In short, our problem, like most every other problem, revolves about such fundamental principles and concepts as: law of evidence, sober judgment, method.

[32] We need not stop here over his "Probleme einer Edition der Septuaginta," in the Paul Kahle Festschrift (1935, pp. 39-46), since this article gives merely a resume of the earlier articles, already discussed above. Nor need be considered here his "New Testament and Septuagint." Where it deals with the problem of the Proto-Septuagint it has nothing essential to add. Thus, e. g., on pp. 273 f. an attempt is made to demonstrate an independent and original Greek translation, otherwise unknown, on the basis of an assumed corruption in this assumed long-lost Greek translation. In Ruth 1: 11 the Old Latin reads *quid uenistis mecum*, for which the masoretic text reads לָמָּה תֵלַכְנָה עִמִּי. Sperber argues that "the perfect tense of *uenistis* is, therefore, an apparent mistake for the corresponding future-form. By referring to a Greek original, the explanation is quite simple: ινα τι πορευεσθε

was misunderstood in ινα τι επορευεσθε." However, in view of the fact that all extant manuscripts of the Septuagint and daughter versions read or imply ἵνα τί πορεύεσθε, the exact equivalent of the Hebrew, is it not more simple and reasonable to assume a corruption within an *existing* manuscript, viz., the Old Latin itself!—an original *venietis*, Sperber's desiderated future form, and the exact equivalent of the reading in the *textus receptus* of the (underlying) Septuagint (πορεύεσθε), became corrupted into the received *venistis*. Note in nn. 1-17 of Sperber's "Wiederherstellung . . ." no less than 17 other inner-Latin corruptions.

The part of the "New Testament and Septuagint" that deals with the asterisked and obelized passages in Origen's Hexapla does not concern our immediate problem. Suffice it here to say that it is without any foundation in itself and ignores or misunderstands early patristic sources and important subsequent discussions. His assumed "Bible of the Apostles" has no more probability than his assumed Greek original of the OL manuscript of Ruth. One may find very instructive and reliable manuals on how to handle the symbolized passages in the Hexapla properly in the *Septuaginta-Studien* of Rahlfs and in Margolis' "The K Text of Joshua," "Specimen," and *The Book of Joshua in Greek.*

[33] Towards the end of n. 25 of my discussion of "The Kings-Isaiah Recensions of the Hezekiah Story" (*JQR* 30 (1939-40) 43) I draw attention to a little known fact noted by Cornill (*Ezechiel*, Proleg., p. 27) that in "17.3 [הַנֶּשֶׁר הַגָּדוֹל] *aquila illa magna* und 26.17 [הָעִיר הַהֻלָּלָה] *civitas illa laudabilis* . . . wo wir, genau wie in allen neueren romanischen Sprachen, das Pronomen *ille* schon ganz als artikel gebraucht sehen."

[34] Not a single Greek manuscript in Brooke-McLean lacks the definite article ταῖς before ἡμέραις. Sperber has overlooked the fact that Latin, lacking a separate definite article, reproduced ταῖς ἡμέραις *exactly and fully* simply by *diebus*. And what sort of concept, in context, is his assumed Hebrew, "In the days of the judge of (the) judges" (or, ". . . of the greatest of judges")?

[35] One may justly wonder why, in view of the deletion of *ταῖς* in his reconstructed Greek, Sperber begins the retroversion with *καὶ ἐγένετο* (= masoretic וַיְהִי) when the OL begins simply with *In diebus* (= . . . בִּימֵי). Do we have here another inner-Latin corruption? An explanatory note of some kind would have been in order. Cf. Rahlfs, p. 105.

[36] In the uncials it is not at all uncommon to meet with corruptions and confusions that involve such letters, and combinations of such letters as Γ, T, H, Π, I.

[37] Cf. Rahlfs' analysis, in keeping with numerous other competent studies of the Old Latin in various books of the Old and New Testaments, *Studie über den griechischen Text des Buches Ruth* (1922). At some future date I hope to discuss such statements as Sperber's "Although he [viz., Rahlfs] admits that he is unable to reconcile [Lagarde's] theory and practice, the theory still seems to him to be true" (*JBL* 54 (1935) 75) and Allgeier's "so unbestreitbar ist die Tatsache, dass sich die LXX-Forschung, indem sie hauptsächlich, ja ausschlieslich so fragte, in eine Sackgasse verrannt hat" (*Biblica* 19 (1938) 18; cf. also the *Einleitung* in his *Die Chester Beatty-Papyri*). The latter (see my review) apparently is unaware of the important work of Montgomery and Margolis on the problem, nor does he see it in its proper light. The former, if he has read the works of these men, certainly has made no use of them.

CHAPTER II

DISCUSSIONS ON THE ORIGIN OF THE SEPTUAGINT

The Septuagint is the Greek version of the Hebrew Old Testament; it was made in Egypt. The Pentateuch was probably translated in the third century B.C., the other parts of the Old Testament in later times. It would be important to know why the translation was made and what principles were applied in its execution. Unfortunately its origin is shrouded in mystery and later reports do not help us to discover the facts.

These reports may record old traditions; but if so, the facts have been obscured by layers of additions through which original fact and legend have become inextricably entwined. It is not intended to analyse these reports here in order to bring to light these different layers in their development and ramifications or to unearth historical facts. In this chapter the story as handed down to us will be treated as a document that has its own value as a piece of literature and as evidence of trends of thought which were current at about 100 B.C., when it was written down. This so-called Aristeas Letter[1] describes how the Hebrew Old Testament, more exactly the Pentateuch, was translated into Greek. It purports to have been written by Aristeas at the time of King Ptolemy II Philadelphus (285–246 B.C.).

[1] Editions: *Aristeae ad Philocratem Epistula cum ceteris de Origine Versionis LXX Interpretum Testimoniis*, ed. P. Wendland (Teubner, 1900); H. G. Meecham, *The Letter of Aristeas*, Publications of the University of Manchester, no. 241 (Manchester, 1935) (Bibliography, pp. xiii–xviii).

Translations into English: R. H. Charles, *The Apocrypha and Pseudoepigrapha of the Old Testament in English*, vol. II (Oxford, 1913), pp. 94–122; *The Letter of Aristeas*, translated by H. St J. Thackeray (London, 1917), whose translation I generally follow; H. G. Meecham, *The Oldest Version of the Bible: 'Aristeas' on its traditional Origin*, the thirty-second Hartley Lecture (London, 1932) (Bibliography, pp. xvii–xxiii). The latest discussion on the LXX and the Aristeas Letter is by P. E. Kahle, *The Cairo Geniza*, The Schweich Lectures of the British Academy, 1941 (London, 1947), pp. 132ff. One of the most valuable papers on the Aristeas Letter is by P. Wendland, 'Zur ältesten Geschichte der Bibel in der Kirche', *Zeitschrift für die neutestamentliche Wissenschaft*, vol. I (1900), pp. 267–90.

Reprinted from *Principles and Problems of Biblical Translation*. Cambridge Univ. Press, 1955; repr. C.U.P. 1970.

The Letter begins with an account of an audience given by the king to his librarian Demetrius Phalereus, at which Aristeas was present. The king intended to collect all the books in the world in his library and Demetrius, telling him of his hope of having 500,000 volumes in his library shortly, gave his opinion that the Jewish Books of the Law should also have a place in it. During this audience Aristeas pleaded for the release of 100,000 Jewish slaves in Egypt, and this request was granted before any further steps were taken leading to the execution of the translation. A memorandum sent by the librarian to the king pointed out that the Books of the Law were written in Hebrew and that they ought to be translated anew; they were of a philosophical nature, but had not been mentioned by authors, poets, and historians because they contained a sacred and holy idea (§ 31). The king thereupon sent a letter to Eleazar, the High Priest in Jerusalem, and asked him to select seventy-two elders, six from each of the twelve tribes, 'men of noble life' (§39) who knew the Law and who were able to translate. This letter, together with gifts for the Temple, was taken to Jerusalem by the chief of the bodyguard and by Aristeas himself.

After a description of these gifts and an account of Jerusalem and Palestine, Aristeas relates how the high priest took leave of the seventy-two translators who, he feared, would be kept in Egypt since Ptolemy II was wont to summon all the wisest men to his court. After an eulogy on the Pentateuch by Eleazar, the scene shifts to Alexandria, where the seventy-two translators were received by the king with great honour. The king first paid reverence to the rolls of the Pentateuch which they had brought to Egypt, and then banqueted with them for seven days, asking every one of them questions about politics, military affairs, kingship, philosophy and so on. They answered all these questions to the greatest satisfaction of the king, who admired their wisdom. Three days later they started upon the translation of the Pentateuch, 'arriving at an agreement on each point comparing each other's work' (§302). The place where they gathered was 'delightful because of its quietness and brightness' (§307); every day before starting with their work the translators washed their hands in the sea and prayed to God. This was an action indicating that they had done no evil. In this way everything was directed towards righteousness and truth (§§305–306). They accomplished their task in seventy-two days 'as though this coincidence had been intended' (§307). The Jews were then called together, the translation was read to them, and

> the priests and the elders of the translators and of the Jewish community[1] and the leaders of the people stood up and said, 'for-as-much as the translation has been well and piously executed and with perfect accuracy, it is right that it should remain in its present form and that no "revision" should take place' (§ 310).

A curse was pronounced upon anybody who should alter the text of this version (§311). The whole translation was read to the king, who was amazed that none of the historians and poets had mentioned these Jewish books which were so enlightened. At this point the beginning of the Letter is taken up where the librarian had drawn attention in his memorandum to the view that these books contain a sacred and holy idea. At the end of the Letter the librarian gave an answer to the king which was more explicit: these books are not mentioned, he said, 'because of the holiness of the Law and because of its origin by God' (§313). He then explained this somewhat obscure answer by saying that it was a dangerous thing to quote the Law and to reveal it to the people. When attempting to do so the historian Theopompos suffered a derangement of the mind which lasted for thirty days, and the poet Theodectes was afflicted with a cataract of the eyes. Both the historian and the poet were healed when they deleted the references to the Pentateuch in their writings (§§314–316). When King Ptolemy had learned this, he ordered that the Books of the Law should be kept with great reverence. The translators were given gifts and allowed to return home.

[1] For this interpretation of the text see R. H. Charles, *The Apocrypha*, vol. II, p. 121 [illegible]

The proceedings, so far as the Bible translation is concerned, are very similar to those of the twentieth century. Expressed in modern words they are: the highest dignitary of the religious community appoints a commission for the translation of the Bible. The members of this commission are of very noble character, they are scholars in theology, and they know the languages necessary for the translation (cf. Aristeas Letter, §121). They meet to compare their individual translations and to hammer out an agreement on the differences. This version, 'well and piously executed and with perfect accuracy', is acclaimed to be final. Nobody is allowed to reprint it in a corrected form, and that means that this version is, as it were, authorized. The writer of the Aristeas Letter comments on the imprecation uttered against anybody who might change the translation: 'And herein they did well, to the intent that the work might for ever be preserved imperishable and unchanged' (§311). In a modern report on a Bible translation this imprecation would naturally not be found and there would be no reference to the danger involved in a rash attempt to render Holy Writ. In the Letter precedents are mentioned warning people not even to quote the Law in any profane writing. There is another difference between modern procedure and that described in the Letter, namely the method of selecting the translators. In modern times the translators are known to be learned men capable of executing their task, in the Letter they must prove their worth in an examination to which they are subjected by the king during the banquets.

Whatever else may have been the intention of the author of the Aristeas Letter, his attitude towards Bible translation is clear. As it is assumed that it was written at about 100 B.C., we can glean very important information about the position of the Bible among the Jews in Egypt at that time: the translation of the Bible as a holy book has to be very carefully executed. For the making of an exact translation a commission is necessary which can discuss every detail. An agreement of the members of this commission which is bent on this holy task, is sufficient proof that the translation is accurate. This is the philological principle of translation. The translators themselves must be learned men and they must approach their work with a pious mind and be free from sin and therefore they purify themselves through washing their hands and through prayer. This, it seems, is not done to seek God's intervention in their task. In the Letter no miracle happens to enlighten the translators. The work of the human mind is sufficient to produce a translation of God's word. There is, however, one sentence which seems to point to some miraculous event. The number of the translators is seventy-two; they completed their work in seventy-two days 'as though this coincidence had been intended' (§307). The author, it seems, is playing with the idea that some miracle might have taken place or referring to another tradition about the origin of the translation.

This other tradition, which scholars consider to be of later origin than the Aristeas Letter, has been preserved by Philo of Alexandria and by the Fathers of the Church. There are differences within this tradition; for example, whether the translators worked separately in different cells without the possibility of communicating with one another or whether they worked together. But such disagreements are of no significance for this study. Only Philo's account will be discussed in detail, not merely because it is the oldest in this group but also because it sets out the principles of inspirational translation more clearly than any other source known to me.

From the very beginning, Philo with great literary skill creates an atmosphere removed from ordinary human life. Every action of the translators is filled with a significance which is important for the success of the rendering. Indeed, the translation is the centre which gives life to those who undertake this difficult task. Thus almost every word gains a new overtone within the narrative. It is impossible to reproduce these qualities of Philo's narration without quoting every word. However, there are more obstacles for the interpreter. By Philo's time neoplatonic philosophy and moral teaching had brought about semantic changes in many Greek words whose full significance it is not always easy to see. Philo's language, however, is even more complex because the connotation of his words is often coloured by both Greek philosophy and Jewish religious conceptions. This blend of different strata of civilization fully corresponds with Philo's attempt to create a union between Greek philosophy and Jewish religion.

This is Philo's account of the origin of the Septuagint:[1] The Jewish Law was, on account of its sanctity, marvelled at by Jews and other peoples. For a considerable time, 'while it had not yet revealed its beauty to the rest of mankind', it was in existence in Hebrew only. 'For a short time', Philo continues, 'envy causes the beautiful to be overshadowed but it shines forth under the benign operation of nature when its time comes' (II, V, 26–7). When the time had come for the Pentateuch to be known among the peoples, Philadelphus, the best of all kings of his own time as of the past, desired to have the Law translated into Greek. He sent messengers requesting the high priest of Jerusalem, who was also king of Judaea, to send translators to him; his wish was fulfilled and many translators arrived who were most esteemed and who had enjoyed an education in Hebrew and Greek. Philadelphus asked them difficult questions to test their wisdom (II, V, 29–33). This story, narrated at great length in the Aristeas Letter, is compressed into a few lines by Philo.

The translators then searched for a place where the rendering could be done. 'Reflecting how great an undertaking it was to render the Law which had been divinely revealed, and reflecting that they could not add or take away or transpose anything but had to preserve the original form of the Law and its character, they proceeded to look for a spot spiritually most pure, outside the city. For, within the walls, it was full of every kind of living creature, and consequently the prevalence of diseases and deaths and the impure conduct of the healthy inhabitants made them suspicious of it' (II, vi, 34). This thought, a perfect blend of

[1] *De Vita Mosis*, II, v–vii, 25–40. The text followed is that by L. Cohn-P. Wendland, vol. IV of Philo's *Opera* (Berlin, 1902). My translation is based on that of F. H. Colson, published in The Loeb Classical Library, *Philo*, vol. VI (1935). But I have changed this translation wherever I thought necessary without indicating my dissent.

Jewish and Neoplatonic ideas on ritual purity, causes the translators to move to the island of Pharos where even the roar of the sea is heard only dimly, in the remote distance. Here, they believed, they would find calm and quietness and their souls would be able to commune with the Law. They raised the sacred books heavenwards asking God to grant them that they might not fail in their purpose. God agreed to these prayers for the benefit of mankind (II, vi, 35–6). Now that God's blessing had been granted to this undertaking, the translators themselves were prepared, and their surroundings and their own disposition fitted to render God's Law. Here Philo's words may be quoted:

Sitting here in seclusion with none present save the elements of nature, earth, water, air, heaven, the genesis of which was to be the first theme of their sacred revelation, for the Law begins with the story of the world's creation, they [the translators] became as it were possessed, and, under inspiration, wrote, not each several scribe something different, but the same word for word, as though dictated to each by an invisible prompter. Yet who does not know that every language, and Greek especially, abounds in terms, and that the same thought can be put in many shapes by changing single words and whole phrases [or: 'by paraphrasing more or less freely'] and suiting the expression to the occasion? This was not the case, we are told, with this Law of ours, but the Greek words used corresponded literally with the Chaldean [i.e. Hebrew], exactly suited to the things they indicated. For, just as in geometry and logic, so it seems to me, the sense indicated does not admit of variety in the expression which remains unchanged in its original form, so these writers, as it clearly appears, arrived at a wording which corresponded with the matter, and alone, or better than any other, would bring out clearly what was meant. The clearest proof of this is that, if Chaldeans have learned Greek, or Greeks Chaldean [i.e. Hebrew], and read both versions, the Chaldean and the translation, they regard them with awe and reverence as sisters, or rather as one and the same, both in matter and words, and speak of their authors not as translators but as prophets and priests of these mysteries, whose sincerity and singleness of thought has enabled them to concur with the purest of spirits, the spirit of Moses.[1]

[1] *De Vita Mosis*, II, vii, 37–40.

Up to his own time, Philo concludes, a feast had been held every year on the island of Pharos to which Jews and many Gentiles came 'to do honour to the place in which the light of that version first shone out, and also to thank God for the good gift so old yet ever so young' (II, vii, 41).

In Philo's view the translation of the Hebrew Pentateuch is no ordinary rendering. It is not due to the endeavour of the human mind to transfer one language into another but to God's direct intervention. The translators cease to be translators, they are prophets and priests who are able to concur with Moses. Moses, however, is the 'purest of spirits', not a human being. The work of the translators was done under inspiration, they were mere instruments writing down their words 'as though dictated to each by an invisible prompter'. There was no necessity for them to discuss differences in their individual versions, for differences there were none. Their work was inspired and thus open to no error. The Pentateuch itself was the result of a revelation, as Philo points out (II, xxxv, 188), and only a new revelation can reproduce the exact wording of Holy Scripture as well as its form and character in a foreign idiom. The new version thus created cannot be compared with any other translation. It is in complete identity with the original, it is truly God's word.

The Greek Pentateuch is therefore the final translation which cannot be changed. Its authenticity is proven by its origin. Nobody who believes in the inspirational origin of the Greek text will attempt to make a new version in Greek. But it is this authenticity which set a new problem, when discrepancies between the texts were discovered: if both the Hebrew and the Greek texts are due to God's revelation, which is the original wording? Which version should be the basis for translations into other languages? This is an important question which was soon to become a burning issue in the Church.

We may round off this short account of the Aristeas Letter with some remarks on Philo's conception of prophecy, which is of importance for the later discussion.

The highest function of the prophet is, in Philo's view, the proclamation of God's word. The prophet is an instrument only, he transmits to man what God has said to him. The prophet himself is not active, he is, as it were, only passive, an 'interpreter' (ἑρμηνεύς) of God's message. It is for this reason that the translators of the Pentateuch could be called prophets. But although praising this kind of prophecy in the highest terms (II, xxxv, 191), Philo maintains that the prophet should not be entirely passive, he should himself take an active part. This may be done in two different ways, and therefore there are in addition to passive prophecy also two kinds of active prophecy. In the one there is 'combination and partnership' (II, xxxv, 190) between God and the prophet. The prophet asks God for advice in a definite situation and thus, as it were, evokes God's help. In the other kind of active prophecy use is made of the gift of foreseeing, a gift which 'God has granted to the prophet' (II, xxxv, 190). The prophet, as a human being, sees, for example, a disaster approaching and then he is 'taken out of himself by divine possession' (II, xlvi, 250) and foretells what will happen. Although in these two cases the prophet is inspired by God, he is not a mere instrument for delivering His message. It is in this connexion that Philo says: 'interpretation and prophecy are of a different nature' (II, xxxv, 191). The meaning of the word 'interpretation' (ἑρμηνεία) includes 'translation'. Thus it could, in later times, be used to connote: 'Translation and prophecy are of a different nature'. In this form it will be found in the writings of St Jerome in his attack upon the theory of inspirational translation.

The philological and inspirational principles of Bible translation had been worked out before Christian renderings were made and before Christian theories on this subject could possibly have been forthcoming. These principles may have influenced the later versions of the Bible into Greek and Latin but many of them have been lost, and even where the names of the translators are known, none of them seems to have discussed these questions in theory.

The references to the origin of the Septuagint in the works of the early Fathers of the Church prove that discussion continued on the questions set by the divergent views contained in the Aristeas Letter and in the works of Philo. It is important to take note of the fact that in the second century A.D. the Old Testament was translated into Latin from the Greek of the Septuagint and not from the Hebrew text. But who can say what was the reason for this? Was it considered that the Septuagint as an inspired version had replaced the original Hebrew text or was it due to the ignorance of the Hebrew language? In the third century A.D. Origen examined the relationship of the Septuagint to the Hebrew in his Hexapla. There he gave the Hebrew text and its transliteration in Greek characters, together with four Greek versions in adjoining columns. Moreover, he clearly marked additions to, and omissions of, the Hebrew wording in the different Greek versions. Although this laborious work was probably never copied in its entirety, it drew the attention of those interested to the fact that the Septuagint and the Hebrew original were not identical, as Philo had maintained. Yet the attestation of these differences, even if it were meant to refute the authority of the Septuagint, did not convince those who believed in the inspirational nature of the Greek version. Thus the divergencies of opinion remained, and at the end of the fourth century they led to an open controversy. The Latin Bible of the Latin-speaking Christian communities at that time was the *Vetus Latina* which, as mentioned above, was a translation from the Septuagint. The disagreement of its various manuscripts necessitated a reconstitution of the Latin text. St Jerome was called upon by Pope Damasus to undertake this task.

As far back as 380/1, before beginning the revision of the Bible, he had made some remarks on the Septuagint while speaking in general terms on translation. In the Preface to his translation of Eusebius' *Chronikon* he did so in a cautious and carefully worded way, not really coming to grips with the issue whether the Septuagint was inspired or not. But even in these short remarks he characteristically finds fault with the style of the translation, stressing the difficulties of a translator who wishes to preserve the elegance of the original without making additions.[1]

Style, indeed, was to be one point of departure for the attack upon the principle of inspirational translation. But before Jerome developed this side of his argument, he discussed the difficulties of Bible translation in the Preface to his revision of the New Testament of 384. In this he foresees that he will be censured by everybody as a falsifier and a sacrilegious person for changing words which everybody knew from earliest childhood. But it must be admitted, he says, that there are almost as many texts as manuscripts.[2] For the reconstitution of the text Jerome advocates the comparison of the Latin version with the original Greek text for the correction of all mistakes made by bad translators or careless copyists. The New Testament was, in his view, originally written in Greek with the exception of Matthew which he believes to have been composed in Hebrew and only later translated into Greek. While dwelling on the difficulties peculiar to the rendering of the New Testament, he mentions the Latin version of the Old Testament as being three degrees removed from the Hebrew original, since it was rendered from the Greek of the Septuagint, and not from the Hebrew text. He refuses to discuss which of the different existing Greek versions is correct. But he gives a rule for discerning the correct Greek text. 'The translation approved by the apostles should be regarded as correct', he writes.[3]

It is difficult to assess the significance of these words, in which Jerome expressly states that he does not wish to discuss the question of the Old Testament. The statement that the Latin is removed by three degrees from the Hebrew may be a statement of fact; it may, however, mean that the Septuagint is not an inspired translation which replaces the original. A confirmation of this latter view may be found in Jerome's doubt whether the

[1] *P.L.* vol. XXVII, cols. 35–6.

[2] 'tot enim sunt exemplaria quot codices.' *P.L.* vol. XXIX, col. 526.

[3] *P.L.* vol. XXIX, cols. 525–7.

Septuagint or any of the other Greek versions contains the correct rendering. He believes that the testimonies of the apostles will throw light on this question.[1]

It will be seen that all these arguments were again used by Jerome at a later stage of his life but that he gradually became more explicit and more outspoken in his views. The sayings of the apostles were to be of decisive weight in assessing the value of the Septuagint and the Hebrew text but they were not used, as they were at this early stage, to distinguish between the values of the translations. The question of the relation between the Hebrew original and the Septuagint came to the fore while the other Greek versions, important though they remained, proved to be of a secondary importance only. When he wrote the Preface to Eusebius' *Chronikon* in 380/1 and the Preface to the New Testament of 384 he may possibly not yet have seen the extent of the differences between the Hebrew Old Testament and the Septuagint. These prefaces were, in all probability, written at a time when he himself had not yet reached clarity in this matter. He was not yet able to judge, and it is a fascinating study to observe how every one of his points is slowly clarified and how the value of the Septuagint is more and more reduced until, at the end, he pronounced judgement against the Septuagint and against the theory of inspiration.

The first step to this end was the discovery of the serious differences existing between the Hebrew text and the Septuagint. This must have been the basis from which all the other results had to be derived. In the Preface to his revision of the Books of Chronicles written not before 395, Jerome discusses the divergencies of varying character and he enumerates the reasons for them. Some of the divergencies between the Hebrew and the Greek texts, he asserts, are due to copyists who, for instance, corrupted many of the Hebrew names. These are errors which

[1] *P.L.* vol. XXIX, col. 527: Neque vero ego de veteri disputo Testamento, quod a Septuaginta senioribus in Graecam linguam versum, tertio gradu ad nos usque pervenit. Non quaero quid Aquila, quid Symmachus sapiant, quare Theodotion inter novos et veteres medius incedat. Sit illa vera interpretatio, quam Apostoli probaverunt.

should not be ascribed to the seventy translators 'who, filled with the Holy Ghost, rendered the truth'. The other discrepancies, however, go back to the translators themselves. These are additions found in the text of the Greek Septuagint only and not in the original Hebrew. They were made, Jerome maintains, 'partly for stylistic reasons, partly on the authority of the Holy Ghost'.[1] This is, at face value, a surprising and even contradictory statement. If the translators were filled with the Holy Ghost, as was asserted some lines earlier, they worked 'on the authority of the Holy Ghost'. But how does the conception of style come into this context? Jerome's words can be understood if it is seen that he had two different kinds of additions in mind. The one has no basis in the original Hebrew text. A word or a whole sentence found in the Septuagint corresponds to nothing of equivalent meaning in the Hebrew. I submit that in Jerome's view additions of this kind are made on the authority of the Holy Ghost and are thus inspired. But matters are entirely different when additions are made for stylistic reasons. In these cases, such differences between Hebrew and Greek as the lack of equivalent words and the presence of idiomatic and syntactical peculiarities forced the translators to add words in order to render the same sense. Additions of this type found in the Septuagint were made for stylistic reasons, they are not the result of inspiration. This method of translation, as Jerome had pointed out in the Preface to Eusebius' *Chronikon*,[2] exceeded the task of the translator.

This theory changes the central conception of inspirational translation. The translator, although inspired, is not like an instrument which is merely used by God to write down the single words and sentences. He does not, as Philo expounded, write as

[1] *P.L.* vol. XXIX, cols. 402, 404. Cf. L. Schade, 'Die Inspirationslehre des heiligen Hieronymus', *Biblische Studien*, vol. XV (1910), pp. 141 ff. Schade sees Jerome's development and he mentions the same examples from Jerome's works as I do. But he neither gives a close interpretation of these sentences nor does he indicate that every one of Jerome's statements on inspiration limits the field where inspiration could have taken place until, at the end, inspiration is entirely discarded.

[2] St Augustine held a similar view, see *P.L.* vol. XLII, col. 1068. For details see D. S. Blondheim, *Les Parlers judéo-romans et la Vetus Latina* (Paris, 1925), pp. cii ff.

if the words 'were dictated by an invisible prompter'. His inspiration, his being filled with the Holy Ghost, ensures that he renders the truth, but he has the liberty to choose the stylistic formulation of his translation. It is the translator, not God, who makes 'additions' to the original for stylistic reasons. He is inspired, but his inspiration is not verbal inspiration. His rendering contains the truth, yet it may differ from the original because of the idiomatic peculiarities of the individual languages. In Philo's account of an inspired version the human element is completely denied, in Jerome's conception it is allowed to find a foothold again; the human brain is not overpowered, but works even during the inspiration.

From this the conclusions for the later translator are obvious: the *contents* of both the original and the inspired translation must be taken into consideration at every step, but so far as the wording is concerned, it is only the original which is binding. The inspired version thus complements but no longer replaces the original.

This interpretation of St Jerome's passage not only dispels any contradiction which might be contained in his Preface to the *Paralipomena*, it also fully agrees with his views on prophecy. The prophet has, according to St Jerome, the faculty to speak and to be silent, he does not speak against his will ('invitus'). He is inspired but retains his intellectual faculties and knows what he says.[1] In the same way the inspired translator knows what he writes and formulates it according to his own judgement.

The above interpretation is also consistent with Jerome's work at this period of his life. He uses the Hebrew text together with that of the Septuagint and informs the reader of the differences between these texts through diacritical signs without rejecting any of these divergencies. Both texts are of value and both must therefore be used together.

Further examination and comparison between the Hebrew and Greek texts may have forced him to modify this position. While working on the revision of the Bible he came to the conclusion

[1] *P.L.* vol. XXV, col. 1274B; cf. L. Schade, *loc. cit.* pp. 21 ff.

that at some places the original Hebrew offers a better wording than the Greek translation. In the Preface to his *Hebraicae Quaestiones in Genesim* of between 389 and 392 he criticizes the Septuagint, asserting that the Seventy translators concealed from King Ptolemy II the meaning of all those passages in which the coming of Christ was promised. A further criterion that could be used to discover the reliability of the Septuagint is contained in the New Testament. According to St Jerome, the apostles' quotations of the Old Testament are testimonies for the soundness of the Hebrew text against the wording of the Septuagint. The conclusion is that an agreement between the Hebrew Bible and the New Testament is a full proof of the authenticity of the Hebrew text and a condemnation of the Greek version whenever the Septuagint disagrees. To this argument Jerome adds that the Seventy translators rendered only the Pentateuch, and not the whole of the Old Testament.[1]

These observations are of the utmost importance for his assessment of the value of the Septuagint for the rendering of the Bible. Jerome does not expressly say that the translators were not inspired. As only the Five Books of Moses were rendered by them, the translation of the other parts cannot claim the same authority. But even in the Pentateuch the intention of the translators played a great part in making the rendering, since they left out passages which should, in their time, not be divulged. The critic is able to discover the purpose of these translators. Their design, praiseworthy though it had been, was destined for their own time and is no longer valid. All traces of their activities had therefore to be removed and to be replaced by that text of the Bible which had been revealed to man in Hebrew.

This is the end of a long development in Jerome's thought. It is difficult to say how much his earlier statements were influenced by considerations of expediency and caution. It is well known that he was heavily attacked by all those who revered the Septuagint and who valued the *Vetus Latina* which had been

[1] *P.L.* vol. XXIII, cols. 936–7.

derived from it.[1] But Jerome was not discouraged in pursuing his way after he had arrived at a full comprehension of the facts. He followed his own investigation and did not hesitate to publish the result of his study. It is the philologist's method to compare the different texts and to rely on the ability of human understanding to find out the truth. In this research there can be no halt. When after a long period of uncertainty he at last found what he believed to be the truth, he drew the logical conclusion, even when this meant a fight against a long tradition and against strong opposition to all new ideas and thoughts.

Jerome had discarded the view that the text of the Septuagint was a faithful translation of the Hebrew original. He no longer believed that the Greek version was inspired, and for this reason identical with the Hebrew text despite differences of detail. This new recognition led necessarily to two conclusions. One was practical: a new Latin translation from Hebrew had to be made. The other was theoretical, derived from the belief in philology: inspirational translation does not exist. 'One thing I know,' he wrote, 'I could translate only what I had understood before.'[2] Translation is based on the comprehension of the original and the command of languages. It is not prophecy. Thus Jerome in his condemnation of the inspirational principle of translation turns Philo's sentence that 'Translation and prophecy are of different nature' against Philo's view about the inspirational origin of the Septuagint.[3] And mockingly he adds that the assumption of the divine revelation of the Septuagint makes it imperative to argue that Cicero's translations, which were rhetorical, were inspired by the rhetorical spirit. In addition, he repeats that the apostles' sayings do not agree with the Septuagint. The inspiration of the apostles is, of course, beyond a shadow of doubt. If the Septuagint

[1] Testimonies are collected by Ferd. Cavallera, *St Jérôme sa vie et son œuvre* (*Spicilegium Sacrum Lovaniense*, Études et Documents, fasc. 2) (Louvain–Paris, 1922), vol. II, pp. 103–15.

[2] *Preface in Job* (*P.L.* vol. XXVIII, col. 1081 A).

[3] It is not known whether Jerome was consciously quoting Philo, but I am sure that Philo was the ultimate source. About Jerome's knowledge of Philo see P. Courcelle, *Les lettres grecques en occident de Macrobe à Cassiodore. Bibliothèque des Écoles Françaises d'Athènes et de Rome*, fasc. 159 (2nd ed. Paris, 1948), pp. 70–1.

too were inspired, the Holy Ghost would have made conflicting statements at different times. This is impossible and thus the Septuagint is not inspired.

These arguments are propounded in the preface to Jerome's new translation of the Pentateuch. He gathers together all the proofs he can find to defend his position and to show the necessity for a new translation. But he also adduces evidence against those who believe in the supernatural origin of the Septuagint. This belief, he points out, cannot be supported by any historical documentary evidence. The cells in which the Seventy translators are supposed to have done their work separated from one another were built by a liar. It is mentioned neither in the Aristeas Letter nor in Josephus. Thus the report about the inspiration of the translators is a legend supported by neither historical evidence nor theological reasoning. Some of Jerome's words may be quoted here:

> I do not know [he says] who was the first who through his lies built seventy cells in Alexandria in which they [the translators] were separated and yet all wrote the same words; whereas Aristeas...and long after him Josephus have said nothing of the sort, but write that they were assembled in a single hall and conferred together, not that they prophesied. For it is one thing to be a prophet and another to be a translator; in one case the Spirit foretells future events, in the other sentences are understood and translated by erudition and command of language.[1]

St Jerome's principle of translation was at this time firmly established in his mind. The Septuagint may be used as any ordinary translation but it cannot replace the original Hebrew. The Latin text of the Old Testament and of the New Testament should be treated in the same way, if the readings in the different manuscripts differ. The correct text will be established through comparison of the Latin translation with the original Hebrew of the Old Testament and the Greek of the New Testament. 'One must go back to the Hebrews', he writes, 'from whose midst

[1] *Praefatio in Pentateuchum* (*P.L.* vol. XXVIII, cols. 150–1); cf. *ibid.* col. 1081.

speaks even the Lord.'[1] Thus the Hebrew text had come back into its own.

The method of Jerome's translation is a matter of considerable dispute. Conflicting statements have been made by Jerome, and there is no possibility of harmonizing them or of proving that he never changed his mind. All his sayings from the very beginning show, beyond all doubt, his interest in style. It will be remembered that in his view lack of elegance in the Septuagint induced later translators to make new renderings of the Bible into Greek. It may be recorded that in his letter to Sunnia and Fretela he wrote that the task of a good translator consists in rendering idiomatic expressions of one language into the modes of expression peculiar to the other.[2] It may be mentioned that in some prefaces of his Bible translation he emphasizes that he does not render word for word, but sense for sense, while in others he maintains that he translates partly the words, partly the sense.[3] Indeed it seems that he made no difference between a translation of a profane book and one of the Bible. From the outset he had proclaimed that the singular characteristics of languages often force the translator to render the sense instead of the word. Even Homer, he points out, would sound incoherent if rendered word for word without regard to metre and contents.[4] Yet at the end of 395 he wrote in a letter that he had always rendered the sense 'with the exception of Holy Scripture where even the order of words is a mystery'.[5] In these words Jerome clearly advocates two different methods of translation. A literary work, he asserts, must be translated according to sense, as the lack of equivalents in the two languages and the preservation of the order of words make the word-for-

[1] *Praefatio in Paralipomena* (*P.L.* vol. XXVIII, col. 1326A): 'Ad Hebraeos igitur revertendum est unde et dominus loquitur.' *Ep.* to Sunnia and Fretela of uncertain date between 393 and 401, *Ep.* CVI, 2, 3 (*P.L.* vol. XXII, col. 838).

[2] *Ep.* CVI, 3, 3 (*P.L.* vol. XXII, col. 839).

[3] *P.L.* vol. XXVIII, col. 1433; *P.L.* vol. XXIX, col. 39.

[4] *Ep.* LVII, 5, 6–8 (*P.L.* vol. XXII, cols. 570–5). No details are necessary since this question has often been discussed. The latest study on this subject is found in P. Courcelle, *op. cit.* pp. 42ff., where also see for literature.

[5] *Ep.* LVII, 5 (*P.L.* vol. XXII, col. 571).

word translation sound ridiculous and incoherent. Such a method destroys all literary qualities.[1] It is therefore necessary to render the sense in its entirety though not the words. In the Bible, however, every word is sacred. 'The revelation of John contains as many mysteries as words', he wrote in a letter of 395.[2] The meaning of the sacred text cannot be exhausted; it is like the ocean, inexhaustible and mysterious.[3] This mystery must be preserved in the translation. As the order of words transcends human understanding, a change in the order of words would not only destroy this mystery but it would also endanger the unfathomable profundity of the sacred text.[4]

It is impossible to know why Jerome advocated the word-for-word method of Bible translation while he himself did not follow it. For this statement is inconsistent with his theory and with his practice. The student always likes to see the person whose activities he is investigating consistent in all his utterances and deeds. It is only too easy to forget that even a Father of the Church was a human being, perhaps irascible and irritated by frequent attacks against him. In such moments he could easily write something contradicting earlier statements without being conscious of any change in his attitude. He may think of a certain example which at a certain moment he makes the pattern for a theory. Inconsistencies and even contradictions sometimes reveal the humanity of an author which it may be difficult to find in his other writings. Documentary evidence cannot, of course, be offered for such explanations, and this is the reason, I believe, why these inconsistencies are confusing. It may be suggested that Jerome's demand for a word-for-word translation is the result of a controversy and that it was written in the heat of it. It is known that the letter in which these words occur was provoked by Rufinus's

[1] *Ep.* LVII, 5, 6–8; *ibid.* 6, 2 (*P.L.* vol. XXII, col. 572). Cf. the Preface to his translation of Eusebius, *Chronikon* (*P.L.* vol. XXVII, cols. 34–5).

[2] *Ep.* LIII, 8, 6 (*P.L.* vol. XXII, cols. 548–9); cf. *Ep.* LVII, 11, 4 (*P.L.* vol. XXII, col. 578). For the date see F. Cavallera, *op. cit.* vol. II, pp. 89–91.

[3] *Comment. in Abacuc*, II, 3 (*P.L.* vol. XXV, cols. 1317–18).

[4] *Ep.* LVII, 5, 2 (*P.L.* vol. XXII, col. 571). Cf. W. Schwarz, 'The Meaning of *Fidus Interpres* in Medieval Translation', *Journal of Theological Studies*, vol. XLV (1944), p. 75.

attacks against him.[1] The prefaces of his Bible revision and his Bible translation prove that from the beginning he was subjected to heavy attacks from all sides. And he felt that all this censure was unjustified. He did not hold himself to be a falsifier of the Bible when correcting the old version or when making a new translation but rather a corrector whose intention it was to produce a faithful text of the Bible. This work, he emphasized over and over again, did not imply the condemnation of earlier translators.[2] But he wished to end a state of affairs where, owing to different readings, there were as many different texts of the Bible as there were manuscripts. He was very conscious of the tendency to retain an old text even though it was faulty and to condemn those as falsifiers who attempted to correct it.[3] Consideration for this attitude may well have been the reason for retaining the text of the earlier Latin version, although he disagreed with the rendering and would have preferred a change.[4] Attacks against him taught him (if he had not been aware of it before) the restrictions to which a translator of Holy Writ has to submit. Sometimes, at least, he gave a literal rendering although, as has lately been shown, the most literal renderings in his version were taken from earlier versions.[5] Thus, I submit, one can understand that writing on his Bible translation at a time when he was censured by everybody, he made this statement on literal translation and was convinced that he was correct. For he had, after all, renounced a great part of the ornamentation of style and paraphrase which he employed in his renderings of profane works.[6]

[1] See, for example, G. Bardy, *Recherches sur l'histoire du texte et des versions latines du 'De Principiis' d'Origène* (*Mémoires et Travaux* fasc. 25) (Paris, 1923), pp. 161–3.

[2] E.g. *P.L.* vol. XXVIII, cols. 463, 1079, 1082 A.

[3] *P.L.* vol. XXIX, cols. 525–6; *P.L.* vol. XXVIII, cols. 147–8. Cf. A. Hauck, *Realencyclopaedie*, s.v. 'Bibeluebersetzung', pp. 36ff.; G. Bardy, *loc. cit.* p. 167.

[4] E.g. *P.L.* vol. XXIX, col. 528 (*Ep.* CVI, 12); *P.L.* vol. XXII, col. 843.

[5] G. Cuendet, 'Cicéron et saint Jérôme traducteurs', *Revue des Études Latines*, vol. XI (1933), p. 383.

[6] G. Cuendet, *op. cit.* pp. 384–6, 387 ff. F. Blatt, 'Remarques sur l'histoire des traductions latines', *Classica et Medievalia*, vol. I (1938), pp. 219ff. P. Courcelle, *op. cit.*, disagrees with Blatt (p. 45, n. 5), but (pp. 45–6) he seems to come to Blatt's conclusion. Nobody has seen that there may be a connexion between this method and Jerome's words in *Ep.* LVII. Cf. G. Bardy, *op. cit.* pp. 158ff., 163.

Jerome's importance for the history of Bible translation is twofold. His advocacy of a word-for-word method of translation for the Bible was, I believe, accepted almost without exception during the Middle Ages. Moreover, the philological principle (as opposed to the inspirational principle) was recognized as being the basis of every translation. His Bible translation was destined to become the authentic version of the Church. His prefaces to the individual books of the Bible were often copied together with his version. Thus it was generally known that 'it is one thing to be a prophet and another to be a translator'.

The inspirational principle found a defender in St Augustine, who took up the challenge contained in Jerome's work.[1] As early as 394 he was opposed to a new version of Holy Scripture unless St Jerome added the diacritical signs for the indication of all the differences found in the Septuagint and the Hebrew texts. He emphasized the authority of the Septuagint whatever its origin, pointing out that he was at a loss to understand how anything could be found in the Hebrew text that had escaped the attention of all the earlier and very learned translators.[2]

In 403, however, Augustine was more outspoken. In the meantime, Jerome had rendered part of the Old Testament and this new version had been read in some churches. Augustine had grave misgivings about this practice. What would the religious communities say, he asks, if they found out the discrepancies between the Bible used before, and Jerome's new version? In North Africa, where there were many Greeks, it would be noticed that Jerome's text disagreed with the Septuagint. But the Hebrew text, from which the new rendering was derived, would not and could not be consulted by those who did not believe in the correctness of the new text. Even if they compared the Hebrew original with Jerome's version, 'who would condemn so many Latin and Greek

[1] A good bibliography is found in P. Courcelle, *op. cit.* pp. 401–20. Courcelle (pp. 144–53) often mentions Augustine's view on translation but without considering *De Civitate Dei*, XVIII, 42, where the inspirational method is discussed.

[2] Augustine, *Ep.* XXVIII, 2, 2 (*P.L.* vol. XXXIII, col. 112).

authorities?' Augustine then continued with a description of disturbances which had taken place at Tripoli (Oea) when the text of Jonah was read in Jerome's new wording. This new version, Augustine maintained, was different from that text which 'was rooted in the affection and memories of all the people [sensibus memoriaque inveteratum] and which had been read during so many succeeding generations'. The Greeks, Augustine records, took an especial part in these disturbances accusing the new wording as being false. The bishop was forced to denounce the new translation fearing that he would be left without a congregation.

Obviously this incident shows the insistence of the people upon the traditional text of their Holy Book. But as this description of the disturbance is coupled with Augustine's opposition to Jerome's translation of the Old Testament it reveals Augustine's fear lest this new text might create a cleavage in Christendom. He clearly saw the dangers arising from Jerome's undertaking. He knew of the discrepancies between the Hebrew text and the Septuagint. But these divergencies had been of little account as long as the Church used one text only, namely the Septuagint and the Old Latin version derived from it. Jerome's new translation of the Old Testament changed the position of the Septuagint through the creation of another text which was in disagreement with the version used until then. The question might easily arise which of the two texts was correct. Would not the acceptance of Jerome's text involve the making of a new translation from Hebrew into Greek? Considerations such as these might underlie Augustine's desire to preserve the Septuagint against all attacks and to ask the question: should one condemn so many Greek and Latin authorities?

Thoughts like these may have been the reason for Augustine's opposition to Jerome's work on the Old Testament, for he is pleased with Jerome's emendations of the New Testament, since, as he points out in the same letter, these are no 'stumbling block'. Anyone can verify the text from the Greek original or, if he has no knowledge of Greek, can easily be instructed. Concluding this letter, Augustine admits that the Latin manuscripts of the Bible abound in different readings and proclaims that Jerome would be of the greatest use if he reconstituted from the Greek a faithful Latin text of 'that part of Scripture which the seventy have translated'.[1]

The polarity between the views of Augustine and Jerome can scarcely be seen in a clearer light. Augustine was not convinced by Jerome's attack on the Septuagint. He could not understand how Jerome could expect to elucidate the meaning of the Hebrew Bible after the attempt of so many learned people before him. 'If the text is obscure, you too will probably be mistaken; if it is clear, it is incredible that the earlier translators were mistaken', he wrote to Jerome in 394. As to the Septuagint, its authority is too great for one man to oppose it.[2]

At first sight two quite separate motives seem to be operating in Augustine's mind, one based on theology, one on Church policy. Which of these should be regarded as primary? Was it belief in the Septuagint and mistrust of man's critical capacity or was it the authority of the Church whose tradition had to be upheld? How could Jerome be more learned than those other than the Seventy who had translated the Bible into Greek? How could he avoid mistakes? Or was it fear lest the unity of Christendom would be destroyed if the old Latin Bible was replaced by a rendering from Hebrew? No positive answer can be given to these questions. Indeed, a closer study of Augustine's thought makes it seem unlikely that he would have considered these two approaches to be incompatible. Any dichotomy can be resolved by the assumption of one firm principle underlying his attitude to this problem. The Septuagint is a faithful translation of God's word, for it is inspired. Only when his belief in the inspirational nature of this translation is taken into account, is Augustine's view of translation coherent and logical in all its details. As far as is known to me there is no recent study on Augustine's thought on

[1] *Ep.* LXXI (*P.L.* vol. XXXIII, cols. 241–3).

[2] *Ep.* XXVIII, 2, 2 (*P.L.* vol. XXXIII, col. 112).

translation that mentions the inspirational principle of translation. Indeed it is typical of the rationalism of the nineteenth and twentieth centuries that it has been forgotten.

Augustine expressed his view on the Septuagint twice, in his *De Doctrina Christiana* of 416/19 and in the *De Civitate Dei* of 410/28.[1] The argument in these two works is the same and has the same purpose: to prove the divine origin of the Septuagint. In both he attacks Jerome's version, but mentions his name only in the *De Civitate Dei.*

Augustine speaks of the miracle of the Septuagint. Although separated from each other, the translators found that all their versions completely agreed in every word and in the order of words. 'There was, as it were, one translator only, for [*ita*] the translation of all of them was one and the same; indeed, one spirit was in all of them', he reports in the *De Civitate Dei.* Because of this miracle, he concludes, the authority of the Septuagint is not human but divine. Augustine follows the tradition which had been so eloquently expressed by Philo. This tradition exalts the importance and excellence of the Septuagint high above all the other translations of the Old Testament. Following this view Augustine is able to dismiss the other versions with a few words and to point out that the Greek and Latin Christians have accepted the Septuagint, the Greeks in its original language, the Latins in a translation, the old Latin version. The decision of the Church to use a text derived from Greek, and not from Hebrew, is thus fully justified. It is necessary to stress this point, for otherwise it escapes the reader that the words following contain a severe censure of Jerome's version from Hebrew:

> However, in our time there was a priest Jerome, a very learned man, knowing all three languages, who translated these Scriptures not from Greek, but from Hebrew into Latin.

The Jews, Augustine goes on, hold that Jerome's is a faithful rendering while the Septuagint is not. Yet the Church should

[1] I follow Courcelle's dating of *De Doctrina Christiana* (*loc. cit.* pp. 149–50). It was generally dated 397.

prefer a work made by so many excellent men to any version executed by one person only.

Having mentioned Jerome, Augustine had to defend his view against all those who did not believe in the inspiration of the Septuagint. It will be remembered that Jerome attacked this assumption on two accounts, first, the translators did not work separately, and secondly, they made omissions and additions according to their own lights. Assuming, answers Augustine, that the translators were not guided by the Holy Spirit and that they had, after a comparison of their versions, decided upon a text, this their agreement is still weightier than the translation of any one person:

> But [he continues] as the sign of divinity was truly manifest in them, it follows that every other translator of those Scriptures from Hebrew into any other language is right only, if he is in agreement with those Seventy translators. If he be not, one has to assume that it is they who are gifted with the true depth of prophecy. For the Spirit that was in the prophets when they spoke, this very Spirit was in the Seventy men when they translated.[1]

From the divergencies between the Hebrew original and the Greek text Augustine draws conclusions contradicting Jerome. It must have been the Holy Spirit who with God's authority changed the words though not the sense. Additions and omissions were made in the Septuagint to prove that 'no human servitude to the words was at work which the translator ought to have but rather a divine power which filled and ruled the translators' minds'. It follows that

> whatever is found in Hebrew and not in the Septuagint, this the Spirit of God wished to say through those prophets and not through these. Conversely, what is found in the Septuagint and not in Hebrew, this the same Spirit intended to say through these prophets rather than those, manifesting in this way that both were prophets.

[1] *De Civitate Dei*, XVIII, 42–3 (*P.L.* vol. XLI, cols. 602–4).

The Holy Spirit, Augustine continues, did indeed not say the same to every one, as witness the fact that he spoke differently to Isaiah and to Jeremiah and to the other prophets. Yet where the prophets and the translators of the Septuagint agree, there the 'one and the same Spirit' wanted both of them to say the same, 'in such a way that the prophets preceded them in time with their prophecies, and that those who made the prophetical translation followed them. For as there was one Spirit of peace among those who spoke true and concordant words, so the same one Spirit was apparent in those who without conferring among themselves nevertheless translated, as if with one mouth.'[1]

Augustine had thus answered Jerome's attacks upon the Septuagint and imbued it with all the qualities found only in an inspired translation. The prophet through his rendering makes a version which replaces the original. This translation must therefore be accepted as God's Word and Jerome's Latin rendering must be wrong, since it was made from the original Hebrew which had been superseded by the new inspired version. From this two conclusions must be drawn: if the Latin text of the Old Testament is corrupt, it must be emended from the Greek of the Septuagint.[2] The other conclusion is that the ordinary translator, unlike the prophetic translator, must be in 'servitude to the words', a phrase found in the *De Civitate Dei*.[3] Augustine must therefore be in favour of the word-for-word technique of translation. A translator who follows the sense often changes not only single words but also whole phrases, he maintains. In the attempt to render idiomatically he often departs from the meaning of the original. A translator, however, who renders word for word retains the meaning of the original. His style may contain barbarisms and solecisms which should be avoided if they lead to ambiguities.

[1] *De Civ. Dei*, XVIII, 43 (*P.L.* vol. XLI, col. 604); cf. *De Doctr. Christ.* II, 15 (*P.L.* vol. XXXIV, col. 46).

[2] *De Doctr. Christ.* II, 25 (*P.L.* vol. XXXIV, col. 46).

[3] *De Civ. Dei*, XVIII, 43 (*P.L.* vol. XLI, col. 604). I wonder if there is any connexion between this phrase and Origen, *Epist. ad Afric.* 2, directed against Aquila: δουλεύων τῇ Ἑβραϊκῇ λέξει (*P.G.* vol. XI, col. 52B).

But if the original can be rendered more faithfully by the use of a style which is not literary, this should be done. Ambiguities should be avoided at all costs.[1] Purity of style is of no importance for him who wishes to recognize the real contents and not only letters and words. Augustine's words are:

> The weaker man is, the more he is offended by impurity of style, and the weaker he is, the more learned he wishes to appear, learned not in the knowledge of those matters which edify man, but in the knowledge of signs only, which most easily inflame the mind, for even the knowledge of those matters which edify man often lifts up man's neck unless it is curbed by the yoke of the Lord.

Augustine elaborates this theme until at the end he quotes: 'Because the foolishness of God is wiser than men; and the weakness of God is stronger than men.'[2]

Here then Augustine emerges as mistrusting human capacity for understanding. It is God who must lead man. It is God who has revealed the Bible twice, to the prophets and to those who, by inspiration, translated the earlier revelation into Greek. It is foolish for a human being to reject this conception of inspirational translation and to undertake a translation of the Bible relying on man's abilities. Even at its best the work created by man must be inferior to the version of the prophet. Only the inspirational translation is binding. It replaces the original, for it is truly God's word.

What was the outcome of this discussion between these two Fathers of the Church whose different points of view reflect not only the differences in the thoughts of these two great personalities but also the clash between inspirational and philological principles? It is obvious that no final answer is to be expected in which either of these theories is condemned. Rather is a solution based on expediency given from time to time. This bridges the gap for

[1] *De Doctr. Christ.* III, 2–3 (*P.L.* vol. XXXIV, cols. 65–9). For details see Courcelle, *op. cit.* pp. 148–9.

[2] *De Doctr. Christ.* II, 13, 19–20 (*P.L.* vol. XXXIV, cols. 44–5); 1 Cor. i. 25.

some time, but is insufficient to prevent another clash from occurring later. In the fifth century the question, it seems, soon lost its importance. In spite of St Augustine's opposition, St Jerome's translation was soon used in churches and thus became the authentic text of the Church.[1]

[1] The Vulgate was officially authorized only by a 'decretum' of 8 April 1546. The reason given then was that the Vulgate 'longo tot saeculorum usu in ipsa ecclesia probata est'.

5. Proto-Septuagint Studies*

J. W. WEVERS

IN 1941 HARRY ORLINSKY published a paper under a similar title which he dedicated to his teacher, the late Max Margolis.[1] The paper was occasioned by a fundamental attack on the positions and methodology of the Lagardian school of Septuagint criticism, of which Margolis was so distinguished a member, on the part of Paul Kahle and his disciple, Alexander Sperber.

Paul de Lagarde devoted a great part of his fabulous career to inaugurating a programme of scholarly textual study and publication which was to eventuate in the recovery of the original text of the Septuagint. From various notices in the Church Fathers[2] it would appear that in the course of the third and early fourth centuries the Greek Old Testament had undergone three extensive revisions. The work of Origen on its text is best known, he himself having described in somewhat cryptic terms his own textual work in his *Commentary on Matthew* and in a letter to Rufinus.[3] His textual work issued in the *Hexapla*, a monument to misguided industry. Origen realized that the Greek Old Testament had undergone extensive corruptions resulting in a text which at times differed widely from the original Hebrew. In order to bring order out of this chaotic state of affairs he prepared his *Hexapla*.

Wherever the Old Greek differed quantitatively from the Hebrew, Origen provided a key. When a word or phrase occurred in the Greek for which no equivalent obtained in his Hebrew text, its onset was marked with an obelus, and its end with a metobelus. Obviously these marks in the text could hardly matter much. Far more serious, however, was Origen's work where the Greek text was shorter than the

*A paper given as presidential address to the Oriental Club of Toronto in March, 1960. In a sense this study is a popular sequel to the author's "Septuaginta-Studien," *Theologische Rundschau*, N.F., XXII (1954), 85–138, 171–90.

[1] Harry M. Orlinsky, "On the Present State of Proto-Septuagint Studies," *JAOS*, LXI (1941), 81–91; incidentally Orlinsky was himself a student of Meek.

[2] E.g., Clement of Alexandria, Eusebius, Jerome.

[3] See also his comments *ad Africanus* 5.

Reprinted from *The Seed of Wisdom. Essays in Honour of T. J. Meek.* Toronto Univ. Press, 1964.

Hebrew. Here Origen would add from one or another of the other three translators,[4] and mark the addition with an asterisk and metobelus as well as with the column(s) from which the reading was borrowed. It is usually presupposed that Origen's work was thus purely quantitative in character. It is also suggested that his knowledge of Hebrew was not overly profound.[5] There is some evidence which seems to suggest that Origen did more than that: that he occasionally changed word order, as well as words where he felt that the Old Greek was in error.[6] One suspects that when the Old Greek was obviously wrong, Origen sometimes changed it to a word found in one of the other three translators. Naturally he could not do this too often, since this would have created a furore in the Church which believed in the inspiration of the Greek Old Testament. Furthermore there was no sign available to indicate changes of this kind.

The *Hexapla* was much too bulky to be copied in its entirety, but some fifty copies of the fifth column were ordered for Constantinople,[7] and this is where real chaos began. Copyists did not always understand Origen's signs; many were thus lost in transcription, others were misplaced, and the resulting work is a field day for modern critics.[8] Somewhat later two other recensions were commissioned, one, in Egypt, and the other in Antioch. About the former little is known; it was undertaken by Hesychius, a shadowy figure reputedly martyred

[4]I.e., Aquila, Symmachus, and Theodotion. For the history of the Septuagint text in greater detail see the author's article, "Septuagint," in *The Interpreter's Dictionary of the Bible*, IV (New York, 1962).

[5]E.g., H. B. Swete, *An Introduction to the Old Testament in Greek*, revised by R. L. Ottley. (Cambridge, 1914), p. 61. For a more recent study, see H. M. Orlinsky, "The Columnar Order of the Hexapla," *Jewish Quarterly Review* N.S., XXVII (1936–7), 137 ff.

[6]An examination of MSS. Alex and x in Samuel-Kings shows a number of instances of word order corrected in the direction of the Masoretic text (MT). Though individually Alex and x show peculiarities, they (together with the Armenian and Syro-Hexaplar) constitute the best evidence in these books for the Hexaplaric recension. It would be interesting to check the text of these MSS. against "the Three" with the possibility of unmarked changes in mind.

[7]Eusebius, *Vita Constantini* iv. 36 f.

[8]Such confusion reigns that even the best manuscripts show mixed readings. For such Hexaplaric materials in Codex Vaticanus (generally considered our best evidence for a pre-Origenian text; cf. S. Silberstein, in *Zeitschrift für die alttestamentliche Wissenschaft* (*ZATW*), XIII (1893), 1–75, XIV (1894), 1–30; H. S. Gehman, "Old Ethiopic Version of I Kings and its affinities," *JBL*, L (1931), 81–114; and note 11 *infra*), but naturally without Origenian signs; see J. W. Wevers, "A Study in the Textual History of Codex Vaticanus," *ZATW*, LXIV (1952), 178–89.

in A.D. 311/2.[9] The latter is universally attributed to Lucian, martyred about the same time as Hesychius.[10] Fortunately for us, two Syrians, Chrysostom and Theodoret, published many of their sermons and commentaries, and since both of them used the Lucianic text as their Greek Bible it is relatively simple to establish which extant manuscripts represent this recensional text. For example, for the books of Samuel-Kings five manuscripts (boc$_2$e$_2$; HP 19, 82, 93, 108, and 127) were well known to Lagarde as being Lucianic in character. To this must now be added MS. r (HP 700) for Samuel.[11] The best evidence among the Fathers for Hesychius is the text of Cyril of Alexandria. Unfortunately for Septuagint scholars Cyril occupied himself largely with the New Testament, the Prophets, and with Nestorianism, and the Hesychian text is therefore not yet established for most of the Old Testament as it is, for example, for Ezekiel.

Returning to Lagarde, we note that his programme entailed the unscrambling of these three recensions as the first step towards restoring the original text of the Septuagint.[12] To that end he published his *Librorum Veteris Testamenti Canonicorum, pars prior* in 1883. This presumed to be the Lucianic text of Genesis through Esther. Lagarde, however, did not fully realize that a manuscript which is Lucianic in one book may change its textual character completely in some other book. The result is that though for Samuel-Kings the Lagarde volume is more or less adequate, it is almost useless for the Pentateuch, since the manuscripts mentioned above as Lucianic for Samuel-Kings are not Lucianic for the Pentateuch. Lagarde, however, simply accepted these manuscripts as represenitive of the Lucianic text throughout.[13]

After the lamented death of Lagarde in 1891, the programme was carried forward by Alfred Rahlfs, and the Goettingen Society has continued to edit various books of the Old Testament in accordance

[9]Eusebius, *Historia ecclesiastica* viii.13.7. Orlinsky wrongly objects to this characterization of Hesychius in "Studies in the Septuagint of the Book of Job, IV," *Hebrew Union College Annual*, XXXIII (1962), n. 6 (pp. 120 f.).

[10]*Ibid.*, ix.6.3. Most of our scanty knowledge about the recensions of Hesychius and Lucian comes from Jerome; for references cf. Swete, *Introduction to Old Testament in Greek*, p. 78 ff.

[11]J. W. Wevers, "A Study in the Hebrew Variants in the Book of Kings," *ZATW*, LXI (1945–8), 46 f.

[12]Cf. his *Ankündigung einer neuen Ausgabe der griechischen Uebersetzung des alten Testaments* (Göttingen, 1882).

[13]Cf. *Librorum Veteris Testamenti Canonicorum*, I, v, vi, where Lagarde quotes with approval Vercellone's statement that HP 19, 82, 93, and 108 "unum idemque *ἀντίγραφον* ad singularem quandam recensionem spectans repraesentare."

with the principles laid down by Lagarde. At present this work is being carried forward by the indefatigable Joseph Ziegler and his associates.[14]

Basic to the work of this school, which included such outstanding textual scholars as the author's academic grandfather, James Montgomery,[15] and his immediate teacher, Henry S. Gehman,[16] is the working hypothesis that eventually some kind of parent text can be restored. In other words, it is held that behind the recensions lies some kind of common text. It is of course not denied that other translations existed for certain parts of the Old Testament. Origen used three anonymous versions beyond those of Aquila, Symmachus, and Theodotion, called simply the Quinta, Sexta, and Septima. Another anonymous version is the famous version of Hab., chapter 3, in the Codex Barberinus (also found in three other manuscripts).[17] Incidentally a colophon attached to Barberinus reads: "I found the Song of Habakkuk agreeing neither with the LXX nor with Aquila, Symmchus, or Theodotion. You might investigate then whether it be the translation of Quinta or Sexta." De Montfaucon states categorically that remnants of Quinta and Sexta are at variance with the text of Anonymous, though he cites only Quinta readings to prove his point, and suggests that it could be the Septima.[18] The fact is: nobody knows. For the books of Judges and Tobit most scholars believe that rival translations are represented in our manuscripts, and the fact that the Theodotion text of Daniel was adopted by the Christian Church as the canonical text in favour of the Septuagint text is well known to Septuagint scholars.[19] In fact, only two manuscripts, a late Chigi MS. and now the Chester Beatty papyrus (968) represent the

[14]Thus far the following critical editions have appeared: I. *Genesis*; IX.1. *Maccab. liber I*; IX.2. *Maccab. liber II*; X. *Psalmi cum Odis*; XIII. *Duodecim Prophetae*; XIV. *Isaias*; XV. *Ieremias, Baruch, Threni, Epistula Ieremiae*; XVI.1. *Ezechiel*; XVI.2. *Daniel, Susanna, Bel et Draco*. For an evaluation of these cf. Wevers, "Septuaginta-Studien," pp. 95 ff.

[15]Especially in the *International Critical Commentary* (*ICC*) volumes on *Daniel* and *Kings*.

[16]Cf. bibliography in Wevers, "Septuaginta-Studien," 86.

[17]E. M. Good, "The Barberini Greek Version of Habbakuk iii," *Vetus Testamentum* IX (1959), 11–30; M. L. Margolis, "Character of the Anonymous Greek Version of Habbakuk 3," *Old Testament and Semitic Studies in Memory of William Rainey Harper* (Chicago, 1908), I, 133–42.

[18]*Hexaplorum Origenis quae Supersunt*. II. *Notae & variae Lectiones ad Cap. III Habacuc. v.1* (Paris, 1713). The actual text of de Montfaucon is "Esse vero septimam Editionem vix est quod dubitemus."

[19]For a thorough discussion of the Greek texts cf. J. A. Montgomery, *Daniel* (*ICC*), 25 ff.

presumably older text. Thus the fact that other translations existed alongside that of the Septuagint is admitted by everyone.

Kahle and his disciples, however, attacked the basic hypothesis of this classical school of Septuagint criticism. In 1915 Kahle published an article in *Theologische Studien und Kritiken* entitled "Untersuchungen zur Geschichte des Pentateuchtextes." The article deals successively with the Samaritan Pentateuch, the Septuagint, and the Hebrew text. In later articles and finally in *The Cairo Geniza* (The Schweich Lectures for 1941) he restates the problem and his own conclusions in greater detail.

Kahle begins with an analysis and reinterpretation of the Aristeas Letter. The story contained in this letter to Philocrates is well known. Since the work of Hody in 1705[20] (that is, for over two and one-half centuries) this Letter has been recognized as a pseudepigraphon. It was certainly written by a Jew as his devotion to Judaism, his interest in the topography of Jerusalem, the temple and its ritual and furnishings, as well as his general Jewish outlook, conclusively prove.[21] Furthermore there are numerous historical inaccuracies in the Letter. Demetrius of Phalerum was never chief librarian at Alexandria, and particularly not under Ptolemy Philadelphus whose displeasure he had incurred. When Philadelphus became king he promptly banished Demetrius for having been so unfortunate as to have supported the wrong son of Soter for the succession, understandably an unpardonable political sin. Another lapse impossible for a contemporary is the representation of Menedemus of Eretria at the royal banquet, a ghostly affair if true since that worthy had died two years before Soter did. Another observation which is often made is the use of Septuagint phraseology throughout Aristeas' description of the temple furnishings and ritual.[22] It would appear that the Septuagint had been in favour and use for some time when this Letter was written.

In fact the whole tone of the Letter militates against its historicity. That Philadelphus may have been interested in adding a copy of the Jewish laws to his library is plausible, but he would hardly have

[20]H. Hody, *Contra historiam LXX, interpretum Aristeae nomine inscriptam dissertatio,* in his *De Bibliorum textibus originalibus. . . .* (Oxon.). The work originally appeared in 1684, but its inclusion in the later work made Hody's formidable attack well-known to Biblical scholars.

[21]Cf. the succinct summary of arguments for its pseudepigraphic character in *Aristeas to Philocrates* (*Letter of Aristeas*), edited and translated by M. Hadas (New York, 1951), pp. 5–9.

[22]*Ibid.*, 182 ff. Interpreted differently by W. W. Tarn, *The Greeks in Bactria and India* (Cambridge, 1938), pp. 414 ff.

engaged in various theological speculations with the translators,[23] or have admitted the superiority of Jewish monotheism.[24] The origins of the Septuagint are to be sought not in the bibliophile interests of the Egyptian ruler but rather in the needs of the Jewish community of Alexandria in the century following Alexander's conquest. Hebrew was becoming more and more difficult for the Greek-speaking members of the diaspora, and the need for a Greek Targum led to the Septuagint.

Kahle has interpreted this Letter somewhat differently.[25] He believes that the Letter was written *circa* 100 B.C. (which may be true, though I think it a bit earlier) as a piece of Jewish propaganda for a standard recension of the Greek Pentateuch rather than for the original translation. He maintains that an official revision of the text was carried out in the second half of the second century B.C., and that this Letter was written to ensure its popular reception. Propaganda, he states, is only written for something that is contemporary; thus fixing the date of the Letter also gives one the date of the recension. He believes that the Letter actually contains evidence for his theory. In Section 30 occurs a passage in Demetrius' report to the king which Kahle translates as follows: "The books of the Law of the Jews (with some few others) are absent. They are written in the Hebrew characters and language and have been carelessly interpreted and do not represent the original text as I am informed by those who know; for they have never had a king's care to protect them."[26] There are two clauses in this translation which need closer examination: "They have been carelessly interpreted" and "they do not represent the original text."

[23]Cf. H. G. Meecham, *The Letter of Aristeas; A Linguistic Study with Special Reference to the Greek Bible* (Manchester, 1935), 316–24. Meecham has collected 24 apparent instances of borrowing by the Letter as well as a number of possible reminiscences and allusions which are by themselves not convincing, since these merely demonstrate familiarity with the biblical (not necessarily the Greek) text. What is of real importance, however, is the demonstration that the Letter was familiar only wih the Greek Pentateuch, and not with the rest of the Greek Old Testament. In my own comparison of the 3 Kingdoms, chapters 6–7, account of the temple and its furnishings with *Aristeas*, 57–82, I could find no evidence of literary relation between the two accounts, whereas the correspondence between *Aristeas* and Exod. 25:23 f. seems completely convincing.

[24]Cf. particularly Demetrius's reply to the king's query concerning the reason for previous silence by historians and poets concerning *τηλικούτων συντετελεσμένων* (312): *διὰ τὸ σεμνὴν εἶναι τὴν νομοθεσίαν καὶ διὰ θεοῦ γεγονέναι καὶ τῶν ἐπιβαλλομένων τινὲς ὑπὸ τοῦ θεοῦ πληγέντες τῆς ἐπιβολῆς ἀπέστησαν* (313).

[25]*The Cairo Geniza* (The Schweich Lectures, 1941; London, 1947), pp. 132 ff.

[26]*Ibid.*, pp. 135 f.

The original text here reads: ἀμελέστερον δὲ καὶ οὐχ ὡς ὑπάρχει σεσήμανται. Kahle maintains that σεσήμανται (from σημαίνω) refers to earlier translations which in itself is possible. The word is certainly ambiguous and can refer either to careless (ἀμελέστερον) transmission of the Hebrew text, or to (careless) interpretations, that is, translations. It is suggested that the reference to careless transmission of the Hebrew text could be of no concern to Ptolemy which is of course quite true but not germane to the argument. It is only germane if the conditions of the Letter are historically genuine, and Kahle quite rightly agrees that they are not. It is a Jewish writer, and such a writer would be very much interested in the state of the Hebrew text. In fact, I would suggest that the poor state of the text to be translated was the actual reason for having a Hebrew text sent for from Jerusalem. Certainly the most natural meaning of σημαίνειν is "to indicate." If the Hebrew laws are rather carelessly "indicated," it would probably refer to their present state.

The argument, however, hinges on the explanatory words which intervene—καὶ οὐχ ὡς ὑπάρχει—and which Kahle loosely renders by "and do not represent the original text." The words literally mean "and not as they really are"—not a particularly clear elucidation of ἀμελέστερον. This to my mind means one of two things: either the Hebrew text is bad and does not represent the pure text as it presumably existed in the holy city, or the Alexandrian Jews are accustomed carelessly to interpret the Hebrew text orally and therefore did not get at the real meaning of the text. As a cornerstone for a theory of diverse translations existing in Alexandra *circa* 100 B.C. this interpretation of Kahle is tenuous.[27]

Kahle also refers[28] to a statement in Section 314 of the Letter where reference is made to Theopompus of Chios, reputedly at home in various exotic literatures. Theopompus "was about to introduce rashly into his history certain material previously translated from the Law"[29]

[27]Hadas, ed., *Aristeas*, translates σεσήμανται by "committed to writing." Meecham, *Letter of Aristeas*, as does Frankel, *Vorstudien zu der Septuaginta* (Leipzig, 1841), p. 24, admits the rendering "interpret" as possible, thus as Kahle making it refer to a former translation. But the most natural interpretation in the context is careless *oral* interpretation, such as a written text would obviate. The passage is certainly obscure and ought not to be used as an argument for anything. Cf. also H. M. Orlinsky, in *Crozer Quarterly*, xxix (1952), 205.

[28]*The Cairo Geniza*, p. 136.

[29]διότι μέλλων τινὰ τῶν προηρμηνευμένων ἐπισφαλέστερον ἐκ τοῦ νόμου προσιστορεῖν—Hadas, ed., *Aristeas*, 314.

and became mentally ill as a result of his tampering with holy things. This is precisely the kind of high-flown fairy tale which one might expect from the writer of this legend. It is hardly proper to press the point of the previously translated material from the Law. Theopompus lived in the time of Soter, and the matter is pure invention. Furthermore in Section 316 the poet Theodectos is related as also having been afflicted. When he was about to put τι τῶν ἀναγεγραμμένων ἐν τῇ βίβλῳ (something recorded in the book) into one of his plays, he was afflicted with a cataract. That too is fancy. It is meaningless as far as Kahle's argument is concerned. But even if such other translations or partial translations were present, it would make no difference. The real point is that they were never accepted.

It should be remembered that Philo records an annual feast held on the Island of Pharos to commemorate the events producing the Septuagint. This feast was not limited to Jews only but also "multitudes of others cross the water, both to do honour to the place in which the light of that version first shone out, and also to thank God for the good gift so old yet ever young."[30] The tradition was apparently an old one, and one feels that more than a recension of the Greek Old Testament was here at stake.

One objection to Kahle's reconstruction which apparently has never been raised is that if the revision was made as late as *circa* 100 B.C. it is extraordinary that the work should have been limited to the Pentateuch. According to the Prologue of the Greek text of Ben Sirach the Prophets were part of the canon. Reference is made to "the Law and the Prophets and the rest of the books." This phrase occurs in the context of a discourse on the difficulties of translation from Hebrew into Greek. The full statement reads: "and not only these, but the Law itself, and the prophecies, and the rest of the books, have no small difference when they are spoken in their original form."[31] This was written in 132 B.C. The Alexandrian canon at this time included the Prophets, and one wonders why, were Aristeas referring to a new revision, he did not include the Prophets. If on the other hand the writer is referring to the event of the original translation, about which by the writer's time all kinds of apocryphal accretions had grown, the reference is clear. The event may well be third century B.C., even

[30] *De Vita Mosis* ii. 41, according to F. H. Colson's translation.

[31] οὐ μόνον δὲ ταῦτα. ἀλλὰ καὶ αὐτὸς ὁ νόμος καὶ αἱ προφητεῖαι καὶ τὰ λοιπὰ τῶν βιβλίων οὐ μικρὰν ἔχει τὴν διαφορὰν ἐν ἑαυτοῖς λεγόμενα—*Prolog. Sir.* 14–16.

though the romance itself was written in the latter half of the second century B.C.

Up to this point the argument between Kahle and the Lagarde school has been purely speculative, Kahle's objections hinging on a rather dubious interpretation of an obscure passage. If Kahle's frontal attack is to stand, some evidence of these presumed translations out of which the "standard" text emerged will have to be forthcoming. Kahle bases his argument mainly on two types of text—that of Philo, and that of the New Testament. The most recent work on Philo's text is that of Peter Katz.[32] Most of the following argument in connection with Philo summarizes and is based on Katz's observations.

It has long been known that the dominant Bible text in Philonic manuscripts is Septuagintal. Certain manuscripts, however, particularly MSS. U and F,[33] have a non-Septuagintal text which has been a constant source of trouble to Septuagint scholars. This aberrant text is on the whole much closer to the Masoretic text but it is not to be identified with that of the literalistic Aquila with which it does have a great deal in common. The real question is which is the text that Philo himself had. Most Philonic scholars from Mangey's edition[34] (over 200 years ago) down to the excellent work of Cohn-Wendland[35] have concluded that the UF text is that of an interpolator, an editor who changed the Bible text of Philo to agree with the particular translator or recension which he followed.

One of the most remarkable books on Philo to appear since the Cohn-Wendland edition was the Greifswald thesis of August Schröder.[36] Schröder was guided in his thesis by the Greifswald classicist, Gehrke, who apparently knew neither Hebrew nor anything about Philo. Gehrke had been stimulated by a shortlived attack on Cohn-Wendland by Eberhard Nestle[37] who had supported the aberrant text on the grounds that it was closer to the Hebrew. The Septuagint, Nestle felt, was a later adaptation to Christian usage. Philo on the other hand

[32]*Philo's Bible: The Aberrant Text of Bible Quotations in Some Philonic Writings and its Place in the Textual History of the Greek Bible* (Cambridge, 1950).

[33]Vat. graec. 381 and Laurent. plut. 85, cod. 10 resp.

[34]*Philonis Judaei Opera*, edited by T. Mangey (2 vols., London, 1742).

[35]*Philonis Alexandrini Opera quae supersunt*, edited by L. Cohn and P. Wendland (6 vols., Berlin, 1896–1915).

[36]*De Philonis Alexandrini Vetere Testamento* (Greifswald, 1907). I am here dependent on Katz, having been unable to find a copy.

[37]"Zur neuen Philo-Ausgabe," *Philologus*, N.F. XIII (1900), 256 ff. with which compare his later reflections in *ibid.*, XIV (1901), 271 ff.

was a Jewish author and would be interested in a text closer to the Hebrew. Therefore the text of UF was the text of Philo.

Schröder set out to prove that the text of UF was earlier than the Septuagint. The result is an excellent example of how a dissertation should not be done. First of all, his work is limited to two treatises, viz., *de sacr. Abel et Cain* and *Quod Deus sit immut.* This is hardly sufficient material for a major thesis. Furthermore, the work is incredibly naïve.[38] After five pages of Preface "of a painfully elementary character," filled with errors, there follows the "magna tabula" for 27 pages in which 108 passages from these two treatises are simply listed in 8 columns. In each case the Philonic text is given with its UF variants, then that of the Septuagint with its variants, the ancient versions, including the Old Latin and Samaritan. The context is never consulted. Katz says: "Obviously the idea never struck him that his task was to obtain from Philo's exposition the standards of decision as to which form of quotation might be Philo's own. Thus he is able to deal with the isolated quotations by themselves, without ever considering that they form part of a context. If we call to mind the meticulous adherence of Philo's exposition to the quoted words, down to the very vocables, from which he extricates his special interpretation, we realize that Schröder has utterly failed to see the real implications of his task."

The conclusions of his fifty-page monograph of which over half is simply a listing of passages without comment were as follows:

1. The two forms of text are so different that only the one could have come by a deliberate modification of the other.

2. If the UF text is secondary, the sources for it must have been the same throughout. This could not have been either one of "the Three" or the Hebrew.

3. Since we know of no Greek text from which that of UF could have been modified, it represents the most ancient known form of the Old Testament in Greek. The other MSS. corrected to the Septuagint.

4. From Josephus, the Old Latin, and Justin we know that there were other translations existing at an early date.

5. A Pauline parallel at Eph. 5:2 based on Num. 28:2 where, for *qorbān*, προσφοράν is used (also occurring in the UF text), whereas in the Septuagint δῶρα occurs. (I might add parenthetically that the verb προσφέρετε governs the word which might independently have given rise to the Pauline προσφοράν.)

[38]What follows here simply summarizes Katz, *Philo's Bible*, 134 ff.

6. This Pauline parallel proves the text of UF to be the most ancient and also the one used by Philo himself.

These conclusions of Schröder are obviously worthless. The aberrant text is to be found in the lemmata which head the expositions, a fact which Schröder neither indicated nor took into consideration. Had he noted the context, that is, read the exposition of the lemmata, he would soon have noted that the text presupposed in the exposition was not that of UF but that of the Septuagint. In other words, the problem of which was the actual text which Philo used could have been simply solved by reading the expositions. The position of serious Philonic scholars, namely that Philo's Bible was Septuagint, would simply have been demonstrated once again instead of being challenged in such a fashion.

The question of the origin of the aberrant text is of course still pertinent. It is clear that the text is at least partially dependent on Aquila though not identical to it. Katz believes that its source is the so-called R (or Reviser) source which Rahlfs found in the book of Ruth.[39] Though independent of Origen's work, it does show the result of methods similar to those used by Origen. That this text was a revision is clear from the sporadic character of its text. Apparently it is a revision of the Septuagint on the basis of an Aquila-like text rather than a separate translation.[40]

But what about Schröder's thesis that the texts of Josephus, the Old Latin, and Justin prove that non-Septuagint translations existed alongside that of the Septuagint at an early date? The problem of Justin's text has long been difficult. Many felt that Justin often adapted his text to his argument; in other words, that there never was a received text at the basis of his *Dialogue* and *Apologies*. This suspicion has at least in part been removed by Père Barthélemy who published some fragments of the Minor Prophets in Greek found by the Ta'amire Bedouin.[41] This text has a peculiar affinity to that of Justin, and what

[39]This suggestion is attractive but difficult to demonstrate since this Reviser text for the Pentateuch has not yet been identified (i.e., if it exists!).

[40]Showing that Origen's approach was not unique. Kahle is undoubtedly right in speaking of the existence of various texts. What is being questioned here is that our Septuagint MSS. reflect a welter of independent texts. There is no doubt that the simple accounts in the Church Fathers fail to do justice to the complexity of the textual problem.

[41]"Redécouverte d'un chaînon manquant de l'histoire de la septante," *Revue Biblique*, LX (1953), 18–29. For a detailed evaluation cf. J. W. Wevers, "Septuaginta-Studien," pp. 136 ff. Cf. also P. Katz, "Justin's Old Testament Quotations and the Greek Dodekapropheton Scroll," *Studia Patristica*, I (1957), 343 ff.; J.-D.

may be even more significant, to the text of Quinta. It is thus quite possible that through this new text the problem of Justin's text may now be partially solved.

The problem of the text of Josephus and that of the Old Latin is actually one problem. At least one of the Old Latin versions (the Afra) and the text of Josephus, as well as parts of the Peshitta (or Syriac) version, reflects the non-Hexaplaric Lucianic text. The only difficulty is that Lucian is supposed to have made his recension *circa* A.D. 310, whereas these texts are all much earlier. There was thus a Lucianic text before Lucian, in fact, at least 200 years before Lucian. There is to my mind no doubt that the Antiochian text was an early revision of the Septuagint text. That it was a revision rather than a separate translation can be demonstrated from a careful study of the Lucianic text. No two separate translations could have made the same peculiar mis-translations in so many places. Kahle believes that the text of Josephus was revised by later Christian revisers who brought the Bible text throughout in line with the Lucianic text. This seems to me to be unlikely. It would have meant a systematic rewriting of Josephus' text, a difficult task to say the least. My own belief, though I have not yet been able to test the proposition, is that the Lucianic revision *circa* A.D. 310 consisted primarily of the addition of the Origenian plusses to the Antiochian text. It is a fact that the best Lucianic manuscripts do have asterisked passages. All in all, the so-called proto-Lucianic text is to my mind the most difficult problem in modern Septuagint work.[42]

But to return to Philo and Schröder's work on his text. Kahle has accepted the conclusions of Schröder without himself examining the evidence. Schröder's conclusion that the aberrant text was the actual text of Philo now becomes evidence that other texts besides that of

---

Barthélemy, "Quinta ou version selon les Hébreux," *ThZ*, XVI (1960), 342 ff.; S. Jellicoe, "Aristeas, Philo, and the Septuagint *Vorlage*," *Journal of Theological Studies*, N.S., XII (1961), 261 ff.

[42]For a discussion of the relation of the Old Latin to the Antiochian text cf. H. Voogd, *A Critical and Comparative Study of the Old Latin Text of the First Book of Samuel* (Unpublished Th.D. dissertation, Princeton Theological Seminary, 1947). An abstract of this thesis appears in *Catalogue of Doctoral Dissertations: Princeton Theological Seminary, 1944-1960* (Princeton, 1962), pp. 15 f., where the author states, "The Old Latin texts of the African Fathers represent the Lucianic or Syrian Greek text tradition. Since the African Fathers antedate the text of Lucian, they furnish independent evidence of an Ur-Lucianic source." For literature on "Proto-Lucian" cf. Orlinsky, "Studies in the Septuagint of the Book of Job, IV," n. 5.

Septuagint existed already in the first century A.D. The further conclusion is then made that the two texts involved are independent, whereas it is equally possible, in fact, probable, that the aberrant text is simply a revision of the Septuagint text.

Kahle also calls attention to a statement in the Philonic treatise *de migratione Abraami* which reads: "his father having died there he departed from it."[43] Terah was 70 years old at the time of Abraham's birth according to Gen. 11:26. Abraham was 75 years old when he left Haran (Gen. 12:4). The last verse of Genesis, chapter 11, states "the days of Terah were 205 years; and Terah died in Haran." The Septuagint text agrees throughout with the Hebrew, but the Samaritan Pentateuch has 145 years for Terah's age instead of 205. Now Stephen's speech in Acts, chapter 7, also recounts the tale but in these words: "Now after his father died, God removed him from there into the land in which you are now living."[44] Stephen, like Philo, took for granted a lifetime of 145 years for Terah. Therefore, says Kahle there must have been a Greek text with a reading like that of the Samaritan Pentateuch as a basis for the statement by these two worthies. This presupposes logical mathematical minds. I doubt whether either Philo or Stephen had any actual text in mind. The fact is that the death of Terah is recorded in the final verse of Genesis, chapter 11, whereas chapter 12 begins with the call of Abraham from Haran. I suspect that if one were asked how long after his father's death Abraham had left Haran most would have said "immediately afterwards," and yet the mathematics of the Genesis account which most readers have often seen is perfectly clear. This is certainly not evidence of a variant text.

Kahle adduces a second kind of evidence for the existence of early variant texts. Much is made of the Old Testament quotations in the New Testament. As is well known some of these are widely divergent from that of the Greek Old Testament as we know it. Many of the proofs adduced by Kahle turn out upon closer scrutiny to be tenuous. Much is made of the plural reading for father in the Samaritan Pentateuch at Exod. 3:6. Here the Masoretic text has "I am the God of *ābīkā* (thy father). The Samaritan Pentateuch has *abōthékā* (thy fathers). In Stephen's speech the reference is ἐγὼ ὁ θεὸς τῶν πατέρων σου. Kahle thinks that this proves the existence of two different translations. Such a conclusion seems hazardous in the extreme to anyone who has dealt with text critical matters. Let us examine further evidence on this

[43]*The Cairo Geniza*, pp. 143 f.
[44]Acts 7:4.

matter. Justin Martyr at one place[45] has ἐγώ εἰμι ὁ ὤν, ὁ θεὸς Ἀβραάμ καὶ ὁ θεὸς Ἰσαάκ καὶ ὁ θεὸς Ἰακώβ καὶ ὁ θεὸς τῶν πατέρων σου. Here the word order is different since in the Masoretic text, "the God of Abraham, and the God of Isaac and the God of Jacob" follows "I am the God of thy Father." Elsewhere[46] Justin quotes the passage again but omits the phrase "and the God of thy Fathers" entirely. (This does not mean that Justin suddenly picked up another translation!) Furthermore two Greek cursives, MSS. k and m, as well as the Bohairic and Codex C of the Ethiopic, codices of Eusebius, and the edited text of Cyprian, have the plural reading. Does this motley lot of witnesses prove a variant text? Of course not. The plural in view of the following genitives "I am the God of Abraham, and the God of Isaac and the God of Jacob" (notice three fathers) is the easier reading. *Lectio difficilior preferendum est!*

Somewhat later in Stephen's speech reference is made to Deut. 18:15. This follows a telescoped account of the exodus and wilderness journey, in fact, an account telescoped into one small verse, verse 36. Later Stephen returns to the story of the rebellion at Mount Sinai. In the Samaritan Pentateuch a number of passages from Deuteronomy are introduced into Exod. 20:15–22. Actually Deut. 18:15 is not there inserted though verse 18 is, and that is much like verse 15. Kahle says "we have to reckon with the possibility that he found in his Greek Tora the passage from Deuteronomy inserted in Exodus 20 which we find today in the Samaritan Pentateuch only."[47] Aside from the fact that the latter actually has verse 18 instead of verse 15, the speech at this point becomes very general, is certainly only the barest of summary statements, and simply proves nothing one way or another.[48]

What Kahle presupposes with respect to New Testament quotations, and he could have used far better examples than he does, is that the New Testament writers actually had a Greek text of the Old Testament and quoted it verbatim. This conclusion I find quite unacceptable. The New Testament writers were Semitic speaking. Greek was

[45] *Apologia* A' 63.17.

[46] *Dialogue* 59.3. Here the text is further abbreviated as ὁ θεὸς Ἀβραάμ καὶ Ἰσαάκ καὶ Ἰακώβ.

[47] *The Cairo Geniza*, p. 145.

[48] Stephen is obviously not quoting a text; he is preaching a sermon. No one would suggest that verse 36 represented a variant text to the detailed account of the exodus, Red Sea, and wilderness wanderings. Homiletically he continues by saying, "This is the Moses who said . . . ," quoting the Deut. verse in question. This is certainly not a textual problem whatsoever.

only their second language. Their Bible was the Hebrew Bible; the translation to which they were accustomed was an oral Aramaic Targum. Paul was trained as a Pharisee, and only secondarily in the Greek translation of the Bible. He and his fellow-writers wrote in Greek, it is true, and quotations from the Old Testament had therefore to be made in Greek. But manuscripts were not readily available to the New Testament writers. One doubts whether Paul took a copy of the Greek Old Testament along with him on his travels. On the other hand, the New Testament writers were well acquainted with the Old Testament in Hebrew, and it would be far simpler to translate *de novo*. What is surprising actually is not how often the quotations depart from the Septuagint text, but rather how often they agree. One further point ought to be mentioned in this connection. Some of the New Testament quotations follow the text of Theodotion, or as the author would prefer to call it, the Palestinian text to which the name of Theodotion was later attached. This is particularly true of the quotations from Daniel in the Apocalypse. Apparently an oral Palestinian interpretation of the book of Daniel arose which Theodotion later adopted and edited and which gradually replaced the Septuagint or Alexandrian version almost completely in the Christian church. That this was an oral Targum is made more likely by the fact that it was known to New Testament writers and quoted by them. An oral Targum seems far more likely than another Ur-Document, in this case an Ur-Theodotion. One Ur-Document, an Ur-Lucian (or better, the Antiochian text) which cannot be avoided, is enough!

In general, Orlinsky's criticism of Kahle's *The Cairo Geniza* is valid. He says: "In his eagerness to find support for his theory of many independent Greek and Hebrew texts, Kahle has ignored the important role that oral tradition, oral quotations and interpretations, played in those days. Thus, e.g., the Nash papyrus is hardly more than some kind of liturgical fragment copied memoriter; the Rabbis in the Talmud cited biblical passages from memory, with the resultant errors and differences. . . ."[49] Memory plays an extremely important role in a manuscript culture. Manuscripts were very expensive, and only the wealthy could afford to have them. Biblical manuscripts would be the property of churches and synagogues rather than of individuals. The kind of manuscript factory which apparently existed at Qumran in Jesus' day was a rarity; from that point of view members of the Qumran community were a privileged group.

[49]A review of *The Cairo Geniza* by Orlinsky in *JAOS*, LXIX (1949), 165.

It should also be kept in mind that biblical manuscripts were not paginated, nor was the text nicely divided into chapters and verses. A modern writer wishing to quote a biblical passage simply looks it up and quotes chapter and verse verbatim. The writers of the gospels and epistles were not so fortunate. They had to depend almost wholly on their memory. Most of these writers would know favourite passages by heart. Paul, for example, in view of his Rabbinic training, knew much of the Hebrew Old Testament and certainly all the Torah by heart. His knowledge of the Greek text would have been somewhat more imperfect, as his quotations from the Old Testament show. This same principle applies to the early Church Fathers. A study of biblical quotations in Justin's *Dialogue with Trypho* will soon convince one of its relevance. Numerous quotations occur more than once. But the quotations are not always word for word the same. I have already mentioned one such quotation: Exod. 3:6 which occurs in different forms in the *Dialogue* and the first *Apology*. Others could be cited with similar results.[50] It is only those Fathers who are commenting exegetically on the Old Testament whose biblical quotations can actually be trusted as textual evidence. Such writers as Cyril of Alexandria on the Prophets, Chysostom and Theodoret, Jerome, Origen, *et al.* have commented on the text and their quotations are solid evidence for textual variants. Why? Because they used manuscripts. They were explaining the text. Hortatory writers such as the apologists simply quoted from memory. The same thing may be true for Josephus. The case of Philo is different. Philo was allegorizing the Torah. His Greek Bible was the Septuagint and he undoubtedly quoted from a manuscript. Thus his text is good evidence. *A priori* the conclusion that all kinds of written translations of the Greek Old Testament existed out of which a "standard" Septuagint eventually emerged is most unlikely. In fact, a standard text did not emerge in the early Christian centuries, but revisions and recensions did.

The Kahle hypothesis has been carried to much greater extremes by his disciples. The story of Franz Wutz and his *Transcriptionstheorie*

[50]E.g., Gen. 19:24 is quoted in the *Dialogue* four times. The quotations are as follows: 56.23– *κύριος ἔβρεξεν ἐπὶ Σόδομα καὶ Γόμορρα θεῖον καὶ πῦρ παρὰ κυρίου ἐκ τοῦ οὐρανοῦ*; 60.5—*κύριον παρὰ κυρίου τοῦ ἐν τοῖς οὐρανοῖς*; 127.5—*καὶ κύριος ἔβρεξεν ἐπὶ Σόδομα πῦρ καὶ θεῖον παρὰ κυρίου ἐκ τοῦ οὐρανοῦ*; 129.1—*ἔβρεξε κύριος πῦρ παρὰ κυρίου ἐκ τοῦ οὐρανοῦ*. All four citations differ. But these readings are largely valueless for textual purposes. Dozens of such variants could be found in the *Dialogue*.

is well-known.[51] At one time it had a great vogue, but his early death brought an end to his brilliant but baseless conjectures. Within a year of his passing almost everyone had abandoned if not forgotten his theories. Another of Kahle's disciples has done far more damage. Alexander Sperber published numerous monographs and lengthy articles on Septuagint studies. His best known work entitled *Septuagintaprobleme*[52] was severely and rightly attacked by Orlinsky.[53] Rather than repeating his criticisms it might be better to review a hundred-page article of Sperber entitled "New Testament and Septuagint."[54] In fairness to Kahle, it should be said that he does not endorse all of his disciple's conclusions.

Sperber begins by pointing out well-known differences between New Testament quotations and the Septuagint. These differences he believes to be based on a "Bible of the Apostles." The article is intended to define this text. Concerning what Swete, in his *Introduction to the Old Testament in Greek*, had to say about the problem (in which he presents the usual solution to the problem more or less as it is discussed in this paper), Sperber comments: ". . . I may say that Swete was far from realizing the problem as such, and that all his remarks are consequently to be put into the discard."[55] After such an auspicious beginning we are prepared for great things, and we are not disappointed. The major part of the article deals not with New Testament quotations but with Origen's *Hexapla*. After dismissing Lagarde's archetype theory in a few words as already refuted by his earlier work, Sperber continues with a statement on the current view of Origen's work and his refutation of it. The refutation consists of four statements. (1) The Septuagint is a translation of Hebrew into Greek, and "like all other ancient translations no doubt follows slavishly the Hebrew original." Since there were great differences in Origen's days, it must mean that the Hebrew had undergone great change.[56] The only thing that can be said about this proposition is that

[51]*Die Transkriptionen von der Septuaginta bis zu Hieronymus.* (*Texte und Untersuchungen zur vormasoretischen Grammatik des Hebräischen* II: BWAT, 2e Folge: Heft 9) (Stuttgart, 1925). It should be noted that Kahle does not necessarily follow Wutz's later absorption "in his special ideas," *The Cairo Geniza*, 233.

[52]*Texte und Untersuchungen zur vormasoretischen Grammatik des Hebräischen* (Herausg. v. P. Kahle; BWANT, 3e Folge, Heft 13) (Stuttgart, 1929).

[53]"On the Present State of Proto-Septuagint Studies."

[54]*JBL*, LIX (1940), 193–293.

[55]*Ibid.*, p. 204, summarizing Swete, *Introduction to Old Testament in Greek*, pp. 392–8.

[56]"New Testament and Septuagint," p. 208.

Sperber's surprising statement does not make it so. (2) The argument of unfairness to the Jews hinges on the presupposition that the Septuagint is more Christian than the Hebrew. But cases can be cited in which the opposite is true, that is, where the Hebrew could be used, much more tellingly than the Greek. Since Christians of the second and third centuries normally could not read Hebrew it is hard to see the relevance of this statement. (3) Origen did not have the "requisite knowledge of Hebrew to restore the Septuagint to its original purity, that is, to the Hebrew veritas." (4) And what is the Hebrew *veritas*? This could only be the Hebrew Bible of Origen, and not the Vorlage of the Old Greek. No one doubts this, but it is an irrelevancy.

Sperber thereupon outlines his own "New Approach." All the evidence about Origen's work in the Church Fathers is set aside and "we shall, therefore, go back to the original sources, and base our conclusions solely on the evidence of Hexaplaric statements themselves." By taking into account only the materials collected by Field, Sperber maintains that "in this fashion *we base our conclusions on Origen's work alone*."[57]

With tremendous industry Sperber has collected and classified materials under the obelus and under the asterisk. From this he concludes that what Origen really did was to compare two Septuagints. One was the obelus Septuagint. This was then compared to the asterisk Septuagint. Divergences were noted with an asterisk on the margin (not in the text). These when eventually copied into the text led to numerous doublets which are particularly apparent in the Old Latin as well as in Theodoret. It does not occur to Sperber, working as he does in lofty isolation, that these texts have long been identified as Lucianic by scholars, and therefore have nothing to do with the work of Origen. All of Origen's work can thus be subsumed under the presupposition that he compared these two Septuagints of his. This thesis is then tested by comparing the texts of MSS. B and A for the Pentateuch. Sperber is naturally able to do this because he has rejected all the work of former Septuagint scholars to whom classification into recensional families was a prior task. This comparison leads Sperber to the conclusion that the texts of these two codices go back to different sources. B is really the product of the obelus text, and A, that of the asterisk type. Similarly for the texts of Judges he says "the only conclusion to be drawn must be that no 'genuine' LXX (in the singular!) existed in Origen's days, but two independent translations

[57] *Ibid.*, p. 209 f.

of the Bible into Greek, both of which held an equal claim to be called 'Septuagint.' "[58] The same conclusion, namely that "B shows close affinity to the obelus type, and A to the asterisk type" is held to be sound for the rest of the Old Testament as well (specifically, Hosea, Ezekiel, I Samuel, and Psalms are examined in a few places).[59] This astounding conclusion is then carried forward to apply to the so-called "Bible of the Apostles." Sperber has thus far concluded that "we saw that as late as in the days of Origen two different translations of the Old Testament into Greek were known as LXX. In combining their variant readings in the fifth column of his *Hexapla* he indicated the source, from which these variants came, by marking them with an obelus or asterisk, respectively. But the very fact that he incorporated these readings in the fifth column proves that he considered the two translations as genuine LXX."[60] The difficulty which Sperber feels has been present with those who concern themselves with Old Testament quotations in the New Testament is that they think of the Septuagint as that of a single text (that of B). The fact is that the "Bible of the Apostles" was really the asterisk Septuagint.

It is quite unnecessary for twentieth-century scholars to refute Sperber's conclusions. Sperber may be able to work in complete isolation of Septuagint scholars on Origen's *Hexapla*, but it is rather too much for him to work in isolation from Origen himself. Origen explains his signs clearly and carefully in his *Commentary on Matthew*.[61] The obelus is put at the beginning of a Septuagint passage for which no equivalent word or words are present in the Hebrew. Whenever the Hebrew had a word or words not found in his Septuagint, he would insert under the asterisk ἀπὸ τῶν λοίπων ἐκδοσέων the necessary phrase. Naturally the passages under the asterisk will be closer to the Hebrew. And of course the so-called "Bible of the Apostles" would seem closer to the later so-called asterisk Septuagint, because the Old Testament quotations in the New Testament which diverged from the Septuagint were simply translations *memoriter*.

Since Origen himself has contradicted Sperber, nothing further need be said on the matter. One doubts whether Kahle would be happy to

[58] *Ibid.*, p. 259.

[59] Section xiv, pp. 263–6 of *ibid.*

[60] *Ibid.*, p. 279.

[61] Ad 19:16 ff. in *Die griechischen christlichen Schriftsteller der ersten drei Jahrhunderte*, Bd. 40, edited by E. Klostermann (Leipzig, 1935). This has now been reprinted in *Bibliotheke Hellenon Pateron kai Ekklesisastikon Sunggraphon*, Vols. XIII f. (Athens, 1957–8). The relevant passage is in Vol. XIII, p. 356, ll. 7–40.

accept some of the wild statements of his disciple, and yet this is the kind of chaos that can result from theories inadequately founded in fact. Kahle has done a service in calling attention once again to the Targumic character of ancient Greek translations. He has, however, not succeded in upsetting the basic approach towards Greek Old Testament textual criticism in which one attempts to classify readings recensionally and thereby tries to determine earlier readings.

Kahle concluded his first major paper on the subject as follows:

Die Geschichte der griechischen Pentateuchübersetzung its gleichbedeutend mit einer allmählichen Angleichung von Uebersetzungen, die dem alten Vulgärtext nahestanden. . . . Die älteste Form dieser Uebersetzung rekonstruieren zu wollen, ist eine Utopie. Man wird im besten Falle eine oder die andere Revision dieser Uebersetzung mit einiger Sicherheit bestimmen können. Die weitere Verbreitung einer Textgestalt ist zumeist erst die Folge von Ueberarbeitungen und steht an Abschlusse einer gewissen Entwicklung, nicht am Anfange. Ich glaube nicht, dass die Uebereinstimmung der hauptsächlichsten, aus dem dritten nachchristlichen Jahrhundert stammenden Textgestalten dem "ursprünglichen" Text der griechischen Uebersetzung nahebringt, trotzdem dies seit Lagarde als ein Art Evangelium gilt.[62]

This Lagarde *Evangelium* has been independently tried in the field of detailed and sustained textual criticism by such great masters as Margolis in his edition of Joshua,[63] by Montgomery in his work on Daniel and Kings,[64] by Ziegler in his editions of the Prophets,[65] and by my own great teacher, Gehman, in his work on various versions,[66] and they have found it true. The future of proto-Septuagint studies depends on the classical line, with some necessary modifications to be sure, rather than on the general lines of Kahle's approach.

[62]"Untersuchungen zur Geschichte des Pentateuchtextes," *Theologische Studien und Kritiken*, LXXXVIII (1915), 399–439.

[63]M. L. Margolis, *The Book of Joshua in Greek*. Pts. I–IV (Paris, 1931–8); for an appreciation of Margolis, cf. H. M. Orlinsky, *Max Leopold Margolis, Scholar and Teacher* (Philadelphia, 1952).

[64]J. A. Montgomery, *A Critical and Exegetical Commentary on the Book of Daniel* (*ICC*) (New York, 1927); *A Critical and Exegetical Commentary of the Books of Kings* (*ICC*), edited by H. S. Gehman (New York, 1951).

[65]Bände XIII, XIV, XV, XVI.1 u. 2 of the volumes listed *supra*, note 14.

[66]E.g., H. S. Gehman, "The 'Polyglot' Arabic Text of Daniel and its Affinities," *JBL*, XLIV (1925), 327–52; "The Sahidic and the Bohairic Versions of the Book of Daniel," *JBL*, XLVI (1927), 279–330; "The Hesychian Influence in the Versions of Daniel," *JBL*, XLVIII (1929), 329–32; "The Old Ethiopic Version of 1 Kings and its Affinities," *JBL*, L (1931), 81–114; "The Armenian Version of I. and II. Kings and its Affinities," *JAOS*, LIV (1934), 53–9; "The Relations Between the Hebrew Text of Ezekiel and that of the John H. Scheide Papyri," *JAOS*, LVIII (1938), 92–102; "The Relations between the text of the John H. Scheide Papyri and that of the Other Greek MSS. of Ezekiel," *JBL*, LVII (1938), 281–7.

(ii) *The Letter of Aristeas*

ARISTEAS AND SEPTUAGINT ORIGINS: A REVIEW OF RECENT STUDIES.

BY

D. W. GOODING

Belfast

In recent years a great deal of work, much of it very valuable, has been done on the so-called Letter of Aristeas, both in extensive studies of the Letter as a whole for its own sake, and in more restricted investigations of the comparatively few paragraphs that purport to relate the origin of the Septuagint, and incidentally refer to pre-Septuagintal translations. Most studies have upheld the common view that Aristeas' story of LXX origins is part of a work of propaganda aimed at glorifying the Jews, their Law, their High Priest, their holy city and country, their temple and scholarly sages; that the details of the story are more romance than history; and that, contrary to what the Letter says, the translation of the Law arose out of the practical needs of Greek-speaking Jews, and not from the policy of Ptolemy's library [1]).

Yet even those who share this view, still disagree as to how many of the details in the story may be accepted as basically true in themselves, and how many are sheer inventions. What is more, there remains wide disagreement on the still more fundamental question, as to how some of the relevant sentences and crucial words should be translated, and how they are to be interpreted within their immediate and wider contexts. It is, therefore, the purpose of this present article to compare the findings of some of the more recent studies, to attempt to assess them and to offer a few slender contributions en passant.

II

There are two passages in Aristeas which have been taken by some to refer to Greek translations of the Law earlier than the LXX.

[1]) Exceptions are E. J. BICKERMAN, *A. Marx Jubilee Volume*, New York, 1950, pp. 156-7 and B. H. STRICKER, "De brief van Aristeas. De hellenistische codificaties der praehelleense godsdiensten". *Verhandelingen der koninklijke Nederlandse Akademie van Wetenschappen, afd. Letterkunde*, Nieuwe Reeks, Deel LXII, No. 4, Amsterdam 1956. The latter is answered by R. HANHART, *VT* XII (1962), pp. 139-63.

Reprinted from *Vestus Testamentum*. Vol. 13, 1963.

The first (para. 30) says: τοῦ νόμου τῶν Ἰουδαίων βιβλία σὺν ἑτέροις τισὶν ἀπολείπει· τυγχάνει γὰρ Ἑβραικοῖς γράμμασι καὶ φωνῇ λεγόμενα, ἀμελέστερον δὲ, καὶ οὐχ ὡς ὑπάρχει, σεσήμανται, καθὼςὑ πὸ τῶν εἰδότων προσαναφέρεται· προνοίας γὰρ βασιλικῆς οὐ τέτευχε.

The questions arise (i) what is it that has been somewhat carelessly done, i.e. what does σεσήμανται mean? and (ii) what are the books that are said to have suffered this fate, whatever it is? Are they carelessly transmitted Hebrew texts, or carelessly made Greek translations?

In the end everything will depend on the meaning of σεσήμανται. If it cannot mean "translated", or even "interpreted", but only "written", there is an end of the argument. But if it could mean, *at least in some contexts*, "interpreted", or "rendered", it would not be fair to say as ZUNTZ does [1]), that since the first (half of the sentence) states that the Law is couched in Hebrew letters and language, the second cannot contain information about any versions but because of the grammatical structure of the sentence is bound to refer, likewise, to the Hebrew Law. ZUNTZ's contention is only true if σεσήμανται means "written" or "copied out"; in which case the first half of the sentence says that the Law is written in Hebrew, and the second half, still referring to the Hebrew text of the Law, says it has been carelessly written out. But if σεσήμανται could mean anything like "translated", then, obviously, the second half of the sentence, while still referring to the grammatical subject, "the books of the Law", would be giving information on the quality of their translation into Greek, and so about the inaccuracy of the Greek versions.

Because of this it is worth while examining a supporting argument, which is frequently brought in by those who argue that the reference is to carelessly made Greek translations. In their estimation carelessly written *Hebrew* texts are out of the question.

M. HADAS [2]), who in his translation (p. 111) renders σεσήμανται "have been committed to writing", nevertheless in his commentary says: "The entire sentence seems intentionally ambiguous. The important question for the history of the Greek translation of the Bible, is whether the existing books referred to are carelessly-transmitted Hebrew texts or carelessly-made earlier translations. It seems unnatural for the king to be interested in the state of the Hebrew text . . ."

[1]) "Aristeas Studies II: Aristeas on the Translation of the Torah". *JSS*, April 1959, p. 117. Hereafter references to ZUNTZ are to this article.

[2]) *Aristeas to Philocrates*, Harper & Brothers, New York, 1951.

P. Kahle, repeating his earlier views, in the second edition of the *Cairo Genizah* [1]) says, "The words 'rather carelessly' (ἀμελέστερον) can only be taken as referring to earlier *translations*, for one can hardly suppose that Demetrius was interested in any form of the Hebrew of the Pentateuch, nor could he suggest that the *Hebrew* copies had been made carelessly". And in a footnote aimed at refuting E. J. Bickerman, who did hold that Demetrius was referring to the original text of the Law, Kahle enlarges the argument: "...the whole letter tends to show the royal sympathy for the Greek *translation*, not for the Hebrew *original*, which after all was imported from Palestine". Subsequently S. Jellicoe [2]) has repeated the argument: "It can hardly be, as Kahle rightly observes, that the state of the *Hebrew* text is here the subject of criticism . . ."

Now this contention that Demetrius would not be interested in the state of the Hebrew text, might carry some conviction if Aristeas' story could be accepted as true: if Aristeas were a Greek as he purports to be; if Demetrius were in fact Ptolemy Philadelphus' librarian, and if the translation were made on his initiative. Then it might, perhaps, be thought a little remarkable that the Greek librarian should be interested in the state of the text of the Hebrew books which he wanted to get translated. Even so, one could reasonably argue that a librarian who habitually examined the textual accuracy of all the Greek works that he collected, might be expected by force of habit to ask himself questions about the textual accuracy of the Hebrew copies of the Law, before he had a translation done. But all this reasoning is in fact needless. Aristeas' story is fictitious as most scholars agree. The author is not a Greek but a Jew; he was not present in Philadelphus' court when Demetrius is supposed to have made his suggestion; Demetrius was not Philadelphus' librarian, anyway. It is obvious, then, that though the author has accurately copied the style of court memoranda for the sake of verisimilitude, he has made Demetrius say whatever he wanted him to say, and in the process has occasionally made him speak more like a Jew than a Greek. It is pointless to complain that it is unnatural for Demetrius to be interested in the Hebrew text; perhaps it is unnatural, but it is equally unnatural for the "Aristeas" of the story, a supposed Greek, constantly to express sentiments and adopt attitudes natural only in a Jew (see Hadas, op. cit., p. 5f.). The unnaturalness is no ground

[1]) Blackwell, Oxford, 1959, p. 213.
[2]) "Aristeas, Philo and the Septuagint *Vorlage*." *JTS*, October 1961, p. 267.

for trying to change the plain sense of what is said; it is merely an indication of the true source of the sentiments.

Moreover, Aristeas makes Demetrius explain where he got his information from on this point; "It is reported by those who know" —Jewish experts, obviously. And it is not altogether implausible for Aristeas to imply that, when Demetrius decided to get a translation of the Hebrew Law, he applied to the Alexandrian Jewish experts, who informed him that some Hebrew manuscripts were carelessly written, and that he had better apply to Jerusalem for a reliable copy.

III.

With the charge of "unnaturalness" removed, the whole case turns on the meaning of σεσήμανται. Disagreement here is wide and continued. L. MENDELSSOHN [1]) translated it "*perscriptae*"; R. MARCUS [2] says "The exact meaning of σεσήμανται in Arist., . . . is a matter of dispute. Some scholars take it to mean "interpreted" and think it refers to previous Greek translations of the Pentateuch, cf. Z. FRANKEL, *Vorstudien zu der Septuaginta*, 1841, p. 61, note k. It seems clear from the context, however, that it refers to Hebrew MSS of the Pentateuch which have been carelessly copied from an original scroll (presumably kept in the Temple at Jerusalem)". E. J. BICKERMAN [3]) takes it to mean *notare*, mark with writing, and claims that Aristobulus uses the term in the same meaning "note down". DIELS suggested that it referred to incorrect vocalisation and THACKERAY [4]) thought his suggestion ingenious. Nonetheless THACKERAY put "interpreted" in his text, meaning it to refer to an earlier translation, though he allowed the possibility that it meant merely "committed to writing". H. G. MEECHAM [5]) follows FRANKEL (see above) with "interpreted" meaning "translated"; HADAS [6]) renders it "committed to writing" but adds a footnote "*sesēmantai* more regularly means "interpreted" i.e. translated. In a review of HADAS, H. M. ORLINSKY [7]) reminds us that "HERZOG (apud F. X. WUTZ, *Die Transkriptionem von der Septuaginta bis zu Hieronymus*, Part I (1925), pp. 128ff.) stated

---

1) *Aristeae quae fertur ad Philocratem epistulae initium*. Dorpat, 1897, p. 35.
2) Loeb, Josephus, *Antiquities*, vol. VII, p. 21 note c.
3) Op. cit., p. 156, n. 25.
4) *The Letter of Aristeas*, SPCK, London, 1917, p. 29 n. 1.
5) *The Letter of Aristeas*, Manchester, 1935, p. 201.
6) Op. cit., p. 111.
7) *Crozer Quarterly*, April 1952, p. 205.

that already the Letter of Aristeas provided support for WUTZ's Greek transcription theory in that *sesēmantai* = 'transkribiert . . . in griechische Buchstaben'." ORLINSKY then continues, "In my review of WUTZ's *Systematische Wege*, etc. (*JBL*, 57 (1938), 216) I wrote that a careful study of the use of sēmeioō [1]) in the *Letter* (as also in Josephus etc.) proves conclusively that it means simply 'make marginal notes, interpret, annotate' etc." On the other hand KAHLE [2]) in his translation puts, "have been carelessly interpreted (ἀμελέστερον σεσήμανται), but in his comments he has, "The words ἀμελέστερον δὲ . . . . . σεσήμανται, 'rather carelessly written', are not clear . . .". It is thus not certain what he believes sesēmantai actually means, though later he makes it clear how he thinks its meaning should be interpreted: "The words 'rather carelessly' (ἀμελέστερον) can only be taken as referring to earlier *translations*", and again "σεσήμανται, is certainly not *copied* . . ." [3]).

In this welter of disagreement it is most helpful to have ZUNTZ's full and, in the present writer's opinion, completely convincing summary of the evidence, both linguistic and contextual, that σεσήμανται means simply "written". He points out (pp. 117-9) that in the context the "careless treatment" is said to have been suffered because the books "have not benefited from royal care". The normal "royal care" given to books entering the library was the establishment of an exact, pure text; the opposite of such careful treatment is not careless translation, but careless writing out. On the linguistic side the decisive piece of evidence is the use made of σημαίνω by Aristobulus in a fragment preserved by EUSEBIUS, *Praep. Evang.* XIII 12 (para. 7 MRAS, but 12 in the older editions). One cannot do better than quote ZUNTZ's comment: "In his endeavour to demonstrate that the Greeks got their best thoughts from Moses he has just quoted the prooemium of Aratus—with a thoroughgoing alteration of the original text, putting throughout "God" in the place of "Zeus" [4]). In dealing with so well-known a text Aristobulus deemed best to confess to his interference. This he did by assuming the pose of rational criticism. "The poem clearly refers to God, whose power permeates the universe" so he argues, "hence I have written as required, eliminating the poetical (fiction) Zeus": καθὼς δὲ δεῖ

[1]) Sic.
[2]) Op. cit., pp. 212-3.
[3]) Op. cit., p. 213 n. 1.
[4]) Older editions print texts in which Aratus' own term, Zeus, has been restored.

σεσημάγκαμεν, περιαιροῦντες τὸν διὰ τῶν ποιημάτων Δία. Περιαιρεῖν is a technical term (Latin *inducere*) of Alexandrian scholars denoting the bracketing of spurious matter. And σημαίνειν is here used for the conscientious writing of a text by a critic—as in Aristeas".

In Aristobulus, then, it is abundantly clear that σημαίνω does not mean "translate", but simply "write". But it should be emphasized that, while σημαίνω means simply "to write", the process of "writing" involved for Aristobulus, not faithful copying of the original, but deliberate change of vocabulary in order to make the author say what Aristobulus "knew" he meant, or ought to have meant. Now the fact that an ancient critic could in the name of careful writing take such liberties with a text, certainly casts light on the phenomena that we see in many LXX manuscripts and particularly the widespread change of vocabulary that is found in the so-called Lucianic recension. These changes, whatever the motive behind them, are not necessarily evidence of the survival and admixture of early, independent translations. They can just as well be accounted for as the result of a careful "writing" out of the LXX. Since, however, σημαίνω means "write" and not "translate", Aristeas 30 is referring to *Hebrew manuscripts* and not Greek translations.

But before we go on to consider the implications of this, we ought briefly to examine another interpretation of Aristeas 30 and 31, that has been proposed more recently by S. JELLICOE [1]). He takes ἀμελέστερον σεσήμανται to refer to the corruptions, intentional and unintentional, which had come into the text between the time of the original translation and that at which the author of Aristeas was writing. There are two parts to his supporting argument and for convenience of reference I number them.

(1) "This surely is the force of ἀμελέστερον δὲ, καὶ οὐχ ὡς ὑπάρχει, σεσήμανται: rather carelessly rendered (i.e. in the course of transmission) and not at all, according to the verdict of those who are well informed on the matter, as it (i.e. the Hebrew text) actually is". (2) "Such a meaning seems to be demanded by the sentence which follows: 'It is fitting, moreover, that these (books) should subsist in the form in which they were accurately rendered under your patronage —δέον δέ ἐστι καὶ ταῦθ' ὑπάρχειν παρά σοι διηκριβωμένα (not, as HADAS, op. cit., p. 111, 'that these books, too, in an emended form should be given a place in your library . . .') for the reason that this legislation is highly philosophical and uncontaminated, as being

[1]) *JTS*, October 1961, p. 267.

divine' (para. 31). Here the accuracy and authenticity of the *original* translation are emphasised—not a revision in the time of Aristeas, the repetition of ὑπάρχειν both stressing the abiding authority of the translation and constituting a plea for its permanent retention".

This new interpretation seems to conflict so violently both with the straightforward meaning of the Greek and with the whole weight of the context, that it is difficult to feel sure that one is interpreting JELLICOE's suggestion fairly. It would be easier, for instance, if the new translation he offers in place of HADAS's, could be taken to mean: "It is necessary that, once these books have been accurately rendered under your patronage, they shall remain in that form"; in other words, if the sentence could be construed as advice against allowing errors to creep into the manuscripts once the translation, which is being proposed, but has not yet been started, has been done. But such does not seem to be JELLICOE's intended meaning. The aorist "were accurately rendered"—suggests that the translation had been done some years before Demetrius' present memorandum. And, in (1), JELLICOE explicitly says that the corruptions, of which Demetrius complains, were corruptions which had come into the Greek text in between the time of the original translation and that at which the author of Aristeas was writing. Since, then, the author represents himself as contemporary with Demetrius and present in court when Demetrius made his original suggestion (para. 10), JELLICOE's interpretation does make Demetrius say that a Greek translation had already been made some years before—long enough for corruptions to have crept into the text—and that it was made under royal patronage; but that, because of the subsequent corruptions, steps must now be taken, not to revise the translation, but to restore its original accuracy.

But if that were Aristeas' meaning, how does he make Demetrius say in para. 11, that the Hebrew books still needed to be translated? And if a translation had been previously made under royal patronage, why was it still wanting in the royal library as paras. 10 and 30 state? And again, if the translation had been made under royal patronage, there must have been an official library copy. How did it happen that within the king's lifetime this copy became so corrupt? And what sense will then attach to the reason given in para. 30 for this corruption: "they (the books of the Law) have not enjoyed royal care"?

Perhaps JELLICOE would take refuge in the plea that Aristeas has forgotten to speak everywhere consistently with the supposed date of his story. Undoubtedly Aristeas has in places been inconsistent as ZUNTZ has so fully demonstrated [1]; but it is impossible to think that he has been *so* inconsistent within such a small space, the more so since, in writing historical fiction, he was free to make his story hang together.

But JELLICOE's interpretation is impossible from the point of view of language as well. To say nothing more, his aorist—were . . . rendered—gives a wrong twist to the perfect διηκριβωμένα, and his translation completely overlooks the significance of the καὶ in the phrase δέον δέ ἐστι καὶ ταῦθ' ὑπάρχειν, these books *too* [2]) . . . Demetrius, in order to complete the library, is proposing the same treatment for the books still missing, as had been given to the books already collected. But if one puts the καὶ into JELLICOE's translation, one makes Demetrius say that the Hebrew law, *as well as all the other books already in the library*, will in future need to be preserved from corruptions.

IV.

But JELLICOE is not alone in holding a view which can only be justified by charging Aristeas with blatant self-contradiction within the space of a few sentences. ZUNTZ, who has so convincingly shown that σεσήμαντια in para. 30 means "written" and that it must grammatically refer, not to any Greek translation, but to the Hebrew manuscripts, nevertheless makes it a major plank in his case against Aristeas that this reference to imperfect Hebrew manuscripts was a "smart" move to create the right atmosphere, which very soon involved Aristeas in a story that was not only incredible but also inconsistent. In the present writer's opinion these allegations are unfair and unnecessary; and because they are unfair they tend to weaken, rather than strengthen, ZUNTZ's otherwise splendid case against founding great theories of LXX origins on this passage of Aristeas. It will, therefore, be worth while examining these allegations in detail.

1. "If we confine ourselves strictly to the context, it still seems strange that Demetrius should assert the poor quality of the Jerusalem text. One may test an alternative interpretation. Could he be referring to Hebrew texts kept by the Alexandrian Jews?

[1]) Op. cit. See also "Aristeas Studies I: 'The Seven Banquets'." *JSS*, January 1959, pp. 21-36.

[2]) HADAS is completely right.

This interpretation runs counter to conclusions previously drawn; even so, it is not beyond possibility that the writer could here be discounting an assumption followed in other parts—and this understanding would be far less improbable on historical grounds. And yet it is, unless I am greatly mistaken, excluded by the wording of this very passage" (ZUNTZ, p. 119).

This contention, that Demetrius is asserting the poor quality of the *Jerusalem* text, is the first part of the argument by which ZUNTZ convicts Aristeas of inconsistency. The second part is the claim that the text that arrives from Jerusalem is, according to Aristeas, the only manuscript of the Law in existence, and therefore any idea of "careless writing" is here completely out of the question (p. 120). First, then, we should observe that Demetrius nowhere asserts the poor quality of the *Jerusalem* text. All he says is:—"the books of the Law of the Jews . . . have been written somewhat carelessly" (para. 30). He does not specify any particular copies; but he does suggest meeting this difficulty (and several others simultaneously) by sending for elders from Jerusalem, who, in the outcome, do bring with them a very special copy of the Law. Now it is perfectly natural for Demetrius to speak vaguely as he does without specifying particular copies. Suppose the early English translators of the OT. had explained the difficulties confronting them to the general public thus: "the OT is written in Hebrew characters and language; moreover it has been copied out rather carelessly; we must therefore get rabbis from Jerusalem to help us". No-one would have supposed that they were referring to the Jerusalem text in particular; or that, on the other hand, they were being deliberately vague about which manuscripts they meant, because they did not really know what they were talking about [1]). People might, in fact, have been excused, if they had taken it for granted that, whereas Hebrew manuscripts in general were poor, Jerusalem was likely to have the best text available.

So we must next examine those "conclusions previously drawn" which make ZUNTZ think that Demetrius *is* complaining about the *Jerusalem* text, although he does not specify it. They are drawn from the wording of para. 3 (not 4-5 as ZUNTZ has inadvertently put): "who (i.e. the High Priest) possesses the greatest usefulness for his countrymen, those with him and those in other places, for the trans-

[1]) "It is only too clear that the writer had no concrete tradition to follow, nor any idea of the real problems facing the real originators of the Septuagint . . .", ZUNTZ, p. 122.

lation (? interpretation) of the divine Law, because of its having been written with them on leather in Hebrew characters". ZUNTZ, after commenting on the apparent lacuna in the text and deciding that the "with them" refers to the inhabitants of Judaea or Jerusalem, continues: "Even so, these fragmentary words yield two important hints. It is stated as a fact of special significance that "with them" the Torah was written "in Hebrew characters"; secondly, this text is supposed to exist there, in Jerusalem, and only there—the wording of this sentence unambiguously implies this, quite apart from the fact that this assumption is indispensable to the story as a whole" (p. 114).

Here one is bound to protest that neither of the last two statements is true. The assumption that the text of the Law exists nowhere outside Jerusalem, is not indispensable to the story as a whole, but only to ZUNTZ's own interpretation, as we shall presently see. And to say that the sentence *unambigously* implies that the text of the Law exists only in Jerusalem, when in fact the sentence is patient of other interpretations, is plainly an exaggeration. To start with, the sentence does not say that the High Priest is the only one who can translate the Law, but simply that he possesses very great (or possibly, the greatest) usefulness in this respect. Secondly, while ZUNTZ agrees with L. COHN in supposing there is a lacuna in the text, his interpretation assumes that the διὰ τὸ clause is somehow explaining the unique *advantage* that the High Priest has—the Judaeans have the Law written down, nobody else has a written copy. Now for a Jew to say such a thing, even under Aristeas' Gentile mask, would be an outrageous misrepresentation of the facts in the eyes of the many Jews for whom he was writing his propaganda. But had he wished to say so *unambiguously* he must have said simply "because with them it has been written down". The fact that he adds "on leather in Hebrew characters" opens the possibility that the intended contrast is not between a written text in Jerusalem and an oral tradition elsewhere, but between a text written, in Jerusalem on leather in Hebrew characters, and in Alexandria on papyrus in Greek. The contrast, of course, would not be fair; the Alexandrian synagogue, too, would have copies of the Law written on leather in Hebrew characters [1]), as well as Greek papyrus copies. But it would be no more unfair than ZUNTZ's interpretation which infers that Alexandria had no copies at all.

---

[1]) Cf. *Sopherim* 1-3 which requires copies of the Law to be written on leather scrolls; and for the early use of leather for writing purposes in Egypt, see *BA*, VI, 1943, pp. 74-5).

Thirdly, it is possible without any over-stretching, to construe the sentence in another, different way, so that it states quite straightforwardly the true facts of the case without any misrepresentation. On this view, (1) one does not need to suppose any lacuna in the text, but would, in fact, insist that the "with them" (παρ' αὐτοῖς) is to be taken to refer, in accordance with strict grammar, to the natural antecedent, "his countrymen, those with him *and* those in other places." In other words "with them" does not refer solely to the inhabitants of Judaea or Jerusalem, and intend a contrast between them and other Jews elsewhere. Aristeas is speaking as a Greek; when he says "*them*" he is thinking of *Jews*, all Jews everywhere, as he explicitly says, "those with the High Priest in Jerusalem and those in other places.

(2) One would then interpret the διὰ τὸ clause as expressing, not the unique *advantage* of Jerusalem Jews, but the common *difficulty* of Jews everywhere: their Law is written in Hebrew. Now no average Jew reads or speaks Hebrew, and therefore their Law has to be interpreted and translated for them. Even the Jews with the High Priest in Jerusalem will need translation, for they speak not Hebrew, but Aramaic; while Jews in Alexandria speak Greek.

(3) One would then suppose a slight ellipse in thought: the High Priest possesses very great usefulness for his fellow-countrymen, both those with him and those in other places, for the translation of the Law: (and it needs translation) because with them it is written on leather in Hebrew characters. The naturalness of this ellipse can be illustrated by an imaginary modern counterpart. A Muslim, interested in the Catholic religion and explaining why he visited the Pope, might quite naturally express himself thus: the Pope possesses the greatest usefulness for his fellow Catholics, both those with him in Italy and those in every other country, for the interpretation of the Mass; for with them the Mass is written in Latin. The inference would be that the Mass, being written in Latin, needs interpretation for Catholics in Italy who speak Italian and not Latin, as well as for Catholics elsewhere.

The general merit, then, of this interpretation is that it fits exactly the historical facts as we know them, whereas the Jews of Alexandria for whom Aristeas was really writing, and who every Sabbath day saw in their synagogue a copy of the Law on leather in Hebrew characters, would not readily read into Aristeas' words what Zuntz does, namely, that there were no written copies of the Law outside

Jerusalem. At least, it would be understandable if *they* did not find the sentence *unambigously* to mean that.

Nevertheless ZUNTZ has a stronger point when he comments on paras. 9-11 (p. 114). "In the context, however, of the scene narrated in 9-11, the king's sudden move, not suggested by Demetrius or anyone else, is understandable only if it is taken for granted that "the laws of the Jews" are to be found only in "the land of the Jews". The inference is borne out by Demetrius' saying (11) that "in Judaea" people use a special kind of writing: this would be pointless, were it not understood that there only the coveted book exists."

But if the king's sudden move is examined more carefully in its context, ZUNTZ's point disappears. The king's suggestion to write to the High Priest comes in reply to Demetrius' complaint, that it was useless obtaining a copy of the Laws and copying it out in the normal way for the library. Demetrius himself could have obtained a copy; as the king pointed out, he had all the necessary means to do it with. The difficulty was that the Law was written in a very peculiar language and would have to be translated. "All right" says the king in effect "let us write to the High Priest and get a translation". The king's suggestion implies, not that Jerusalem is the only place where one can get a copy of the Law, but that only there can one get a proper translation. And in so saying the king is expressing a sentiment to which many Alexandrian Jews would have assented.

If, then, the difficulty was that copies of the Law were available only in Jerusalem, Demetrius would not have troubled to mention it to the king. Was he not used to sending to Athens for official texts of the Greek classics? But if Demetrius' difficulty is supposed to have been, as ZUNTZ suggests, that there was only one copy of the Law in existence, must he not have said so in his reply to the king? The simple fact is that neither here nor elsewhere does Demetrius ask for "the Law", or for a copy of it, but only for translators (see paras. 11, 32, 39). He obviously anticipated no difficulty in getting a good copy.

And further to emphasise that the difficulty is one of language, Aristeas makes Demetrius stress the difference between Aramaic and Hebrew. "In the Jews' country they use a peculiar script . . . They are supposed to use Syrian (Aramaic), but that is not the case, for theirs is another dialect" (11). These words surely re-echo the frustration of many an Aramaic-speaking Jew on examining a copy of the Law and hearing it read [1]). Josephus in his paraphrase of Aristeas expands the point: "though their (the books of the Law) script seemed to be similar to the peculiar Syrian (Aramaic) writing and their language to sound like the other, it was, as it happened, of a distinct type" [2]). This many Aramaic-speaking Jews must have discovered to their disappointment, though at the same time it must have increased their patriotic admiration for the experts in their nation who could read the "real" Hebrew. While, therefore, it is very natural for Aristeas, as a Jew, to make Demetrius present the difficulty as one of language, and stress the fact that Hebrew is not Aramaic, it would be quite unnatural for him to make Demetrius imply that Jerusalem was the only place where copies of the Law existed.

Zuntz, admittedly, has a strong point when he calls attention to Demetrius' expression that "in Judaea" people use a special kind of writing, and argues that this would be pointless, were it not understood that there only the coveted book exists (pp. 114-5). It is, perhaps, the more obvious way to fill out Demetrius' train of thought: translation is required, because in Judaea they use a special script; and the Law is to be found only in Judaea. But it is not the only way. One could just as easily complete his thought thus: translation is required, because in Judaea they use a special script; and copies of the Jews' Law, wherever found, are naturally written in the language of the Jews' country of origin [3]).

But Zuntz is hardly being fair to Aristeas when he argues: "And so Ptolemy gives orders to write to the High Priest . . . What does he want from him? A copy of the "laws of the Jews"? "Interpretation of its stange letters? A translation? The pompous last words of this section leave the reader in the dark. This much only is clear: he who wants the "Laws of the Jews" must apply to Jerusalem (p. 116). Admittedly Ptolemy himself does not say explicitly what is the exact purpose of writing to the High Priest; but the sequence is: Demetrius says "Translation (ἑρμηνεία) is needed. Ptolemy replies "Well, let us write to the High Priest". Can there be any doubt what Ptolemy was after? Or if there can be, the matter is settled by the fact that

[1]) Cf. modern Greeks, if they try to read the classics without knowing ancient Greek.

[2]) *Ant.* XII, 15.

[3]) And this interpretation finds, perhaps, some support in the reading of all the MSS, "in the land of the Jews", not "in Judaea". Zuntz regards the MSS reading as a fault; but the phrase is natural, if Demetrius meant "in the land where Jews come from".

Aristeas, who after all is the author both of Demetrius' and Ptolemy's remarks, has already told us a few lines earlier (para. 3) why he himself gladly offered to go on this embassy to the High Priest: the High Priest possessed the greatest usefulness . . . for the translation of the Law. We are not left in the dark; Aristeas has stated the purpose of the embassy as explicitly as anyone could wish.

V.

We are now free to return to the crucial passage, paras. 30-32, and in particular to the words, "the books of the Law . . . have been somewhat carelessly written". So far we have argued against ZUNTZ's plea that the reference is to the Jerusalem text, to the one and only manuscript in existence. We have suggested that the more natural interpretation is to understand it as a reference to Hebrew texts in general and in particular to Hebrew texts available in Alexandria. But ZUNTZ is not to be disposed of so easily. He has considered the latter view, which he admits would be far less improbable (than his "Jerusalem" view) on historical grounds, but he rejects it for two reasons which must now be faced.

(1) "And yet it (the view that Demetrius is referring to Hebrew texts kept by Alexandrian Jews) is, unless I am greatly mistaken, excluded by the wording of this very passage. If the books were supposed to be available in Alexandria, why does not Demetrius say so? How could he say that they are "wanting"? The observation that they were of inferior quality, because unimproved by "royal care", applied to every single book he acquired; it did not cause them to be "absent" from the library. Not even Aristeas would suppose Demetrius to describe an Alexandrian copy of, say, Homer or Euripides to be "absent" because it had not been edited by the scholars of the Museion" (p. 119f.).

Once again, one must protest that this is being unfair to Aristeas. "Wanting" in para. 30 (the books of the Law are wanting) must surely mean the same as "wanting" in the previous sentence (the books that are wanting for the completion of the library). It has nothing to do with the geographical location of the desired books—wanting in Alexandria, existent only in Jerusalem—; it simply means that they are not yet in the library. Secondly, Demetrius does not say that the books of the Law are wanting because unimproved by "royal care". The reasons for their absence, explicit and implicit in his memorandum, are:—

(1) They are written in a strange language and strange characters;
(2) the text is of poor quality because of careless copying; (It has been carelessly copied because it has not benefited from royal care).
(3) the contents are divine and very well worth having; but it would require holy men to edit them for the public;
(4) in addition to being holy, the men would have to be expert exponents of the Law:
(5) and not one expert, but a whole body of experts would be needed.

The phrase "because they have not benefited by royal care" is meant to explain, not the absence of the books, but the poor quality of their text. Their absence from the library is accounted for by the *combination of difficulties*, 1-5. Difficulty no. 2, with the reason given for it, was true of Greek works as well; but by itself it would not have kept Greek works out of the library, for Demetrius could have coped with that difficulty, even if it meant sending to Athens for official copies. All the other difficulties were peculiar to the Hebrew Law, and they would have effectively caused these books to be absent from the library hitherto, even though there were copies enough in Alexandria.

(2) This argument ZUNTZ regards as decisive. "What is more, and in my view decisive, is the conclusion Demetrius derives from his premiss. If he really meant that Alexandrian copies of the Torah were not good enough for his library, then his point in suggesting applying to Jerusalem must be to get a better copy from there. In fact, however, a manuscript to be obtained from there is, strangely enough, not even mentioned. He suggests the dispatch, from Jerusalem, of seventy-two worthy men, outstanding in character and well versed in their Law. Are they to correct the faulty Alexandrian manuscripts? That is not what he says, not what actually happens afterwards. Eleazar, in his reply to Ptolemy, states (46) that he is dispatching the seventy-two "with the law", ἔχοντας τὸν νόμον. The impression is confirmed that the only place from which it can be had is Jerusalem; indeed, that there is only one manuscript of it in existence; the one which Eleazar is sending for "copying" (μεταγραφή 46 and 47). And the uniqueness of this manuscript is powerfully stressed in the elaborate and fairy-tale-like description of the reception, in Alexandria, of this wonderful book, written in golden letters (χρυσογραφίᾳ τοῖς Ἰουδαικοῖς γράμμασιν) on marvellous parchment (175-9)" (p. 120).

These arguments seem, to say the least, a trifle difficult to follow. The point at issue, after all, is whether, in complaining that the books of the Law had been written carelessly, Demetrius was talking of Alexandrian copies or of the Jerusalem text. Put more directly ZUNTZ's arguments seem to be:—

(1) If Demetrius were complaining about the Alexandrian manuscripts, he would have asked Eleazar for a better copy. Instead he asks for elders and makes no mention of a manuscript. Therefore he must have been complaining about the Jerusalem text [1]).

(2) Had his complaints been referring to the Alexandrian texts, his point in asking for elders would have been to get them to correct the faulty Alexandrian manuscripts. This was not his point. His point was to get the elders to bring on loan from Jerusalem the only copy of the Law in existence, the Jerusalem copy. This can be deduced from what he says and from what actually happened. And from the "conclusion" one can deduce what he meant in his "premiss": he was there complaining, not about Alexandrian texts, but about the unique Jerusalem text.

Immediately we must observe that argument (2) completely invalidates argument (1). If he did request, by implication, the Jerusalem copy of the Law, it is no longer of any significance to say "In fact, however, a manuscript to be obtained from there is strangely enough not even mentioned".

1) Here the whole argument turns on the observation that Demetrius *makes no request* for a copy of the Law; for if a request for a copy of the Law from Jerusalem were so much as implicit inter alia in his request for elders, then his request would show that it was not Jerusalem, but Alexandrian, copies that he was complaining about.

So then he did not want a manuscript from Jerusalem, he wanted elders. What for? To translate the Heb. law, obviously; but since they were not asked to bring a copy from Jerusalem, they must have been expected to translate local Alexandrian copies. And since, ex hypothesi, Demetrius has complained about the poor quality of the Jerusalem text, we must assume that the Alexandrian text is all right; for as ZUNTZ observes no mention is made of correcting faulty Alexandrian manuscripts.

The Librarian's proposition then runs: "the books of the law are wanting because they are spoken in Hebrew, and the Jerusalem copies have been somewhat carelessly copied out. I suggest we send to Jerusalem and get seventy-two elders to translate the local Alexandrian copies.

This of course is absurd; but its absurdity springs from insisting that the request for elders means elders only and does not include a (better) copy of the Law. But one cannot understand a copy of the Law as included in his request without thereby making it evident that his complaints were against Alexandrian copies.

But further, if it was the Jerusalem text that he complained of in the premiss, then we reach the absurd contradiction, that he made *that* premiss the ground for suggesting, as a cure, sending for the very Jerusalem text he had just complained of.

Zuntz, of course, sees the contradiction and proceeds to charge Aristeas with inconsistency. But Aristeas is surely hard done by. One cannot fairly maintain at one and the same time that,

(1) the conclusion logically shows what was the intention of the premiss; and

(2) the conclusion so contradicts the premiss as to make it evident that the author, by the time he reached his conclusion, has conveniently "dropped" his premiss.

Next we may question whether the story of the reception of the Jerusalem scrolls in Alexandria, for all its fairy-tale character, is really intended to create the impression that these scrolls were the only manuscript of the Law in existence. Elsewhere (46, 123-127, 318) the High Priest makes a tremendous fuss about his reluctance to let the *translators* go; he begs Ptolemy to send them back as soon as the work is done, and further enlists the aid of Andreas and Aristeas to make certain that they return. But there is no sign of reluctance at letting go "the only copy of the law in the world", nor is there a single request for the return of this "unique" copy; in fact Aristeas does not trouble to tell us what happened to it. For all that, this Jerusalem copy is obviously meant to be a superb copy of the Law, and we may agree with Zuntz that "any idea of careless writing" and lack of scholarly treatment is here completely out of the question". But with a sudden turn of argument Zuntz, whose words I have just quoted adds "whether we think of the Jerusalem text or for that matter of an Alexandrian one" (p. 120). And so it seems that in order to establish his charge of inconsistency against Aristeas, Zuntz argues:

(1) Demetrius must have been complaining about the Jerusalem text, for there were not any texts in Alexandria; there was only one copy in the world, the marvellous Jerusalem scroll. It was inconsistent for him to complain about that copy.

(2) Even if there were a copy in Alexandria, the same grand story would have been told about it, as about this unique copy from Jerusalem. Therefore it was inconsistent for Demetrius to complain about any imperfect Heberew manuscripts, Jerusalem copies or Alexandrian copies.

VI.

But having "established" glaring inconsistency in Aristeas by these arguments, ZUNTZ then examines in the light of this inconsistency, what Demetrius did actually say was his purpose in sending for the elders, and finds in it a *double entendre* designedly ambiguous, in order to cover up the contradictions inherent in his story. He was trying to represent the work of translation as if it were a work of the normal Alexandrian critical procedure of collecting and collating manuscripts, and establishing a correct text. He was therefore obliged to devise an excuse for dragging in the Alexandrian procedure for establishing exact (ἀκριβῆ) texts by collating (ἀντιβάλλειν) different copies; which he does by smartly introducing his passing reference to imperfect manuscripts. Thereafter, to quote ZUNTZ, "Continuing in the terminology of Alexandrian scholarship, he (Demetrius) proposes (32) that the exact wording (τὸ ἀκριβές) is to be reached by the "examining" of — here the identification threatens to break down. For, after all, what is to be compared is not as in scholarly work, various manuscripts, but various translations of one text set forth by various elders. But Aristeas endeavours to keep up appearances. Leaving the reader to trace his ingenuity in every detail we may single out but one. If he intended unequivocally here to have the task of translation proposed, why does he not say so unequivocally? In fact, this concept is kept entirely outside this whole section—until the very end. And there, this is telling, Demetrius is not made to say: "thus we shall obtain an exact translation", but τὸ κατὰ τὴν ἑρμηνείαν ἀκριβές . . . As it (this paraphrastic clause) stands, it involves the *double-entendre* "what is exact according to" either "(scholarly) interpretation" or "translation" (p. 121).

Now it is quite clear that Aristeas has deliberately used the terms of textual criticism to describe the work of translation; but it is seriously to be doubted that he has done so from the motives which ZUNTZ imputes to him. Let us examine the alleged motives in detail. (1) The fact is clear enough that Aristeas makes no attempt at keeping up appearances that the work was textual criticism. At the very point where according to ZUNTZ "the identification threatened to break down", and Aristeas had to strain ingenuity to keep up appearances (at the very point, indeed, where ZUNTZ breaks off his quotation of the text) Aristeas is making Demetrius say that they should examine τὸ σύμφωνον ἐκ τῶν πλειόνων. The reader does not have to search around suspiciously to discover that the πλειόνων are not manuscripts after all, but men; Demetrius is openly referring to elders, and is explaining the purpose of having such a large number, "so that we may examine wherein the majority agree and thus obtain accuracy is the interpretation (i.e. translation). There is no attempt here to lead the reader to think that a collation of manuscripts is being made. In fact Demetrius' suggestion ("the conclusion" as Zuntz calls it) does not so much as mention manuscripts. Aristeas then was not trying to keep up false appearances.

Nor is there any attempt anywhere else to create or maintain the impression that the elders were doing textual criticism. The manuscripts that they bring from Jerusalem are marvellously made and written; and though we may not believe with Zuntz (now gone to the other extreme, which makes all textual criticism impossible) that these manuscripts are the only copy of the Law in existence, the manuscripts are obviously meant to contain the authoritative text: textual criticism is plainly unnecessary.

When the work of translation is finally related (para. 302), Aristeas says "And they proceeded to carry it out, making all details harmonise among themselves by the collations (ἀντιβολαῖς). Zuntz comments: "'Αντιβάλλειν, as noted above, is the technical term for the "collating" of manuscripts. The "imperfect manuscripts" have been out of view for a long time; what is "collated" is the views of the elders; and they themselves collate them; to Demetrius falls the lot of acting as secretary" (p. 122). It is only fair to add that, if by "imperfect manuscripts" Zuntz refers to the remark about carelessly written Hebrew manuscripts (30), those manuscripts fell out of view at once; they are not mentioned thereafter in the rest of Demetrius' speech, nor anywhere else after para. 30. But if by "imperfect manuscripts" Zuntz wishes to infer that by para. 302, Aristeas has dropped the earlier, subtly introduced, *impression* that the elders were collating "imperfect manuscripts", and now frankly admits that it was translators' views and not manuscripts that were being collated, it is only fair to repeat that Aristeas made it clear right from the start (para. 33) that it was the elders' views that were to be collated and has nowhere ever talked of collating manuscripts, though he has both in 30-32 and again in 302 deliberately used the terms of textual criticism and collation to describe the collating of the elders' views.

(2) As for the *double-entendre* which is supposed to lurk in the paraphrastic τὸ κατὰ τὴν ἑρμηνείαν ἀκριβές, we may first doubt

whether this neuter, τὸ .... ἀκριβές is any more sinister than the neuter used in the previous phrase: ὅπως τὸ σύμφωνον ἐκ τῶν πλειόνων ἐξετάσαντες καὶ λαβόντες τὸ κατὰ τὴν ἑρμηνείαν ἀκριβές. The two phrases show a like construction. And then we may notice that the ambiguity is not in the paraphrase, but in the term ἑρμηνεία, which can mean both (scholarly) interpretation and translation (as Zuntz himself points out, p. 112, and makes evident in his translation, p. 122). When Zuntz asks "If he intended unequivocally here to have the task of translation proposed, why does he not say so unequivocally", we may quote Zuntz in reply: "Where the noun (for "Translation") was required, even Greek usage reduced him to the simple ἑρμηνεία (3, 11, 32, 120, 301, 308)" (p. 112). The noun ἑρμηνεία was the only noun available for "translation" and grammatically it fitted his participial construction. To remove all ambiguity and say "translation", not "interpretation", he would have to have used a compound verb, which would not have suited the structure of his sentence. In other words, he would have to have gone out of his way to remove from the phrase any idea of interpretation, when it doubtless suited his meaning better (though not for the reason Zuntz alleges; see below) to leave the idea "interpretation" mingling with "translation".

(3) But when Zuntz complains "In fact, this concept (i.e. the concept of translation) is kept entirely outside this whole section—until the very end", this is most unfair. Demetrius' proposal to the king naturally comes last in the memorandum. The long preamble has been necessary to explain the many difficulties and to prepare the way for his extreme proposal of fetching seventy-two elders from Jerusalem. It was moreover a matter already decided (para. 11) that there should be a translation, and that a letter should be sent to the High Priest about it. What was not decided then, and what therefore forms the new proposal now, is what the High Priest shall be asked to do by way of meeting the need. Naturally enough, when Demetrius does come, at the end of his memorandum, to make his proposal, prominence is given, not to the suggestion that a translation should be made, but to the method of producing it. Even so, the desired ἑρμηνεία finds mention in the same sentence as the rest of the proposal, so that it cannot fairly be said to have been deliberately "kept entirely outside this whole section—until the end", unless one is prepared to say that the proposal to send for elders to do the ἑρμηνεία has likewise been kept entirely outside this whole section—until the end.

(4) But if Aristeas, contrary to the charges brought against him, everywhere advertises so openly that the "collating" done by the translators was a "collating" of their views and not of manuscripts, can the passing reference to carelessly written copies of the Law (30) be explained as anything else than a smart, but irrelevant, remark, designed to create the 'atmosphere' of Alexandrian scholarly procedure? And is the fact that Demetrius in his proposal nowhere so much as mentions manuscripts, good or bad, attributable to anything else than Aristeas' wish now conveniently to "forget" that he had three sentences earlier mentioned imperfect manuscripts? Our answer will depend in part on how much we think was involved in the process that Aristeas describes as ἀμελέστερον δὲ, καὶ οὐχ ὡς ὑπάρχει, σεσήμανται. If this process covered nothing more than ordinary scribal errors, we shall have to say that in Demetrius' application to Jerusalem the smaller request for an error-free, authoritative text was implicit in the larger request for official interpreters. But the process may have involved more. As we have seen (p. 362), when Aristobulus carefully wrote (σημαίνω) Aratus' prologue, it involved, not so much accurate copying of Aratus' original text, but a substituting, here and there, of different vocabulary to make Aratus say what Aristobulus "knew" he meant. Such "writing" involves "interpretation". It is not, perhaps, too much to say that similar, well-intentioned, "writing" lies behind some of the variants in the different Hebrew textual traditions; not all Hebrew scribes in those early days worked according to Masoretic principles, as Qumrân has plainly showed us [1]). If then Demetrius is referring to some such process "carelessly done", when he complains about copies of the Hebrew law, it is even more natural that he should ask, not for an exact manuscript, but for elders to give the exact interpretation; for if accuracy in writing out a manuscript meant to Aristeas, not merely copying exactly what you saw in the text, but giving what you "knew" to be the accurate "meaning" of what you saw, how much more would "interpretation" be involved, when it came to translating the Hebrew into Greek. And that ability to interpret the exact meaning of the Law was of greater importance to Aristeas than the

[1]) "Skehan points out that the St. Mark's manuscript illustrates the effect of an "exegetical process" in the transmission of the text; that is, the scribe who copied a manuscript was at the same time an interpreter, who felt free to expand and modify the text in order to bring out what he believed to be its meaning". M. Burrows, *More Light on the Dead Sea Scrolls*, London, 1958, p. 147. Cf. also *VT Supplement*, Vol. IV, pp. 151-3.

ability to express the meaning in Greek, we may judge from the way he everywhere advertises the elders' ethical wisdom and theological knowledge, and scarce says anything about their linguistic ability. All seventy-two were experts in their law—but, apparently, they did not have a sub-committee of non-theologians to advise them on matters of style.

Aristeas, then, has certainly exploited the double meaning of ἑρμηνεία to the full; or, at least, he has emphasised the exegetical and interpretative element in it far more the translation element. But he has done so, not because, in ignorance of what was involved in translation, he tried to describe it as if it were Alexandrian textual criticism, but because, to his mind, interpretation was the biggest and most important element in translation.

And anyway this ability to interpret the Law was far more to Aristeas' purpose than linguistic ability. To have seventy-two men from Jerusalem so proficient in Greek that they could translate Hebrew into Greek, was of no particular propaganda value to Jews living in Alexandria. But to have a translation that must be right, and must represent exactly what the Law meant, because it was made by seventy-two experts in the interpretation of the Law, straight from Jerusalem and with the confidence of the High Priest, would be a great comfort for Jews who were disturbed by rumours and reports that not all Hebrew MSS agreed. According to F. M. Cross [1]), Cave 4 at Qumrân has produced not only at least three sharply defined textual traditions, but among them one tradition that is far nearer to the text type underlying the Septuagint than to the proto-Masoretic text [2]). Now it is altogether likely that knowledgeable Jews in Alexandria would be aware, if only vaguely, that their Hebrew text, and in consequence, their LXX translation derived from it, differed from Hebrew texts elsewhere. While then, we are not obliged to believe Aristeas' wonderful story of LXX origins, we can readily accept his reference to carelessly written Hebrew manuscripts as reflecting the true state of affairs, of which he himself was aware; and we can understand why he should create a story of LXX origins that would not only glorify the Law and the wisdom of its translators in comparison with Greek literature and sages, but would also incidentally assure Alexandrian Jewry that their Hebrew text, and the Greek translation made from it, were true representatives of the Law; they

[1]) *The Ancient Library of Qumran*, Duckworth, London, 1958, p. 135f.
[2]) See also W. F. Albright, *BASOR*, December 1955, p. 27f.

came direct from the High Priest in Jerusalem with his authority and blessing.

VII

On p. 357 we noticed that there were two crucial passages in Aristeas that have been taken by some to refer to Greek translations of the Law earlier than the LXX. So far we have discussed the first. The second can be dealt with far more quickly. It comes in para. 314, where Demetrius explains why the wonderful contents of the Law had not been mentioned by historians and poets before. He knows, so he assures Ptolemy, of two men who did attempt it, but were stopped by God. The first, Theopompus, was smitten, when he was μέλλων τινὰ τῶν προηρμηνευμένων ἐπισφαλέστερον ἐκ τοῦ νόμου προσιστορεῖν.. Jellicoe [1]) has well presented the case for taking the adverb ἐπισφαλέστερον with προσιστορεῖν and not with προηρμηνευμένων; in other words, he shows that Demetrius is not complaining about the imperfections of previous translations, but about Theopompus for rashly trying to quote from them. Nevertheless it still leaves Demetrius asserting that previous translations had been made. What then is the historical value of this assertion? Very little or none! Zuntz has brilliantly demonstrated its worthlessness by tracing this piece of propaganda to its source in the fiction of Jewish tradition, and then setting it side by side with other completely contradictory fictions in the same tradition (pp. 123-5). The case for translations of the Law earlier than the LXX must rest on evidence other than Aristeas'.

---

[1]) *JTS*, October 1961, 267-8.

THE IDEOLOGY OF THE LETTER OF ARISTEAS *

V. TCHERIKOVER
THE HEBREW UNIVERSITY, JERUSALEM

MODERN scholars commonly regard the "Letter of Aristeas" as a work typical of Jewish apologetics, aiming at self-defense and propaganda, and directed to the Greeks. Here are some instances illustrating this general view. In 1903 Friedländer wrote that the glorification of Judaism in the Letter was no more than self-defense, though "the book does not mention the antagonists of Judaism by name, nor does it admit that its intention is to refute direct attacks." [1] Stein sees in the Letter "a special kind of defense which practices diplomatic tactics," [2] and Tramontano also speaks of "an apologetic and propagandist tendency." [3] Vincent characterizes it as "a small apologetic novel written for the Egyptians" (i.e. the Greeks in Egypt).[4] Pfeiffer says: "This fanciful story of the origin of the Septuagint is merely a pretext for defending Judaism against its heathen denigrators, for extolling its nobility and reasonableness, and for striving to convert Greek speaking Gentiles to it." [5] Schürer classes the Letter with a special kind of literature, "Jewish propaganda in Pagan disguise," whose works are "directed to the pagan reader, in order to make propaganda for Judaism among the Gentiles." [6] Andrews, too, believes that the rôle of a Greek was assumed by Aristeas in order "to strengthen the force of the argument and commend it to non-Jewish readers." [7] And even Gutman, who rightly recog-

* The present study is based on my article published in Hebrew in Dinaburg Festschrift, Jerusalem, 1949, p. 83 sqq. For the preparation of the English text my thanks are due to my wife and to Dr. Hedva Ben-Israel.

[1] M. Friedländer, Gesch. d. jüdischen Apologetik, 1903, p. 97. The opinion that the Letter of Aristeas is intended for the pagan reader is repeated several times in the chapter devoted to this book, p. 84–104.

[2] M. Stein, The author of the Letter of Aristeas as a defender of Judaism, Zion, I, 1936, p. 132 (Hebrew).

[3] R. Tramontano, La Lettera di Aristea a Filocrate, 1931, p. 104, cf. p. 132.

[4] Vincent, Rev. Bibl., 17, 1908, p. 523.

[5] Pfeiffer, History of New Testament Times, 1949, p. 225.

[6] Schürer, Gesch. des jüdischen Volkes, III, p. 554; especially on the Letter of Aristeas: "All is directed in the first place towards the pagan readers," p. 610.

[7] Andrews in Charles' The Apocrypha and Pseudoepigrapha, 1923, II, p. 84.

Reprinted from *Harvard Theological Review*, Vol. 51, 1958.

nizes that the Letter sprang "from an inner need of the educated Jew," sees in it "a strong means for making Jewish propaganda in the Greek world." [8]

In this article an attempt will be made to prove that the Letter of Aristeas was not written with the aim of self-defense or propaganda, and was addressed not to Greek, but to Jewish readers. This suggestion is made on the following grounds:

1.) In the second century B.C.[9] Alexandrian Jewry attained a sufficient degree of Hellenization to create Jewish literature in Greek. The aim of this literature was to present Jewish subjects in an attractive Greek form (for instance, epic poetry or tragedies on Jewish themes) or to comment on some special item of Jewish history or religion. In this way the first representatives of Jewish Hellenistic literature, such as the historian Demetrios, the poet Philo, the tragedian Ezekiel and others made their appearance. There is no doubt that all those authors wrote for the Jewish public.[10] It is my opinion that other authors (like Artapanos and Aristobulos) also had the Jewish readers in mind, but this is not the place to discuss the tendencies of Alexandrian literature as a whole.[11] For our purpose here it is sufficient to state the fact that in the second century B.C. there were Jewish writers in Alexandria who wrote on Jewish subjects for the Jewish reader in Greek.

2.) Those who emphasize the apologetic tendency of Alexandrian literature often confuse the time limits and read the views of the

[8] J. Gutman, The origin and the main purpose of the Letter of Aristeas, Ha-Goren, 10, 1928 (Hebrew) p. 54; cf. p. 59: "The Letter of Aristeas contains clear and frank propaganda for the basic doctrines of Judaism and for spreading the knowledge of the Torah in the Greek world."

[9] On the date of the composition of the Letter of Aristeas see the article of Bickerman in ZNTW 29, 1930, p. 280 sqq. Bickerman dates the composition of the Letter in the second half of the second century B.C. He bases his suggestions on formal data (such as the greeting formula in the official letters, the names of certain court offices, etc.), familiar to scholars from the papyri of this period. This approach makes it possible to fix a date within a range of a few decades, and although it is always possible that new sources might change Bickerman's chronological framework by a number of years, it seems to me that on the whole it is justified. Cf. M. Hadas, Aristeas to Philocrates, 1951, pp. 9 sqq., 54.

[10] This is admitted also by other scholars. See Freudenthal, Alexander Polyhistor, 1875, p. 81 (on Demetrios); Schürer, III, p. 502 (on Ezekiel).

[11] I discuss this question in detail in my article: "Jewish apologetic literature reconsidered," Eos, 48, fasc. iii ("Symbolae Taubenschlag").

Roman period into the early Ptolemaic period. We have to bear in mind that Jewish defensive writings were an answer to antisemitism, and we have no evidence of the existence of Greek antisemitic writings before the Hasmonaean period.[12] On the contrary, the first Greek writers who mentioned Jews (Theophrastos, Hekataios, Klearchos of Soloi) spoke of them without hate and even with a certain amount of favor and appreciation. Although antisemitic literature appears in the second century B.C., it only reaches its climax toward the end of the Hellenistic and the beginning of the Roman period. We cannot, therefore, attribute to a Jewish writer of the second century the psychology of Philo and Josephus. The time of the Letter of Aristeas is not that of "Against Apion."

3.) The same confusion appears with regard to the question of propaganda. Preaching the Torah is obviously one of the most effective methods of self-defense, but if in the second century there was not any need for defense, there was even less ground for a widespread Jewish propaganda among the Gentiles or for a direct attack on paganism. As for the glorification of Judaism, which is the main subject of the Letter, why should we see it as a means of propaganda? Is it not possible to imagine that this glorification of Judaism could have found more favor and understanding in the heart of a Jew, than it could have influenced a Greek reader?

4.) Schürer sees in the very Greek pseudonym of Aristeas a means of propaganda among the Gentiles. Against this opinion we may argue: first, is it not naïve to suppose, that an educated Greek would be taken in by so crude a fiction and believe that it was a genuine Greek praising Judaism so highly? [13] Secondly, the name of Aristeas was probably taken by the author out of the legend on the origin of the Septuagint, whence he also got other details, such as the invitation of seventy-two Elders, and the active participation of King Philadelphos in the whole enterprise. And since, to a certain Aristeas was ascribed a book "on

[12] Manetho was not a Greek, but an Egyptian priest. His antisemitism is limited to the discussion of one single topic, that of Exodus, which was of special interest to the Egyptians.

[13] For a detailed discussion of this question, see below.

the Jews," we may suppose that the author of the Letter thought it desirable to ascribe to him also his own work.[14] And, finally, the Greek pseudonym does not exclude the possibility that the book was intended for the Jewish reader; on the contrary, we shall see below, that it enforces this view.

5.) In paragraphs 130–169 the High Priest Eleazar discusses in detail the precepts of the Torah, and it is particularly in this exposition that scholars see apologetic tendencies. We have, however, to ask: why did the author, if he truly intended to preach the Torah to the Gentiles, choose, of all things, the difficult chapters of "animals chewing the cud and parting the hoof"? Did the Gentiles have a special interest in this question? It is well known that the precepts and customs which attracted their special attention and aroused their curiosity, were the circumcision, the Sabbath, the main holidays, and the prohibition of pork. But Eleazar passes over these questions in silence. In addition to the precepts dealing with forbidden foods, the High Priest touches only those on "Tefilin and Mesusot" (158–159). Neither of these questions could have been of any interest to the Gentiles.[15] It is hard to imagine that the Gentiles were such experts in the Torah that for them only these minor precepts required further clarification. Is it not possible that the Jewish reader himself felt the need for explanations of this kind? This question will also be discussed below.

These are the arguments which, in my opinion, justify the attempt to approach the Letter of Aristeas from a different point of view. We shall analyze this book on the assumption that it was composed not for propaganda among the Greeks, but for the

[14] Cf. Hadas, op. cit., p. 4.

[15] In order to keep the literary form which the author chose (a Jewish sage explaining the Torah to Aristeas, "the Greek") Eleazar opens his exposition with the idea of monotheism and criticizes paganism, but this is no more than an introduction; he soon passes to the main subject, that of clean and unclean animals, and discusses it at length. Speaking of his basic subject, the author pretends that his discussion is merely an example (143: χάριν δὲ ὑποδείγματος), but he forgets that it was not by accident that Eleazar touched the subject of unclean animals, but as an answer to a question of Aristeas "the Greek" (128–9). Aristeas had not enquired about the main doctrines of the Torah, but only asked for an explanation of this particular question, claiming that it arouses the curiosity of "most men" (τοὺς πολλούς). Tramontano's interpretation, that "most men" means the Gentiles, especially the Alexandrian Greeks, cannot be proved.

needs of the Jewish reader. If this approach raises problems which have not been noted as yet, or have not found their full explanation, we can claim that our method of research has been justified.

I.

The author of the Letter of Aristeas [16] writes Greek; he assumes a Greek disguise; his attitude toward Greeks is full of respect and praise; his book testifies to his thorough familiarity with Greek culture. On the other hand, the Letter is an ardent panegyric upon Judaism; long and enthusiastic passages are devoted to the description of Jerusalem, of the Temple and the High Priest. The practical prescriptions of the Torah are regarded by the author as a "wall of iron" to separate the Jews from the Gentiles and to preserve the purity of Judaism. In this duality of the general outlook lies the riddle of Aristeas.

Let us start with the Greek aspect of the book. There are two sides to this problem: the extent to which the author was imbued with Greek culture; and, his attitude toward Greeks and Hellenism.

There is no doubt that the Hellenistic influence on the author was very strong. The language, the literary form and the philosophical ideas of the Letter — all testify to this. As far as the language is concerned, I shall limit myself to a few remarks, since this subject has already been amply dealt with.[17] The Letter is written in the ordinary Greek language of the Hellenistic period (*κοινή*) and shows no influence of Semitic tongues. In the narrative, and especially in the documents, one can trace the influence of the Ptolemaic offices. Many words, expressions and certain subtleties of style are repeated in the same form as in the papyri of that period. In the exposition of abstract ideas the style grows heavier, and the sentences turn into long complicated periods. The vocabulary is rich and the author skilfully uses numerous

[16] I call the book of Aristeas a "letter," as it is commonly styled so by scholars, though I am fully aware of the weight of the arguments put forth by Hadas (op. cit., p. 56) against the epistolary character of the book. The denomination "Letter" has in the present article only the aim of facilitating reference. — The numbers in brackets refer to the paragraphs of the Letter. My thanks are due to Professor M. Hadas for his kind permission to use his translation of the Letter.

[17] See Tramontano, p. 148 sqq.; H. G. Meecham, The letter of Aristeas, 1935.

synonyms in order to add color and interest to the narrative. We may say, on the whole, that the author has perfect mastery of the Greek language, official (Ptolemaic usage) as well as literary, and that he reveals a certain skill (talent would perhaps be too flattering a word) in narrating various events in a manner attractive to the reader.

The Hellenistic influence is also apparent in the literary form of the composition. Aristeas (we shall refer to the anonymous author of the Letter by this name, since it was obviously his own wish) included in his work a great variety of topics, accounts of historical events, documents, an account of a journey, discussions of abstract themes, etc. It is, indeed, difficult to find another literary work in ancient literature which would, on the whole, be like the Letter of Aristeas. Still, if we examine every part separately, we will have no difficulty in tracing its dependence on the standard works of Greek literature. Gutman justly remarked that the description of the journey to Palestine (83–120) is a kind of "Utopia," composed in the style of Euhemeros and other writers.[18] Even more evident is the Greek influence in that part of the Letter which is devoted to a Symposium (182–294). From Plato on, the form of the Symposium became a favorite among the authors of dialogues, although Plato's treatment of it, at once light and profound, was above the capacity of the epigoni. The dialogues composed in the Hellenistic period deal with insignificant topics or contain pedantic complicated discussions, in which all the participants in turn expressed their opinions on specific problems in philosophy, morals, etc.[19] The Symposium, described in the Letter, is of this latter kind, but it goes beyond all other Symposia in its lack of any poetic feeling, and in its dry didactic manner.[20] The documents, again, were clearly composed

[18] On the Greek "Utopias" see E. Rhode, Der griechische Roman², 1900, p. 210 sqq.; W. W. Tarn, Hellenistic Civilization³, p. 112 sq.

[19] On the Dialogues in general and on the Symposia in particular see Hirzel, Der Dialog 1895, I, pp. 274, 341, 355; II, p. 141. It is worth noting that Hirzel does not mention at all the Symposium in the "Letter of Aristeas," although we have here a unique example of a Symposium composed in the Hellenistic period and preserved in full up to our time.

[20] The King asks each of the seventy-two Elders one question on an abstract subject and receives suitable answers. Aristeas felt that it was impossible to prolong the Symposium until all the seventy-two Elders gave their answers, and so he divided it into seven days. The classical dialogue demanded that the discussion

in the usual manner of the Ptolemaic offices.[21] If we add that the allegorical commentaries to the precepts of the Torah were also influenced by Hellenistic examples, we might rightly conclude that the book of Aristeas in all its parts followed the patterns of Greek literature.

And now a few words about the influence of Hellenism on the philosophical ideas of the book, a few words only, since here too others have anticipated me.[22] The ideas of Greek philosophers on ethics and politics are mainly reflected in the Symposium part of the Letter. Aristeas says, for instance, that the typical features of a good political ruler are love for mankind, generosity, magnanimity (*φιλανθρωπία, ἐπιείκεια, μακροθυμία*), and the basic moral qualities for every human being are prudence, justice, temperance (*σωφροσύνη, δικαιοσύνη, ἐγκράτεια*). All this is drawn from the ethics and politics of the contemporary philosophers, especially of the Stoics (cf. e.g. Diod. I, 70, 6). Again, it is in the true spirit of Greek philosophy that the questions are asked: "What is philosophy?" (256), "Which is the highest rule?" (221), "How he (sc. the King) might be beyond outbursts of wrath?" (253), "How may one avoid yielding to pride?" (262). When one of the Elders mentions the "Lawgivers" (240), he does not have Moses in mind (for, if he did, he would use the singular form), but the great political reformers of Greece, such as Solon, Lykourgos, etc. The high respect for the Law (*νόμος*), to which even kings had to submit (279), reflects the political views of the Greeks of the Classical period.[23] Other questions and answers

should not last more than one day. Aristotle, however, had already divided his dialogues into several days, and Cicero followed his example. Cf. Hirzel, I, p. 299. As for the answers given in turn, the same method is applied by Plutarch in his "Symposium of seven sages," where the sages gave their answers to the questions put before them by Amasis, King of Egypt, one after the other in turn. But the literary talent of Plutarch is, of course, incomparably superior to that of Aristeas.

[21] In speaking of documents, I have in mind those which were obviously composed by Aristeas, like the memorandum of Demetrios to the King (29 sqq.), or the King's letter to Eleazar (35 sqq.). The edict of Philadelphos freeing the Jewish prisoners (22 sqq.) is now considered by some scholars as genuine. Cf. Wilken, Archiv für Papyrusforschung 12, 1937, 221 sqq.; Wilhelm, ibid., 14, 1941, 30 sqq.

[22] Cf. numerous notes in Wendland's edition of the Greek text and in the commentaries of Tramontano and Hadas.

[23] Of the Classical period only, since in the Hellenistic period the King himself became in a certain sense the source of the law. See Goodenough, The political philosophy of Hellenistic Kingship, Yale Class. Stud., I, 1928, p. 53, sqq.; Schubart,

obviously point to the political background of the Ptolemaic kingdom.[24] Occasionally a question sounds strange, coming from the King, and it seems obviously composed for the sake of an answer which sounds clearly like a quotation from a Greek work on ethics, or from one of the numerous books "on the Kingship" (περὶ βασιλείας) so widely known in the Hellenistic period.[25] Tramontano, in his commentary on the Letter, tries to stress the Jewish character of the questions and answers; yet all the parallel sentences enumerated by him, are drawn either from the later books of the Bible (Proverbs, Psalms, Daniel) or from the Apocrypha (Sirach, The Books of Maccabees, and especially The Wisdom of Solomon), all written in a period in which Jewish literature was already greatly influenced (directly or indirectly) by Hellenism. Tramontano's examples, therefore, do not prove anything. On the other hand, it is worth noting, that several passages in the Symposium have no counterpart at all in Jewish literature. There is little doubt, therefore, that the Greek ideas in the Symposium of Aristeas are drawn directly from the great stock of Hellenistic literature without Jewish intermediaries.

To sum up: Aristeas was a learned Jew who had a Greek education and was influenced by the Greek philosophical literature of that period. The attitude of a Jew of this kind toward Hellenism was naturally very favorable, and it will be important for our study to discuss this question in greater detail.

In speaking about Greek education, Aristeas uses two terms:

Das hellenistische Königsideal nach Inschriften und Papyri, Arch. für Papyr. 12, 1937, p. 1 sqq.

[24] For instance, the questions on the attitude of the King toward different nations in his Kingdom (267), on the duties of the officials, and so on. Schwartz (in his article Hekataeos von Teos, Rheinisches Museum, 40, 1885, p. 258 sqq.) has already stressed the idea that the Letter reflects the official views of the Ptolemaic monarchy on the royal power. And, indeed, when we compare passages from the Symposium of Aristeas with Hekataeos' account on the way of life of the ancient Egyptian Kings (as a matter of fact, the Ptolemies are meant), and on their attitude toward the Kingdom and their subjects, we find several points of contact and parallel ideas (cf. Diod. I, 70 sqq.).

[25] Cf. e.g. the questions: How he might render due thanks to parents?" (238), "How he might avoid doing anything contrary to Law?" (240), "How he might obtain acceptance in a sojourn abroad?" (257), "Which is best for the people, that a commoner be set over them as king, or a king of royal descent?" (288). Cf. Andrews, p. 87, when he speaks about a compendium of "moral sayings" as a possible source for the discussions in the Symposium. Goodenough, in his study quoted above, often mentions works "on Kingship" published in the Hellenistic period.

παιδεία and καλοκἀγαθία, the first one meaning education in the widest sense of the word and the second designating the cultural ideal to which the élite of Greek society aspired.[26] These two notions are so deeply involved with the very conception of Hellenism that it is difficult to consider them apart from the Hellenistic background or to apply them to persons of another nation. Aristeas, however, uses these terms without any reservations when speaking not only about the Greeks (43.8) but also about the Jews; e.g. he refers to the High Priest Eleazar (3) as καλὸς κἀγαθός ("the true gentleman") and he makes him use the very same word for describing the seventy-two Elders. The characterization given by Aristeas for these Elders is especially remarkable: "Eleazar then selected men most excellent and of outstanding scholarship," who had a thorough knowledge not only of Jewish literature, "but had bestowed no slight study on that of the Greeks also" (121). They were therefore, he adds, best suited for the purpose of the delegation to the King, being great experts in the Torah and at the same time well prepared to answer the King's questions and to hold speeches. "They zealously cultivated the quality of the mean (and that is the best course) and eschewing a crude and uncouth disposition, they likewise avoided conceit and the assumption of superiority over others." Whom did Aristeas have in mind, when speaking about the "crude and uncouth disposition of mind"? Stein, in his article already mentioned (p. 134) thinks that Aristeas meant the "Hasidim." His opinion is essentially sound, if we understand the term "Hasidim" in its widest sense. Aristeas does not oppose any particular sect, but a certain state of mind which existed mostly in Palestine, but not only there. It seems as if Aristeas here anticipated the skeptic smile of his enlightened readers, members of the Hellenized Jewish community in Alexandria, who might ask: Those Jews coming from Palestine, what have they in common with modern culture? And he answers: A great deal, since they

[26] Aristeas does not explain precisely the meaning of the term παιδεία, and it may be suggested that he meant ἐγκύκλιος παιδεία, i.e. "the general education." Cf. Philo, Vita Mosis I, 23. The term παιδεία, however, has a wider sense as well, viz. the creation of a harmonious personality by developing equally the faculties of the body and the soul. Cf. J. Stenzel, Plato der Erzieher, 1928, p. 120 sqq. On the term παιδεία in its historical development see W. Jaeger, Paideia, I–III.

differ basically from their "crude and uncouth" brethren; they have acquired a Greek education and can therefore be received among the καλοὶ κἀγαθοί.

Aristeas' favorable attitude toward the ideals of Greek education explains his attitude to the Greeks themselves, as it appears in the Letter. It is an attitude of exceptional favor, such as could be shown to the most faithful friends of the Jews. Many scholars see in this attitude a typical apologetic feature; in order to extol Judaism in the eyes of the Greeks, it was necessary to emphasize the high respect paid to Jews by the most important rulers of the Hellenic world.[27] Now, it is true that such apologetic features do exist in Jewish literature (e.g. in Josephus), but an examination of the picture drawn by Aristeas shows clearly that, in this case, the alleged "apologetics" grew far beyond the needs of propaganda among the Greeks. The gifts sent to Jerusalem were the most precious ones in the Royal Treasury, and the King himself supervised their selection (80, 81); when the Elders arrived in Alexandria, the King ordered their immediate reception, although he usually received people only on the fifth day after their arrival, and the envoys of kings and cities had to wait thirty days before they were presented to the King (174–175). The day of the Elders' arrival was fixed as a holiday for the whole of King Philadelphos' reign (180); in his letter to Eleazar the King acknowledged that the highest of gods (i.e. the God of Israel) preserved his kingdom in peace and honor (37); seven times did the King prostrate himself before the rolls of the Torah and he wept with joy (177–178). Did not the author here offend the taste of the pagan reader? Was he so simple as to think that such propaganda would be successful among educated Greeks? No, such a thought was indeed far from his mind. His intention was to influence the Jewish, not the Greek, reader. There is nothing that makes you love people more than the knowledge that they love you. Aristeas' reader was expected to deduce from the King's and the courtiers' affectionate attitude toward Jews that he himself ought to develop an affection toward Greeks.

[27] Cf. Thackeray Translation of the Letter of Aristeas, JQR 15, p. 338, and Sterling Tracy, III, Macc. and Arist., Yale Class. Stud. I, p. 250.

To bring the Jews nearer to the Greeks and their culture — this was the aim of Aristeas.

But what if the Jews say: Those Greeks are pagans; how can we approach them? Aristeas is ready with his answer. Very cautiously he tries to impress upon his readers the idea that no abyss separates Judaism from Hellenism. With some good will on both sides, it would be easy to bridge the two worlds. Has he not already shown that the Greek King and his courtiers had fully acknowledged the superior power of the God of Israel and lowered their heads before the Law of Moses? How significant does it now appear that the author puts on a Greek disguise: the glorification of the Jewish religion, coming from a Jew, would not have made the necessary impression upon the reader, while its praise by Aristeas, supposedly a Greek of high standing, may arouse much hope in the hearts of the Jews. They are approaching us, let us go and meet them! But how could a Jew come near to the pagan without betraying his monotheism? Aristeas, well versed as he was in Greek philosophy, had no difficulty in dissipating these doubts. The time of naïve polytheism had passed long since. Educated Greeks knew that the gods were merely symbols, and from the beginning of the Hellenistic era Euhemeros' theory gained force. According to this theory, the gods were kings and heroes of ancient times whose various actions for the benefit of mankind earned them the honor due to gods. Aristeas too sees paganism through the eyes of Euhemeros. The idols made of wood and stone are "images of persons who made discoveries useful in life" (135), and it would obviously be foolish to worship those idols. Aristeas makes the High Priest Eleazar use three times the words "foolishness" and "ignorance" in characterizing idolatry (135/8: *κενὸν καὶ μάταιον, ἀνόητοι, ματαίως*). He obviously abstains from using sharper words, and no attempt is made to emphasize the moral and religious depravity of paganism (as we find it, e.g. in the "Wisdom of Solomon," XIV, 22, 99). Now, ignorance is not an unforgivable sin, it is merely an error which can be corrected through rational explanation. And, indeed, the elect among the Greeks understand this. In one of the most important passages in the Letter, Aristeas tells the King: "God, the creator of all things, whom they (sc. the Jews) worship, is

He, whom all men worship (ὃν καὶ πάντες), and we too, Your Majesty, though we address him differently, as Zeus" (16). Here is the final answer given to the wavering Jewish reader: Know that the Greeks in fact worship the same Highest God, and the difference lies only in names. Thus Aristeas found the synthesis between Judaism and Hellenism, and the way was now open, he must have hoped, for the two nations to approach one another — for peace and mutual benefit.

This, however, was not so simple, and Aristeas knew it. In Greek education, in close intercourse with Greek society, in the breaking of the boundaries between Judaism and Hellenism, in all these lay serious danger for the Jews, the danger of losing their national character and assimilation among other nations. Did Aristeas really aspire to this? Certainly not. He was not a preacher of assimilation. On the contrary, his intention was to preserve Judaism against any alien attack, and he was ready even to surround it with an iron wall. How could these apparently conflicting notions be reconciled?

II.

The answer lies in the analysis of Aristeas' conception of Judaism. Let us start with a detailed examination of the Symposium. We have already seen that the answers of the seventy-two Elders were composed in the spirit of Greek philosophy. What part then does Judaism play in the Symposium? The strange thing is that in all the seventy-two answers there is no trace of any Jewish elements. The Torah, Moses, Sinai, the Jewish nation, Palestine — none of these appears. Moreover, there is not, in all the answers, a single hint at the nationality of the Elders. It is as if bodyless souls and not human beings were conversing with the King. Now, it is clear that Aristeas could not have intended to conceal the nationality of the Elders. The Symposium is an integral part of the story about the invitation of the Elders from Palestine for the purpose of translating the Torah. Why then this perplexing anonymity? Surely, the author did not simply forget to mention anything really Jewish! Moreover, it is clear that the dialogues with the Elders of Jerusalem were supposed to reveal to the King (and in fact to the reader) the very essence of Judaism. If they do not fulfill this purpose, what else were they meant for? There is, indeed, no doubt that the author did his best to make them serve this aim, for he included the word "God" in *all* the seventy-two answers. Sometimes God is mentioned at the beginning of an answer, but usually at the end and, occasionally, even in an additional sentence.[28] Now, if we also say that these answers were composed in the true spirit of Greek philosophy (which was, at this time, conceived as the universal human wisdom), then the basic idea which the author was trying to prove in the Symposium will be clear: *Judaism is a combination of a universal philosophy with the idea of monotheism.* Here, then, lies the explanation for the author's strange silence concerning the national and historical aspects of Judaism. These aspects of Judaism appear elsewhere in the Letter, but it was obviously the wish of the author that at the moment of the climax, when the Elders appeared before the King and preached their faith and doctrines, all trifling and casual historical events should be banished from the reader's mind in order that Judaism should reveal itself in its ideal purity.

This ideal aspect of Judaism, as it appears in the Symposium, gives us the key to the understanding of the general outlook, the "Weltanschauung," of the author.[29] Ideal Judaism is pure monotheism, in no way at variance with the common Greek conception of the world. One's attitude to one's neighbor, family life, questions of state and power — all remain the same, but above them rises in all its splendor the crowning idea of One God. I have, however, said that in the Symposium Aristeas draws a picture of *ideal Judaism.* He could not, of course, stay on this high level, in a vacuum so to speak, for a long time. In the first place, he was writing a literary work and not a philosophical treatise and, besides, he was, after all, only human, and he definitely belonged to a certain nation and to a certain period. He could not ignore matters of daily life for he had to provide his readers

[28] Cf. e.g. the paragraphs 194, 199, 205–9, 219 sqq. This additional sentence can easily be omitted, and the sense of the answer would not suffer.

[29] The ideas expressed in the Symposium, in particular the idea concerning the power of God over the King, is reflected also in other parts of the book. Cf. e.g. 17, 20, 132 sqq.

with answers to some of the problems which troubled them. Those problems naturally concerned the Law, the Land and the people of Israel. It is easy to understand why Aristeas occasionally departed from the ideal Judaism of the Symposium, though we may safely say that nowhere does he actually contradict himself.

The Torah is of special interest to Aristeas. In a sense the Torah is his main subject, since his narrative is entirely based on the story of how the Torah was translated into Greek. In Aristeas' time there existed already several commentaries on the Torah. The Jewish philosopher Aristobulos wrote under Ptolemy VI Philometor an exegetic work on the Torah, and Aristeas (144) refers with some anger to a particular comment of Aristobulos on some precepts of the Torah which did not agree with his own opinion.[30] The main passage devoted to the Torah in the Letter is the dissertation of the High Priest Eleazar on forbidden food (128 sqq.). Let us note the way in which Eleazar explains the practical prescriptions of the Law of Moses. He sees the regulations concerning forbidden food as mere allegories given by Moses in a symbolic manner (*τροπολογῶν*, 150). The practical prescriptions of the Torah, he explains, have a profound meaning (*λόγον βαθύν*, 143). For instance, the prescription concerning animals "chewing the cud and parting the hoof" was not chosen at random or by some caprice of the mind, but with a view to truth and as "a token of right reason" (*καὶ σημείωσιν ὀρθοῦ λόγου*, 161). And what is this right reason? The fowls which may be eaten are pure since they feed on grain, whereas the forbidden birds are birds of prey, and the Lawgiver called them "unclean" to indicate that those who accept the prescriptions of the Torah have to practice righteousness and not to use violence against others (147–148). It is permissible to eat animals chewing the cud and parting the hoof since this "is a symbol to discriminate in each of our actions with a view to what is right" (150). Again, each animal chewing the cud and parting the hoof is a symbol of memory, "for the chewing of the cud is nothing else than recalling life and its subsistence" (154). These examples, as

[30] It is quite clear that Aristeas had in mind a *Jewish* commentator, because it cannot be supposed that in the second century B.C. the Gentiles wrote commentaries on the Torah.

well as many others, show how in his commentaries Aristeas used the allegorical method, of which the first representative, as far as we know, was the Jewish philosopher Aristobulos, and which reached its climax in Philo's writings about one hundred and fifty years after Aristeas. This is not the place for a detailed analysis of the allegorical commentary, and only those of its qualities will be mentioned here which may help us to understand Aristeas.[31]

The prescriptions of the Torah are nothing but symbols. Behind the simple words of the Torah a profound meaning is concealed which can be revealed only by an allegorical interpretation. This meaning is of a moral-religious nature and is open to any man who strives to acquire a profound philosophical knowledge; it is devoid of any specific Jewish feature. The allegorical commentary turns the Torah into a universal doctrine which may be accepted by every enlightened mind, especially by those who had a Greek education. Aristeas, indeed, was still a long way from the time when the obvious sense of the Torah was completely rejected in order to retain the concealed sense only, a tendency which provoked strong opposition on the side of such a religious Jew as Philo. Aristeas stands at the beginning of this long process; his commentary is of a symbolical rather than of an allegorical nature.[32] The tendency to universalism is, however, beyond doubt, since the endeavor to attain moral perfection and the attempt to bear in mind the moral commandments with the help of external symbols are principles of ethics and logical thought in the widest sense of the word. Here we confront again the ideas of the Symposium, but this time the direction is indicated which the Torah is to follow, if it is to attain "Ideal Judaism." The Torah ought to be imbued with the general human (i.e. Greek) philosophy and the teaching of Moses ought to adapt itself to the school of Plato. Then, and only then, could Moses be accepted by the educated Alexandrian Jew as a Lawgiver and Prophet.

A Torah with a universal teaching ought to be written in a universal language. Hence the importance of the translation,

[31] For the allegorical method of Biblical commentaries see Wolfson, Philo, I, p. 115 sqq.

[32] Cf. E. Stein, Die allegorische Exegese des Philo aus Alexandrien. 1929, p. 10 sqq.

which is Aristeas' main subject in the Letter. He makes every effort to prove the sanctity of the translation. In the first place, the translation receives the sanction of Palestinian Jewry. The seventy-two Elders were selected "six from each tribe" (32, 46, 51), i.e. they represented the whole Jewish nation; they were selected by the High Priest who was the head of the nation, and the entire people (τὸ πᾶν πλῆθος) was assembled in order to approve their selection (42, 45, 46). In the second place the translation received the approval of Alexandrian Jewry. The "Jewish masses" (τὸ πλῆθος τῶν Ἰουδαίων) were assembled at the place where the translation was accomplished and listened to its first reading (308). "When the rolls had been read, the priests and the elders of the translators and some of the corporate body (πολίτευμα) and the leaders of the people rose and said: Inasmuch as the translation has been well and piously made and is in every respect accurate, it is right that it should remain in its present form and that no revision of any sort take place" (310). After this solemn announcement no wonder that an imprecation was pronounced upon those who would try to introduce any additions or alterations into the text of the translation (311), and so the translation received its third and most sublime sanction — the sanction from Heaven. The imprecation lent to the translation the nature of a Revelation, like that on Mount Sinai, and not unjustly do modern commentators point out the corresponding places in the Bible, such as Num. 4,2; 13,1; 28,15 sqq. And, finally, we have to mention the fourth sanction, that of the King and the Court; indeed, the whole work of translation was initiated by the King and his Greek courtiers, and after its execution the King prostrated himself before the sacred rolls and gave orders that they should be watched with the greatest care. Aristeas especially emphasizes that the Septuagint is the only authentic translation. Twice before had attempts been made to publish the Holy Law in Greek, but those who dared to do so did not receive God's sanction and were even severely punished by him (312 sqq.). More important, however, than the polemics against other translators is the attempt at criticism of the original Hebrew text of the Bible. In the report, allegedly prepared for Philadelphos by the head of the library, Demetrios, the Holy Scriptures are referred to in the following words (30): "It happens that they are written in Hebrew characters and in the Hebrew tongue, and they have been committed to writing somewhat carelessly and not adequately." [33] Aristeas, we assume, had in mind those copies of the Hebrew Torah which were in use in Alexandria. The Elders must have brought from Jerusalem the authentic text of the Torah, since otherwise the very basis of the Septuagint would fall to pieces. But Jerusalem was far away and Aristeas, after all, wrote for the Alexandrian reader. And, since the Septuagint with all the sanctions mentioned above undoubtedly reflected God's Law in all its purity and truth, it had obviously some advantage over the Hebrew Torah, the text of which had been preserved in Alexandria only in imperfect copies. And, indeed, we find in one place in the Letter (57) an explicit preference for the text of the Septuagint over that of the original Hebrew.[34] We ought not lightly to dismiss this point, for it is not a mere philological remark of a scholar studying the texts with cool objectivity, but an echo of a lively debate within the Alexandrian community. Fortunately, one passage of the contemporary Hellenistic literature was preserved revealing an opposite opinion. The grandson of Sirach, in the introduction to his translation of his grandfather's Book of Wisdom, emphasizes the fact that the translation cannot reflect with precision the original

[33] This sentence is not sufficiently clear and it was interpreted in different ways. "The Torah is written in Hebrew characters and in the Hebrew tongue, *ἀμελέστερον δέ, καὶ οὐχ ὡς ὑπάρχει, σεσήμανται.*" The word *σεσήμανται* serves as a bone of contention between scholars. Some explain it as referring to the Greek translations of the Torah (cf. Thackeray, JQR 15, p. 347, and Andrews, p. 98). But the verb *σημαίνω*, as used in the Letter, never does mean "translation." "To translate" is rendered always by the word *ἑρμηνεύω*, while the usual meaning of *σημαίνω* is *to mark*, *to note*, *to indicate*; and since the subject is a book, it is quite clear that the meaning of the word is *to mark in writing*, i.e. *to write*, *to copy*, etc. And, indeed, it was understood in this way by Wendland (Kautzsch, Apokr. und Pseudoepigr., II, p. 7), L. Mendelssohn (Aristeae epistolae initium, 1897, p. 35), Tramontano (p. 51), Hadas (p. 111) and Bickerman, Alexander Marx Jubilee Volume, 1950, p. 156, note 25.

[34] In describing the golden table sent by the King to Jerusalem as a sacred gift Aristeas emphasizes that the table was made of *pure gold* and not only *overlaid* with gold. Since the pious King strove to keep in full the precepts of the Torah concerning the sacred utensils intended for use in the Temple (cf. 55/56 on the measurements of the table), it is clear that here too he followed the Torah, yet not the Hebrew text which speaks only of a table overlaid with gold (Ex. 25, 24; 37, 11), but the Greek text which speaks of a table made of pure gold (LXX, Ex. 25, 22: *καὶ ποιήσεις τράπεζαν χρυσῆν χρυσίου καθαροῦ*).

Hebrew text, and adds that this statement applies not only to Sirach's works, but to all the books of the Bible. This was probably the opinion of the newly arrived emigrants from Palestine who had not yet become acclimatized in Alexandria, and this opinion contradicted that of native Alexandrian Jews who saw in the Septuagint the perfect version of the Bible. Aristeas expressed the opinion of the native Alexandrian Jews. It is as if he transferred the holiness of Mount Sinai from the original Hebrew text to the Greek translation.

What is the nature and the purpose of this idealization of the Septuagint? It seems clear that it was not prompted merely by the wish to prove to Alexandrian Jews that the Septuagint was faithful to the original text, since for that purpose it would not have been necessary to show its advantage over the Hebrew text.[35] If we note that the day the translation was accomplished was fixed in Alexandria as a holiday for generations to come (Philo, Vita Mosis II, 41), it would appear that Alexandrian Jewry attached exceptional importance to this achievement and that Aristeas merely expressed a prevalent opinion. Aristeas himself gives us the key for understanding the true value of the translation, in the letter of Philadelphos to Eleazar: "Now, since we desire to show favour (*χαρίζεσθαι*) to these (i.e. to the Egyptian Jews) and to all the Jews in the world and to their posterity, we have resolved that your Law should be translated into Greek" (38). Why should the permission to translate the Bible be granted as a special favor? The reason is this: from now on the Jews would not need the Hebrew language any more, even in their religious service; Greek, the language of the King and the State, would serve for all their spiritual needs, and there would be no language barrier between the Jews and the Greeks. The Greeks would be able to read the Bible and to realize how sublime are its ideas and how high is the culture of the Jewish nation, chosen

[35] In Andrew's opinion, Aristeas tried to defend the translation against the attacks of the critics and also wished to "secure appreciation for it in the minds of the Greek readers." I do not think that the interest of the Greek reader in the Torah of the Jews was so profound that the question of the preciseness of the translation could have had a decisive significance for him. It is advisable to take care not to exaggerate the extent to which the Septuagint was known among the Greeks. (See H. B. Swete, An Introduction to the Old Testament in Greek, 2nd ed., 1914, p. 22.)

by God to receive the Torah. The Torah in Greek would serve the Jews as a ticket of admission into the world of Greek culture and Greek society. To use a modern parallel, the Septuagint fulfilled in Aristeas' opinion a rôle similar to that which Mendelssohn's translation of the Bible into German did in the eyes of the enlightened Jews of the eighteenth century: it served as a first step toward the intellectual emancipation of the Jews.

Aristeas devoted much space in his book to the account of his journey to Jerusalem (83–120). Those chapters present, as is well known, a "hard nut" to the scholars. My intention here is not to examine the various scholarly opinions on the subject, since that would require a special work of research. There is, however, one point in Aristeas' story which has not been sufficiently stressed by scholars, although it was lightly noted in the commentary of Tramontano and in the study of Vincent. I mean Aristeas' dependence on the Biblical tradition.

Jerusalem, says Aristeas, lies in the center of the Land of Judaea (83); this is not exact, but it is the version of the Jewish legend from the time of Ezekiel on.[36] The Temple, according to Aristeas (84), stands on the top of a mountain. This is certainly not true, but it corresponds to a well known prophecy in Isaiah 2, 2 and Micah 4,1. Aristeas, like Ezekiel (47,1), thinks that the edifice "looks towards the east" (88) and again like Ezekiel (ib.), he speaks about a "natural spring within the Temple area" (89).[37] The remark about the apparel of the priests when ascending the altar ("the priests were swathed in coats of fine linen reaching to the ankles") (87), is based on Exodus 20,26 ("Neither shalt thou go up by steps unto mine altar, that thy nakedness be not discovered thereon"), and it may be suggested that the detailed description of the High Priest in all his glory (96–99) is no more than an elaboration of Exodus 28 and 39, and not a true image of the High Priest at the time of the Second Temple.[38] The description of Palestine (107 sqq.) is not a true

[36] Vincent, Rev. Bibl. 17, p. 530.

[37] Vincent, ibid. 18, p. 559. ("There never was a natural spring within the Temple area.")

[38] If we compare this description in the Letter with that in LXX Ex. 28 and 39, we shall easily realize that almost all the details concerning the attire of the High Priest, as given by Aristeas, have their parallels in the Biblical story.

account of Judaea under the Hasmonaeans, but of "Palaestina Biblica," as Tramontano (p. 112) rightly notes. The reference to the overflowing of the Jordan in summer is not an error made by the Egyptian writer and induced by the overflowing of the Nile at that season, but an expansion of the remark in Joshua 3,15 ("for Jordan overfloweth all his banks all the time of harvest"). The statement that the area of the Land of Israel is about 60 million arourai (a figure out of all proportion) is based on the figure of 600,000 Jews of the Exodus (Ex. 12,37,Num. 11,21), every one of whom, Aristeas fancied, received a lot of *100 arourai.*[39] These are examples, which were noted by commentators on the Letter who had no special intention of stressing Aristeas' dependence on the Biblical tradition; so it is possible, that a detailed examination would reveal more examples of this kind. The very fact that Aristeas divides the seventy-two Elders equally among the twelve tribes without any reservation or comment, shows that he lived in the atmosphere of Biblical tradition, and that every piece of information about the land, town and Temple which came from the Holy Scriptures was in his eyes an historical truth. We have therefore to introduce an important correction into the common opinion of scholars about chapters 83–120. It may be that the very idea of the journey to Palestine and its description as a land of an ideal order were influenced by the Greek utopias, as Gutman thinks. It may be that single pieces of information were taken from an account of a Greek or Jewish tourist, as Wendland and Vincent suggest. Yet the main point is, that the author's intention was to describe Palestine as a Holy Land, where the sublime ideal of Biblical theocracy was fulfilled. For Aristeas, the most important part of the Holy Land is Jerusalem, and of Jerusalem the Temple, its High Priest and its religious service. Here is the center of his interest and for it the whole account was written. The Jewish reader in Alexandria

[39] This last figure had a special meaning for the Egyptian Jews. Foreign soldiers, including Jews, received from the Ptolemaic authorities lots of 30, 40, 80, and even 100 *arourai* (Egyptian *aroura* equals 2.756 sq. meters). A lot of 100 arourai was the biggest lot a soldier could ever get. Soldiers who received 100 arourai constituted a kind of aristocracy within the Ptolemaic army. Aristeas, in giving to every one of the 600,000 Jews of the Exodus the maximum number of arourai, expressed by this the dream of every Jewish soldier of Egypt to belong to this aristocracy.

learned from those chapters that his heart should be attracted not by Hasmonaean Palestine, with its wars and political aspirations, but by the pure and beautiful Holy Land, as it appears in the pages of the Holy Scriptures — the Land of Israel as an integral part of the Torah of Israel.

Thus we return to the Torah, the main subject of Aristeas' book, the Torah which contains a treasure of sublime religious and moral ideas, understandable to every man, and which appeared at last in a civilized dress having been translated into Greek.[40] Aristeas is convinced that the Torah alone opens before the Jews of Egypt the gate to the world of culture and authority, because the Torah reveals to the Greeks the advantage of the Jews over the barbarians. And if this is so, the Jew ought to keep the practical prescriptions of the Torah with utmost care and punctuality, *even if it leads to the isolation of the Jews from other nations*. This idea is expressed by Aristeas in the following sentence: "When therefore our Lawgiver, equipped by God for insight into all things, had surveyed each particular, he fenced us about with impregnable palisades and with walls of iron (ἀδιακόποις χάραξι καὶ σιδηροῖς τείχεσιν) to the end that we should mingle in no way with any of the other nations, remaining pure in body and in spirit" (139). How very strange it is to hear this sentence coming from Aristeas, of all people! Is this not a negation of the author's favorable attitude toward the Greek world? At first sight it is, but if we call to mind the ideology of Aristeas as a whole, we shall easily be convinced that this strong statement is more fitting here than in any other book. I have already noted above the *duality* which is a basic feature of Aristeas' outlook. He never preached assimilation among the Greeks. On the contrary, the whole Letter is nothing if not a eulogy to Judaism. Not assimilation among the Gentiles is Aristeas' aspiration, but the opening of the world of culture before Jews and Judaism. He would like to enter this world with his head held high, like a man who has mighty cultural values in his possession, open to everyone, Jews and Gentiles alike. But these values are inseparably connected with the Torah. The estrangement of the Jew from the Torah would cause only a degradation

[40] Cf. Philo, Vita Mosis II, 26 sqq.

of his cultural value in the eyes of the Gentiles. Hence the strong emphasis on the idea of isolation, in which we can already hear one of the leading ideas of Philo: The Jewish nation is a nation of priests whose destiny is to preserve, for the advantage of the whole world, the eternal truth of the religion of One God (de Abrah. 98; Vita Mosis I, 149).

III.

I have already mentioned more than once the question of the reading public of the Letter. We have now to deal with this question in greater detail.

The Jewish community in Alexandria was established as early as the time of the first Ptolemies. Mercenary soldiers and prisoners of war, freed from slavery, were, it seems, its first members. The big and busy city attracted emigrants from all sides, and the Jewish community developed at a rapid pace. The growth of the community brought with it great wealth, since trade with other countries, ship-building, financial affairs played a considerable part in the life of the capital. At the beginning of the second century B.C. the Jewish community in Alexandria (and perhaps the Jewish population in other parts of Egypt) reached a degree of development which permitted it to appear on the political stage as an active factor. The young King Ptolemy VI Philometor (180–145 B.C.) and his wife Kleopatra appointed Jews as military commanders and civil servants, admitted Jews to the Court and settled a Jewish army on Onias' Land; it is even possible that some Alexandrian Jews were attached to the Macedonian garrison which guarded the capital.[41] The increase in wealth and influence brought the Jews a rise in their standard of life and drew them nearer to the Greeks. The Greek language dominated the Jewish community and became the language of culture and of everyday life alike. Educated Jews read Plato and Homer and probably sent their sons to the gymnasium, and if a writer appeared among the Jews, he would certainly write his books in Greek. The wealthy Jews gradually approached the circles of

[41] For further details concerning the economic position of the Jewish community in Alexandria and the Jewish army in Egypt, cf. Corpus Papyrorum Judaicarum, vol. I, pp. 10 sqq., 48 sqq.

Greek intelligentsia, and some of them acquired Alexandrian citizenship. This approach toward Greek society and culture did not, however, break their ties with the ancestral tradition. There were, of course, individual cases of Jews abandoning their religion,[42] but on the whole, they remained faithful to their ancestral laws and customs. This is quite natural, since, first and foremost, the Jewish community in Alexandria consisted not only of wealthy people, but of poor elements as well, and these workers, craftsmen, small merchants, and so on, came nowhere near the Greeks and their culture. Secondly, the ties with Palestine, which was imbued with the spirit of ancestral tradition, remained strong during the whole Hellenistic period. And, thirdly, the Jewish community in Alexandria was an official body, recognized by the Government and authorized to live according to the ancestral laws of the Jews, and no one would question these rights. The Jewish Diaspora in Egypt, with its various communities and numerous synagogues, which numbered among its members soldiers and officers, officials and courtiers, bankers and merchants, was not likely to drive its members to desertion. The rich Jews in Alexandria were not inclined toward assimilation; numerous ties — social, juridical and cultural — attached them to their nation and religion. On the other hand, it was quite impossible, living among the Greeks and enjoying the splendid works of Greek literature, to be enclosed in a spiritual Ghetto and to be reckoned among the "barbarians." It was a necessity to find a compromise, a synthesis, which would permit a Jew to remain a Jew and, at the same time, to belong to the elect society of the Greeks, the bearers of world culture.

This duality, which we have already recognized as the basic feature of the Letter, is therefore a characteristic not of Aristeas alone, but of the whole class to which he belonged. Several details in the Letter would be more understandable, if we considered them as the views of a whole class and not as the private opinion of an individual writer. How typical is, e.g., the yearning of the Jewish aristocracy in Alexandria for Greek education, or the desire to belong to the *καλοὶ κἀγαθοί*. These were the same Jews who sent their sons to the Greek gymnasium and were anxious to

[42] Cf. Corpus Papyrorum Judaicarum, vol. I, No. 127.

acquire Alexandrian citizenship and against whom the Greek reaction turned fiercely at the beginning of the Roman period.[43] How typical of these circles is the cautious attitude toward Greek religion and the desire to convince themselves, that "we all have one Father and one God has created us." Did not the Septuagint give the translation of Exodus 22,27 as follows: "Thou shalt not revile the gods," translating the Hebrew form "Elohim" as *gods*, and not as *God*? The Jewish writer Artapanos, who was probably a contemporary of Aristeas, did not even hesitate to attribute to Abraham, Jacob and Moses the foundation of the pagan cults of Egypt. How well did Aristeas understand the spirit of the rich Jews in Alexandria, who wavered between two worlds, when he depicted the highly favorable attitude of the Ptolemaic King and his courtiers toward the Jews. Not without purpose did Aristeas turn the pagan King almost into a proselyte, and make him and his courtiers bow their heads before the Law of Moses. Such a description helped the readers to overcome the feelings of inferiority which gnawed at the heart of the rich Alexandrian Jews at the sight of the brilliant life of the Court and of the Greek "polis," so close to them, but, alas, so remote. It is clear, on the other hand, that Aristeas' opinion on the Jews and the Jewish religion also reflects the views of the same social group, since they recur several times in Alexandrian literature from Aristobulos to Philo. We meet Aristeas' views on the Septuagint again about one hundred and fifty years later in Philo (Vita Mosis II,41) when the latter speaks of the holiday fixed in honor of the translation. Philo adds that, in this feast, not only Jews, but also Gentiles participated, and here again we recognize Aristeas' views that the Torah does not separate the Jews from the Greeks but, on the contrary, brings the two nations together. The Torah, of course, was to be interpreted in an allegorical spirit, in order that it might fulfill its rôle as a means of synthesis. This was the opinion of Aristeas as well as of Philo and of many other Alexandrian commentators. As for the other national values of Judaism, Aristeas did not esteem them highly, and here too, certainly, he was in accord with his own class. The Hebrew language, for instance, exists for Aristeas only as

[43] Cf. ibid. p. 64 sqq.

the language of the Torah; and, indeed, it ceases to be necessary at the moment, when the translation was accomplished. It is worth noting that all the Alexandrian writers (including Philo) quote the Torah from its Greek translation and do not use the original text at all. Palestine is, in Aristeas' eyes, only the Holy Land, and there, too, he probably expresses the opinion current among the rich Alexandrian Jews.[44] And, indeed, what did those rich Jews, who were so strongly attracted by the Greeks and their culture, have in common with the Hasmonaeans, who fought stubbornly against the Greeks and Hellenism? Could their attitude toward the Hasmonaeans be other than that of reservation, or even of open hostility?

We would not, however, do justice to Aristeas, if we estimated him only as a representative of a certain social group and not as a personality who fights for his own ideals. Scholars have rightly noted that the Letter contains some sort of propaganda, but they were mistaken in assuming that this propaganda was directed to the Gentiles. It was directed to the Jews. His preaching has two tendencies, corresponding to the duality of the cultural ideals of Aristeas and of his social class. In the first place, he turns against those Jews who have not yet freed themselves from the "lack of education and stubbornness" of their Palestinian brethren. Those were people who continued to use the Hebrew Torah in spite of the fact that it was preserved in Alexandria only in bad copies (30), and who commented on the Torah in a rational way and not in the fashion of allegorical interpretation (144). For the benefit of these Jews in particular, Aristeas exerted himself to depict the pleasant characters of the King and his courtiers and to emphasize the advantages of a Greek education. The idea of turning the seventy-two Elders, and even the High Priest himself, into a symbol of Greek education, was an especially powerful propagandist idea. The aim of Aristeas' propaganda was to bring up a generation of educated Jews, who would be able to live on equal terms with the Greek citizens of Alexandria and possibly to occupy high positions in the Ptolemaic army, at the court of the

[44] But surely not the opinion of the whole of the Egyptian Jewry, who more than once showed their sympathy for the Hasmonaean Palestine; cf. Corpus Papyr. Jud., I, p. 46 sqq.

King and in the administration of the realm. On the other hand, Aristeas' propaganda was directed against those who intended, if not to reject Judaism (those were few) then at least, to ease the burden of the practical prescriptions of the Torah. Aristeas' care was well timed, for it is easy to imagine that within the Hellenized society of the rich Alexandrian Jews the neglect of some of the prescriptions was gradually spreading. This neglect, however, had not yet touched the main customs of Israel — circumcision, the keeping of the Sabbath and abstention from eating pork. Aristeas, therefore, does not see any need to defend those prescriptions. But it is quite natural that the educated Alexandrian Jew was inclined to neglect the prescriptions of minor importance, not because he spurned the ancestral customs, but simply because he did not understand their purpose. There was a vital need to explain to these Jews the purpose of the prescriptions concerning "the parting of the hoof" and the "cloven foot," as well as those concerning the "tefilin" and "mesusot." If young people were allowed to neglect the minor prescriptions, they were bound to end by neglecting the major ones as well, and thus to undermine the very foundations of the Jewish communities in Alexandria and in the whole of Egypt. The famous sentence of Aristeas about the "impregnable palisades" and "walls of iron" (139) sounds as a warning against the danger hidden in the future: Do not neglect the Torah, do not reject it, for it is your only true stronghold!

To sum up: The Letter of Aristeas appears as a typical work of Alexandrian Jewry in the Ptolemaic period. There is no unity in the book, as there was no unity either in the heart of the author or in the social class to which he belonged. Like most of the people who strive to be "citizens of two worlds," Aristeas did not actually belong to either of them. It is difficult to class Aristeas among the nationalist Jews; his Judaism is pale and colorless, imbued with foreign influences, and it lacks the inner warmth of a genuine national feeling. Even less does Aristeas belong to the Hellenes. His aspirations to be like the Greeks only emphasize the great distance between him and the *καλοὶ κἀγαθοί* of the true Greek intelligentsia. But it is precisely this duality which is most important for the scholar studying the cultural aspect of Hellenistic Jewry. Aristeas wanted to write history, but in fact he depicted his own times. Aristeas' small book serves as one of the most important sources for the study of the spirit of Alexandrian Jewry in the Ptolemaic period, when anti-semitism had not yet blocked the way to cultural emancipation before the Egyptian Jew, and the life of the Jewish nation in Egypt appeared to be tranquil and safe.

ARISTEAS STUDIES II: ARISTEAS ON THE TRANSLATION OF THE TORAH

By G. Zuntz, Manchester

I

To be assessed correctly, Aristeas' story of the translation of the Torah has to be interpreted carefully and in detail. At the same time, this story forms the framework of the whole book; in consequence, any interpretation is liable to miss the mark which fails to see it within the context of which, at least in size, it forms but one small section. We may therefore begin by surveying the structure of Aristeas' novel, paying particular attention to the manner in which the author connected its constituent parts.

After the preface, the narrative begins with the plan to have the Torah translated (9–11); the execution of the plan makes the end of the book (301 ff.). This frame is filled by the following main items: the liberation of the Jewish prisoners (12–27); the exchange of letters between Ptolemy and Eleazar (34–50); the description of the royal presents (51–82) and of Jerusalem and its vicinity (83–120); Eleazar's apologia for the Jewish Law (128–71); the arrival of the translators (172–81) and, finally, the "Seven Banquets" (182–300). It is very clear that by far the greater part of the book has no factual connexion with the translation and that, really, the wish to stir interest in, and admiration for, the Jews is the common denominator of these heterogeneous parts. As a story, however, they could be interconnected only by Aristeas' telling them, one by one, as successive events witnessed by himself; it is therefore appropriate that, in the very first words of the preface, his "embassy", and not the translation of the Law, is described as the subject of the book.

The author, however, lacked the capacity to make this plan work and to give a semblance of reality to an imagined story. This judgement will be substantiated by the following detailed interpretation; it is in accordance with observations made in considering the "Seven Banquets" [1] and may here be illustrated by some further points.

After the translation has first been suggested by Demetrius, the king is stated (11) to have "commanded writing to the high-

[1] Cf. above, pp. 21 ff. (On p. 22, l. 10, for "with" read "from"; *ibid.*, l. 25, read "investigation"; p. 32, n. 3, l. 2, for "god" read "God".)

Reprinted from *Journal of Semitic Studies*. Vol. 4, 1959.

priest of the Jews in order that the aforesaid matter be carried out". Nothing comes of this royal command but, rather, the same measure is suggested again in 32, ordered again 33 and, finally, executed in 35 as though it had not been mentioned before. The well-disposed reader is expected to infer—it is nowhere stated—that the king's original order was countermanded in view of Aristeas' intercession on behalf of the Jewish slaves; the attentive critic will conclude that the scene 9–11 was duplicated by the author in order to fit in his tale of the liberation of these slaves.[1] The duplication is veiled by the nice invention of presenting it as an official memorandum presented by Demetrius following his first, informal suggestion and by the addition of some new traits (on which later), but his wish to give reality to it has tempted the writer into the incredible assertion that, in the brief intervening time, the able librarian has managed to secure almost all of the 300,000 volumes which he had described as still wanting at the preceding meeting.[2]

There follows the exchange of letters between king and high-priest. Aristeas seeks to establish his ability to present these documents, as well as Demetrius' memorandum, by that reference to the "*Schreibwut*" of "the kings of yore" (28) which has long since been paramount in disproving his assumed identity. In the letters it is stated (40 and 43) that he has been sent to, and arrived in, Jerusalem; Eleazar moreover professes that he has dispatched the translators (46–50); the reader is not informed that all this is said in anticipation of what actually is going to be implied by the next hundred, or so, paragraphs (not until para. 172 do the translators actually leave Jerusalem). Implied, but not told. A writer of moderate imagination could have embodied what Aristeas desired to tell in a coherent report about his embassy, and this is what Aristeas describes as his purpose, not only in the preface but again in 83. He did not achieve it. He poses as the conveyor of Ptolemy's precious gifts—but traces their description to documents in the royal archives (28, end; cf. 34 and 51). There is not a word about the journey accomplished by the embassy; suddenly they are, one does not see how, in Jeru-

[1] He who attentively compares this tale with the sources on which it is based—namely the royal order preserved, largely, in the papyrus published by H. Liebesny in *Aegyptus*, XVI (1936), 257 and, secondly, pseudo-Hecataeus' report (summarized by Josephus, *c. Ap.* I. 186) about the many Jews following Ptolemy I into Egypt after the battle at Gaza in 312—will gain an instructive insight into Aristeas' attitude towards history. [2] Compare 30 with 10.

salem; and matters are made worse by the promise, at this point (83), of a report about their "way". Observing that in the same, unaccountable manner the translators are finally transferred to Alexandria (173) we are entitled to conclude that consistency and realistic concreteness are not among the virtues of this writer. He elaborates individual scenes unable, or unconcerned, to organize them into a sustained and credible unity. These observations will prove useful in the interpretation of the passages bearing directly upon the production of the Septuagint to which we now turn.

II

The interpretation of these passages is hampered by some vagueness of the terminology bearing upon the concept, here central, of "translation". This vagueness is connected with certain peculiarities of language and usage both Jewish and Greek; we shall see that it is enhanced by the absence, in Aristeas, of a concrete mental picture of the facts he was aiming to narrate. Here, again, his imagination was not strong and consistent enough to make up for the lack of a substantial, historical tradition.

In Aramaic—there are no instances in ancient Hebrew—two verbs fill the place of our notion of "translating", *targēm* and *parēsh*.[1] Neither of them is confined to this connotation; on the contrary, both retain the wider and more frequent meaning of "explaining" and "elucidating" (apart from still other shades of meaning not here relevant). This accounts for the fact that Greek-speaking Jews developed the habit of using ἑρμηνεύω for the first, and διασαφέω for the second verb. The effect was, in the context of Greek speech, an unidiomatic and ambiguous usage, for with Greeks διασαφέω and διασάφησις never conveyed the notion of "version from one language to another"; as to ἑρμηνεύω, this root had indeed early covered the two notions of the English "interpreter", especially so the noun ἑρμηνεύς, but in the Hellenistic period the specific notion of "translating" was expressed unambiguously by the compounds δι- and μεθερμηνεύω. Aristeas uses these verbs (in 15, 308, 310 the first, and in 38 the second). In 39, though, the simple takes the place of the compound verb,

[1] I am in the following utilizing, and in part correcting, what I had written in *H.T.R.* XXXVI (1943), 303 ff. In particular, I wish to retract the assertion (p. 304) that "the Greek conception remained basically monoglot". On the contrary, from the time, at least, of Polybius onward the notion of "translating" has its specific equivalent in Greek speech.

and where the noun was required, even Greek usage[1] reduced him to the simple ἑρμηνεία (3, 11, 32, 120, 301, 308) which once he varied by using the Jewish coinage διασάφησις (305). These stylistic facts deserved stating because the ambiguity of the words used may in part account for the ambiguity of the facts related.

Beside the ambiguity in the notions of "translating" and "explaining" there is the interchangeability, or nearly so, of the notions of "translating" and "transcribing", or "copying". Aristeas does indeed expressly distinguish between the two in 11 and 15, and only there; for the rest, the task proposed by Demetrius is termed ἑρμηνεία at the five other places just adduced, but μεταγραφή stands for the same, twice, in 45 f. and again in 307, while in 28 we find the synonym ἀντιγραφή.[2] Relevant details will come up later; here it may be observed that comparable *quid pro quo*'s (to our mode of thinking) occur elsewhere in Greek literature (I cannot say if also in Semitic speech). Here are the passages known to me:

(1) Darius, according to Herodotus VII. 87, had "all the people over whom he ruled" inscribed on two columns at Byzantium, in "Assyrian letters" (that is cuneiform) on the one, "in Greek" on the other ("letters", not "language").

(2) Thucydides IV. 50: the Athenians intercept a Persian ambassador carrying a letter to Sparta. "They transcribed it from the Assyrian letters and read it"—τὰς μὲν ἐπιστολὰς μεταγραψάμενοι ἐκ τῶν 'Ασσυρίων γραμμάτων ἀνέγνωσαν. Nothing is said about "translating".

(3) Eumenes, according to Diodorus XIX. 23. 2, forged a letter which "was written in Syrian letters"—and, presumably, in Syriac; this however is not said. In the same book, 96. 1, the Nabataeans are said to have written a letter to Antigonus—ἐπιστολὴν γράψαντες Συρίοις γράμμασιν (surely not in the Greek language).

(4) The same mode of expression recurs in several of the reports about the inscription on the monument of Sardanapalus. Thus in Athenaeus 530B: "...on it was written in Assyrian

[1] I cannot quote an instance, from literary Greek, of the noun ἑρμηνεία meaning "translation"; for instances from the papyri see, e.g., Bauer's *Wörterbuch zum N.T.* It does not occur in the Sirach prologue. The salient point is that the compound verbs did not yield a noun which could have conveyed their specific connotation.

[2] This compound is rare. Josephus and Philo, in quoting the present passage, have ἀναγραφή instead. This compound is normal, but its connotation does not fit the context, for νόμων ἀναγραφή is the standing term for the "writing down" of laws previously transmitted orally.

letters" (the text follows in Greek). Strabo 672 reproduces the same author (the Alexander-historian Aristobulus) in the same manner, while Arrian (*Anab.* II. 5. 4) distinguishes between the "Assyrian letters" and their "meaning". Finally, schol. Aristoph. *Aves* 1022, quoting Apollodorus, uses the same form as the first two.

(5) According to the longer text of Luke xxiii. 38, the inscription on the Cross was "in letters Greek, Roman and Hebrew" (the Greek wording follows); Jn. xix. 20 avoids this form.

(6) The very last royal edict of the Hellenistic world, issued by Cleopatra,[1] begins with the words: "The subjoined...is to be copied in Greek and demotic letters"—μεταγραφήτω τοῖς τε Ἑλληνικοῖς καὶ ἐγχωρίοις γράμμασιν.

For our present purpose the texts quoted under nos. (2) and (6) are the most significant, the rest pointing in the same direction. To our way of thinking it seems odd that in Greek it was possible (though by no means necessary) to speak as though letters Assyrian or Syrian, etc., conveyed, *sans plus*, a Greek meaning, and that "transcribing" them into Greek letters could imply translation into Greek. The reason for this "oddity" may be in the fact that reading, in antiquity, meant reading aloud; in consequence, when one read something written in, for example, Syrian letters, one sounded Syriac speech; when their meaning was rendered understandably, that is in Greek, one either felt that one was still "reading out" the Syrian letters or, when being more specific, one conceived of Greek sounds (= letters) as being put in the place of Syrian sounds (= letters). Thus the notion of "transcribing" could unconsciously take the place of "translating".[2] This understanding of letters, γράμματα,

[1] Published by Lefèbvre in *Mélanges Holleaux*; cf. W. Schubart in *Archiv für Pap.* VI, 341.

[2] The word μεταγραφή then does not bear the specific meaning of the modern "transcript" implying that merely the signs of another alphabet are put in the place of a foreign one in still rendering the foreign wording. The practice is likely to have existed in antiquity; its use in the preparation of the Septuagint is not excluded; but this meaning cannot in Aristeas be foisted on the Greek word, since he uses it as a synonym for ἑρμηνεία. The only explicit reference, in Greek, to this practice—which is different from the transition from the Ionian to the Attic alphabet, called μεταχαρακτηρισμός—is, as far as I know, in Strabo 730, where the word μεταγραφή is not used. Strabo quotes two Hellenistic historians, Aristobulus and Aristus, to the effect that the grave monument of Darius was inscribed with a Greek epigram written in Persian letters, as well as with a Persian one. If this statement is materially wrong, still the meaning is unambiguous.

as implying sound led to the use of the word γράμμα to mean "articulate sound" already in the time of Plato; a letter is so to speak a frozen sound, until it is read out.[1]

The acknowledgement of this, to us strange, mode of thinking should make some oddities in Aristeas seem less odd, even though it will hardly dispose of them entirely.

III

The preface (1–8) makes astonishingly little reference to the version of the Torah which almost all later readers have supposed to be the central subject of the book; to make matters worse, the one passage which does refer to it, is corrupt. It makes no sense when, in 4–5, it is added to the glowing description of the virtues of the Jerusalem high-priest that "he possessed the greatest usefulness for his citizens at home and abroad towards the 'translation' of the Law, since with them (whom?) it was written on leather in Hebrew letters". As L. Cohn saw, there is a lacuna after the word "Law" in which, among other things, the noun to which the following "with them" refers has disappeared. No one will doubt that "the inhabitants of Judaea", or "of Jerusalem", are meant. Even so, these fragmentary words yield two important hints. It is stated as a fact of special significance that, "with them", the Torah was written "in Hebrew characters"; secondly, this text is supposed to exist there, in Jerusalem, and only there—the wording of this sentence unambiguously implies this, quite apart from the fact that this assumption is indispensable to the story as a whole.

This conclusion at once imposes itself again when, at the end of 11, Ptolemy is stated to have given order to write to "the high-priest of the Jews". It has already been observed that the author had to put in this trait already at this point in order to give his double in the story the opportunity to raise the question of the Jewish slaves. In the context, however, of the scene narrated in 9–11 the king's sudden move, not suggested by Demetrius or anyone else, is understandable only if it is taken for granted that "the laws of the Jews" are to be found only in "the land of the Jews". The inference is borne out by Demetrius' saying (11) that "in Judaea" people use a special kind of writing:

[1] Cf. the Platonic school-definition of λόγος ("speech") as φωνὴ ἐγγράμματος (*Def.* 414D), that is "articulate sound".

this would be pointless, were it not understood that there only the coveted book exists.

This passage also shows that concern with letters rather than with language on which we have commented. I believe that the text requires the transposition which Mendelssohn proposed (or at least a part of it); even though Wendland marked it "*vix recte*" while other editors do not even mention it.[1] Thereafter it reads: "In Judaea[2] people use a kind of writing of their own, as do the Egyptians. They are supposed to use Syrian letters; this

[1] As transmitted in the MSS. and also by Eusebius, the text raises the following difficulties. After the words "in Judaea, people use a particular kind of letters" it is tolerable that Ptolemy should be reminded of the similar state of affairs in his own realm, where his Egyptian subjects use a different kind of writing from the Greeks; the short phrase "as do the Egyptians", καθάπερ Αἰγύπτιοι, if not very lucid, may therefore stand. The following τῇ τῶν γραμμάτων θέσει however is intolerable. Not only do these words duplicate the preceding χαρακτῆρσι...ἰδίοις, but this phrase has now to be made dependent on the verb χρῶνται; the resulting sentence "as the Egyptians use the order of the letters" is meaningless. Γράμματα cannot be supposed to have the pregnant meaning "hieroglyphs", nor does θέσις refer to the direction of the writing (this would anyhow spoil the context): it ought to have been noted, from a comparison with 64, 70, 78, that Aristeas uses this word all but periphrastically in connexion with various nouns in the plural, so that γραμμάτων θέσις about equals mere γράμματα. Moreover, if the words are left in their transmitted order, it becomes doubtful to whom the following words "as also they have a language of their own" refer: the Jews or the Egyptians? At least, then, the words τῇ...θέσει are out of place. If the following reference to language is left standing, what follows has to be taken to refer to the distinction between Hebrew and Aramaic speech. This is, in itself, materially possible; but seeing that Demetrius started by commenting on the peculiarity of the letters used by the Jews, and in view of the persistent concern with them, one would expect, rather, now to be told what the peculiarity of the letters consisted in. Here it becomes important, or even decisive, that Josephus in his paraphrase (*Ant.* XII. 2. 14) makes the distinction between "Syrian" (that is Aramaic) and Hebrew with respect, not to language but to writing: δοκεῖ μὲν γὰρ τῇ ἰδιότητι τῶν Συρίων γραμμάτων ἐμφερὴς ὁ χαρακτὴρ αὐτῶν. Josephus is careless; but carelessness could not induce him to invent a wording which so well fits the trend of the argument. Mendelssohn healed the two shortcomings by a single operation: he transferred the words τῇ τῶν γραμμάτων θέσει to follow ...Συριακῇ χρῆσθαι. He would, moreover, transfer the words καθὸ καὶ φωνὴν ἰδίαν ἔχουσιν to the very end of Demetrius' speech, after τρόπος. This no doubt results in the most satisfactory progression; but this second transposition is not supported by Josephus. Perhaps these words may be left standing, as a mere aside (which would be suitable) at their present place.

[2] Ἰουδαίων is a fault of the archetype of our manuscripts, here as well as in 83; read Ἰουδαίας with Eusebius.

however is not so; it is a different kind; as also they have a language of their own." Even if Mendelssohn's cure is rejected, the characteristic fact remains that the primary reason why the Torah cannot, like other books, simply be copied is found, not in the fact that it is couched in a foreign language but because "in Judaea people use peculiar letters" (cf. 38 and 176).

The argument, then, of this first section, which raises the proposal to have the Torah translated, is this. Demetrius has brought together many books for the royal library by either purchase or copying (μεταγραφή). It has been reported to him that "the laws of the Jews", too, deserve copying (μεταγραφή).[1] The difficulty about it is, at least primarily, in the letters in which they are written; hence ἑρμηνεία is needed. In this context, the rendering "translation" clearly would not exhaust the implications of the Greek word; the strange letters will have to be "elucidated", or "interpreted". And so then Ptolemy gives order to write to the high-priest.... What does he want from him? A copy of the "laws of the Jews"? "Interpretation" of its strange letters? A translation? The pompous last words of this section leave the reader in the dark. This much only is clear: he who wants the "laws of the Jews" must apply to Jerusalem.

IV

The questions left open in 9–11 are only very partially cleared up by Demetrius' "memorandum" 29–32; instead, new motifs are brought in, the notion of "translating" being all but absent. The subject, according to the introduction (28), is still the "copying" (here ἀντιγραφή) of the Jewish books.

In a preamble (29) Demetrius sums up the king's wishes which, so he reports, he has made it his business keenly to fulfil. Among them is one not before mentioned; namely the task of repairing damaged volumes (we may here naturally recall the work of Acacius and Euzoius in the Caesarean library; a much more relevant parallel though is II Macc. ii. 13 (Nehemiah)).

[1] Who has "reported" this to Demetrius? We had better not ask. How was this Greek to know of the existence, and excellence, of the laws of that strange people—unless somebody had told him? Hence the author puts this "somebody" in, careful not to divulge his identity. He does exactly the same again in 30, and for the same reason. "It is learned on reliable authority": he who is met by this phrase knows all he is expected to know.

Evidently the author is at pains to give a suitable "local colour" to his story—and what could be more natural, in a librarian, than this task? After this slight display he hurries on to his real concern. "The books of the laws of the Jews are wanting, *for* they are spoken in Hebrew letters and language" (the last sentence, in oddity, exceeds what our previous discussion could hope to account for). The reasoning seems odd, too; previously, the "Hebrew letters and language" had been said to make "elucidation" or "translation" necessary—rather than being, in themselves, the cause of the absence, from the library, of the Hebrew books. The reasoning here seems incomplete; one may anticipate the continuation: "they will first have to be translated"; or, perhaps, "copies are hard to come by". Either argument could have led on to the suggestion to turn to Jerusalem, but neither of them is produced. Instead, the sentence goes on: ἀμελέστερον δὲ καὶ οὐχ ὡς ὑπάρχει σεσήμανται. These words require careful interpretation, for various bold conclusions have been based upon them.

Meecham observes: "σεσήμανται: 'have been interpreted'.... If σεσήμανται here means 'interpret' (so Frankel, *Vorstudien zur Septuaginta*, p. 24), the reference is probably to an earlier translation of the Law than the LXX." P. Kahle concurs.[1] Scholars who maintain this view ought at least clearly to state that they suppose this verb here to mean "to translate", for their argument hinges on this assumption. It is contradicted, first, by the structure of the sentence. One need not know Greek to see that its second half completes the first; since the first states that the Law is couched in Hebrew letters and language, the second cannot contain information about any versions but is bound to refer, likewise, to the Hebrew Law. The second point requires knowledge of Greek: σημαίνω does not mean "to translate"; not even *via* the—likewise inadmissible—connotation of "interpreting". Misinformation may be derived even from the great Liddell–Scott. What, then, is here said to have been done "rather carelessly" about the books of the Hebrew Law? A definite hint is given by what follows: "for they have not benefited from royal care". In the mouth of the Royal Librarian this can only mean that they have not been treated as were those Greek works which entered the Alexandrian library: these were treated, not "carelessly" but carefully. The following words make plain what this

[1] H. G. Meecham, *The Letter of Aristeas* (1935), p. 201; P. Kahle, *The Cairo Geniza* (1947), p. 135.

care aimed at; namely the establishment of an exact, pure text (διηκριβωμένα). Books benefit from scholarly care in Alexandria but not in Jerusalem: the author has here supplied another dash of local colour to heighten the effect of the scene he pretends to have witnessed.

It follows that σημαίνειν must here mean, simply, "to write". This has been observed, more than sixty years ago, by Mendelssohn and again, more recently, by E. J. Bickerman.[1] They have failed to convice their opponents; perhaps the truth will impose itself when the simple case is argued a third time and in detail. Σημαίνειν, "to betoken" or "indicate", very often *implies* writing. In the many instances in the papyri where the recipient is urged σήμαινέ μοι, "inform me" (about this or that), the translation "write to me" would often be natural, but in such cases it is still possible to argue against this specific meaning. At any rate this usage could easily lead to σημαίνειν meaning unambiguously "to write". Instances of this unambiguous kind occur, as far as I can see, only in books written by Jews (like Aristeas).[2] Two are in the Septuagint: I Esdras viii. 48 πάντων ἐσημάνθη ἡ ὀνοματογραφία "the catalogue of all the names has been written", and II Macc. ii. 1 ὡς σεσήμανται "as has been written". The decisive parallel to Aristeas occurs in a fragment of Aristobulus, the literary predecessor of Aristeas, preserved by Eusebius, *Praep. Evang.* XIII. 12 (para. 7 Mras, but 12 in the older editions). In his endeavour to demonstrate that the Greeks got their best thoughts from Moses he has just quoted the prooemium of Aratus—with a thoroughgoing alteration of the original text, putting throughout "God" in the place of "Zeus". In dealing with so well-known a text Aristobulus deemed best to confess to his interference. This he did by assuming the pose of rational criticism. "The poem clearly refers to God, whose power permeates the universe," so he argues, "hence I have written as required, eliminating the poetical (fiction) Zeus": καθὼς δὲ δεῖ σεσημάγκαμεν, περιαιροῦντες τὸν διὰ τῶν ποιημάτων Δία. Περιαιρεῖν

[1] Mendelssohn in the posthumous edition of Aristeas (1897), p. 35 ("*perscriptae*"); Bickerman in *J.B.L.* LXIII (1944), 343 with note 24 ("Aristeas 30...speaks of the original text") and *A. Marx Jubilee Volume*, I (1950), 156 ("σεσήμανται means *notare*, 'mark with writing'...Aristobulus uses the term in the same meaning 'note down'": this, I think, is not quite correct).

[2] The passage which Meecham *loc. cit.* quotes in evidence of the meaning "commit to writing" (this translation is anyhow not exact) proves nothing, for there (Plutarch, *Mor.* 204E) the dative γράμμασιν is added to σημαίνειν.

is a technical term (Latin *inducere*) of Alexandrian scholars denoting the bracketing of spurious matter. And σημαίνειν is here used for the conscientious writing of a text by a critic—as in Aristeas.[1]

Demetrius then is made to say that "the books of the Jewish laws" are written rather carelessly, καὶ οὐχ ὡς ὑπάρχει. The meaning of these last words is none too obvious. "Not as they (really) are" (this is how Josephus, too, understood these words, whose synonym ἔχει therefore ought not to be altered);[2] apparently some standard of correctness of the text of the Torah is supposed to exist or, rather, the Torah has a real existence of its own which is but imperfectly represented by "the books of the Jews"—because these have not been critically edited. Here, as throughout, the reader is perfectly free to protest that all this is historically improbable or impossible; but the present task is to understand the writer and not, as yet, to criticize him.

If we confine ourselves strictly to the context, it still seems strange that Demetrius should assert the poor quality of the Jerusalem text. One may test an alternative interpretation. Could he be referring to Hebrew texts kept by the Alexandrian Jews? This interpretation runs counter to conclusions previously drawn; even so, it is not beyond possibility that the writer could here be discounting an assumption followed in other parts—and this understanding would be far less improbable on historical grounds. And yet it is, unless I am greatly mistaken, excluded by the wording of this very passage. If the books were supposed to be available in Alexandria, why does not Demetrius say so? How could he say that they are "wanting"? The observation that they were of inferior quality, because unimproved by "royal care", applied to every single book he acquired; it did not cause

[1] A few lines later, para. 12 (15), Aristobulus uses the verb σημαίνω again; there, too, the connotation of "writing" seems required, since the actual wording of Genesis is contrasted with its philosophical meaning; hence the verb cannot be translated by the vaguer English "to indicate".

[2] As an alternative, the possibility may be considered that ὑπάρχειν here has the meaning "to be possible", indicating that the Jewish books "are written rather carelessly and not as is (would be) possible"; namely if Alexandrian scholarship were applied to them. Several objections, though, can be raised against this understanding: the absence of a *dativus personae* which is normally present where ὑπάρχειν has this connotation; the different rendering by Josephus; and the implied over-condensation of the meaning. Anyhow, the general interpretation of the passage would be the same even if this alternative were preferred.

them to be "absent" from the library. Not even Aristeas would suppose Demetrius to describe an Alexandrian copy of, say, Homer or Euripides to be "absent" because it had not been edited by the scholars at the Museion. What is more, and in my view decisive, is the conclusion Demetrius derives from his premiss. If he really meant that Alexandrian copies of the Torah were not good enough for his library, then his point in suggesting applying to Jerusalem must be to get a better copy from there. In fact, however, a manuscript to be obtained from there is, strangely enough, not even mentioned. He suggests the dispatch, from Jerusalem, of seventy-two worthy men, outstanding in character and well-versed in their Law. Are they to correct the faulty Alexandrian manuscripts? That is not what he says, nor what actually happens afterwards. Eleazar, in his reply to Ptolemy, states (46) that he is dispatching the seventy-two—"with the Law", ἔχοντας τὸν νόμον. The impression is confirmed that the only place from which it can be had is Jerusalem; indeed, that there is only one manuscript of it in existence: the one which Eleazar is sending for "copying" (μεταγραφή 46 and 47). And the uniqueness of this manuscript is powerfully stressed in the elaborate and fairy-tale-like description of the reception, in Alexandria, of this wonderful book, written in golden letters (χρυσογραφίᾳ τοῖς 'Ιουδαϊκοῖς γράμμασιν) on marvellous parchment (175–9).

Any idea of "careless writing" and lack of scholarly treatment is here completely out of the question (whether we think of the Jerusalem text or, for that matter, of an Alexandrian one). Aristeas' story, in short, is not only incredible from the historical point of view but, moreover, inconsistent in itself. This particular feature was introduced not for any reason of fact or tradition but as a literary motif, utilized where it could serve and forgotten when the story reached a stage which it did not fit. We had already inferred that the reference to "royal care" for books in Alexandria stands out as a dash of "local colouring"; in pursuing this inference, the puzzling features of this section find their explanation.

The writer had decided to present the production of the Septuagint under this twofold aspect: devised in the interest of Philadelphus' library and executed by the Jerusalem elders. He was roughly aware of the goal and procedure of the Alexandrian scholars who edited the authoritative texts of the Greek classics; after all, he lived in the century of the great Aristarchus.

Those critics, he knew, aimed at establishing exact (ἀκριβῆ) texts and their most evident method consisted in the comparing, or collating (ἀντιβάλλειν), of different copies. The production of a translation is, in fact, a very different matter; yet, under the circumstances (and in the absence of any tradition or precedent) he saw no choice but of presenting it, for better or worse, in the light of this analogy. A completely authentic text leaves no scope for the scholar's endeavour; hence the author smartly introduces his passing reference to imperfect manuscripts (leaving their identity suitably undefined and thus causing his critics an unrewarding task). Therewith the scholarly ideal of an "exact" text is appropriately evoked (31). How is it to be achieved? Traditionally, by collating and selecting; and selection must largely be determined by "interpretation" (ἑρμηνεία). And who was to carry out the task? Here, if anywhere, the Jewish elders had to be brought in. The goal envisaged, however, was not really the establishment of a critical text of the Hebrew scriptures, but their Greek translation. These two endeavours then had to be described, as far as possible, as one. In doing this, the writer was helped by those idiosyncrasies of ancient thought which have been mentioned before. "Transcription", μεταγραφή, can imply "translation", and so can "interpretation", ἑρμηνεία. He utilized these linguistic ambiguities—and surely not unconsciously. The task in hand is described as μεταγραφή (28, 46 f.), and ἑρμηνεία comes in at the end of Demetrius' proposal (32); if rather obliquely. Continuing in the terminology of Alexandrian scholarship, he proposes (32) that the exact wording (τὸ ἀκριβές) is to be reached by the "examining" of—here the identification threatens to break down. For, after all, what is to be compared is not, as in scholarly work, various manuscripts, but various translations of one text set forth by various elders. But Aristeas endeavours to keep up appearances. Leaving to the reader to trace his ingenuity in every detail, we may single out but one. If he intended unequivocally here to have the task of translation proposed, why does he not say so unequivocally? In fact, this concept is kept entirely outside this whole section—until the very end. And there, this is telling, Demetrius is not made to say: "thus we shall obtain an exact translation", but τὸ κατὰ τὴν ἑρμηνείαν ἀκριβές. It is well known that Hellenistic Greek abounds in periphrases replacing the case-ending by a preposition. This usage is of limited relevance here; it does not really account for this wording. As it stands, it involves the *double-entendre* "what is exact according to", either, "(scholarly) interpretation" or "translation".[1]

When at last the execution of the translation is narrated, in 301–7, we are given proof that our effort at determining the author's intention has been on the right lines; however abstruse it may seem that he should have chosen to represent the translators' task as a work of critical scholarship; with the individual elders, or at least their detailed views, taking the place of manuscripts collated. But he had no choice.

Of the 322 paragraphs of his book, seven are, on a generous reckoning, devoted to the actual work of translation (301–7). From these, however, no less than six have to be deducted as irrelevant. The first describes the idyllic place of work, and the way thither; 303–5 tell what the elders did when they were not translating; from the last of these, an occasion for expounding the allegorical meaning of the washing of hands is derived (306), and the last duplicates the idyll described in the first, adding the astounding fact that the seventy-two completed their work in seventy-two days (this, by the way, I suspect to be an alternative, traditional way of accounting for the designation of the translation). Actually, then, it is the one para. 302 which really tells of the central event.

"They carried out (the interpretation-translation), making every point agreed among themselves by the 'collations'." Ἀντιβάλλειν, as noted above, is the technical term for the "collating" of manuscripts. The "imperfect manuscripts" have been out of view for a long time; what is "collated" is the views of the elders; and they themselves collate them; to Demetrius falls the lot of acting as a secretary.

It is only too clear that the writer had no concrete tradition to follow, nor any idea of the real problems facing the real originators of the Septuagint, nor the imagination to devise a substantial

[1] The last two words of 32, θῶμεν εὐσήμως, are obscure. Mendelssohn rendered it *in loco conspicuo reponamus*. This rendering, accepted by many students, is proved possible by the parallels adduced in commentaries and by Liddell–Scott, *s.v.* εὔσημος II. These very parallels, however, show that the current connotation would be "written in big letters which can be distinguished easily and from afar". It is a far cry from there to the assumption that the meaning is "place the books in our distinguished library". The alternative is worth considering that the meaning "that we may put it down (in writing; cf. L.–S. *s.v.* τίθημι A.9) clearly" is intended; the implication being that the wording critically established is both true (and hence worthy of the king's intention) and plain.

and plausible scene. The one thing, meagre enough, left to him was once again to utilize the analogy, suggested by the framework of his story, between Alexandrian scholarship and the production of the Alexandrian Bible.

He who strives to elicit historical facts from this narrative is building on foundations very much less solid than sand. The question remains: for what purpose was it ever put forth?

V

Enlightenment on this point has variously been sought in the next two sections (308–11 and 312–16), which tell of the reception of the completed work by, first, "the Jews" and, secondly, the king; these therefore we have to examine.

The enthusiastic approval by the former conveys an assurance of the perfect quality of the translation by the only competent judges imaginable; hence "the Jews"—presumably of Alexandria—here make their first and only appearance. The work, they proclaim, has been done "well, piously and throughout accurately" (once more the scholarly ἀκρίβεια, 310); hence they insure its unaltered preservation by applying to it the rigid injunctions of Deut. iv. 2 and xii. 32. The reader of Aristeas is therewith assured that any copy of the Septuagint which he may take to hand will be literally identical with the one produced for Philadelphus—which, in turn, is the perfect rendering of the venerable original. This, by the way, is the inescapable refutation of the view (recently revived by P. Kahle) which would describe "Aristeas" as a piece of propaganda for a revision promulgated at, or about, the time when the pseudepigraphon was actually written. You cannot commend a revision known to have been produced today or yesterday by solemnly prohibiting any alteration of a perfect and sacrosanct original created 150 years ago.

This section precedes the report about Ptolemy's reaction, not because it entails some dim recollection of the role actually played by the Alexandrian Jews, but for literary reasons. The judgement of the experts justifies his enterprise; besides, he had to play the leading part right to the end of the book; a part which would have been unsuitably broken up by a later reference to "the Jews". He is duly impressed by the profundity of the book revealed to him in the translation, and this admiration makes him ask Demetrius "why no historian or poet had made mention of things so grand". Therewith Demetrius is led to continue exactly where he had broken off when first proposing the translation (31). Then, he had spontaneously obviated the question with which Greeks were bound to react to the assertion of the excellence and antiquity of Jewish traditions; namely "why then has one never heard thereof"? The riposte was: because they contain a philosophy holy, sublime, divine. This somewhat perplexing rejoinder is now elaborated; after some introductory words the close similarity of which with the earlier passage precludes any doubt that we are not continuing in the earlier context; or, to say the same thing in other words, the author continues utilizing the same source. We now learn what the earlier, perplexing hints meant: God did not want his words (τὰ θεῖα) to be wantonly spread among common men (315). In confirmation, Demetrius relates the amazing experiences of two famous Greeks who had tried to act against this divine intention.

The particular absurdity of this passage has frequently been noted and need not be elaborated again; what matters in the present context is its origin and purpose. In 31, Demetrius described Hecataeus of Abdera as his informant, and though in the continuation (314 ff.) Theodectes and Theopompus are, with ruthless disregard of chronological possibility, alleged likewise, and even more explicitly, to have personally imparted their experiences to him, it is clear that the whole context is taken from a book that went under the name of Hecataeus. It ought not to be necessary to repeat that the real Hecataeus cannot possibly be credited with this nonsense and that, on the other hand, Josephus, *c. Ap.* I. 183 ff. preserves the fairly detailed outline of the Jewish pseudepigraph fathered on him into which this fragment easily inserts itself. It serves the same tendency; namely propaganda—not for the Septuagint, still less for a revision of it, but—for the Jews. The Greek objection against the excellence and antiquity of the Torah is met by the assertion that some famous Greeks had indeed endeavoured to quote from it, but the deity punished their impious attempts in the same way as, long ago, the offence of the poet Stesichorus. It was a traditional motif; it had previously been transferred to Demetrius of Phaleron and was to be applied, later on, to the apostle Paul and others. In the present instance it necessitated the invention that some partial and unauthentic version of the Torah had been attempted at an early date; God, though, prevented it from becoming known—that is to say, it never existed. This invention has as little basis in fact as has the similar one attested for Aristobulus by Eusebius, *Praep.*

Ev. XIII. 12. According to him, all the most famous Greeks, from Homer and Orpheus down to Pythagoras and Plato, derived their ideas from the Torah; necessarily therefore translations of it must be supposed to have existed. It may be felt to be mildly funny that strictly opposite lines of propaganda led to one and the same fiction ((*a*) the Greeks did not know of the Torah, for God prevented them from reading the old translations, and (*b*) the Greeks derived all their ideas from the Torah, for it had early been translated, and read). But once the origin of the invention has been recognized, one will refrain from drawing from it any conclusions about the prehistory of the Septuagint. In "Aristeas" it serves the same purpose as it had done in pseudo-Hecataeus; namely, Jewish propaganda.

VI

"The purpose of the narration", so E. Schürer long ago summarized his analysis of the *Ad Philocratem*,[1] "is by no means in the story as such, but in its showing the respect and admiration for the Jewish Law and for Judaism generally on the part of pagan authorities." The preceding discussion, I trust, confirms this judgement and shows that any historical reality or any relation to a specific point in the history of the Septuagint is sought in it in vain. The writer appears to have met with a legendary tradition current among Alexandrian Jews according to which the Torah had been translated on Pharos in the days of "King Ptolemy" (uncertain which) and with the aid of Demetrius of Phalerum. The existence of this legend is likely because our author is not the man whom one would easily credit with so substantial an invention; moreover, the reference to it in Aristobulus can hardly be dated after "Aristeas"; finally, Philo's report about an annual feast celebrated on Pharos in commemoration of the translation seems genuine and points to an ancient tradition.

This legendary tradition suggested itself as a suitable, if slender, bond to hold together a number of chapters designed to impress pagan readers with the high qualities of Judaism. These chapters surely were not of the writer's own devising; the helplessness evidenced where he had no substantial tradition to follow—namely in the sections bearing upon the translation—suggests his faithful adherence to some literary model in more substantial sections; such as the description of Jerusalem and the "apologia"

[1] *Geschichte des Jüdischen Volkes*, 3. Aufl., III, 468.

for the Law. Moreover it has, I hope, been demonstrated that he followed a literary source even in a section where so competent a critic as P. Wendland would credit him with some, moderate originality; namely, in the "Seven Banquets". If this is true there, it would apply *a potiori* to the rest (the ecphrasis of the royal gifts, though, may be due to his unaided pen—hence its failure). To identify these sources seems hard except in the section on the liberation (fifty years after their capture!) of the Jewish prisoners. It would obviously be tempting to trace the sections just instanced to pseudo-Hecataeus, in whose book they could quite as well have figured as did the model of Ar. 31 and 312–16; but the thorough differences in the figures quoted for the size of Palestine and its capital (Ar. 105 and 116; pseudo-Hec. *ap.* Jos. *c. Ap.* I. 195–7) is an obstacle hard to overcome.

Too little survives of Hellenistic-Jewish literature to admit of such questions of detail to be confidently settled. But the outline of pseudo-Hecataeus is, thanks to Josephus, sufficiently distinct to admit of describing his book as the model, in a general way, of "Aristeas".[1] There he found Jewish propaganda given special effect by presenting it as the utterance of an outstanding Greek; the latter as the deeply impressed witness of Jewish excellence; the High-priest expounding Jewish lore; and other Jews outshining and humbling a circle of Hellenes. "Aristeas" endeavoured to surpass this model by presenting the most glorious of Hellenistic kings as the devout admirer of Jewish wisdom and by inviting the Greeks to study the Torah which, according to his tale, was available for them in a "transcript" of complete and authoritative authenticity.

It is not its literary merit which caused this little book to survive; it alone from among a probably vast number of similar productions. Josephus (*Ant.* XII, iv) summarizes a novel written to extol the Tobiad family. One may sympathize with E. Meyer who turned with indignation from this immoral laudation of brutal but successful tax-farmers; even so one will have to admit that in liveliness and interest this piece of propaganda appears to have been far superior to "Aristeas"; and yet it, too, has failed to survive. Joseph and Hyrcanus the Tobiads could not hold the interest of posterity; while in "Aristeas" the Christian Church found the story of its Scripture.

[1] Cf. the most valuable commentary of F. Jacoby in his edition of the fragments of Hecataeus and pseudo-Hecataeus in the third volume of his *Fragmente der Griechischen Historiker*.

(iii) *Qumran and the Septuagint*

REDÉCOUVERTE D'UN CHAÎNON MANQUANT DE L'HISTOIRE DE LA SEPTANTE

Pendant la répression du mouvement insurrectionnel de Ben Kosebah — si nous en croyons la mise en scène du « Dialogue » — Justin se plaignait auprès du juif Tryphon de l'attitude du rabbinat contemporain à l'égard de la vénérable version des Septante. Non seulement ils avaient l'audace de soutenir que l'interprétation donnée par leurs soixante-dix anciens réunis chez le roi d'Égypte Ptolémée n'était pas exacte en tous points (1), mais ils allaient jusqu'à prétendre donner eux-mêmes leur propre interprétation de l'Écriture (2), osant ainsi dénaturer ce vénérable héritage (3) et remplacer l'exégèse messianique traditionnelle des prophéties par des interprétations misérables, « qui se traînent à ras de terre » (4). Justin affirme sans ambages que c'est pour ôter une arme essentielle à la propagande chrétienne que les rabbins ont falsifié ainsi les prophéties en en retranchant maints passages qui laissaient entrevoir trop nettement la figure de Jésus-Christ (5).

Ne se bornant pas à ces accusations globales, Justin prétend nous donner en plusieurs cas, face à face, des exemples de l'interprétation traditionnelle des LXX et de celle du rabbinat contemporain (6). Il accepte même à contre-cœur la situation faite ainsi à la controverse chrétienne antijudaïque et s'efforce de n'argumenter qu'à partir de textes acceptés par ses adversaires (7). En plusieurs cas, il nous prévient incidemment qu'il les cite sous la forme où les lisaient ceux-ci (8).

Si l'on pouvait faire toute confiance à Justin, nous aurions donc en lui un témoin précieux d'une phase très importante de l'histoire du

(1) LXVIII, 7; LXXI, 1; LXXXIV, 3 (divisions et texte selon l'éd. d'ARCHAMBAULT, *Textes et Documents*, Picard, Paris, 1909).
(2) LXXI, 1.
(3) LXXXIV, 3.
(4) CXII, 4.
(5) LXVIII, 8; LXXI, 2; LXXII, 3; CXX, 5.
(6) CXX, 4; CXXIV, 2 et 3; CXXXVII, 3.
(7) LXXI, 2.
(8) CXXIV, 4; CXXXVII, 3.

Reprinted from *Revue Biblique*. Vol. 60, 1953.

texte grec de l'Ancien Testament. Ses innombrables citations souvent très longues, tirées de livres bibliques fort divers, nous auraient conservé le texte grec courant dans les milieux juifs orthodoxes du début du Second siècle. Mais certaines considérations ont empêché la critique contemporaine de se laisser entraîner par cet espoir. Même ceux qui ne nient pas, à la suite de Preuschen et de Schäder, l'authenticité du « Dialogue » sont forcés d'y reconnaître une bonne part de fiction et de repousser sa composition dans la seconde moitié du siècle. Aussi envisage-t-on volontiers le texte biblique très original attesté par Justin comme une recension personnelle de la LXX à partir des premières grandes traductions juives du Second siècle et spécialement de celle d'Aquila. Il importe enfin de faire remarquer que nous ne connaissons l'œuvre de Justin que par un unique ms. du XIVe siècle, et que la forme de ses citations bibliques a pu être sérieusement affectée par son passage à travers cette longue et étroite filière. Il semblait donc, jusqu'à une date toute récente, que le plus prudent fût de souscrire à ces lignes déçues et décevantes par lesquelles Rahlfs concluait une étude du texte biblique de Justin : « Für den LXX-Forscher ist unser Resultat insofern lehrreich als es wieder einmal zeigt wie vorsichtig man bei der Verwertung von Kirchenväter-Zitaten sein muss. » (1).

Mais au cours de la seconde quinzaine d'août 1952, les infatigables bédouins Taʿamré ont découvert dans une nouvelle grotte du désert de Juda d'importants fragments d'un rouleau de parchemin qui y avait été déposé lors de la révolte de Ben Kosebah (2). Ces fragments ont été acquis par le Musée Archéologique Palestinien, avec l'assentiment de Mr. Harding, Directeur des Antiquités de Jordanie, et nous sommes autorisés à en faire une première présentation aux lecteurs de la *Revue Biblique.* Il s'agit d'un texte grec des Petits Prophètes dont les parties conservées appartiennent à Michée, Jonas, Nahum, Habacuc, Sophonie et Zacharie. Comme on pourra s'en rendre compte par la planche ci-jointe (pl. I), la très belle onciale de notre ms. se situe au mieux vers la fin du Ier siècle après J.-C. (3), ce qui concorde avec le fait que

(1) *ZNW.*, 1921, p. 198.

(2) C'est ce qu'indique de façon suffisamment certaine l'écriture des petits fragments de papyri hébréo-araméens trouvés dans la même grotte ainsi que les monnaies et documents datés trouvés en deux autres grottes toutes proches.

(3) Des *apices* inférieurs vigoureusement lancés vers la droite constituent la caractéristique la plus frappante de cette onciale au caractère très ferme. Ni l'*alpha* ni le *mu* ne présentent les signes de fléchissement qui apparaissent au début du second siècle. Le centre de gravité de l'écriture n'est ni surélevé ni surbaissé. Les apices obliques supérieurs qui apparaissent parfois dans le *delta*, l'*alpha* et le *lambda* ne manifestent aucune tendance à s'incurver.

le ms. était déjà très usagé lorsqu'il fut abandonné. L'abondance de textes découverts cette année ne nous permet pas d'aborder tout de suite la publication intégrale de ces nouveaux fragments bibliques, aussi me bornerai-je pour cette fois à situer cette nouvelle recension du texte grec dans son contexte littéraire et historique.

Voici tout d'abord un passage qui recouvre partiellement une importante citation faite par Justin au ch. CIX du « Dialogue » : il s'agit de *Michée* IV, 3-7.

		]πολλω[
		]κρανκαισυνκοψου
	]μαχα[	]νεισαροτρακαιτασ
	σιβυ[ ]υτων[	]ανακαιουμηανθα
	ρηεθν[ ]φεθνοσ[	]καιουμημα
4	θωσινετιπολεμει[	]ονταιανηρ
	υποκατωαμπελουαυ[	]υκησ
	α[ ]ιουκεστινο[	]οτ τοστομα
5	(tetr.)[ ]νδ[	]οτιπαν
	τεσοιλα . . πορε[	]ουαυτων
	ημεισδεπορε[	](tetr.) θεου
	ημω . ειστον[	]
6		]συνα
		]ξωσ
7		]ηνεκα[ ]θησω
		]νεισυ[ ]μμα
		]νηνεισεθνοσισχυρον
		](tetragr.) επαυτωνεντωορεισει
		]ωστουαιωνοσ

Il suffit de comparer ce texte à celui de la citation de Justin pour constater qu'il lui est substantiellement identique. Voici les seules variantes qui les distinguent : v. 3. : ανθαρη/αρη Just.; v. 4 : καθι]σονται/καθισεται Just.; ibid. : εστιν/εσται (1) Just.; ibid. : το στομα/στομα Just.; v. 5ª : θε]ου/θεων Just. Aucune de ces variantes, on le voit, n'excède ce que l'on est en droit d'attendre des abâtardissements d'une tradition manuscrite aussi longue et étroite que l'est celle du texte de Justin.

La dimension des lettres est régulière, bien calibrée. Toutes ces caractéristiques s'accordent au mieux avec la Seconde moitié du Premier siècle; date qu'aucune particularité de détail ne vient contredire, bien qu'il soit difficile de trouver des parallèles parfaitement typiques.

(1) En CX, 4, Justin reprenant ce passage lit εστιν comme notre ms.

Les points où notre texte concorde avec celui de Justin contre les LXX sont beaucoup plus nombreux et typiques (1) : v. 3 : συνκοψουσι/κατακοψουσι LXX; ibid. ; μαχαιρας/ρομφαιας LXX; ibid. : τας ζιβυνας/τα δορατα LXX; ibid : ου μη/ουκετι μη (1er) LXX; ibid. ου μη...ετι/ουκετι μη (2e) LXX; v. 4 : ανηρ/εκαστος LXX; ibid. : των δυναμεων/παντοκρατωρος LXX; v. 6 : ην εκακωσα/ους απωσαμην LXX; v. 7 : θησω/θησομαι LXX; ibid. : επ'αυτων εν τω ορει/επ'αυτους εν ορει LXX; ibid. : εως του αιωνος/εως εις τον αιωνα LXX.

Notons de plus que les lacunes du ms. sont beaucoup plus aisément remplies avec le texte de Justin qu'avec celui des LXX. Mais les concordances formelles qui viennent d'être relevées paraissent suffisamment démonstratives : en argumentant contre Tryphon, Justin citait Michée selon notre texte.

Je n'ai relevé dans le « Dialogue » qu'un autre passage très bref où ses citations des Petits Prophètes recoupent encore une fois nos fragments : il s'agit de *Zac.* II, 12 où tous deux sont d'accord pour lire ἐκλέξεται contre αἱρετιεῖ de la LXX. Remarquons enfin, pour éviter une méprise, que le texte que donnent nos fragments pour *Mic.* v, 2 est très différent de celui que cite Justin. Cela tient seulement à ce que ce dernier ne cite pas directement Michée, mais en réalité reproduit la citation libre qu'en fait l'évangile de S. Matthieu.

Que nous ayons ainsi retrouvé dans une grotte de la Seconde Révolte le texte des Petits Prophètes cité par Justin, cela nous amène déjà à une première conclusion : c'est que Justin cite un texte juif réel, en vogue au moment où il situe son dialogue avec Tryphon. Nous n'avons donc pas affaire, comme on pouvait le craindre, à une mixture tardive et arbitraire : il n'invente rien. Seuls ses copistes peuvent être rendus responsables de quelques modifications facilitantes ou assimilantes. De là nous pouvons inférer que les autres citations de Justin, et elles sont aussi amples que variées, représentent très vraisemblablement, dans ce qu'elles ont d'original, une recension rabbinique de la Septante qui avait cours entre 70 et 135.

Il est en effet assez aisé de prouver, sur la base des fragments qui nous en sont parvenus, premièrement que notre texte n'est qu'une *recension de la Septante*, et deuxièmement que cette recension est l'œuvre de *lettrés juifs*.

Que notre texte ne soit pas une version originale mais une recension, un simple exemple suffira à le prouver en permettant de saisir sur le

(1) Pour l'établissement du texte de la LXX, je me base sur l'édition de J. Ziegler (Göttingen, Vandenhoeck & Ruprecht, 1943).

vif les procédés du recenseur. Voici deux versets d'Habacuc. On pourrait trouver nombre d'autres passages typiques dans nos fragments. Le seul privilège de ces deux versets est de ne pas avoir été rendus trop lacunaires par la dent des rats :

Hb. II, 7 : **οὐχὶ** ἐξαί[φνη]ς ἀναστήσονται δάκνοντες **σε** καὶ ἐγνή[ψουσ]ιν οἱ **ἀλεύοντες** σε καὶ ἔσῃ εἰς διαρπαγὰς αὐτ[οῖς].

Hb. II, 18 : τί ὠφέλ**ησεν** γλυπτόν ὅτι [ἔγλυψε]ν αὐτό **ὁ πλάσας** αὐτὸ χώνευμα [**καὶ** φα]ντασίαν ψευδῆ ὅτι πέποιθεν ὁ πλάσας ἐπὶ τὸ πλάσμα αὐτοῦ **ἐπ' αὐτό** [π]οιῆσαι εἴδωλα κωφά.

Il suffit de comparer ces deux versets au texte de la LXX et à l'hébreu pour se rendre compte que toutes les modifications (en caractères gras) du texte grec traditionnel s'expliquent par un souci de le modeler plus exactement sur l'hébreu.

Il convient cependant d'ajouter qu'à côté de centaines de variantes de ce type, on en trouve aussi un certain nombre où notre texte semble s'éloigner à la fois de la LXX et du T.M. Cela peut vouloir dire alors que le texte hébreu sur lequel le recenseur s'est base différait du nôtre. Ainsi en Hab. I, 17 où εκκεν]ωσει μαχαιραν αυτου (qui remplace αμφιβαλει το αμφιβληστρον αυτου de la LXX) suppose qu'il lisait avec le Pesher d'Habacuc de Qumrân חרבו au lieu de חרמו du T. M. Peut-être faut-il faire entrer dans la même catégorie la substitution de αρτος à μερις en *Hab.* I, 16. Notre recenseur aurait lu dans son texte hébreu probablement abâtardi לחם au lieu de חלק, modification que paraît supposer aussi le targum de Jonathan.

Lorsqu'il quitte la base de la LXX pour essayer de rendre par ses propres moyens le texte hébreu, il se montre souvent fort inconséquent. Il lui arrive de faire preuve d'un littéralisme extrême qui violente la syntaxe grecque : ainsi lorsqu'il ajoute επ' αυτο en *Hab.* II, 18 (cf. *supra*) ou bien lorsqu'il laisse au nominatif sans aucun lien syntactique des substantifs dont il a supprimé, par fidélité à l'hébreu, la préposition introductive : ainsi en *Hab.* II, 6 : οὐχὶ ταῦτα πάντα παραβολὴν κατ' αὐτοῦ λήμψεται (1) καὶ πρόβλημα **διήγησις** αὐτοῦ. Ailleurs au contraire il traduit de façon assez large. C'est ainsi que ערות est traduit εξε]κενωσας en *Hab.* III, 13, ou חבש : περιεσχ[ε]ν en *Jon.* II, 6, ou encore בריאה : στερεον en *Hab.* I, 16.

Je ne puis, dans les limites de cette simple présentation, m'attarder à étudier une à une chaque option de notre réviseur anonyme. Notons plutôt une conclusion intéressante qui semble se dégager du fait qu'il

(1) Le texte hébreu de notre recenseur supprime le *waw* final par haplographie.

ait pris pour base la LXX au lieu de se lancer dans une traduction entièrement personnelle. Il est difficile de ne pas voir là un hommage tacite rendu à la très grande diffusion dont jouissait alors, jusqu'en Palestine, citadelle du Judaïsme orthodoxe, la grande traduction alexandrine. Cela correspond bien à la situation suggérée par Justin et me paraît s'opposer à l'hypothèse d'une diffusion essentiellement chrétienne de la LXX (1). Partout l'Église naissante a dû trouver entre les mains de la Diaspora juive de langue grecque un texte grec essentiellement identique à celui dont l'autorité traditionnelle s'appuyait sur le récit merveilleux que nous rapporte la lettre d'Aristée. Je ne nie évidemment pas que la tradition de ce texte ait pu se nuancer de façon caractéristique en tel ou tel grand centre juif; mais il semble bien que dès le Ier siècle il avait évincé tous les autres targums grecs locaux, s'il y en eut jamais de vraiment consistants.

Essayons d'établir maintenant que cette recension est bien, comme le pretend Justin, l'œuvre de lettrés juifs.

Le fait que le rouleau dont proviennent nos fragments ait été en possession de réfugiés de la Seconde Révolte est déjà un indice, d'autant plus que, dans ce nouvel ensemble de grottes, on a trouvé des fragments hébreux de la Thôrah et des Psaumes ainsi qu'un phylactère parfaitement orthodoxe (avec suppression du Décalogue en signe de raidissement anti-chrétien). Mais ce sont plutôt des arguments de critique interne qui nous apporteront, je pense, une preuve suffisante.

Précisons tout d'abord que, dans ce qui nous a été conservé de son œuvre, le recenseur ne peut être accusé d'avoir agi en polémiste gauchissant les textes. Il a seulement fait de son mieux pour rendre la LXX plus fidèle à l'hébreu qu'il avait sous les yeux. Ce n'est donc pas à des indices doctrinaux que nous reconnaîtrons une main juive. Mais le fait décisif est que Aquila, le grand champion de l'orthodoxie rabbinique, a pris pour base notre recension. Pour établir cela, envisageons les vingt-huit cas où notre recension diffère de la LXX et où, par ailleurs, la leçon d'Aquila nous a été conservée (2) :

L :	*Mic.* I, 4 σαλευθησεται;	II, 7 εισι καλοι;	*ib.* πεπορευνται;
R :	]σον[;	]θυναν;	]ενου;
A :	τακησονται;	αγαθυνουσι;	πορευομενου;

(1) Ceci contre ma concession à Kahle en *RB.*, 1952, p. 191.
(2) Sigles : L = LXX; R = Recension récemment découverte; A = Aquila.

L :	IV, 5 την οδον;	V, 3 αυτων;	℣. 5 δηγματα ;
R :	]ου;	αυτου;	αρχοντας ;
A :	εν ονοματι θεου;	αυτου;	κατεσταμμενους;

L :	℣. 6 τη ταφρω;	℣.7 αγρωστιν;	*Jon.* III, 10 μετενοησεν;
R :	παρα[;	χο[;	]ληθηι;
A :	σειρομασταις;	ποαν;	παρεκληθη;

L :	*Nah.* III, 8 ετοιμασαι μεριδα;	℣. 9 της φυγης;	℣. 14 πλινθον;
R :	μη αγαθυνεις υπ[;	φουδ;	]λινθε.ου;
A :	μητι αγαθυνης υπερ;	φουδ;	πλινθιου;

L :	*Hab.* I, 8 Αραβιας;	℣. 10 εντρυφησει;	*ib.* παιγνια;
R :	]ρας;	]παιξει;	γ[;
A :	εσπερας;	πομπευσει;	γελασμα;

L :	II, 3 εις κενον;	*ib.* υστερηση;	℣. 4 εαν υποστειληται ουκ ευδοκει;
R :	]ιαψευσεται;	στραγ[;	σκοτια ουκ ευθεια;
A :	διαψευσεται;	μελληση;	ιδου νωχελευομενου ουκ ευθεια;

L :	*ib.* εκ πιστεως μου;	℣. 15 σπηλαια;	℣. 17 ασεβεια;	℣ 19 εν αυτω;
R :	εν πιστει αυτου;	]υνην;	αδικια;	εν μεσω αυ- [του;
A :	εν πιστει αυτου;	γυμνωσιν;	αδικια;	in medio [ejus;

L :	III, 9 ποταμων;	℣. 10 λαοι;	℣.14 διανοιξουσι χαλινους ;
R :	]μοι;	ορη;	του σκο.... αι ημας το γαυριαμα;
A :	ποταμους;	ορη;	του διασκορπισαι γαυριαμα;

L :	*ib.* πτωχος λαθρα;	*Soph.* I, 4 ιερέων;	℣. 15 αωριας.
R :	πτωχον κρυφη;	]ρειμ;	αποριας.
A :	πενητα εν αποκρυφω;	τεμενιτων;	συμφορας.

Comme on le voit, Aquila présente des contacts plus ou moins nets avec notre texte en *Mic.* I, 4; II, 7 *a* et *b;* IV, 5; V, 3; *Jon.* III, 10; *Nah.* III, 8, 9, et 14; *Hab.* I, 8 et 10 *b;* II, 3 *a*, 4 *a* et *b*, 17 et 19; III, 10 et 14 *a*, c'est-à-dire 18 fois sur 28. Les témoignages de *Jon.* III, 10; *Nah.* III, 8; *Hab.* II, 3 *a* et III, 14 *a* paraissent particulièrement formels (1). Il semble bien que ce contact ne puisse s'expliquer que par

(1) On notera encore un point de contact entre Aquila et notre recension : l'écriture du tétragramme en lettres « phéniciennes ». A propos d'un petit fragment de Psaumes sur parchemin provenant du Fayyûm et publié par Wessely en 1910 comme faisant partie de la

Une ancienne recension de la LXX des Petits Prophètes.
Hab. I, 14-II, 5 et II, 13-15.

une dépendance d'Aquila a l'égard de notre recension. En effet les inconséquences du recenseur anonyme suggèrent qu'il ne s'agit que d'une ébauche dont l'œuvre d'Aquila présente l'aboutissement achevé. Si l'on voulait au contraire voir dans notre texte une recension tardive partiellement inspirée d'Aquila, il faudrait expliquer premièrement comment ce texte peut se trouver déjà très usagé dans une grotte de la Seconde Révolte, deuxièmement comment il a pu acquérir au cours du Second siècle une assez notable diffusion dans les communautés juives de la Diaspora (cf. *infra*) alors qu'il est beaucoup moins fidèle à l'hébreu que la recension d'Aquila supposée existante, et enfin troisièmement pourquoi au siècle suivant Origène ne le connaît plus comme une version en circulation, mais témoigne par contre de la grande vogue d'Aquila.

L'existence de cette première recension juive nous oblige donc à envisager l'œuvre d'Aquila sous un jour un peu différent : il s'agit d'une surrecension et non d'une traduction originale. Aquila eut le mérite d'étendre à toute la Bible sous une forme infiniment plus systématique un effort de recension qui s'était déjà fait jour dans le judaïsme palestinien avant la Seconde Révolte, très vraisemblablement en liaison avec la réforme intégriste et unificatrice qui suivit 70. Mais certaines initiatives que l'on considérait jusqu'ici comme des originalités d'Aquila doivent être restituées au premier recenseur, ainsi par exemple les créations de mots du genre de ποταμωθησονται reconnu par Rahlfs dans la citation que fait Justin de *Mic.* IV, 1.

Symmaque lui aussi manifeste une connaissance directe de notre recension. Il suffit pour s'en persuader d'envisager plusieurs cas où il reproduit, souvent sans changements, certaines de ses leçons caractéristiques alors qu'Aquila avait éprouvé le besoin de les éliminer. Ainsi en *Mic.* V, 7 il a χορτον (cf. χο[ ); en *Hab.* I, 10 *a* εμπαιξεται (cf.]παιξει); en *Hab.* II, 3 *b* στραγγευσηται (cf. στραγ [); en *Hab.* II, 15 ασχημοσυνην (cf.]υνην); en *Hab.* III, 14 *b* πτωχον κρυφαιως (cf. πτωχον κρυφη). A ces cas s'en ajoutent dix autres où la leçon d'Aquila ne nous est pas connue mais où celle de Symmaque trahit une dépendance très probable à l'égard de notre recension :

L :	*Mic.* II, 8 εξεδειραν;	V, 4 αχρων;	℣. 6 τον Ασσουρ;	*Jon.* II, 5 εξ;
R :	εξεδυσ[;	περατων;	την γην Ασσουρ;	εξ εναντιας;
S :	εξεδυσατε;	περατων;	terram Assur;	απεναντι;

version d'Aquila — attribution contestée par Mercati (*RB.*, 1911, pp. 266-272) — je suggère la possibilité de son appartenance à notre recension dont la diffusion atteignit l'Égypte (cf. *infra*). Le tétragramme y figure aussi en « phénicien ».

L :	*ib.* προς τον ναον τον αγιον σου;	IV, 1 συνεχυθη;
R :	προς ναον αγιον σου;	η..μησεν;
S :	προς ναον αγιων σου;	ηθυμησεν;

L :	*Nah.* III, 7 καταβησεται;	*Hab* I, 9 συντελεια;
R :	αποπ[;	παντα εις;
S :	recedet ;	παντα εις;

L :	*ib.* προσωποις αυτων εξ εναντιας;	III, 10 σκορπιζων;
R :	του προσωπου αυτων καυσων;	εντιναγμα;
S :	του προσωπου αυτων ανεμος καυσων;	εντιναγματα;

En règle générale, Symmaque présente moins d'indépendance qu'Aquila par rapport à notre recension. Lorsqu'il s'en éloigne, c'est pour des motifs littéraires plutôt que littéraux.

Quant à Théodotion, on ne trouve mentionnées que très rarement des leçons caractéristiques de lui pour les passages qui nous intéressent. Cependant, à propos de *Soph.* I, 4 que nous avons mentionné au sujet d'Aquila, il est le seul à avoir conservé la transcription χωμαρειμ de notre recension (Symmaque a βεβηλων). Mais la meilleure façon d'étudier son comportement par rapport à notre texte est de comparer sa recension de Daniel à la longue citation que Justin fait de *Dan.* VII, 9-28 au ch. XXXI du « Dialogue ». Si nous supposons, ce qui est très probable, que Justin témoigne ici encore pour notre recension, nous ne manquerons pas d'être frappés par le fait que Théodotion ne manifeste, ici du moins, aucune connaissance directe de la LXX non-recensée, mais semble avoir pris pour base notre texte. Tout comme Aquila et Symmaque il ne serait donc qu'un surrecenseur et leur base commune serait cette vieille recension palestienne de la fin du Ier siècle. Une telle conclusion suppose, sans doute, que l'on puisse attester par d'autres indices que notre recension a joui, en son temps, d'une diffusion et d'une autorité appréciables.

Si l'on ne veut pas se laisser convaincre par Justin qui se met en scène à Éphèse utilisant notre recension comme un texte reçu par les Juifs du lieu, il nous est loisible de consulter les versions coptes qui nous attesteront qu'elle fut considérée jusqu'en Égypte comme un exact témoin de la « veritas hebraica ». W. Grossouw a prouvé en effet que les très nombreuses assimilations à l'hébreu qui caractérisent le Dodécaprophéton copte (surtout sous sa forme achmimique) ne peuvent s'expliquer adéquatement ni par un recours direct au texte hébraïque, ni par une utilisation constante de l'une ou l'autre des trois grandes versions du Second siècle (1). Si l'on veut établir que c'est de notre recension que les versions coptes tirent tous leurs hébraïsmes, il faut pouvoir prouver qu'aucun de ces hébraïsmes n'est absent de notre recension. J'estime que cette preuve peut être faite. Pour aujourd'hui je me bornerai à relever un certain nombre de coïncidences particulièrement typiques en me servant de l'apparat critique de Grossouw (2). On se rendra compte aisément que notre recension est le seul témoin grec aujourd'hui connu qui groupe toutes ces leçons (3) :

Mic.	IV,	6	ην εκα[κωσα (cf. Grossouw p. 45 n. 3).
	V,	6	εν παρα[ξιφισιν
	V,	7^{a}	χο[ρτον
Jon.	II,	6^{f}	η ελος περιεσχεν την κεφαλην μου
	IV,	1	η[θυ]μησεν
Nah.	III,	7^{a}	αποπ[ηδησεται
Hab.	I,	9^{b}	]του προσωπου αυτων καυσων
	I,	17	εκκεν]ωσει μαχαιραν αυτου
	II,	3^{d}	ενφανησετ[...]ιαψευσεται (cf. Gr. p. 68 n. 3)
	II,	14^{d}	θαλασσ[
	II,	15^{d}	ασχημοσ]υνην
	III,	13^{b}	κε]φ[αλ]η εξ οικου ασεβ[
	III,	13^{e}	εξε]κενωσας θεμελιους
Soph.	II,	10	επι λαον κυριου

Mais ce n'est pas seulement en Egypte, patrie de la LXX, que notre recension a pris pied. Nous pouvons peut-être suivre sa trace jusqu'en Grèce (ce qui rendrait toute la vraisemblance désirable à l'attestation par Justin de sa présence à Éphèse). On sait en effet, par le témoignage d'Origène lui-même (4), que ce fut « à Nicopolis près d'Actium » que la Quinta fut découverte. Or les quatre seules variantes connues de la

(1) *The Coptic Versions of the Minor Prophets*. Rome, Pontifical Biblical Institute, 1938, pp. 112 sq.

(2) *Op. cit.*, pp. 18-97. Lorsque Gr. a plusieurs notes critiques sur un même verset, je les distingue par *a*, *b*, *c*...

(3) Notons que l'hypothèse d'une dépendance des versions coptes à l'égard de notre recension est confirmée par la chronologie. On admet en effet généralement que l'origine des versions coptes est à chercher au cours du IIe siècle. Or c'est justement à cette époque que se situe la plus large diffusion de la recension palestinienne. Reste a préciser si le milieu copte où se fit la traduction des Petits Prophètes était déjà purement et simplement chrétien ou s'il ne gardait pas encore quelque attache au judaïsme.

(4) Voir la discussion des textes d'Origène et d'Eusèbe dans *The Cairo Geniza* de P. Kahle, pp. 161 sqq.

Quinta qui recoupent le contenu de nos fragments leur sont substantiellement identiques :

Q : *Mic.* v, 5 principes hominum; *ib.* εν παραξιφισιν
R : αρχοντας ανθρωπων; εν παρα[

Q : *Hab.* ii, 15 ignominias eorum; iii, 13 evacuasti fundamentum
R : ασχημοσ]υνην αυ[τω]ν; εξε]κενωσας θεμελιους

Q : usque ad collum sela.
R : εως τραχ[ηλου] σελε.

Les très légères variantes qui, dans les deux derniers exemples, distinguent le texte de nos fragments de la Quinta telle qu'elle est citée par Jérôme n'excèdent pas les divergences que l'on est en droit d'attendre à l'intérieur de la tradition manuscrite d'un même texte. Si l'on veut encore un argument convergent pour l'identification de notre recension avec la Quinta d'Origène (1), on remarquera que, selon les statistiques de Grossouw (2), les hébraïsmes des versions coptes concordent douze fois de façon indubitable avec des leçons de la Quinta et ne s'y opposent *jamais* formellement, alors qu'il leur arrive de contredire quatre fois Théodotion, onze fois Aquila et onze fois Symmaque.

Je ne voudrais pas grossir l'importance de cette recension juive de la fin du Premier siècle. Il ne s'agit, répétons-le, que d'une première tentative encore tâtonnante et pleine d'illogismes, certainement limitée à quelques livres de la Bible. Il n'est pas étonnant que les grandes recensions du Second siècle l'aient entièrement éclipsée et qu'au début du siècle suivant Origène ait dû déjà, comme nous aujourd'hui, la « redécouvrir ». Elle joua cependant en son temps un rôle appréciable : celui d'amorcer l'œuvre de révision de la LXX qui allait être la grande tâche des générations qui suivirent. Le travail de l'ancêtre anonyme d'Aquila et d'Origène mérite donc une publication que nous espérons pouvoir aborder sans trop tarder. De cette publication nous pouvons attendre un triple témoignage : premièrement sur l'état du texte de base de la LXX, deuxièmement sur l'état du texte hébreu utilisé par le recenseur, troisièmement sur l'exacte originalité de chacun des trois

(1) Je parle ici de la Quinta telle qu'elle est citée par Jérôme et je laisse de côté la question délicate des citations attribuées à la Quinta par le second glossateur marginal du *codex Barberini*... qui mériterait une étude spéciale.
(2) *Op. cit.*, p. 112.

grands recenseurs du Second siècle. Ce témoignage se trouvera encore élargi si on accepte la quadruple identification que nous proposons aujourd'hui : premièrement avec le texte cité par Justin, deuxièmement avec la base commune d'Aquila, Symmaque et Théodotion, troisièmement avec la source des hébraïsmes des versions coptes, et quatrièmement avec la Quinta d'Origène. Tant que le texte n'est pas édité il ne peut s'agir que de suggestions. Elles appelleront certainement telles ou telles nuances notables, mais j'espère qu'elles pourront servir au moins d'hypothèses de recherche .

Jérusalem, 19 septembre 1952. D. BARTHÉLEMY, O. P.

Appendice :

Une des parties les mieux conservées de notre recension portant sur les deux premiers chapitres d'Habacuc pour lesquels nous nous trouvons posséder deux textes hébraïques assez différents : celui du *Pésher* de Qumrân (Q pH) et celui de la Bible massorétique (T. M.), voici un très bref apparat critique où j'ai seulement relevé les appuis donnés par la Septante originale (LXX) et sa recension palestinienne (Rec), lorsque leurs témoignages respectifs les départagent nettement, aux deux formes susdites du texte hébraïque. Nombre de cas plus complexes demanderaient toute une discussion. Dans cet aperçu provisoire, je les ai délibérément omis.

	T.M.		QpH	
I, 8	יבאו	: Rec	om.)	: LXX
I, 17	העל כן	: Rec	על כן	: LXX
ibid.	חרמו	: LXX	חרבו	: Rec
II, 2	קורא	: Rec	הקורא	: LXX
II, 6	ויאמר	: Rec	ויומרו	: LXX
ibid.	עליו	: Rec	עלו	: LXX
II, 8	ישלוך	: LXX	וישלוכה	: Rec
II, 19	דומם	: Rec	רומה	: LXX

En six cas sur huit nous trouvons donc la recension palestinienne aux côtés du T. M, tandis que la LXX originale témoignait pour le texte de Qumrân. Cela semble indiquer que la date de 70 ap. J.-C. marque une étape importante dans le processus de recension du texte hébreu, ce que confirme pleinement une comparaison des textes bibliques de la Seconde Révolte avec ceux de Qumrân.

CHAPTER FIVE

The Textual Criticism of the Old Testament*

HARRY M. ORLINSKY

THE PAST SEVERAL DECADES have witnessed a flowering of Old Testament research under the influence largely of archaeological discovery. The Biblical lands, Iraq, Syria, Lebanon, Palestine, and Egypt, coming as they did under the control of England and France, became fertile ground for the rediscovery by excavation of the Fertile Crescent of old. And though the economy and social structure of the various parts of the Near East—as of the European powers—began to change in the twenties, thirties, and forties, so that England and France have been all but replaced by the authority of the United States and the Soviet Union, and such new political groupings as the United Arab Republic, the Hashemite Kingdom of Jordan, and Israel have come into being, with even the immediate end not yet in sight, enough archaeological work is still going on—in Israel more than in Transjordan and Iraq—to satisfy the desires of Biblical scholars, if not the needs of specialists in Biblical archaeology.

At about the same time, however, a new trend began to make itself felt in higher education on both sides of the Atlantic Ocean: the humanities and the social sciences began to give way to the applied sciences. The curricula of high schools and colleges generally became increasingly bereft of Latin and Greek and grammar—shades of the days when a public school was sometimes called Latin school or grammar school!

The consequences for the textual criticism of the Old Testament were soon felt. Here, on the one hand, the written and unwritten documents un-

* The second section of this article was published in *Journal of Biblical Literature* (March 1959), pp. 26–33, under the title of "Qumran and the Present State of Old Testament Text Studies: the Septuagint Text" © 1959, Society of Biblical Literature and Exegesis.

Reprinted from *The Bible and the Ancient Near East* [Festschrift W. F. Albright]. Garden City, New York. 1961.

covered by archaeology were attracting the attention of the students of the Biblical world; and there, on the other, students of this same field of research found themselves more and more unable to handle the textual criticism of the Hebrew Bible, for they were entering and leaving their seminaries and Semitics departments with less direct knowledge of Hebrew, Aramaic, Greek, and Latin than the students of earlier decades. We have gone a long way since Ezra Stiles, president of Yale University, himself taught the freshman and other classes Hebrew, and in 1781 delivered his commencement address in Hebrew.[1] To such a low state has our discipline fallen that among the several volumes that have appeared during the past few decades constituting surveys of Old Testament research, virtually the only one that contained a chapter on "The Textual Criticism of the Old Testament" was *The Old Testament and Modern Study* (Oxford, 1951),[2] pp. 238 ff., ably contributed by D. Winton Thomas (with useful bibliography in the footnotes and on pp. 259–63).[3]

There was also a subjective factor that, quite unintentionally, helped to bring down the textual criticism of the Old Testament to its present low level. Back in 1905–6 Rudolf Kittel brought out *Biblia Hebraica*², superseding *Textus Hebraici emendationes quibus in Vetere Testamento Neerlandice vertendo,* ed. H. Oort (usi sunt A. Kuenen, I. Hooykaas, W. H. Kosters, H. Oort).[4] The *apparatus criticus* in *BH*² was soon recognized, to quote from that great master, S. R. Driver (*Notes on . . . Samuel*², 1913, "Introduction," p. xxxv, n. 6), as containing "the best collection both of variants from the versions and of conjectural emendations." Most unfortunately, however, scholars began to regard this apparatus as more sacred and authoritative than the preserved Masoretic text itself: between the preserved reading and its emended form in *BH*², students of the Bible tended to accept the latter. They ignored the vigorous *caveat* in Driver (ibid.), "but in the acceptance of both variants and emendations [in *BH*²—to which Driver contributed the notes for Deuteronomy], considerable discrimination must be exercised."

For this is the crux of the matter. The convenient collection of notes in *BH*² (save Driver's)—and the situation was not substantially improved in *BH*³ (1937)—in "nearly every line . . . swarms with errors of commission and omission, as regards both the primary and the secondary versions."[5]

I

It took a bit of time for scholarship to express publicly its discontent with *BH*. In 1928 C. C. Torrey made this sweeping attack (*The Second Isaiah,* New York, pp. 214 f.): "The apparatus of Kittel's *Biblia Hebraica* contains very many readings erroneously supposed to be attested by the Greek version, readings gathered blindly from the commentaries. . . ." A sober scholar such as J. A. Montgomery, in working up *The International Critical Commentary on the Book of Daniel* (1927), criticized and bypassed the apparatus in *BH,* and went directly to the manuscripts and editions of the Hebrew text and the versions of it, both the primary and the secondary.[6]

Following up his previous studies, especially the "Specimen of a New Edition of the Greek Joshua,"[7] with his erudite and monumental reconstruction of *The Book of Joshua in Greek* (Paris, 1931—),[8] Max L. Margolis made it clear enough not only that the careful scholar should ignore the data in *BH* but also that he must wherever possible check the readings of the Septuagint in H. B. Swete's editions, and even the apparatus in the Larger Cambridge Septuagint[9]; to rely on the data in *BH* is to seek support from the "bruised reed" made proverbial by Isaiah.

Joseph Ziegler, the expert editor of Septuagint texts, criticized *BH*'s apparatus very severely. In preparing his model edition of the Septuagint of the Minor Prophets in the Göttingen series, Ziegler had occasion to check the use of the Septuagintal material in *BH*³. At the end of his "Kritische Bemerkungen zur Verwendung der Septuaginta im Zwölfprophetenbuch der Biblia Hebraica von Kittel,"[10] Ziegler wrote, "Bei einer Neuausgabe der Biblia Hebraica des Dodekapropheton muss das gesamte G-material, wie es die eben erschienene Göttinger Septuaginta-Ausgabe vorlegt, neu bearbeitet werden."

The present writer has long been especially critical of *BH*'s so-called *apparatus criticus.* Ever since he began serious work on his doctoral dissertation, "Studies in the Septuagint of the Book of Job," and published his first article as a result of it,[11] there was scarcely a line in the apparatus, whenever he had occasion to examine it, that he did not find in error, be it in commission or in omission. Thus in 1944, in an extensive article on "The Hebrew Root *ŠKB*" (*JBL* 63, pp. 19–44), he wrote (p. 33), "We note once more how unreliable and inadequate is the *apparatus criticus* for most of the books in Kittel's *BH*³ . . . Rudolf Kittel, whose forte was not textual criticism. . . ," and in n. 18 (ibid.) he listed seven other articles in which he had taken *BH* to task at numerous points.

Six years later, in the first of a number of articles on the complete Isaiah scroll and some of the Biblical fragments among the Dead Sea scrolls,[12] he wrote, ". . . it has long been my contention that no single publication has had such detrimental effect on the lower textual criticism of the Hebrew Bible as Kittel's *Biblia Hebraica*²·³; cf. . . . when M. Burrows' edition of the St. Mark's Isaiah scroll will appear, the chances are that utter confusion will be introduced in the revived study of the Hebrew text of Isaiah by those who will use Kittel's convenient collection of what amounts to *Addenda et Corrigenda.* . . . The careful scholar will distrust these footnotes, and go to the sources whence they are alleged to derive" (p. 153, n. 5). By 1953 it was, unfortunately, possible to state,[13] "There can be little satisfaction in the knowledge that even my worst fears have been exceeded. . . . One doesn't know which is more treacherous for those who do not study critically the data at their source, the text of SM [St. Mark's Isaiah scroll] or the so-called critical apparatus in Kittel. . . ." (pp. 330, 340). At one point, dealing with sing. *yāḵol* in Isaiah 7:1 vs. the plur. *yāḵ*^{e}*lū* in the Isaiah scroll, he wrote (p. 332, § 5), "Unbelievable as it may seem . . . Kittel . . . emended the plural *yāḵ*^{e}*lū* in II Ki. 16.5 into the singular . . . on the basis of the sing. in MT of Isa. 7.1, having forgotten that he had emended the sing. in the Isaiah passage into the plur., on the basis of the plur. in the Kings passage! Verily the right hand of Kittel in Isaiah did not know what the left hand in Kings was doing." This is how "textual criticism" was made to support the reading in the scroll as the original, as against the reading in the Masoretic text.[14]

In his fine survey of "Septuagintal Studies in the Mid-Century,"[15] Peter Katz wrote *inter alia* of how "Duhm and his school"[16] misused Lagarde's understanding of the textual criticism of the Masoretic and Septuagint texts, so that "One may say with truth: Never was the LXX more used and less studied! Unfortunately much of this misuse survives in *BH*^{3}. I have long given up collecting instances. Ziegler, after ten pages of corrections from the Minor Prophets alone, rightly states that all the references to G must be rechecked. H. M. Orlinsky, who comes back to this point time and again, is not very far from the truth when he says that not a single line in the apparatus of *BH*^{3} in free from mistakes regarding G. . . ."

After all this,[17] it seems unbelievable that instead of scrapping the apparatus in *BH*^{3} and beginning to prepare the groundwork for a new apparatus, one that could claim scholarly respect for reliability and comprehensiveness, the Privilegierte Württembergische Bibelanstalt decided to sponsor a work that would help the student understand and accept the apparatus in *BH*^{3}! In 1951 it published E. Würthwein, *Der Text des alten Testaments, eine Einführung in die Biblia Hebraica von Rudolf Kittel,* and in 1957 an English version of it (translation by P. R. Ackroyd), *The Text of the Old Testament, an Introduction to Kittel-Kahle*[sic!]*'s Biblia Hebraica.* The German version had been criticized severely by a reviewer[18] as follows: "Würthwein furthermore identifies himself so completely with *BH*^{3} that he fails to realize that serious misgivings have been felt about the app. crit. of this edition." Würthwein rejected this devastating criticism ("Foreword to the English Edition," p. XI) as "clearly a misunderstanding," for he had added a special chapter (IV) on "Textual Criticism" which, he claimed, included a criticism of the principles of textual criticism in *BH*^{3} and encouraged "its intelligent and at the same time *critical* use." Yet the simple fact is "that not a single work critical of *BH*^{3} is referred to in Chapter IV, and no one of the three introductory paragraphs (A, B, C) and eight sections warns the student of the misleading and harmful character of the apparatus in *BH*^{3}."[19] The chapter, brief as it is (thirteen pages), can but mislead and harm the unwary student; the scholar certainly does not need to resort to it.

II[20]

The direct effects of the largely uncritical reliance on *BH* can be observed in the study of the Biblical fragments among the Dead Sea scrolls, and these effects, to this writer, are little short of depressing—"depressing" because the average Biblical scholar knows about the textual criticism of the Dead Sea scrolls, and more especially about the relationship between the Septuagint (hereinafter LXX) and the Biblical texts among the scrolls, not what he has learned from a direct study of the Hebrew and LXX texts, nor even for the most part from what other scholars who have published analyses of these texts learned from a direct study, but from what these published analyses derived from the critical apparatus in Kittel's *BH*. Let me cite two illustrations of the point.

In Isaiah 49:17 the Masoretic text (hereinafter MT) of the Hebrew Bible tells us that the prophet assures his fellow Judean exiles in Babylonia that מִהֲרוּ בָּנָיִךְ מְהָרְסַיִךְ וּמַחֲרִבַיִךְ מִמֵּךְ יֵצֵאוּ, "Your sons will hasten, your destroyers and those who laid you waste will depart from you." Kittel's note urges the reader to emend MT בָּנָיִךְ "your sons" to בֹּנַיִךְ "your builders," with Codex Petropolitanus, the LXX, Vulgate, Targum, and Arabic ("l c Var^{P} (G) V T (A) בֹּנַיִךְ"). So when the Isaiah scroll came along with the reading בוניך (=בּוֹנַיִךְ) "your builders," it was natural for scholars to accept the scroll's reading, fortified by the data in Kittel, as against the Masoretic reading. Disregarding the relative merits of the two readings in the context,[21] a direct consultation of the sources gave us this picture: (1) Codex Petropolitanus (A.D. 916) does not read בֹּנַיִךְ "your builders" but בָּנָיִךְ "your sons," exactly as MT does. (2) The Arabic evidence for בֹּנַיִךְ "your builders" is no independent evidence whatever; for the Arabic is but a secondary version that helps to prove that the LXX text from which it derived read "your builders." It has no bearing at all on the original Hebrew text. (3) There are, in reality, two traditions in the Targum, not one as claimed by Kittel; one reads "your builders" and the other "your sons." (4) Kittel erred grievously in not telling the reader that two of the Minor Versions, Theodotion and Aquila, read "your builders," whereas a third, Symmachus, read "your sons." These versions are far more important than, say, the Vulgate. Regardless of whether Masoretic "your sons" or the scroll's "your builders" is the original reading, how could scholars decide in favor of the scroll's reading, and of what value was their decision, when the data that they employed consisted of what Kittel offered them?

Or take, as the second case in point, Isaiah 15:9. The prophet, in delivering himself of "The Burden of Moab," enumerates a number of places that will be laid waste, among them "Dimon." But "Dimon" is unknown otherwise, and the Vulgate reads the well-known place name "Dibon." So when the Isaiah scroll exhibited "Dibon" in place of MT "Dimon," some scholars took one look at Kittel's reference to the Vulgate ("al loc דיבון

[V]") and pronounced the scroll's "Dibon" as the original reading, MT "Dimon" being but a corruption of it. But the evidence is not limited to the Vulgate and our scroll. (1) All the earlier witnesses to the LXX (the Chester Beatty Papyrus, Codices Sinaiticus, Vaticanus, Alexandrinus, and the like), translation of the LXX into Bohairic and the Syro-Hexapla, the Targum, all three major Minor Versions (Theodotion, Aquila, Symmachus), the *Hebraios* in Origen's Hexapla—all these early witnesses testify to MT "Dimon." (2) Some time after the turn of the era, "Dibon" came into being alongside "Dimon"; thus such fourth-fifth century sources as Eusebius (*Onomastica Sacra*), the Vulgate, and Codex Venetus, and a number of tenth-eleventh century MSS of the LXX, and the commentary by Basil the Great, read "Dibon." To single out Vulgate "Dibon," as Kittel did, and to ignore all the other textual data and their chronological sequence, is but to make a farce of the textual criticism of the Hebrew Bible and the Isaiah scroll. Yet some scholars did exactly that when the scroll's reading "Dibon" came to light.[22]

But let us get to the Isaiah scroll as a whole, in relation to the LXX text. As is well known, scholars generally tended in the first years after the scroll's appearance to find numerous instances where the reading in the scroll agreed with that found in the LXX, as against the reading preserved in the so-called MT. This was the tenor of the otherwise sober survey article on the scrolls by W. Baumgartner in 1951, in *Theologische Rundschau.* Virtually no scholar bothered to take up these alleged instances in detail, in part because they were blinded by the dazzling antiquity of the scroll, and in part—as mentioned previously—because scholars generally had ceased to work at the discipline of lower textual criticism after World War I and could no longer handle it properly. Your present lecturer was almost the only one who devoted himself to a detailed analysis of a number of these instances. He found most of them lacking all justification, and none convincing. These studies appeared from 1950 to 1954. Interestingly, the tidal wave of scholarly and public opinion, according to which there could be no doubt of both the great antiquity of the scrolls and their superiority to any other existing texts, was such that the scholarly literature on the Isaiah scroll and the LXX largely ignored these caveats, that is to say, it did not attempt to demonstrate the argumentation erroneous, or even to refer to it, but contented itself with making reference to those who had claimed scroll-LXX identification, and let it go at that.[23]

By 1953–54 this attitude had begun to change. Scholars now, at last, were less inclined to identify the Isaiah scroll with the LXX; indeed, the scroll's text was rapidly becoming something of a major disappointment. Thus in October 1954, Professor James Muilenburg published in *BASOR* (No. 135) "Fragments of another Qumran Isaiah Scroll," containing parts of approximately from 12:5 to 13:16 and from 22:13 to 23:6, and he stated flatly (p. 32), ". . . 4Q nowhere diverges in favor of the LXX. This is by no means a unique situation, for many other texts follow the Masoretic tradition. . . ." This was the tenor, too, of Frank M. Cross's article in *The Christian Century,* in August 1955—though I should not have minded it one bit if Muilenburg and Cross had referred specifically to those articles on the scroll and the LXX that had led them to turn their backs on the opinion that had prevailed during the preceding few years.

It was not merely the Isaiah scroll, however, that was involved in this changing attitude. In 1953 Karl Elliger, in the most detailed study of the Biblical text of the Habakkuk scroll (*Studien zum Habakuk-Kommentar vom Toten Meer*), reached the same conclusion. In addition, the new Biblical texts, fragmentary as they were, tended to confirm this conclusion. Thus in 1952, J. T. Milik published in *Revue biblique* "Fragments d'un Midrash de Michée dans les Manuscrits de Qumran," and the editor claimed agreement at two points between the Qumran text and the LXX, as against MT. However, in one instance, at Micah 1:3, he was misled by the critical note in Kittel's *BH*³.[24] Had he consulted, say, Ziegler's critical (Göttingen) edition of the LXX of the minor prophets, he would have learned that the LXX did not unequivocally support the scroll's text, but constituted an inner-Greek problem. In the second instance, also in 1:3, involving the scroll's במו]תי האר[ץ and LXX ἐπὶ τὰ ὕψη τῆς γῆς, as against MT בָּמֳתֵי אָרֶץ, without the definite article, the editor overlooked the fact that במתי ארץ is precisely the idiom elsewhere in the Bible (in Deuteronomy, Isaiah, and Amos), analogous to במתי עָב in Isaiah, and to במתי יָם in Job—all without the definite article, as befits ancient Hebrew poetry—and that in every one of these half-dozen instances the LXX employed the definite article—simply because that was Greek idiom, exactly as all our English versions employ the definite article, "the *bamoth* of *the* earth," or "of *the* cloud," or "of *the* sea."[25]

The same general situation is true also of "A Qoheleth Scroll from Qumran" covering parts of chapters 5–7, published in *BASOR* in October 1954 (No. 135, 20–27). The editor, J. Muilenburg, found a single instance where a reading in the scroll coincided with the LXX against the MT correspondent. I myself found reason to believe that even in this case the LXX did not justify a reading in its Hebrew *Vorlage* that agreed with that of the scroll; perhaps a decision can be reached only after other parts of this scroll should come to light.[26]

There are other fragments that might be referred to here, e.g., the "Fragment of the 'Song of Moses' (Deuteronomy 32)," published by Father Skehan in *BASOR,* December 1954 (No. 136, 12–15). But since I should like to get on to the most significant Biblical text among the scrolls, that of Samuel, I shall content myself here with quoting from pp. 150–53 of Father Skehan's published paper read at the International Congress for OT Studies at Strasbourg, in 1956.[27] "For Isaias, the complete scroll from cave 1 remains textually the most interesting document, and there is nothing among the 13 manuscripts of cave 4 which is recensionally different from the received consonantal text, or yields improved readings in any significant degree. . . . Now, 1QIsa^a and the LXX of Isaias are not recensionally connected, though they have an occasional reading in common; but they are mutually illustrative, because the cave 1 manuscript gives us, for the first time in Hebrew, the kind of glossed and reworked manuscript that the LXX prototype must have been. . . . It has been in conjunction with the text of Isaias that the writer has examined to some extent the likely effects of the extrabiblical documents at Qumran in providing us with text-critical materials for the OT itself . . . the conclusion thus far is largely negative: allusions and *lemmata* in the extrabiblical documents may yield some points of detail, but will not alter our understanding of the textual history of the book. . . ."

It is in dealing with the Samuel text published by Cross in *BASOR*, December 1953 (No. 132, 15–26), that we come to something significant in the *Uberlieferungsgeschichte* of the Hebrew text in relation to the LXX. Back in 1871 Julius Wellhausen, in my judgment the most brilliant and penetrating textual critic of the OT, wrote the finest analysis of the Hebrew and Greek texts of Samuel; and several decades later, S. R. Driver wrote the most balanced study, his model commentary, *Notes on the Hebrew Text . . . of Samuel*. These two constitute the best pair of commentaries in our field. That the MT of Samuel is incomplete and difficult has long been recognized. That the LXX text has what might be called "addenda et corrigenda" to the MT has generally been recognized too—as may be seen from Driver's widely used and followed commentary, where so many of Wellhausen's insights were accepted. The new scroll text has so far been published only in small part, so small, as a matter of fact, that I for one have been most hesitant and reluctant to accept it as a basis for any positive statement, or even for a negative conclusion.[28] After all, photostatic reproduction of parts of a total of twenty-three verses in the first two chapters of I Samuel do not yet justify conclusions about the character of the Hebrew text of the scroll of all 1506 verses in I and II Samuel. We all remember the embarrassment of Univac in the national elections a few years ago, when—on the basis of incomplete returns—it elected the "wrong" (or should I say, the "right") man for the presidency. But I have recently made a closer study of these twenty-three verses, and I can but agree with Cross that the scroll's text may well be of considerable importance in the reconstruction of the history of the MT of Samuel, as well as help to determine the character of the LXX translation of Samuel and the kind of Hebrew *Vorlage* from which it derived. If I say "may well be" instead of "will be," it is merely because I have not seen the unpublished Samuel material to which Cross makes reference, most recently in his book on *The Ancient Library of Qumran and Modern Biblical Studies*.

Another Biblical text that may be of great importance for LXX studies is the bit of a fragment of Jeremiah, described by Cross in his book just mentioned. As is well known, the LXX text of Jeremiah and Job are respectively one eighth and one sixth shorter than MT. I first began to work on the problem in Job almost 25 years ago, and I had concluded that the

LXX translator did not curtail a Hebrew text that coincided in length with MT, but had a shorter Hebrew *Vorlage* before him.[29] Whether this shorter Hebrew version is closer to the original than the longer MT, I have as yet not reached any definite conclusion. The problem in Jeremiah has not yet received competent study. I have a student who has just begun to work on the problem; he is currently devoting himself to trying to comprehend the character of the LXX of Jeremiah. Now in the case of Chapter 10, vss. 5–10 of the MT, the LXX lacks vss. 6–8 and 10, and reads vs. 5 after vs. 8. It is precisely this sequence that is present in the Jeremiah fragment. And, finally, Cross has noted that, "The longer recension is also present at Qumran."[30]

A few LXX fragments have been discovered in Qumran, of leather and papyrus, containing parts of verses in Leviticus 2–5 and 26; and in Numbers 3 and 4; and parts of the Minor Prophets.[31] However, since these materials have as yet received but preliminary study it is best not to take them up at this point. But this much may be said: the LXX translation, no less than the MT itself, will have gained very considerable respect as a result of the Qumran discoveries in those circles where it has long—overlong—been necessary. And the LXX translators will no longer be blamed for dealing promiscuously with their Hebrew *Vorlagen;* it is to their *Vorlagen* that we shall have to go, and it is their *Vorlagen* that will have to be compared with the preserved MT. This is true not only of anthropomorphisms and other theological matters, but even of minor and non-tendentious items.[32]

This much, too, may be said. The theory of one original Greek translation of each of the various books of the Hebrew Bible, which in turn gave rise to the various recensions, the theory which has long been associated with Lagarde, Rahlfs, Montgomery, and especially Margolis, has been demonstrated beyond reasonable doubt by the Hebrew and Greek materials from Qumran. Those who have opposed this theory, notably Kahle, have received nothing but opposition from the Dead Sea scrolls.[33]

In fine, it is clear that much work remains to be done by the textual critic of the Hebrew Bible and its LXX version and recensions—although more, and more extensive, Biblical texts from Qumran will first have to be made available to the scholar for a broad enough base to work on. It is something worth looking forward to.

III

While the present essay was being written there appeared an article by P. Wernberg-Møller, "Studies in the Defective Spellings in the Isaiah-Scroll of St. Mark's Monastery."[34] It may be worth-while to analyze this article with special reference to the problem of methodology.

The author begins with the assumption that wherever the scroll failed to use the defective spelling, it may well have been due to a pronunciation that differed from that preserved in the Masoretic text. He then lists some twoscore instances (§ III, pp. 254 ff.) where, in his judgment, the LXX rendering coincided with, and demonstrated, the pronunciation of the word in question in the scroll. We shall deal here with the first two of these instances.

The author has noted (p. 254) that since the MT at 1:29 reads מֵאֵילִים as against the scroll's מאלים, the LXX's ἐπὶ τοῖς εἰδώλοις "shows that מאלים of 1QIsa[a] means 'of the gods,' and not 'of the terebinths,' as MT has it. Symmachus follows MT." But let us delve into the matter a little more closely.

First of all, it is only a conclusion hastily reached that εἴδωλον "idol; false god" in the LXX of Isaiah, or anywhere else in the Bible, represents אֵל(ים) "god(s)." Indeed, the combination εἴδωλον/אֵלִים occurs only here and in Isaiah 57:5 in the entire LXX.[35] All that one has to do to prove this conclusion wrong is to run down every occurrence of אל(ים) "god(s)" in Isaiah (e.g., *via* Mandelkern's *Concordance,* pp. 85c–86c) as reproduced in the LXX—and he will find that, whether the Hebrew term is used for "God" or for "god(s), idol(s)," the Greek equivalent is invariably a form of θεός. On the other hand, our אילים is clearly (as elsewhere, e.g., Hosea 4:13) a "terebinth" used in idolatrous worship, i.e., an idol, and it is paralleled by גַּנּוֹת—exactly as in the identical sort of passage, Isaiah 57:5 (not mentioned by our author), אֵלִים//תַּחַת כָּל־עֵץ רַעֲנָן. Accordingly, LXX "idols" represents an excellent interpretation of Masoretic אֵ(י)לִים[36] (so also, e.g., Targum, Symmachus, Aquila, Rashi, Malbim, H. Ewald, Franz Delitzsch, B. Duhm, K. Marti, J. Skinner, G. H. Box, G. B. Gray, O. Procksch, E. J. Kissane; and others)—what else could א(י)לים mean here? Indeed, our author would scarcely have included 1:29 in his article had he consulted J. F. Schleusner's *Novus Thesaurus Philologico-Criticus sive Lexicon in LXX et reliquos Interpretes Graecos ac Scriptores Apocryphos Veteris Testamenti* (5 vols., Lipsiae, 1820),[37] *s.* ειδωλον (Vol. II, p. 246), "אילים:אלים, plur. ex אֵלָה, *querceta, in quibus idola colebantur,* ut adeo per metonymian etiam *ipsa idola* significare possit. Ies. I, 29, LVII, 5. Male nonnulli statuunt, LXX utrobique legisse צְלָמִים. . . ."[38] As to the scroll's מאלים, it should teach the student not to rely on the orthography of that idiosyncratic manuscript, to the point where a different pronunciation (and morphology) or a different interpretation is glibly achieved and then readily identified with the LXX's Hebrew *Vorlage.*[39]

In his second case in point (pp. 254 f.), our author advances the opinion that 1QIsa[a] ונשא (פנים) and LXX καὶ θαυμαστὸν (σύμβουλον) and καὶ τοὺς (τὰ πρόσωπα) θαυμάζοντας in 3:3 and 9:14 point to אָנֹשֵׂא (פנים) for Masoretic וּנְשׂוּא (פנים)—for "In neither of the two parts of 1QIsa[a] can we imagine a passive participle Qal [נשוא] spelt defectively." However, since no Hebrew form וְנָשָׂא makes any sense in context, our author has to fall back on the theory that "the Greek translator connected [assumed נָשָׂא] with Aramaic נְפָא 'wonder'. . . ."

1: First of all, our author has failed altogether to note that *θαυμαστὸν σύμβουλον* in 3:3 (unlike the LXX reading in 9:14) does not correspond to ונשא פנים; *συμβουλος* represents וְיוֹעֵץ immediately following (so already Schleusner, *s.v.* [v, 159]; *θαυμ. συμβ.* is Aquila's rendering of פֶּלֶא יוֹעֵץ in 9:5, cf. J. Reider *JQR,* 4 [1913–14], p. 592).[40] In his study of *The Septuagint Version of Isaiah* (p. 23 and n. 21), I. L. Seeligmann followed up the discussions and proposed solutions of LXX *θαυμάζειν πρόσωπον* by G. Bertram (*Theologisches Wörterbuch zum Neuen Testament* 3 [1938], pp. 29 f.), Schleusner (*s. θαυμαστός*/נשוא פנים, III, 47), and Ziegler (*Untersuchungen zur Septuaginta des Buches Isaias* [*Alttestamentliche Abhandlungen,* XII, 3; 1934], p. 136), with one of his own.[41]

2: But regardless of *σύμβουλον,* there is no reason to vocalize ונשא as anything but the passive participle Qal because of LXX *θαυμαστός*. Is alleged נִשָּׂא more, or less, "passive" than נָשׂוּא? And would נִשָּׂא (פנים) have to be assumed also in II Kings 5:1 because of LXX *τεθαυμασμένος* (. . . *πρόσωπον*)—incidentally also Theodotion's rendering in our 3:3?[42]

3: Furthermore, what is the evidence that Aramaic נִפָּא "wonder" was involved? Indeed, the Targum reproduced נְשׂוּא (פנים) by נְסִיב (אַפִּין) in 3:3; 9:14; II Kings 5:1; סְבִיר in Job 22:8. And where, in Isaiah, is alleged נִפָּא "wonder" used in the Targum even for root פלא?

4: Moreover, our author has erred in restricting LXX *θαυμάζω/θαυμαστός* to "wonder." One has but to consult the Hebrew equivalents for the various forms of this Greek root (conveniently in Schleusner, III, 45–48; Hatch-Redpath, I, 626–27), or the various translations of this root in the Old Latin and other daughter versions, and he will realize at once that it is quite unnecessary to look for the meaning "wonder" for a root resembling Hebrew נשא in some Semitic language. Thus in Leviticus 19:15 (לֹא תִשָּׂא פְנֵי־דָל) וְלֹא תֶהְדַּר פְּנֵי (גָדוֹל) was reproduced (*οὐ λήμψῃ πρόσωπον πτωχοῦ*) *οὐδὲ θαυμάσεις πρόσωπον* (*δυνάστου*); cf., e.g., *ἐθαύμασα* (*σου τὸ π.*) for נָשָׂאתִי (פָנֶיךָ) in Genesis 19:21. In Job 22:8 *ἐθαύμασας* (*δέ τινων*) *πρόσωπον* (or, —*πα*), for נְשׂוּא פָנִים, was translated in the Old Latin (ed. P. de Lagarde, *Mittheilungen,* II [Goettingen, 1897], pp. 189 ff.) (*aut*) *miratus es personam* (*aliquorum*); in 32:22, *θαυμάσαι π.* (either for אֲכַנֶּה in v. 22 or [with E. Dhorme, *Le Livre de Job* (Paris, 1926), ad loc.] for [פְּנֵי אִישׁ] נִשָּׂא in v. 21) was reproduced (*non enim scio*) *mirari faciem;* and in 34:19 *θαυμασθῆναι π.* was rendered *admirari facies* (*eorum*). In all these cases, "respect, admire," or the like, suits the context admirably.

5: Last, but very far from least, the Isaiah scroll should not be taken so seriously even in matters of *scriptio defectiva,* at least not until every aspect of it has been studied *per se,* without regard to "superiority" to the Masoretic text, or "identity" with the LXX-*Vorlage;* and the like.[43] This scroll literally cries out for a thorough analysis by a competent textual critic. What should one do with the alternate *plena* and *defectiva* spelling for Pharaoh, פרעה . . . פרעוה, in both 19:11 and 30:2–3 (*plena* in 36:7); should one vocalize the *defectiva* differently from the *plena?* Or again, how would the defective spelling in the scroll at 8:10 change—or more correctly, should it be used for changing—the vocalization of MT עֻצוּ (עֵצָה) וְתֻפָר. Or, getting back to our root, would the scroll's נשא (עוון) at 33:24 for MT נְשֻׂא require the vocalization נָשֻׂא? Or would the scroll's כנשא at 18:3 for MT כִּנְשֹׂא point to a vowel other than *holem?* If so, what about SM נשוא for MT (נִלְאֵיתִי) נְשֹׂא in 1:14? In our very verse (3:3), MT וִיוֹעֵץ was written defectively (ויעץ) in our scroll; would that point to a different vocalization or, rather, to the unreliable character of the scroll's scribe as a speller? Or one may note, in the immediate vicinity of נשא (פנים) in 9:14, the spelling ראש . . . ראוש (9:13–14), where the scribe ignored his frequent *plena* spelling and then "corrected" (i.e., he or another scribe) the second instance alone, by inserting the "missing" *waw* over the *'āleph* of the word. The same thing happened in 9:16, where the scribe's defectively spelled יחמל was later "corrected" by means of an additional *waw* above the *mem*.

The grammar, as well as the text, of Biblical Hebrew is sometimes revised because of the Isaiah scroll's spelling. Thus, because Masoretic דֹּב/דֻּבִּים is written דב/דבים rather than דוב/דובים in 1QIsa[a] at 11:7 and 59:11, it is assumed to prove that the scribe of the scroll was "preserving a pronunciation found in the cognate languages . . . cf. Syr. *debbā* and Eth. *deb*" (Wernberg-Møller, p. 252). Similarly, 1QIsa[a] חטר (instead of the *plena* חוטר) for MT חֹטֶר at 11:1 recalls Arabic *ḥiṭr*^{un}. The scroll's חרש (instead of חורש for MT חֹרֶשׁ) at 17:9 coincides with Arabic *ḫirš*^{un}. The spelling צורך (for MT צַוָּארֵךְ) at 52:2 reflects Syriac *ṣaurā*. The spelling קדקד (instead of קדקוד, for MT קָדְקֹד) at 3:17 points to Accadian *qaqqadu*. And so on (pp. 252–53).[44]

To the writer it would seem that, at best, all that the *scriptio defectiva* in such instances as the above might help to prove is that some of the Jewish "cavemen" of Qumran spoke a dialect of Hebrew that at times coincided with Arabic or Aramaic or Babylonian-Assyrian or Samaritan or Syriac or Ethiopic, etc. However, since such a dialect is *a priori,* shall we say, absurd, it is far more likely that most of these defectively written words in the Isaiah scroll point to nothing more than just that, viz., *scriptio defectiva.* It is one thing to assume for the sake of argument that the above words point to a vocalization different from that preserved in the Masoretic text; but when this line of assumption leads to what is obviously a nonexistent dialect of Hebrew (*reductio ad absurdum* is probably a good technical term for this kind of "reasoning"), then the assumption should be scrapped. If not, then the scroll's קראתי will play havoc with the good sense of MT (אֲנִי) קַרְתִּי (וְשָׁתִיתִי מָיִם) at 37:25.[45]

IV

On the surface, one might not think that the attempted reconstruction of the territorial history of any part of ancient Israel would have much to do with the textual criticism of the Biblical texts involved. That the opposite can be true is evident from Albright's detailed analysis of the archaeological-topographical data in combination with the pertinent documentary sources in the attempt to date the list of Levitic towns in Joshua 21 and I Chronicles 6.[46] His treatment of the Hebrew and Greek forms of the place names (see the commentary on pp. 66 ff.) is something of a tour de force and has gone a long way toward helping to disprove the opinion of Wellhausen and others that the list was essentially unhistorical from the very beginning.[47]

Considerable advance has been made in the textual criticism of the Hebrew Bible as a result of the discovery and sober analysis of the proto-Hebrew Ugaritic texts, along with numerous Aramaic and other Northwest Semitic documents of the Late Bronze and Early Iron periods. These documents have enabled the student of the Old Testament not only to get at the original meaning of the Masoretic text better than ever before, but also to respect its integrity. Here and there in the Bible these Canaanite documents have led to the justified emendation of a reading that has come down to us in corrupted form; far more frequently, however, they have nullified other proposed and sometimes popularly accepted emendations, and have shed light on the preserved text to the point where it often becomes clear and acceptable.

A typical case in point is his analysis of "The Oracles of Balaam" (*JBL* 63 [1944], pp. 207–33). In his brief but detailed introductory statement (pp. 208–11), he noted that the "new text and translation of the poems" (Numbers 23:7–10, 18–24; 24:3–9, 15–24) that he was presenting was

> *based on cautious use of the versions and especially on full use of the mass of material now available for early Northwest Semitic grammar, lexicography and epigraphy. Since very little of this material has yet been employed by biblical scholars, it is only natural that we are able to progress beyond older commentators in the interpretation of some passages. It is to be noted that our date for the first writing down of these poems depends wholly on the inductive agreement of textual criticism with the spelling of epigraphic documents. In our subsequent sketch of the geographical and historical background of the poems* [*pp. 227–33*] *we shall utilize new material from the traditional age of Balaam. . . . Our reconstruction of the consonantal text endeavors to recapture the original orthography with the aid of archaisms in the Masoretic and Samaritan text, hints from the Greek version, and parallels in Northwest Semitic epigraphy. . . .*

Albright's study was so well done that his dating of the Oracles ("we must date the first writing down of the Oracles in or about the tenth century B.C. . . . ," p. 210) and his insistence "that there is no reason why they may not be authentic" (p. 233), together with the textual analysis proper, have gained wide acceptance in the scholarly world.[48]

There is much more that remains to be surveyed critically in the field of textual criticism. The renewed study of the Tell el-Amarna tablets—in which Albright has played a prominent role[49]—along with the appearance of the various Northwest Semitic inscriptions,[50] have shed useful light on the grammar and text of Biblical Hebrew. And the Mari tablets that have already appeared indicate clearly that the continued publication and study of these texts will add very considerably to that knowledge.

There is also the matter of the studies and editions of the Septuagint and other versions of the Old Testament. Thus J. Ziegler has been making available a mass of reliable data, much of it well digested in his useful *Einleitungen,* in his editions of *Septuaginta, Vetus Testamentum Graecum* (Auctoritate Societatis Litterarum Gottingensis editum): Isaiah (1939), the minor prophets (1943), Ezekiel (1952), Susannah, Daniel, and Bel and the Dragon (1954), and Jeremiah, Baruch, Lamentations, and the Epistle of Jeremiah (1957).[51] Additional parts of the Larger Cambridge Septuagint have made their appearance, constituting the beginnings of Vol. III in this notable series: Esther, Judith, and Tobit (1940).

There are also the editions of the Old Latin and Vulgate translations of the Old Testament. In 1941 J. Schildenberger published his searching study, *Die altlateinischen Texte des Proverbienbuches untersucht und textgeschichtlich eingegliedert.* Erste Teil: *Die alter afrikanische Textgestalt*[52]; in 1949 the first fascicle, *Verzeichnis der Sigel,* appeared in connection with *Vetus Latina. Die Reste der altlateinischen Bibel nach Petrus Sabatier neu gesammelt und herausgegeben von der Erzabtei Beuron;* the following four fascicles (1951–54; ed., B. Fischer) constitute the text of Genesis; and this erudite and important work goes on.[53] One cannot leave the Old Latin without at least mentioning two scholarly works by R. Weber, *Les anciennes versions latines du deuxième livre des Paralipomènes* (Rome, 1945) and *Le Psautier Romain et les autres anciens Psautiers latins: Edition critique* (Rome, 1953)—respectively Vols. VIII and X in *Collectanea Biblica.* As for the Vulgate, the monks of St. Jerome's Monastery in Rome have been putting out a critical edition of this landmark in Biblical exegesis, *Biblia Sacra iuxta Latinam Vulgatam versionem ad codicum fidem iussu Pii PP. XI–XII cura et studio monachorum Abbatiae Pontificiae Sancti Hieronymi in urbe Ordinis Sancti Benedicti* (Rome, 1926—). J. O. Smit has written a fine study of *De Vulgaat, Geschiedenis en Herziening van de Latijnse Bijbelvertaling* (Roermond, 1948).

A promising career was cut short when H. C. Gleave died at the age of twenty-eight; C. Rabin helped in getting his manuscript published, *The Ethiopic Version of the Song of Songs* (London, 1951).

As this survey comes to a close, only brief reference can be made to other surveys and reference works. The fine work by D. Winton Thomas, mentioned above, may be recalled here, as well as the writer's survey in *The Study of the Bible,* etc., likewise mentioned above (n. 2). P. Katz's "Septuagintal Studies in the Mid-Century," as well as such other studies of his as *Philo's Bible* and "The Recovery of the Original Septuagint: a Study in the History of Transmission and Textual Criticism"[54] should be noted. Much useful material is available in J. W. Wevers's survey, "Septuaginta-Forschungen," *Theologische Rundschau,* 22 (1954), pp. 85–138, 171–90.[55] And, finally, up-to-date references are available in B. J. Roberts, *The Old Testament Text and Versions* (Cardiff, 1951), *passim* and "Bibliography" (pp. 286–314); and O. Eissfeldt, *Einleitung in das alte Testament*[2] (1956), *passim* and "Der Text" (pp. 822–75; and the "Literaturnachträge" on pp. 876 ff.).

New York; Summer, 1958; revised, January, 1959

NOTES TO CHAPTER FIVE

1. See Orlinsky, "Jewish Scholarship and Christian Translations of the Hebrew Bible," *Yearbook of the Central Conference of American Rabbis* 63 (1953), p. 248.
2. Essays by members of the Society for Old Testament Study, edited by H. H. Rowley. Mention may be made here of the writer's chapter on "Current Progress and Problems in Septuagint Research," in H. R. Willoughby, ed., *The Study of the Bible Today and Tomorrow* (Chicago, 1947), pp. 141–61.
3. Thus H. H. Rowley, in *Book List* 10 (1955), p. 640, noted that in H. F. Hahn's survey, *The Old Testament in Modern Research* (Philadelphia, 1954), "Philology and textual criticism are left unsurveyed . . ." Or cf. E. C. Colwell's presidential address, "Biblical Criticism: Lower and Higher," *JBL* 67 (1948), pp. 1 ff., "Biblical criticism today is not the most robust of academic disciplines. . . ."
4. Lugduni Batavorum, 1900.
5. See Orlinsky, op. cit. (n. 2 above), p. 151 in the section, "The Use of the LXX and its Daughter-Versions in the Textual Criticism of the Hebrew Bible." Or his discussion of "The Septuagint—Its Use in Textual Criticism," *The Biblical Archaeologist* IX (1946), pp. 21–34.
6. See the valuable section (III) on "Ancient Versions" in the "Introduction" (pp. 24–57); also pp. 3–24 of the "Introduction" to his commentary on *Kings* in the same series (1951; ed. H. S. Gehman). Professor Gehman himself (followed by his student, J. W. Wevers) has frequently objected to *BH*'s collection of emendations; for bibliography, see Wevers, *Theologische Rundschau* 22 (1954), pp. 86, 90.
7. *Jewish Studies in Memory of Israel Abrahams* (New York, 1927), pp. 307–23.
8. Parts I–IV cover Joshua 1:1–19.38. Part V and the all-important introduction are apparently lost forever—a tragedy.
9. Cf. Margolis (*AJSL* 28 [1911–12], p. 3), "For the uncials [of Joshua] I have used the phototypic editions . . . I say this because I have discovered numerous inaccuracies in Swete's edition"; "Corrections in the Apparatus of the Book of Joshua in the Larger Cambridge Septuagint," *JBL* 49 (1930), pp. 234–64. On Margolis' attempt at "The Recovery of the Original Septuagint Text" see Orlinsky, "Current Progress . . . ," (pp. 144 ff.) and "Margolis' Work in the Septuagint," pp. 34–44

in *Max Leopold Margolis: Scholar and Teacher* (Dropsie College Alumni Assoc., Philadelphia, 5712 = 1952).

10. Pp. 107–20 in "Studien zur Verwertung der Septuaginta im Zwölfprophetenbuch," *ZAW* 60 (1944), pp. 107–31.
11. "Job 5.8, a Problem in Greek-Hebrew Methodology," *JQR* 25 (1934–35), pp. 271–78; G. Beer in *BH*[2,3] had failed to note that for Masoretic אלהים the LXX read—only here in the book of Job—*τὸν πάντων δεσπότην* (G[A] *παντοκράτορα*; ordinarily = שַׁדַּי), and that Kenn 223 actually read שדי. Chapters I ("An Analytical Survey of Previous Studies") and II ("The Character of the Septuagint Translation of the Book of Job") of the dissertation have now appeared: *HUCA* 28 (1957), pp. 53–74; 29 (1958), pp. 229–71.
12. "Studies in the St. Mark's Isaiah Scroll," *JBL* 69 (1950), pp. 149–66.
13. Orlinsky, "Studies in the St. Mark's Isaiah Scroll, IV," *JQR* 43 (1952–53), pp. 329–40.
14. For additional details, and bibliography, on "the footnotes in Kittel's *Biblia Hebraica*—the standard and monotonous source of variants (and conjectural emendations) for those who have no conception or standard of scholarship," see Orlinsky, "Notes on the Present State of the Textual Criticism of the Judean Biblical Cave Scrolls," in *A Stubborn Faith* (the W. A. Irwin *Festschrift*), ed. E. C. Hobbs (Dallas, 1956), pp. 117–31.
15. Subtitled: "Their Links with the Past and their Present Tendencies," in *The Backgrounds of the New Testament and Its Eschatology* (the C. H. Dodd volume), ed. W. D. Davies and D. Daube (Cambridge, 1956), pp. 176–208.
16. Cf. C. C. Torrey, *The Second Isaiah,* pp. 208 ff., for sharp criticism of Duhm, as of those scholars from whom the *Handwörterbuch* of Gesenius-Buhl so freely culled emendations and the like (p. 215 and n.*).
17. One could go on to cite similar opinions by other scholars: e.g., J. B. Payne, "The Relationship of the Chester Beatty Papyri of Ezekiel to Codex Vaticanus," *JBL* 68 (1949), pp. 251 ff., "More care must be employed in the use of the phrase often found in the Kittel Editions of *M,* 'Lege cum Graeco' " (p. 262); A. M. Honeyman, *VT* 5 (1955), p. 223, "Again the reviewer has become increasingly aware of the dangers which Kittel's *Biblia Hebraica,* in spite of its many merits, may constitute for the incautious user, for the *apparatus criticus* is not always as careful or systematic as it should be. . . ."; D. Winton Thomas, op. cit., p. 248, n. 1, "As has already been pointed out (p. 243, n. 1 [*in re līḳ*[e]*hat*/*γῆρας*, Prov. 30.17]), the critical apparatus of *BH*[3] calls for careful use; see Orlinsky's warning . . . and Sperber's criticism, *P.A.A.J.R.* xviii, 1948–49, pp. 303 ff."
18. P. Katz, *VT* 4 (1954), pp. 222–23.
19. From the writer's review of Würthwein, *Journal of Semitic Studies* 4 (1959), pp. 149–51. On the Hebrew text edited by P. Kahle for Kittel's *BH*[3] being no more valuable to the scholar than that of *BH*[2] or of any carefully printed edition of the Bible, see Orlinsky, "The Import of the Kethib-Kere and the Masoretic Note on *L*[e]*ḵāh,* Judges 19.13," *JQR* 31 (1940–41), pp. 59–66.
20. This section of the chapter originally appeared as a separate article in *JBL* 78 (1959), pp. 26–33.
21. For the writer's argument in favor of the priority of the MT reading, see "Studies in the St. Mark's Isaiah Scroll, VII" (in Hebrew), *Tarbiz,* XXIV, 1 (Oct. 1954), 4–8 (English summary, pp. I–II).
22. The writer's detailed discussion of *Dimon-Dibon* constitute "Studies . . . V," *Israel Explor. Jour.,* IV (1954), 5–8.
23. M. Burrows, *The Dead Sea Scrolls* (New York, 1955), and now his *More Light on the Dead Sea Scrolls* (1958), constitute a notable exception; see Chapter XIV

(pp. 301–25) in the former, and Part Three: "Results for Old Testament Studies" (pp. 135 ff.) in the latter.

24. MT reads כִּי־הִנֵּה יהוה יֹצֵא מִמְּקוֹמוֹ וְיָרַד וְדָרַךְ עַל־בָּמֳתֵי־אָרֶץ. O. Procksch in *BH*[3] notes *ad* ודרך: "dl c G V"; and the Micah fragment lacks ודרך. Burrows (*More Light . . .*, pp. 155–56) has suggested that only one of ירד ודרך is original, and that "The reading of the Qumran commentary may indicate which of the two verbs was original." However, in the light of the use of דרך with עַל־בָּמֳתֵי־עָב / אֶרֶץ / יָם in Isaiah 14:1; Amos 4:13; Job 9:8—and cf. וְאַתָּה עַל־בָּמוֹתֵימוֹ תִדְרֹךְ (Deuteronomy 33:29) and וְעַל־בָּמוֹתַי יַדְרִיכֵנִי (Habakkuk 3:10; where Albright would insert ים if it is not actually to be understood elliptically, "The Psalm of Habakkuk," pp. 12–13 and n. *m'* on p. 18, ad loc., in *Studies in O. T. Prophecy*, ed. H. H. Rowley [Edinburgh, 1950])—and even יַרְכִּבֵהוּ עַל־בָּמֳתֵי אָרֶץ (Deuteronomy 32:13) /וְהִרְכַּבְתִּיךָ (Isaiah 58:14) and וְעַל־בָּמ(וֹ)תַי יַעֲמִ(י)דֵנִי (II Samuel 22:34 // Psalms 18:34; where Albright, loc. cit., would restore or understand במתי־ים), it would seem more likely that the Micah fragment has preserved the secondary of the two readings; in other words, the fragment derives from the text-tradition that gave rise to the so-called MT.

The verb (על במתי) ירד finds a parallel in אֶעֱלֶה עַל־בָּמֳתֵי עָב in Isaiah 14:14 only superficially; the prophet there, in mocking the king of Babylonia, speaks on several occasions of his downfall (e.g., vss. 11–12, הוּרַד שְׁאוֹל גְּאוֹנֶךָ . . . אֵיךְ נָפַלְתָּ מִשָּׁמַיִם הֵילֵל בֶּן־שָׁחַר) after his attempts to rise up against the Lord (e.g., vss. 13–15, . . . וְאַתָּה אָמַרְתָּ בִלְבָבְךָ הַשָּׁמַיִם אֶעֱלֶה . . . אֶעֱלֶה עַל־בָּמֳתֵי־עָב אֶדַּמֶּה לְעֶלְיוֹן אַךְ אֶל־שְׁאוֹל תּוּרָד. Note the pun in עֶלְיוֹן . . . אֶעֱלֶה).

25. Burrows (*More Light . . .*, 156–57) has accepted this argument. The two readings in Micah 1:3 were discussed by the writer on pp. 122–23 of his chapter, "Notes on the Present State of the Textual Criticism of the Judean Biblical Cave Scrolls," in the W. A. Irwin volume, *A Stubborn Faith*, ed. E. C. Hobbs (Dallas, 1956).

26. In 7:9, many scholars, e.g., F. Horst in *BH*[3] (but contrast S. R. Driver in *BH*[2]) held that LXX βοηθήσει derived from a reading תַּעֲזֹר חָכָם, as against MT (הַחָכְמָה) תָּעֹז לֶחָכָם. This Qoheleth fragment reads תעזור. But a careful study of the root עזז and of LXX βοηθέω (cf. my "Notes on . . . Scrolls," pp. 121–22) shows clearly how frequently a form of the latter is used for the former. Cf. Burrows's discussion (pp. 144–45).

27. "The Qumran Manuscripts and Textual Criticism," *VT Supplement* IV (1957), 148–60.

28. See my "Notes on . . . Scrolls," pp. 124–25.

29. See my "Studies in the Septuagint of the Book of Job," *HUCA*, XXVIII (1957), 53–74; XXIX (1958), 229–71; XXXI (1960); to be continued.

30. *The Ancient Library of Qumran . . .*, p. 139 and nn. 37–38.

31. Cf. P. W. Skehan, "The Qumran Manuscripts . . . ," pp. 155–60 (the Lev and Num fragments from cave 4); D. Barthélemy, "Redécouverte d'un chaînon manquant de l'histoire de la Septante," *RB*, LX (1953), 18–29 (covering parts of verses in Micah, Jonah, Nahum, Habakkuk, Zephaniah, and Zechariah). Some literature on the minor prophets material is cited in Cross, op. cit., p. 21, n. 35; I note also P. Katz, "Justin's Old Testament Quotations and the Greek Dodekaprophreton Scroll," *Studia Patristica*, I (1957), 343–53.

32. Cf. most recently, e.g., M. S. Hurwitz, "The Septuagint of Isaiah 36–39 in relation to that of 1–35, 40–66," *HUCA*, XXVIII (1957), pp. 75–83; A. Soffer, "The Treatment of Anthropomorphisms and Anthropopathisms in the Septuagint of Psalms," pp. 85–107; on these aspects of the LXX of Isaiah see Orlinsky, *HUCA*, XXVII (1956), pp. 193–200; on Job, XXXI (1960).

33. Cf., e.g., Orlinsky, "On the Present State of Proto-Septuagint Studies," *JAOS*, LXI

(1941), pp. 81–92 (= AOS Offprint Series, 13); the chapter on "Margolis' Work in the Septuagint," *Max Leopold Margolis, Scholar and Teacher* (Philadelphia, 1952), 33–44 (note on p. 43 a list of scholars who have accepted the recensional hypothesis of the LXX as against the theory of independent translations, among them Albright, R. Marcus, B. J. Roberts, O. Pretzl, Mercati); Skehan, op. cit., p. 158 (*in re* the Leviticus fragments), "The more general impression with which the writer is left is that we have here one more book of the OT in which a single early Greek rendering seems to have undergone a good deal of what we would today call critical revision, in the period even before Origen"; P. Katz, op. cit. (cf. p. 353, where reference is made to the "wealth of supporting arguments in Kahle's comprehensive paper, among them some which have long been shown to be gravely mistaken. . . . Although there is little hope to convince Kahle, I would conclude by putting right one of his fresh mistakes. . . ."); Cross, op. cit., pp. 124 ff., especially n. 13 (on pp. 125–27) and pp. 128–130 and n. 19; cf. n. 13 (pp. 126–27), ". . . It may be noted that in his article devoted precisely to this new recension, Kahle failed to deal with this point, that the scroll is a Jewish revision, *not* [italics in original] translation, which takes the pre-Christian Septuagint as its base. The failure is most curious, since this is easily the most significant characteristic of the text, as well as most damaging evidence against Kahle's theories of Septuagint origins."

34. *Journal of Semitic Studies* 3 (1958), pp. 234–64. It may be remarked that the Isaiah scroll here referred to, along with the Pesher on Habakkuk, the Manual of Discipline, and the so-called Genesis Apocryphon ceased legally to be the property of the monastery of St. Mark and its archbishop in July 1954, when they were sold to the state of Israel; see the writer's "Notes on the Present State," etc., p. 126, n. 1; Y. Yadin, *The Message of the Scrolls* (New York, 1957), pp. 39–52.

35. Actually, there is at least a third instance. In 41:28 LXX *καὶ ἀπὸ τῶν εἰδώλων αὐτῶν* represents a form of וּמֵאֵלִים for Masoretic (וְאֵרֶא וְאֵין אִישׁ) וּמֵאֵלֶּה (וְאֵין יוֹעֵץ).

36. I. L. Seeligmann, *The Septuagint Version of Isaiah: a Discussion of its Problems* (Leiden, 1948), p. 20, regards Lucianic *γλύπτοις* "as a correction" of LXX *εἰδώλοις* (in turn, a "misunderstanding" of אילים). But apart from the fact that *γλύπτοις* represents *εἰδώλοις* very well, it may be that *γ.* constitutes a "correction" of LXX *κήποις* for גַּנּוֹת (see the apparatus in *Isaias*, ed. Ziegler; Schleusner, II, 29, *s. γλυπτός*).

37. On the importance of this shamefully neglected scholar, see, e.g., p. 71 of the writer's "Studies in the Septuagint of . . . Job," *HUCA* 28 (1957).

38. At this late date it is only a distortion of the facts to state blandly, "Scholars have already noticed cases of agreement between 1QIsa[a] and LXX, see. . . ." (Wernberg-Møller, p. 254, n. 1). How many of these alleged instances—usually merely asserted to be so—have been subject to careful analysis? In all fairness to the problem, reference should have been made to the several articles in which the present writer disproved such alleged instances; cf., e.g., O. R. Sellers, *JNES* 7 (1958), p. 219 (in reviewing the W. A. Irwin volume), "Harry M. Orlinsky . . . has been the foremost defender of the Masoretic text against proposed emendations based on the Dead Sea Scrolls . . . or . . . their having a *Vorlage* of the Septuagint or any other ancient version."

39. There can no longer be any doubt that parts of the Isaiah scroll and other Biblical manuscripts among the scrolls were copied from dictation, and probably also from memory—for numerous readings in these texts are due to a *hörfehler*, e.g., in the Psalm fragment (37:20; see Orlinsky, § v, p. 124, of "Notes on the Present State," etc.): "The wicked shall perish//And the lovers of the Lord shall be as thē fat of lambs. . . ." where incongruous ואוהבי "and the lovers" in the scroll stands for Masoretic וְאֹיְבֵי "and the enemies" (//"the wicked"). Yet our author (p. 254)

makes mention only of "1QIsa[a], or the original from which it was copied . . ." without warning the reader that there may frequently not have been any text before the scribe. For some cases in point in Isaiah, cf. Orlinsky, *JBL* 69 (1950), pp. 156–57 and nn. 8–9 (with reference to S. R. Driver and Burrows).

40. It is good to learn that P. Katz and J. Ziegler, an excellent team of Septuagint experts, have "Ein Aquila-Index in Vorbereitung," as described in *VT* 8 (1958), pp. 264–85.

41. The problem is most complicated: cf., e.g., the data at 3:3, 9:5, 14 in the full apparatus in Ziegler's ed. of the LXX. The present writer would tentatively propose as the original LXX reading approximately *καὶ θαυμαστὸν* (or the like) *τὰ πρόσωπα* (*καὶ*) *θαυμαστὸν σύμβουλον*, deriving from a *Vorlage* (שַׂר־חֲמִשִּׁים) וּנְשׂוּא פָנִים (ו)פֶּלֶא (וַחֲכַם חֲרָשִׁים וּנְבוֹן לָחַשׁ) יוֹעֵץ—or under the influence of פֶּלֶא יוֹעֵץ in 9:5. In favor of this are: (1) the original LXX became the present, corrupt text by simple haplography (the scribe's eye going from the end of the first *θαυμαστὸν* (or the like) to the end of the second; note the accusative ending in the nouns in vv. 1b–3); (2) our verse in the Hebrew would then consist of five two-word expressions, so that וְיוֹעֵץ does not stand out like something of a sore thumb. Note also that in this section the Lord threatens to remove from Judah, *inter alia*, the גִּבּוֹר and the זָקֵן (v. 2), and the שַׂר־חֲמִשִּׁים and the [*פֶּלֶא] יוֹעֵץ (v. 3), and according to 9:5 he will bring restoration through the lad who is to be named: פֶּלֶא יוֹעֵץ אֵל גִּבּוֹר אֲבִי־עַד שַׂר־שָׁלוֹם; and nine verses farther on (9:14) reference is again made to the זָקֵן וּנְשׂוּא־פָנִים.

42. Our author is content with the parenthetic statement, "Aquila follows M.T. in both passages"—whatever that was meant to indicate. Aquila rendered *αἰρόμενος* (*προσωπ*[*ω*]; so Ziegler, but perhaps pl. *προσωπ*[*οις*] as in 9:14) in both verses. Symmachus employed *αἰδέσιμος* in both, Theodotion *ἐπῃρμένος* in 9:14.

43. The Masoretes noted on our word (פָנִים) וּנְשֻׂא at II Kings 5:1: ד׳דין חס׳, i.e., the word ונשא occurs four times in the Bible, and in this instance is written defectively. But with the aid of the Masoretic elaboration in the margin of the Rabbinic Bible and the explanation in *Massora Magna*, ed. S. Frensdorff (Hannover und Leipzig, 1876), Part I, *s.* נשא (p. 125 and n. 2), it seems clear that what the Masoretes originally meant to convey was this: the word (פנים) ונש(ו)א—with conj. *waw*—occurs four times in the Bible (II Kings 5:1; Isaiah 3:3; 9:14; Job 22:8), being written *plena* three times, and defectively once (II Kings 5:1); the form נְשֻׂא—without conj. *waw*—occurs only once, and is written defectively (Isaiah 33:24). The Masoretic note in Kahle's text in Kittel's *BH*[3] reads simply ל̇ and gives the reader no idea of what is really involved; see my note 19 above.

44. I do not understand the reference in this section to "M.T.: שִׁבֹּלֶת (twice: xvii.5, xxvii.12), 1QIsa[a]: defective spelling in both passages, cf. Aram. . . . Syr. . . . Arab. . . ." (p. 253 and n. 2). Both MT and the scroll read שִׁבֳּלִים twice—not שבלת—in 17:5, and the scroll reads משבל for MT מִשִּׁבֹּלֶת in 27:12, and שוליך for MT שֹׁבֶל in 47:2; in short, 1QIsa[a] has preserved no form of שִׁבֹּלֶת. As to the discussion in n. 2, how many linguists and textual critics would argue with confidence on the basis of a hapaxlegomenon (שֹׁבֶל) and so meager data otherwise?

The author singled out anomalous צורך in 52:2 (he could have done so, e.g., with MT צַוְּרֵם in Neh. 3:5), but he should have told the reader that the word is spelled with the *'āleph* in the other three instances in the Isaiah scroll (8:8; 10:27; 30:28). I suppose that one would assume—on this manner of reasoning—two morphologies for עִוֵּר, because it is spelled as in MT eight times (29:18; 35:5; 42:7, 16, 18, 19; 56:10; 59:10), but עואר in 42:19 (*bis:* עור . . . עואר . . . עואר) and 43:8; or two morphologies for forms of עָוֹן, because it is usually written plene (with two *wāws*) throughout the scroll (עוון), but with one *wāw* alone in 43:24 and 65:7 (ועונות for expected ועוונות = MT וַעֲוֹנֹת; and right after בעונותיכמה

for MT עֲוֹנֹתֵיכֶם). In 50:1 שלחה (for MT שִׁלַּחְתָּהּ) was "corrected" by addition of *wāw* over the *shin* (שׁולחה). But such inconsistencies should not be made the basis for a new grammar of Biblical Hebrew.

45. The Septuagint and Targum proved most useful in a recent attempt to distinguish in Biblical Hebrew between the Qal inf. const. and the noun used verbally; cf. Orlinsky, "Notes on the Qal Infinitive Construct and the Verbal Noun in Biblical Hebrew," *JAOS* 67 (1947), pp. 107–26 (= No. 22 in the AOS Offprint Series).
46. "The List of Levitic Cities," *Louis Ginzberg Jubilee Volume* (English section; New York, 1945), pp. 49–73.
47. See now M. Haran, "The Levitical Cities: Utopia and Historical Reality" (in Hebrew), *Tarbiz* 27 (1958), pp. 421–39 (with English summary, pp. I–II).
48. Among other poems in the Bible treated by Albright from this angle, cf., e.g., "The Psalm of Habakkuk" (*Studies in Old Testament Prophecy* [the T. H. Robinson volume], ed. H. H. Rowley [Edinburgh, 1950], pp. 1–18) and "A Catalogue of Early Hebrew Lyric Poems (Psalm LXVIII)" (*HUCA* 23, I [1950–51], pp. 1–39).
49. Cf., e.g., his "Amarna Letters" (with G. E. Mendenhall) in *ANET*, pp. 483–90; and articles (with W. L. Moran) in *Journal of Cuneiform Studies* (from 1948 on).
50. See F. Rosenthal, "Canaanite and Aramaic Inscriptions," in *ANET* (2nd, revised edition, 1955), pp. 499–505, with extensive bibliography.
51. Ziegler has offered us also numerous important studies, some of monographic proportions, arising from his work on these editions of the LXX; most of these are listed in J. W. Wevers, op. cit., pp. 90–91.
52. In the series, *Texte und Arbeiten herausgegeben durch die Erzabtei Beuron*, I. Abteilung, pp. 32–33.
53. See H. Kusch, "Die Beuroner Vetus Latina und ihre Bedeutung für die Altertumswissenschaft," *Forschungen und Forschritte* 29 (1955), pp. 46–57.
54. *Philo's Bible: the Aberrant Text of Bible Quotations in some Philonic Writings and its Place in the Textual History of the Greek Bible* (Cambridge, 1950); "The Recovery," etc., in *Actes du Ier Congrès de la Fédération Internationale des Associations d'Etudes Classiques* (Paris, 1951), pp. 165–82 (cf. "Das Problem des Urtextes der Septuaginta," *Theologische Zeitschrift* 5 [1949], pp. 1–24).
55. Mention should be made of I. Soisalon-Soininen, *Die Textformen der Septuaginta-Übersetzung der Richterbuches* (*Annales Academiae Scientiarum Fennicae*, LXXII, 1; Helsinki, 1951), and his *Vanhan Testamentin alkuteksti* (Helsinki, 1953). G. Zuntz has been adding to our scholarly understanding of things Septuagintal; cf., e.g., "Die Antinoe Papyrus der Proverbia und das Prophetologion" (*ZAW* 68 [1956], pp. 124–84) and "Das Byzantinische Septuaginta-Lektionar 'Prophetologion'" (*Classica et Mediaevalia* 17 [1956], pp. 183–98).

III. TRANSMISSION HISTORY

(i) *Translations and Recensions*

TWO HITHERTO UNKNOWN BIBLE VERSIONS IN GREEK.

By Professor Dr. SAMUEL KRAUSS,
CAMBRIDGE.

I. Ben La'ana and Ben Tilga Probably Identified.

THE observation of a single word in the 'Arukh, the famous and most reliable Rabbinical Dictionary written by Rabbi Nathan of Rome (11th century), helped me, so I hope, to throw some light on a problem in Rabbinical literature which until now has seemed to defy every explanation. This problem is associated with the two names בן לענה, בן תלגה = Ben La'ana and Ben Tilga (hereafter signed B.L. and B.T. respectively).

The two names occur, as is known, in several Midrashic passages and in one passage of the Jerusalem Talmud, to the effect that their writings were banned along with those of Ben Sira. The Midrashic text (Qoheleth Rabbah) to Eccles. XII. 12[1] runs as follows: "And further, by these, my son, be admonished"—"for everyone who brings into his house more than twenty four books,[2] confusion[3] he brings into his house, for example: the Book of Ben Sira and the Book of Ben Tigla,"[4] "and much study is a weariness of the flesh"—"they are

[1] Folio 31*a* in ed. Wilna. I am laying this passage as base. Comp. Pesiqta Rabbathi c. 3 (p. 9*a* ed. Friedmann), and Bacher, *Agada der pal. Amoräer*, III, 357 and 757. Parallel passages are Threni Rabbah I, 1 (p. 42 ed. Buber) and Cant. Rabbah IV, 12 (folio 28*b* ed. Wilna). By Talmud Jerusalem is meant: Yerushalmi Sanhedrin X, 1 (folio 28*a* ed. Krotoschin). The passages Gen. R. c. 8 and c. 91, as quoted by J. Levy (*Neuhebr. Wörterbuch* I. 240) to this point, belong properly to Ben Sira. See also Kohut, *Aruch completum*, II, 119, and Jastrow, *A Dictionary of the Targumim, the Talmud Babli and Yerushalmi, and the Midrashic Literature*, p. 714.

[2] The 24 canonical books are meant.

[3] מְהָמָה of the text was read, מהומה.

[4] "Ben Sira"—the well-known apocryphal book. Yerushalmi has ספרי in the plural, and the same with B.L. On the contrary, Babli Sanhedrin 100b and all Midrash texts have ספר in the singular.

Reprinted from *Bulletin of the John Rylands Library*. Vol. 27, 1942-3.

destined to study, but not destined to weariness of the flesh." [1]

Hitherto it has been entirely overlooked that the name תלגא occurs once elsewhere in our Rabbinical literature. I have in mind the quotation in 'Arukh s.v. פלקט (ed. Kohut VI. 358, which is the best and standard edition), showing the following Midrashic text: ואלבישך רקמה, רב סיסי אמר פורפירן, תלגא עקילס [פוקרטין] פולקטן, the translation of which will be made evident below.

From the 'Arukh it is not clear whether the quotation concerns the Threni Rabbah or the Canticum Rabbah passage. It can be assumed that he had both passages in mind which might have had in his text the same sequence, as indeed there is no real difference between them. As by the Greek rendering the Bible word רקמה is to be interpreted, Kohut rightly supplements 'Arukh's quotation with other Bible words which in the LXX have the same Greek rendering; this task has been more conspicuously executed in the Hexapla work of Field [2] and in the Concordance of Hatch and Redpath.[3]

What meaning can be claimed for the word תלגא in the Midrash text as quoted in 'Arukh? Kohut sets it in brackets and remarks (see his note 7): " Not to be found in Cant. R. and in Threni R. at the beginning, nor is it in 'Arukh ed. Amsterdam ".

In opposition to this verdict I have remarked in my 'Arukh Supplement [4] that a series of reliable texts do have it: 'Arukh ed. Venice 2, ed. Pesaro, ed. Basel, MSS. Elkan Adler 2 and 3

[1] The meaning is not clear, see commentaries, especially that of מהרז״ו, printed in the Wilna edition. Roughly the meaning is: you may study these books, but not in the way of the canonical books, which alone are destined to lead to " weariness of flesh ".

[2] Field, *Hexapla*, II, 803. Cp. *ib.* also the rendering of Syr. Hexapla.

[3] Hatch and Redpath, *Concordance*, s.v. ποικιλία. We learn that the same Greek word serves also to render the Hebrew חשב, מעשה מחשבת. *Ib.* also ποικίλλειν. The occurrence of the same Greek word is registered in my *Griechische und Lateinische Lehnwörter in Talmud, Midrasch und Targum* II, 112 and 475. The word בקילים *ib.* 162 rendered by ποικιλός turns out false, as Imm. Löw remarks. So also *ib.* 452, פיקיילה does not belong there, a word for which I now show to Juḥasin (ed. London, p. 49*b*): פי׳ כובעו it means: his hat (or cap).

[4] Hebrew title תוספות הערוך השלם. In Latin: *Additamenta in librum Aruch completum* Al. Kohut (Vienna, 1937), p. 327.

(now in the Jewish Theological Seminary in New York). The mere presence of this word in this passage cannot be an accident or a mistake of copyists. It is so entangled with the threat of the sentence that it cannot be separated from it. To have it crossed out would be a great philological error. By a little adjustment in the Midrash text as quoted in the 'Arukh the true meaning would be easily restored: תלגא תרגם פוקרטון, עקילס תרגם פולקטון (or you can put Akylas and Tilga in inverted order).

By way of this an important discovery is made: a Bible word interpreted by T. appears side by side with that of Akylas! From this we learn that T. was known as the author of a translation of the Bible in Greek, and as the Bible passage quoted is taken from Ezekiel, he must have translated at least as far as this chapter, because it seems unlikely that there would be attributed to him the translation of this single book only.

That the Midrash passage as quoted in the 'Arukh must indeed be divided between *two* authors, in addition to R. Sisi's saying, deduces from the content itself. The one Biblical word רקמה has been interpreted by Sisi [1] with a single word: purple (purplish, pertaining to purple); the same proceeding is to be expected also in respect of the "Targum" Akylas; why should it be that *his* interpretation is given in *two* words פוקרטין, פולקטין as the text runs *now* in our editions? [2] To see in them only a variant would be a very delusive argument.[3] The parallel *lemmata* in 'Arukh, numbering three, indicate only *one* word, as is clearly studied by Benjamin Mussaphia, the learned interpreter of 'Arukh's intentions, who indeed glosses only one word. His reading is right, but T. does not appear in his text; it was extant in the original 'Arukh; the usual Midrashic texts and

[1] Correctly to be spelled סוסי and transcribed Σώσσιος Sosius, s. *Lehnwörter, ib.* 377. That is clearly demanded by the word's ending in double Jod in the Yerushalmi, as shown in *Lehnwörter, ib.;* cp. also Y. Ma'aseroth 48*d*. A Σωσᾶ (genitive form) occurs in Josephus, B.J. IV, 4. 2 (§ 235). "Sisi" is, however, 'Arukh's spelling, while our texts have "Simai".

[2] See, for example, 'Arukh ed. Lemberg, 1870.

[3] Jastrow, *Dictionary*, p. 104, writes (rendering Threni R., beginning) corr. acc. by striking out one of the two words as *var. lect.* that came into the text. In the main so also Kohut and before him also Mussaphia. The proceeding of Levy (*l.c.* IV, 57), honouring both loan-words, seems more justified.

their commentators did, however, simplify. In later times it seemed impossible to have a Bible translator named Tigla; so they let his name drop out. This was done in all our texts, even in Threni Rabbah and Cant. R., both having been quoted above, and in Pesiqta di R. Kahana (ed. Buber, p. 84*b*), where, however, only one Greek word is given,[1] and Tigla's word has been preserved only in 'Arukh's *lemma* פלקט. The later writers, very little interested in Greek words, inclined, furthermore, to eliminate even such a name as that of Akylas (it is omitted in Yalqut, the big collection of all Midrashim), and it so happens, that where the name Akylas ought to be, now we find ת"י (= Targum Jonathan) instead,[2] which is altogether a great puzzle.

As T. is named first, even before Akylas, he seems the earlier, though that is not definite.

II. Doublets in Greek Bible Versions.

Both, T. and Akylas, translate and interpret this single word similarly, almost indeed by the same Greek word, as do also the LXX. This feature of interrelation can indeed be observed amongst our Greek translators, the LXX included,[3] as has already been observed by scholars. This lies in the nature of the case, and we have also other examples of it. In his valuable investigation in ὁ Συρός and the Peshitta[4] Joshua Bloch adduces many such cases, e.g. Ezekiel viii. 16, אולם, which ὁ Συρός renders by *κιγκλίς*, while the usual word would be *κάγκελλον*, but it is evident that the two Greek words are synonymous terms. The use of one of them by this or that author is only a matter of style or taste. So also in our case. Between *ποικίλα* of the LXX, *ποικιλτά* of T., and *ποικιλτόν* of Akylas there is no difference whatever, and the variety shows only that a great fashion of rendering in Greek must needs have existed.

Can it be said that there have existed Bible translations in

[1] This text is accompanied by a very learned and exhaustive note of Solomon Buber, the editor of this Midrash, where the whole *Leidensgeschichte* of these Greek glosses is registered.

[2] In *Additamenta* quoted from the " short " 'Arukh (ערוך הקצר).

[3] Of course, this is true for Theodotion and Symmachus, too.

[4] *Jewish Studies in Memory of Israel Abrahams*, New York, 1927, p. 68.

Greek which remained unknown to us or survived only in feeble traces? That must be admitted. The aforementioned ὁ Σύρος is clearly such an example. Dr. Alexander Sperber, a successful inquirer in the field of Greek Bible translations, asserts that the so-called "recensions" of Lucian and Hesychius are rather to be regarded as independent "translations," thus indicating that the texts in question do not represent two recensions of one single Greek text (a meaning associated with the word recension), but two entirely different texts.[1] It may have some interest for our own investigation that what is singled out by the same author (*ib.* p. 82) regarding בְּשִׁבְטֶךָ in Mic. vii. 14, which is rendered in Cyril's commentary ῥάβδῳ φυλήν, that is by *two* words, should rightly be rendered by *one* word, "for I suppose that originally Lucian had here φυλήν and Hesychius ῥάβδῳ, and Cyril combined both readings". This is closely analogous to what the present writer asserts: the Greek rendering of רקמה was contaminated by the rendering of *two* authors! In our case, however, by two expressions which are closely akin to each other.

Again, Joseph Reider in his "Prolegomena"[2] makes the observation that in such cases "the signatures may be wrong, or the notes may have been attached to the wrong word". "Then we meet with doublets, one element in which alone can belong to Aquila." In a note he gives a list "which is fairly complete," unfortunately our case is not dealt with, as Rabbinics—Græca sunt, non leguntur. "Quite another matter are parallel renderings ascribed to Aquila which go back to two editions of his work; the subject is adequately dealt with by Field in his Prolegomena" (pp. xxiv ff.). In our case the thesis of *secunda editio* is not needed, as we have seen that the two renderings are to be attributed to two different authors; the case is similar to that of the two renderings by Cyril.

In the category of Bible translators whose works are almost lost to us I place also this T. named in 'Arukh's quotation side by side with Akylas. In this quotation he is not named *Ben T.*,

[1] "The Problems of the Septuagint Recensions," in *Journal of Biblical Literature*, Vol. LIV, Part II, 1935, p. 80.

[2] *Prolegomena to a Greek-Hebrew and Hebrew-Greek Index to Aquila*, Philadelphia, 1916, p. 12.

as we might have expected, perhaps by reason of his name to conform to that of Akylas, or by the fault of the copyist, or even by that of R. Nathan himself, who shortens his texts drastically. The name " Tigla " is so singular and is nowhere else to be met with in the vast Rabbinic literature that it cannot be doubted that it is the name of one and the same person.

Having found, in this way, at least evidence, however faint, to identify T., it is to be regretted that for Ben La'ana even this support is missing. But I don't hesitate to claim for B.L. the same place in Jewish literature, as the two seem to be a sort of couple and cannot be separated; it must be assumed that the one source (Talmud Jerusalem) cites, as example, B.L., whereas the other (Midrash) prefers, also as example and for the same purpose, to allude to B.T. The view of one scholar [1] that the two are identical, I cannot share. As to the name T. itself, reference can be made to the view of the same scholar who proposes to read תלגא = שלג = snow, which by no means gives a plausible sense; if a light emendation might be allowed, I would read [2] חָגְלָה, known as the name of a daughter of Zelophḥad (Num. xxvi. 33, etc.), the meaning of which may be a bird (like Zipporah, the wife of Moses); it does not matter that this would be a feminine name, because this man, for some reason or other, was rather associated with his mother than with his father. The word לַעֲנָה has certainly a feminine character; it denotes, as an appellative, " wormwood," cp. the phrase " gall and wormwood," a name which, perhaps, has been purposely deflected towards the unpleasant Greek writer. This mood of detraction would account also for the use of חָגְלָה, a wild bird. But it is better not to touch the transmitted form תִּגְלָה " Tigla " or תִּלְגָה " Tilga "; it may be that the Rabbis derived it from the root גִּלָּה in Pi'el, to reveal something in the Torah which was not according to their heart.

[1] S. Klein in the Hebrew periodical לשוננו (= Our Language), I, 344. Cp., however, Hareubeni, *ib.* II, 46. Both scholars have for Ben Sira the explanation סירה - הקוץ - thorn; long years ago (see *Jewish Quarterly Review*, XI, 1898, pp. 150-158, " Notes on Sirach ") I tried to prove that the true meaning is אסירא, prisoner. My view has been duly registered in *The Wisdom of Ben Sira*, by Schechter-Taylor, Cambridge, 1899, p. liii.

[2] See my *Sanhedrin-Makkōt*, Giessen, 1933, p. 269.

But how does it happen that these authors are named in the same breath with Ben Sira? Shall this juxtaposition not rather imply that as with Ben Sira so also T. and L. are to be taken for ethical writers and not for translators? It may be supposed that for the aggadic author who is concerned with Eccl. xii. 12 the couple T. and L. are viewed only as ethical writers, after the fashion of Ben Sira, while to the author who comments upon רקמה in Ez. xvi. 10, they are known as Bible translators, and they figure by the side of Akylas. Naturally, the one would not exclude the other.

We cannot be certain why they or their work are condemned, as in the case of Ben Sira, whose work, we know, reflects a high moral standing. Regarding T. and L. we are perplexed once more. In their capacity, however, as Bible translators they had to endure the ostracisms of Rabbinic circles on all works of this kind. It is well known that in the Rabbinic schools of those days there was a bias under which every Bible translation was condemned. Even the Aramaic "Targum" of Jonathan ben Uzziel to the Prophets was no exception.[1] And what was said against the LXX is too well known to be repeated. Even such scientific work as Origenes' Hexapla found no mercy in the eyes of the severe Rabbis who never cite it, and it can be conjectured that they and their zeal are responsible for the work being now so mutilated. Even Akylas, the pious proselyte, must needs suffer disguise as "Onkelos" to be tolerated in the synagogue, and it has already been shown by us that in later times there existed a tendency to substitute for his name that of ת"י, i.e. a genuine Jewish author.

III. The Greek Glosses in Question—Genuine or Spurious?

The preceding considerations do stand or fall, consequent on the Akylas glosses contained in Talmud and Midrash, to which are attached those of B.T. too, being held genuine or spurious. Since 'Azaria de Rossi,[2] who, four hundred years ago, first dealt

[1] See my article, "The Jews in the Works of the Church Fathers," *J.Q.R.*, V and VI (1892 and 1893), and "Church Fathers," in *The Jewish Encyclopedia*, IV 80-86.

[2] In his Me'or 'Ena'm, ch. 45.

with the matter scientifically, nobody has doubted the genuineness of these glosses, and Jewish scholars duly collected them and transliterated them into proper Greek,[1] and the mere fact that their work resulted in good " biblical " Greek, has been regarded as a proof of the authenticity of these glosses. It was reserved for the hypercriticism of our time to deny and reject this philological work.

Pinkas Churgin (*Targum Jonathan to the Prophets*, New Haven, 1907) attempted this destructive task, to the benefit—of his hero, Jonathan. In order to do him full justice, in order, too, to enable the reader to judge for himself, I am quoting his opinion in his own words: " The quotation in Yerushalmi Shabbath 6, 4 from Akylas on Is. iii. 20 is not found in the Hexapla. The case of Ez. xvi. 10 (Lam. R. 1, 1) containing a double rendering, may even be a quotation from Jonathan. The LXX might as well be meant, which here, as also in Ex. xxvii. 16, agrees with Akylas, as recorded in the Hexapla, and also disagrees, just as Akylas, with its version in the Midrash. Similarly, the citation from Akylas on Gen. xvii. 1 in Gen. R. 46, 2; in this case also there is no telling which Greek translation was meant, for the LXX contains also such a rendering (comp. Field, *Hex. l.c.*). The ascription again, to Akylas, of citations from other sources was demonstrated above. This might have been the case with the quotations from Akylas on Dan. v. 5 (Y. Yoma 3, 8 Gemara) and Esth. R. 6. In the former, Akylas is preserved in the LXX only."

On the preceding page (12, n.) Churgin was already keen enough to write a final judgment: . . . " and all assumptions by De Rossi . . . and Krauss . . . in this case deserve little consideration ".

The present writer is constrained to meet this bold attack by the following arguments: (1) A thing not found in the Hexapla

[1] In the valuable article *Bibelübersetzungen*, by Eb. Nestle, in *Realencyklopädie für protest. Theologie und Kirche* (I am using the reprint, Leipzig, 1897), the following two works are duly mentioned (p. 82): M. Friedmann, *Onkelos und Akylas*, Vienna, 1896—S. Krauss-Budapest (that was previous to my Vienna time), in the Jubilee Volume in honour of M. Steinschneider, Leipzig, 1896. Since all Greek glosses attributed to Akylas in Talmud and Midrash have found place in my *Lehnwörter*, as mentioned above.

does not cease to exist, as in Field's *Hexapla* there have been collected remnants in Greek[1] sources only, and later discoveries have augmented considerably the Hex. material as collected by Field (1867 ss.) (2) Soon in his next sentence Churgin is speaking of "double rendering," and this fact alone, that is the existence of double renderings, destroys his former argument. (3) Everything granted—how can Churgin ascribe *Greek* quotations to Jonathan, whose "Targum" is entirely Aramaic? (4) That LXX renderings coincide with those of Akylas, or *vice versa*, nobody will deny, and "coincidence" was plainly stated concerning the glosses dealt with above. We found also that Akylas, as indeed LXX and Origenes' Hex., have existed in a second edition. Slight differences only attest that there was already a fixed schematisation in rendering in Greek, a feature which easily could be demonstrated in the various English versions which are in public use to-day, and as a matter of fact also in the various renderings in other languages. (5) If the citation in Gen. R. 46, 2 is stated there to be from Akylas, as it is, how can Churgin say "there is no telling which Greek translation was meant"? (6) Churgin's next two arguments have been disposed of by what I said above: quite naturally Akylas sometimes *does* coincide with LXX.

[1] What was collected from the Syriac and other sources, see by Eb. Nestle, *l.c.*

CHAPTER ONE

THE LUCIANIC RECENSION OF THE GREEK BIBLE[1]

B.M. METZGER

Among the several scholars of the ancient Church who occupied themselves with the textual criticism of the Bible, one of the most influential was Lucian of Antioch. Though not as learned or as productive in a literary way as either Origen or Jerome, Lucian's work on the text of the Greek Bible proved to be of significance both in his own day and, to an even greater extent, during the centuries following. In fact, his recension of the text of the New Testament, with only minor modifications, continued to be used widely down to the nineteenth century, and still lives on in the so-called Ecclesiastical text of the Eastern Orthodox Church.

Little is known of the life of Lucian of Antioch. Born probably at Samosata in Syria about the middle of the third century, he was educated at Edessa under a certain Macarius, who, according to Suidas, was a learned expounder of holy Scripture. After a period when he may have studied at Caesarea, Lucian transferred to the famous theological school of Antioch, of which he and Chrysostom, Diodorus, Theodoret, and Theodore of Mopsuestia were to be some of the more distinguished alumni.

Apparently Lucian was in sympathy with the theological views of his fellow townsman, Paul of Samosata, and when Paul was deposed for Christological heresy in A.D. 268 (or 270), he too withdrew from the Church. During his later years Lucian seems to have become more orthodox, and under the episcopate of Cyril of Antioch (A.D. 283-304) he was restored to ecclesiastical fellowship. He died in the peace of the Church, suffering martyrdom for the faith at Nicomedia, Bithynia, probably on January 7, 312.

Many are the historical and theological problems connected with the person and influence of Lucian of Antioch. The question has even been raised as to whether Lucian the excommunicated heretic was the same person as Lucian the martyr and Biblical scholar.[2]

[1] The substance of this chapter was presented as a lecture at the Symposium on Antioch of Syria held during May, 1959, at the Dumbarton Oaks Research Library and Collection, Washington, D.C.

[2] This view, suggested earlier by Ceillier, Fleury, De Broglie, and Oikonomos, has been revived by D. S. Balanos in Πρακτικὰ τῆς 'Ακαδημίας 'Αθηνῶν,

Reprinted from *Chapters in the History of New Testament Textual Criticism.* [*N. T. Tools & Studies,* ed. B. M. Metzger, Vol. 4.]

There is no need, however, to suppose the existence of two Lucians, one orthodox and one heretical; the somewhat conflicting reports can be easily reconciled by the assumption that Lucian was a critical scholar whose views on the Trinity and on Christology differed from what was later defined at Nicea as the orthodox position, but that he wiped out all stains of doctrinal aberrations by his heroic confession and martyrdom.[1] It is quite understandable that during his connection with the school at Antioch he exerted a pervasive influence upon the theological views of those who came to adopt Arian theology. Indeed, Arius himself, a former pupil of Lucian's, declared (in a letter to Eusebius of Nicomedia) that he was merely following Lucian's views regarding Christology. Along with Arius, other sympathizers of Lucian's point of view—such as Eusebius of Nicomedia, Maris of Chalcedon, Leontius of Antioch, Eudoxius, Theognis of Nicaea, Asterius—became a closely-knit group that were dubbed "Collucianists."

It is, however, not the vicissitude of doctrinal disputes[2] that is our concern here, but the part that Lucian played in editing the text of the Greek Bible. Though not a little has been written on the subject, it is unfortunate that, with only a few exceptions,[3] scholars have confined their attention either to problems relating to his recension of the Greek Old Testament or to those relating to the New Testament. Such restrictions of interest have worked to the disadvantage of both groups of scholars. Just as the grammarian and the lexicographer of the New Testament can learn much from an examination of the language of the Septuagint, so too the tex-

VII (1932), 306-311, and by Gustave Bardy, *Recherches sur saint Lucien d'Antioche et son école* (Paris, 1936).

[1] So, for example, Albert Ehrhard, *Die Kirche der Märtyrer* (Munich, 1932), pp. 304f., and Adhémar d'Alès, "Autour de Lucien d'Antioche," *Mélanges de l'université Saint Joseph* (Beyrouth), XXI (1937), 185-199, who point out that it is extremely unlikely that two persons of the same name should have played important roles in Antioch at the same time without leaving in the sources a trace of their differentiation from each other.

[2] For discussions of Lucian from a doctrinal point of view, reference may be made to E. Buonaiuti, "Luciano martire, la sua dottrina e la sua scuola," *Rivista storico-critica delle scienze teologiche*, 1908, pp. 830-836, 909-923; 1909, pp. 104-118; Friedrich Loofs, *Das Bekenntnis Lucians, des Märtyrers* (= *Sitzungsberichte der königlich preussischen Akademie der Wissenschaften*, Berlin, 1915), pp. 576-603; Adolf von Harnack, *Dogmengeschichte*, 5te Aufl., II (Tübingen, 1931), 187-190; and, especially, Bardy, *op. cit.*

[3] E.g. M. Spanneut's recent study, "La Bible d'Eustathe d'Antioche — Contribution à l'histoire de la 'version lucianique,'" *Studia Patristica*, ed. F. L. Cross, IV (*TU*, LXXIX [Berlin, 1961]), 171-190.

tual critic of the New Testament will profit from considering the problems and tasks of Septuaginta-Forschung. As an exploration in methodology, therefore, the aim of the present chapter is to shed light upon the text of the New Testament by giving attention to one specific type of text common to both Old and New Testaments, the Lucianic text.

The following pages will present, first, a résumé of ancient testimonies relating to Lucian and his work as textual critic; second, a survey of research on the Lucianic or Antiochian text of the Greek Bible; third, the influence of this text outside the Greek Church; and fourth, a critical evaluation of the Lucianic recension. The chapter will conclude with a list of some of the problems that remain to be solved.

I. Ancient Testimonies to Lucian and his Textual Work

The earliest references to Lucian are two brief and highly favorable estimates which Eusebius includes in his *Church History*. Here Lucian is described as a presbyter of Antioch, "whose entire life was most excellent (ἄριστος)" (VIII.xiii.2), and as "a most excellent (ἄριστος) man in every respect, temperate in life and well-versed in sacred learning" (IX.vi.3).

Later in the fourth century Jerome makes three references to Lucian which differ considerably in temper and appreciation of his work. The differences are no doubt to be accounted for by considering the several contexts and Jerome's immediate purpose in referring to Lucian. On the one hand, when Jerome is comparing his own work as reviser of the Old Latin text with similar work by others in Greek, he is rather severe in his judgment of Lucian. Thus in his Preface to the Four Gospels, which takes the form of an open letter addressed to Pope Damasus and which was composed perhaps about the year 383, he refers somewhat contemptuously to the "manuscripts which are associated with the names of Lucian and Hesychius, the authority of which is perversely maintained by a few disputatious persons." Continuing in the same vein Jerome condemns the work of Lucian and Hesychius as infelicitous: "It is obvious that these writers could not emend anything in the Old Testament after the labors of the Seventy; and it was useless to correct the New, for versions of Scripture already exist in the languages of many nations which show that their additions are false."[1]

[1] Praetermitto eos codices quos a Luciano et Hesychio nuncupatos paucorum hominum adserit peruersa contentio: quibus utique nec in ueteri in-

Subsequently, in the Preface to his translation of the books of Chronicles, Jerome makes a more temperate allusion to the work of Lucian and other Biblical scholars. In referring to the diversity of the editions of the Greek Old Testament, he declares that three are current in various parts of the Empire: "Alexandria and Egypt in their [copies of the] Septuagint praise Hesychius as author; Constantinople to Antioch approves the copies [containing the text] of Lucian the martyr; the middle provinces between these read the Palestinian codices edited by Origen, which Eusebius and Pamphilus published."[1]

In his valuable *Lives of Illustrious Men*, written soon after A.D. 392, Jerome is still more generous in his description of Lucian. Here, in a biographical sketch devoted to the martyr from Antioch, he characterizes him as "a man of great talent" and "so diligent in the study of the Scriptures that even now certain copies of the Scriptures bear the name of Lucian."[2] What is of special importance is the declaration that copies of the Scriptures (and not just of the Septuagint, as Jerome is sometimes quoted) passed under the name of *Lucianea*.

strumento post septuaginta interpretes emendare quid licuit nec in nouo profuit emendasse, cum multarum gentium linguis scriptura ante translata doceat falsa esse quae addita sunt (edita sunt, ms. E; John Wordsworth and H. J. White, *Novum Testamentum Domini Nostri Iesu Christi Latine*, I [Oxford, 1889], 2). There has been a curious reluctance among many scholars to admit that Jerome here refers to any more than the Lucianic text of the Old Testament. But, as B. H. Streeter pointed out, "seeing that Jerome is writing a careful and considered Preface to a revised version of the Four Gospels, and that he only mentions the Lucianic and Hesychian versions in order to contrast their inferior text with that of the 'ancient codices' he himself has used, I simply cannot understand why some scholars have raised doubts as to whether the Lucianic and Hesychian recensions included the New Testament as well as the Old" (*The Four Gospels* [London, 1936], p. 591). As regards the much more nebulous figure of Hesychius, whom no Greek author mentions, the situation is different. Despite the popularity of Wilhelm Bousset's suggestion that the so-called "Neutral" text is to be attributed to Hesychius, most scholars today are inclined to agree with Sir Frederic G. Kenyon, who concluded his study of "Hesychius and the Text of the New Testament" (*Mémorial Lagrange* [Paris, 1940], pp. 245-250) with the words: "The title of 'Hesychius' rests in fact upon what is little more than a shadow of a shade."

[1] Alexandria et Aegyptus in LXX suis Hesychium laudat auctorem; Constantinopolis usque Antiochiam Luciani martyris exemplaria probat; mediae inter has provinciae Palaestinos codices legunt, quos ab Origene elaboratos Eusebius et Pamphilus vulgaverunt (Migne, *PL*, XXVIII, 1392 A, and Friedrich Stummer, *Einführung in die lateinische Bibel* [Paderborn, 1928], p. 239).

[2] Lucianus, vir disertissimus, Antiochenae ecclesiae presbyter, tantum in Scriptuarum studio laborat, ut usque nunc quaedam exemplaria Scripturarum Lucianea nuncupentur (*de Viris inlustribus*, 77 [*TU*, XIV, pp. 41f., ed. E. C. Richardson]).

Information of the widespread use of Lucian's recension of the Psalter is contained in Jerome's letter to Sunnias and Fretela (about A.D. 403). These two Gothic churchmen had inquired of Jerome why his own Latin Psalter (the so-called Roman Psalter) differed so frequently from the Septuagint. In his reply Jerome points out that they have been misled by their edition of the Septuagint, which varied widely from the critical text of Origen given in the Hexapla and used by himself. Jerome writes: "You must know that there is one edition which Origen and Eusebius of Caesarea and all the Greek commentators call κοινή, that is common and widespread, and is by most people now called Lucianic; and there is another, that of the Septuagint, which is found in the manuscripts of the Hexapla, and has been faithfully translated by us into Latin."[1] Here Jerome distinguishes the Lucianic text from that of the Hexapla, and indicates that the former met with such universal acceptance that it received the name of the Vulgate or common text.

Later testimonies refer to Lucian's competence in Hebrew. For example, Suidas and Simeon Metaphrastes (in the *Passio S. Luciani martyris*) assert that "he translated [literally, renewed] them all [i.e. the books of the Old Testament] again from the Hebrew language, of which he had a very accurate knowledge, spending much labor on the work."[2] Though Lucian may have consulted the Hebrew in connection with his revision of the Septuagint, this statement is obviously exaggerated in the manner of hagiographers. More sober, and doubtless nearer to the truth of what Lucian attempted to do, is the description of pseudo-Athanasius in his *Synopsis sacrae scripturae*: "Using the earlier editions [i.e. of Aquila, Theodotion, and Symmachus] and the Hebrew, and having accurately surveyed the expressions which fell short of or went

[1] Illud breuiter admoneo, ut sciatis aliam esse editionem, quam Origenes et Caesariensis Eusebius omnesque Graeciae tractatores κοινήν—id est communem—appellant atque uulgatam et a plerisque nunc Λουκιάνειος dicitur, aliam septuaginta interpretum, quae et in ἑξαπλοῖς codicibus repperitur et a nobis in Latinum sermonen fideliter uersa est (*Epist.* 106, § 2, 2 [*CSEL*, vol. LV, p. 248, ed. Hilberg]).

[2] Both Suidas and Simeon, who here agree (except in inconsequential details) in their accounts of Lucian, depend upon earlier hagiographical sources. The variant ἐπανεσώσατο, which Adler adopts into her text of Suidas, is clearly the inferior reading; either Simeon's ἀνενεώσατο or ἐπανενεώσατο is to be preferred. For the text of both see Joseph Bidez's ed. of Philostorgius, Anhang VI (= *Griechische christliche Schriftsteller*, 1913, p. 187).

beyond the truth, and having corrected them in their proper places, he published them for the Christian brethren."[1]

Among testimonia of uncertain origin there is an unequivocal statement that Lucian concerned himself with the New Testament as well as the Old. Under the date of October 15, the Menaeon of the Greek Church (this is a liturgical volume which includes short accounts of saints and martyrs to be read on their festivals) states that Lucian made a copy with his own hand of both the Old and New Testaments, written in three columns, which afterwards belonged to the Church in Nicomedia.[2] Substantially the same information in a more extended hagiographical context is contained in the Synaxarium ecclesiae Constantinopolitanae for October 15.[3]

This list of testimonies may be brought to a close[4] with a reference to the condemnation of Lucian in the so-called *Decretum Gelasianum*, where mention is made of *Evangelia quae falsavit Lucianus, apocrypha, Evangelia quae falsavit Hesychius, apocrypha* (V, iii, 8-9). It is generally agreed that this statement rests upon a misunderstanding of the critical remarks of Jerome.[5]

By way of summarizing ancient testimonies concerning Lucian's textual work, we find that his contemporaries generally regarded him as an able scholar, entirely competent to undertake such a recension. As a native Syrian he could, of course, have consulted the Syriac version; he also appears to have had some acquaintance with Hebrew. As would have been expected, he made use of previous Greek translations of the Old Testament, and sought to adjust the Greek to the underlying Hebrew text. But we are told nothing as to the amount of revision which he undertook in either Old or

[1] Theodor Zahn dated this document not later than the fifth or sixth century; see his *Geschichte der neutestamentlichen Kanons*, II (Erlangen, 1890), 311. The text is printed in Migne, *PG*, vol. XXVIII, col. 433; see also H. Dörrie's discussion of the textual transmission of this passage in his article, "Zur Geschichte der Septuaginta im Jahrhundert Konstantins," *ZNW*, XXXIX (1940), 79-87.

[2] The relevant passage is a follows: εἰς κάλλος δὲ γράφειν ἐπιστάμενος βιβλίον κατέλιπε τῇ Νικομηδέων ἐκκλησίᾳ, γεγραμμένον σελίσι τρισσαῖς (εἰς τρεῖς στήλας διῃρημένης τῆς σελίδος), περιέχον πᾶσαν τὴν παλαιάν τε καὶ τὴν νέαν διαθήκην.

[3] Edited by Hippolyte Delehaye, *Propylaeum ad Acta Sanctorum, Novembris* [vol. LXI], 1902, pp. 138ff.

[4] For several other ancient testimonies to Lucian, see M. J. Routh, *Reliquiae sacrae*, 2nd ed., IV (Oxford, 1846), 5-10.

[5] See Ernst von Dobschütz, *Das Decretum Gelasianum* (= *TU*, XXXVIII, 4), pp. 51 and 292.

New Testament text, the nature of the manuscripts which he consulted, the relation of his work to the Hexapla, and other similar matters. For information bearing on such problems, we must turn to the manuscripts which have been thought to contain the Lucian recension.

II. Survey of Research on the Lucianic or Antiochian Text

A. *The Old Testament*

Our account begins with the first printed edition of the entire Greek Old Testament; namely, that contained in the famous Complutensian Polyglot Bible sponsored by the Spanish Cardinal Francisco Ximenes de Cisneros (1437-1517), Archbishop of Toledo, and published at Complutum (now Alcalá de Henares). The four folio volumes containing the Old Testament in Hebrew, Latin, and Greek were printed between 1514 and 1517. As it happened, one[1] of the two manuscripts of the Greek Old Testament which Pope Leo X sent from the Vatican Library for the use of the editors of the Polyglot, and which forms the basis of a large part of their text, contains the type of text now thought to be Lucianic, at least in Samuel and Kings. In other parts of the Old Testament, however, this manuscript departs from the Antiochian type of text. Furthermore, the Spanish editors frequently adopted readings from several other Greek witnesses, and occasionally even conformed the Greek to the Hebrew without any manuscript authority. This Complutensian text was followed on the whole in subsequent Polyglot Bibles (those published at Antwerp, 1569-72; Heidelberg, 1586-1616; Hamburg, 1596; and Paris, 1645).

During the seventeenth and eighteenth centuries scholars laid the basis for subsequent investigations by collecting variant readings from manuscripts of the Greek Old Testament, from the early versions, and from the quotations of the Fathers. Brian Walton's Polyglot Bible (London, 1654-57), Humphrey Hody's valuable researches into the text of the Septuagint (Oxford, 1703), and the collection by Bernard de Montfaucon of the remains of Origen's Hexapla (Paris, 1713) were climaxed by the publication of the monumental *Vetus Testamentum Graecum cum variis lectionibus* edited by Robert Holmes and James Parsons (5 vols., Oxford, 1798-1827). The variant readings of about three hundred separate

[1] Namely, Cod. Vat. gr. 330 (= Holmes 108).

codices, of which twenty are uncial, are given. In addition to patristic citations, evidence is also supplied from the Old Latin, the Coptic, Arabic, Slavonic, Armenian, and Georgian versions, obtained partly from manuscripts, partly from printed texts. This immense apparatus now made it possible to group manuscripts by families; indeed, it became necessary to do so if only to bring some kind of order out of the chaotic mass of evidence.

During the latter part of the nineteenth century, through the researches of Ceriani, Field, and that polymathic scholar, Lagarde,[1] a beginning was made in the assigning of extant manuscript witnesses to each of the major recensions of antiquity. In the case of the Lucianic text, two touchstones were available for identifying the paternity of variant readings. One was the frequent agreement between this text and the quotations of the Fathers of the fourth and fifth centuries who almost certainly used the Antiochian Bible, in particular Chrysostom and Theodoret. A second means of identifying certain individual readings was supplied by the presence of the siglum καὶ λ̥ which is found prefixed to marginal readings in several Greek manuscripts, as well as the letter lomadh (ܠ) marking variants in certain Syriac manuscripts. Although in some instances the Greek siglum is to be interpreted as meaning καὶ λοιποί, most scholars are agreed that in other instances it is to be resolved as καὶ Λουκιανός. The key to this resolution of the siglum was discovered in the nineteenth century in a note[2] prefixed to the Arabic translation of the Syro-Hexaplar, which states, "Lucian compared with the greatest care these Hebrew copies, and if he found anything different or superfluous he restored it to its place, prefixing to the part which he emended the initial letter L." In the same passage reference is made to the marks by which the readings of Aquila,

[1] The literary activities of this scholar were immense. He published books in no less than ten languages. As the Prorector of the University said at his funeral, probably no one of his colleagues could spell out the alphabets of all the languages in which Lagarde had edited texts; see p. 170 of the address delivered by George Foot Moore, entitled "Paul Anton de Lagarde," on the occasion of the opening of the Lagarde Library in the University of the City of New York, April 29, 1893 (*The University Quarterly*, July, 1893, pp. 166-179). An (incomplete) bibliography of his publications, compiled by R. J. H. Gottheil (*Proceedings of the American Oriental Society*, 1892, pp. ccxi-ccxxix), includes 297 major publications.

[2] A Latin translation of this Arabic note is found in Field, *Origenis Hexaplarum quae supersunt ... fragmenta* (Oxonii, 1875), pp. lxxxiv sq.; cf. Giovanni Card. Mercati, "Di alcune testimonianze antiche sulle cure bibliche di San Luciano," *B*, xxiv (1943), 1-17, especially pp. 7ff.

Symmachus, Theodotion, and the other Greek versions are denoted; and then the writer proceeds: "but if [the letters] elif, vaw, ra are used, these are Origen's readings; if the letter lomadh, that is Lucian's."

Making use of this aid in identifying Lucianic readings, scholars were able to isolate and classify witnesses to the Antiochian recension. Thus, for the historical books of the Old Testament Ceriani[1] and Field[2] discovered that the text of the cursive Greek manuscripts 19, 82, 93, 108 agrees frequently with the form of text quoted by the Antiochian Fathers, and that these same manuscripts contain readings marked as Lucianic in the Syro-Hexaplar. Working independently Lagarde had come to almost the same results, and on the basis of evidence from these four manuscripts plus another, codex 118, he reconstructed the Lucianic recension of about one half of the Old Testament (Genesis to II Esdras, and a double text of Esther).[3] Unfortunately, except for the Book of Esther and, in another publication, the first fourteen chapters of Genesis, Lagarde provided no *apparatus criticus*. Thus, the scholar who wishes to check the variants in order to evaluate Lagarde's judgment must still go to Holmes and Parsons' thesaurus of variant readings.

In the Prophets another group of manuscripts has been found to contain the text of Lucian. Field satisfied himself that codices 22, 36, 48, 51, 62, 90, 93, 144, 147, 233, 308 offer in more or less pure form the Antiochian text. Later scholars, however, have criticized Field's grouping, and some of the manuscripts have been removed from his list of Lucianic witnesses. Thus, Cornill[4] struck out four (62, 90, 147, 233), and in this he was supported by Lagarde. In the Minor Prophets, the doctoral research of a young Dutch scholar, Schuurmans Stekhoven, indicated a slightly different grouping of manuscripts (22, 36, 42, 51, 62, 86, 95, 147, 153, 185, 238, 240, and in Zech. ch. 13 also 231).[5] He also pointed out that they do not all supply the Lucianic text in an equally pure form.

During the first decade of the twentieth century a group of scholars in Germany, many of them under the leadership of Alfred

[1] *Monumenta sacra et profana*, II, 2 (1864), pp. 76, 98, 102; *Rendiconti del R. Istituto Lombardo*, Ser. 2, vol. XIX (1886), 206 ff.

[2] *Op. cit.*, p. lxxxvii.

[3] *Librorum Veteris Testamenti canonicorum pars prior graece* (Göttingen, 1883).

[4] C. H. Cornill, *Das Buch des Propheten Ezechiel* (Leipzig, 1886), pp. 65-66.

[5] J. Z. Schuurmans Stekhoven, *De alexandrijsche vertaling van het Dodekaprofeton* (Leiden, 1887), p. 44.

Rahlfs, Lagarde's successor at Göttingen, began a systematic investigation of the Lucianic text within certain books of the Bible. For example, Johannes Dahse attempted a classification of the manuscripts in Genesis, and assigned codices 53, 56, 129 to Lucian.[1] His reasons for this assignment, however, rested on a narrow selection of evidence, and subsequent scholars have indicated their dissatisfaction with his judgment. On the basis of a large induction of evidence, Ernst Hautsch found that, for the Book of Joshua, the quotations of the Antiochian Fathers agree with codices 44, 54, 75, 76, 84, 106, 134, while in the Book of Judges, the Bible of Theodoret (and Chrysostom) is most purely represented in codices 54, 59, 75, with which group 44, 82, 84, 106, 134 are frequently jointed.[2] For the books of the Pentateuch, Hautsch found no overwhelmingly clear distribution of manuscripts that had previously been considered to be Lucianic; indeed, the most assured conclusion he could draw is that certain manuscripts which had been previously thought to be Lucianic (e.g., b, w, 108) do not in fact represent this recension. Procksch continued the research on the history of the Septuagint text of the Prophets.[3] He concluded that in Isaiah the Lucianic text is represented in manuscripts 22, 36, 48, 51, 93, 144, 308; that in Jeremiah it is in manuscripts 22, 36, 48, 51, 96, 144, 229, 231; that in Ezekiel it is in manuscripts 36, 48, 51, 231; and that in the Minor Prophets it is in 22, 36, 48, 51, 93, 95, 96, 114, 130, 153, 185, 240, 308, 311.

The most vigorous and thorough-going investigation of the Septuagint text during the twentieth century was that undertaken by Alfred Rahlfs. His aim, like that of his master, Lagarde, was to distinguish among the mass of manuscripts the three principal recensions (those of Origen, Hesychius, and Lucian), and, from the agreements among these, to recover the original pre-hexaplaric Septuagint text. In the first of his *Septuaginta-Studien* he examines in minute detail Theodoret's quotations from the Books of Kings and from II Chronicles.[4] Though in general his findings confirm the

[1] "Textkritische Studien," *Zeitschrift für die alttestamentliche Wissenschaft*, XXVIII (1908), 1-21, 161-173.

[2] *Der Lukiantext des Oktateuch* [= Mitteilungen des Septuaginta-Unternehmens der königlichen Gesellschaft der Wissenschaften zu Göttingen, vol. 1] (Berlin, 1909).

[3] O. Procksch, *Studien zur Geschichte der Septuaginta: Die Propheten* (Leipzig, 1910).

[4] *Septuaginda-Studien*; Heft 1, *Studien zu den Königsbüchern* (Göttingen, 1904).

view of previous critics (namely, that Theodoret commonly quoted a text of the type represented in Lagarde's edition), Rahlfs discovered that in a considerable number of passages Theodoret's text does not agree with that of Lucian. In answer to the question of the nature of the text underlying the recension of Lucian, he found that it stands closest to Vaticanus (13) and to the Ethiopic version in the older and purer form represented by Dillmann's codices S and A. Thus Lucian is sometimes, especially in I Kings, an important witness to this old, "pre-hexaplaric" form of text.

Rahlfs gave attention next to an examination of the text of the Greek Psalter.[1] With rigorous and scrupulously careful weighing of evidence, his research is a model of patient and exact scholarship. In the chapter devoted to Lucian's text,[2] beginning with the hint given in Jerome's letter to the Gothic churchmen Sunnias and Fretela,[3] Rahlfs examines the quotations from the Psalter in Jerome, Theodoret, and Chrysostom, and concludes that the Lucianic Psalter was widely used throughout the East, where it, indeed, had obtained the status of the "official" text of the Greek Church. This text also circulated, in more or less pure form, even in the West, and at Milan influenced a revision of the Old Latin Psalter. As it happens, however, no manuscript is extant today which contains a pure Lucianic text of the Psalter (codex Alexandrinus, for example, presents a mixed text).

In a subsequent part of *Septuaginta-Studien*, Rahlfs criticizes Lagarde's edition of the Lucianic text of the books of Samuel and Kings.[4] Nowhere in his edition did Lagarde set forth the principles which he had followed in constructing the text. From Lagarde's *Nachlese*, Rahlfs shows that in the Books of Kings Lagarde depended primarily on codex 93, but here and there introduced into a transcript of this manuscript readings from other witnesses, besides making certain changes in proper names and in grammatical details without support in any manuscript whatever. Moreover, several inadvertent and arbitrary departures from the tradition also found their way into his text. The value of Lagarde's edition, therefore, as

[1] *Septuaginta-Studien*; Heft II, *Der Text des Septuaginta-Psalters* (Göttingen, 1907).

[2] *Op. cit.*, pp. 169-182.

[3] See p. 5 above.

[4] *Septuaginta-Studien*; Heft III, *Lucian's Rezension der Königsbücher* (Göttingen, 1911); the substance of this monograph was awarded a prize by the Göttingen Academy.

Rahlfs points out, is that it gives in convenient form a general view of the character of the recension which it represents, but for the detailed study of the Lucianic text it is quite inadequate.

Using Lagarde's collations, checked by Holmes and Parsons, Rahlfs found that in the Books of Kings four manuscripts, which fall into two sub-groups, preserve the Lucianic text; they are codices 19, 108, and 82, 93. Tested by internal probability of readings, the second of these sub-groups proves itself to be markedly superior to the other group. (It will be recalled that 108 played a considerable part in the construction of the Greek text in the Complutensian Polyglot, while Lagarde's text was based largely on 93). Rahlfs added as a major Lucianic witness codex 127. Related manuscripts are 56, 158, 245.

In subsequent publications Rahlfs continued to investigate the tangled history of the transmission of the Septuagint. In what is one of the most searching contributions ever made to the textual criticism of the Septuagint, in 1922 Rahlfs published 117 pages devoted to the textual history of the little Book of Ruth.[1] In the same year he issued in pamphlet form a *Probe-Ausgabe* of the Greek text of Ruth,[2] which opened a new era in the century-long work on the Septuagint. Rahlfs found the Lucianic recension to be preserved in codices 54, 59, 75, 82, 93, 314, and (from 4.11 to the end of the book) in 19 and 108.

Four years later the text of Genesis was published, being the first of a proposed sixteen-volume edition of the Septuagint.[3] Here the enormous mass of material and, more particularly, the lack of distinct lines of text-type prevented the editor from assigning in clear-cut fashion any codices to the Lucianic recension. The most that he was able to say is that in Genesis codex 75 is a representative of the text of Lucian, but that it contains strands of other text-types as well.[4] Rahlfs turned next to the task of editing the Psalms, and

[1] *Studie über den griechischen Text des Buches Ruth* (= *Mitteilungen des Septuaginta-Unternehmens*, III, 2-3).

[2] *Das Buch Ruth griechisch, als Probe einer kritischen Handausgabe der Septuaginta* (Stuttgart, 1922).

[3] *Septuaginta*; Societatis Scientiarum Gottingensis auctoritate edidit Alfred Rahlfs; I, *Genesis* (Stuttgart, 1926). For a discerning essay on the proposed edition see P. L. Hedley in *HTR*, XXVI (1933), 57-72.

[4] It is instructive that in his Preface to the edition of Genesis Rahlfs makes the statement that, though Lagarde's program of first reconstructing the three great ancient recensions of the Septuagint is correct in principle, yet in practice the enormous magnitude of the task prevents the attainment of

in 1931, as part X of the large edition, his *Psalmi cum Odis* appeared. The volume contains an extensive introduction, in which the author supplements and modifies the second part of his *Septuaginta-Studien* (1907). The great bulk of witnesses fall into the category of the Lucianic recension, which, as has been mentioned earlier, was extremely widespread and which, in fact, became the authoritative text of the Psalter for the Greek Church.

Subsequent fascicles of the Göttingen Septuagint were prepared by Werner Kappler, Joseph Ziegler, and Robert Hanhart. The manuscripts which they found to be Lucianic in the several books thus far edited are as follows:

In I Maccabees (ed. Kappler, 1936) the Lucianic manuscripts are 64, 236, 381, 536, 728. A sub-group of Lucianic manuscripts includes 19, 62, 93, 542.

In the XII Prophets (ed. Ziegler, 1943) the Lucianic manuscripts are 22, 36, 48, 51, 231 (only a fragment), 719, 763. Two sub-groups of Lucianic manuscripts are: (1) 62, 147, and (2) 46, 86, 711.

In Isaiah (ed. Ziegler, 1939) the Lucianic manuscripts are 22, 48, 51, 231, 763. Three sub-groups of Lucianic manuscripts are (1) 62, 142; (2) 90, 130, 311; (3) 36, 93, 96. Other manuscripts show sporadic Lucianic readings, e.g. 46, 233, 456, and 926.

In Ezekiel (ed. Ziegler, 1952) the Lucianic manuscripts are 22, 36, 48, 51, 96, 231, 763. Two sub-groups of Lucianic manuscripts are (1) 311, 538, and (2) V, 46, 449.

In Susanna, Daniel, Bel and the Dragon (ed. Ziegler, 1954), the Lucianic manuscripts are 22, 36, 48, 51, 96, 231, 763. Two sub-groups of Lucianic manuscripts are (1) 311, 538, and (2) 88, 449.

In Jeremiah, Baruch, Lamentations, and the Epistle of Jeremiah (ed. Ziegler, 1957), the Lucianic manuscripts are 22, 36, 48, 51, 96, 231, 311, 763. A sub-group of Lucianic manuscripts includes 62, 198, 407, 449.

In II Maccabees (ed. Kappler and Hanhart, 1959), the Lucianic

that ideal. For discussions of the problems by two scholars who are critical of the Lagardian program, see Alexander Sperber's "Probleme einer Edition der Septuaginta," in *Studien zur Geschichte und Kultur . . . Paul Kahle* (Leiden, 1935), pp. 39-46; the same author's study of "The Problems of the Septuagint Recensions," *JBL*, LIV (1935), 73-92; as well as Paul Kahle in *The Cairo Geniza* (London, 1947), pp. 154 ff.; 2nd ed. (1959), pp. 231 ff. For a criticism of Kahle's position, see the article by Peter Katz, "Septuagintal Studies in the Mid-Century," in *The Background of the New Testament and its Eschatology*, edited by W. D. Davies and D. Daube (Cambridge, 1956), especially pp. 205-208.

manuscripts are 64, 236, 381, 534, 728. A sub-group of Lucianic manuscripts includes 19, 62, 93, 542.

In III Maccabees (ed. Hanhart, 1960) the Lucianic manuscripts are 64, 236, 381, 534, 728. A sub-group of Lucianic manuscripts includes 19, 62, 93, 347 (1.1-2.19), 542.

The above survey of scholarly attempts to identify and study the Lucianic text suggests something of the magnitude and complexity of the problem. It will be understood that the Septuagint is not a unified version of the Old Testament, but a collection of independent translations of the several books or groups of books made at different times and places. Of some books there was more than one translation, and even in the case of individual books the hand of more than one translator can be discerned.[1] It was inevitable that during the centuries these translations should have been corrected, one by another, and all of them occasionally by the Hebrew—which may or may not have been the same form of Hebrew text as that from which the book was originally translated. Possibilities for additional contamination were accelerated by the publication in the second Christian century of three new Jewish translations, those of Aquila, Theodotion, and Symmachus.[2] Furthermore, the three recensions of the Septuagint prepared by Christian scholars—Origen, Lucian, and Hesychius—in the third century, so far from putting an end to the confusion, gave it a new impulse. It is therefore not surprising that today the manuscripts of the Greek Old Testament present a mixed form of text. Nor should the investigator imagine that it will be possible in every case to distinguish neatly ordered families of witnesses; in his search for the Lucianic text he must be prepared to acknowledge that for some of the books of the Old Testament it has left no recognizable trace among extant manuscripts.[3]

[1] See, e.g., H. St. J. Thackeray in *JTS*, IV (1902/03), 245-266, 398-411, 578-585; VIII (1906/07), 262-278; IX (1908), 88-98.

[2] According to Samuel Krauss two other Jewish translations into Greek were prepared by Ben La'ana and by Ben Tilga (see "Two Hitherto Unknown Bible Versions in Greek," *Bulletin of the John Rylands Library*, XXVII [1942-43], 97-105).

[3] For the difficulties involved in the contamination of recensional and non-recensional manuscripts, see the incisive comments of Heinrich Dörrie in his monograph, "Zur Geschichte der Septuaginta im Jahrhundert Konstantins," *ZNW*, XXXIX (1940), 57-110. Raymond Thornhill, in his discussion of "Six or Seven Nations; a Pointer to the Lucianic Text in the Heptateuch with Special Reference to the Old Latin Version" (*JTS*, N.S. X [1959], 233-246), finds that on the whole the Lucianic text of the Pentateuch has been preserved in relatively few manuscripts.

It appears to the present writer, however, that these unfavorable estimates of the value of the Antiochian text must be at least partially revised in the light of critical study of what may be called (for the want of a better name) the Ur-Lucianic text. Let us begin first with the Old Testament.

A. *The Old Testament*

It is a curious fact that certain readings which have been generally regarded as typical of Lucian's recension of the Greek Old Testament occur in texts and authors that are earlier than Lucian. The following is a list of seven such pre-Lucianic witnesses to a form of text which, at least in part, resembles the Lucianic recension.

(1) Although not all scholars who have investigated the subject are in agreement as to how to explain the data, there seems to be substantial evidence to prove that various parts of the Old Latin version of the Old Testament contain Lucianic readings. This was noticed first by Ceriani in connection with Lamentations,[1] and then by Vercellone,[2] who observed that when the glosses in the margin of the Leon manuscript depart from the ordinary Septuagint text they agree with the readings of the Lucianic group 19-82-93-108. Other scholars have called attention to the same type of text in other parts of the Old Latin Bible. Thus, Burkitt found that "the Old Latin in the Prophets sometimes supports 'Lucianic' readings. This fact proves that among the constituents of the eclectic text most used by the Antiochene Fathers of the fourth century there was an ancient element akin to the Old Latin, but quite independent of our leading MSS codd. A ℵ B."[3] For the Books of Samuel, S. R. Driver wrote, "The Old Latin is a version made, or revised, on the basis of manuscripts agreeing closely with those which were followed by Lucian in framing his recension. The Old Latin must date from the second century A.D.; hence it cannot be based on the recension of Lucian as such; its peculiar interest lies in the fact that it affords independent evidence of the existence of MSS. containing Lucian's characteristic readings (or renderings), considerably before

[1] A. M. Ceriani, *Monumenta sacra et profana*, I, i (Milan, 1861), p. xvi (addenda).

[2] Carlo Vercellone, *Variae lectiones Vulgatae latinae Bibliorum editionis*, II (Rome, 1864), xxi-xxii, 179; cf. I, pp. xciii-xcv.

[3] F. C. Burkitt, *The Book of Rules of Tyconius* (= *TS*, III, 1; Cambridge, 1895), p. cxvii.

the time of Lucian himself."[1] The Belgian scholar, Dieu, sought to explain these parallels in terms of scribal activity in replacing the original form of the Old Latin quotations with a form that resembles the text of Lucian.[2] Although a certain number of Lucianic glosses may have been introduced here and there into one or more Old Latin witnesses, the wide variety of evidence makes it difficult to explain all the data in this way. According to the investigation of Montgomery,[3] the Old Latin text of Daniel likewise displays Lucianic readings, and Haupert, one of Montgomery's students, found that the situation is similar for the Books of Kings.[4]

These phenomena in Old Latin manuscripts appear to be corroborated by quotations of the Bible made by Latin authors who lived prior to Lucian. Although Rahlfs had concluded that no Latin author before Lucifer of Cagliari (died 371) cited characteristic Lucianic readings in the Books of Kings,[5] Capelle, in a monograph on the text of the Latin Psalter in Africa, discovered that both Tertullian and Cyprian show a certain amount of acquaintance with a pre-Lucianic form of text of the Psalms.[6] In a recent analysis of Cyprian's citations from the four Books of Kings, Fischer[7] found that Cyprian agrees with Lucian in those readings which are linguistic corrections or which otherwise improve the Greek text according to the Hebrew, but that, quite understandably, he does not agree with Lucian when the latter takes over hexaplaric variants. Furthermore, in many cases where Cyprian agrees with Lucian, other Old Latin witnesses are corrected to the Septuagint.

[1] S. R. Driver, *Notes on the Hebrew Text and the Topography of the Books of Samuel*, 2nd ed. (Oxford, 1931), p. lxxvi.

[2] L. Dieu, "Retouches Lucianiques sur quelques textes de la vieille version latine (I et II Samuel)," *RB*, n.s., XVI (1919), 372-403.

[3] James A. Montgomery, *A Critical and Exegetical Commentary on the Book of Daniel* (New York, 1927), pp. 54-55.

[4] R. S. Haupert, *The Relation of Codex Vaticanus and the Lucianic Text in the Books of the Kings from the Viewpoint of the Old Latin and the Ethiopic Versions* (Univ. of Penna. Diss., 1930), pp. 36 f. Whether these data prove that the Old Latin Version was made originally at Antioch in Syria, as some have thought, need not be examined here; for a classic discussion of the problem, see H. A. A. Kennedy, "Latin Versions, the Old," Hastings' *Dictionary of the Bible*, III (New York, 1900), p. 54.

[5] *Lucians Rezension der Königsbücher* (Göttingen, 1911), pp. 158 ff.

[6] Paul Capelle, *Le texte du Psautier latin en Afrique* (= *Collectanae biblica latina*, IV; Rome, 1913), p. 204.

[7] Bonifatius Fischer, "Lukian-Lesarten in der Vetus Latina der vier Königsbücher," *Miscellanea biblica et orientalia R. P. Athanasio Miller ... oblata* (= *Studia Anselmiana*, XXVII-XXVIII; Rome, 1951), 169-177.

The wide distribution of Old Latin evidence and the general consensus among scholars that the origin of the Old Latin version of the Old Testament dates from about the second century A.D. make the conclusion inevitable that the Greek text lying behind the Old Latin was one element, and perhaps one of the more important elements, from which the composite Lucianic text was constructed.

(2) The Peshitta version of the Old Testament also exhibits numerous readings which find a parallel in the recension associated with Lucian. At the end of the last century Stockmayer[1] found more than a score of readings in I Samuel where Lucian agrees with the Peshitta against the Masoretic text and the current Septuagint text. Although the exact date of the translation of the Old Testament Peshitta is not known, most scholars believe that it was made in the second or third century of the Christian era. Thus, at least in the Books of Samuel, it too affords evidence of Ur-Lucianic readings.

One is not limited, however, to versional evidence testifying to the existence of an Ur-Lucianic text. Several pieces of Greek evidence point in the same direction; they are the following:

(3) A papyrus fragment (Rahlfs' no. 2054),[2] dating from the third (or possibly the second) Christian century, contains the Greek text of Psalm 77.1-18 in a form which exhibits several significant agreements with the Lucianic text, some of which are against all other witnesses cited by Rahlfs in his edition of *Psalmi cum Odis*. In other words, fully half a century before Lucian made his recension in Syria, a Greek text circulated in Egypt which anticipated certain of Lucian's characteristic readings.

(4) At the middle of the second century Justin Martyr cited the Old Testament in a form which Bousset found to agree frequently with the Lucianic recension; moreover, this agreement, Bousset declared, is "nicht nur in einzelnen Stellen, sondern in weiterem Umfange."[3] Puzzled as to how to explain the apparent anachronism, Bousset felt compelled to suppose that scribes in transmitting Justin's works brought his quotations into harmony with the pre-

[1] Theodor Stockmayer, "Hat Lucian zu seiner Septuagintrevision die Peschito benützt?" *Zeitschrift für die alttestamentliche Wissenschaft*, XII (1892), 218-223.

[2] The fragment, which is 240 in the Greek and Roman Museum in Alexandria, was edited by M. Norsa in *Bulletin de la Société royale d'archéologie d'Alexandrie*, XXII (1926), 162-164.

[3] Wilhelm Bousset, *Die Evangeliencitate Justins des Märtyrers in ihrem Wert für die Evangelienkritik* (Göttingen, 1891), p. 20.

vailing Antiochian text of the Old Testament. Schürer, however, in his review of Bousset's monograph pointed out that not every reading which is found in Lucianic manuscripts is later than Justin.[1]

(5) At the end of the first Christian century Josephus had before him a Greek copy of the Books of Samuel which, according to the research of Mez, diverged widely from codices A and B and habitually agreed with the text of Lucian, following this text even against the Hebrew.[2] Rahlfs re-examined with great care the evidence presented by Mez, extending the scope of the investigation to Josephus's text of the Books of Kings. His conclusion was that Mez exaggerated the measure and significance of the agreement between Josephus and Lucian, but that, particularly in the Books of Samuel, some readings which appear in the Lucianic recension were current at a much earlier time.[3] Going far beyond this cautious evaluation, Thackeray (who showed no acquaintance with Rahlfs's monograph) asserted roundly: "The Josephan Biblical text is *uniformly* of this Lucianic type from I Samuel to I Maccabees."[4]

(6) In an analysis of the Old Testament quotations in the New Testament, Staerk discovered that here and there New Testament citations diverge from all the major codices of the Septuagint and agree with the Lucianic text.[5] It must be admitted, however, that this evidence is not conclusive, for we can never be sure on which side the borrowing may lie (i.e., the Byzantine scribe of the Lucianic codices may have conformed the Old Testament text to the Antiochian form with which he was familiar in the New Testament quotations). Nevertheless, it is pertinent to observe that the very widespread interpolation of the Pauline catena in Romans 3.13-18

[1] *Theologische Literaturzeitung*, XVI (1891), 67.

[2] Adam Mez, *Die Bibel des Josephus untersucht für Buch V-VII der Archäologie* (Basel, 1895), p. 80.

[3] Rahlfs, *Lucians Rezension der Königsbücher*, pp. 80-111.

[4] Henry St. John Thackeray, *Josephus, the Man and the Historian* (New York, 1929), p. 85. In the Preface to the Cambridge edition of the Septuagint text of the Books of Samuel, Thackeray declares that from I Sam. 8 onwards "Josephus becomes a witness of first-importance for the text of the Greek Bible . . . His main source is a Greek Bible containing a text closely allied to that of the 'Lucianic' group of MSS., but anterior by more than two centuries to the date of Lucian" (p. ix).

[5] W. Staerk, "Die alttestamentlichen Citate bei den Schriftstellern des Neuen Testaments," *Zeitschrift für wissenschaftliche Theologie*, XXXV (1892), 464-485; XXXVI, 1 (1893), 70-98.

after Psalm 13 (14).3, an addition which Jerome says[1] was current in the widely-used text of his day and which Rahlfs even prints as part of the Septuagint text, did not appear in the Lucianic recension, nor did the scribes of these manuscripts succumb to the temptation to add it.

(7) In the John Rylands Library at Manchester there are fragmentary remains of a papyrus scroll containing Deuteronomy 23.25; 25.2-3; and 26.18 in Greek.[2] The text of these tiny fragments, which date from about the middle of the second century B.C., appears to be related to the Lucianic form of the Greek Bible.[3]

From these seven items it can be seen that various texts and authors earlier than Lucian of Antioch present readings which agree with what is believed to be the Lucianic recension of the Greek Old Testament.[4] The conclusion which one must draw is that, despite the numerous secondary features which Lucian introduced into his recension of the Old Testament, one may expect to find here and there in it certain readings, not extant in the other forms of the Septuagint, which will be useful in ascertaining the most ancient form of the Hebrew text.

B. *The New Testament*

In evaluating the critical worth of the Antiochian text of the

[1] For a discussion of the correct text of Jerome's comment on this interpolation, see E. F. Sutcliffe, "The κοινή, 'diversa' or 'dispersa'? St. Jerome, P.L. 24, 548 B," *B*, XXXV (1955), 213-222. It is curious that elsewhere Jerome calls the Lucianic recension the κοινή text; see p. 5 above.

[2] It was edited by C. H. Roberts, *Two Biblical Papyri in the John Rylands Library, Manchester* (Manchester, 1936).

[3] So Albert Vaccari, "Fragmentum Biblicum saeculi II ante Christum," *B*, XVII (1936), 501-504; compare P. E. Kahle, "Problems of the Septuagint," in *Studia Patristica*, ed. by Kurt Aland and F. L. Cross, I (= *Texte und Untersuchungen*, LXIII; Berlin, 1957), 328-338.

[4] It may be mentioned here that Paul Wendland's careful examination of the Old Testament quotations in one of Philo's tractates and his conclusion that in a large proportion of cases the text of Philo agrees with Lucian and seldom joins other manuscripts against Lucian, cannot be accepted without being re-examined ("Zu Philos Schrift *de posteritate Caini*. Nebst Bemerkungen zur Rekonstruktion der Septuaginta," *Philologus*, LVII [1898], 248-288). Wendland naturally made use of Lagarde's edition of the Lucianic text, but since this begins to be Lucianic only on p. 259, line 3, with Ruth 4.11 (so Rahlfs, *Studie ... Ruth*, pp. 77 f.), a comparison of Philo's Penteteuchal quotations with this edition counts for nothing. See Peter Katz, "Das Problem des Urtextes der Septuaginta," *Theologische Zeitschrift*, V (1949), 19 f., and his monograph, *Philo's Bible* (Cambridge, 1950), p. 12, note 1.

above the Antiochian text is necessarily the original text. The lesson to be drawn from such evidence, however, is that the general neglect of the Antiochian readings which has been so common among many textual critics is quite unjustified.[1] It is equally unsatisfactory to utilize the evidence of the Koine text in a purely mechanical fashion, as von Soden did. On the contrary, the only proper methodology is to examine the evidence for each variant impartially, with no predilections for or against any one type of text. In the case of the Antiochian recension, very many readings will no doubt continue to be judged to be the result of the editorial labors of Lucian and those who shared his preference for a smooth and often composite reading, but here and there a discriminating criticism will discover ancient and perhaps original readings which the Antiochian revisers took from the texts on which they worked. The possibility should even be left open that a reading which happens to be preserved in only the Lucianic recension may commend itself as the original.[2]

V. Problems Relating to the Lucianic Recension

In the course of his discussion of "The Antiochian Recension of the Septuagint," George Foot Moore declared, "Every serious bit of investigation in any spot in the Greek Bible reveals in some new way the immense variety and baffling complexity of the problems it presents."[3] A few of the problems and tasks which clamor for attention from both Old Testament and New Testament scholars include the following.

(1) The text of Codex Y (Cod. Macedonianus, Gregory 034, von Soden ε 073), a manuscript dating from the ninth century and containing the Four Gospels (with lacunae), deserves to be studied

[1] Compare G. Zuntz, "The Byzantine Text in New Testament Criticism," *JTS*, XLIII (1942), 25-30; and *The Text of the Epistles; a Disquisition upon the Corpus Paulinum* (London, 1953), pp. 49-57 and 150 f.

[2] For several examples of readings peculiar to Lucian, which nevertheless so sober a critic as Ropes was disposed to accept as original, see his discussion in *The Text of Acts*, p. cclxxxv. For an attempt to prove the originality of six Antiochian variants in Matthew, see J. M. Bover, "Variantes semíticas del texto antioqueno en san Mateo," in *Miscellanea biblica B. Ubach*, curante Dom Romualdo M.ª Días (*Scripta et documenta*, 1; Montisserrati, 1953), pp. 323-327. H. Greeven argues cogently for the originality of ἱερεῖς in Lk. 20.1, which is supported by the Koine text alone (*NTS*, VI [1960], 295 f.).

[3] *American Journal of Semitic Languages and Literatures*, XXIX (1912-1913), 50.

more thorougly than has hitherto been the case.[1] It is inadequately cited by Tischendorf, while a collation made by Gregory is buried in the "Nachträge" to his *Textkritik*.[2] According to von Soden, the manuscript belongs to his K^a-text.[3] Mrs. Lake found that this manuscript shares with Fam. Π and A some readings not preserved elsewhere.[4]

(2) According to Mrs. Lake, in both Testaments codex Alexandrinus contains a large number of misspellings or itacisms of a consistent character. A thorough study of these by a Greek philologist would no doubt lead to worthwhile and interesting results.

(3) It is generally believed that John of Damascus used the Ecclesiastical text, but this has never been either proved or refuted.

(4) Though it is commonly said that Chrysostom's New Testament text was Antiochian, partial studies of the problem suggest that further analysis of his text is much to be desired.

(5) It is not to the credit of textual critics of the Greek Bible that they have been so slow in utilizing information derived from the iconography of Byzantine manuscripts in determining their date, provenance, and textual relationships.[5]

(6) What principles, if any, controlled the formation of the texts of those manuscripts (such as B, ℵ, A, etc.) which contain both Old and New Testament?

(7) Is it possible on palaeographic or iconographical grounds to prove that this or that New Testament manuscript belongs to this or that Old Testament manuscript of Lucianic derivation and that both were originally one and the same complete Bible? (It does not necessarily follow, of course, that the textual complexion of both Testaments would be the same or even similar.)

(8) In view of the research published by the Lakes on certain

[1] For relatively brief accounts of this manuscript see W. C. Braithwaite, "A New Uncial of the Gospels," *Expository Times*, XIII (1901-02), 114-117, and "The Lection-System of the Codex Macedonianus," *JTS*, V (1904), 265-274.

[2] Vol. III (Leipzig, 1909), pp. 1028-1037.

[3] *Op. cit.*, I, ii, 1161.

[4] *Family* Π, p. 57, note 5.

[5] Cf. Kurt Weitzmann, "The Relation between Text Criticism and Picture Criticism," in *Illustrations in Roll and Codex, a Study of the Origin and Method of Text-Illustration* (Princeton, 1947), pp. 182 ff., and also "Die Illustration der Septuaginta," *Münchner Jahrbuch der bildenden Kunst*, Dritte Folge, III/IV (1952/53), 96-120, especially pp. 113-114.

parts of the Byzantine text, precisely how far is von Soden's classification of the Koine text in need of correction?

(9) Why did the Lucianic Old Testament fail to gain the same acceptance as the corresponding Antiochian text of the New Testament?

(10) What precisely was the textual basis of the Lucianic recension, and to what extent can readings of that recension be accepted as probably inherited, and not produced, by Lucian and his fellow-workers?

Kleine Mitteilungen aus dem Septuaginta-Unternehmen.

II. Quis sit ὁ Σύρος.

Von

Alfred Rahlfs.

Die Frage „Quis sit ὁ Σύρος" hat Frid. Field, Origenis Hexaplorum quae supersunt I (1875), S. LXXVII—LXXXII in seiner gründlichen und klaren Weise behandelt. Im wesentlichen Anschluß an ihn berichte ich zunächst kurz über den bisherigen Stand der Frage.

Der „Syrer" wird zitiert von Melito (nur einmal zu Gen. 22 13), Didymus, Diodor, Eusebius von Emesa, Polychronius und

Reprinted from *Mitteilungen des Septuaginta-Unternehmens*. Vol. 1:7. Berlin, 1915.

Apolinarius (zu Dan.), Chrysostomus, Theodoret (zu Ier. und Ez.), Prokop u. a., und zwar zur Gen. 30 mal, zu Ier. 26 mal, zu Ez. 12 mal, zu den Ps. 7 mal, zu Thr. 5 mal, zu Exod., Dan. und Os. je 2- oder 3 mal, zu Reg. III und Is. je 1 mal. In den übrigen Büchern des A. T. hat Field keine Erwähnung des Syrers gefunden.

Die Ansichten über den Syrer gingen seit Montfaucon sehr auseinander. Man könnte zunächst daran denken, daß der Syrer nichts anderes sei als die alte syrische Übersetzung des A. T., die Peschita, und in der Tat haben diese Ansicht Ioan. Wichelhaus, De Novi Testamenti versione syriaca antiqua quam Peschitho vocant (1850), S. 63—68, und etwas modifiziert Jos. Perles, Meletemata Peschitthoniana (Diss. Breslau 1859), S. 49—51 vertreten; letzterer sagt S. 50: „Verisimillimum igitur videtur, Syri denominatione interpretationes eas, quae a Peschittho profectae viva voce circumferebantur, indicari. Etenim Syrus cum Pesch. multis locis congruit, ubi vero differt, ex ipsius Pesch. corruptione aut eorum, qui auribus percipiebant, errore quocunque differentia illa nasci potuit". Die häufige Übereinstimmung des Syrers mit der Peschita leugnet auch Field nicht; er selbst führt S. LXXVIII eine größere Anzahl von Stellen auf, an denen beide aufs beste übereinstimmen. Aber diese Stellen beweisen nichts für ihre Identität, da die Übereinstimmung sich auch aus Benutzung derselben hebräischen Grundlage erklären läßt. Gegen die Identität beweist aber, wie Field S. LXXVIII f. zeigt, eine andere Reihe von Stellen, an denen der Syrer von der Peschita abweicht. Zu ihnen gehört auch eine Stelle, welche Perles S. 49 f. zum Beweis dafür verwendet hatte, daß es sich beim Syrer um eine semitische Übersetzung handle: Gen. 22_{13}, wo Diodor zu dem ἐν φυτῷ σαβέκ der LXX = בסבך bemerkt, daß der Syrer nicht φυτῷ, sondern bloß σαβέκ habe. Dürfte man, wie Perles tat, schon aus dem Vorkommen des semitischen Wortes σαβέκ auf eine semitische Übersetzung schließen, so wäre derselbe Schluß z. B. auch bei Theodotion erlaubt, der so viele hebräische Wörter einfach transkribiert (Field I, S. XL f.). Mit der Peschita aber hat der Syrer hier gar nichts gemein; denn diese hat nicht das hebräische Wort סבך beibehalten, sondern es durch ܣܘܒܟܬܐ übersetzt. Aus diesem und ähnlichen Fällen schließt Field S. LXXIX mit Recht, „Syrum nostrum anonymum cum versione Peschito (quae dicitur) nihil commune habere". Und mit demselben Rechte lehnt er den Vorschlag von Perles ab, die Abweichungen des Syrers von der Peschita aus Verderbnis der Peschita in ihrer schriftlichen Fixierung oder mündlichen Überlieferung zu erklären. Wie sollte man es sich

28*

auch vorstellen, daß aus dem eben angeführten ܣܘܒܟܐ durch irgendeine Verderbnis gerade σαβέκ entstanden wäre, das dem סבך des hebräischen Textes ganz genau entspricht?

Noch weit verfehlter ist eine andere Annahme, die besonders von Döderlein verfochten und von Eichhorn akzeptiert wurde, daß der Σύρος die von Sophronius ins Griechische übertragene lateinische Übersetzung des Hieronymus (Vulgata) sei. Field hat sie S. LXXIX—LXXXII eingehend widerlegt. Damit ist sie endgültig abgetan und kann der verdienten Vergessenheit anheimfallen.

Field selbst stimmt mit Montfaucon darin überein, daß es sich beim Σύρος um eine von einem Syrer verfaßte griechische Übersetzung handelt. Nur in der genaueren Formulierung dieser Annahme gehen Montfaucon und Field auseinander. Montfaucon, Hexaplorum Origenis quae supersunt 1 (1713), Praeliminaria S. 20f. hatte es für das Richtigste gehalten, in dem Σύρος „versionem aliquam Graecam ex Syro factam“ zu sehen. Nach Field ist die Übersetzung, wie sich oben zeigte, nicht aus dem Syrischen, sondern aus dem Hebräischen gemacht; doch schließt er eine Mitbenutzung der Peschita nicht aus, sondern sagt auf S. LXXXII, daß der Σύρος seine neue griechische Übersetzung „adhibita etiam versione Syriaca simplici“ angefertigt habe.

Dafür, daß es sich um eine griechische, nicht um eine syrische Übersetzung handle, hatte Montfaucon S. 20 zwei Beweise angeführt: 1) In Ez. 8_{16} hat der Syrer nach einem in der Sixtina mitgeteilten Scholion אולם durch κιγκλίς wiedergegeben, wofür man, wie der Scholiast bemerkt, gewöhnlich κάγκελλον sagt („ὁ Σύρος τὴν κιγκλίδα καλεῖ, ἥτις λέγεται παρὰ τοῖς πολλοῖς κάγκελλον“). κιγκλίς und κάγκελλον sind aber Synonyma, die man nur im Griechischen unterscheiden kann. 2) In Gen. 39_2 hatte der Syrer nach Diodor für מצליח nicht ἐπιτυγχάνων wie die LXX, sondern κατευοδούμενος. Auch dies sind Synonyma, die sich im Syrischen nicht unterscheiden würden[1]).

Field S. LXXXII übernimmt diese Beweise, findet aber den ersten nicht bündig, da die Syrer, wie sie ܩܢܩܠܐ = κάγκελλον brauchen (mehrfach belegt, s. R. P. Smith, Thesaurus Syriacus Sp. 3671f.), so auch ܩܝܓܟܠܝܣ (bisher nicht belegt) = κιγκλίς gebraucht haben könnten. Den zweiten Beweis dagegen findet Field „majoris, immo maximi momenti“, und er führt zur Bekräftigung desselben sehr gut an,

1) Montfaucon fügt hier noch die gleichfalls synonymen Übersetzungen des Symmachus (εὐοδούμενος) und Aquila (κατευθυνόμενος) hinzu. Diese läßt Field mit Recht aus dem Spiele, da Diodor sie nicht erwähnt.

daß die syrohexaplarische, also eine sehr genaue Übersetzung ἐπιτυγχάνων Gen. 39 2 und κατευοδούμενος Ps. 36 7 in genau derselben Weise durch ܡܨܠܚ wiedergibt.

Indessen ist auch dieser zweite Beweis nicht ganz unanfechtbar. κατευοδούμενος wird zwar von Diodor und auch von Prokop, der nur etwas abweichend statt dessen κατευοδῶν bietet (s. Field zu Gen. 39 2), dem Σύρος zugeschrieben. Aber εὐοδούμενος oder κατευοδούμενος wird auch als Übersetzung des Symmachus überliefert: εὐοδούμενος in den hexaplarischen Noten der Sixtina und in den Hss. M und Brooke-McLean „j" = HoP 57, κατευοδούμενος in den Hss. HoP 127 und Brooke-McLean „v" = Rahlfs 344, s. Field und Brooke-McLean z. St. Daher könnte man bei einiger Zweifelsucht eine Verwechselung von Σύρος und Σύμμαχος, etwa hervorgerufen durch falsche Auflösung der für Σύμμαχος vorkommenden Abkürzung „Συ" (Field I, S. XCV), annehmen. Und man könnte sich dafür sogar auf den Vorangang Fields berufen, der S. LXXVII Anm. 17 konstatiert, daß Chrysostomus eine Lesart des Symmachus (muß hier allerdings richtiger heißen: des Theodotion) irrtümlich dem Syrer zuschreibt. Daß nicht nur Diodor, sondern auch Prokop den Syrer als Autor von κατευοδούμενος oder -δῶν nennt, würde nicht sicher gegen die Annahme einer solchen Verwechselung sprechen, da Prokop sehr häufig seine Vorgänger einfach abschreibt; nur müßte der Fehler, wenn er nicht auf Diodor selbst zurückginge, schon in der Zeit zwischen Diodor und Prokop entstanden sein.

Zum Schlusse führt dann Field S. LXXXII noch Ier. 48 33 an, wo der Syrer κελεύειν nach einem Brauche der „exquisitissima Graecitas" für das die Arbeit begleitende und zu ihr anfeuernde Singen im Takte braucht („οὐκέτι οἱ ληνοβατοῦντες κελεύσουσι λέγοντες· ἰά, ἰά"), und schließt daraus, daß „etiam stylus Syri nostri anonymi Graecam potius quam Syriacam originem arguit". Aber hiermit ist nichts bewiesen. Denn der echt griechische Stil würde auch dann erklärbar sein, wenn die Kirchenväter, welche den Syrer zitieren, eine syrische Vorlage ad hoc ins Griechische übersetzt hätten.

Unter diesen Umständen freut es mich, eine von Montfaucon und Field übersehene Stelle anführen zu können, die, wie mir scheint, einen vollständig sicheren Beweis für Fields Auffassung des Σύρος liefert und überhaupt für die Frage nach der Beschaffenheit dieser immer noch recht rätselhaften Größe besonders wichtig ist. Sie findet sich in Theodorets Quaestiones in Octateuchum in der 19. Frage zum Richterbuche (Opera ed. Schulze 1 [1769],

S. 337), und es wird dadurch zugleich zu den oben S. 421 aufgezählten biblischen Büchern, in welchen man bisher Erwähnungen des Syrers gefunden hatte, ein neues Buch hinzugefügt. Gehandelt haben über die Stelle E. Hautsch, Der Lukiantext des Oktateuch (Nachr. d. K. Ges. d. Wiss. zu Gött., Philol.-hist. Kl. 1909, S. 538 = Mitteilungen des Sept.-Untern. 1, S. 23) und ihn verbessernd (vgl. unten S. 429. 431f.) George F. Moore, The Antiochian recension of the Septuagint (American Journal of Semitic languages and literatures 29 [1912—13], S. 43 f.); doch haben beide sich auf die für ihren Zweck abseits liegende Frage „Quis sit ὁ Σύρος" nicht eingelassen. Schon vor ihnen hat P. de Lagarde, Übersicht über die im Aramäischen, Arabischen und Hebräischen übliche Bildung der Nomina (Abh. d. K. Ges. d. Wiss. zu Gött., 35. Bd., 1889), S. 91 Anm. ** die Stelle angeführt und auf ihre Wichtigkeit für die aramäische Dialektologie hingedeutet; für den Σύρος verweist er „vorläufig" auf Field [1]).

Theodoret behandelt a. a. O. die berühmte Stelle Iud. 12_6, wo Jephthas Leute die Ephraimiten das Wort „Schibboleth" sprechen lassen, diese aber statt dessen „Sibboleth" sagen. Der LXX-Text, welchen Theodoret zugrunde legt, hat, da sich der Unterschied der Aussprache im Griechischen nicht wiedergeben ließ, verständigerweise auf eine wörtliche Übertragung verzichtet und für שבלת und סבלת einfach σύνθημα „eine Parole" eingesetzt: καὶ ἔλεγον αὐτοῖς Εἴπατε δὴ σύνθημα· καὶ λέγοντες σύνθημα οὐ κατηύθυνον τοῦ λαλῆσαι οὕτως (oder ähnlich; der Text ist nach der Gruppe 54 etc., mit der Theodoret gewöhnlich zusammengeht [vgl. Hautsch und Moore a. a. O.], rekonstruiert) = ויאמרו לו אמר נא שבלת ויאמר סבלת ולא יכין לדבר כן. Hierzu bemerkt nun Theodoret, dessen Kenntnisse sich nicht auf den LXX-Text beschränkten, jene Parole habe in einem Worte bestanden, bei dem schon die Aussprache den Beweis für die Herkunft des Sprechenden lieferte („τινὰ λόγον ὃς ἐπέφερε διὰ τῆς γλώττης τὸν ἔλεγχον"). Und um dies deutlicher zu machen, fährt er fort:

> ὥσπερ γὰρ Ὀσροηνοὶ καὶ Σύροι καὶ Εὐφρατήσιοι καὶ Παλαιστινοὶ καὶ Φοίνικες τῇ Σύρων χρῶνται φωνῇ, πολλὴν δὲ ὅμως ἡ διάλεξις ἔχει διαφοράν, οὕτως Ἑβραῖοι μὲν ἦσαν αἱ δυοκαίδεκα φυ-

1) Lagarde sagt: „Die Stelle wird vielleicht von nun an — ohne den Namen Lagarde — oft angeführt werden". Beinahe wäre dieser Fall hier wirklich eingetreten; denn obwohl ich die „Übersicht" seinerzeit, als ich das Register zu ihr anfertigte, sehr genau kannte, war mir doch jenes Zitat inzwischen vollständig entfallen, und ich fand es erst jetzt, nachdem ich die Bedeutung der Theodoretstelle erkannt hatte, halb zufällig wieder.

λαί, εἶχον δέ τινα ὡς εἰκὸς ἰδιώματα, ὥσπερ ἀμέλει καὶ αὕτη[1]. ὡς γὰρ ὁ Σύρος φησί, τῶν ἄλλων τὸν ἄσταχυν σεμβλὰ[2]) καλούντων οἱ τοῦ Ἐφραὶμ ἔκ τινος συνηθείας σεμβελὼ[3]) ἔλεγον. τοῦτο γινώσκων Ἰεφθάε λέγειν ἐκέλευσε καὶ διελεγχομένους ἀνῄρει.

Theodoret führt also zunächst als Parallele zu dem Vorhandensein verschiedener Dialekte bei den alten Hebräern die gleiche Erscheinung bei den heutigen Syrern an. Zu der Aufzählung der verschiedenen Abteilungen der Syrer bemerkt Lagarde treffend, daß Theodoret die Provinznamen seiner Zeit braucht, wie sie uns durch das Staatshandbuch jener Zeit, die Notitia dignitatum, authentisch überliefert sind, vgl. in der Ausgabe O. Seecks (1876) z. B. S. 49, wo unter den Provinzen des Orients „Palaestina secunda, Palaestina salutaris, Foenice Libani, Eufratensis, Syria salutaris, Osrhoena“ aufgezählt werden. Weniger vermag ich Lagarde beizustimmen, wenn er meint, daß Theodoret hier gerade von „fünf Dialekten des Aramäischen“ spreche; denn daß die Dialekte sich nach den römischen Provinzgrenzen gerichtet haben sollten, ist doch höchst unwahrscheinlich[4]). Meines Erachtens soll die Aufzählung nur darauf hinweisen, daß es eine ganze Reihe Syrisch redender Provinzen gibt, und daß dementsprechend auch manche dialektische Unterschiede im Syrischen vorhanden sind.

Sodann führt Theodoret noch den Σύρος zu der in Frage stehenden Stelle Iud. 12₆ an. Allerdings zitiert er ihn offenbar nicht wörtlich; dazu weicht der Wortlaut von dem der Bibelstelle gar zu weit ab. Aber wenn wir auch den genauen Wortlaut des Σύρος aus dem Zitate Theodorets nicht rekonstruieren können, so viel können wir doch mit Sicherheit sagen: auf jeden Fall hat der Σύρος den hebräischen Dialektunterschied שבלת : סבלת durch einen syrischen Dialektunterschied ersetzt; denn σεμβλά und σεμβελώ sind nur zwei verschiedene Aussprachen desselben syrischen Wortes ܫܒܠܐ, das dem hebräischen שבלת entspricht. Hieraus folgt:

1) Zu αὕτη ergänze ἡ φυλή. Gemeint ist der Stamm Ephraim.

2) Sirmond und Schulze haben im Texte ἐμβλά, aber Picus und die von Schulze verglichene Hs. (s. Rahlfs, Verzeichnis der griech. Hss. des A. T. [1914], S. 380 Anm. 1) haben σεμβλά.

3) Sirmond und Schulze haben im Texte ἐμβελώ, aber Picus σεμβὲλ ὡς, die von Schulze verglichene Hs. σεμβελός. Über das hieraus herzustellende σεμβελώ s. unten S. 428.

4) Auch sind es, da es zwei Palaestinae gibt, nicht fünf, sondern sechs Provinzen. Allerdings sind die beiden Palaestinae unter demselben Dux vereinigt, aber dasselbe gilt auch für Eufratensis und Syria, s. Seeck S. 69—74.

1) Der Σύρος ist nicht die Peschita. Denn diese hat den hebräischen Dialektunterschied getreu nachgeahmt, indem sie zu dem syrischen Worte ܫܒܠܐ ad hoc eine sonst nirgends vorkommende Nebenform ܣܒܠܐ bildete: ܐܡܪܝܢ ܠܗ ܐܡܪ ܫܒܠܐ. ܐܡܪ ܣܒܠܐ ܡܛܠ ܕܠܐ ܡܫܟܚ ܗܘܐ ܠܡܬܩܢܘ ܗܟܢܐ.

2) Der Σύρος hat überhaupt nicht Syrisch, sondern, wie Montfaucon und Field mit Recht annahmen, Griechisch geschrieben. Denn der Unterschied zwischen σεμβλά und σεμβελώ wäre in der syrischen Schrift gar nicht zum Ausdruck gekommen; sowohl σεμβλά als σεμβελώ hätte man syrisch ܫܒܠܐ schreiben müssen. Im Griechischen dagegen konnte man umgekehrt den Unterschied der semitischen Zischlaute שׁ und ס nicht wiedergeben und mußte daher, wenn man nicht wie die LXX ganz frei übersetzen wollte, einen anderen Unterschied an die Stelle setzen, der sich in der griechischen Schrift ausdrücken ließ.

3) Da im Syrischen neben dem Status emphaticus ܫܶܒܶܠܬܳܐ auch ein Status emphaticus ܫܶܒܠܳܐ vorkommt (Th. Nöldeke, Kurzgefaßte syr. Grammatik § 87), so können σεμβλά und σεμβελώ Transkriptionen dieses ܫܶܒܠܳܐ sein. Wahrscheinlicher jedoch stellen sie den ebenso lautenden Status absolutus zu ܫܶܒܶܠܬܳܐ dar; denn der Status absolutus der Substantiva, welcher bekanntlich in der syrischen Literatursprache fast völlig vom Status emphaticus aufgesogen ist, hat sich in den Dialekten, z. B. dem syropalästinischen, noch viel länger gehalten und kann für die Zeit des Σύρος ohne weiteres als noch sehr üblich angenommen werden. In diesem Falle entsprechen σεμβλά und σεμβελώ auch hinsichtlich der grammatischen Form ganz genau dem artikellosen שבלת des hebräischen Textes. Aber auch wenn sie den Status emphaticus von ܫܒܠ darstellen sollten, würden sie immer noch Singulare sein und insofern dem hebräischen Urtexte entsprechen, nicht der Peschita, die hier zwar auch dasselbe Wort hat, aber nach allgemeiner Überlieferung als Plural (ܫܒ̈ܠܐ und ܣܒ̈ܠܐ). Also dürfen wir es auf jeden Fall als sehr wahrscheinlich bezeichnen, daß der Σύρος an unserer Stelle nicht aus der Peschita, sondern aus dem hebräischen Urtexte übersetzt hat.

4) Der Σύρος war in der Tat von Herkunft ein Syrer. Denn nur ein solcher konnte auf den geistreichen Einfall kommen, den im Griechischen unausdrückbaren hebräischen Dialektunterschied durch einen im Griechischen ausdrückbaren syrischen Dialektunterschied zu ersetzen, der mit dem hebräischen weiter nichts zu tun hat, als daß er sich bei demselben Worte findet.

So viel über die Bedeutung der Stelle für die Frage „Quis sit ὁ Σύρος“. Zum Schluß wollen wir noch sehen, was sie, abgesehen von der allgemeinen Nachricht, daß es zur Zeit Theodorets dialektische Unterschiede im Syrischen gegeben hat, noch weiter für die Geschichte der syrischen Sprache abwirft. Hierfür kommt folgendes in Betracht:

1) Es ist ein bekannter Unterschied zwischen dem Ost- und Westsyrischen, daß sich im Ostsyrischen das altsemitische *ā* rein erhalten hat, während es im Westsyrischen zu *ō* getrübt ist. Der Prozeß war vollendet, als um 700 n. Chr. im Westsyrischen die Bezeichnung der Vokale durch griechische Buchstaben eingeführt wurde; denn dabei wurde das griechische ο, dessen Quantitätsunterschied von ω im Griechischen bereits geschwunden war, zur Bezeichnung des alten *ā* gewählt. Dagegen wurde im I. Jahrh. n. Chr. wenigstens in Palästina noch *ā* gesprochen; denn in den neutestamentlichen Transkriptionen μαραναθά = מָרַנָא תָא (noch bei Nestle und v. Soden falsch μαρὰν ἀθά getrennt!), ἀββᾶ = אַבָּא, ταλιθά = טַלְיְתָא, Κηφᾶς = כֵּיפָא u. s. w. erscheint das alte *ā* noch überall als α. Das σεμβελώ unseres Σύρος beweist nun, daß der Übergang des *ā* in *ō* mindestens in gewissen Gegenden des westlichen Syriens schon recht früh erfolgt ist. Wenn das dem Melito zugeschriebene Zitat aus dem Σύρος (vgl. oben S. 420 Z. 2 v. u.) wirklich auf Melito zurückgeht, so müßte der Σύρος noch dem II. Jahrh. n. Chr. angehören; andernfalls wäre er spätestens dem IV. Jahrh. n. Chr. zuzuweisen.

2) Die Wiedergabe des syrischen *bb* durch μβ sowohl in σεμβλά als in σεμβελώ beweist, daß der Übergang der Doppelkonsonanten in einfache Konsonanten mit vorhergehendem Nasal in den syrischen Dialekten weiter verbreitet war, als die Orthographie der aus Edessa stammenden Literatursprache ahnen läßt. Dafür haben wir auch sonst Beweise, s. C. Brockelmann, Grundriß der vergleichenden Grammatik der semit. Sprachen I (1908), S. 245; besonders bemerkenswert ist, daß jene Erscheinung, wie Brockelmann unter „δ“ zeigt, auch in dem nordsyrischen Dialekte, dem die Armenier ihre aramäischen Fremdwörter entlehnten, sehr verbreitet gewesen sein muß. Genau derselbe Übergang findet sich übrigens bei demselben Worte auch im Arabischen, wo سُنْبُلَة dem hebr. שבלת und syr. ܫܒܠܐ entspricht. (Über analoge Erscheinungen im Griechischen und Lateinischen s. W. Schulze, Samstag: Ztschr. f. vergl. Sprachforschung 33 [1895], S. 366—386 und Ath. Buturas, Über den irrationalen Nasal im Griechischen: Glotta 5 [1914], S. 170 ff.)

3) Ich habe seinerzeit, als Hautsch die oben erwähnte Besprechung der Theodoretstelle niederschrieb, ihm auf seine Anfrage gesagt, aus den für die zweite Aussprache des Wortes überlieferten Varianten ἐμβελώ, σεμβὲλ ὡς, σεμβελός [1]) sei als ursprünglich wahrscheinlich σεμβλώ herzustellen, sodaß also der Unterschied der beiden Dialektformen σεμβλά und σεμβλώ nur in dem auslautenden Vokal läge, und dementsprechend sagt auch Hautsch: „wahrscheinlich ist σεμβλὼ zu schreiben“. In der Tat würde dieser eine Unterschied für den Zweck des Σύρος vollständig genügen, und es würde dann eine genaue Parallele zum Hebräischen vorliegen, wo der Unterschied der beiden Formen sich gleichfalls auf einen einzigen Laut beschränkt. Anders jedoch stellen Lagarde, dessen oben S. 424 zitierte Stelle mir damals nicht im Gedächtnis war, und Moore σεμβελώ her [2]), und ich gestehe gern, daß dieses wegen seines engeren Anschlusses an die Überlieferung, die in allen drei Varianten zwischen β und λ ein ε aufweist, entschieden den Vorzug verdient. Das ε ist auch sehr wohl erklärlich: es ist das Schwa mobile, zu welchem das ursprüngliche *ă*, das in ܫܒܠܬܐ noch erhalten ist, in ܫܒܠܐ abgeschwächt wurde. Wenn dieses ε in σεμβλά fehlt, so ist das daraus zu erklären, daß der hinsichtlich des *ā* auf älterer Sprachstufe stehen gebliebene Dialekt, welchem σεμβλά angehört, in der Abschwächung des *ă* umgekehrt noch weiter als der σεμβελώ-Dialekt fortgeschritten war und auch das Schwa mobile nicht mehr deutlich aussprach; vgl. ähnliche Fälle bei Th. Nöldeke, Kurzgefaßte syrische Grammatik § 21 B und 23 D.

---

1) Siehe oben S. 425 Anm. 3.

2) Daneben wirft Lagarde noch die Frage auf, ob die Variante σεμβελός auf ein ursprüngliches σεμβέλθε zurückzuführen sei. σεμβέλθε soll offenbar = ܫܒܠܬܐ sein, aber eine Wiedergabe des -*ā* des Status emphaticus durch -ε ist ganz unwahrscheinlich und die Zurückziehung des Akzentes auf die vorletzte Silbe, durch welche Lagarde dieses -ε anscheinend erklären will, für so alte Zeit schwerlich anzunehmen. Überdies ist die Hs., welche σεμβελός bietet, so jung (XV. Jahrh., vgl. Rahlfs, Verzeichnis der griech. Hss. des A. T. [1914], S. 154 f. Nr. 351), daß man nicht, wie Lagarde tut, mit einer Unzialverwechselung (ΟϹ statt ΘЄ) rechnen darf, wenn eine andere Erklärung (σεμβελος aus σεμβελως) möglich ist.

PROLEGOMENA TO A GREEK-HEBREW AND HEBREW-GREEK INDEX TO AQUILA*

INTRODUCTION

1. THE Oxford Concordance to the Septuagint and the other Greek Versions of the Old Testament by Hatch and Redpath, completed in 1897[1] and with its two supplements in 1906,[2] follows a double plan with regard to the two

* [The Indexes to which allusion is made in the present work have been completed and the manuscript has been deposited in the Library of Dropsie College. Another student in the Biblical Department of the College is engaged in preparing similar Indexes to Theodotion, and it is hoped that the work of indexing Symmachus and the other translators recorded in the Oxford Concordance, as well as the Hexaplaric matter found in Field but not excerpted in the Concordance, will be shortly undertaken by members of the College. All these Indexes when completed will be issued in one volume, which it is hoped will be welcomed by scholars as a useful supplement to Hatch and Redpath.—Professor Margolis has appended a few notes in brackets signed with the initial M.]

[1] *A Concordance to the Septuagint and the other Greek Versions of the Old Testament (including the apocryphal books)*, by Edwin Hatch and Henry A. Redpath, assisted by other scholars. 2 vols. Oxford, 1897.—Hatch and Redpath have been preceded by Konrad Kircher *Concordantiae V^{tis} T Graecae, ebraeis vocibus respondentes πολυχρηστοι*, Frankf. a. M., 1607, 2 vols.; Abraham Tromm, *Concordantiae graecae versionis, vulgo dictae LXX interpretum, cujus voces secundum ordinem elementorum sermonis graeci digestae recensentur.* Amsterdam, 1718. 2 vols.; G. M[orrish], *A Handy Concordance of the LXX.* London, 1887. Mention must also be made of J. F. Schleusner, *Novus Thesaurus philologico-criticus sive lexicon in LXX.* London, 1829. In the last-named work there are found instructive observations which I have turned to good purpose.

[2] Fasc. I containing a concordance to the proper names occurring in the

I B

Reprinted from *Prolegomena to a Greek-Hebrew and Hebrew-Greek Index to Aquila.* Philadelphia, 1916. (Extracts.)

main sources upon which it is based. In the case of the Septuagint, under every word the citations for all the passages in which the word occurs are given with 'as far as possible enough of the context to show (1) the grammatical construction of the word, (2) the words with which it is ordinarily associated'.[3] At the head of each article an alphabetically arranged list of Hebrew (Aramaic) equivalents is found, to which throughout the article reference is made by number.[4] This plan has been deviated from in case of numerals, prepositions, and conjunctions: instead of full citations we have merely an index of passages, and furthermore the Semitic equivalents are not given. This latter method has been followed throughout for the 'other'

Septuagint. Oxford, 1900. Fasc. II containing a concordance to Ecclesiasticus, other addenda and Hebrew index to the whole work. Oxford, 1906.

[3] Preface, p. v, end. The editor goes on to say: 'But to have combined in each quotation all its points either of grammatical interest or of analogy with other passages would have made the work inordinately long: and consequently it will frequently be found that the quotations under a single word are made on different principles in order to illustrate different points relating to it.'

[4] For a criticism of the arrangement of the work, cp. Margolis, 'Entwurf zu einer revidierten Ausgabe der hebräisch-aramäischen Äquivalente in der Oxforder Concordance to the Septuagint and the other Greek Versions of the Old Testament,' *ZAW.*, XXV (1905), pp. 311 ff.; see also Smend, *Griechisch-Syrisch-Hebräischer Index zur Weisheit des Jesus Sirach.* Berlin, 1907, pp. x ff. Both Margolis and Smend object to the quid pro quos or unidentified Greek words marked by a dagger, claiming that this lack of identification impairs the usefulness of the work for lexical purposes and textual criticism. Smend, furthermore, considers altogether impractical the arrangement of the Greek citations according to the order of the books of the Bible and not (as Tromm) according to the Hebrew equivalents. He also considers it unfortunate that the Hebrew index contained in the second Supplement gives reference to the pages in which the Greek equivalents occur and not to the equivalents themselves [similarly Glaue-Rahlfs, *Fragmente e. griech. Übersetzung d. samarit. Pentateuchs*, 52. M].

Greek versions.[5] Both for the Septuagint and the other versions certain pronouns and particles of frequent occurrence have been omitted altogether, such as, for example, *καί* and the definite article *ὁ, ἡ, τό*.[6]

2. The work to which the following pages are introductory is intended to supplement Hatch-Redpath on the sides in which the editors have left room for improvement. While the Oxford Concordance has been taken as a basis for a new double index, Greek-Hebrew and Hebrew-Greek, to Aquila, who heads the list of the 'other' versions, it has been sought to supply two main deficiencies. In the first place references are given also for words of frequent occurrence omitted in the Oxford work.[7] In the second place every article contains the Hebrew (Aramaic) equivalents both for the articles found and those not found in Hatch-Redpath. The need for a registration of these equivalents has been felt by all students of the Greek versions. In giving these equivalents it has been deemed advisable to deviate from the method adopted by the Oxford editors. The equivalents are presented not in alphabetical order, but with regard to frequency. Another feature is

[5] Smend, *l. c.*, considers this as one of the weak points in the Concordance.

[6] Cp. Schmiedel, *Georg Benedict Winer's Grammatik des neutestamentlichen Sprachidioms*[8], Göttingen, 1894, p. xv. Schmiedel not only criticizes the omission of certain prepositions and particles in the Concordance, but also the failure to reproduce the whole phrase in connexion with the prepositions and particles, for 'es kann doch keinen Augenblick zweifelhaft sein, dass hier das Ausschreiben des Textes 100 Mal wichtiger ist als z. B. bei *ἄνθρωπος* oder *ἀνήρ*'. He considers this 'den schwersten Fehler des Werkes'.

[7] That such words are important and have a bearing on Aquila's manner of translation and exegesis may be seen from his use of the definite article, cp. Burkitt, *Fragments of the Books of Kings according to the translation of Aquila*. Cambridge, 1897, p. 12 f. See also below.

B 2

the arrangement of compounds and derivatives under the head of the *simplicia*, though the former are also entered in the alphabetical place with cross-references.[8]

3. So far as the 'other' versions and in particular Aquila, the subject of the present effort, is concerned, the material gathered together in the Oxford Concordance is based chiefly on Field's monumental work,[9] but incorporates also later material contained in the printed works of Pitra,[10] Swete,[11] Klostermann,[12] Morin,[13] Burkitt,[14]

[8] This plan of arrangement was outlined fully by Margolis, *l. c.* It is justified by the fact that it is in the nature of the Hebrew to ignore the shades of meaning brought out by a preposition attached to the verb in Greek; e. g. יָשַׁב may be rendered by either *οἰκεῖν*, *ἐνοικεῖν*, *κατοικεῖν*, or *παροικεῖν*; and hence it is more practical to have them all grouped together.

[9] 'Monumentum exegit, hisce diebus, Fredericus Fieldius, in summum decus utriusque Academiae Oxoniensis et Cantabrigiensis,' Pitra, *Analecta Sacra Spicilegio Solesmensi Parata*, Tom. III, p. 551. The full title of Field's work is: *Origenis Hexaplorum quae supersunt; sive Veterum Interpretum Graecorum in totum Vetus Testamentum Fragmenta.* Post Flaminium Nobilium, Drusium, et Montefalconium, adhibita etiam versione Syro-Hexaplari, concinnavit, emendavit, et multis partibus auxit Fridericus Field. Tom. II. Oxonii, 1875.

[10] *Analecta Sacra Spicilegio Solesmensi Parata.* Tom. III. E Typographeo Veneto, 1883, pp. 551 ff.

[11] *The Old Testament in Greek according to the Septuagint.* 3 vols. Cambridge, 1887-94. Of especial value are the excerpts from Q (Codex Marchalianus).

[12] *Analecta zur Septuaginta, Hexapla und Patristik.* Leipzig, 1895, pp. 47 ff.

[13] *Anecdota Maredsolana seu Monumenta Ecclesiasticae Antiquitatis* ex MSS. codicibus nunc primum edita aut denuo illustrata. Vol. III, Pars I: Sancti Hieronymi Presbyteri Commentarioli in Psalmos. Vol. III, Pars III: Sancti Hieronymi Presbyteri Tractatus novissime reperti. Maredsoli, 1895–1903. Valuable material bearing on the later Greek versions is found in these works of Jerome.

[14] *Fragments of the Books of Kings according to the translation of Aquila.* Cambridge, 1897.

Taylor,[15] and, in one instance, unpublished fragments discovered by Dr. Mercati of the Vatican Library, who 'very kindly lent the Editor . . . a transcript of the fragments'.[16]

4. It is to be regretted that the excerpting of Field has been done with little attention to the Hebrew,[17] and betrays occasionally a mechanical haste which has resulted in the incorporation of words which never formed part of the text in question.[18] But another disappointing feature

[15] *Hebrew-Greek Cairo Genizah Palimpsests from the Taylor-Schechter collection, including a Fragment of the Twenty-second Psalm according to Origen's Hexapla.* Cambridge, 1900.

[16] See on this find Klostermann, *ZAW.*, XVI (1896), 336 f. It is to be regretted that the important publication is still due.

[17] Thus under the article *κόρος* (*satietas*) the references Exod. 8. 14 (10) *bis*; 3 Kings 5. 11 (25) are to be taken out and transferred to the preceding article *κόρος* (*corus*). The Hebrew equivalents are חֹמֶר in Exodus and כֹּר in Kings. Another grave error of a similar character is found in the article *εὑρίσκειν*, where Ps. 77 (78), 26 is entered for Symmachus. Field has correctly *εὖρον*, which the excerpter misread as *εὗρον*; the Hebrew is קָדִים. Hence insert on p. 579 at the head of column 3

εὖρος

[Sm., Ps. 77 (78). 26].

Under the article *κέρδος* delete the α′ reference (Ezek. 27. 24). Field has correctly *κέδρος* which is duly entered in the Concordance *s.v.*—The α′ reference *s. v.* *ἁδρύνειν* should be placed under the article preceding (*ἁδρός*); at the same time write σ′ for α′.—The α′ reference *s. v.* *ἠχεῖν* Ps. 67 (68). 18 should be transferred to σ′. Delete the α′ reference 3 Kings 3. 3 *s.v.* *θύειν*.—The article *κίτρις* should be credited to Al. instead of α′. In the article *κοσκίνωμα* add: α′ σ′ θ′ Exod. 27. 4. This is a plain omission, the accompanying adjective *δικτυωτός* being duly entered *s.v.*

[18] *Sub* *ἐκδιδόναι* the Concordance has: α′ θ′ Jer. 37 (44). 12 (which reference is repeated under σ′). Field gives (*Auctarium*, p. 47 f.) from codd. 86. 88 a rendering of ver. 11 f., attributed to Joannes (see Field's *Prolegomena*, pp. xciii f.), which he follows up by the scholion (from cod. 88) *Καὶ οἱ λοιποὶ ὁμοίως ἐξέδωκαν.* The excerpter took this to mean: And the remaining [translators] likewise [have] *ἐξέδωκαν*. Of course, the correct English is: And the remaining [translators] have rendered in a like

consists in the fact that the excerpter appears to have considered his task done when he paid attention to Field's text, disregarding on the whole Field's illuminating notes below, which in many instances serve to modify the text above in essential points.[19]

manner. The reference is to לחלק, for which Joannes has *εἰς τὸ νείμασθαι τὸν κλῆρον* (to obtain possession of the lot), and so similarly *α' θ' τοῦ μερισθῆναι σ' μερίσασθαι* (on the exegesis of the Hebrew as well as on the variant reading underlying the Septuagintal rendering *ἀγοράσαι*, see Margolis, *JAOS.*, XXX (1910), 308 f.). On p. 1503, col. 2, *ἐκζεῖν α' σ'*, Ezek. 24. 13 (from Swete) is to be struck out. Swete adduces from Q: * *θ' εν τη ακαθαρσια σου ζεμμα* (*ζεμα* with one *μ*, Q[a]) and from Q[mg] *ad ζεμ(μ)α* : *α' σ' συνταγη ζεμα εξεζεσε*. The excerpter took the whole phrase as coming from *α' σ'*, whereas it is clear that only *συνταγη* belongs to the two; what follows is a gloss on *ζεμα* (*θ'*'s rendering) which is erroneously combined with Greek (*ἐκ*)*ζεῖν* 'boil over'.—*Sub ἔσω* strike out the references *α' σ' θ'* 1 Kings 26. 19, and *θ'* 1 Kings 25. 1. In the latter place Field has (from the margin of 243) *ο' ραμα θ' το εσω* 'h. e. *quod intus* (in textu) *habetur*' (so Field explicitly below the text). The purport of the marginal note is to say that Origen wrote in the Septuagint column *ραμα* = רָמָה, whereas *θ'* had the same as in the text, i. e. *'Αρμαθαίμ*. In the other passage λ̥· *τὸ ἔσω* means that they read as in the text *ἐν κληρονομίᾳ*. Accordingly two additional entries are obtained for *α' σ' θ'* under *ἐν* and *κληρονομία*. A clear example of superficial haste is the ignoring of a period (.). Job 2. 9, Field prints: *α' θ' καὶ εἶπεν αὐτῷ ἡ γυνή*. ÷*χρόνου δὲ πολλοῦ προβεβηκότος* ✓. *Οὐ κεῖται ἐν τῷ 'Εβραϊκῷ*. The whole means that in the place of the Septuagintal *χρόνου δὲ πολλοῦ προβεβηκότος* (a free expansion) which, as is expressly noted, is not found in the Hebrew, *α' θ'* had merely the conjunction *καί*. The excerpter's eye overlooked Field's period after *γυνή* and thus included *χρόνου* (see *s. v.*) in the phrase ascribed to *α' θ'*; curiously enough there is no reference to Job 2. 9, *α' θ' s. vv. πολύς* and *προβαίνειν*!

[19] A case in point has been met at the end of the previous note, where surely a glance at Field's notes would have made impossible the error of citing *sub ἔσω* the meaningless references there given. Had the notes been consulted, a further faulty reference should have been added: *α' θ'* 1 Kings 25. 31 (see foot-note 45). But here Field wisely kept out of his text the phraseology of the gloss and merely registered the result. Obviously it was the excerpter's duty in every case to square the text with the notes, which, however, he failed to do. The examples are so numerous that only a selection can be pointed out here. Thus *sub ἀναθεματίζειν*, Deut. 3. 3 and 6, are attri-

5. Much valuable instruction as Field's notes offer, the scope of the present work would have been incomplete

buted to α'. Now Field (foot-note 1) correctly records the tradition according to which α' had ἀνεθεματίσαμεν for 𝔊 ἐπατάξαμεν = ונכ(הו) and just as rightly remarks 'invitis Regiis tribus . . . , qui lectionem ad ver. 6 recte retrahunt'; on the basis of the latter authority he prints in ver. 6 α' ἀνεθεματίσαμεν for 𝔊 ἐξωλοθρεύσαμεν = ונחרם. The Editors of the Concordance were free either to adopt Field's suggestion and therefore to quote 3. 6 or to follow tradition implicitly and hence to record 3. 3. Only by disregarding the notes was it possible for them to register both 3. 3 and 3. 6. In my own Index 3. 3 is of course deleted. Similarly the reference 4 Kings 2. 14 (for α' σ' θ') *sub* κρύφιος should be eliminated: Theodoret ascribes the rendering to 'the other ἑρμηνευταί', but Field (note 22) expressly adds 'ubi ἑρμηνευταί de *enarratoribus*, non de *interpretibus* intelligendum videtur'. We are dealing here merely with a fanciful etymology which combined αφφω with Hebrew חבא and is no worse than αφφω πατέρες (combined with אב) in the Onomastica Vaticana; see Lagarde, *Onomastica Sacra*², 187. 43. As a matter of fact, α' wrote καίπερ αὐτός and σ' καὶ νῦν (see Field). Strike out also the first reference *sub* φύλαξις (α', Isa. 26. 3). See Field, under note 8; the emendation φυλάξεις (of which φυλαξις is an itacistic error) εἰρήνην is self-evident. See further my Greek Index, *s.v.* εἰς, εἷς, ἐν, ἐπικαλύπτειν, εὑρίσκειν, ζωοῦν, ἰά, καλεῖν, σύντονος, τοῖχος. Many words and references have been incorporated by the Editors where Field has indicated his doubt by printing the phrases in question in brackets. In my Index they are omitted. Such are, for instance, Job 27. 20 ἐν περιστάσει μὴ ἐκφύγοι; Prov. 31. 3 τὰ σὰ χρήματα; Isa. 3. 8 κατὰ τοῦ κυρίου γέγονεν; *ibid.*, 40. 24 ἄνεμος; Jer. 20. 9 φέρειν; *ibid.* 31 (38). 22, ἐν τῇ σωτηρίᾳ; *ibid.* 44 (51). 29 εἰς κακά; Amos 1. 2, προβάτων. In nearly all of these cases there is no Hebrew to correspond in the MT. Field's notes, if they had been at all consulted, would have led to the transfer of several references from α' to σ', θ', or **Al.** The Editors' point of view may have been to follow the traditional signature and to refrain from criticism however justified. In my own Index I have thought it advisable, with due reference to what Field has to say in the notes, to indicate a reasonable doubt in tradition by printing all such words or references in brackets. See *s.v.* ἀνευλαβής; ἀπόθετος Ps. 30 (31). 20; ἀποθνήσκειν Job 14. 14; ἄφοβος; διαμένειν; δυσωπεῖσθαι; μέγας 2 Kings 5. 10; πάλιν; παρά Jer. 52. 8; πρόσωπον Job 20. 25. I have similarly included in brackets words and references which tradition ascribes to α' and where the signature has been rightly enclosed by Field in brackets; in his notes are found the reasons upon which he bases his doubts. For examples, see my Index, *s.v.* εὐθύτης Jer. 13. 10; ἐν 1 Kings 14. 18; θεός *ibid.*; καρδία Jer. 13. 10;

had not an attempt been made to transcend Field in the application of critical canons to the mass of fragments which tradition ascribes to Aquila. At the time when Field published his work (1875) no continuous text of Aquila's Greek version had come to light. Foremost among the new finds exhibiting a continuous Aquila text stand Taylor's Cairo and Mercati's Milan Palimpsests of the remains of the Hexapla Psalter. In both Aquila occupies the (third) column immediately after the (second) column containing the Greek transliteration of the Hebrew. This is in conformity with the testimony of Eusebius, Jerome, and Epiphanius concerning the order of the Hexaplaric columns.[20] On comparing the text[21] with the data in Field we find that though on the whole there is agreement there are nevertheless more or less important divergencies; and above all we are taught to distrust the signatures which Field faithfully copied from his sources.[22]

μετά Gen. 16, 6; *παρεμβολή* 1 Kings 14. 18; *πονηρός* Jer. 13. 10; *ὑπαναχωρεῖν*; *φυγή*.

[20] See Swete, *Introduction to the OT. in Greek*, 1900, 64.

[21] Ps. 21 (22). 20–27, Taylor; 45 (46). 1–4, Mercati *apud* Klostermann, *ZAW.*, XVI (1896), 336 f. (Swete, *l. c.*, 62 f.).

[22] Here is a collation in detail (including also the data for *σ′ θ′*): Ps. 21. 15 *σ′ (καὶ) διέστη* F(ield) = *και διεστη* T(aylor): 17 *σ′ ὅτι ἐκύκλωσάν με θηραταί* F contrast *περιεκυκλω* (*sic*) *γαρ με κυνες* T; 21 *α′ μοναχήν* (*μου*) *σ′ τὴν μονότητά μου* (in part based on Syrohex.) F = *α′ μοναχην μου σ′ την μονοτητα μου* T; Ps. 45. 1 *α′ τῷ νικοποιῷ τῶν υἱῶν Κορὲ ἐπὶ νεανιοτήτων μελῴδημα* F = M(ercati) with the exception of the last word which is *ασμα* in M (see my Index, *s. v. μελῴδημα*: it is used for שִׁיר only in this place, while in the other twenty instances it invariably renders מִזְמוֹר; while *ᾆσμα* = שִׁיר in all cases but one); on the other hand *σ′*'s rendering in F tallies in every particular with that in M; 2 *α′ σ′ εὑρέθη σφόδρα.* Ἄλλος· *ἐν θλίψεσιν εὑρισκόμενος* (Field's sources are Syrohex. ܐ. ܣ. ܐܫܬܟܚܬ ܛܒ—Field adds that the Syrian must have followed a faulty reading *εὑρέθης σφόδρα*—and Chrysost.:

Next in order come the Palimpsests from the Taylor-Schechter Genizah Collection edited by Burkitt and Taylor, which show us manuscripts of Aquila as they were current among Greek-speaking Jews in a form which in its origin is older than the Hexapla. The portions extant cover 3 Kings 21 (20). 9–17; 4 Kings 23. 12–27; Ps. 89 (90). 17; 90 (91); 91 (92). 1–10; 95 (96). 7–13; 96 (97); 97 (98). 3; 101 (102). 16–29; 102 (103). 1–13; and the text is continuous (barring lacunae owing to the imperfect condition of the manuscript). In designating the version as Aquila's no external evidence such as the Hexapla Fragments revealed was available, and the editors were thrown back upon the scanty citations in Field, but in the main upon the internal character of the version which comports with the general statements concerning it in patristic literature.[23]

Αλλος· *ἐν θλ. εὑρισκόμενος*; Nobil.: *Οἱ λοιποί· εὑρέθη εὑρισκόμενος*, which Field rightly divides into *εὑρέθη* and *εὑρισκόμενος*) F comp. *α′ εν θλιψεσιν ευρεθης* (the actual faulty reading presupposed by Syrohex.) *σφοδρα σ′ εν θλιψεσιν ευρισκομενος σφοδρα* M (while *σ′* rightly took נִמְצָא to be a participle, *α′* rendered it as a perfect); 3 *α′ σφάλλεσθαι σ′ κλίνεσθαι* F = M; 4 *α′ ὑπερηφανίᾳ* F = M; the long quotation from *σ′* in F agrees with M except that *αὐτῶν* is omitted in M (see Field's note). It is interesting in this connexion to study the bearing of the new texts on the Syrohex. material which Field has done into Greek. 21. 17 *σ′ ἐκύκλωσαν* F contrast *περιηλθον* T (the Syriac has ܐܬܟܪܟܘܗܝ both for *α′* and *σ′*; but ܐܬܟܪܟ corresponds to *κυκλοῦν*, comp. for instance Joshua 6. 3, 4, 15, and also to *περιέρχεσθαι*, comp. Joshua 6. 7, 11, 15); *σ′ ὡς ζητοῦντες δῆσαι χεῖράς μου καὶ πόδας μου* F contrast *ως λεοντας χειρας μου και τους ποδας μου* T; 18 *σ′* only *ἐμοῦ* is to be corrected into *μου* and *καί* excised; 20 *α′ σ′ σπεῦσον* F = T; 22 *α′ εἰσήκουσάς με* F contrast *εισ]ακουσον μου* T, *σ′ τὴν κάκωσίν μου* F = T; 25 *α′ ἀπ' αὐτοῦ* F contrast *εξ αυτου* T; 26 *α′ πολλῇ* F = T; 27 *πραεῖς sine nomine* (strike out the article) F = *α′* T; 45. 3 *α′ σ′ ἐν τῷ ἀλλάσσεσθαι τὴν γῆν* F contrast *α′ εν τωι ανταλλασσεσθαι γην* (note the compound and the omission of the article) *σ′ εν ταις* (r. *τωι*) *συγχεισθαι γην* M; *ibid.*, in *α′* strike out the article (*ὄρη*); 4 according to M *α′* has *αε[ι* for סֶלָה.

[23] See the references below (Chapter I).

Now in comparing these texts with Field we find again notable agreement, but also differences and untrustworthy signatures.[24] It is therefore clear that where Field is our sole authority for an Aquila rendering the whole force of internal evidence must come into play if we are minded to give to Aquila what is his and not perchance the property of another. Field's sources, whether we consider the stores collected by his predecessors[25] or his own notable additions, are ultimately patristic citations or excerpts from the Hexaplaric columns found between the lines or on the margin of codices of the Septuagint, or again asterisked elements of the fifth Hexaplar column to which a signature is attached. Aside from the fact that Field will bear

[24] Thus, to mention only important deviations, Ps. 90. 6 *ῥήματος* (which would presuppose דָּבָר for דֶּבֶר) F contrast *λοιμου* T (which reading Field postulates in note 12 on the basis of Syrohex.) ; 11 T has *σε* after *εντελειται* (r. *σοι* = לְךָ) ; 91. 4 *εβλη* F contrast *ναβλη* T ; 7 the first *και* in F is rightly missing in T (comp. Hebr.). T frequently omits the article where F has it (so Ps. 90. 1, 2, 7, 12 ; 95. 7 *bis*, 11, 12 *bis*) ; the matter has some importance in dealing with *α'*'s manner of translation.

Thus F's doubt as to the correctness of the signature 90. 4 end is substantiated by T : in the place of *ὡς πανοπλία α'* has simply *ασπις* ; *ibid.*, 7 the double signature *α' σ'* is to be taken *a parte potiori* ; according to T *α'* has not *εκ* but *απο* ; as for the article see preceding note.

[25] The first to collect Hexaplaric fragments was Petrus Morinus who incorporated them in annotations to the so-called editio Sixtina or Romana of the Greek Bible, published in 1587 at Rome. After him Joannes Drusius published the same material under the title: *Veterum Interpretum Graecorum in totum V. T. Fragmenta, collecta, versa et notis illustrata a Johanne Drusio*, Arnhem, 1622. Drusius's work was followed by Lambertus Bos, *Vetus Testamentum ex versione LXX interpretum secundum exemplar Vaticanum Romae editum, una cum Scholiis ejusdem editionis, variis MSS. codicum veterumque exemplarium lectionibus, necnon Fragmentis versionum Aquilae, Symmachi et Theodotionis*, Franequerae, 1709. A more complete edition was that of D. Bernardus de Montfaucon, the immediate predecessor of Field. His work is entitled : *Origenis Hexaplorum quae supersunt, multis partibus auctiora quam a Flaminio Nobilio et Joanne Drusio edita fuerint.* Tom. II. Parisiis, 1713.

correction from an ocular inspection of the codices he quotes on the authority of his predecessors or the 'schedae Holmesianae'—the margin of the Larger Cambridge Septuagint, as well as the works of Pitra and Swete, yield important material—caution is requisite even where there is no ground to suspect that the manuscripts have in any way been departed from. In the first place the signatures may be wrong,[26] or the notes may have been

[26] There is particular cause for doubt where a rendering is ascribed to α′ in common with other translators. Comp. Ps. 48 (49). 18 *α′ θ′ ε′ σ′ ἀκολουθοῦσα*; this is true enough so far as σ′ goes, comp. the phrase in full preserved in another source *οὐδὲ συγκαταβήσεται ἀκολουθοῦσα αὐτῷ ἡ δόξα αὐτοῦ*, whereas according to the same source α′ wrote *οὐδὲ συγκαταβήσεται ὀπίσω αὐτοῦ δόξα αὐτοῦ*. Now *ἀκολουθεῖν* is never elsewhere used by α′, while σ′ apparently is very fond of the verb (see *Concordance, s.v.*). Very likely the ascription to α′ rests on an error.—Isa. 22. 14 אָמַר אֲדֹנָי יֱהוִֹה צְבָאוֹת *α′ θ′ εἶπεν κύριος κύριος τῶν δυνάμεων*. Montfaucon referred it rightly to σ′ θ′, stating as his reason that α′ always puts *στρατιῶν* for צְבָאוֹת. See furthermore below.—Examples with α′ included in the generic signature *οἱ λοιποί*: 1 Kings 20. 19 וְשִׁלַּשְׁתָּ *οι λ̥· καὶ τῇ τρίτῃ*, but we have for α′ with specific ascription *καὶ τρισσεύσας*; 4 Kings 15. 5 בְּבֵית הַחָפְשִׁית *οι λ̥· κρυφαίως* (Theodoret), but contrast *α′ ἐν οἴκῳ τῆς ἐλευθερίας* (cod. 243 supported by the Syrohex.); Job 21. 23 בְּעֶצֶם תֻּמּוֹ *οι λ̥· ἰσχύων ἄμωμος* but contrast *α′ ἐν ὀστεώσει ἁπλότητος αὐτοῦ* so characteristically in conformity with α′'s diction; Ps. 36 (37). 37 f. *οι λ̥· τὰ μέλλοντα* (ver. 37) *τὰ ἔσχατα* (ver. 38) (Procop.; this is the meaning of his remark though it is a trifle confused) which is true enough for σ′ who writes *μέλλοντα* in ver. 37 and *τὰ ἔσχατα* in ver. 38, while α′ is expressly credited with *ἔσχατον* (note the sing.) in both verses; Ezek. 1. 24 שַׁדַּי *λ̥· θεοῦ σαδδαί* but contrast *α′ ἱκανοῦ* (α′ nowhere else transliterates שַׁדַּי); 12. 10 הַנָּשִׂיא הַמַּשָּׂא הַזֶּה *θ′ και λ̥· ὁ ἄρχων ὁ ἀφηγούμενος οὗτος* but contrast *α′ τὸ ἐπηρμένον τὸ ἄρμα τοῦτο* and *σ′ περὶ τοῦ ἄρχοντος τὸ λῆμμα τοῦτο*; Hos. 10. 15 בַּשַּׁחַר *οι λ̥· ὡς ὄρθρος* but contrast *α′ ἐν ὄρθρῳ*. While in all these cases the conflicting testimony may be explained as going back to the two editions of Aquila (see below), it is just as likely, and in many instances much more probable, that the inclusion of α′ under *οἱ λοιποί* rests on an error. Important in this connexion is the remark of Prof. G. F. Moore (*AJSL.*, XXIX (1912), 39, n. 9) that 'Field, in the greater part of his Hexapla, follows Montfaucon in the error' of resolving the construction λ̥, which is found on the margin of codd. of the

attached to the wrong word.[27] Then we meet with doublets, one element in which alone can belong to Aquila.[28] Quite another matter are parallel renderings

Septuagint, by λοιποι, whereas in reality Lucian (Λουκιανός) was meant. Comp., e. g., Num. 3. 22 in BM, where α′ σ′ render פקודיהם by επεσκεμμενοι, while to λ̥ (as well as ο′) is attributed επισκεψις.

[27] Thus Job 38. 7 Field cites α′ θ′ ἅμα υἱοὶ θεοῦ to the words of the text כָּל־בְּנֵי אֱלֹהִים 𝔊 πάντες ἄγγελοί μου; but while ἅμα is found for כל (ἡ ἐκκλησία ἅμα כל הקהל) 2 Chron. 30. 23 𝔊, it is unlikely that α′ would indulge in such freedom; it is more probable that ἅμα in Field's source was misplaced from the line above and belongs in front of ἄστρα, where indeed Syrohex. places it (see Field).—Isa. 30. 33, I am inclined to think that α′ κέδρινα does not belong to מְדֻרָתָהּ but to גָּפְרִית, comp. עֲצֵי גֹפֶר Gen. 6. 14 εν τω εβραιω εξ ξυλων κεδρινων i^{m} (BM); but it ought to be stated that α′ has there ασηπτων τεθε⟨ι⟩ωμενων.—Zeph. 1. 12 אֲחַפֵּשׂ οἱ λοιποί· καὶ ἐκδικήσω: not only καί is puzzling here but also ἐκδικεῖν, which is used by α′ σ′ θ′ Ἑβραῖος and Ἄλλος for נקם only and is not so easy as an equivalent for חפש; hence Schleusner may be right with his suggestion that καὶ ἐκδικήσω belongs to the following וּפָקַדְתִּי [Schleusner is wrong. 𝔊 has itself καὶ ἐκδικήσω; hence the marginal note would have been purposeless. Moreover, according to Dr. Reider's own Index, פקד is rendered uniformly in α′ ἐπισκέπτειν. M].

[28] Here is a list which is fairly complete: Exod. 28. 33 BM register for α′ διαφορου διβαφου for שָׁנִי, but the former alone belongs to α′, who uses it four more times for שָׁנִי (which he derives from שָׁנָה = be different), while the second is peculiar to σ′ alone, who employs it also 28. 5; 35. 23, 35.—Judges 18. 7 α′ καὶ οὐκ ἐνῆν καταισχύνων οὐδὲ διατρέπων, Field casts suspicion on the derivation of the rendering as a whole from α′, pointing to Job 11. 3, where α′ has ἐντρέπων for מַכְלִים, and to Isa. 29. 22, where the rarer verb διατρέπεσθαι is used by σ′ (for Hebr. חָוַר, θ′ has ἐν-); to which may be added that καταισχύνων and διατρέπων are apparently parallel renderings for Hebr. מַכְלִים and that the same doublet, only in an inverted order, occurs in the B text of the Septuagint (which also has a doublet for עֶצֶר: ἐκπιέζων θησαυροῦ; the second element would appear to have been introduced from Origen, see Field); there is no reason therefore to discard the entire rendering as not belonging to α′; it is true, ἐνῆν does not sound as an α′ rendering; but of the two verbs used for מַכְלִים καταισχύνων might credibly be assigned to α′, and it should be excised in the B text as a foreign element.—2 Kings 3. 22 מֵהַגְּדוּד α′ ⟨ἀπὸ⟩ τοῦ γεδδοὺρ μονοζώνου, Field calls the whole rendering in question in view of the express citation α′ ἀπὸ τοῦ εὐζώνου in cod. 243 and parallel passages where α′ consistently writes εὔζωνος for גְּדוּד; still the case may be disposed of in this way: in the

ascribed to Aquila which go back to the two editions of his work; the subject is adequately dealt with by Field in his Prolegomena.[29]

Naturally enough the text of Aquila is here and there handed down in a faulty condition. No mention shall be made here of errors set right by Field; but a few which have escaped his attention are given below.[30] Lastly, an

doublet *μονοζώνου* represents a textual variant of *ευζωνου*, while the transliteration cannot possibly come from α′, *γεδδούρ* for גְּדוּד being found in the Septuagint of Kings and Chronicles (see 1 Kings 30. 8, 15, 15, 23; 1 Chron. 12. 21 (22); [2 Chron. 22. 1, 93^mg; comp. also 1 Ch. 12. 7 (8) *γεδ(δ)ωρ*. M]).—Jer. 20. 2 *οἱ γ′ καὶ ἐνέβαλεν καὶ ἔδωκεν*: this note should be corrected in accordance with Q^mg *καὶ ἐνέβαλεν οἱ γ′ καὶ ἔδωκεν*, Hebr. וַיִּתֵּן.—Add from Pitra, Exod. 8. 7 (3) בְּלָטֵיהֶם *α′ ἐν ἠρεμαίοις ἀποκρύφοις*, where the second element does not belong to α′, see Field *ad loc.* and comp. 7. 11, 22; also Ps. 20 (21). 12 *α′ ἐλογίσαντο ἐννοίας βουλὴν ἣν οὐ μὴ δύνωνται ἀδυνάτους*; *σ′ διελογίσαντο βουλὰς ἃς οὐ μὴ δύνωνται*; *θ′ ἐλογίσαντο ἀπ′ ἔννοιαν οὐ μὴ δύν.*: there is much confusion here, one is tempted to vindicate for α′ what is ascribed to θ′ (comp. *ἀπ′* = מ of מְזִמָּה taken as a preposition, but it exercises no influence on the construction, the noun being placed in the accusative; furthermore, absence of the relative exactly as in Hebrew); in the rendering attributed to α′ *ἀδυνάτους* and *ἐννοίας* belong to σ′ (see Field).

29 pp. xxiv ff.

30 Thus Job 21. 17 אֵיד *α′ ἐπικλυσμός* is probably to be emended to *ἐπιβλυσμός*: the former is found only once in the Greek Bible (σ′ for Hebrew שֶׁטֶף Dan. 9. 26), while the latter is exclusively an α′ word and is used uniformly for אֵ(י)ד; the interchange of κ and β is a usual occurrence in cursive script.—Ps. 34 (35). 28 תְּהִלָּתֶךָ *α′ ὑμνήσει σε* read perhaps *υμνησῑ σου* = *ὕμνησίν σου*; certainly it is unlikely that α′ read תְּהַלֶּלְךָ.—82 (83), 3 *ὤκλασαν* is probably miswritten for *ὤχλασαν*; see Index, *s. v.* *ὀχλάζειν*.—Isa. 7. 20 בְּמֶלֶךְ אַשּׁוּר *α′ ἐν βασιλείᾳ Ἀσσυρίων* read *ἐν βασιλεῖ Ἀσσυρίων* (α dittographed).—Jer. 5. 31 יִרְדּוּ *α′ ἐπεκρότουν* has been emended by Cappellus and L. Bos (*apud* Schleusner) to *ἐπεκράτουν*; the same error underlies *ἐπεκρότησαν* in the Septuagint, comp. also 3 Kings 9. 23 A.—6. 25 לְאוֹיֵב *α′ τῶν ἐθνῶν* read *τῶν ἐχθρῶν*.—Ezek. 19. 7 אַלְמְנוֹתָיו *α′ χώρας* read *χήρας*.—26. 4 חוֹמוֹת צֹר *α′ σ′ θ (τὰ τείχη) σου* read *σόρ*, comp. 𝔊.—Hos. 12. 8 (9) אוֹן לִי *α′ ἀνωφελὲς αὐτῷ* read *ἐμαυτῷ* like 𝔊.—From Pitra: Gen. 14. 23 *α′ ἱμάτιον* read *ἱμάντος*, so j^m s^m according to BM (see also Field, n. 23), Hebr. שְׂרוֹךְ; 15. 12 תַּרְדֵּמָה *α′ κάρσος σ′ κάρος*, comp. *α′ κορος* (*κορσος* C_2)

important point, to which as far as I know scant attention has been paid, deserves on that very account to be emphasized. It follows from the nature of the majority of notes, be they patristic or marginal, that the aim is to contrast a rendering of the later Greek versions with that in the Septuagint. Where the rendering consists of a whole phrase the tendency was to be accurate in the point of difference which was essential for the moment, and to be less exact with non-essentials which were therefore accommodated to the diction of the Septuagint. In other words, renderings ascribed to the Three are frequently to be understood *a parte potiori*. To illustrate by an example: Joshua 1. 1 אֶל־יְהוֹשֻׁעַ בִּן־נוּן, 𝔊 *τῷ* Ἰησοῖ *υἱῷ* Ναυῇ. *α′ σ′ πρὸς* Ἰησοῦν *υἱὸν* Ναυῇ; the salient point is that whereas 𝔊 construed *εἶπεν* with the dative, both *α′* and *σ′* wrote *πρός* c. acc. for Hebr. אֶל; that much may be relied upon; but it would be hazardous to follow the source for the other parts of the phrase; *α′* at least cannot be credited with the graecized Ἰησοῦν, for well-understood reasons; Deut. 1. 38 we know from the margin of M that *α′* wrote Ιωσουα (so BM; Field has Ιησουα); accordingly *α′* must have written here *προς* Ιωσουα, and we may even go farther and complete the phrase to read *υιον* Νουν (we find Exod. 33. 11 *νυν* in F^{b} and Deut. 1. 38 *νουη* in F^{b} M^{m}, read in both places Νουν, comp. 𝔊 1 Chron. 7. 27 where Νουμ BA should of course be corrected into Νουν, so Lagarde's text). Instructive is also the following example: Job 5. 5 וְאֶל־מִצִּנִּים יִקָּחֵהוּ,

σ′ καρος j^{m} s^{m} v^{m} c$_{3}^{m}$ in BM who also quote *α′ σ′ nausea* from Barh.; Field prints in the text *α′ κόρος σ′ κάρος*, he adds in a note that though the *α′* reading which he prints is best attested it is nevertheless unsatisfactory; it would seem to me that both *α′* and *σ′* wrote *κάρος*, which alone corresponds to the Hebrew.

𝔊 αὐτοὶ δὲ ἐκ κακῶν οὐκ ἐξαίρετοι ἔσονται, α' αὐτὸς δὲ πρὸς ἐνόπλων ἀρθήσεται, σ' αὐτοὶ δὲ πρὸς ἐνόπλων ἀρθήσονται. It is evident at a glance that personal pronoun + δέ, common to all these versions, really belongs to 𝔊 (and σ'): apart from the fact that α' could not have used it because it has no equivalent in MT, the phrase itself is foreign to α''s diction while being peculiar to the Septuagint; note the use of δέ, whereas α' would employ καί. This being of less moment they were not exact in quoting it, while quoting carefully the point of difference: πρὸς ἐνόπλων ἀρθήσεται.

6. It is obvious that my own Index, constructed as it is with due regard to the critical points just enumerated, will in turn furnish a means by which many questions of detail will solve themselves. For naturally the double Index, Greek-Hebrew and Hebrew-Greek, resolves itself into a complete storehouse of observations concerning the various sides of Aquila as a translator and student of the Scriptures. By way of summing up the material which is necessarily scattered in the Index itself, I propose to present in the following chapters a study of

I. Aquila's Manner of Translation;
II. Aquila's Knowledge of the Hebrew Grammar and Lexicon;
III. Aquila's Exegesis;
IV. The Hebrew Text underlying Aquila's Version.

In the concluding pages some unsolved problems will be laid before the reader.

CHAPTER IV

THE HEBREW TEXT UNDERLYING AQUILA'S VERSION

33. It is a well-known thesis propounded by Lagarde[88] that all our manuscripts of the Hebrew text of the Bible belong to the same recension and are descended from the same imperfect archetype dating from the times of Hadrian (Akiba). The corollary which Lagarde saw fit to append to his thesis, to the effect that the archetype in question represented a recension 'doctored up in the interest of the most violent hatred of Christianity', has been disposed of in a masterly criticism by Kuenen ('Der Stammbaum des masoretischen Textes des Alten Testaments' in *Gesammelte Abhandlungen*, übersetzt von Budde, 82 ff.). The thesis itself, however, has been accepted with more or less of modification by serious scholars like Nöldeke,[89] Wellhausen,[90] W. R. Smith,[91] Cornill,[92] and Driver.[93] On the other hand,

[88] The first part of Lagarde's thesis was enunciated in the introduction to his *Anmerkungen zur griechischen Übersetzung der Proverbien*, 1863 (reprinted in his *Mittheilungen*, I, 19 ff.), while the second part was formulated casually on p. xii of the preface to his *Materialien zur Kritik und Geschichte des Pentateuchs*, I, 1867, and more fully in his *Symmicta*, I, 1877, 50 ff. A similar view was given expression to by Olshausen in the introduction to his *Commentary on the Psalms*, 1853, 17 ff. On the question of priority see Lagarde, *Symmicta*, II, 120 f.; *Mittheil.*, I, 22–6.

[89] The citations are given by Lagarde, *Symmicta*, II, 120 f.

[90] Bleek-Wellhausen, *Einleitung in das A.T.*[6], pp. 574, 578.

[91] *The Old Testament in the Jewish Church*, New York, 1900, p. 57, note 2.

[92] Prolegomena to Ezekiel, p. 10; *Einleitung in das Alte Testament*, 1892, § 51.

[93] *Notes on the Hebrew text of the Books of Samuel*[2], p. xxxiv: '*All MSS.*

R. G

the thesis as a whole has been subjected to criticism at the hands of König,[94] and rejected by Strack.[95]

34. Whatever be the genesis of the recension of the Scriptures known as Masoretic—in point of date it may ascend to a period much older than the Hadrianic—this much is certain that after a period coinciding with the date of the earlier parts of the Septuagint, during which time the text was more or less in flux, there followed one of gradual uniformity culminating in the stereotyped condition immediately preceding the Masorah.[96] For when all deduction is made of variations due to the exigencies of translation or to unsatisfactory exegesis, there still remains in the Septuagint a body of variants having their undoubted origin in the divergence of the Hebrew text underlying the version.[97] Also the Samaritan recension of the Pentateuch

belong to the same recension, and are descended from the same imperfect archetype. Existing MSS. all represent what is termed the *Massoretic* text' (italics by author).

94 *Einleitung in das Alte Testament*, p. 88 f.

95 *Einleitung in das Alte Testament*[6], p. 192, where it is maintained that even after the close of the canon the Hebrew text continued in a state of fluctuation.

96 The beginnings of the Masorah are shrouded in darkness. The passage in Ketubbot 106 a that a standard text was preserved in the court of the Temple from which all copies were prepared, would lead to the assumption of an early origin, but on the other hand we must not forget that as late as the second century C. E. the Rabbis warn against incorrect copies of the Bible. Thus while it is true that already the Mishnah and the Talmud generally (particularly the post-talmudic tracts *Maseket Sefer Torah* and *Maseket Soferim*) contain Masoretic material, still the Hebrew text continued in fluctuation and was not fixed in its final form before the close of the talmudic era. Comp. on this subject Elias Levita, *Massoret ha-Massoret*, ed. Ginsburg, London, 1867; C. D. Ginsburg, *Introduction to the . . . Hebrew Bible*, London, 1897; Strack, *Prolegomena Critica in V. T.*, Leipzig, 1873; Bacher in Winter und Wünsche, *Jüdische Literatur*, ii, 121-32; Buhl, *Kanon u. Text*, p. 94 ff.

97 Comp. Wellhausen's *Text der Bücher Samuelis*; Driver's *Notes on the*

with which the Septuagintal version shows marked affinity,[98] no matter what one may think of certain dogmatic changes, proves that more than one recension of the Law was current in pre-Maccabean times. As for the Hebrew upon which the oldest parts of the Alexandrine version rest, the recensional character of the 'Vorlage' reveals itself on the one hand in a more developed form of diaskeue, bent upon harmonizing the unevennesses of composition, and on the other hand in faithfully preserving a cruder and more archaic text laying bare incongruities which the Masoretic text has covered up.[99]

There is just as little doubt in turn that in the times of Akiba, when Aquila and his congeners lived and laboured, the Hebrew text had, roughly speaking, assumed the form of our Masoretic text. Thus Origen, when engaged in rectifying the Septuagint in a manner so as to square it with the 'Hebrew truth', was in a position to fall back upon the Three for supplying lacunae which he was neither competent nor willing to translate afresh.

35. When the fragments of Aquila are compared with the parallel translation of the Septuagint the textual identity

Hebrew Text of the Books of Samuel; Cornill's *Ezechiel*; Graetz's *Kritischer Commentar zu den Psalmen*, and his *Emendationes in plerosque Sacrae Scripturae Vet. Test. Libros*, edited by Bacher; for a list of monographs comp. Buhl, *Kanon u. Text*, p. 125 f. A list of characteristic variants may be found in Swete, *Introduction to the Old Test. in Greek*, p. 442 ff.; comp. also Margolis, 'Studien im griechischen Alten Testament' in *ZAW.*, XXVII (1907), 212 ff. The most complete collection of variants based on both recensions and Hebrew manuscripts is found in the foot-notes of Kittel's *Biblia Hebraica*, whose reconstruction of the Hebrew, however, is not always successful.

[98] Comp. Geiger, *Urschrift*, p. 98 ff.; against Frankel, *Vorstudien*, p. 32 ff., and esp. *Einfluss*, p. 238. See, furthermore, König, *Einleitung*, p. 95 ff.

[99] Comp. Wellhausen, *Composition*², p. 126, for the first instance; as to the second, see *ibid.*, p. 53.

G 2

of Aquila's Hebrew and our own, as far as consonants are concerned, is proved in a preponderating number of cases.[100]

[100] A list of telling examples is not without interest: Job 3. 5 יבעתהו כמרירי יום α′ *ἐκθαμβήσαισαν αὐτὴν ὡς πικραμμοὶ* (*ἡμέρας*), 𝔊 *καταραθείη* (variants *καταραχθείη, καὶ ταραχθείη*) *ἡ ἡμέρα*, evidently omitting כמרירי; *ibid.*, v. 18 יחד אסירים שאננו α′ *ἅμα δέσμιοι εὐθήνησαν*, 𝔊 *ὁμοθυμαδὸν δὲ οἱ αἰώνιοι*, omitting the last word and reading אשרים *beati* (L. Cappellus in *Critica Sacra*); 5. 5 ושאף צמים חילם α′ *ἀφειλκύσαντο διψῶντες εὐπορίαν αὐτῶν*, 𝔊 *ἐκσιφωνισθείη αὐτῶν ἡ ἰσχύς*, צמים wanting; 6. 9 יתר ידו α′ *ἐπιβαλὼν τὴν χεῖρα* . . ., 𝔊 *εἰς τέλος δέ*, reading ותמיד or more likely its Aramaic equivalent ותדיר; 7. 15 ותבחר מחנק נפשי α′ *καὶ αἱρεῖται ἀγχόνην ἡ ψυχή μου*, 𝔊 *ἀπαλλάξεις ἀπὸ πνεύματός μου τὴν ψυχήν μου*, as if ותברח מרוחי נפשי; 13. 9 אם כהתל באנוש תהתלו בו α′ *εἰ ὡς παραλογισμῷ ἐν ἀνθρώπῳ παραλογίζεσθε* . . ., 𝔊 *εἰ γὰρ τὰ πάντα ποιοῦντες προστεθήσεσθε αὐτῷ*, which certainly a different Hebrew text underlies; 18. 19 לא נין לו ולא נכד α′ *οὐ γονεῖς αὐτῷ καὶ οὐκ ἔγγονοι*, 𝔊 *οὐκ ἔσται ἐπίγνωστος* = לא נכר; 19. 20 בעורי ובבשרי דבקה עצמי α′ *ἐν δέρματί μου καὶ ἐν κρέᾳ μου ἐκολλήθη τὸ ὀστοῦν μου*, 𝔊 *ἐν δέρματί μου ἐσάπησαν αἱ σάρκες μου τὰ δὲ ὀστᾶ μου* = בעורי בשרי רקבה ועצמי; 20. 26 טמון לצפוניו α′ *ἀποκέκρυπται τοῖς ἐγκεκρυμμένοις αὐτοῦ*, 𝔊 *αὐτῷ ὑπομεῖναι* = טמון ל; 24. 5 משחרי לטרף α′ *ὀρθρίζοντες εἰς ἅλωσιν*, wanting in 𝔊; 28. 13 ערכה α′ *τάξιν αὐτῆς*, 𝔊 *ὁδὸν αὐτῆς* = דרכה; 30. 15 וכעב עברה α′ . . . *παρῆλθεν*, which is missing in 𝔊; 37. 21 ורוח עברה ותטהרם α′ *καὶ πνεῦμα παρῆλθε καὶ ἐκαθάρισεν αὐτάς*, 𝔊 *ὥσπερ τὸ παρ᾽ αὐτοῦ ἐπὶ νεφῶν*, in which עב alone is recognizable; 39. 21 לקראת נשק α′ *εἰς ἀπάντησιν ὅπλου*, 𝔊 *συναντῶν βασιλεῖ*, perhaps נָשִׂא; Ps. 27 (28). 3 אל תמשכני עם רשעים ועם פעלי און α′ *μὴ ἑλκύσῃς* (*με*) *μετὰ ἀσεβῶν καὶ μετὰ κατεργαζομένων ἀνωφελές*, 𝔊 *μὴ συνελκύσῃς μετὰ ἁμαρτωλῶν τὴν ψυχήν μου καὶ μετὰ ἐργαζομένων ἀδικίαν μὴ συναπολέσῃς με*, which, it must be admitted, may be a paraphrastic rendering of our Hebrew; 31 (32). 5 עון חטאתי α′ *ἀνομίαν ἁμαρτίας μου*, 𝔊 *ἀσέβειαν τῆς καρδίας μου*; 49 (50). 11 זיז שדי α′ *παντοδαπὰ χώρας*, 𝔊 *ὡραιότης ἀγροῦ*, as if זיו; 71 (72). 14 דמם α′ *τὸ αἷμα αὐτῶν*, 𝔊 *τὸ ὄνομα αὐτῶν* = שמם; Prov. 2. 6 מפיו α′ *ἀπὸ στόματος* (*αὐτοῦ*), 𝔊 *ἀπὸ προσώπου αὐτοῦ* = מפניו; 4. 4 וחיה α′ *καὶ ζῆθι*, wanting in 𝔊; 8. 26 עד לא עשה α′ *πρὶν ἢ ἐποίησε*, 𝔊 *κύριος ἐποίησε*; 10. 7 ירקב α′ *σαπήσεται*, 𝔊 *σβέννυται*, which, according to some exegetes, would correspond to ידעך; 10. 21 ירעו רבים α′ *ποιμαίνουσι πολλούς*, 𝔊 *ἐπίσταται ὑψηλά* = ידעו רמים; 15. 22 וברב יועצים α′ *καὶ ἐν πλήθει συμβουλευόντων*, 𝔊 *ἐν δὲ καρδίαις βουλευομένων*, as if ובלב; 27. 13 כי ערב זר α′ *ὅτι ἐνεγυήσατο ἀλλότριον*, 𝔊 *παρῆλθε γὰρ ὑβριστής* = כי עבר זר; Isa. 3. 24–5 כי תחת יפי: מתיך α′ *ὅτι ἀντὶ κάλλους ἄνδρες σου*, 𝔊 *καὶ ὁ υἱός σου ὁ κάλλιστος ὃν ἀγαπᾷς*; 11. 4 במישור α′ *ἐν εὐθύτητι*, wanting in 𝔊; 30. 28 ורסן מתעה על לחיי עמים α′ *καὶ χαλινὸν πλανῶντα ἐπὶ σιαγόνας*

36. Instances, however, are not lacking in which Aquila is at variance with the received text. Before proceeding to

λαῶν, 𝔊 καὶ διώξεται αὐτοὺς πλάνησις καὶ λήψεται αὐτοὺς κατὰ πρόσωπον αὐτῶν, as if ורצן מתעה על לחייהם (לחייהם being construed as פניהם); 33. 20 קרית מועדנו α′ πόλις ἑορτῶν . . ., 𝔊 πόλις τὸ σωτήριον ἡμῶν, as if ישועתנו; 35. 2 והשרון α′ καὶ τοῦ Σαρών, wanting in 𝔊; 38. 12 מיום עד לילה α′ ἀφ᾽ ἡμέρας ἕως νυκτός, 𝔊 ἐν τῇ ἡμέρᾳ ἐκείνῃ = ביום ההוא; 38. 14 עגור α′ ἀγούρ, wanting in 𝔊; Jer. 6. 11 חמת יהוה α′ θυμοῦ κυρίου, 𝔊 θυμόν μου = חמתי; 25. 38 (32. 24) חרון היונה α′ ὀργῆς . . ., 𝔊 μαχαίρας = חרב; 30 (37). 16 כלם בשבי ילכו α′ πάντες αὐτοὶ ἐν αἰχμαλωσίᾳ πορεύσονται, 𝔊 κρέας αὐτῶν πᾶν ἔδονται = כל בשרם יאכלו; 31 (38). 12 כגן רוה α′ ὡς κῆπος μεθύων, 𝔊 ὥσπερ ξύλον ἔγκαρπον = כעץ פרי; 34 (41). 18 לפני העגל אשר כרתו לשנים ויעברו בין בתריו α′ ἐνώπιον τοῦ μόσχου οὗ διεῖλον εἰς δύο καὶ διῆλθον ἀναμέσον τῶν διχοτομημάτων αὐτοῦ, 𝔊 κατὰ πρόσωπόν μου τὸν μόσχον ὃν ἐποίησαν ἐργάζεσθαι αὐτῷ; 46 (26). 12 קלונך α′ τὴν ἀτιμίαν σου, 𝔊 φωνήν σου = קולך; 49 (30). 2 ובנתיה α′ καὶ αἱ θυγατέρες αὐτῆς, 𝔊 καὶ βῶμοι αὐτῆς = ובמתיה; 49. 25 (30. 14) עיר תהלה α′ (πόλιν) ἐπαινετήν, 𝔊 πόλιν ἐμήν = עירי; Ezek. 1. 13 ודמות α′ καὶ ὁμοιώσεις, 𝔊 καὶ ἐν μέσῳ = ובתוך; 5. 14 ולחרפה בגוים α′ καὶ εἰς ὄνειδος ἐν τοῖς ἔθνεσι, 𝔊 καὶ τὰς θυγατέρας σου = ובנותיך; 13. 3 הנבלים α′ ἀπορρέοντας, 𝔊 ἀπὸ καρδίας αὐτῶν = מלבם; 18. 11 והוא את כל אלה לא עשה α′ καὶ αὐτὸς σύμπαντα ταῦτα οὐκ ἐποίησεν, 𝔊 ἐν τῇ ὁδῷ τοῦ πατρὸς αὐτοῦ τοῦ δικαίου οὐκ ἐπορεύθη, which, however, may be a paraphrase of the Hebrew; 22. 25 קשר נביאיה α′ σύστρεμμα . . ., 𝔊 ἧς οἱ ἀφηγούμενοι = אשר נשיאיה; 23. 34 ושדיך תנתקי α′ καὶ τοὺς μαστούς σου κατατιλεῖς, wanting in 𝔊; 28. 13 מלאכת תפיך α′ ἔργον τοῦ κάλλους σου, 𝔊 ἐνέπλησας τοὺς θησαυρούς σου = מלאת תכיך (Cornill); 29. 7 כל כתף α′ πάντα ὦμον, 𝔊 πᾶσα χείρ, as if כף; Hos. 6. 8 עקבה מדם α′ περικαμπὴς ἀπὸ αἵματος, 𝔊 ταράσσουσα ὕδωρ, as if מים; 11. 12 (12. 1) רד עם אל α′ ἐπικρατῶν . . ., 𝔊 ἔγνω αὐτοὺς ὁ θεός = ידעם אל; Amos 7. 1 והנה לקש אחר גזי המלך α′ καὶ ἰδοὺ ὄψιμος ὀπίσω τῆς γάζης τοῦ βασιλέως, 𝔊 καὶ ἰδοὺ βροῦχος εἷς Γὼγ ὁ βασιλεύς, as if והנה ילק אחד גג המלך; Mic. 1. 10 אל תגידו α′ μὴ ἀναγγείλητε, 𝔊 μὴ μεγαλύνεσθε = אל תגדילו; Hab. 1. 5 ראו בגוים α′ *aspicite in gentibus* (Jer.), 𝔊 ἴδετε οἱ καταφρονηταί, as if בגדים; Zeph. 3. 18 נוגי ממועד α′ *translatos* . . . (Jer.), 𝔊 ὡς ἐν ἡμέρᾳ ἑορτῆς = כיום מועד. [Dr. Reider might have readily enlarged his list by citing cases of variation in the Hebrew underlying 𝔊 which admit of no doubt; attention is directed to passages where 𝔊 has clearly preserved the superior reading, while α′ clings to the received text. There are enough examples in the list, however, to substantiate the statement in the text. M.]

It was thought expedient to omit from this list as too evident those Aquila words and passages which serve to fill up gaps and lacunae in the Septuagint. These, as a rule, follow our consonantal text very closely, enumerate them it is well to state that my own efforts bear out the statement of Cornill to the effect that the three minor versions though extant in small remains 'reveal a series of renderings which can be explained only as due to a divergent text; even in Jerome who flourished about 400 some minor differences of pointing and word-division and here and there even consonantal variants may be detected'.[101] The same scholar has gleaned a goodly number of consonantal variants from the Targum to Ezekiel.[102] Similar lists may be made in other books, and it is a source of regret that no comprehensive monograph on this subject is available, though noteworthy contributions on a smaller scale have been made.[103] Of course, in dealing with the Targum, and for that matter with the other versions not greatly removed from it in time, the differences between the two Masoretic schools, the Orientals and the Occidentals, must not be lost sight of. Especially is this true of the marginal readings or קְרָיָן on which subject there is notable divergence between the two schools. On the whole it may be said that Aquila goes with the margin (קְרִי); but instances to the contrary are not wanting. Interesting are those

while, on the authority of Origen, they were wanting in the Alexandrine version.

[101] See Prolegomena to his edition of Ezekiel, p. 11. Likewise Nestle in *Realencyclopädie für protestantische Theologie und Kirche*[3], III, 22: 'Aquila's translation shows that even in the school whence our Masoretic text is descended the latter was not yet fixed in all its particulars in the first third of the second century.' Contrast Burkitt, *JQR.*, X (1898), 214 note, who speaks of 'the exact agreement of the translation of Aquila with the present Masoretic text'.

[102] See *ibid.*, p. 126 ff.

[103] See the literature in Strack's *Einleitung*[6], § 84; comp. especially Geiger, *Urschrift*, Excurs II on the Palestinian Targum to the Pentateuch, p. 451 ff.

cases where Aquila follows the כְּתִיב, while the Septuagint goes with the קְרִי. The conclusion is forced upon us that Aquila's adherence to the כְּתִיב in opposition to the older version is but another instance of his literalism.

37. In grouping the consonantal variants I only cite those that have a high degree of probability as having existed in Aquila's archetype. Thus Ruth 1. 12 גַּם הָיִיתִי הַלַּיְלָה לְאִישׁ = καίγε . . . βεβηλωμένη ἀνδρί, implying חֲלוּלָה 'profaned, polluted' (𝔊 and 𝔖 omit the word altogether); 1 Kings 2. 5 συνετρίβησαν shows that α′ read נִשְׁבָּרוּ for נִשְׁכָּרוּ; 28. 16 עָרֶךָ = κατὰ σοῦ, so α′ θ′ and in a citation by Origen, Field conjectures עָלֶךָ, comp. indeed *BDB.*, *s.v.* על 6 d (it is more probable, however, that the signatures are faulty and that α′ θ′ wrote what is now ascribed to σ′, ἀντιζηλός σου, see Index *s.v.*); 2 Kings 23. 19 מִן הַשְּׁלֹשָׁה הֲכִי נִכְבָּד = παρὰ τοὺς τρεῖς, ὅτι ἔνδοξος, hence α′ read כִּי; Ps. 77 (78). 33 ὡς ἀτμόν implies כַּהֶבֶל for בַּהֶבֶל, but 𝔊 reads MT; 88 (89). 51 כָּל־רַבִּים = πάσας ἀδικίας, hence רִיבֵי (= רִבֵי), so Jer. *omnes iniquitates*, who is followed by Duhm, while Baethgen suggests כְּלִמַּת and Perles (*Analekten zur Textkritik des A. T.*, p. 14) derives the same word from כל abbreviated; 118 (119). 119 διελογίσω corresponds to חִשַּׁבְתָּ which α′ read for הִשְׁבַּתָּ with σ′ and Jer., while 𝔊 reads חִשַּׁבְתִּי, ἐλογισάμην; 120 (121). 3 μὴ δῴης which is common to all the Greek versions yields אַל־תִּתֵּן for אַל־יִתֵּן; Prov. 21. 28 לָנֶצַח יְדַבֵּר, α′ σ′ θ′ εἰς νῖκος πορεύσεται, implies יַעֲבֹר; 30. 1 וְאֻכָל καὶ τέλεσον implies וְכַלֵּה or וְכַלֵּא (comp. Dan. 9. 24), possibly וְכַל; Eccles. 7. 23 (22) יָדַע πονηρεύσεται, hence יֵרַע was read with 𝔊 and σ′; 8. 12 מְאַת ἀπέθανεν α′ σ′ θ′, all of whom read מֵת, while 𝔊's ἀπὸ τότε = מֵאָז, the latter more in style of α′; 11. 5 כַּאֲשֶׁר ἐν ᾧ, implying בַּאֲשֶׁר; 12. 6 גֻּלַּת הַזָּהָב λύτρωσις τοῦ χρυσίου, pointing to גְּאֻלַּת = גְּאֻלַּת; Cant. 3. 6 כְּתִמְרוֹת ὡς ὁμοίωσις, points

to כִּתְמֻנַת;[104] Isa. 14. 32 מַלְאֲכֵי βασιλεῖς α′ θ′, hence both read מַלְכֵי with 𝔊; 16. 7 τοῖς πολυχρονίοις μου implies לִישִׁישַׁי for לַאֲשִׁישֵׁי, 𝔊 and 𝔗 read לְאַנְשֵׁי by analogy with Jer. 48 (31). 31; a similar variant is also found Hos. 3. 1 where אֲשִׁישֵׁי = παλαιά implies יְשִׁישֵׁי; 61. 6 תִּתְיַמָּרוּ was read תִּתְחַמָּרוּ = πορφυρωθήσεσθε, der. from חָמַר 'to be red'; Jer. 6. 6 הָעִיר הָפְקַד = ἡ πόλις ἄδικος, in the same sense also 𝔊 (ἡ ψευδής), 𝔗 דאיתפקידו לה חובהא, Duhm suggests הָעִיר הַבּוֹגֵדָה, Giesebrecht עִיר הַפֶּרֶק, Cornill עִיר הַשֶּׁקֶר, the latter is the most probable for both 𝔊 and α′; *ibid.*, v. 11 סוֹד בַּחוּרִים σύστρεμμα πονηρευομένων, hence סוֹד מְרֵעִים, comp. Ps. 63 (64). 3 where מְרֵעִים is so rendered; 9. 21 (20) בְּחַלּוֹנֵיכֶם for בְּחַלּוֹנֵינוּ with 𝔊 𝔏 σ′, and בְּאַרְמְנוֹתֵיכֶם for בְּאַרְמְנוֹתֵינוּ with σ′; 15. 11 שֵׁרוּתִךָ τὸ ὑπόλειμμά σου, hence שְׁ(אֵ)רִיתְךָ with σ′ 𝔗 𝔙; 17. 1 מִזְבְּחוֹתֵיהֶם for ־תֵיכֶם with 𝔗 𝔙 𝔖, but perhaps assimilated to the preceding לִבָּם; *ibid.*, ver. 4 καὶ διαβιβάσω σε points to וְהַעֲבַרְתִּיךָ instead of וְהַעֲבַדְתִּיךָ, comp. 15. 14 where וְהַעֲבַרְתִּי = (καὶ) παραβιβάσω σε also implies the same reading וְהַעֲבַרְתִּיךָ though 𝔙 read MT *et adducam*, 𝔊 𝔗 𝔖 read והעברתיך in both places; 20. 11 עַל־כֵּן οὐχ οὕτως implies לָכֵן dissolved into לֹא כֵן, a process frequent in the Septuagint; 21. 14 כִּפְרִי מַעַלְלֵיכֶם = κατὰ τὰ πονηρὰ ἐπιτηδεύματα, hence α′ and θ′ read כְּרֹעַ for כִּפְרִי by analogy with ver. 12; 26 (33). 18 αὐτός = הוּא for הָיָה; 34 (41). 5 κατὰ τοὺς ἐμπυρισμούς points to וּכְמִשְׂרְפוֹת inst. of וּבְמִשְׂרְפוֹת, so 𝔊 𝔖 𝔙; 41 (48). 17 ἐν τοῖς φραγμοῖς implies בִּגְדֵרוֹת inst. of בְּגֵרוּת, comp. 49 (30). 3 where בַּגְּדֵרוֹת is rendered by α′ similarly, comp. also Josephus, *Antiq.*, X, 95 where Μάνδρα supports α′'s reading; 48 (31). 30 בַּדָּיו τὰ ἐξαίρετα αὐτοῦ (Syro-Hex. ܓܒܝܬܐ ܕܝܠܗ), hence בָּרָיו, similarly 50 (27). 36 where אֶל־הַבַּדִּים is rendered ܠܘܬ ܓܒܝܐ (Syro-Hex.); *ibid.*, ver. 37 גְּרֻעָה κατατετμημένος would imply גְּרֻעָה, but Syro-Hex.

[104] But more likely *ομοιωσις* is a corruption of *θυμιασις*.

records [illegible]; *ibid.*, גְּדֵרֹת *καταπεπληγμένος*, did *α′* read חֲרָדֹת? 51 (28). 10 צִדְקֹתֵינוּ *δικαιοσύνην αὐτοῦ*, hence צִדְקֹתָיו with 𝔊; *ibid.*, ver. 64 וְיָעֵפוּ עַד־הֵנָּה דִּבְרֵי יִרְמְיָהוּ *καὶ ἐστάθησαν ἕως ἐνταῦθα οἱ λόγοι Ἱερεμίου*, which implies perhaps וַיַּצִּיבוּ and a different division than MT, but it must be remarked that Syro-Hex. records ܘܢܠܐܘܢ and that the same word in ver. 58 is rendered *καὶ ἐκλυθήσονται*, both in agreement with MT; Ezek. 3. 9 מִצְחֵךְ *νῖκός σου*, hence נִצְחֵךְ; 12. 11 לָהֶם *ὑμῖν*, hence לָכֶם, possibly assimilation to the context, see also Ken. and De Rossi; 19. 7 *καὶ ἐκάκωσε* implies וַיָּרַע for וַיֵּדַע comp. 𝔊 *ἐνέμετο* = וַיִּרַע; 21. 12 (17) *συγκεκλεισμένοι* implies סְגוּרֵי for מְגוּרֵי, similarly, 35. 5 *καὶ συνέκλεισας* = וַתַּסְגֵּר inst. of וַתַּגֵּר; *ibid.*, ver. 30 (35) *εἰς τὸν κολεόν σου* points to תַּעְרֵךְ inst. of תַּעְרָהּ, but perhaps assimilated to the context; 22. 16 וְנִחַלְתְּ *καὶ κατακληροδοτήσω*, hence וְנִחַלְתִּי with 𝔊 𝔙; 23. 15. 23 שָׁלִישִׁים is made to correspond to *σκυλευτῶν* (those that strip a slain enemy), hence Cornill suggests the reading שֹׁלְלִים; *ibid.*, ver. 35 שְׂאִי *πίε*, did *α′* read שְׁתִי?; 24. 12 תְּאֻנִים does not fit *ταπεινωθήσεται*, hence Cornill suggests תְּעֻנֶּה; 27. 11 וְגַמָּדִים = *τετελεσμένοι* accord. to the second edition of *α′*, hence he read וּגְמָרִים, 𝔗 also had the same consonants, comp. Lagarde, *Onom.*, II, 95, who considers this the original reading referring to גֹּמֶר; *ibid.*, ver. 16 Ἐδώμ points to אֱדֹם inst. of אֲרָם, so 𝔖, while the same consonants underlie also 𝔊's *ἀνθρώπους*; *ibid.*, *συναλλαγήν σου* cannot stand for בְּנֹפֶךְ, it is not improbable that *α′* read בְּנַאֲפֵךְ, deriving it from נָאַף and construing it as בְּנַאֲפֻפַיִךְ; *ibid.*, ver. 19 *σπαρτίον* (cord) probably refers to קָוֶה which *α′* read for קִדָּה, comp. the Ketib 3 Kings 7. 23; Jer. 31. 39; Zech. 1. 16; *ibid.*, ver. 32 כְּדֻמָּה was read כְּרָמָה = *ὡς ὕψος αὐτῆς*, comp. Judges 15. 17 where רָמַת is rendered by *ὕψωσις* (comp. also 𝔊 Isa. 38. 10 בִּדְמִי יָמַי = *ἐν τῷ ὕψει τῶν ἡμερῶν μου* where we have the opinion of Jerome that they read *rame* for *dame*, comp. Field note); 28. 13 מְלֶאכֶת תֻּפֶּיךָ is rendered by α′ θ′ ἔργον τοῦ κάλλους σου, hence they may have read מְלֶאכֶת יָפְיֵךְ, likewise 𝔙 *decoris*; *ibid.*, ver. 16 καὶ πτερύγια χερούβ impl. וְאֵבֶר כְּרוּב for וָאַבֶּדְךָ כְּרוּב, comp., however, the variant (καὶ) ἀπολέσω σε (Field); 30. 22 for הַנִּשְׁבֶּרֶת which makes no sense, α′ probably read הַנִּשֵּׂאת = ὑψηλόν; 40. 2 ἐξ ἔναντι renders מִנֶּגֶד inst. of מִנֶּגֶב, so 𝔊, comp. Hitzig *ad loc.*; Mic. 6. 14 καὶ καταφυτεύσω cannot correspond to וְיֶשְׁחֲךָ, Margolis (*Micah*, p. 67) suggests that α′ read ואשתלך (from שתל): and I will plant thee, 𝔊 θ′ have συσκοτάσει = ויחשך, σ′ διαφθερεῖ σε = וישחתך.

38. Some variants depending on ו and י and hence of less importance are as follows: Deut. 28. 20 α′, like Sam. 𝔊 𝔗^Jon 𝔙 and MSS., reads את המארה ואת המהומה, σπάνιν καὶ φαγέδαιναν; *ibid.*, ver. 53 יָצִיק was read יָצוּק = ἐπιχύσῃ; Judges 5. 21 καυσώνων points to קְדִימִים for קְדוּמִים; Job 41. 4 καὶ δωρήσεται impl. יָחֹן for וְחִין, comp. Deut. 28. 50 where יָחֹן is so rendered; Ps. 21 (22). 17 ᾔσχυναν impl. כָּאֲרוּ (on the meaning comp. above, § 23) inst. of כָּאֲרִי, which is supported by most versions, Midr. Tillim, and Complut., comp. Taylor, pp. 42 ff., see also Graetz *ad loc.* (Perles, *Analekten*, p. 50, emends כארי to כִּתְּרוּ claiming that this underlies α′'s second translation ܟܒܠܘ and Jerome's *vinxerunt*); 73 (74). 5 ὡς εἴσοδος points to כִּמְבוֹא inst. of כְּמֵבִיא, so 𝔊 𝔖 σ′ θ′ and Jer.; Cant. 7. 9 (10) χείλεσι καὶ ὀδοῦσι impl. שְׂפָתַיִם וְשִׁנַּיִם inst. of שִׂפְתֵי יְשֵׁנִים, so 𝔊 and 𝔖 who only vary in reading שְׂפָתַי, comp. Geiger, *Urschrift*, p. 405; Isa. 52. 5 παρανομοῦσιν impl. יְהוֹלְלוּ inst. of יְהֵילִילוּ, but contrast Jerome's *flebunt* = ὀλολύζουσιν; Jer. 6. 18 καὶ γνῶτε = וּדְעוּ for וּדְעִי; 31 (38). 24 וְנָסְעוּ בָּעֵדֶר = καὶ αἴροντες ἐν ποιμνίῳ, hence α′ read וְנֹסְעֵי with σ′ 𝔗 𝔖 𝔙, which also yields a better sense; Ezek. 27. 25

ἐλειτούργει σοι impl. שֵׁרְתוּךָ for שָׁרוֹתַךְ, the versions have various readings none of which is as satisfactory as that of our translator, comp. Cornill *ad loc.*; Dan. 10. 1 συνήσει points to יָבִין inst. of וּבִין, similarly 𝔊 διανοηθήσεται; Hab. 2. 4 ἡ ψυχή μου impl. נַפְשִׁי inst. of נַפְשׁוֹ, so also 𝔊.

39. Another class of variants are those which may be based on metathesis. Thus Judges 5. 22 εὐπρέπεια impl. הֲדָרַת inst. of דַּהֲרוֹת; Ps. 17 (18). 46 וְיַחְרְגוּ is rendered by συστέλλεσθαι making it evident that α′ read וְיַחְגְּרוּ, so 𝔊 and some Jewish commentators, among them Ibn Ǧanaḥ; Prov. 17. 10 תֵּחַת was read חִתַּת = πλῆξις; Ezek. 16. 61 μιμήσασθαι does not correspond to בְּקַחְתֵּךְ but בְּחַקֹּתֵךְ, comp. 23. 14 where α′ renders מְחֻקֶּה by μίμημα; 21. 14 (19) οἱ θάμβοι (astonishment) yields הַחֲרָדֹת for הַחֹדֶרֶת, 𝔊 similarly read וְהַחֲרַדְתָּ, 𝔗 דמזיעא, so also Jer.; Hab. 2. 4 עֻפְּלָה was probably read עֻלְּפָה = νωχελευομένου with some Bible manuscripts; 2. 16 καὶ καρώθητι, as Field already remarked, corresponds to וְהֵרָעֵל inst. of וְהֵעָרֵל, 𝔊 and 𝔖 derive it likewise from רעל, and so also many commentators; Zeph. 3. 18 הָיוּ was read הוֹי = οἴ, so 𝔊 οὐαί and 𝔗 וַי.

40. Still another set of variants are those which may go back to a phonetic similarity of two or more sounds, resp. letters, in which case we must assume that the translator sometimes translated by ear.[105] Thus Gen. 41. 43 γονατίζειν = הַבְרֵךְ inst. of אַבְרֵךְ; Exod. 5. 4 *et al.* ἀποπετάζειν (πετάζειν = spread out, fly) for הִפְרִיעַ, assuming הִפְרִיחַ (comp. 9. 9); Deut. 26. 14 (also 3 Kings 22. 47 and 4 Kings 23. 24) ἐπιλέγειν does not correspond to בִּעֵר but בָּחַר; 1 Kings 21. 13 (14) καὶ προσέκρουεν points to וַיְתָף for וַיְתָו, likewise 𝔊 𝔙; Job 4. 2 μήτι ἐπαροῦμεν points to הֲנִשָּׂא for הֲנִסָּה, so also σ′ and θ′; *ibid.*, ver. 13 ἐν παραλλαγαῖς (change, variation)

[105] Comp. Graetz, *Kritischer Commentar zu den Psalmen*, p. 121 ff.

impl. בִּסְעִפִּים for בִּשְׂעִפִּים ; 28. 11 ἐξερεύνησεν of both α′ and θ′ implies חִפֵּשׂ for חִבֵּשׁ, likewise 𝔊 ἀνεκάλυψεν and 𝔙 *scrutatus est*; 41. 7 σῶμα αὐτοῦ implies גֵּוֹה for גַּאֲוָה, so also 𝔊 𝔙; Ps. 4. 7 ἔπαρον of α′ and θ′ yields נְשָׂא for נְסָה; 26 (27). 12 καὶ ἐξεφάνη corresponds to וַיִּפַע inst. of וִיפֵחַ, likewise ϛ′; 89 (90). 10 חִישׁ was translated ἀνήρ, hence אִישׁ, in the first recension of α′ (Field note); Prov. 22. 19 ζωήν = חַיִּים for הַיּוֹם; Jer. 6. 28 ἄρχοντες points to שָׂרֵי for סָרֵי, so 𝔗 𝔖 𝔙 and many Hebr. MSS.; Ezek. 13. 22 ἠμαυρώθη points to הַכְהוֹת (der. from כהה) for הַכְאוֹת, 𝔊 𝔗 𝔙 הַכְאִיב; 27. 9 εἰς πλῆθος points to לְרֹב for לַעֲרֹב; 31. 15 ἐπένθησεν αὐτόν implies וְהִקְדִּר for וָאַקְדִּר; Mic. 4. 8 σκοτώδης implies אֹפֶל for עֹפֶל, the same is implied by σ′ ἀπόκρυφος.

41. While it is not strange to find some consonantal variants in Aquila's version it is rather surprising to find in it a number of words and even phrases which are either extant in Aquila but missing in the Hebrew or extant in the Hebrew and missing in Aquila. To account for this we must assume that in most of these cases he certainly had a text different from our own, while in others he may have been made to agree with the Septuagint by later scribes or copyists. In enumerating these cases all doubtful ascriptions have been kept out. Extant in Aquila but missing in Hebrew: 2 Kings 3. 27 εἰς τὸν ἐνοπλισμόν impl. הַחֹמֶשׁ (or עַל) אֶל, so also 𝔊 and σ′; Cant. 6. 5 (6) . . . τῆς κόκκου, hence α′ must have read like 𝔊: כְּחוּט הַשָּׁנִי שִׂפְתוֹתַיִךְ וּמִדְבָּרֵךְ נָאוֶה, which is missing in MT at this place but is found in 4. 3 and by the nature of the discourse should have existed also here; 8. 4 ἐν δορκάσιν ἢ ἐν ἐλάφοις τῆς χώρας which corresponds to בִּצְבָאוֹת אוֹ בְּאַיְלוֹת הַשָּׂדֶה, a phrase found 2. 7 in connexion with הִשְׁבַּעְתִּי, perhaps it is a mistake of the copyist who thought of 2. 7 (comp. Frankel,

Vorstudien, p. 68 f.), but it is also possible that α′'s Hebrew text had it, it is interesting that also 𝔊 has this addition; Jer. 16. 5 αὐτῶν with 𝔊; a superfluous πᾶς is found Jer. 44 (51). 23: Ezek. 18. 10: Zeph. 3. 9 to which comp. Frankel, *ibid.*, p. 67; a superfluous ἐκεῖνος is found Jer. 45. 4 (51. 34) and Ezek. 20. 40; Ezek. 13. 2 τοῖς προφητεύουσιν credited to α′ and θ′ has no equivalent in MT; 20. 14 οὐκ probably later addition; 28. 13 ἐν σοί; 40. 3 ἐν τῇ χειρὶ αὐτοῦ which is supported by 𝔊^A θ′ 𝔏 𝔙 and 𝔖 *sub asterisco.*—Extant in Hebrew but missing in Aquila: 1 Kings 13. 18 הַנָּבִיא; 3 Kings 8. 24 לוֹ וַתְּדַבֵּר, likewise 𝔊 and σ′; 21 (20). 7 וַיֹּאמֶר; 4 Kings 23. 18 עַצְמֹתָיו 2°; Ps. 60 (61). 8 מַן accord. to Eus. and Syro-Hex. (also σ′ and Jer. omit it); 61 (62). 12 זוּ, so σ′; 105 (106). 7 בְּיָם, so σ′; 140 (141). 3 דַּל, found in the other versions; Prov. 12. 14 no translation for אָדָם unless αὐτοῦ is a corruption of ἀνθρώπου; Ezek. 32. 1, 17 ἐν τῷ δεκάτῳ ἔτει renders בִּשְׁתֵּי עֶשְׂרֵה שָׁנָה, hence שְׁתֵּי was not read, so 𝔊 σ′ θ′; Hos. 10. 15 נִדְמֹה, found in 𝔊, is κατεσιωπήθη a free rendering of נִדְמֹה נִדְמָה?

42. More frequent are minor variants such as the addition or omission of the connective particle, the article, the *nota accusativi* את, or the substitution of sing. for pl. and *vice versa.* These are often due to the carelessness of the scribe or copyist and hence great care must be exercised before stamping them as real variants.[106]

[106] On such minor variants in the Talmud comp. Aptowitzer, 'Das Schriftwort in der rabbinischen Literatur' in the *Sitzungsberichte der Akad. der Wiss. in Wien* cliii (1906), Abhandl. VI; *ibid.* clx (1908), Abhandl. VII; in the *XVIII. Jahresbericht der Isr.-Theol. Lehranstalt in Wien*, 1911. [Comp. also Rosenfeld, משפחת סופרים, Wilna, 1883. M.]—These too are not always real variants owing to the fact that the Rabbis were wont to quote from memory and hence misquotations arose; comp. Geiger, *Nachgelassene Schriften*, IV, 30, and Margolis, *The Columbia College MS. of Megilla*, New York, 1892, p. 11 ff. The Church Fathers too quoted Bible

43. Aquila follows the Ketib in the following passages: Exod. 21. 8 אֲשֶׁר לֹא (לוֹ ק׳) יְעָדָהּ = ὃς οὐ καθωμολογήσατο αὐτήν, so σ′ θ′ and other versions, as well as Bab. Kiddushin 19 a and Mekilta *ad loc.*, the latter not without a compromise מכלל לאו הין[107]; 4 Kings 25. 12 καὶ εἰς βοθυνώτας = וּלְגָבִים (וּלְיֹגְבִים Kere), so 𝕲 transliterating γαβίν; 1 Chron. 25. 1 τῶν προφητῶν = הַנְּבִיאִים (Kere הַנִּבָּאִים); Ps. 9. 31 (10. 10) ܘܕܟܐ = ודכה (pointed וְדָכָה), so σ′ ὁ δὲ θλασθείς, but Kere יִדְכֶּה; 70 (71). 20 ἔδειξας ἡμῖν = הִרְאִיתָנוּ, while Kere requires -נִי; 143 (144). 2 ܠܥܡܐ = תַחְתָּי, Kere תַחְתָּיו; Prov. 6. 16 βδελύγματα = תּוֹעֲבוֹת; 21. 29 ἑτοιμάσει α′ σ′ yields יָכִין, which is also adopted by 𝕿 𝕾 𝖁, while 𝕲 follows Kere יָבִין; Isa. 9. 3 (2) οἱ λ̥ read הַגּוֹי לֹא instead of לוֹ, which lends support to Krochmal's emendation הַגִּילָה = הַגִּילָא (|| הַשִּׂמְחָה); Jer. 9. 8 (7) τιτρῶσκον implies שׁוֹחֵט, so 𝕲 σ′ 𝖁, but 𝕿 and 𝕾 follow the Kere in reading שָׁחוּט or שָׁחֻט; 40 (47), 8 עוֹפַי = ܥܘܦܝ on the margin of the Syro-Hex., Kere עֵיפַי; Ezek. 43. 26 *manum eius* (Jer.) = יָדוֹ; Dan. 11. 10 מָעֻזּהֹ ܠܡܥܫܢܘܬܗ ܕܝܠܗ, hence הּ- inst. of Kere וֹ-.

The Kere is followed Gen. 30. 11 where ἦλθεν εὐζωνία corresponds to בָּא גָד, so most versions except 𝕲 ἐν τύχῃ = בְּגָד; 2 Kings 20. 23 Χερηθί = כְּרֵתִי (Ketib כָּרִי); 21. 20 ἀντίδικος or ἀντιλογίας = מָדוֹן; 3 Kings 1. 33 ܠܘܬ = אֶל; 4 Kings 12. 9 (10) ܡܢ ܝܡܝܢܐ ܕܡܥܠܢܐ = מִיָּמִין; Ps. 21 (22). 30 וְנַפְשׁוֹ לֹא חִיָּה . . . αὐτῷ ζῇ, hence לוֹ[108] with 𝕲 σ′ θ′ 𝕾 Jer. and חַיָּה with almost all the versions[109]; 29 (30). 4 ἀπὸ τοῦ

passages from memory, and hence incorrectly, comp. Cornill, *Ezechiel*, pp. 58–61, and Rahlfs, *Septuaginta-Studien*, I, 16 f. and 49.

[107] It is noteworthy that Aquila's interpretation disagrees with the rabbinic tradition that a Hebrew maid, when engaged as a servant, is to be married by her employer, comp. Mekilta and Kiddushin, *loc. cit.*

[108] On this Kere comp. Baer, *Liber Psalmorum*, p. 91.

[109] Just how he construed the phrase it is difficult to say, since

καταβῆναί με corresponds to מִיָּרְדִי in which *α′* is followed by *σ′* 𝔗 and Jer., but 𝔊 *θ′* 𝔙 𝔖 have מִיּוֹרְדֵי; 54 (55). 16 *ἐπάξει θάνατον* corresponds to יַשִּׁיא מָוֶת (Ketib יְשִׁימוֹת), so most versions; 99 (100). 3 ܘܠܗ = וְלוֹ; Isa. 36. 12 צוֹאָתָם וּמֵימֵי רַגְלֵיהֶם; 49. 5 *ei* points to לוֹ; Jer. 7. 22 *ἐξαγαγόντος μου* = הוֹצִיאִי, Ketib הוֹצִיא; 17. 19 *τοῦ λαοῦ* = הָעָם, Ketib עָם; 32 (39). 23 ܒܡܥܘܗܝ ܕܠܒܝ = בְּתוֹרָתְךָ; 50 (27). 11 from *ἐπεχάρητε* = תִּשְׂמְחוּ it can be seen that *α′* like most other versions followed the Ḳere throughout the sentence; Ezek. 23. 43 *πορνεύουσιν* = יִזְנוּ (Ketib יִזְנֶה); Dan. 9. 24 *καὶ τοῦ τελειῶσαι* = וּלְהָתֵם, so most versions, Ketib ולחתם.

44. The preceding study of Aquila, though dealing with details, does not claim to be exhaustive. In the course of the work many problems presented themselves which could not be solved for the moment, and hence had to be left to the future. To begin with, there is the paramount problem confronting every student of the ancient versions as to how much Aquila material entered into the Septuagint. Doubts have been cast on certain books of the Alexandrian Version as being contaminated with Aquila readings: thus

the equivalent of the first word has not been preserved, but we may safely assume that like *σ′ θ′* 𝔗 and Jer. he read וְנַפְשׁוֹ. However that may be, there is reason to suppose that our translator wished here to emphasize the belief in immortality of the soul among the Jews, so that this would be a further proof for the view of M. Zipser (*Ben Chananja*, 1863, 182 f.) that *α′*'s translation of עַל־מוּת Ps. 47 (48). 15 by *ἀθανασία* was due to an effort to prove that the term and idea of immortality existed in the Hebrew Bible. Further proof for this view lies in the fact that *α′* actually had עַל־מוּת or עַלְמוּת, for in the very same passage the Syrohex. credits him with ܥܠ ܡܘܬܐ, while 9. 1 he renders the same word by *νεανιότης* (= עַלְמוּת). Hence the contention of M. Stössel (*ibid.*, p. 693) that *α′* had a faulty text before him, with אַל־ instead of עַל־, is quite untenable. Comp., furthermore, Anger, *De Aquila*, p. 17 f., who likewise assumes that *α′* here followed MT.

it appears that wherever the B text is defective in Joshua and Kings 3–4 the lacunae have been supplied in the A text from the third column of Origen's Hexapla[110]; furthermore, the books of Canticles and Ecclesiastes remind strikingly of the method of Aquila[111]; while Cornill speaks of an Oxford codex to Ezekiel which is highly influenced by Aquila.[112] Now, in order to get to the original Septuagint—and this is a *conditio sine qua non* for obtaining ultimately the pre-Masoretic text of the Hebrew Scriptures—it is essential to separate out the Hexaplaric material which crept in through the influence of Origen.[113] Before this attempt is made, however, the style and vocabulary of the three translators, Aquila, Symmachus, and Theodotion, from whom Origen supplied the lacunae in the Septuagint, have to be determined unequivocally. With a critical index of Aquila at hand the process of eliminating Aquila readings from the Septuagint can now go on. Let us hope that also Symmachus and Theodotion

[110] Comp. Thackeray, *Grammar of the O. T. in Greek*, I, 3 f.

[111] See Buhl, *Kanon und Text*, p. 123.

[112] *Ezechiel*, pp. 64, 104 f.

[113] Comp. the three axioms of Lagarde in his *Anmerkungen zur griechischen Ubersetzung der Proverbien*, 1863, p. 3: 'I. die manuscripte der griechischen übersetzung des alten testaments sind alle entweder unmittelbar oder mittelbar das resultat eines eklektischen verfahrens: darum muss, wer den echten text wiederfinden will, ebenfalls eklektiker sein. sein maasstab kann nur die kenntniss des styles der einzelnen übersetzer, sein haupthilfsmittel muss die fähigkeit sein, die ihm vorkommenden lesarten auf ihr semitisches original zurückzuführen oder aber als originalgriechische verderbnisse zu erkennen. II. wenn ein vers oder verstheil in einer freien und in einer sklavisch treuen übertragung vorliegt, gilt die erstere als die echte. III. wenn sich zwei lesarten nebeneinander finden, von denen die eine den masoretischen text ausdrückt, die andre nur aus einer von ihm abweichenden urschrift erklärt werden kann, so ist die letztere für ursprünglich zu halten.'

will receive an adequate treatment in the near future, so that they too may become links in the long chain of textual criticism.

45. Another problem arising from this work is the identification of such anonymous Hexaplaric readings as belong to Aquila. There can be no doubt that many of these nameless passages belong to either Aquila, Symmachus, or Theodotion, but particularly to the first. Thus Cornill has gleaned for Aquila some readings which are quoted by Field under Ἄλλος,[114] and the same may be done in the other books of the Bible. It is certainly not without reason why Ἄλλος coincides with Aquila in many places to the exclusion of the other translators, and peculiarly enough in characteristic words[115] and passages; it simply proves that no care was taken in quoting signatures.[116] But not only under Ἄλλος are to be found Aquila readings: they are also imbedded in Hexaplaric passages quoted under an asterisk * and *sine nomine*.[117] Under a close scrutiny such

[114] *Ezekiel*, p. 104 ff.

[115] The following is a list of such words: *ἀκριβοῦν, ἄνθιμον, ἀντιδικία, γονατίζειν, δολιεύεσθαι, ἐναλλάσσειν, ἐπίσχεσις, ἐσπευσμένως, ἑστίασις, ζεστός, μελῳδημα, μονοῦσθαι, ὄφλημα, παρατανυσμός, παρεκτός, σικχαίνειν, σκύλαξ, σκωλοῦσθαι, συσκιασμός, ὑπουργεῖν, ὑφή.*—A good illustration is furthermore afforded by a comparison of Field with the larger Cambridge Septuagint with reference to *α′* and Ἄλλος: Thus Exod. 13. 4 הָאָבִיב = *τῶν νεαρῶν* is quoted under Ἄλλος in F but under *α′* in BM; likewise הָאֵיפָה = *τοῦ οἰφί*, *ibid.*, 16. 36 and מְשַׁכֵּלָה = *ἄτεκνος*, *ibid.*, 23. 26; וְהִסְגִּירוֹ = *χωρίσει* . . . Lev. 13. 21; הַמָּסָךְ = *τοῦ παρατανυσμοῦ*, Num. 4. 5; זֵיתְךָ לֹא תְפָאֵר = *ἐλαίαν σου οὐ στεφανώσεις*, Deut. 24. 22 (20). Note also Jer. 10. 10 where Field quotes in the body of the Hexapla a whole sentence under Ἄλλος while the Auctarium credits the same sentence to *α′*, thus justifying Field's note in the body of the book.

[116] Comp. above, § 5.

[117] It is to be regretted that Hatch-Redpath failed to include such passages in their Concordance, and the work still remains to be done.

R. H

readings may often be identified and referred to their originator. With an adequate index this process of identification becomes comparatively easy.

46. There is, moreover, an intimation that the so-called Ἑβραῖος, to whom several readings are referred in the Hexapla, is none other but Aquila, who on account of his close adherence to the Hebrew was probably so styled. To quote but one example in favour of this view: Exod. 29. 22 καὶ τὴν κέρκον is placed under Ἑβρ. in Field, but the larger Cambridge Septuagint puts it under α′ on the authority of MS. v. [Compare, however, Gen. 4. 26. The whole subject is now undergoing a detailed examination, in connexion with which Dr. Reider's Index is proving a great help. M.]

47. On the other hand, it is as much of a problem to eliminate from Aquila readings which, though referred to him, cannot belong to him by force of style and diction. Thus many quotations in Klostermann's *Analecta*[118] under signature α′ hardly belong to him, and hence great caution must be exercised in excerpting them. Furthermore, every reading bearing the generic signature οἱ λοιποί is necessarily an eclectic reading containing elements from each one of the Three, and hence should be differentiated from a reading bearing the distinct signature of α′ and possibly classed by itself as at least doubtful. There is also sufficient reason to suspect the fourteenth chapter of 3 Kings which Field wisely questions, putting the Aquila signature in parentheses. Of course, there can be no doubt that it contains passages belonging to Aquila, but that the chapter as a whole goes back to Aquila is very doubtful (comp. below, Appendix IV).

48. A further problem of great moment is the identifi-

[118] pp. 47-68.

cation of talmudic and midrashic Greek quotations as originating in Aquila's translation of the Bible. Anger,[119] Zipser,[120] Brüll,[121] and Friedmann[122] have delved into this problem, trying to identify such quotations given expressly under Aquila's name (comp. below, Appendix III). But Zunz, to my mind, was the first to suggest[123] that some anonymous Greek quotations in the Midrash may belong to Aquila's version. Recently this question was taken up by Samuel Krauss,[124] who endeavoured to prove that certain Greek passages in Talmud and Midrash, among them the long passage p. Shab. 8 a containing an anonymous Greek translation of Isa. 3. 18 ff., go back to Aquila's version. As to the thesis itself, there is no doubt that it holds good; from Aquila's popularity among the Jews we expect some renderings of his to have crept into the Talmudim and Midrashim. But the method pursued by Krauss invites criticism; having started out with the idea of finding Aquila renderings in the talmudic literature he goes so far as to ascribe to him words which are foreign to Aquila's vocabulary, as, for inst., νεανίσκοι and ἄφεσις, his only pretence being that presumably Aquila used them in his *editio secunda*, or that because Symmachus has it Aquila too must have had it. In only one case is he supported by Hexaplaric evidence: τελαμῶνας for שְׁבִיסִים. The only way to identify talmudic passages as belonging to Aquila would be to examine them in the light of the evidence from all the Greek versions, and by a process of elimination to determine which words actually belong to him because

[119] *De Aquila*, p. 13 ff.

[120] *Ben Chananja*, 1863, pp. 162, 181. [121] *Ibid.*, pp. 233, 299.

[122] *Onkelos und Akylas*, p. 44 ff.

[123] *Gottesdienstliche Vorträge*, p. 83, note *a*.

[124] Steinschneider's *Festschrift*, German division, p. 155 ff.

H 2

they could not belong to any other translator. Furthermore, if a passage contains at least one word peculiar to Aquila (and by peculiar I mean words known to belong to Aquila and to no other translator, comp. below, Appendix I), then we may say with some certainty that it belongs to our translator as a whole. Only in pursuing such methods can we hope to glean new material for the fragmentary version of Aquila.

The Hesychian Recension of the Septuagint (*)

Alberto VACCARI, S.J. - Rome

In the *Journal of Biblical Literature* 82 (1963) Professor Sidney Jellicoe of Bishop's University has a contribution entitled "The Hesychian Recension Reconsidered" (pp. 409-418). At issue is a clarification of a statement of St. Jerome in his foreword to the books of Chronicles:

> Alexandria and Egypt give as author of their Septuagint Hesychius; from Constantinople to Antioch the approved text is that of Lucian the Martyr; the provinces in between read Palestinian codices edited by Origen and spread by Eusebius and Pamphilus. The whole world is thus split three ways in the matter (1).

In this statement Jerome is clearly placing emphasis on the Old Testament as distinguished from the New. Of the Hesychian recension of the New Testament and especially of the gospels, he had written a dozen years before: "I pass over those codices going under the names of Lucian and Hesychius which the warped controversy of a few men has claimed for its own ... inasmuch as previously translated versions of Scripture in many language indicate that the additions are false" (2).

(*) I wish to express my gratitude to Rev. James Swetnam, S.J. for translating my Italian original into English.

(1) "Alexandria et Aegyptus in Septuaginta suis Hesychius laudat auctorem, Constantinopolis usque Antiochiam Luciani martyris exemplaria probat, mediae inter has provinciae palestinos codices legunt, quos ab Origene elaboratos Eusebius et Pamphilius [*sic*] vulgaverunt, totusque orbis hac inter se trifaria varietate compugnat" (*Biblia Sacra iuxta latinam vulgatam lectionem ad codicum fidem* ... cura et studio monachorum Abbatiae Pontificiae S. Hieronymi in Urbe, vol. VII [Romae 1958], p. 4).

(2) "Praetermitto eos codices quos a Luciano et Hesychio nuncupatos paucorum hominum adserit perversa contentio ... cum multarum gentium linguis Scriptura ante translata doceat falsa esse quae addita sunt". The quotation is taken from the well-known letter written to Pope St. Damasus in 383 when Jerome was in Rome correcting at the Pope's request the Old Latin version of the gospels on the basis of the most ancient Greek manuscripts he could find. In his letter of presentation to the pontiff ("Novum opus facere me cogis ex vetere" it begins) he makes a number of clear and energetic observations on the differences between the New and the Old Testament in regard to the two languages. As examples of subsequent additions corrupting the text we may cite: at Mk 4,9 "et intellegens intellegat"; Lk 6,17 "et trans fretum"; Lk 7,5 "in bono"; Lk 8,42 "ut suffocarent eum". See H. J. VOGELS, *Vulgatastudien* (Neutestamentliche Abhandlungen, XIV/2-3; Münster 1928).

Reprinted from *Biblica*. Vol. 46, 1965.

But this distinction made by Jerome between the two Greek Testaments is apparently unknown to Prof. Jellicoe, for he writes: " For our present purpose we are concerned only with Hesychius, and here the monk of Bethlehem helps us little " (1).

This attitude is not surprising. Two outstanding Septuagint scholars of the present century, Alfred Rahlfs and Joseph Ziegler, have been quite pessimistic about the possibility of discerning the Hesychian recension on the basis of existing evidence. In his brief " History of the Septuagint Text " in his *Septuagint, id est Vetus Testamentum graece iuxta LXX Interpretes* (Stuttgart 1935), Rahlfs wrote: " Jerome mentions yet a third recension [sc., other than those of Origen and Lucian]. This is to be traced back to a certain Hesychius, about whom we know little, and it prevailed in Egypt at about 400 A.D. It had been presumably by that time in existence for about a century. No conclusive information is yet to be had with regard to this third recension " (2). Ziegler's position is even more negative (3).

It may not be out of place here to point out that the Pontifical Biblical Institute's *Institutiones Biblicae scholis accommodatae* from the very first edition of 1923 on has made some detailed observations on the Hesychian recension. I translate from the sixth edition (1951):

> Apart from Jerome, no author or document tells us anything about Hesychius. It is thought that he is the Hesychius who Eusebius says (*Historia ecclesiastica* 8,13) was martyred in the persecution of Diocletian (circa 300 A.D.?). Scholars have not succeeded in discovering in what witnesses (especially codices) his recension is contained, and hence what its distinctive traits were. But since it is highly probable that from the Hesychian recension depend to a large extent both the Coptic versions and the Egyptian Fathers (above all, the Alexandrians) of the fourth and fifth centuries, we may use this criterion to state that the recension for the historical books is to be found in codices M. V. 55, 56, 119, 158 and related mss; for the prophets, in codices A. Q. 26, 86, 106, 198, 233 (4).

(1) *Art. cit.*, p. 409.

(2) P. XXXI.

(3) " Den Text der alexandrinischen Gruppe wollte man bis jetzt gewöhnlich mit der von Hieronymus genannten Rezension des Hesychius in Verbindung bringen. Jedoch ist diese Rezension nur an einer einzigen Stelle, nämlich in der Praefatio des Hieronymus zu den Paralipomena, geschichtlich bezeugt; dann ist sie zu blass und kaum greifbar, und schliesslich ist sie zeitlich nicht einreihbar " (*Septuaginta* Vetus Testamentum Graecum auctoritate Societatis Litterarum Göttingensis editum. XIV. *Isaias* [Göttingen 1939], p. 23). Cf. Ziegler's opinion as expressed in *Septuaginta* ... XVI/2. *Susanna — Daniel — Bel et Draco* (Göttingen 1954), p. 47, note 1.

(4) A. VACCARI, S. J., " De Textu ", *Institutiones Biblicae scholis accommodatae*. Vol. I: *De S. Scriptura in universum*. 6a ed. recognita (Rome 1951), p. 287. The codex numbers refer to the Oxford edition of HOLMES-PARSONS, the same ones used by the editors of the Göttingen

We propose this view with all due caution. But it is noteworthy that the Prussian scholar Johann Ernst Grabe, a convert to Anglicanism, known for his edition of the Codex Alexandrinus (A) of the Septuagint (Oxford 1707-1720), held that the Hesychian recension was identical with Vaticanus (B). In his edition of the Codex Alexandrinus Grabe aimed at reconstructing, with the help of other manuscripts and documents, Origen's recension with its asterisks and obeli in the text and in the margin. In 1705 he had published a lengthy tract, the title of which contains the conclusions drawn from his investigations: " A Communication in Which It Is Demonstrated That the Genuine Septuagint Version of the Book of Judges Is That Which MS Codex Alexandrinus Exhibits, While the Roman Edition, [i.e., the Sistine, based on Codex Vaticanus] As Regards the Said Book Is in Opposition and Is the Same as the Hesychian Version " (1).

The question of the Hesychian recension was studied by R. R. Ottley in the introduction to his two translations of Isaias (2). These translations are published in the same volume, on facing pages: on the left, the translation from the Hebrew; on the right, from the LXX. To the Hesychian recension he assigned the codices Q. 26, 49, 87, 91, 106, 198, 306 (3). Three of these codices coincide with three codices in my listing (26, 106, 198).

With regard to the problem of isolating in an Egyptian manuscript a distinctive reading that could indicate the Hesychian recension, St. Jerome offers a helpful lead in his commentary on Isaias 58,11:

> The following has been added at the beginning of this verse in the Alexandrian manuscripts: " and still will your praise be always in you "; and at the end: " also your bones will rise as grass and will grow flesh and will possess the inheritance from generation to generation ". This is not in the Hebrew nor even in the corrected and faithful copies of the Septuagint; hence is should be marked with an obelus (4).

---

edition today. On the whole question of identification of Greek codices cf. A. RAHLFS, *Verzeichnis der griechischen Handschriften des Alten Testaments* (Berlin 1914).

(1) " Epistola qua ostenditur libri Judicum genuinam LXX Interpretum versionem eam esse quam MS codex Alexandrinus exhibet; romanam autem editionem, quod ad dictum librum ab illa prorsus adversam eamdem cum Hesychiana esse ". Cf. F. VIGOUROUX (ed.), *Dictionnaire de la Bible*, Voll. III (Paris 1903), col. 289.

(2) R. R. OTTLEY, *The Book of Isaiah according to the Septuagint* (*Codex Alexandrinus*) *translated and edited*. 2. vols. (Cambridge 1906).

(3) *Ibid.*, vol. I (2nd. ed. 1909), p. 14.

(4) " Quod in Alexandrinis exemplaribus in prooemio huius capituli additum est: *Et adhuc in te erit laus mea semper*; et in fine: *et ossa tua quasi herba orientur, et pinguescent, et hereditate possidebunt in generationem et generationes*, in Hebraico non habetur, sed ne in Septuaginta quidem emendatis et veris exemplaribus; unde obelo praenotandum est " (*S. Hieronymi Presbyteri Opera*. Pars I, *Opera exegetica*. 2 A *Commentarium in Esaiam Libri XII-XVIII. In Esaia parvula adbreviatio* (Corpus christianorum, Series Latina, 73 A; Turnholti 1963),

One has only to turn to Rahlf's edition of the Septuagint at this text to read: *καὶ τὰ ὀστᾶ σου ὡς βοτάνη ἀνατελεῖ καὶ πιανθήσεται καὶ κληρονομήσουσι γενεὰς γενεῶν.* These words, which correspond exactly to the quotation of St. Jerome, are stated as occurring only in Alexandrian mss. as over against Vaticanus and Sinaiticus (1).

Using this distinctive reading of Is 58,11 as a clue, further evidence of an Egyptian and even Alexandrian provenance of a distinctive Greek recension is obtained from an examination of translations from Greek into Arabic and Coptic-Arabic. By two independent sources, one, Arabic mss, the other, Coptic-Arabic mss, the translation of the Old Testament prophets from Greek into Arabic is available to us in the famous Polyglot of Walton, vol. 3 (1657). Pursuing the line of transmission of the text in accordance with the careful colophons in use among the oriental scribes, we arrive at an archtype from the year 1356. The following is a translation from a photocopy of the Vatican Arabic Ms 445, copied in the year 1583 from an exemplar dating from 1356:

> Here ends the prophecy of the prophet Malachias and with it ends the book of the sixteen prophets. From an accurate copy of the original in the possession of the late Reverend Father George, son of the venerable priest Abu'l Mufaddal, with the date 1072 of the Martyrs [= 1356 A.D.]. There it is recorded that the translation was made by the reverend priest of blessed memory, El ʿAlam the Alexandrian, from an ancient original in parchment of the Greek writing *λιτόν* (2). The Arabic copy from which the present copy was made is in the library of the Church of Our Lady the Virgin Pure and Immaculate Martamariam (3) in the quarter Zuwailat 'el kubrâ (4). The copyist is the lowest and most despised of men, unworthy to raise his head owing to the great number of his sins — by name, Fadlallāh, priest in charge of the above-mentioned church and of the church of the great martyr, Barbara at Qasr eggiamaʿ in Old Cairo, which may God preserve always in priests and deacons and clerics in general. Amen. And whoever prays for the copyist, may God repay him two-fold. In the year 1299 of the Martyrs.

A careful comparison of the Arabic translation contained in ms 445 with the Greek of the Codex Alexandrinus (photocopy, London 1936)

---

p. 671. Cf. also PL 24 [1845], 570c. Note that in the 1865 edition of Migne the " ne " in " sed ne in Septuaginta quidem " has been omitted.

(1) Rahlfs, *Septuaginta* (cf. above, p. 61), vol. II, p. 645.

(2) On the meaning of this technical term, which corresponds in the language of paleography to the word " uncial ", cf. the numerous proofs presented in Biblica 2 (1921) 412-418.*

(3) This is the word with which the Copts referred to the Blessed Virgin Mary (cf. the Italian " la Madonna ").

(4) On this church, the oldest in Cairo, cf. Alfred J. Butler, *The Ancient Coptic Churches in Egypt*, I (Oxford 1884), pp. 271-277; *Les guides bleus: Égypte* (Paris 1956), p. 107.

shows that the Greek manuscript used by el ʿAlam for his translation was notably freer from copyists' errors or the influence of harmonization that the classic Alexandrinus of the fifth century (¹). Despite this, but in line with St. Jerome's clue, the superfluous words of Is 58,11 are to be found in the version of el Alam as it appears in the London Polyglot (p. 155): وعظامك تشرق مثل النبات وتستدسم وترث جيل الاجيال It would seem that we have here an indication of the Hesychian recension.

This is my opinion on the significance of the el ʿAlam translation. A confirmation as remarkable as it is unexpected comes from the studies of two Orientalists working independently of each other on el ʿAlam's translation of the Book of Daniel (²). Their mutually confirmatory research shows that el ʿAlam was using manuscripts that were distinctively Egyptian.

Henry L. Gehman, of the University of Pennsylvania, writing in *JBL* 44 (1925) 327-352, made a study precisely on the question at issue here: "The 'Polyglot' Arabic Text of Daniel and Its Affinities". After indicating the previous works on the subject he cites the opinion of Walton himself:

> ... in his Prolegomena XIV, 18, on the testimony of Augustinus Justinianus Episcopus Nebiensis, [Walton] states that there were two arabic versions of the Old Testament in vogue among the Christians. He has used both of them and calls the one recension the Syriac, and the other the Egyptian from the two regions in which they were respectively read. Cornelius a Lapide names the one the Antiochian and the other the Alexandrian. This view is quited by Döderlein, Eichhorn's Repertorium, IV, 60-61 ... Cornill, *opere citato* (³), p. 49 also makes reference to the Egyptian and the Syriac recensions of the Arabic (⁴).

(¹) For justification of this assertion cf. BIBLICA 2 (1921) 418-423. Included in this article is an unedited page of the excellent Vatican Arabic Codex 445.

(²) The translation of el ʿAlam of the Book of Daniel is not from the Septuagint but from Theodotion. But it can be used here to show that el ʿAlam was working with manuscripts that were distinctively Egyptian. Worth recalling here are the words of St. Jerome in the Praefatio to his translation of Daniel from the original Semitic into Latin: " Danielem prophetam iuxta Septuaginta interpretes Domini Salvatoris Ecclesiae non legunt, utentes Theodotionis editione; et hoc cur acciderit, nescio ..... Hoc unum affirmare possum, quod multum a veritate discordet, et recto iudicio repudiatus sit, etc. " (PL 28 [ed. 1845], 1291 b). The unfortunate custom (or better, carelessness) of the modern editions of omitting completely the pertinent *Praefatio* of St. Jerome to each of the books he translated forces me to refer the reader to the Patrologia of Migne, where they were brought together (at the end of the Old Testament) by Maurin MARTIANAY out of deference to the arrangement of TEODULF OF ORLEANS.

(³) Henrich CORNILL, *Das Buch des Propheten Ezechiel* (Leipzig 1886), p. 49.

(⁴) GEHMAN, *art. cit.*, pp. 328-329.

There were other Arabic versions, too, as Gehman notes. But the important thing is the existence of a major Arabic version of Egyptian provenance.

Gehman then goes on to establish the relation of the Arabic recension of Daniel in the London and Paris Polyglots, i.e., the relation of the recension of el 'Alam to the Greek codices. He bases his argumentation on the division of the Greek codices of Daniel made by his teacher, Professor James A. Montgomery:

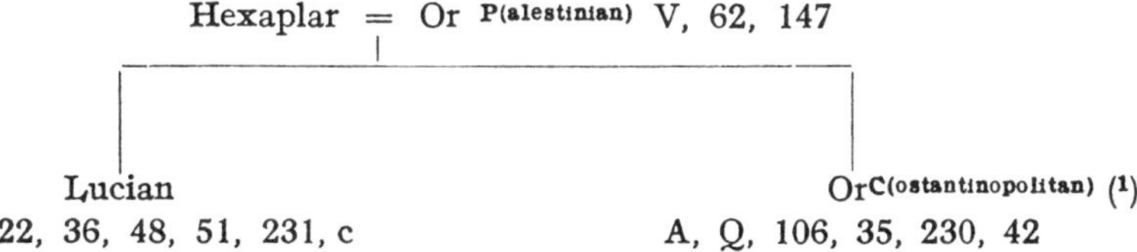

Then he reports that " the Arabic recension [sc., of Daniel] as published in the two Polyglot Bibles is a representative of the Origenian Constantinopolitan texts. The evidence of the collations is so overwhelming that there is no doubt about this matter. In many cases it corrects A and also 106, but it consistently follows the group. In fact it is one of the best representatives of the OrC group that we have; in making any study of the Constantinopolitan text the Arabic stands on a par with the Greek and cannot be left out of account (2). This is a completely independent confirmation of the importance of the el 'Alam version as a witness to the Greek text of Alexandria.

The second independent testimony in favor of our view on the distinctively Egyptian provenance of el 'Alam's source comes from the Swedish scholar Oscar Löfgren of the University of Uppsala. He has written a book of over one hundred pages on the Arabic versions of the Book of Daniel, examining the entire textual tradition, whether in Arabic or Coptic-Arabic (3). For the establishment of the text he chose twenty codices, 13 Arabic, 3 Coptic-Arabic, and 4 from psalters and miscellaneous items (the latter for the canticle of the three youths in chapter 3, a section omitted by the majority of the manuscripts) (4). The classification

(1) It should be noted that though J. A. MONTGOMERY classified Alexandrinus as belonging to a Constantinople parent text, he considered it Egyptian: " ... Codex A is not, I believe, physical Constantinopolitan; it is Egyptian, an Alexandrian copy of the Textus Receptus of the Melchite Church in Egypt, the faithful daughter of Byzantium " (" The Hexaplaric Strata in the Greek Texts of Daniel ", *JBL* 44 [1925] 300).

(2) GEHMAN, *art. cit.*, p. 333.

(3) Oscar LÖFGREN, *Studien zu den arabischen Danielübersetzungen*, mit besonderer Berücksichtigung der christlichen Texte, nebst einem Beitrag zur Kritik des Peschittatextes (Uppsala Universitets Årsskrift 1936: 4; Uppsala 1936).

(4) This had already been noted by the able scholar Georg GRAF, *Geschichte der christlichen arabischen Literatur* (Studi e Testi, 118; Vatican City 1944), pp. 131-135.

he was constrained to by the evidence was a division into two series, a clear-cut one of the Alexandrian el ʿAlam, and a less well-defined one by the Syrian Pethion, influenced by the Peshitta (pp. 28 ff.). Löfgren knew of 41 manuscripts (pp. 5-8) and of these he chose 20 for establishing the text (pp. 9-27). Of these 20 he lists 6 as the sources for the London Polyglot (pp. 28-29) (1).

With such a varied basis of research to rest upon I think that we are justified in saying that there are indications of the Hesychian recension of the Septuagint in the textual tradition of the Old Testament.

(1) LÖFGREN calls attention to a little known work, a reprint edited by J. D. Carlyle of the Arabic section of the London Polyglot of WALTON: *The Holy Bible*, containing the Old and New Testaments in the Arabic language (Newcastle upon Tyne 1811).

(ii) *The Hexapla*

Origen's aims as a Textual Critic of the Old Testament

S. P. Brock, Cambridge

Modern textual critics of the LXX, bearing in mind only their own difficulties in the face of the confusion in the manuscript tradition brought about by the influence of the Hexapla, have often been unfair to Origen in their assessment of his work. To quote but one recent example: Wevers[1] dismisses the Hexapla as 'a monument to misguided industry'.

What I propose to do here is to reconsider briefly Origen's aims as a textual critic in the compilation of the Hexapla, in particular, of course, the fifth – LXX – column, in the light of his own explicit statements on the purpose for which he intended that monumental work to serve.

Origen speaks of his revised Septuagint text in two famous passages, in the *Letter to Africanus*, and in his *Commentary on Matthew*. In the former of these he talks chiefly about the purpose of the work, while in the latter he is more concerned with explaining how he went about it. From the *Letter to Africanus* it becomes quite clear that Origen's purpose in compiling the Hexapla was primarily apologetic. As he himself puts it[2]: *ἀσκοῦμεν δὲ μὴ ἀγνοεῖν καὶ τὰς* (sc. *ἐκδόσεις*) *παρ' ἐκείνοις ἵνα πρὸς 'Ιουδαίους διαλεγόμενοι μὴ προφέρωμεν αὐτοῖς τὰ μὴ κείμενα ἐν τοῖς ἀντιγράφοις αὐτῶν καὶ ἵνα συγχρησώμεθα τοῖς φερομένοις παρ' ἐκείνοις*. The Hexapla was thus designed first and foremost as the tool for the Christian controversialist with the Jews, and, in that it is Origen's way of replying to the old Jewish charge – especially common in the second century – that Christians had falsified their biblical texts, it provides a parallel to another great controversial work of Origen's, I mean of course the *Contra Celsum*, in that that work too was a rebuttal of a second century, rather than a contemporary, attack on Christianity.

Looked at in this light, the Hexapla is of course an ideal tool, showing at a glance the readings of all the Jewish editions for any given passage, and giving in the fifth column a Septuagint text revised[3] in accordance with the Hebrew – a text which the Christian could thus safely and authori-

---

[1] Proto-Septuagint Studies, in: The Seeds of Wisdom. Essays in honour of T. J. Meek, ed. W. S. McCullough (Toronto, 1964), p. 58.

[2] §5, = PG 11, cols 60–61.

[3] That the fifth column already contained a revised text, with the asterisks and obeli, I have argued (against Lietzmann, Mercati and Kahle) in The Recensions of the LXX Version of I Samuel (D. Phil. thesis on deposit in the Bodleian Library, Oxford), pp. 37–42.

Reprinted from *Studia Patristica*. Vol. 10. Berlin, 1970.

tatively use in his controversies with Jews, a text, moreover, which, by means of the asterisks and obeli, conveniently showed him which passages were missing in the Christian LXX, and which were redundant, when compared with the Jewish editions.

It is this apologetic purpose of the Hexapla that one must always keep in mind when considering Origen's practice as a textual critic. He was not interested in constructing any 'original text' of the LXX, in the way that modern scholars are, but simply in providing the Christian controversialist with a text that would be acceptable in the authoritative eyes of contemporary Jewish scholars. Yet all too often modern scholars, blinded by their own exclusive interests in the 'hebraica veritas' on what one may call a diachronic plane, have consciously or unconsciously accredited Origen with the same interests. Origen's own interests, however, were on quite a different plane, on what may be called the synchronic one; for he was only concerned with finding out what was the text of the Old Testament as used by Jews *of his own day*, and since contact between Christians and Jews would naturally mean Greek speaking Jews, Origen's chief interest lay in the *ἐκδόσεις* of the Old Testament current in the Greek speaking Diaspora, that is to say 'the Three', Aquila, Theodotion and Symmachus. It is for this reason that one frequently finds that when Origen discusses textual points in his homilies or commentaries, he will speak of a reading primarily as being present or not in 'the Three', only mentioning, rather as an afterthought, their concurrence with the Hebrew. To give but two examples: in one of his homilies on Jeremiah[1] Origen speaks of 'another prophecy mysteriously not to be found in the LXX...', *εὕρομεν δὲ ἐν ταῖς λοιπαῖς ἐκδόσεσι, δῆλον ὅτι κειμένην ἐν τῷ Ἑβραικῷ...* And in his *Commentary on John*[2] he quotes Ps x 7 in a form on which he comments: *οὕτω γὰρ ἐν τοῖς ἀκριβέσιν ἀντιγράφοις εὕρομεν καὶ ταῖς λοιπαῖς παρὰ τοὺς ἑβδομήκοντα ἐκδόσεσι, καὶ τῷ Ἑβραικῷ.* Often no mention at all of the Hebrew is made, only of the Jewish editions; thus, commenting on the quotation in I Cor xiv 21[3], Origen says: *ταῦτα δὲ τὰ ῥήματα εὕρομεν παρὰ Ἀκύλᾳ καὶ ταῖς λοιπαῖς ἐκδόσεσι, οὐ μὴν παρὰ τοῖς ἑβδομήκοντα.* Another instructive case occurs in the *Commentary on Numbers*[4], where he quotes Dan i 17, 19, 20 and goes on: *et haec quidem in exemplaribus septuaginta interpretum habentur; in hebraeorum vero codicibus aliquid etiam vehementius repperi, quibus quamvis non utamur, tamen agnoscendi gratia dicemus...* Likewise, in a homily on Genesis[5], he discusses Moses's words in Ex vi 30 with an imaginary Jewish interlocutor: *in Exodo ubi nos in codicibus ecclesiae habemus scriptum respondentem ad Dominum Moysen et dicentem 'provide, Domine, alium quem mittas; ego enim gracili*

[1] Hom. XVI § 10 = GCS Origenes III, p. 141.
[2] Comm. Jn I.19 (Bk VI.6) = GCS Origenes IV, p. 115.
[3] Comm. I Cor. = JTS X, p. 38.
[4] Hom. XVIII § 3 = GCS Origenes VII, p. 172.
[5] Hom. III. § 5 = GCS Origenes VI, p. 45.

voce sum et tardus lingua', vos in hebraeis exemplaribus habetis 'ego autem incircumcisus sum labiis'. ecce habetis circumcisionem labiorum secundum vestra quae veriora dicitis exemplaria. And elsewhere the Jewish texts are simply referred to as 'the more accurate manuscripts'[1].

All too often modern scholars have thoughtlessly misinterpreted Origen's practice in this matter, claiming that it was his lack of knowledge of Hebrew that caused him to rely on the Jewish Greek editions[2]. But this, as I have tried to show, is to give quite the wrong emphasis: Origen uses the Three as a *κριτήριον* (a word he himself employs in the Commentary on Matthew[3]) primarily because it is they that are the authoritative texts in Jewish Greek circles – and only incidentally because his knowledge of Hebrew was not very great[4].

To Origen, then, it was the contemporary, living, biblical text that really mattered, whether that current in the synagogue, or that of the church. Thus, in his homilies he will sometimes expound both if they happen to be divergent; as he says in one of his homilies on Jeremiah[5]: *δεῖ οὖν καὶ τὸ καθημαξευμένον καὶ φερόμενον ἐν ταῖς ἐκκλησίαις διηγήσασθαι, καὶ τὸ ἀπὸ τῶν Ἑβραικῶν γραφῶν ἀδιήγητον μὴ καταλιπεῖν.* But for the Christian community it is of course the LXX that necessarily holds pride of place, even when it disagrees with the Hebrew[6]. Evidently to Origen, as to his contemporaries, a belief in the verbal inspiration of scripture applied to the Greek translation, as well as to the original: as far as I know Origen never makes any explicit statement on this, and indeed it seems that one must wait until Agobard of Lyons in the ninth century for any clear comment on the implications of such a belief for translations of the Old Testament[7]. It was for this reason that, in his *Letter to Africanus* (§ 4), Origen expressly states that the revised LXX text of his fifth column

---

[1] E. g. Hom. Jer. VIII 1 = GCS Origenes III, p. 55: *ὡς ἐν τοῖς ἀκριβεστέροις ἀντιγράφοις εὕρομεν.*

[2] Thus Swete (Introduction to the Old Testament in Greek², p. 61) quite misunderstands Origen's intentions when he speaks of Origen as not possessing 'the requisite knowledge of Hebrew' to make an entirely new Greek version.

[3] Comm. Mt. XV. 14 = GCS Origenes X, p. 388.

[4] I am in substantial agreement here with (e. g.) Bardy, Les traditions juives dans l'œuvre d'Origène, R. Bibl. 34 (1925), pp. 219–20; R. P. C. Hanson, Allegory and Event (London, 1959), pp. 167–72 (Hanson's examples of Origen's poor knowledge of Hebrew are however often presented in a grossly unfair way).

[5] Hom. XIV §2 = GCS Origenes III, p. 107.

[6] Precedents, as Origen points out, are already provided by St Paul, cf Comm. Rom. VIII § 8 = PG 14, cols 1171, 1175.

[7] PL 104, col 162f. Philo had evidently seen the problem when he stated that the translators were themselves inspired (Vita Mos. II. vii. 40). Likewise a realisation of the difficulties raised explains Ps. Aristeas's stress on the eminently respectable Jerusalem origin of the Hebrew *Vorlage* used by the translators. The other solution to the problem was to 'correct' the LXX in accordance with the Hebrew, a process evidenced notably in Barthélemy's 'Palestinian Recension', and culminating in Aquila.

was not intended for public use in the Christian community. He puts it in the form of a rhetorical question: *ὥρα τοίνυν . . . ἀθετεῖν τὰ ἐν ταῖς ἐκκλησίαις φερόμενα ἀντίγραφα, καὶ νομοθετῆσαι τῇ ἀδελφότητι ἀποθέσθαι μὲν τὰς παρ' αὐτοῖς ἐπιφερομένας ἱερὰς βίβλους, κολακεύειν δὲ 'Ιουδαίους καὶ πείθειν ἵνα μεταδῶσιν ἡμῖν τῶν καθαρῶν καὶ μηδὲν πλάσμα ἐχόντων;*

This ruling concern for the contemporary text does not mean that Origen was not interested in, or not aware of, the historical textual problems involved. Indeed he quite frequently speaks of the current LXX text as being corrupt[1]. Nevertheless he is careful not to let these – to him, purely scholarly – interests interfere with his duty as an exegete of the current Greek *textus receptus*, except of course, when the former can do service to the latter. In the same way, when creating the revised LXX text of the Hexapla's fifth column, he keeps rigidly to his intention of producing a text that will be acceptable in Greek speaking Jewish circles of his day, a text that could serve as a sound basis for Christian Jewish dialogue.

In both cases Origen's attitude is alien to the modern scholar, whose main aim is to recover the original text of a work; and so, judged – quite unfairly – by this standard, Origen of course appears as a very unsatisfactory textual critic[2]. What I have tried to do here is to show that, given Origen's own confessed aims, he carried out his task in a thoroughly scholarly and reputable way. Indeed I should like to end by pointing out that Origen has something to teach the modern textual critic of the LXX: such a scholar, influenced by classical scholarship, exerts all his energy on recovering the original texts of the translators, forgetting that the LXX was a living and ever changing entity, and forgetting too that many scholars outside his own field – and here I have in mind the patristic scholar in particular – would like to see an edition of the LXX as current, say, in fourth century Antioch – to give but one example that might actually be feasible[3].

---

[1] Cf. especially Comm. Jn I § 28 (Bk VI. 41) = GCS Origenes IV, p. 150; discussing the variants *Γαδαρα/Γερασα/Γεργεσα* (Mk v 1 and parallels), he points out a similar liability to corruption in LXX proper names: *ὡς ἠκριβώσαμεν ἀπὸ 'Εβραίων μαθόντες, καὶ τοῖς ἀντιγράφοις αὐτῶν τὰ ἡμέτερα συγκρίναντες, μαρτυρηθεῖσιν ὑπὸ τῶν μηδέπω διαστραφεισῶν ἐκδόσεων 'Ακύλου καὶ Θεοδοτίωνος καὶ Συμμάχου.*

[2] E.g. (for the NT) B. M. Metzger, Explicit References in the Works of Origen to Variant Readings in New Testament Manuscripts, in: Biblical and Patristic Studies in Memory of R. P. Casey, Freiburg etc., 1963, p. 94: "On the whole his treatment of variant readings is most unsatisfactory from the standpoint of modern textual criticism".

[3] As indeed attempted by de Lagarde, with, alas, lamentable results!

THE PURPOSE OF THE SECOND COLUMN OF THE HEXAPLA

THE object of this paper is to suggest that the most probable purpose of the second column of the Hexapla was to enable those who knew both the Hebrew language and alphabet to vocalize a consonantal text in Hebrew characters. The chief argument in favour of this suggestion is that a transliterated text would have been useless to those who knew no Hebrew, whereas those who understood Hebrew are unlikely to have been ignorant of the Hebrew script. The suggestion is compatible with either of two commonly held views of the origin of the second column: that it was prepared by Origen independently of any previous tradition of transliteration, and that he adopted a system already in use among Jews. Although this study is concerned primarily with the purpose of the second column rather than with its origin, it is clearly impossible to discuss the one without reference to the other.

I

Several theories have been advanced to explain the purpose of transliterated texts. Most of them fall into one of two classes—those which suppose that transliterations were for readers who knew no Hebrew at

[1] For *gargĕrōth-*, see ibid., p. 120.

Reprinted from *Journal of Theological Studies.* N. S., Vol. 7, 1956.

all, and those which suggest that they were used by readers who knew the Hebrew language but not its script. Each class will be examined in turn to see how it fails to provide a satisfactory explanation.

1. It has been suggested that transliterated texts were originally prepared to be used by Jews who knew no Hebrew but wished to read the sacred language in the synagogue. Halévy[1] claims to find evidence for this in rabbinic literature, but Cardinal Mercati has shown that the passages in question do not refer to Greek transliterations.[2] Another analogy has been found in the modern practice of transliterating the Aramaic Qaddish.[3] Hebrew was certainly used in synagogues where not all the congregation understood the language. It was because many, even in Palestine, failed to understand the Hebrew scriptures that a Targum in Aramaic was provided as well.

There are good reasons for rejecting this theory. When a lesson was read in Hebrew from Hebrew characters in a Palestinian synagogue, it is probable that there would usually have been some at least who understood without waiting for the Aramaic translation. If, however, the scriptures were read from transliterated texts in the synagogues of the dispersion, they must often have been incomprehensible even to those who understood Hebrew.

The chief difficulty in the way of reading intelligible Hebrew from a transliterated text is the failure of the Greek alphabet to represent adequately all the Hebrew consonants. *Sigma* must stand for *samekh*, *sadhe*, *sin*, and *shin*.[4] More important is the inability of the Greek letters adequately to represent the gutturals. There are many examples in the Hexapla of attempts to represent Hebrew gutturals—or at least to represent their influence on adjacent vowels.[5] For example, in βεειρ for בעיר (Ps. xxx. 22) the second *epsilon* represents the guttural and is un-

[1] *Journal Asiatique*, 9th ser., xvii (1901), pp. 335–41.

[2] *Biblica*, xxviii (1947), pp. 181 ff.

[3] H. M. Orlinsky in *Jewish Quarterly Review*, N.S. xxvii (1936–7), pp. 140, 142.

[4] It has been argued that in the time of Jerome *sin* and *shin* were not distinguished. See A. Sperber in *Hebrew Union College Annual*, xii–xiii (1937–8), pp. 114 f. But in view of the distinction between these two letters in the Massoretic Text they cannot everywhere have been confused. In any case the Origenic transliterations are at least a century earlier than the time of Jerome.

[5] Sperber, op. cit., pp. 110 ff., 128 ff., and P. E. Kahle, *The Cairo Geniza*, 1947, pp. 88 ff., argue that the gutturals were no longer pronounced as consonants. The opposite view is stated by W. E. Staples in *Journal of the American Oriental Society*, lix (1939), pp. 74 f. Staples goes too far in arguing that every guttural is represented. See also E. Brønno, *Studien über hebräische Morphologie und Vokalismus*, 1943, pp. 146 f., 275–7, 326, and *Z.D.M.G.* c (1950), pp. 527–31; G. Dalman, *Grammatik des Jüdisch-Palästinischen Aramäisch*, 1894, pp. 43–45.

likely to be a dittograph or merely part of a diphthong *ει* which had become identical in sound with *ι*.[1] This is confirmed by the fact that a vowel corresponding to a *ḥireq* in the Massoretic Text is regularly represented by a simple *iota* whereas *ει* regularly represents a guttural with an i-vowel. Frequently the transliterated text fails to represent a guttural at all.

There are further difficulties. *Iota* represents sometimes a vowel and sometimes a consonant, as does the diphthong *ου*. It would have been impossible for one who was ignorant of Hebrew to know when *alpha* was to be read as a long vowel and when it should be short. Similarly, his accentuation would have been wrong.

The reading of a transliterated text by a Jew who knew only Greek would therefore have led to the production of sounds which bore little relation to Hebrew and which would have been incomprehensible even to hearers who understood that language. It is unlikely that devotion to the sacred tongue was of such a character that it led to the paradoxical result that a debased pronunciation was used which was nonsense to those proficient in Hebrew no less than to those who knew only Greek. If, however, synagogues had no members who knew any Hebrew it is doubtful whether they would still have troubled to read the scriptures in anything but translation.

2. Theories of the second class maintained that transliterations were intended for Jews who knew their language fairly well but not its script.[2] If, however, a Jew's knowledge of Hebrew was good enough to enable him to read a transliteration he would almost certainly have been able to read a text in Hebrew characters. The Hebrew alphabet is not a particularly difficult one to learn, and any Jew who had sufficient zeal to keep alive a dead language for religious purposes must surely have been willing to devote an afternoon to learning the sacred script. As well as being a sign of piety it would have been easier to learn the Hebrew script than to learn to read Hebrew from a transliterated text. On the other hand, it is doubtful whether Jews would have been willing to go to the immense trouble of transliterating the Old Testament in order to save some of their compatriots the small but meritorious task of learning the national alphabet.

These arguments render most improbable the theory of W. E. Staples[3]

[1] The example comes from the tenth-century manuscript of the Hexapla in the Ambrosian Library at Milan. On this manuscript see E. Klostermann in *Z.A.W.* o.s. xvi (1896), pp. 334 f. This material is published in the supplement to the Septuagint concordance of Hatch and Redpath.

[2] See Staples, op. cit., and F. Wutz, *Die Transkriptionen von der Septuaginta bis zu Hieronymus*, 1933, pp. 123–32.

[3] See p. 80, n. 5.

that the transliterated texts in the second column of the Hexapla were intended to show only the consonantal text and that this explains why vowels are often omitted or written inconsistently. He believes that they were used by Jews who were ignorant of the Hebrew alphabet but knew the language well enough to be able to read it once the transliterated texts had given them the consonants. He claims that this view is supported by the fact that the consonants are carefully and regularly transcribed in contrast to the omissions and inconsistencies of the vowels.

Staples's arguments break down on careful examination. It is only necessary to refer to Brønno's excellent studies[1] to realize that the vocalization is not as haphazard as Staples maintains. Staples is wrong to expect these transliterations to show the same vocalization as the Massoretic Text centuries later, and there is external evidence for the correctness of some of the forms in the second column of the Hexapla as an adequate representation of the current pronunciation.[2] On the other hand, gutturals, which are consonants, are not regularly, consistently, or clearly shown as they would have to be if Staples's theory were correct.

In addition to these two classes of theories another hypothesis has been advanced. H. M. Orlinsky[3] suggests that, although transliterated texts were used by Jews long before the time of Origen, the specific purpose of the Hexapla was to serve as a textbook for Christians who wished to learn the Hebrew language. He believes that Origen wanted other Christians to follow his example of learning to read the Old Testament in the original tongue. It was not always easy for a Christian to find a Jewish teacher and so Origen prepared the Hexapla to make it possible to learn the language without one. The first column showed what the Hebrew looked like in the original, the second how it was to be pronounced, and the other columns provided translations to make the meaning plain.

This view too must be rejected—at least in the form in which Orlinsky states it. It is most unlikely that Origen was unrealistic enough to hope that a Christian could thus learn Hebrew without a teacher. Before such a student could make use of the reading book he would need to know certain things about Hebrew. He would have to know that the alphabet was only consonantal and that not all of its sounds could be adequately represented in transliteration. Some account of the gutturals and sibilants

[1] See p. 80, n. 5.

[2] It is, for example, wrong to question the absence of the final a-vowel of the second person singular masculine of the perfect and of the pronominal suffix. See Kahle, op. cit., pp. 95 ff.

[3] See p. 80, n. 3.

would have to be given. In the early stages Hebrew is not an easy language to learn without a teacher or at least a detailed written explanation of certain matters. It has already been seen how many difficulties would have to be overcome before transliterations could be used to give some idea of the pronunciation.

Orlinsky's theory would be tenable only if it were modified to say that the Hexapla was not intended to teach Hebrew without further aids, but was to be used in conjunction with a teacher or a textbook on the language. With such help a student would soon learn to read the Hebrew alphabet, and the consonants of the transliteration would be of use to him only in the early stages as an aid to the memory. Why should he use such inadequate representations of the Hebrew sounds when a much more reliable indication was to be found in the first column? On the other hand, the vowels of the second column would be of use to him for a much longer period—for as long as he made a study of the Bible text. When thus modified Orlinsky's hypothesis has become but a variety of another theory—the theory which it is the purpose of this paper to advance and which may now be considered.

II

The great defect of the Hebrew script is its failure to show with any precision how words are vocalized. This was not a very serious problem in the days when Hebrew was still a living language—at least for those who spoke it as their vernacular. In later times, however, the lack of vocalization was a source of great trouble. Even Jews who were brought up from infancy to know large parts of the Old Testament by heart must often have found that their memories failed them. How much less was Origen, who learned the language later in life, to make out the vocalization of the consonants in every place? This must have been a matter of great concern to him in days when Jewish exegesis regarded the traditional text with great awe. If Origen were to meet Jewish scholars on anything like an equal footing he must have some means of knowing the right vowels. Lesser scholars among the Christians would stand in even greater need of knowing how to vocalize the Hebrew in order both to make sense of it and to know which of several possibilities was correct in an ambiguous passage.

It has been seen that anyone who knew enough Hebrew to be able to make use of the second column of the Hexapla would also have known the Hebrew alphabet. For one who knew a little Hebrew the transliterated consonants would soon become superfluous for showing the pronunciation of the Hebrew consonants. The vowels of the transliteration would always be useful for filling in the deficiencies of the consonantal text. It is therefore suggested that transliterated texts were never intended to be used without reference to consonantal texts in Hebrew characters, and that their purpose was to indicate the vocalization. The chief value of the transliterated consonants was to show in which part of the word vowels should be read. The only other purpose may have been to show when consonants were doubled.[1] In the transliterated text of Origen long and short Greek vowels seem to be clearly distinguished even though they were probably confused in the speech of Origen's day. Similarly it has been seen that ι and ει are distinguished. This is adequately accounted for on the supposition that it was a scholarly archaism deliberately introduced in order to add precision; another explanation, involving the hypothesis that Origen borrowed the transliterations from Jews, is that they had been prepared long before the time of Origen.[2]

The hypothesis that transliterated texts were intended to be used alongside texts in Hebrew characters in order to supply the vowels thus offers a satisfactory explanation of the evidence, whereas the other theories fail to do this. Obviously in the Hexapla the texts in Hebrew and Greek letters were set side by side for the purpose of comparison, but it has not been generally realized that the only purpose of the second column was to show how to vocalize the consonants of the first. In time this purpose was forgotten—there do not seem to have been many who followed Origen's example in making a study of Hebrew. It was therefore possible for the famous tenth-century manuscript of the Hexapla in the Ambrosian Library to omit the column in Hebrew characters though without it the column in transliteration must have been singularly useless.[3]

III

The theory outlined above holds good whether the transliterations in the second column originated with Origen or whether he borrowed a system which was already in use among Jews. Mercati has challenged the view that transliterations were used by Jews before the time of Origen,[4] but even if the theory is questionable it has still to be taken into consideration as a possibility. It is not difficult to see how well the above view of the purpose of the transliterated texts would fit a theory of their origin among Jews.

It is probable that in ancient times, as today, synagogue readings were given from a consonantal text with comparatively few *matres lectionis*.

[1] See Brønno, op. cit., pp. 383 ff.

[2] Ibid., pp. 6–8; E. A. Speiser, *Jewish Quarterly Review*, N.S. xvi (1925–6), p. 365.

[3] See p. 81, n. 1.

[4] See p. 80, n. 2.

The correct vocalization was determined largely by tradition, but it is doubtful whether purely oral tradition would have been enough—especially for Jews whose vernacular was Greek and whose knowledge of Hebrew was not very extensive. The longer Qumran Isaiah scroll has a number of *matres lectionis* not found in the Massoretic Text, presumably to help those whose knowledge of Hebrew or of the traditional vocalization was defective.[1] Yet even this use of *matres lectionis* did not meet all the difficulties. Today the need would be met by the use of a pointed text which the reader could consult before the service. In ancient times there were no pointed texts, but the fact that systems of pointing were developed proves that a great need was felt for something of the kind. It is suggested that the place now filled by pointed texts was then filled by transliterations used in conjunction with consonantal texts in Hebrew characters; the need to fix and show the vocalization which gave rise to the Tiberian and other systems gave rise in an earlier period to transliterations.[2] The system was clumsier than that of the Massoretes since it meant using two texts instead of one, but it served the same purpose. Doubtful words were looked up in a transliterated text laid at the side of a consonantal text and the vocalization was learned. The transliterations could not always indicate the precise value of the vowels as far as such matters as length are concerned—though they could give greater precision than could *matres lectionis*. The reader's knowledge of Hebrew was good enough for him to recognize the right pronunciation once he was given the help of the transliteration.

This seems to have been one of the ways in which the deficiencies of a consonantal script were remedied without giving up the script in favour of another. There were other attempts to solve the same problem. The Tiberian system of vocalization is the final form which Hebrew manuscripts have taken, but this was preceded by a long history of experiment in Palestine and Babylonia. More akin to the system discussed in the present paper is that adopted by the Jacobite Syrians who wrote Greek vowels over or under the Semitic consonants. This method may not have occurred to Origen or to any predecessors that he may have had, or it may have been rejected in favour of transliteration. Possibly it was

[1] See also *Bulletin of the American Schools of Oriental Research* for October 1954, pp. 20 ff.

[2] An essentially similar explanation seems to be offered by M. Noth in *Die Welt des Alten Testaments*[2], 1953, p. 253. Others have compared the use of transliterated texts to that of modern pointed texts, but, as far as I am aware, everyone else has supposed that transliterations were used without reference to texts in Hebrew characters. Kahle has an interesting reference to the use of Hebrew scriptures by second-century Christians on pp. 135 f. of *Alttestamentliche Studien Friederich Nötscher zum 60 Geburtstag gewidmet*, 1950.

thought irreverent to annotate the sacred text in this way even though it was permissible to make a separate transliteration.

IV

In confirmation of the arguments advanced above reference may be made to several non-Jewish analogies in the ancient world. At the beginning of the Christian era the Demotic script was used in Egypt. It was a cumbersome script and was almost entirely consonantal. Eventually it was superseded by the Coptic script which is a modification of the Greek alphabet. The Greek alphabet lacked certain consonants which were needed in Egypt and so it had to be supplemented. Similarly there is an Egyptian papyrus of the second century A.D. which is transliterated into Greek letters, but this transliteration has had to be supplemented by certain letters not found in the Greek alphabet.[1] This serves the negative purpose of confirming the argument advanced above against the view that Jews used transliterated texts without reference to texts in Hebrew characters. The Greek alphabet was as inadequate for the Jews as it was for the Egyptians.

The London and Leiden Papyrus of the third century A.D.[2] offers a more positive analogy. This papyrus is written in Demotic but has the difficult words glossed in the Greek alphabet. The obscure word is written in Demotic and has the Greek gloss above it. For example, the word written *ʿg'nʿgwp* in Demotic has the gloss *AKANAKOYП*,[3] and *nyptwmykh* is glossed *NIΠTOYMIK*.[4] The words glossed are almost exclusively inventions of the magicians and not Egyptian words. The pronunciation would be unknown to readers of the Demotic script but would have to be communicated to them in a precise form if the spells were to be efficacious. The Demotic script could show the consonants but not the vowels. The scribe therefore transliterated the words into Greek characters which could indicate the vowels. The whole word, and not just the vowels, was written in Greek letters to indicate the exact position of the vowels in relation to the consonants.

The parallel to Greek transliterations of Hebrew is not quite complete because the glosses are written above the original instead of as a separate text, and also because only selected words are glossed. But, as has been

[1] W. E. Crum, *Journal of Egyptian Archaeology*, xxviii (1942), pp. 20 ff.; A. Volten in *Studia Orientalia Iohanni Pedersen Dicata*, 1953, pp. 364 ff.

[2] F. Ll. Griffith and H. Thompson, *The Demotic Magical Papyrus of London and Leiden*, 1904. According to Volten, op. cit., p. 375, there is other material as yet unpublished. I am indebted to Professor T. W. Thacker for drawing my attention to this papyrus and for help in preparing the first three paragraphs in this section.

[3] Griffith and Thompson, op. cit., vol. ii, plate 23, line 28.

[4] Ibid., plate 16, line 8.

seen, it may have been thought more reverent not to annotate the sacred Hebrew text. Whereas many Hebrew vocalizations may have been obscure, Egyptian scribes were thoroughly familiar with Demotic apart from these unusual magical terms. There is thus a clear similarity of purpose in a semi-religious text of the same age as Origen.

A further analogy may be found in Mesopotamia. In the first or second century B.C. certain cuneiform texts were transliterated into Greek letters; they are concerned with such matters as lists of places in Babylon, a prayer, and perhaps a hymn.[1] On one side of each tablet is the text in cuneiform and on the back is a transliteration into Greek. Pinches argues that the transliterations were made by a Greek since such help would not have been needed by a native Babylonian.[2] Halévy is, however, surely right in holding that a Greek would have needed translations as well as transliterations, whereas transliterations would have been a great help to a Babylonian in enabling him to read ideograms and to determine the value of polyphonous signs.[3] The fact that cuneiform is written on the other side of the tablets shows that it is likely that the transliterations were never intended to serve as texts in themselves but only as aids to the reading of texts in a non-Greek script. The problems of the cuneiform script were not, of course, the same as those of the Hebrew, but there may be found in these texts yet another example of the attempt to determine ambiguous or uncertain readings in a sacred script by the provision of a transliterated text to be compared with it.

J. A. EMERTON

1 T. G. Pinches, A. H. Sayce, and F. C. Burkitt in *Proceedings of the Society of Biblical Archaeology*, xxiv (1902), pp. 108–25, 143–5; W. G. Schileico in *Archiv für Orientforschung*, v (1928), pp. 11–13; P. E. Van der Meer in ibid. xiii (1940), pp. 124–8.

2 Op. cit., p. 113.

3 *Revue Sémitique*, x (1902), pp. 247 f.

THE TREATMENT OF THE HEXAPLARIC SIGNS IN THE SYRO-HEXAPLAR OF PROVERBS

CHARLES T. FRITSCH

PRINCETON THEOLOGICAL SEMINARY

IT IS a well-known fact that there are many variations between the Greek and Hebrew texts of the Book of Proverbs. The order of the chapters in the latter part of the book in Greek is quite different from that in the Hebrew: 30 1–14 follows 24 22, and 30 15—31 9 follows 24 34, giving the arrangement 22 17—24 22; 30 1–14; 24 23–34; 30 15—31 9; 25—29; 31 10–31. The order found in the Greek text is probably older than that of the Hebrew.[1] The Greek text also has a different order of verses at the end of ch. 15 and at the beginning of ch. 16, as well as in ch. 20. In the acrostic poem of 31 10–31, vs. 26 [פ] precedes vs. 25 [ע] in the Greek.

Besides these differences in general arrangement the LXX has important textual variations from the Hebrew. In it is found new material which has no Hebrew counterpart in the MT (7 1, 9 12, 24 22, etc.), as well as numerous double translations of verses or single stichoi (see below for examples). It also omits numerous verses and stichoi which are found in the Hebrew (1 16; 4 7, 7 25b, 8 33, 20 14–19, etc.).[2]

Then, too, the Greek translation of Proverbs is characterized by a certain freedom of expression and by certain peculiarities in the mode of translating. Hebrew sentences are recast in an entirely new form in the Greek by taking liberties with grammatical forms and syntax, or by

[1] See Pfeiffer, R. H., *Introduction to the Old Testament.* (N. Y.: Harper & Brothers, 1941), p. 646.

[2] These problems of the relationship between the Hebrew and Greek texts of Proverbs are treated most thoroughly in the following works:

Lagarde, P. de, *Anmerkungen zur griechischen Uebersetzung der Proverbien.* Leipzig, 1863.

Baumgartner, A. J., *Étude critique sur l'état du texte du Livre des Proverbes.* Leipzig, 1890.

Delitzsch, F., *Das Salomonische Spruchbuch.* (Biblischer Commentar ueber die Poetischen Buecher des Alten Testaments. Dritter Band) Leipzig, 1873, pp. 540–547.

Mueller, A. & E. Kautzsch, *The Book of Proverbs.* (The Sacred Books of the Old Testament. English trans. of notes by D. B. Macdonald) Leipzig, 1901, pp. 70–85.

Toy, C. H., *A Critical and Exegetical Commentary on the Book of Proverbs.* (The International Critical Commentary) New York, 1904.

Reprinted from *Journal of Biblical Literature.* Vol. 72, 1953.

simply guessing at the meaning of the Hebrew expression (1 18, 5 5, 10 18, 21 30, etc.). With the exception of a few important terms,[3] Hebrew words which recur throughout the book are usually translated by a variety of Greek words, showing that in general there was no set pattern of translation. In the Greek text there are frequently added such moralizing terms as *κακός* (1 18, 28, 6 11, 14 25, 18 3, 21 26), *δίκαιος* (10 17, 12 25, 16 11, 20 8, 28 21, 28), and others.

However one may account for these serious deviations in the Greek text of Proverbs, it is clear that the translator(s) was not bound by any well-established translation-tradition, or by a sacrosanct attitude toward the Hebrew text.

The problem discussed in this paper grew out of an exhaustive study of the doublets in the Greek text of Proverbs. 76 examples of these double translations have been found, and are classified as follows:

1. Double translations of verses: 1 7, 2 21, 3 15, 6 11, 14 22, 15 6, 18, 18 22, 22 8, 29 25.
2. Double translations of a single stichos of a verse: 1 14, 27, 2 2, 3, 19, 4 10, 5 23, 6 25, 8 10, 9 10, 14 35, 16 17, 26, 29 7, 31 27, 29, 30.
3. Double translations of phrases: 2 18, 6 3, 10, 20 11.
4. Double translations of words: 3 10, 18, 23, 5 19, 11 30, 15 15, 17, 17 9, 14, 15, 18, 23 (2), 28, 21 1, 19, 24, 26, 22 13, 23 20, 21, 29, 31(4), 32(2), 24 7(2), 10, 23, 31, 25 10, 27 24, 29 25, 30 14, 16(2), 28, 30, 33, 31 3, 23, 29.

It should also be mentioned that the following examples are doubtful, and so have not been included in the above list: 1 4, 21, 6 10, 11, 9 2, 6, 12 26, 14 23, 15 22, 22 3, 23 2, 16, 25 20, 28, 30 15.

To the list of doublets given above there may be added 15 more examples which have come to light by comparing the variant readings found in the different uncials, minuscules, in the early Church Fathers, and other sources: 9 7, 8, 11 1, 18, 26, 29, 15 32, 33, 16 4, 17 27, 19 10, 23, 24 26, 28 10, 30 15.

When faced with this mass of doublet material in the Greek translation of Proverbs, one's first reaction is to ask, Where does it come from? and, Why is it there? In order to find an answer to these questions the translation of Proverbs in the Syro-Hexaplar (SH) was carefully studied, and there certain evidence came to light which has helped to solve the problem.

[3] רָשָׁע is translated by *ἀσεβής* 65 out of the 73 times it occurs in Proverbs, צדיק by *δίκαιος* 57 out of 63 times (*δικαιοσύνη* 5 times), חָכְמָה by *σοφία* 30 out of 33 times (*σοφός* 2 times), and אויל by *ἄφρων* 10 out of 13 times. These figures do not bear out the statement of W. Frankenberg when he says, "the expressions for the same things, even for the main ideas (צדיק, רָשָׁע, אויל, etc.) change continually and to be sure most of the time without any observable reason." (*Die Sprueche.* [Handkommentar zum Alten Testament, Goettingen, 1898] p. 11).

According to Swete,[4] "the Origenic signs were scrupulously retained" in the SH. These signs consisted of the obelus which was prefixed to words or lines which were wanting in the Hebrew and found in the Greek, and the asterisk, which noted words or lines wanting in the Greek but present in the Hebrew. In 31 of the examples of the doublets noted above in the Greek text, SH has retained either the obelus or the asterisk from the fifth column of Origen's Hexapla, leaving 45 doublets without any sign at all. Thus we can see that SH did not "scrupulously" retain all of the Origenian signs from the fifth column of the Hexapla, and we shall note later on that the wrong sign was used in a good many instances in SH. These inaccuracies in the use of the Origenian signs in SH may have crept into the text between the time of Origen (d. ca. 250 A. D.) and Paul of Tella, who translated SH in 616 A. D., or mistakes may have come about in the transmission of the text of SH after the time of Paul of Tella.

The doublet material in the Greek text of Proverbs will be divided into three groups: I. Examples with the Origenian signs correctly noted in SH; II. Examples with the Origenian signs incorrectly noted in SH; III. Examples which have no signs in SH. In the last group an attempt will be made in certain cases to indicate the signs which should have been used according to the principles discovered in the first group.[5]

I. *Examples with the Origenian signs correctly noted in SH.*

1 7 M "The fear of Yahweh is the beginning of knowledge,
Wisdom and instruction fools despise."

LXX a *᾿Αρχὴ σοφίας φόβος θεοῦ*
b *σύνεσις δὲ ἀγαθὴ πᾶσι τοῖς ποιοῦσιν αὐτήν.*
c *εὐσέβεια δὲ εἰς θεὸν ἀρχὴ αἰσθήσεως,*
d *σοφίαν δὲ καὶ παιδείαν ἀσεβεῖς ἐξουθενήσουσιν.*

SH a and b with obelus = OG.
c and d, which are closer to the Hebrew, are accordingly Hexaplaric. In this example, a and b, or the OG, are taken from Ps 110 (M 111) 10.

[4] Swete, H. B., *Introduction to the Old Testament in Greek.* Cambridge, 1914, p. 112.

[5] Besides the commentaries, the following works have been used in this study:

Ceriani, A. M., *Monumenta Sacra et Profana ex Codicibus Praesertim Bibliothecae Ambrosianae.* Vol. VII. Mediolani, 1874.

Field, F., *Origenis Hexaplorum quae supersunt, sive Veterum Interpretum Graecorum in totum Veterum Testamentum fragmenta.* Vol. II. Oxonii, 1875.

Holmes R., and J. Parsons, *Vetus Testamentum graecum cum variis lectionibus.* Vol. III. 1819.

2 2b M "Apply thine heart to understanding."

LXX a καὶ παραβαλεῖς καρδίαν σου εἰς σύνεσιν,
b παραβαλεῖς δὲ αὐτὴν ἐπὶ νουθέτησιν τῷ υἱῷ σου.

SH b with obelus = OG.
a, which is closer to the Hebrew, is accordingly Hexaplaric.

2 19b M "And not do they attain unto the paths of life."

LXX a οὐδὲ μὴ καταλάβωσιν τρίβους εὐθείας.
b οὐ γὰρ καταλαμβάνονται ὑπὸ ἐνιαυτῶν ζωῆς.

SH b with obelus = OG.
a, which is closer to the Hebrew, is accordingly Hexaplaric. εὐθείας for חַיִּים in a is probably due to inner Greek corruption.

2 21 M "For the upright shall dwell in the land,
And the perfect shall remain in it."

In A and a number of minuscules the following double translation is found:
a χρηστοὶ ἔσονται οἰκήτορες γῆς,
b ἄκακοι δὲ ὑπολειφθήσονται ἐν αὐτῇ,
c ὅτι εὐθεῖς κατασκηνώσουσι γῆν,
d καὶ ὅσιοι ὑπολειφθήσονται ἐν αὐτῇ.

Bℵ only c and d.

SH has the four stichoi. a and b with obelus = OG.
c and d, which are closer to the Hebrew, are accordingly Hexaplaric.

3 15 M "More precious is she than rubies,
And all thy desires are not comparable to her."

LXX a τιμιωτέρα δέ ἐστιν λίθων πολυτελῶν,
b οὐκ ἀντιτάξεται αὐτῇ οὐδεν πονηρόν.
c εὔγνωστός ἐστιν πᾶσιν τοῖς ἐγγίζουσιν αὐτῇ,
d πᾶν δὲ τίμιον οὐκ ἄξιον αὐτῆς ἐστιν.

SH b and c with obelus = OG.
a and d, which are closer to the Hebrew, are accordingly Hexaplaric.

4 10b M "And the years of thy life shall be many."

LXX a καὶ πληθυνθήσεται ἔτη ζωῆς σου,
b ἵνα σοι γένωνται πολλαὶ ὁδοὶ βίου.

SH b with obelus = OG.
a, which is closer to the Hebrew, is accordingly Hexaplaric.

5 19 The Hebrew word יְרַוֻּךָ is translated twice in LXX:
ἡγείσθω σου καὶ συνέστω σοι.
'A, literally, μεθυσκέτωσάν (σε)

SH The first of the two expressions in LXX has the obelus = OG.

According to Lagarde the double translation of LXX is due to two different readings of the Hebrew word. ἡγείσθω σου corresponds to יורוך, and συνέστω σοι to יְרֵעוּךָ or יְרָעוּךָ. In both renderings LXX avoided the literal meaning of the Hebrew word. Perhaps, as Toy suggests, they are allegorizing phrases which were so rendered in order to avoid the sensuous physical expression of the Hebrew.

Since neither translation in LXX is close to M, we can infer only on the basis of the markings in SH that ἡγείσθω σου is OG, and συνέστω σοι is Hexaplaric.

6 25b M "Neither let her take thee with her eyelids."

LXX a μηδὲ ἀγρευθῇς σοῖς ὀφθαλμοῖς
b μηδὲ συναρπασθῇς ἀπὸ τῶν αὐτῆς βλεφάρων.

SH a with obelus = OG.
b, which is closer to the Hebrew, is accordingly Hexaplaric.

9 7b M "And he that reproveth a wicked man, [getteth] himself a blot."

ABℵ read: ἐλέγχων δὲ τὸν ἀσεβῆ μωμήσεται ἑαυτόν.
V, 68, 109, etc. read: οἱ δὲ ἔλεγχοι τῷ ἀσεβεῖ μώλωπες αὐτῷ.

SH has both readings, with the second one under obelus = OG.

The uncial reading, which is closer to the Hebrew, is accordingly Hexaplaric.

9 8 M "Reprove not a scoffer lest he hate thee,
Reprove a wise man, and he will love thee."

B reads: μὴ ἔλεγχε κακούς, ἵνα μὴ μισῶσίν σε·
ἔλεγχε σοφόν, και ἀγαπήσει σε.

ἀγαπήσει σε]+ἄσοφον καὶ μισήσει σε A, 161 (mg.), 248, etc.
+ἄφρονα καὶ προσθήσει τοῦ μισῆσαί σε 254
+ἔλεγξον ἄφρονα καὶ μισήσει σε 296

Of these additional lines, which seem to be double translations of the first stichos of B, only the second (254) occurs in SH, where it is under the obelus=OG. The first stichos of B, which is closer to the Hebrew, is accordingly Hexaplaric.

9 10b M "And the knowledge of the Holy One is understanding."

LXX a καὶ βουλὴ ἁγίων σύνεσις·
b τὸ γὰρ γνῶναι νόμον διανοίας ἐστὶν ἀγαθῆς·

SH b with obelus=OG.
a, which is closer to Hebrew, is accordingly Hexaplaric.

11 26a M "The one who withholds grain shall the people curse."

LXX ὁ συνέχων σῖτον ὑπολίποιτο αὐτὸν τοῖς ἔθνεσιν.
τοῖς ἔθνεσιν]+ ὁ τιμιουλκῶν σῖτον δημοκατάρατος V, 161
'Α . . . . καταράσονται αὐτὸν φυλαί
Σ ὁ κωλύων (σῖτον) λαοκατάρατος
Θ ὁ κωλύων (σῖτον) δημοκατάρατος

SH has two readings of this verse. The first corresponds to LXX and is under the obelus=OG. The second, "he who seizes grain is cursed by the multitude," is obviously closer to the Hebrew, and so Hexaplaric; it is markedly similar to 'ΑΣΘ.

14 22 M "Do not the devisers of evil err?
But mercy and truth [shall be] to them that devise good."

LXX a πλανώμενοι τεκταίνουσι κακά,
b ἔλεον δὲ καὶ ἀλήθειαν τεκταίνουσιν ἀγαθοί.
c οὐκ ἐπίστανται ἔλεον καὶ πίστιν τέκτονες κακῶν,
d ἐλεημοσύναι δὲ καὶ πίστεις παρὰ τέκτοσιν ἀγαθοῖς.
הֲלוֹא־יִתְעוּ] 'Α μήτι οὐ πλανηθήσονται; Θ ἰδοὺ πλανηθήσονται.

SH c and d with obelus=OG.
a and b, which are closer to the Hebrew, are accordingly Hexaplaric. The one expression in the Hexaplaric addition is markedly similar to 'ΑΘ as given above.

14 35b M "But his wrath shall be against him who causeth shame."

LXX a τῇ δὲ ἑαυτοῦ εὐστροφίᾳ ἀφαιρεῖται ἀτιμίαν.
b ὀργὴ ἀπόλλυσιν καὶ φρονίμους (15 1a)

SH b with obelus = OG.
a, which is closer to Hebrew, is accordingly Hexaplaric. וְעֶבְרָתוֹ was probably read וְעָרְמָתוֹ (τῇ δὲ ἑαυτοῦ εὐστροφίᾳ), or there may have been a different text.

15 6 M "In the house of the righteous is much treasure,
But in the revenues of the wicked is trouble."

LXX a ἐν πλεοναζούσῃ δικαιοσύνῃ ἰσχὺς πολλή,
b οἱ δὲ ἀσεβεῖς ὁλόρριζοι ἐκ γῆς ἀπολοῦνται.
c οἴκοις δικαίων ἰσχὺς πολλή,
d καρποὶ δὲ ἀσεβῶν ἀπολοῦνται.

SH has for b, λογισμοὶ δὲ ἀσεβῶν ἐκριζωθήσονται, with LXX b in the margin. V also has this reading, found in SH, for b. In SH, a and b with obelus = OG. c and d, which are closer to Hebrew, are accordingly Hexaplaric.

15 18 M "A wrathful man stirreth up contention;
But he that is slow to anger appeaseth strife."

LXX a ἀνὴρ θυμώδης παρασκευάζει μάχας
b μακρόθυμος δὲ καὶ τὴν μέλλουσαν καταπραΰνει.
c μακρόθυμος ἀνὴρ κατασβέσει κρίσεις,
d ὁ δὲ ἀσεβὴς ἐγείρει μᾶλλον.

SH c and d with obelus = OG.
a and b, which are closer to Hebrew, are accordingly Hexaplaric.

15 33b M "And before honor [is] humility."

Bℵ read, καὶ ἀρχὴ δόξης ἀποκριθήσεται αὐτῇ.
πάντα τὰ ἔργα] praemitt. προπορεύεται δὲ ταπεινοῖς δόξα. 68, 296. προσπορεύεται . . . . A, 252, 254.

ΣΘ, καὶ ἔμπροσθεν δόξης πραΰτης.

SH has only the reading found in Bℵ, which is under the asterisk, and which is accordingly Hexaplaric. The other reading, found in the minuscules and A, is OG.

16 4 M "Yahweh hath made everything for its own end;
Yea, even the wicked for the day of evil."

LXX πάντα τὰ ἔργα τοῦ κυρίου μετὰ δικαιοσύνης, φυλάσσεται δὲ ὁ ἀσεβὴς εἰς ἡμέραν κακήν. (16 9)

SH has LXX translation under the obelus = OG.

The Greek text is hopelessly confused in these opening verses of ch. 16. SH not only shares in this confusion, but also adds material which is not found in LXX. In this additional material another translation of the first stichos of LXX is found: *πάντα εἰργάσατο ὁ κύριος δι' ἑαυτόν*. This is under the asterisk and is attributed to Theodotion. It is Hexaplaric, and its origin is definitely attested.

16 17b M "He who guards his soul keeps his way."

LXX a ὃς φυλάσσει τὰς ἑαυτοῦ ὁδοὺς τηρεῖ τὴν ἑαυτοῦ ψυχήν·.
b ἀγαπῶν δὲ ζωὴν αὐτοῦ φείσεται στόματος αὐτοῦ.
Θ τηρεῖ ψυχὴν αὐτοῦ φυλάσσων ὁδοὺς αὐτοῦ.

SH b with obelus = OG.
a, which is closer to Hebrew, is accordingly Hexaplaric. The Hexaplaric material is obviously derived from Theodotion's translation.

16 26b M "For his mouth urgeth him thereto."

LXX a καὶ ἐκβιάζεται ἑαυτοῦ τὴν ἀπώλειαν·
b ὁ μέντοι σκολιὸς ἐπὶ τῷ ἑαυτοῦ στόματι φορεῖ τὴν ἀπώλειαν.

SH a with obelus = OG.
b, which is closer to the Hebrew, is Hexaplaric.
פִּיהוּ was probably read פידו (τὴν ἀπώλειαν).

18 22 M "He who finds a wife finds a good thing,
And obtaineth favor from Yahweh."

LXX a ὃς εὗρεν γυναῖκα ἀγαθὴν εὗρεν χάριτας,
b ἔλαβεν δὲ παρὰ θεοῦ ἱλαρότητα.
c ὃς ἐκβάλλει γυναῖκα ἀγαθὴν ἐκβάλλει τὰ ἀγαθά·
d ὁ δὲ κατέχων μοιχαλίδα ἄφρων καὶ ἀσεβής.

SH c and d are with obelus = OG.
a and b, which are closer to the Hebrew, are accordingly Hexaplaric.

20 10b At the end of this stichos M has "even the both of them" (גַּם־שְׁנֵיהֶם).

LXX reads: *καὶ ἀμφότερα*, and begins vs. 11 with *καὶ ὁ ποιῶν αὐτά*, which Lag. seems to think is the result of reading גַּם־שְׁנֵיהֶם again as גַּם־עֹשֵׂיהֶם.

SH has this second reading, together with three additional words not in Greek here, under the obelus, which means it is the reading of OG. The first reading in the Greek and in SH is closer to the Hebrew, and therefore Hexaplaric.

24 23b The word הַכֵּר (to have respect [of persons]) in M is translated twice in LXX: a *ἐπιγινώσκειν*; b *αἰδεῖσθαι*.
'ΑΣΘ *ἐπιγινώσκειν*.

SH b is with obelus = OG.
a, which is the more literal Hebrew, is accordingly Hexaplaric, which corresponds with the translations of 'ΑΣΘ.

28 10c M "But the perfect shall inherit the good."

LXX a *οἱ δὲ ἄνομοι διελεύσονται ἀγαθά*
b *καὶ οὐκ εἰσελεύσονται εἰς αὐτά.*
οἱ δὲ ἄνομοι] praemitt. *οἱ δὲ ἄμωμοι διελοῦνται ἀγαθά* V, 106, 261.
'ΑΘ (*καὶ*) *οἱ ἄμωμοι κληροδοτηθήσεται ἀγαθόν.*
Σ *καὶ οἱ τέλειοι κληρονομήσουσιν ἀγαθόν.*

SH has the three readings in V, 106, 261. LXX a and b are under obelus = OG. The additional stichos, found in V, etc. is closer to the Hebrew, and accordingly Hexaplaric. LXXb seems to be a further expansion of 10c.

31 29a M "Many are the daughters who have done worthily."

LXX a *πολλαὶ θυγατέρες ἐκτήσαντο πλοῦτον,*
b *πολλαὶ ἐποίησαν δυνατά,*
ἐκτήσαντο πλούτον] *ἐποίησαν δύναμιν* V, 68, 106, 109, 147, 157, 161 (mg.) 252, 295, 297.
πολλαὶ ἐποίησαν] *πολλαὶ ἐκτίσαντο* V, and substantially the same in 68, 106, 252, 295, 297

SH a *πολλαὶ θυγατέρες ἐποίησαν δύναμιν,*
b *πολλαὶ δὲ ἐκτήσαντο πλοῦτον.*

In this case, SH seems to reflect the correct Greek text, as shown by the variants in the large number of minuscules above. In SH, b is with obelus = OG. Here a, which is closer to Hebrew, is accordingly Hexaplaric.

Out of the 25 examples of the double translations of Hebrew verses, stichoi, phrases, or words just given, 24 have one of the members of the double translation written with the obelus in SH. The rendering in each case under the obelus is that of OG, whereas the unmarked member is always closer to the Hebrew, and therefore Hexaplaric. In five of these 24 examples (11 26a, 14 22, 16 4, 17b, 24 23b) the Hexaplaric material is obviously dependent upon the translations of 'ΑΣΘ. It may be concluded, therefore, from this evidence, not only that one member of the doublet material in the Greek text of Proverbs is Hexaplaric, but that it had its origin in 'ΑΣΘ, or the manuscripts of Greek translations referred to as Quinta, Sexta, (Septima), in Origen's Hexapla.

In one example (15 33b) the Hexaplaric translation is marked with the asterisk. The double translation, not found in SH, is accordingly OG. (Cf. 16 4).

II. *Examples with the Origenian signs incorrectly noted in SH.*

1 14b M "One purse shall be to all of us."

LXX a *κοινὸν δὲ βαλλάντιον κτησώμεθα πάντες,*
b *καὶ μαρσίππιον ἓν γενηθήτω ἡμῖν.*
b is omitted in V.

SH only the first three words of b are marked with the asterisk. The marking itself is correct, since b is closer to the Hebrew, and accordingly Hexaplaric, and a is OG; but all of b should be included under the Origenian signs. In other words, the metobelus should come at the end of the stichos, and not in the middle.

In checking the use of the Origenian signs in SH, the writer has found eleven other examples like this, where the obelus or asterisk-metobelus do not cover the full verse or stichos. They are 1 12b, 6 11, 11 2b, 4, 16, 13 6, 16 17, 17 4, 19 7, 22 9, 25 10.

2 3b M "For understanding lift up thy voice."

B *καὶ τῇ συνέσει δῷς φωνήν σου,*

A a *καὶ τῇ συνέσει δῷς φωνήν σου,*
b *τὴν δὲ αἴσθησιν ζητήσῃς μεγάλῃ τῇ φωνῇ.*

SH b with asterisk. Certainly a looks to be closer to the Hebrew than b, and so it should have the asterisk according to the conclusions of Section I. Here a is Hexaplaric, and b is OG.

Twelve other examples like this have been found in SH where the wrong signs have been used. They are 7 19, 9 12, 15 33, 16 32, 17 21, 18 14, 19 7, 25, 24 27, 25 11, 29 25, 30 15.

6 11 M "And thy poverty shall come like a robber,
And thy want as an armed man."

LXX a εἶτ' ἐμπαραγίνεταί σοι ὥσπερ κακὸς ὁδοιπόρος ἡ πενία
b καὶ ἡ ἔνδεια ὥσπερ ἀγαθὸς δρομεύς.
c ἐὰν δὲ ἄοκνος ᾖς, ἥξει ὥσπερ πηγὴ ὁ ἀμητός σου,
d ἡ δὲ ἔνδεια ὥσπερ κακὸς δρομεὺς ἀπαυτομολήσει.

SH only d is under obelus. Certainly both c and d should be, as they are OG. a and b, which are closer to Hebrew, are accordingly Hexaplaric. Cf. 1 14b above.

29 25 M "The fear of a man bringeth a snare,
But he who trusts in Yahweh shall be safe."

LXX a φοβηθέντες καὶ αἰσχυνθέντες ἀνθρώπους ὑπεσκελίσθησαν.
b ὁ δὲ πεποιθὼς ἐπὶ κύριον εὐφρανθήσεται.
c ἀσέβεια ἀνδρὶ δίδωσιν σφάλμα·
d ὃς δὲ πέποιθεν ἐπὶ τῷ δεσπότῃ σωθήσεται.

SH c and d under obelus. But they are closer to Hebrew than a and b. There is here again a mistake in the use of the Origenian signs. c and d should be under the asterisk, or a and b should be under the obelus.

In a, the doublet of חֶרְדַּת is also wrongly marked. αἰσχυνθέντες is under the asterisk, which is certainly a freer translation of חֶרְדַּת than φοβηθέντες. The asterisk should be written with φοβηθέντες, or the obelus with αἰσχυνθέντες. Cf. 2 3b above.

30 15b M "There are three things that are never satisfied."

LXX καὶ αἱ τρεῖς αὗται οὐκ ἐνεπίμπλασαν αὐτήν.

'ΑΣΘ τρία δέ ἐστιν ἃ οὐ πλησθήσεται.

SH has two translations of this line:
a καὶ αἱ τρεῖς αὗται οὐκ ἐνεπίμπλασαν αὐτήν
b τρία δέ ἐστιν ἃ οὐ πλησθήσεται.

b is under the obelus, and yet that is the translation of 'ΑΣΘ, which is certainly closer to the Hebrew. Therefore the asterisk should be placed with b, or the obelus with a.

It is clear from this evidence that the Origenian signs cannot always be trusted. Mistakes in the use of these signs may have crept into the text during the 400 years between the time of Origen and Paul of Tella, or they may have come about in the transmission of the text of SH after the time of Paul of Tella.

III. *Examples which have no signs in SH.*

In the remaining forty-five examples of doublets in LXX, the Syro-Hexaplar shows no Origenian signs, or it may not even have the double translation in the text. On the basis of the conclusions reached in Section I, however, it is possible in some cases to see clearly what is the OG, and what is Hexaplaric in the doublet material. Only those examples are given here where there seems to be no doubt concerning the nature of the double readings.

2 18 M has the phrase וְאֶל־רְפָאִים, "and to the Rephaim, or, shades," which is translated twice in the Greek:

καὶ παρὰ τῷ ᾅδῃ μετὰ τῶν γηγενῶν

'ΑΣ (μετὰ) ῥαφαείν

Θ (μετὰ) τῶν γιγάντων

παρὰ τῷ ᾅδῃ is therefore OG; μετὰ τῶν γηγενῶν is Hexaplaric, with its origin clearly seen here in the translation of Θ.

8 10b M "And knowledge rather than choice gold."

B καὶ γνῶσιν ὑπὲρ χρυσίον δεδοκιμασμένον.

A, with numerous minuscules having substantially the same reading: ἀνθαιρεῖσθε δὲ αἴσθησιν χρυσίου καθαροῦ.

B, which is closer to Hebrew, is probably Hexaplaric; the other reading is OG.

11 18b M "But he who soweth righteousness [has] a sure reward."

LXX σπέρμα δὲ δικαίων μισθὸς ἀληθείας

Another reading is: ὁ σπείρων δικαιοσύνην ἐργάζεται πίστιν (Clem)

LXX seems to be closer to Hebrew, and therefore Hexaplaric; the other reading is OG.

17 18 For M תֹּקֵעַ LXX reads: ἐπικροτεῖ καὶ ἐπιχαίρει.

Θ ἐπικροτήσει

ἐπιχαίρει is therefore OG; ἐπικροτεῖ is Hexaplaric, with its origin clearly seen in Θ.

17 23 M "to pervert the ways . . ."

LXX οὐ κατευοδοῦνται ὁδοί . . . ἐκκλίνει ὁδούς

Σ ἐκκλίνειν ὁδούς

The first translation in LXX is OG; the second, which is closer to the Hebrew, is Hexaplaric, with its origin clearly seen in Σ.

19 10b M "Much less for a servant to rule over princes."

LXX *καὶ ἐὰν οἰκέτης ἄρξηται μεθ' ὕβρεως δυναστεύειν.*
Another reading: *οὐδὲ δούλῳ ἐξουσιάζειν ἀρχόντων* 248, 252, Θ.

LXX is OG; the other reading is closer to Hebrew, and so Hexaplaric, with its origin ascribed to Θ.

24 26b M "Who returns right words."

LXX *ἀποκρινόμενα λόγους ἀγαθούς.*
λόγους ἀγαθούς]+*ὃς δὲ ἀποκρίνεται λόγους ἐνωπίους* V, 149, 260

LXX is OG; the other reading is closer to Hebrew, and so Hexaplaric.

29 7b M "The wicked does not understand to know it."

LXX a *ὁ δὲ ἀσεβὴς οὐ νοεῖ γνῶσιν,*
b *καὶ πτωχῷ οὐχ ὑπάρχει νοῦς ἐπιγνώμων.*

a is closer to Hebrew, and so Hexaplaric. b=OG. In b, רָשׁ (*πτωχῷ*) was read for רָשָׁע.

THE COLUMNAR ORDER OF THE HEXAPLA*

By Harry M. Orlinsky

Baltimore Hebrew College

The purpose of the present study is to suggest a motive on the part of Origen for drawing up his six-columned Bible, the Hexapla, and especially for arranging the six columns in the order that he did, that has escaped notice hitherto.

As is well known, the Jews of Alexandria and other centers in Egypt had forgotten their mother tongue Hebrew to so great an extent that already in the third century B. C. E. they could no longer read or study the Bible in the original. In the course of the next century or so a Greek translation of the Old Testament, the Septuagint, was made for them, and they used it in study and in prayer much the same as the preceding generations had used the Hebrew original.[1]

But after the Roman conquest of Palestine and the rise of Christianity, certain conditions arose whereby the Septuagint fell into great disfavor in the eyes of the Jews. The most important reasons, for our present purpose, for this complete change of attitude were three in number: (1) Christians from the very beginning adopted the Septuagint as their own, thereby compelling the Jews to fall back upon

*Read at the meeting of the American Oriental Society in Ann Arbor, Mich., April 25, 1935. The present writer wishes to take this opportunity to thank Profs. Speiser, Sperber and Montgomery for their interest and suggestions in connection with this study.

[1] See in general, Swete, *An Introduction to the Old Testament in Greek*[2], part 1, chaps. II–III; Driver, *Notes on the Hebrew Text . . . of the Books of Samuel*,[2] Introd., §3.

Reprinted from *Jewish Quarterly Review*. New Series, Vol. 27. 1936-7.

the Hebrew Bible, which they were no longer able to read in the original; (2) the Septuagint, spread among the many Jewish and Christian communities of Africa, Palestine, Syria, Asia Minor and Mesopotamia, without a central authority to preserve its original text and to censor reproductions and translations therefrom, fairly rapidly became colored by the theological and political beliefs of each of these communities, especially in the course of the many fierce theological battles among Christian groups and between Christians and Jews; (3) a more or less fixed text of the Hebrew Canon had been drawn up, probably by Rabbi Akiba or his school, about the middle of the second century C. E., a text by and large identical with that preserved in the Masorah to-day, but differing considerably from the Hebrew texts in use four centuries earlier upon which the Septuagint had been based.[2]

As a result of these developments, it became apparent in Jewish circles that a new Greek translation to conform to the current Hebrew text and to their own traditions and exegesis had become absolutely imperative. In a short time at least three new translations of the Old Testament came into existence, those of Theodotion,[3] Aquila and Symmachus.[4] Aquila's translation was slavishly literal, reproducing every dot and tittle of the Hebrew text, even the etymology of many words.[5] Symmachus, on the other

[2] See in general, Swete, op. cit., 197–230; 381–432; 462–77; Buhl, *Canon and Text of the Old Testament*, 50–75. Cf. also the Introductions, e. g., Bleek-Wellhausen, Driver.

[3] On the relative order of these three, see note 14 below.

[4] For discussions of these three as well as of other translations, see Field, *Origenis Hexaplorum*, vol. I, Prolegomena, Chaps. II–V, VIII; Swete, op. cit., 53 ff.; Rahlfs, *Psalmi Cum Odis*, Göttingen, 1931, p. 60; "Quis Sit ὁ Σύρος" in *König. Gesell. der Wiss. zu Göttingen*, 1915, 420–28; Bloch, "ὁ Σύρος and the Peshitta," in *Jewish Studies in Memory of Israel Abrahams*, New York, 1927, 66–73.

[5] Cf. Reider, *Prolegomena to a Greek-Hebrew and Hebrew-Greek Index to Aquila*, Philadelphia, 1916, ch. I.

hand, willingly sacrificed literalness for the sake of Greek idiom. Theodotion supplied the golden mean between the other two, adhering to the Hebrew text faithfully and yet turning out a Greek version that was quite readable.

Now so far as the Jews were concerned, their task was completed. They had a Bible for those comparatively few who understood Hebrew, and Greek translations based upon the current text of that Bible for those who knew Greek only. But for the Christians the task had just begun, for not only did their Bible, the Septuagint, differ from the current Hebrew text, or as they called it, the *ueritas hebraica*, but the very term "Septuagint" had become meaningless in that hardly any two of the numerous Greek Mss. of the Old Testament, each one claiming to represent the original Greek translation, agreed with each other.[6]

To a methodical and pious character like Origen[7] the situation was unbearable. As scholar he could not depend with any degree of confidence upon any one Greek Ms. of the Old Testament as opposed to the other, and upon none as opposed to the current Hebrew text. As theologian he, and so too his fellow Christians, found himself at a great disadvantage in polemizing against the Jews. The latter on the one hand had at their disposal passages in their Hebrew Bible that were lacking in the Septuagint, and on

[6] It should be pointed out that it was not a question of a single authoritative original Greek translation having undergone "corrections" and corruptions. There must have been numerous "original" translations, contemporaneous perhaps, but independent of each other. Cf. Sperber, "Septuagintaprobleme" (in *Beitr. zur Wiss. von A. u. N. T.*, Dritte Folge, Heft 13) 1929; *Tarbiz*, VI (1934–35), 1–29; *JBL*, LIV (1935), 73–92. The present writer hopes to discuss this problem in the near future.

[7] Cf. Wescott, article "Origenes" in *Dict. of Christian Biography*, vol. IV, 96–142; E. de Faye, *Origen and His Work*, New York, 1929, p. 171 f., "so remarkable a scholar . . . from beginning to end of his work, we find the purest Christian spirit."

the other scorned to accept as evidence passages found in the Septuagint to which the Hebrew Bible had nothing to correspond.[8]

And so it is commonly accepted to-day that it was only to satisfy the scholarly and theological wants of himself and of his Christian contemporaries that Origen set before himself the prodigious task of recovering and fixing the true text of the Septuagint of the entire Old Testament,[9] and that for these purposes alone he arranged in six parallel columns: (i) the current Hebrew text in Hebrew characters; (ii) column (i) transliterated in Greek characters;[10] (iii)

[8] It was not at all a question of it being "*unfair* [italics ours] to the Jew to quote against him passages from the LXX. which were wanting in his own Bible . . . " (Swete, op. cit., p. 61). Origen himself admits in his *Epistola ad Africanum*, ed. Lommatzsch, vol. XVIII, §5, τοιαύτης γὰρ οὔσης ἡμῶν τῆς πρὸς αὐτοὺς ἐν ταῖς ζητήσεσι παρασκευῆς, οὐ καταφρονήσουσιν, οὐδ', ὡς ἔθος αὐτοῖς, γελάσονται τοὺς ἀπὸ τῶν ἐθνῶν πιστεύοντας, ὡς τ' ἀληθῆ καὶ παρ' αὐτοῖς ἀναγεγραμμένα ἀγνοοῦντας, "For if we are so prepared for them in our discussions, *they will not, as is their manner, scornfully laugh at Gentile believers* [italics ours] for their ignorance of the true reading as they have them."

[9] Cf., e g., Schürer, *Geschichte des Jüdischen Volkes*, vol. III, p. 429, "Es sollte damit eine sichere Grundlage geschaffen werden für gelehrte theologische Exegese . . . ;" Swete, op. cit., p. 61, "Origen held that Christians must be taught frankly to recognise the divergences between the LXX. and the current Hebrew text . . . (and that it was) injurious to the Church herself to withhold from her anything in the Hebrew Bible which the LXX. did not represent."

[10] As demonstrated long ago by Blau, *Zur Einleitung in die Heilige Schrift*, Budapest, 1894, pp. 80–99 (cf. also Schürer, op. cit., vol. III, 140 ff.), transliterations into Greek of the Hebrew text of the Pentateuch and of those sections of the Prophets and Hagiographa that were read in the synagogue as Haftarahs and Megillot, had been in existence for centuries for the use of those Jews who could not read or pray from the Bible in Hebrew characters and yet did not wish to do so from a Greek translation; for their purpose a Greek transliteration would be quite adequate, since they would then be uttering the prayer in the sacred tongue.

Tychsen (*Tentamen de Variis Codicum Hebraicorum Vet. Test. Mss Generibus*, Rostochii, 1772) and more recently and far more fully Wutz

Aquila; (iv) Symmachus; (v) the text of the Septuagint corrected by himself with the aid primarily of Aquila, Symmachus and Theodotion, to agree as closely as possible with the current Hebrew text in columns (i) and (ii); (vi) Theodotion.

But a few problems arise at this point. (A) Why should Origen have gone to the trouble of reproducing the Hebrew text in his six-columned Bible? There were plenty of copies available for anybody in need of one. And if the motive were his scholarly sense of completeness, then the question could be posed: of what value would the Hebrew text in his Hexapla be to any of his Christian colleagues when hardly a single one of them had any knowledge of Hebrew?[11]

("Die Transkriptionen von der Septuaginta bis zu Hieronymus," in *Beitr. zur Wiss. vom A. u. N. T.*, 1925, 1933. See also his *Die Psalmen*, München, 1925) developed the theory that the Septuagint of the Old Testament was a translation made from a Hebrew text written not in Hebrew but in Greek characters. This theory has been subjected to such thoroughgoing criticism that ere long it will be remembered as nothing more than a curiosity. The present writer recently completed a doctoral thesis at the Dropsie College on "The Relationship between the Septuagint and Masoretic Texts of the Book of Job," in which Wutz's Job passages are discussed in detail. For the best use of the second column in reconstructing the pronunciation of Hebrew, see Speiser's thesis, *JQR*, XVI (1926), 344–82; XXIII (1932), 233–65; XXIV (1933), 9–46 (to be continued). On the morphology, see Prof. Sperber's forthcoming monograph.

[11] Cf. Elliot's extensive article, "Hebrew Learning," in *Dict. of Christian Biography*, vol. II, p. 872, "With the exception of Jerome, and perhaps of Origen, none of the early Christian writers appear to have possessed any knowledge of Hebrew which was worthy of the name." Edmund Stein, in his *Alttestamentliche Bibelkritik in der Späthellenistischen Literatur*, Lwów, 1935, 30 ff. [reprinted from *Collectanea Theologica*, XVI (1935)] states that " . . . Porphyrius sich ausschliesslich auf Theodotion [of Daniel] stütze. Hätte er die Kenntnis des Hebräischen besessen, so würde es ihm kaum entgangen sein, dass das Wort מעזים in dem Modin [Μαωζειμ>Μωδεμ/ν] keinen Sinn geben würde." But surely Porphyry's non-use of the Hebrew was due not to the fact that "für das Buch Daniel das Griechische als die Sprache des Originals

(B) The same difficulties raised by the presence of col. (i) apply to the presence of col. (ii) also. True, Origen's fellow Christians would be enabled to pronounce the Hebrew of col. (i) through the medium of the Greek alphabet in the column immediately following, but the mere uttering of the Hebrew would in nowise help them understand what they were reading.[12] It is not too much to assume, therefore, that the presence of cols. (i) and (ii) would be of practically no assistance to non-Jews, who knew very little or no Hebrew, in squaring the Septuagint with the current Hebrew text.

And when we turn to examine the relative order of each of the six columns of the Hexapla, we find ourselves confronted by problems no less perplexing. That chronology did not enter into the columnar make-up of the Hexapla[13] is evident from the fact that the Septuagint of col. (v) antedated cols. (ii), (iii) and (iv), and that Theodotion in

angenommen hat," but to his inability to make use of a Hebrew or Aramaic original. The statement of Sutcliffe, "The Venerable Bede's Knowledge of Hebrew," *Biblica*, XVI (1935), p. 305, "Bede (died 735) had no knowledge of Hebrew beyond the few scraps of information he was able to glean from the writings of St. Jerome . . . Hebrew in the seventh and eighth centuries was not a tongue that could be learnt without oral assistance," holds good for the preceding centuries also.

It goes without saying, of course, that the fact that many Church Fathers reveal midrashic sources and rabbinic interpretations in their writings (for examples, and bibliography, cf. Gordon, *JBL*, XLIX (1930), 384 ff.), in no way implies that they were intimately acquainted with Hebrew or Aramaic. Oral tradition played an overwhelming rôle in these cases.

[12] For a striking analogy, compare the *Kaddish* of to-day. Many of the younger generation of Jews are unable to read the Hebrew alphabet. For their purpose, this prayer has been transliterated in some Prayer Books into English. Now although this enables them to utter the *Ḳaddish* as if they were reading directly from the Aramaic original, they do not know the meaning of the words they utter.

[13] So already Swete, op. cit., p. 64, "With regard to the order, it is clear that Origen did not mean it to be chronological."

col. (vi) flourished prior to Symmachus in col. (iv) and almost certainly even to Aquila in col. (iii).[14]

The explanation universally accepted is that "Aquila is placed next to the Hebrew text because his translation is the most verbally exact, and Symmachus and Theodotion follow Aquila and the LXX. respectively, because Symmachus on the whole is a revision of Aquila, and Theodotion of the LXX."[15] This statement, however, because of the fact that it is descriptive rather than explanatory, and that Symmachus is hardly "on the whole . . . a revision of Aquila,"[16] does not seem convincing. Moreover, it would have been far more logical for Origen to have placed his revision of the Septuagint in col. (iii), immediately after the Hebrew, so that the reader could most readily compare

[14] There is absolutely no evidence other than that based upon the column order of the Hexapla that Aquila antedated Theodotion. All evidence extant definitely points to the priority of Theodotion to Aquila. Cf. Schürer, op. cit., vol. III, 435 ff., 442; Montgomery, *Inter. Crit. Comm. on Daniel*, New York, 1927, 46 f. Yet, e. g., Rahlfs, *Septuaginta id est Vetus Testamentum Graeca Juxta LXX Interpretes*, Stuttgart, 1935, p. xi, "Bald *nach* [italics ours] Aquila . . . entstanden zwei andere griechische Übersetzungen, die des Theodotion . . ."

[15] Swete, op. cit., p. 65. For older explanations, cf. the unfortunately generally neglected work of Hody, *De Bibliorum Textibus Originalibus*, etc., Oxonii, 1705, Lib. IV, Cap. II, § 10, p. 604 f., "De ratione ordinis editionum variarum in Hexaplis." In Hody's opinion, ibid., "Aquilae et Symmachi versiones ante LXX. disposuit Origenes, qui proprius ad Heb. accedebant; Theodotioni vero post LXX. sedem tribuit, quia licet Hebraeo magis consonabat, ex ipsa tamen LXX. Versione verbatim permulta descripsit." Cf. Schürer, op. cit., p. 440, n. 15, "Die Anordnung in der Hexapla ist lediglich durch sachliche Gesichtspunkte bedingt. Origenes gibt zuerst den hebräischen Text, dann Aquila und Symmachus weil diese sich am engsten an den hebräischen Text anschliessen, darauf die LXX und neben ihnen den Theodotion, weil seine Arbeit eigentlich nur eine Revision der LXX ist." So also Rahlfs, op. cit., p. xi f.

[16] Cf. Rahlfs, ibid., "Symmachos lieferte eine ganz neue Übersetzung des A. T." See also note 27 below.

the two. Certainly the mere fact that Aquila's version, "the most verbally exact" of them all, was placed after the Hebrew text would be of little if any significance to Origen's co-religionists, for Aquila's version was only too often unintelligible to them,[17] and no comparison between it and the Hebrew text would yield anything substantial, for they knew no Hebrew.[18]

It would seem that the clue to these problems is to be found in a letter that Origen wrote to one of his contemporaries, Africanus.[19] In this Epistle, Origen strongly urged his Christian colleagues to acquaint themselves with the contents of the Hebrew text,[20] and modestly relates how difficult it was for him to carry out the investigation and

[17] It should be noted that when Origen and Jerome, for instance, praise Aquila's version, they do so only because of his extreme fidelity and ingenuity in adhering to the Hebrew text, and not at all because of his ability to make the latter, or his own version for that matter, popular amongst non-Jews. Cf. Jerome's *Epistola LVII ad Pammachium*, ed. Vallarsi, vol. I, col. 316, "Aquila autem, qui non solum verba, sed etymologias quoque verborum transferre conatus est . . . (et syllabas interpretatur et literas) . . . jure projicitur a nobis." Cf. also Rahlfs, op. cit., p. xxvi, "Aquila's translation of the Bible must on occasions have proved altogether incomprehensible to non-Jews."

[18] I note the very interesting passage in Margolis, *The Story of Bible Translations*, Philadelphia, 1917, p. 41, "Origen transcribed them [Aqu., Symm., Theod.] (as well as the other anonymous versions) in his monumental edition of the Greek Bible, where Aquila occupied the third column next to the Hebrew in the original square characters and in Greek transliteration, thus enabling the student to pronounce every Hebrew word and at once to ascertain its meaning; then came the free Symmachus, then the text of the Septuagint, then Theodotion, then in the remaining columns the other versions wherever they were available." This statement is presumably based upon the Latin scholium quoted in part in n. 25 below. See also Field, op. cit., vol. I, p. x, and note 8.

[19] *Epistola ad Africanum*, ed. Lommatzsch, vol. XVII, § 5.

[20] *τοιαύτης γὰρ οὔσης ἡμῶν τῆς πρὸς αὐτοὺς ἐν ταῖς ζητήσεσι παρασκευῆς*, "for if we are so prepared for them in discussion." Cf. also Wescott, op. cit., p. 132, "He [Origen] recognized the necessity of learning Hebrew that he might be confident as to the original form of the records of the Old Testament."

how hard he had to labor over the Hebrew text.[21] And even then he had to have frequent recourse to Jewish Rabbis.[22] Now since it was manifestly impossible for Church Fathers to consult Rabbis on every occasion that difficulties arose, especially when the difficulties were due to differences between texts to which each group adhered tenaciously, and since practically the only means of learning Hebrew was by studying under Rabbis, and since in Origen's day there was hardly a Rabbi who would be willing to teach a Church Father Hebrew in order that the latter might later on wage theological battle against the Jews with his intimate knowledge of the Hebrew text as one of his most effective weapons,[23] it would not be too much to expect from Origen,

[21] *καὶ ταῦτα δέ φημι, οὐχὶ ὄκνῳ τοῦ ἐρευνᾷν καὶ τὰς κατὰ Ἰουδαίους γραφὰς, καὶ πάσας τὰς ἡμετέρας ταῖς ἐκείνων συγκρίνειν, καὶ ὁρᾷν τὰς ἐν αὐταῖς διαφοράς. Εἰ μὴ φορτικὸν γοῦν εἰπεῖν, ἐπὶ πολὺ τοῦτο, ὅση δύναμις, πεποιήκαμεν· γυμνάζοντες αὐτῶν τὸν νοῦν ἐν πάσαις ταῖς ἐκδόσεσι καὶ ταῖς διαφοραῖς αὐτῶν,*
"Nor do I say this because I shun the labor of investigating the Jewish scriptures and comparing them with ours, and noticing their various readings. This, if it be not arrogant to say it, I have already to a great extent done to the best of my ability, laboring hard to get at the meaning in all the editions and various readings."

[22] Cf. *Epis. ad Afric.*, § 6, *οὐκ ὀλίγοις Ἑβραίοις ἀνεθέμην*; § 7, *μέμνημαι μέντοι γεφιλομαθεῖ Ἑβραίῳ*; § 8, *καὶ ἕτερον δὲ οἶδα Ἑβραῖον.*

[23] Cf. Elliot, op. cit., p. 855, "Extreme jealousy which the Jews displayed toward the Christians in regard to the acquisition of the Hebrew language was strong." Cf., e g., Sanh. 59a, ואמר ר' יוחנן עכום שעוסק בתורה חייב מיתה "R. Joḥanan [contemporary of Origen, taught in Sepphoris and Tiberias] said, 'A heathen who studies the Torah is deserving of death.'" (Cf. on this passage, Lauterbach, "The Attitude of the Jew towards the Non-Jew," in *Yearbook of the Central Conference of American Rabbis*, vol. XXXI, 1921, p. 215, " . . . R. Johanan is strongly objecting to the heathen studying the Torah and in expressing his objection in such an emphatic manner, had in mind just such heathen slanderers and enemies of the Jews who with malice and evil intent were trying to study the Torah merely in order to misinterpret its teachings so as to lend a semblance of truth to their false accusations and libellous charges against the Jews and Judaism!") Cf. also Ḥag. 13a, ואמר ר' אמי אין מוסרין תורה לגוי, "And R. Ami

about if not the only Church Father in those days to be in possession of a working knowledge of Hebrew,[24] to provide his contemporaries with the much needed facilities to learn Hebrew, and thus to be able to make use of all six columns of his Hexapla.[24a]

Nor did Origen fail his readers. The Hexapla among other things was extremely practicable for text-book purposes. The first column supplied the text in Hebrew characters; the second column taught the reader how to

[pupil of R. Johanan, contemporary of Diocletian] said, 'You must not impart the Law to a heathen.' " I owe this last reference to the kindness of Prof. Zeitlin.

[24] Cf. Wescott, op. cit., p. 132, "He [Origen] seems to have contented himself with being able to identify the Hebrew corresponding with the Greek texts before him." Even then, Jerome expresses great surprise that Origen was able to acquire in those days as much as he did. Cf. also note 11 above. In this connection, the following passage from Eusebius, *Historia Ecclesiastica*, ed. Lake-Oulton in the *Loeb Classical Library*, Book VI, § XVI, is very significant: "And so accurate was the examination that Origen brought to bear upon the divine books, that he even made a thorough study of the Hebrew tongue;" apparently an unusual phenomenon in those days. Eusebius follows this statement with, "and got into his own possession the original writings in the actual Hebrew characters which were extant among the Jews." It seems to the present writer that this passage offers additional proof that the Christians of Origen's day did not know much, if any Hebrew. The reason "the original writings in the actual Hebrew characters . . . were extant among the Jews" and not among Christians, was primarily, if not exclusively, because the latter were unable to use them due to their ignorance of Hebrew.

[24a] It would seem worth while emphasizing that a man of Origen's character and training would be just the type who would wish to provide his many disciples and friends with the means of learning Hebrew. Numerous passages in Eusebius, op. cit., bear this out amply. Cf., e. g., Book VI, §§III, VIII, XIV, XV, the last section particularly, which gives us an idea of Origen's modern pedagogic method. Origen was up-to-date in other matters also; for instance, "as he dictated [his commentaries on the Sacred Scriptures] there were ready at hand more than seven shorthand-writers, who relieved each other at fixed times, and as many copyists, as well as girls skilled in penmanship" (§XXXIII).

pronounce the Hebrew;[25] Aquila's version provided a "crib" that gave the reader not only a slavish word-for-word and even letter-for-letter "Greek or quasi-Greek equivalent for every fragment of the original," but quite often also its etymology.[26] Symmachus' version could be used and indeed was indispensable as a translation in normal Greek of the otherwise often unintelligible "Aquilanic" Greek.[27] And equipped with the knowledge gained from the first four columns, the reader was ready to tackle the most important column of them all, the Septuagint in col. (v). Theodotion in col. (vi) was not placed before the Septuagint simply because it was not necessary there for Origen's text-book purposes. It had to be included somewhere however, since it was a superior translation to Aquila and Symmachus, and was used by Origen in revising the fifth column far more frequently than these two translators together. The only position left for it was in column (vi), immediately after the Septuagint.[28]

[25] Hody, op. cit., p. 597, quotes a Latin scholium found in an Arabic Ms. of the Pentateuch, concerning the Hexapla. The second column is described as follows, "Scripturam Graecam, sermonem vero plane Hebraicum instar praecedentis, ut ita Graece ea legerent, qui scripturam Heb. nequaquam callerent."

[26] Cf. Taylor, article "Hexapla" in *Dict. of Chris. Biog.*, vol. III, p. 18. See also Jerome's statement, note 17 above. For some examples, cf. Reider, op. cit., § 10, p. 340 ff.

[27] Cf. note 17 above, "Aquila . . . jure projicitur a nobis." It should be noted that even though Symmachus' version was an independent one (cf. note 16 above), nevertheless, because it followed the Hebrew text closely, differing from Aquila's translation only in that it "was distinguished by the purity of its Greek and its freedom from Hebraisms," it could be used in the majority of cases to clarify Aquila's renderings. It was probably because of this that the belief arose that "Symmachus on the whole is a revision of Aquila."

[28] Similarly Quinta, Sexta, Septima, etc. They had to be included because they were authoritative Greek versions, but for text-book purposes they were superfluous before column (vi). The problem of the relationship between the Tetrapla and the Hexapla, the present writer hopes to discuss separately.

Nor is this all the evidence available that Origen had pedagogic reasons for the composition and arrangement of the Hexapla. Confirmation of this theory is fortunately forthcoming from an entirely different and independent angle. As a result of his analysis of the transliterations in the Hexapla,[29] Prof. Speiser arrived at the conclusion "that Origen frequently transcribed his words as he heard them instead of blindly following some particular system of transliteration,"[30] and that he endeavored "to reproduce in sound the Hebrew text current in his own days as faithfully as he knew how."[31] In other words, Origen devoted a goodly portion of time and energy[32] to developing a system whereby the Hebrew could be reproduced through the medium of Greek consonants and vowels as perfectly as was possible. That he wished thereby to preserve the current pronunciation of the Hebrew is quite clear. But that Origen at the same time provided his contemporaries with the current pronunciation of the Hebrew text as opposed to the older transliterations of portions of the Old Testament, which at best reproduced the antiquated pronunciation inadequately, is equally clear.

From the above then, it would seem reasonable to conclude that behind the formation of the Hexapla, and

[29] "The Pronunciation of Hebrew Based Chiefly on the Transliterations in the Hexapla," quoted at end of note 10 above.

[30] *JQR*, XVI (1926), 361.

[31] Idem, 363.

[32] Elliot, op. cit., p. 858, bearing in mind the fact that Origen's knowledge of Hebrew was not very extensive, concludes that col. (ii) as well as col. (i) must have been "the exclusive work of Origen's Jewish amanuenses." However, since Origen worked out his own system of transliteration [cf. *JQR*, XXIII (1932), 238; XXIV (1933), 27 f.], it is safest to agree with Swete [op. cit., p. 73; so Speiser, *JQR*, XVI (1925–26), 363] that "a large part of the labour of transcription may have been borne by . . . copyists . . . but the two Hebrew columns . . . were probably written by his [Origen's] own hand."

certainly the only reason for the order in which the six columns were drawn up, was the desire of Origen to provide his fellow Christians with a text-book wherewith to learn the Hebrew language.[33]

[33] It should be added that it is far from unlikely that one of the reasons that Origen wrote usually only one or two Hebrew words to the line was to facilitate comparison between each Hebrew word and its Greek correspondent. For specimens of the Hexapla, see Swete, op. cit., p. 62 f.; Field, op. cit., vol. I, p. xiv f.

H. M. Orlinsky, New York צ. מ. אורלינסקי, ניו־יורק

ORIGEN'S TETRAPLA — A SCHOLARLY FICTION?

About 240 C. E. the Christian scholar Origen, living in Caesarea, Palestine, compiled a Bible which consisted usually of six columns, occasionally of seven or eight or nine columns. In the days of the well-known Church Father, Eusebius (3rd — 4th cent.), this Bible came to be known popularly as the Hexapla ("six-columned Bible").

In 1934, at a meeting of the American Oriental Society, I discussed the columnar order of the Hexapla, and suggested that Origen had in mind a pedagogic motive when he arranged the first six columns as he did: The first column supplied the consonantal text in Hebrew characters; the second column, consisting of the transliteration of the Hebrew consonantal text in Greek characters (consonants and vowels), taught the Christian reader, who knew little or no Hebrew, how to read the Hebrew of column I; Aquila's version in column III gave the reader not only a slavish word-for-word and sometimes even a letter-for-letter Greek, or quasi-Greek, equivalent for every fragment of the original Hebrew in columns I and II, but quite often also its etymology; Symmachus' Greek version could be used, and indeed was often indispensable as a translation in normal Greek for the otherwise often unintelligible Aquilanic Greek; and equipped with the knowledge gained from the first four columns, the reader was ready for the most important column of them all, the Septuagint in column V; Theodotion in column VI was not placed before the Septuagint simply because it was not necessary there for Origen's textbook purposes. (See my paper on "The Columnar Order of

173[1]

Reprinted from *Proceedings of the First World Congress of Jewish Studies.* 1947, Vol. 1. Jerusalem, 1952.

the Hexapla," *Jewish Quarterly Review*, 27 [1936-37], 137-149.)

It is commonly asserted that in addition to the Hexapla, Origen compiled also a Tetrapla, that is, a four-columned Bible, consisting of the four Greek translations of the Hexapla: Aquila, Symmachus, the Septuagint, and Theodotion. In the course of time, it came to be asserted almost as commonly that Origen compiled the Tetrapla after he had compiled the Hexapla— merely deleting the Hebrew texts of columns I and II to produce the four Greek columns which constituted the Tetrapla. In a paper read before the Society of Biblical Literature in 1936, I argued, contrary to this widely accepted opinion, for the priority of the Tetrapla to the Hexapla. However, this paper was never published, because while I believed that the Tetrapla could not possibly have come into being later than the Hexapla, I was not so certain of the nature and scope of the Tetrapla: again and again I was struck by the vagueness and lack of first-hand knowledge in regard to the Tetrapla, even in the source material, a situation which does not exist at all in regard to the Hexapla. In 1937, while reviewing the primary and secondary literature on the subject, it occurred to me that there never did exist a Tetrapla as a separate work; and this is what the present paper will try to demonstrate.

It goes without saying that Eusebius and Jerome, in the fourth and fifth centuries, both of whom tell us that they saw and used Origen's Hexapla in Caesarea, would have made every effort to make use of the Tetrapla. The Tetrapla would have been a very bulky work, not much smaller than the Hexapla; thus Nestle has conservatively estimated the latter's size to have been anywhere from about 2,000 to 3,500 leaves. Eusebius and Jerome, in working on the Hexapla in Pamphilus' library, could hardly have avoided bumping into such a gigantic work. It would seem not unreasonable to infer from this that already in the days of Eusebius and Jerome the Tetrapla was not to be found along with Origen's Hexapla in the Caesarean library.

Neither was the Tetrapla apparently to be found anywhere else. Already one such as Epiphanius, Bishop of Constantia (Salamis) in Cyprus (367 — 402), whose uncritical imagination is responsible for so many curious embellishments to the Letter of Aristeas, the origin of the LXX, the origin of the Hexapla, and even the reasoning for its columnar order, the nature and significance of Origen's aristarchian signs, and the like, not even Epiphanius has anything more to say about the Tetrapla, its origin aud purpose, and its temporal relationship to the Hexapla, than this extremely vague sentence: "For the Greek is a Tetrapla when the translations of Aquila and Symmachus and the Seventy-two and Theodotion are drawn up together." I shall have to content myself here with the bare statement that actually Epiphanius knew nothing whatever concerning the Tetrapla except what he read in Eusebius.

As one reads what Origen himself, Eusebius, Jerome, and Epiphanius have to say about Origen's many-columned Bible(s), he notices at once a decided lack of precision and consistency as regards their names. So far as Origen himself is concerned, nowhere in any of his extant writings, including his more than 100 letters which Eusebius used in his Church History, do we find any name at all for his many-columned Bible. Eusebius' reference to Origen's columned work is to be found in his Church History (VI, 16), "...Thus, too, Origen traced the editions of the other translators of the Sacred Writings besides the Seventy; and besides the beaten track of translations, that of Aquila and Symmachus and Theodotion, he discovered certain others which ...in the Hexapla of the Psalms, after the well-known editions, he placed besides them not only a fifth but also a sixth and a seventh translation... and so he has left us the copies of the Hexapla, as it is called...". Thus it is clear that when referring to Origen's nine-columned

Bible in the Psalms, Eusebius does not talk of an Enneapla or the like, but of a Hexapla; such terms as Heptapla and Octopla are not used by him.

As to Jerome, it is significant that in none of his rather extensive writings do we find any term applied to Origen's columned Bible, or Bibles, other than the term Hexapla. Thus he refers to what came to be called later on, and so called today, namely, the Heptapla, Octopla, and Enneapla, on at least six widely separated occasions, simply as the Hexapla. On no less than eleven occasions in his *Epistle to Sunnia and Fretela*, in discussing the Hebrew text and the numerous Greek translations of tha book of Psalms, he makes mention of the "four well-known translations" [namely, Aquila, Symmachus, LXX, Theodotion] along with Quinta, Sexta, and Septima, and again only the term Hexapla is employed by him.

Of great importance, hitherto overlooked, is Rufinus, the younger contemporary of Eusebius and the translator into Latin of his *Church History*. For one thing, Rufinus leaves untranslated and skips over completely the vague statement in Eusebius about the Tetrapla. But of greater significance is this fact: Whereas Eusebius writes "...[Origen] has left us copies of the so-called Hexapla," Rufinus' Latin translation (made about 402) reads, "...and on account of which he [Origen] named it the Hexapla." In other words, Rufinus, without any basis and authority whatever, created a fictitious tradition that Origen himself named his columned Bible the Hexapla.

It should come as no great surprise to learn that it is none other than Epiphanius who is responsible for Origen's many-columned Bible acquiring a name in addition to that of Hexapla. Here is what Epiphanius has to say in his sort of Introduction to the Bible, popularly known as *De Mensuris et Ponderibus* ("Concerning Measures and Weights"): "For when [Origen] had placed the six translations and the Hebrew writing, in Hebrew letters and words, in one column, he placed another column over against the latter, in Greek letters but in Hebrew words... and so, in the Hexapla or Octopla..." (§7); "And Origen set forth the Scripture, placing the six columns [of the Greek] and the two columns of the Hebrew side by side... calling the books the Hexapla..." (§ 18); "When people happen upon the Hexapla or Octopla — for the Greek [columns] are a Tetrapla when the translations of Aquila, Symmachus, the Seventy-two. and Theodotion are placed together; but when these four columns are joined to the two Hebrew columns they are called the Hexapla, and when the fifth and sixth also are joined successively to these, they are called the Octopla..." (§ 14). It is clear then, that Octopla, not found in the writings of Epiphanius' predecessors and contemporaries, was just coming into use as an alternative term for Hexapla.

It was asserted above that nowhere in any of Origen's writings is there found any name for his columned Bible (or Bibles). I think that we can go even farther than that, and make this, perhaps startling statement: there is no evidence that Origen made reference to any columned Bible! It is true that all scholars in the field have stated that in Origen's writings reference is made to a columned Bible; but let us go back to the original record.

Origen touches on our general subject in three extant works; in his *Epistle to Africanus* (§ 2), in his *commentary on Matthew* (Book XV, § 14), and in some of his more than one hundred letters preserved and used in Eusebius' *Church History*. Now in both the *Epistle* and the *Commentary* Origen states merely that he compared the Septuagint translation of the Holy Scriptures with the Hebrew, noting the differences between them, marking the plus-es and the minus-es with special symbols, and paying special attention to the readings in the other Greek translations. If Origen had had in mind a columned Bible, he would surely have in some way indicated the fact that he had arranged in parallel columns the various Hebrew and Greek forms of the Scriptures. We are justified, it seems to me, in being very sceptical towards the popularly accepted assumption, derived from a rather hastily drawn conclusion, that Origen's Epistle and Commentary refer to a columned Bible. But we have more than this feeling of scepticism to go by.

In his Epistle, Origen refers twice to Aquila and Theodotion (§§ 2,3), and refers frequently to the Hebrew and Septuagint texts. Not once, however, does Origen make mention of Symmachus. Thus, with regard to a passage in Daniel (§ 2), Origen gives the Hebrew reading, points out that Aquilo agrees with it, and remarks that one Septuagint manuscript in his possession follows the Septuagint, while another follows Theodotion. Or again (§ 3), in dealing with Job, Origen points out that the Hebrew and Aquila lack a certain passage, but that it is to be found both in the Septuagint and in Theodotion. Surely Origen would have made mention in connection with these two passages of such an important Greek translation as Symmachus, if the latter were available to him at the time. It seems to me not unreasonable to infer that Origen did not have Symmachus' translation before him when he wrote the Epistle to Africanus.

Let us delve a bit into the history of Symmachus' translation. Already about 180 C. E., in his work Against the Heresies (Book III, 24), Bishop Irenaeus of Lyons, in discussing the prophecy in Isa. 7: 14, mentions and attacks the renderings of Theodotion and Aquila; he makes no reference to Symmachus. It is scarcely possible to believe that Irenaeus knew and ignored Symmachus, for this simple and sufficient reason, among others, namely, in discussing Isa. 7: 14 Irenaeus makes a violent attack on the Ebionite sect. Symmachus was an Ebionite. Had Irenaeus known Symmachus, he would surely have cited his "Ebionite" rendering and attacked it.

The clue to the problem of Symmachus is provided clearly

in Eusebius' Church History (VI, 17). Eusebius tells us that Symmachus was an Ebionite, and follows with this statement: "And memoirs too of Symmachus are still extant, in which by his opposition to the Gospel according to Matthew, he seems to hold the above-mentioned heresy. These, along with other interpretations of the Scriptures by Symmachus, Origen indicates that he had received from a certain Juliana, who, he says, inherited in her turn the books from Symmachus himself." Now we know from Palladius (Historia Lausiaca, Ch. 147), who quotes an entry allegedly made by Origen himself, that Juliana was a wealthy widow of Caesareas in Cappadocia who sheltered Origen in her house during the three years between 235 and 238 C.E. when Origen had to flee from his workshop in Caesarea in Palestine from before Emperor Maximinius who persecuted the Christians. It is clear beyond all doubt, therefore, that Origen could not have begun to compile any columned Bible before 238 C.E., for such a Bible could not have come into being without Symmachus, and Symmachus was not available before that time. (And it might be added here, neither were Quinta, Sexta, and Septima available before the same date). For lack of space, the date of the Epistle to Africanus cannot be analysed here; the bare assertion will have to suffice that no columnar Bible and no Hexaplaric text are involved (cf. §11 of the Epistle where I Kings 3: 16-28 is cited).

Three questions now ask themselves, and they require an answer: (1) If there never did exist a Tetrapla, how then did such a notion come into being already, as we saw above, in the Church History of Eusebius? (2) When Origen wrote in his Epistle and Commetary about his revision of the current Septuagint text, with the use of such aristarchian signs as the obelus, metobelus, and asterisk, if he did not have in mind any columned Bible, be it the Tetrapla or the Hexapla, what then did he have in mind? (3) When numerous marginal notes and scholia in Septuagint manuscripts make mention of a reading as deriving from the Tetrapla, whence their origin? As to (1), it will be recalled that Origen himself made no mention of any such term as Tetrapla or Hexapla; also that in the days of Eusebius, by whom Origen's nine-columned Psalter is called "the Hexapla of the Psalter," the term Hexapla was just coming into being. Jerome, too, when talking of the 6 or 7 or 8 or 9 columns, speaks usually of the term Hexapla. However, to both Eusebius and Jerome, as to their contemporaries and to those who came after them, e.g. Epiphanius, the most important columns by far were not columns I and II with their Hebrew text, but columns III-VI with their Greek text. Again and again, both Eusebius and Jerome speak of "the four well-known editions," i.e., the Greek columns of II-VI. So all-important were these four Greek columns, that the three anonymous Greek translations which Origen placed in the seventh, eighth, and ninth columns of his columned Bible came to be called not "Seventh," "Eighth," and "Ninth," but "Fifth," "Sixth," and "Seventh" (Quinta, Sexta, and Septima). Jerome frequently talks not only of the four Greek columns of Aquila, Symmachus the Septuagint, and Theodotion and calls them Hexapla, bu also makes mention of Origen's six-columned Bible and calls it simply "the four editions" (quatuor editionum; e.g. in his Prologue to the Book of Chronicles). Interesting too is the passage in his Book Concerning Illustrious Men (§ LIV), where Jerome describes the importance and characte of Origen's nine-columned Bible, and while he mentions columns III-IX specfically, he does not make mention of the Hebrew columns I and II. In short, the idea of a four-columned Bibl had its origin in the loose terminology commonly used fo Origen's six-columned Bible, when it was the all-importar four Greek columns ("Tetrapla") which were stressed rathe than all six (Hexapla). Eusebius saw and used the six-fol Bible, and tells us about it in detail. He was acquainted wit the term "Four-fold Bible" (Tetrapla); he never saw or used such a Bible; he assumed it to be a separate work of Origen's consisting of the six-columned Bible without the first two Hebrew columns, and describes it as such in the briefest and vaguest manner. Rufinus skipped over this sentence altogether in his Latin translation. and Jerome knows the term "four editions" as only another term for the Hexapla. It is thanks to Epiphanius, who took up the sentence in Eusebius, that we owe the fiction that Origen compiled a Tetrapla as well as the Hexapla. As to the second question (2): What Origen described in his Epistle to Africanus and Commentary on Matthew was his first attempt to revise the current Septuagint text to conform to the current Hebrew text. He indicated the correction and revisions in Septuagint text by the use of the obelus, metobelus, and asterisk. What Books and how much of the Bible Origen revised in this fashion, we shall probably never know. After his return from Caesarea in Cappadocia to Caesarea in Palestine, during or shortly after 238, in possession for the first time of Symmachus and some, if not all, of Quinta, Sexta, and Septima, he set about compiling his many-columned Bible. In this new Bible of his, Origen revised the Septuagint text more thoroughly than he did the first time. Since the many-columned Bible was too bulky for popular use, the fifth column alone, the revised Septuagint with all the symbols, was copied by itself and soon became the only column of the nine to remain effective and alive. And, to go on to question (3), once it came to be believed, even if erroneously, that Origen had compiled a Tetrapla apart from and later than the Hexapla, what was more natural than that this first and incomplete revision, consisting of only one column and with the same sort of symbols, should have become known as from the Tetrapla, just as the Septuagint column which circulated apart from the other columns came to be known as Hexaplaric. And because the Tetrapla was considered the later and more authoritative work of Origen, this earlier revision came to be regarded as the later and more mature revision; that is why the scribes and scholia cite the "corrected" readings in the Septuagint manuscripts as from the Tetrapla. But when they cite the Minor Versions (Aquila, Symmachus, Theodotion, Quinta, Sexta, Septima), they naturally cite them from the Hexapla; for neither they nor anyone else ever saw, for there never existed, any columns on both sides of the so-called "Tetraplaric" Septuagint text.

IV. TEXT; TRANSLATION TECHNIQUE

THE TREATMENT OF ANTHROPOMORPHISMS AND ANTHROPOPATHISMS IN THE SEPTUAGINT OF PSALMS*

ARTHUR SOFFER, New York

MUCH work has been done during the past fifteen years or so on the attitude of Septuagint translators to their Hebrew text in relation to those terms and expressions that tended to treat God as though He were a human being. The most recent discussion of this phase of Septuagint criticism, dealing with the book of Isaiah, is that by Harry M. Orlinsky (in *HUCA* 27 [1956], 193–200). Reserving for another occasion a detailed analysis of the problem in general, and of the work — albeit meager — done hitherto on the Septuagint (hereafter LXX) of Psalms in particular, we turn our attention at once to the following anthropomorphisms in the Masoretic text (hereafter MT) of Psalms and their translation in the LXX: פָּנִים, רֹאשׁ, שְׂפָתַיִם, קוֹל, פֶּה, אָזְנַיִם, עֵינַיִם, יָד, זְרוֹעַ, יָמִין, כַּף, אֶצְבָּעַת, אֶבְרָה, חֵיק, פְּעָמִים רַגְלַיִם and כְּנָפַיִם. To conclude this chapter we shall investigate those words which Edwin Hatch, in his *Essays in Biblical Greek*, has classified as "psychological terms," i. e., רוּחַ and לֵב. These terms represent the borderline cases lying between anthropomorphism and anthropopathism. They are associated in the Hebrew language with the material world or with a specific organ; consequently they are closer to anthropomorphisms than to the anthropopathisms that we will study in the following chapter, i. e., אַף, חָרוֹן, חֵמָה, עֶבְרָה, זַעַם, קֶצֶף, כַּעַס, קִנְאָה and שִׂנְאָה.

* This article constitutes the essential part of a study that was accepted by the New York School of Hebrew Union College - Jewish Institute of Religion in partial fulfilment of the requirements for the degree of Master of Hebrew Letters (1956). The writer plans to continue with the subject so as to cover other aspects of the Septuagint of Psalms in relation to the Hebrew. Here he would express his indebtedness to Prof. Harry M. Orlinsky not only for suggesting this subject to him and for the numerous and invaluable suggestions made by him in the course of the research and the composition, but also for his constant encouragement and limitless patience.

The writer should like to express his gratitude to Rabbi I. Edward Kiev, Librarian of the New York School of the College-Institute, for his generous help in matters of bibliography and research; and to Mrs. Susan Tabor of the Library staff for her assistance in finding a number of the bibliographical items.

Reprinted from *Hebrew Union College Annual,* Vol. 38, 1957.

Because so many of the Psalms are highly personal prayers directed at a God who is felt to be near, and because they include some of the most poetic passages in the Bible, the Hebrew text of the Book of Psalms abounds in anthropomorphisms and anthropopathisms. Since the Psalter was an integral part of the public worship, it would seem that the LXX translator would have taken great care to reproduce this text properly. It was this combination of factors that has led the writer to assume that the Book of Psalms lends itself admirably to an inquiry such as the one projected in this introduction.

Chapter I. Anthropomorphisms

1. (a) The פָּנִים of the Lord appears 41 times in our Book.[1] In every case but one (9.20; see below), the translator uses some form of *τὸ πρόσωπον*, even in 42.6 (see below) where the Hebrew and Greek do not coincide. Typical of פנים/*το προσωπον* are 22.25 פָּנָיו מִמֶּנּוּ (וְלֹא הִסְתִּיר)/ (*οὐδὲ ἀπέστρεψεν*) *το π. αὐτοῦ ἀπ' ἐμοῦ* and 95.2 פָּנָיו (נְקַדְּמָה) (בְּתוֹדָה)/(*προφθάσωμεν*) *το π. αὐτοῦ* (*ἐν ἐξομολογήσει*).

We might compare the literalness of the translation in the passage just given, where it is the "face" of the Lord that is involved, with the paraphrase of a similar expression in 17.13 קַדְּמָה פָנָיו (קוּמָה יְהוָה)/(*ἀνάσθητι, κύριε,*) *πρόφθασον αὐτοὺς*. Note that it is the "face" of the wicked that is paraphrased.

Now let us turn our attention to the sole instance involving the "face" of the Lord which the translator has rendered without using *το π.*, 9.20 יִשָּׁפְטוּ גוֹיִם עַל־פָּנֶיךָ / *κριθήτωσαν ἔθνη ἐνώπιόν σου*. The sense has not been changed, עַל־פָּנֶיךָ has merely been rendered idiomatically. This use of עַל־פְּנֵי is discussed by Driver in *BDB*, p. 818. It is noted that this phrase may have one of three connotations: "before," "in preference to," or "in addition to." Our example falls into the first category, which, Driver says, is more definite and distinct than לִפְנֵי. *ἐνώπιον* which the translator used here, is regularly used to translate the various forms of לִפְנֵי. Clearly, the translator was not anti-anthropomorphic when he chose to translate עַל־פָּנֶיךָ with a word which accords more closely to the meaning of the phrase than with one that is merely literal and doesn't convey the idea. One may compare here *πρότερός σου* for עַל־פָּנֶיךָ in Ex. 33.19, where the "face" is Moses', not God's.

[1] 4.7; 9.20; 10.11; 11.7; 13.2; 16.11; 17.15; 21.7, 10; 22.25; 24.6; 27.8 (*bis*), 9; 30.8; 31.17, 21; 34.17; 42.3, 6; 44.4, 25; 51.11; 67.2; 69.18; 80.4, 8, 17, 20; 88.15; 89.15, 16; 90.8; 95.2; 102.3; 104.29; 105.4; 119.58, 135; 140.14; and 143.7.

In 11.7: (כִּי־צַדִּיק יהוה צְדָקוֹת אָהֵב) יָשָׁר יֶחֱזוּ פָנֵימוֹ / *εὐθύτητα εἶδεν τὸ πρόσωπον αὐτοῦ*, the anthropomorphism inherent in פָּנֵימוֹ has been reproduced literally with *τὸ π.*; but the translator has taken it to be the subject of the verb, not its object. E. Kissane[2] says that "both Heb. and the Versions (except Targ.) make 'face' subject and 'upright' the object." Rashi takes פָּנֵימוֹ to be the subject: ואוהב אותם שפנימו יחזו ישר, "He loves those whom His face sees (as) righteous." Ibn Ezra, however, points out the difficulty involved: ולא מצאנו הפנים רואים רק העינים שהם בם "We do not find (any instance of) the face seeing, only of the eyes which are in it." He also takes exception to the idea that the plural verb could possibly have the Lord as its subject. Consequently, he takes פָּנֵימוֹ to be the object of the verb. It is apparent that the meaning of this verse is far from clear in the Hebrew; the LXX translator was faced with a problem that was essentially textual, not theological as others assert (e. g., Fr. Baethgen, "Der textkritische Wert der alten Uebersetzungen zu den Psalmen," in *Jahrbücher für protestantische Theologie*, 8 [1882], 405–459, 593–667). The plural verb of the Hebrew suggested that פָּנֵימוֹ be taken as the subject; its Greek counterpart, *τὸ πρόσωπον*, necessitated the singular *εἶδεν*. Under these circumstances, one can hardly consider his translation to be motivated by the desire to avoid an anthropomorphism — one which he did not avoid!

Nor is there any anti-anthropomorphic tendency in 42.6, 7 כִּי־עוֹד אוֹדֶנּוּ יְשׁוּעוֹת פָּנָיו: אֱלֹהַי / *ὅτι ἐξομολογήσομαι αὐτῷ. σωτήριον τοῦ προσώπου μου ὁ θεός μου.* MT פָּנָיו appears as *τοῦ προσώπου μου* i. e., the face of the Psalmist rather than of the Lord. However, one is not justified in jumping to the conclusion that the translator deliberately mistranslated his Hebrew text in order to avoid an anthropomorphism. Rather, it is clear that he read or understood: יְשׁוּעוֹת פָּנַי וֵאלֹהָי, which (together with the entire verse) actually is the closing refrain of Psalms 42 and 43 (42.12; 43.5), מַה־תִּשְׁתּוֹחֲחִי נַפְשִׁי וּמַה־תֶּהֱמִי עָלָי הוֹחִילִי לֵאלֹהִים כִּי־עוֹד אוֹדֶנּוּ יְשׁוּעוֹת פָּנַי וֵאלֹהָי: *ἵνα τί περίλυπος εἶ, ψυχή, καὶ ἵνα τί συνταράσσεις με; ἔλπισον ἐπὶ τὸν θεόν, ὅτι ἐξομολογήσομαι αὐτῷ. σωτήριον τοῦ προσώπου μου ὁ θεός μου.*

In 17.15 the Greek translation does not correspond exactly with

[2] Kissane, Monsignor Edward J., *The Book of Psalms* (Dublin 1953), Vol. I, p. 48. He adds: "But this reading is generally regarded as a correction made by the scribes for dogmatic reasons." This probably refers to the plural form of the verb, which Ibn Ezra takes as definitely precluding the idea that God's face is the subject. In spite of Kissane's assertion that 'face' is the subject in the Hebrew, the Hebrew text is still obscure.

MT. But this cannot be accounted for by an anti-anthropomorphic tendency. For, as in 11.7, whatever the other difficulties, the anthropomorphism is literally reproduced rather than paraphrased: אֲנִי בְּצֶדֶק אֶחֱזֶה פָנֶיךָ אֶשְׂבְּעָה בְהָקִיץ תְּמוּנָתֶךָ: / *ἐγὼ δὲ ἐν δικαιοσύνῃ ὀφθήσομαι τῷ προσώπῳ σου, χορτασθήσομαι ἐν τῷ ὀφθῆναι τὴν δόξαν σου*. Since the translator has reproduced פָּנֶיךָ literally with *τῷ προσώπῳ σου* it would be strange if his rendering of תְּמוּנָתֶךָ by *τὴν δόξαν σου* were motivated by an objection against attributing form to the Deity. This being the sole instance of תְּמוּנָה in Psalms, it would be difficult to demonstrate that anti-anthropomorphism is involved in its translation by *δόξα*. It would be equally difficult to prove the contrary; but certainly the burden of the proof does not rest on those who aren't able to see that anti-anthropomorphism is involved. The burden of the proof rests on those (such as Baethgen, p. 605) who advance that hypothesis. Methodologically, the fact that *δόξα* is generally used to translate כָּבוֹד has no bearing on the question. The use of *δόξα* would be pertinent only if it could be demonstrated that the translator has used *δόξα* in this case of the תְּמוּנָה of the Lord instead of using another word, one which he generally uses to translate תְּמוּנָה when the Lord is not involved. Furthermore, for the evidence to be really convincing, it ought to come from the same Book, presumably the work of a single translator. Since this is the sole instance of תְּמוּנָה in Psalms, it is manifestly impossible to prove that anti-anthropomorphism is involved in its translation by *δόξα*.

However, we shall still consider the possibility. Since Psalms affords only one example of תְּמוּנָה, we turn our attention to the Pentateuch, where it appears 8 times. In 7 instances it is translated by *ὁμοίωμα*. *ὁμοίωμα* is used to translate the תְּמוּנָה of the Lord in Deut. 4.12, 15 as well as the תְּמוּנָה not involving the Lord in Ex. 20.4; Deut. 4.16, 23, 25; and 5.8. It appears that the translators of Exodus and Deuteronomy did not feel constrained to avoid the translation of the תְּמוּנָה of God as *ὁμοίωμα*, or to choose an especially anti-anthropomorphic word with which to translate תְּמוּנָה when it involved the Lord.

There is, however, one more instance of תְּמוּנָה in the Pentateuch. It occurs in Numbers 12.8, where God is said to have spoken with Moses "mouth to mouth," פֶּה אֶל־פֶּה אֲדַבֶּר־בּוֹ וּמַרְאֶה וְלֹא בְחִידֹת וּתְמֻנַת יְהוָה יַבִּיט / *στόμα κατὰ στόμα λαλήσω αὐτῷ ἐν εἴδει καὶ οὐ δι' αἰνιγμάτων, καὶ τὴν δόξαν κυρίου εἶδεν*. We might note that the use of *δόξα* here may have been recalled by the translator of Psalms when he came to תְּמוּנָה in Ps. 17.15; on the other hand, the similarity may be pure coincidence, both translators having independently understood that the תְּמוּנָה of the Lord is His *δόξα*. In connection with this use of δόξα in the Pentateuch, C. T. Fritsch (*The Anti-Anthropomorphisms of the Greek Pentateuch* [Princeton, 1943], 9) says that "the very idea of ascribing form to God is carefully avoided in the Greek of Num. 12.8"; and he uses the latter part of the verse as his third example in the chapter on anti-anthropomorphisms, examples which he defines as instances where "in their attempt to spiritualize the conception of God, the translators of the Greek Old Testament avoided, to some extent, those representations which invested the deity with human form." Had Fritsch considered and cited the first part of the verse, where פֶּה אֶל־פֶּה אֲדַבֶּר־בּוֹ is literally reproduced as στόμα κατὰ στόμα λαλήσω αὐτῷ, he could hardly interpret the use of δόξα for תְּמוּנָה as an anti-anthropomorphism. To use his own phrase, "the very idea of ascribing form to God" and one of "those representations which invested the Deity with human form" is carefully reproduced in the Greek of Num. 12.8. Whatever the translator's reason for using δόξα in Num. 12.8 or in Ps. 17.15, it was clearly not anti-anthropomorphism. Moreover, we have no basis for assuming that he considered using ὁμοίωμα and rejected it in favor of δόξα; δόξα may have been the first word that suggested itself to him. Even if he did reject ὁμοίωμα, a better explanation can be found than that of anti-anthropomorphism which involves us in the inconsistency of the translator's being anti-anthropomorphic at the end of a verse in the earlier part of which he reproduced a glaring anthropomorphism literally. For instance, it may be that he felt that ὁμοίωμα didn't properly represent the meaning of תְּמוּנָה in Num. 12.8, because תְּמוּנָה here meant the very presence of God, not a representation. ὁμοίωμα does mean a representation as it is used in Ex. 20.4; Deut. 4.16, 23, 25; and 5.8. Even in Deut. 4.12 and 15, ὁμοίωμα may mean a representation. But in Num. 12.8 and in Ps. 17.15 תְּמוּנָה means God's own physical manifestation,[3] for which the translator chooses to use δόξα. Fritsch came close to the point but missed it. By using δόξα in Num. 12.8, what the translator avoided was not "the very idea of ascribing form to God," but the very idea that Moses gazed on a representation of the Deity rather than on God Himself. Similarly, in Ps. 17.15 :אֶשְׂבְּעָה בְהָקִיץ תְּמוּנָתֶךָ / χορτασθήσομαι ἐν τῷ ὀφθῆναι τὴν δόξαν σου, the translator has correctly communicated the idea that the Psalmist will be satisfied when God Himself appears; not with an

[3] Cf. Ioh. Fr. Schleusner, *Novus Thesaurus Philologico-Criticus sive Lexicon in LXX . . . Veteris Testamenti* (Lipsiae, 1820), s. δόξα. He points out that δόξα is used in Ps. 17.15 because in that instance תְּמוּנָה "non solum *imaginem* sed etiam *faciem* notat . . ."

ὁμοίωμα of Him, but with His *δόξα*. This is similar to that which Moses requested (Ex. 33.18), וַיֹּאמַר הַרְאֵנִי נָא אֶת־כְּבֹדֶךָ׃ / *καὶ λέγει Δεῖξόν μοι τὴν σεαυτοῦ δόξαν*, and to which God replied (v. 19), וַיֹּאמֶר אֲנִי אַעֲבִיר כָּל־טוּבִי עַל־פָּנֶיךָ / *καὶ εἶπεν Ἐγὼ παρελεύσομαι πρότερός σου τῇ δόξῃ μου* and vv. 22, 23 וְהָיָה בַּעֲבֹר כְּבֹדִי וְשַׂמְתִּיךָ בְּנִקְרַת הַצּוּר וְשַׂכֹּתִי כַפִּי עָלֶיךָ עַד עָבְרִי׃ וַהֲסִרֹתִי אֶת־כַּפִּי וְרָאִיתָ אֶת־אֲחֹרָי וּפָנַי לֹא יֵרָאוּ׃ / *ἡνίκα δ' ἂν παρέλθῃ μου ἡ δόξα, καὶ θήσω σε εἰς ὀπὴν τῆς πέτρας καὶ σκεπάσω τῇ χειρί μου ἐπὶ σέ, ἕως ἂν παρέλθω. καὶ ἀφελῶ τὴν χεῖρα, καὶ τότε ὄψῃ τὰ ὀπίσω μου, τὸ δὲ πρόσωπον μου οὐκ ὀφθήσεταί σοι.* In passing, we might note the fidelity with which the translator has reproduced the anthropomorphisms כַּף, אָחוֹר and פָּנִים in these verses from Exodus. It is also apparent that *δόξα*, which is used for כָּל־טוּבִי as well as for כְּבֹדִי, represents the פָּנִים of God; and it is in this sense that it is used for תְּמוּנָה by the translator of Numbers (12.8) and also in Ps. 17.15.

Our excursus to Exodus 33 is not so much a digression as it may seem at first. For it is in that chapter that we can find our translator's reason for rendering אֶחֱזֶה פָנֶיךָ in Ps. 17.15 as *ὀφθήσομαι τῷ προσώπῳ σου*, with the verb in the passive rather than in the active voice. Before explaining *ὀφθήσομαι* with the hypothesis of a deliberate, theologically motivated exegesis, it is the responsibility of the scholar to exhaust the less striking possibilities. To begin with, one must recognize that the idea of man's seeing the "face" of the Lord conflicted with the Pentateuchal theology as expressed specifically in Ex. 33.20 וַיֹּאמֶר לֹא תוּכַל לִרְאֹת אֶת־פָּנָי כִּי לֹא־יִרְאַנִי הָאָדָם וָחָי׃ / *καὶ εἶπεν οὐ δυνήσῃ ἰδεῖν μου τὸ πρόσωπον· οὐ γὰρ μὴ ἴδῃ ἄνθρωπος τὸ πρόσωπόν μου καὶ ζήσεται.* With unmistakable reference to the first clause, the translator glossed the suffix of יִרְאַנִי with *τὸ πρόσωπόν μου*. The denial of man's ability to see the "face" of God is reflected in Ex. 23.15, 17; 34.20, 23, 24; Deut. 16.16 and 31.11, in all of which MT vocalizes as *Niphal* rather than *Qal* the various forms of the phrase לראת (את־) פני יהוה, and the Greek appears with the appropriate form of the passive *ὁρᾶν* (*ὀφθήσομαι*). It would still be unwarranted to conclude that the passive *ὀφθήσομαι* is used for MT אֶחֱזֶה in Ps. 17.15 as the result of a deliberate exegesis on the part of the translator. Even F. W. Mozley, who believes that "a neuter sense is given to the verb to avoid seeming irreverence," (*The Psalter of the Church* [Cambridge, 1905], p. 30), is constrained to add immediately "but in Exod. 10.28, 29 twice out of 3 times is the same change in the case of men." Moreover, it is not unlikely that the translator understood the unvocalized אחזה to mean *ὀφθήσομαι*; because of the numerous precedents in the Pentateuch, concerning which he was in possession of the tradition of reading them as verbs in the *Niphal*, he may well have thought that אחזה in Ps. 17.15 was also in the *Niphal*. Our translator was dealing with an unvocalized text; he could have understood the verb in either of two ways, both of which were justified by his Hebrew text. To say that he understood it in the way that presented no theological difficulties is not the same as saying that he deliberately chose one over the other (which would imply that if the sole reading justified by his Hebrew text conflicted with his theological ideas, he would ignore the text and proffer an unobjectionable paraphrase as a conscientious translation of scripture).

In 63.3 we have another instance of the verb חזה being translated as a passive although it appears in MT in the *Qal* voice: כֵּן בַּקֹּדֶשׁ חֲזִיתִ֑יךָ לִרְאוֹת עֻזְּךָ וּכְבוֹדֶךָ: / *οὕτος ἐν τῷ ἁγίῳ ὤφθην σοι τοῦ ἰδεῖν τὴν δύναμίν σου καὶ τὴν δόξαν σου*. Here it is not specifically the "face" of the Lord that is involved, but the Lord in His totality. Before we take *ὤφθην σοι* as an anti-anthropomorphic paraphrase of חֲזִיתִיךָ (as Baethgen [p. 420] and Mozley [p. 100] do), we should pause to recognize that this entire verse, but especially the first verb, poses a problem. The problem is one that caused difficulties not only for the LXX translator, but also for modern translators who were not at all concerned with avoiding anthropomorphisms. In the King James version, for example, the second strophe is made to precede the first: "O God, Thou art my God; early will I seek Thee, my flesh longeth for Thee as a dry and thirsty land, where no water is; To see Thy power and Thy glory, so as I have seen Thee in the sanctuary." The Revised Standard Version keeps the order of MT intact. However, חֲזִיתִיךָ appears as "I have looked upon Thee," but לִרְאוֹת is reproduced as a participle, "beholding." In the Jewish Publication Society version, חֲזִיתִיךָ appears as "I have looked for Thee." The problem is this: if חֲזִיתִיךָ means "I have seen Thee," then לִרְאוֹת cannot be a complementary infinitive meaning "to see." Kissane[4] solves the problem by emending חֲזִיתִיךָ to שִׁחַרְתִּיךָ, "So in the sanctuary do I seek Thee, to see Thy strength and Thy glory." Oesterley,[5] who translates חֲזִיתִ֑יךָ as "I beheld Thee," had to render לִרְאוֹת as "and saw." The LXX translator of our Book solved this problem by understanding חזיתיך as *ὤφθην σοι*, which allowed

[4] *Op. cit.*, pp. 268–9. "Heb. has '*I beheld Thee.*' The text is probably corrupt The context suggests something like 'I long for Thee.' " So, in his Critical Notes, he emends to שִׁחַרְתִּיךָ! F. Buhl, in *Biblia Hebraica*[3], offers: "prps בַּק' אִוִּיתִךָ; melius בִּקַּשְׁתִּי חֲזוֹתְךָ." As for myself, I am inclined to keep the problem, rather than try to justify such emendations.

[5] W. O. E. Oesterley, *The Psalms*, etc. (London, 1953), p. 305.

לִרְאוֹת to appear as a complementary infinitive, *ἰδεῖν*. Why he did not choose to reproduce חזיתיך with *εἶδόν σε*, and לִרְאוֹת as *ὀφθῆναι*, cannot be explained with any degree of certainty. But to force an explanation based on anti-anthropomorphism would be difficult in view of the unmistakable anthropomorphisms literally reproduced in verses 8 and 9 of this very chapter: וּבְצֵל כְּנָפֶיךָ אֲרַנֵּן: דָּבְקָה נַפְשִׁי אַחֲרֶיךָ בִּי תָּמְכָה יְמִינֶךָ: / *καὶ ἐν τῇ σκέπῃ τῶν πτερύγων σου ἀγαλλιάσομαι. ἐκολλήθη ἡ ψυχή μου ὀπίσω σου, ἐμοῦ ἀντελάβετο ἡ δεξιά σου.* Finally, as even Mozley points out (p. 30), in 84.8 the LXX is less "reverent" than MT: יֵרָאֶה אֶל־אֱלֹהִים / *ὀφθήσεται ὁ θεὸς τῶν θεῶν.*

(a) The compound מִפְּנֵי and its various derivatives occur 8 times in our Book with reference to the Lord (9.4; 38.4; 68.2, 3, 9; 96.9; 102.11; and 139.7). In every case it is translated literally *ἀπὸ προσώπου*, e. g., 139.7 וְאָנָה מִפָּנֶיךָ אֶבְרָח: / *καὶ ἀπὸ τοῦ προσώπου σου ποῦ φύγω;*

(b) The compound לִפְנֵי and its various derivatives do not really fall within the scope of this paper, since they can hardly be considered anthropomorphisms; they are included for the sake of completeness in the various forms of פָּנִים, and because of what we may learn about the style of the translator. There are 34 instances of לִפְנֵי, or its derivatives, involving the Lord. In 2 of these instances the translator uses some form of *πρόσωπον*: 96.13 לִפְנֵי יְהוָה כִּי בָא / *πρὸ προσώπου κυρίου ὅτι ἔρχεται*; 98.9 לִפְנֵי־יְהוָה כִּי בָא / G^A^ (G^B^ is lacking here) *ἀπὸ προσώπου κυρίου ὅτι ἔρχεται.*

The translator used *ἐνώπιον* 22 times (18.7; 19.15; 22.28; 41.13; 56.14; 61.8; 62.9; 68.4, 5; 72.9; 79.11; 86.9; 88.3; 96.6; 98.6; 100.2; 106.23; 119.169, 170; 141.2; 142.3b; and 143.2). In 22.28 וְיִשְׁתַּחֲווּ לְפָנֶיךָ כָּל־מִשְׁפְּחוֹת גּוֹיִם: / *καὶ προσκυνήσουσιν ἐνώπιόν σου πᾶσαι αἱ πατριαὶ τῶν ἐθνῶν*, Duhm, Briggs, Oesterley, and many others, may be justified in emending MT לפניך on the basis of G^BSA^ (*αὐτοῦ*), Vulgate, etc., to לְפָנָיו. On the other hand, Rahlfs, following Cyprian, reads *ἐνώπιον σου*. But whether *αυτου* or *σου*, the reference is still to the Lord.

The translator used also *ἐναντίον* 8 times (50.3; 85.14; 95.6; 97.3; 102.1; 116.9; 119.169; and 142.3a), e. g., 50.3 (יָבֹא אֱלֹהֵינוּ וְאַל־יֶחֱרַשׁ) אֵשׁ־לְפָנָיו תֹּאכֵל / (*ἥξει ὁ θεὸς ἡμῶν, καὶ οὐ παρασιωπήσεται·*) *πῦρ ἐναντίον αὐτοῦ καυθήσεται.*

There are 2 instances of periphrasis: 76.8 וּמִי־יַעֲמֹד לְפָנֶיךָ (מֵאָז אַפֶּךָ:) *καὶ τὶς ἀντιστήσεταί σοι* (*ἀπὸ τότε ἡ ὀργή σου*). Similar periphrasis is found in Esther 9.2 where וְאִישׁ לֹא־עָמַד לִפְנֵיהֶם appears as *οὐδεὶς γὰρ ἀντέστη*. That there is no objection to the idea involved (such as the denial of "place" to God) is apparent from the literal translation of Ps. 106.23: לוּלֵי משֶׁה בְחִירוֹ עָמַד בַּפֶּרֶץ לְפָנָיו / *εἰ μὴ* Μωυσῆς *ὁ ἐκλεκτὸς αὐτοῦ ἔστη ἐν τῇ θραύσει ἐνώπιον αὐτοῦ*.

The other instance occurs in 102.29: (בְּנֵי־עֲבָדֶיךָ יִשְׁכּוֹנוּ) וְזַרְעָם לְפָנֶיךָ יִכּוֹן: / (*οἱ υἱοὶ τῶν δούλων σου κατασκηνώσουσιν*,) *καὶ τὸ σπέρμα αὐτῶν εἰς τὸν αἰῶνα κατευθυνθήσεται*. As Schleusner points out, *εἰς τὸν αἰῶνα κατευθυνθήσεται* is simply a free translation of the MT reading; the supposition of לָעַד in the translator's *Vorlage* (so, e. g., Buhl in *BH*[3]) is hardly necessary.

(c) To translate מִלִּפְנֵי, *ἀπὸ προσώπου* is used, the reason being that the translator wanted to render the prefixed מִן as well as לִפְנֵי. To have used *ἐνώπιον* or *ἐναντίον* alone would not have been enough. There are 6 instances of מִלִּפְנֵי in which the Lord is involved (17.2; 51.13; 97.5 [*bis*]; and 114.7 [*bis*]). Our word is reproduced literally in every instance, e. g., 17.2 מִלְּפָנֶיךָ מִשְׁפָּטִי יֵצֵא / *ἐκ προσώπου σου τὸ κρίμα μου ἐξέλθοι*; 97.5 [*bis*]: מִלִּפְנֵי יְהוָה מִלִּפְנֵי אֲדוֹן כָּל־הָאָרֶץ / *ἀπὸ προσώπου κυρίου, ἀπὸ προσώπου κυρίου πασῆς τῆς γῆς*.

2. The ראשׁ of the Lord occurs twice in our Book, both times in the phrase מָעוֹז ראשִׁי. In 60.9 it is reproduced *κραταίωσις τῆς κεφαλῆς μου*; in 108.9, *ἀντίλημψις τῆς κεφαλῆς μου*. It goes without saying that when ראשׁ means "top," "chief," or "beginning," it is translated by *ἄκρος* (72.16), *ἄρχων* (24.7, 9), or *ἀρχή* (137.6; 139.17). As a matter of fact, in the last three instances cited, Aquila translates ראשׁ with *κεφαλή*. The LXX translator used better judgment in avoiding this literalism. But note that this occurs only in passages where the ראשׁ is not that of the Lord.

3. The שְׂפָתַיִם of God are mentioned twice in Psalms, and in both cases the translation is literal: 17.4 בִּדְבַר שְׂפָתֶיךָ / *διὰ τοὺς λόγους τῶν χειλέων σου*; 89.35 (לֹא אֲחַלֵּל בְּרִיתִי) וּמוֹצָא שְׂפָתַי לֹא אֲשַׁנֶּה: / *καὶ τὰ ἐκπορευόμενα διὰ τῶν χειλέων μου οὐ μὴ ἀθετήσω*.

4. The קוֹל of the Lord occurs 13 times in our Book (18.14; 29.3, 4 *bis*, 5, 7, 8, and 9; 46.7; 68.34; 81.12; 95.7; and 106.25) and is always translated literally by *φωνή*, e. g., 18.14 (וַיַּרְעֵם בַּשָּׁמַיִם יְהוָה) וְעֶלְיוֹן יִתֵּן קֹלוֹ / *καὶ ὁ ὕψιστος ἔδωκεν φωνὴν αὐτοῦ*; 29.5 (שֹׁבֵר אֲרָזִים) קוֹל־יהוה / *φωνὴ κυρίου* (*συντρίβοντος κέδρους*). When the translator does, however, paraphrase קוֹל — by *προσευχή* — the voice is the Psalmist's, not God's, e. g., 64.2 שְׁמַע־אֱלֹהִים קוֹלִי בְשִׂיחִי / *εἰσάκουσον, ὁ θεός, τῆς φωνῆς* (G[B] *τῆς προσευχῆς*) *μου*; 130.2 אֲדֹנָי שִׁמְעָה בְקוֹלִי / *κύριε, εἰσάκουσον τῆς φωνῆς* (G[A] *τῆς προσευχῆς*) *μου*. Were there any strong objection to this anthropomorphism, he might well have used *λόγος*, which appears for קול in Jer. 38.20[6] and which would have accorded well with Alexandrian philosophical terminology. It may be noted that although the attribution of speech and voice to the Lord constitutes anthropomorphism, even the Targums do not paraphrase or employ hypostases of God when these terms are used in reference to Him.

5. There are 7 instances of the פֶּה of the Lord (18.9; 33.6; 105.5; 119.13, 72, 88; and 138.4) in our Book. It is regularly translated by *τὸ στόμα* except in 18.9, (עָלָה עָשָׁן בְּאַפּוֹ) וְאֵשׁ־מִפִּיו תֹּאכֵל / (*ἀνέβη καπνὸς ἐν ὀργῇ αὐτοῦ,*) *καὶ πῦρ ἀπὸ προσώπου αὐτοῦ κατεφλόγισεν*. פיו appears as *πρόσωπον* here and also in 55.22, which is discussed in § **19** below. In MT of this verse the Lord is not the subject, but He is taken as such by the LXX translator, חָלְקוּ מַחְמָאֹת פִּיו (וּקֲרָב־לִבּוֹ) / *διεμερίσθησαν ἀπὸ ὀργῆς τοῦ προσώπου αὐτοῦ* (*καὶ ἤγγισεν ἡ καρδία αὐτοῦ*). That neither anti-anthropomorphism nor any theological consideration is involved in 18.9 and 55.22 would seem clearly indicated by the literalness of the other 6 instances, e. g., 33.6 (בִּדְבַר יהוה שָׁמַיִם נַעֲשׂוּ) וּבְרוּחַ פִּיו כָּל־צְבָאָם: / (*τῷ λόγῳ τοῦ κυρίου οἱ οὐρανοὶ ἐστερεώθησαν*) *καὶ τῷ πνεύματι τοῦ στόματος αὐτοῦ πᾶσα ἡ δύναμις αὐτῶν*.

Some scholars would explain *ἀπὸ τοὺ προσώπου αὐτοῦ* in these two verses as from מִלְּפָנָיו (for MT (וּ)מִפִּיו), but this is not likely. (1) Two independent instances are involved, in the second of which (55.22) מִלְּפָנָיו would be senseless; (2) In Prov. 2.6 (כִּי־יהוה יִתֵּן חָכְמָה) מִפִּיו דַּעַת וּתְבוּנָה is likewise reproduced by (*ὅτι κύριος δίδωσιν σοφίαν*) *καὶ ἀπὸ προσώπου αὐτοῦ* (*γνῶσις καὶ σύνεσις*) — where some would assume "G וּמִפָּנָיו vel וּמִלְּפָנָיו" (e. g., Beer, in *BH*[3]). Three such instances of *πρόσωπον* / (מִ)פִּיו render מִ(לְ)פָנָיו most unlikely.

6. There are 11 instances in our Book of the "ear(s)" (אֹזֶן־אָזְנַיִם) of the Lord (10.17; 17.6; 18.7; 31.3; 34.16; 71.2; 86.1; 88.3; 102.3; 116.2; and 130.2). It is always translated as *οὖς–ὦτα*, e. g., 10.17 תַּקְשִׁיב אָזְנֶךָ: / *προσέσχεν τὸ οὖς σου*; 116.2 כִּי־הִטָּה אָזְנוֹ לִי / *ὅτι ἔκλινεν τὸ οὖς αὐτοῦ ἐμοί*.

The verb הֶאֱזִין occurs 15 times in Psalms. To translate it, *ἐνωτίζεσθαι* is used 11 times. Of these eleven, the verb occurs with the Lord as subject 9 times (5.2; 17.1; 39.13; 54.4; 55.2; 84.9; 86.6; 140.7; and 143.1), once with man as the subject (49.2), and once, with the idols (135.17). For the remaining 4 instances of הֶאֱזִין, *προσέχειν* is

[6] LXX 45.20, where שְׁמַע־נָא בְּקוֹל יהוה appears as *ἄκουσον τὸν λόγον κυρίου*.

used. Of these four instances, it occurs with the Lord as the subject 3 times (77.2; 80.2; and 141.1) and with man as the subject, once (78.1). The following examples should suffice to illustrate: 55.2 הַאֲזִינָה אֱלֹהִים תְּפִלָּתִי / *ἐνώτισαι, ὁ θεός, τὴν προσευχήν μου*; 77.2 (קוֹלִי אֶל־ אֱלֹהִים) וְהַאֲזִין אֵלָי / (*φωνῇ μου πρὸς τὸν θεόν,*) *καὶ προσέσχεν μοι.*

προσέχειν also occurs in a case involving the Lord, where the anthropomorphic verb does not appear in the Hebrew but has been added by the translator for stylistic effect: 22.2 אֵלִי אֵלִי לָמָה עֲזַבְתָּנִי / *ὁ θεὸς, ὁ θεός μου, πρόσχες μοι· ἵνα τί ἐγκατέλιπές με.*

7. There are 12 instances in MT Psalms of the עֵינַיִם־עַיִן ("eyes") of the Lord. Of these, 10 are translated literally by *ὀφθαλμός* (5.6; 11.4; 17.2; 18.25; 31.23; 32.8; 33.18; 34.16; 90.4; and 139.16). Some examples are: 11.4 עֵינָיו יֶחֱזוּ (עַפְעַפָּיו יִבְחֲנוּ בְּנֵי אָדָם:) / *οἱ ὀφθαλμοὶ αὐτοῦ εἰς τὸν πένητα ἀποβλέπουσιν, (τὰ βλέφαρα αὐτοῦ ἐξατάζει τοὺς υἱοὺς τῶν ἀνθρώπων)*; 31.23 נִגְרַזְתִּי מִנֶּגֶד עֵינֶיךָ / *ἀπέρριμμαι ἄρα ἀπὸ προσώπου τῶν ὀφθαλμῶν σου.* In the remaining 2 instances, both cases of prepositional בְּעֵינֵי, the translator correctly used the preposition *ἐνώπιον, ἐναντίον*: 51.6 וְהָרַע בְּעֵינֶיךָ עָשִׂיתִי / *καὶ τὸ πονηρὸν ἐνώπιόν σου ἐποίησα*; 116.15 יָקָר בְּעֵינֵי יְהוָה (הַמָּוְתָה לַחֲסִידָיו:) / *τίμιος ἐναντίον κυρίου (ὁ θάνατος τῶν ὁσίων αὐτοῦ).*

In 17.2 עֵינֶיךָ תֶּחֱזֶינָה מֵישָׁרִים: becomes *οἱ ὀφθαλμοί μου ἰδέτωσαν εὐθύτητας*, and it is not unlikely that the LXX translator based his reading on an original עֵינַי, which accords well with the context; cf. e. g., Buhl in *BH*[3], "G עֵינַי prb recte."

90.4, which is cited above, is an instance where the translator is more literal in rendering an "anthropomorphism" in a case involving the Lord than he is with the same phrase when God is not involved. Although בְּעֵינֵי is generally reproduced *ἐνώπιον* or *ἐναντίον*, in 90.4, where it is the Lord that is addressed, the figure of speech is literally spelled out: *ἐν ὀφθαλμοῖς σου.* Of course, in view of 51.6 and 116.15, one can hardly say that the translator is especially literal in cases involving God; and it is hardly more than coincidence that in every instance of בְּעֵינֵי with reference to *man* the "anthropomorphism" is avoided by the use of *ἐνώπιον* (15.4; 36.3; and 72.14) or *ἐναντίον* (73.6 and 98.2).

8. The יָד־יָדַיִם of the Lord occur 38 times in our Book,[7] and in every instance it is reproduced literally by the appropriate form of *ἡ χείρ*,

[7] 8.7; 10.12, 14; 17.14; 19.2; 28.5; 31.6, 16; 32.4; 38.3; 39.11; 44.3; 74.11; 75.9; 78.42; 80.18; 81.15; 88.6; 89.14, 22; 92.5; 95.4, 5, 7; 102.26; 104.28; 106.26; 109.27; 111.7; 119.73, 173; 136.12; 138.7, 8; 139.10; 143.5; 144.7; and 145.16.

e. g., 10.12 (קוּמָה יְהוָה אֵל) נְשָׂא יָדֶךָ / ὑψωθήτω ἡ χείρ σου; 32.4 (כִּי יוֹמָם וָלַיְלָה) תִּכְבַּד עָלַי יָדֶךָ / ἐβαρύνθη ἐπ' ἐμὲ ἡ χείρ σου; 89.14 (לְךָ זְרוֹעַ עִם גְּבוּרָה) תָּעֹז יָדְךָ (תָּרוּם יְמִינֶךָ:) / (σὸς ὁ βραχίων μετὰ δυναστείας·) κραταιωθήτω ἡ χείρ σου, (ὑψωθήτω ἡ δεξιά σου).

In 55.21 there is an instance of יָדָיו which the translator takes to be the hand of the Lord although it would hardly seem proper to say this of Him: שָׁלַח יָדָיו (בִּשְׁלֹמָיו חִלֵּל בְּרִיתוֹ:) / ἐξέτεινεν τὴν χεῖρα αὐτοῦ (ἐν τῷ ἀποδιδόναι· ἐβεβήλωσαν τὴν διαθήκην αὐτοῦ). Cf. further **§5** (פֶּה) above and **§19** (לֵב) below. The entire passage, 55.20–22, is very difficult to understand in MT, and the pronominal references are uncertain. But the LXX translator, in trying to clarify it, seems to take the Lord to be the subject of יָדָיו, and of פִּיו and לִבּוֹ in v. 22.

9. There are 8 instances of the זְרוֹעַ of the Lord in our Book (44.4b; 71.18; 77.16; 79.11; 89.14, 22; 98.1; and 136.12) and 1 instance (89.11) of בִּזְרוֹעַ עֻזְּךָ. In all 9 cases, זְרוֹעַ is literally rendered *βραχίων*, e. g., 71.18 עַד אַגִּיד זְרוֹעֲךָ לְדוֹר (לְכָל־יָבוֹא גְּבוּרָתֶךָ:) / *ἕως ἂν ἀπαγγείλω τὸν βραχίονά σου πάσῃ τῇ γενεᾷ*; 79.11 כְּגֹדֶל זְרוֹעֲךָ / *κατὰ τὴν μεγαλωσύνην τοῦ βραχίονός σου*; 89.11 בִּזְרוֹעַ עֻזְּךָ (פִּזַּרְתָּ אוֹיְבֶיךָ:) / *καὶ ἐν τῷ βραχίονι τῆς δυνάμεώς σου*.

In passing, it may be noted that there is one instance where the translator paraphrased זְרוֹעַ; but the verse does not involve the Lord: 83.9 (גַּם־אַשּׁוּר נִלְוָה עִמָּם) הָיוּ זְרוֹעַ לִבְנֵי־לוֹט / (*καὶ γὰρ καὶ Ἀσσουρ συμπαρεγένετο μετ' αὐτῶν*,) *ἐγενήθησαν εἰς ἀντίλημψιν τοῖς υἱοῖς Λωτ*.

10. The *יָמִין of the Lord occurs 22 times in our Book (16.11; 17.7; 18.36; 20.7; 44.4; 48.11; 60.7; 63.9; 74.11; 77.11; 78.54; 80.16, 18; 89.14; 98.1; 108.7; 110.1; 118.15, 16 (*bis*); 138.7; and 139.10). The translator always uses *δεξιά*, e. g., 63.9 בִּי תָּמְכָה יְמִינֶךָ / *ἐμοῦ ἀντελάβετο ἡ δεξιά σου*; 118.16 יְמִין יְהוָה רוֹמֵמָה יְמִין יְהוָה עֹשָׂה חָיִל: / *δεξιὰ κυρίου ὕψωσέν με, δεξιὰ κυρίου ἐποίησεν δύναμιν*.

In this connection, mention might be made of a passage in which the "right hand" of the Lord occurs in the LXX and does not occur in MT: 90.12 לִמְנוֹת יָמֵינוּ כֵּן הוֹדַע / *ἐξαριθμήσασθαι τὴν δεξιάν σου* (= יְמִינוֹ) *οὕτος γνώρισον*.

11. Reference is made to the כַּף of the Lord only once in Psalms: 139.5 וַתָּשֶׁת עָלַי כַּפֶּכָה: / *καὶ ἔθηκας ἐπ' ἐμὲ τὴν χεῖρά σου. χείρ* is also used for כַּף in 19 other instances in Psalms, where the Lord is not involved. In the sole remaining instance, 128.2, *καρπός* is used; but the כַּף is not the Lord's.

12. The אֶצְבָּעוֹת of the Lord are mentioned once, and translated literally: 8.4 (כִּי אֶרְאֶה שָׁמֶיךָ) מַעֲשֵׂי אֶצְבְּעֹתֶיךָ / (ὅτι ὄψομαι τοὺς οὐρανούς,) *ἔργα τῶν δακτύλων σου.*

13. There is one instance of the אֶבְרָה ("pinion") of God: 91.4 בְּאֶבְרָתוֹ יָסֶךְ לָךְ / *ἐν τοῖς μεταφρένοις αὐτοῦ ἐπισκιάσει σοι.* Μετάφρενον is also used in the only other instance of אֶבְרָה in Psalms, 68.14, where the reference is to a dove.

14. The חֵיק ("bosom") of the Lord is rendered literally in the LXX of the following verse: 74.11 (לָמָּה תָשִׁיב יָדְךָ וִימִינֶךָ) מִקֶּרֶב חֵיקְךָ כַלֵּה: (Kethib = חוקך ;Qre =) / (ἵνα τί ἀποστρέφεις τὴν χεῖρά σου καὶ τὴν δεξιάν σου) *ἐκ μέσου τοῦ κόλπου σου εἰς τέλος.*

15. There are 2 instances of the פְּעָמִים ("steps") of God. In both cases, the translator has reproduced the anthropomorphism literally, though differently in each case: 74.3 הָרִימָה פְעָמֶיךָ / *ἔπαρον τὰς χεῖράς σου*; 85.14 וְיָשֵׂם לְדֶרֶךְ פְּעָמָיו: / *καὶ θήσει εἰς ὁδὸν τὰ διαβήματα αὐτοῦ.* *Διάβημα* is the most common translation of פְּעָמִים in Psalms (cf. 17.5; 85.14; 119.133; and 140.5. In none of these cases is the reference to God). Χείρ, usually the translation for יָד, is used not only in 74.3 but also in 58.11 (where God is not involved): (יִשְׂמַח צַדִּיק כִּי־חָזָה נָקָם) פְּעָמָיו יִרְחַץ בְּדַם הָרָשָׁע: / (εὐφρανθήσεται δίκαιος, ὅταν ἴδῃ ἐκδίκησιν ἀσεβῶν·) *τὰς χεῖρας αὐτοῦ νίψεται ἐν τῷ αἵματι τοῦ ἁμαρτωλοῦ.*

In the Hatch-Redpath *Concordance to the Septuagint*, p. 1463, these instances of *χείρ* are followed by an obelus, which would indicate "that the identification of the Greek and Hebrew is doubtful" (*ibid.* vi). However, it would seem clear that the translator used *χείρ* in both 58.11 and 74.3 for פְּעָמִים and no other word. We might not agree with his translation; but we have no grounds for questioning the identification in the translator's mind. Nor is it necessary to assume כַּפָּיו (so, e. g., Buhl in *BH*[3]) in the LXX-*Vorlage* in 58.11 and 74.3; cf. Schleusner, s. *χείρ*, p. 515. To conclude this matter of פְּעָמִים, it might be noted that our translator also uses *πούς* in 57.7. But, whether *πούς*, *χείρ*, or *διάβημα*, the anthropomorphism remains.

16. Our Book affords 3 examples of the רַגְלַיִם of the Lord; all of them are literally translated with *πούς*: 18.10 (וַיֵּט שָׁמַיִם וַיֵּרַד) וַעֲרָפֶל תַּחַת רַגְלָיו: / *καὶ γνόφος ὑπὸ τοὺς πόδας αὐτοῦ*; 99.5 (רוֹמְמוּ יְהוָה אֱלֹהֵינוּ) וְהִשְׁתַּחֲווּ לַהֲדֹם רַגְלָיו / *καὶ προσκυνεῖτε τῷ ὑποποδίῳ τῶν ποδῶν αὐτοῦ*; 132.7 (נָבוֹאָה לְמִשְׁכְּנוֹתָיו) נִשְׁתַּחֲוֶה לַהֲדֹם רַגְלָיו: / *προσκυνήσομεν εἰς τὸν τόπον οὗ ἔστησαν οἱ πόδες αὐτοῦ.*

Both 18.10 and 132.7 should be enough to negate the premise that motion and place are denied God in the LXX (cf. Fritsch, *op. cit.*, chap. IV). The entire idea is not to be included in this paper for a number of reasons: the ascription or denial of motion and place to God has little to do with anthropomorphism; it is patently incorrect to explain away any paraphrases by means of such an hypothesis in view of the numerous examples in the LXX of the Psalter of the literal translation of such phrases as בֵּית יְהוָה / אֱלֹהִים and other instances of suffixed forms of בַּיִת, etc., where the reference is to God, etc.; cf. my "Critical Note" in *JBL*, 75 (1956), 144–5.

17. There are 6 references to the כְּנָפַיִם of the Lord in our Book, all of which are literally reproduced by *πτέρυξ*: 17.8; 36.8 בְּצֵל כְּנָפֶיךָ; 63.8; 57.2 וּבְצֵל כְּנָפֶיךָ / *καὶ ἐν τῇ σκέπῃ* (57.2 *σκία*) *τῶν πτερύγων σου*; 61.5 בְּסֵתֶר כְּנָפֶיךָ / *ἐν σκέπῃ τῶν πτερύγων σου*; 91.4 וְתַחַת כְּנָפָיו תֶּחְסֶה / *καὶ ὑπὸ τὰς πτέρυγας αὐτοῦ ἐλπιεῖς*.

18. In translating רוּחַ the LXX generally used either *πνεῦμα* or *ἄνεμος*. 'Ανεμος, which occurs 7 times in Psalms, and always as a translation of רוּחַ, means simply "wind." The passages are: 1.4; 18.11, 43; 35.15; 83.14; 104.3; and 135.17. However, it must be noted that *πνεῦμα*, too, is used in passages where the meaning is obviously "wind," e. g., 11.6; 48.8; 103.16; 104.4; 107.25; and 148.8. *Πνεῦμα* is usually translated into English as "spirit." But since the meaning of *πνεῦμα* includes the idea of "wind," it ought not be taken in a thoroughly non-material sense, but as, approximately, "breath."

There are 5 instances of the רוּחַ of the Lord in our Book. In every case רוּחַ appears as *πνεῦμα*: 51.13 וְרוּחַ קָדְשְׁךָ (אַל־תִּקַּח מִמֶּנִּי:) / *καὶ τὸ πνεῦμα τὸ ἅγιόν σου*; 104.30 תְּשַׁלַּח רוּחֲךָ (יִבָּרֵאוּן) / *ἐξαπεστελεῖς τὸ πνεῦμά σου*; 139.7 מֵרוּחֶךָ (אָנָה אֵלֵךְ) / *ἀπὸ τοῦ πνεύματός σου*; 143.10 רוּחֲךָ טוֹבָה (תַּנְחֵנִי) / *τὸ πνεῦμά σου τὸ ἀγαθὸν*; 147.18 יַשֵּׁב רוּחוֹ (יִזְּלוּ מָיִם:) / *πνεύσει τὸ πνεῦμα αὐτοῦ*.

Had רוּחַ been translated *ἄνεμος* in any of the above verses, the figure of speech would have been somewhat more material, almost palpable. But anthropomorphic is one thing it would not have been. Let us put it this way: "His wind" (רוּחַ / *ἄνεμος*) is in the same category as "His ice" and "His cold" (147.17 מַשְׁלִיךְ קַרְחוֹ כְפִתִּים לִפְנֵי קָרָתוֹ מִי יַעֲמֹד: / *βάλλοντος κρύσταλλον αὐτοῦ ὡσεὶ ψωμούς, κατὰ πρόσωπον ψύχους αὐτοῦ τίς ὑποστήσεται*), material things which are His, and which He sends to the world. But His *πνεῦμα*, His "breath," is a part of Him. Although the figure of speech is less material, it is anthropomorphic in a way in which His *ἄνεμος* is not. That is, the *πνεῦμα* is a part of man; it is that which is present in a living man and departs from him at his death (146.4 תֵּצֵא רוּחוֹ יָשֻׁב לְאַדְמָתוֹ / *ἐξελεύσεται τὸ πνεῦμα αὐτοῦ, καὶ ἐπιστρέψει εἰς τὴν γῆν αὐτοῦ*). It is in this sense that we can say that when the Lord is said to have a *πνεῦμα* we have a kind of anthropomorphism, equivalent to the Hebrew רוּחַ, which we do not have in an instance of the Lord's *ἄνεμος*.

With the idea clearly in mind that *πνεῦμα* is not the non-material "spirit," but bears the meaning "breath," we now turn to the two remaining verses in our Book in which *π.* bears a relation to the Lord: 18.16 :מִגַּעֲרָתְךָ יְהוָה מִנִּשְׁמַת רוּחַ אַפֶּךָ / *ἀπὸ ἐπιτιμήσεώς σου, κύριε, ἀπὸ ἐμπνεύσεως πνεύματος ὀργῆς σου*; 33.6 (בִּדְבַר יְהוָה שָׁמַיִם נַעֲשׂוּ) וּבְרוּחַ פִּיו כָּל־צְבָאָם: / *καὶ τῷ πνεύματι τοῦ στόματος αὐτοῦ πᾶσα ἡ δύναμις αὐτῶν*. The translation of אַף by *ὀργή* in 18.16, instead of *ῥίς*, will be discussed later (§ **20** below). The translation of 18.16 shows no sign of any anti-anthropomorphic tendency; גַּעֲרָתְךָ is literally reproduced *ἐπιτιμήσεως*, and נִשְׁמַת, *ἐμπνεύσεως*. Obviously *πνεῦμα*, rather than *ἄνεμος*, is used here and in 33.6 because in both passages רוּחַ means "breath" rather than the "wind" which is not part of the Lord. We might compare the translation of וּבְרוּחַ פִּיו in 33.6 with a similar expression in 135.17, where אַף־אֵין־יֶשׁ רוּחַ בְּפִיהֶם — the idols are described here — is rendered by *οὐδὲ γάρ ἐστιν πνεῦμα ἐν τῷ στόματι αὐτῶν*. It is a sign of their nothing-ness that idols do not have a *πνεῦμα*. To have avoided the use of *πνεῦμα* in connection with God would have been much worse than anthropomorphism.

19. There are 2 instances in MT Psalms of the לֵב of God: 33.11 (עֲצַת יְהוָה לְעוֹלָם תַּעֲמֹד) מַחְשְׁבוֹת לִבּוֹ (לְדֹר וָדֹר:) / *λογισμοὶ τῆς καρδίας αὐτοῦ*; 27.8 (אֶת־פָּנֶיךָ יְהוָה אֲבַקֵּשׁ:) לְךָ אָמַר לִבִּי בַּקְּשׁוּ פָנָי / *σοὶ εἶπεν ἡ καρδία μου Ἐζήτησεν τὸ πρόσωπόν μου, (τὸ πρόσωπόν σου, κύριε, ζητήσω)*. *Ἐζήτησεν* . . . is the rendering preferred by Rahlfs. However, in Vaticanus (B) and Alexandrinus (A) the verse appears as *ἐξεζήτησα τὸ πρόσωπόν σου, (τὸ πρόσωπόν σου, κύριε, ζητήσω)*. By taking the verb as *ἐξεζήτησα, ἡ καρδία μου* is to be taken as the heart of the Psalmist. Yet, inasmuch as the פָּנִים of the Lord is literally reproduced twice (and in the first of these two instances פָּנַי is rendered *τὸ πρόσωπόν σου* so that there can be no mistake as to whose "face" is meant,) it would be futile to attempt to see any anti-anthropomorphic tendency in accounting for the differences between BA and MT.

In 55.22 there is an instance of לִבּוֹ which the LXX translator takes to be the heart of the Lord although the pronominal reference is by no means certain in MT. This verse can be best understood in the context of the preceding verses: 55.20 יִשְׁמַע אֵל וְיַעֲנֵם וְיֹשֵׁב קֶדֶם סֶלָה אֲשֶׁר

אֵין חֲלִיפוֹת לָמוֹ וְלֹא יָרְאוּ אֱלֹהִים: / *εἰσακούσεται ὁ θεὸς καὶ ταπεινώσει αὐτούς ὁ ὑπάρχων πρὸ τὸν αἰώνων διάψαλμα. οὐ γάρ ἐστιν αὐτοις ἀντάλλαγμα, καὶ οὐκ ἐφοβήθησαν τὸν θεόν.* 55.21. שָׁלַח יָדָיו בִּשְׁלֹמָיו חִלֵּל בְּרִיתוֹ: / *ἐξέτεινεν τὴν χεῖρα αὐτοῦ ἐν τῷ ἀποδιδόναι. ἐβεβήλωσαν τὴν διαθήκην αὐτοῦ.* 55.22 . . . חָלְקוּ מַחְמָאֹת פִּיו וּקְרָב־לִבּוֹ / *διεμερίσθησαν ἀπὸ ὀργῆς τοῦ προσώπου αὐτοῦ καὶ ἤγγισεν ἡ καρδία αὐτου* . . .

Periphrasis is apparent in 36.2, where בְּקֶרֶב לִבִּי = *ἐν ἑαυτῷ*; but it is the *παράνομος* rather than God, whose "heart" has been "avoided." In such a case everyone will agree that what we have here is simply good style; had the case involved God, however, it would have been an example of "anti-anthropomorphism" to more than a few.

Chapter II. Anthropopathisms

In this chapter we shall investigate the various instances of anthropopathisms in the masoretic text of Psalms and their translation in the LXX. Our list includes only those words meaning "anger," "jealousy," "zealousness," and the like. We have not included the numerous references to the "benign" emotions of pleasure, gladness, etc., because there would certainly be no theologically motivated objection to them at the time of the translation of Psalms into Greek.

We shall investigate the following anthropopathisms: אַף, אָנַף, חָרָה, חָרוֹן, חֵמָה, עֶבְרָה, זַעַם, קָצַף, כַּעַס, קִנְאָה, שִׂנְאָה and שָׂנֵא.[8]

20. There are 29 references to the אַף of the Lord in Psalms: it appears as *ὀργή* in 2.5; 7.7; 18.9, 16; 21.10; 27.9; 56.8; 69.25; 76.8; 77.10; 78.21, 31, 50; 85.6; 90.7, 11; 95.11; and 110.5; and as *θυμός* in 2.12; 6.2; 30.6; 74.1; 78.38, 49; 85.4; and 106.40. אֶרֶךְ אַפַּיִם appears in 86.15; 103.8; and 145.8; and it is always reproduced *μακρόθυμος*.[9] There is

[8] Since the idea of anti-anthropomorphism is not involved in M. Flashar's "Exegetische Studien zum Septuagintapsalter," *ZAW*, 21 (1912), especially 259–265, we shall treat separately his analysis of *ὀργή* and *θυμός*.

[9] In the following example, an anthropopathism is afforded by the translator's understanding of רֶגַע as "anger." 30.6 כִּי רֶגַע בְּאַפּוֹ / *ὅτι ὀργὴ ἐν τῷ θυμῷ αὐτοῦ.* Buhl's suggestion (BH^3) of רֹגֶז or נֶגַע in the *Vorlage* is unwarranted since in 35.20 *ὀργή* is used for רגעי. On the other hand, רֶגַע is translated differently in 6.11, where יֵבֹשׁוּ רָגַע: appears as *καταισχυνθείησαν σφόδρα διὰ τάχους*. The fact is that רֹגֶז does not appear anywhere in Psalms. Curiously, Buhl does not make the same suggestion for רגעי in 35.20. But Briggs anticipated the "oversight"; see *ICC on Psalms*,

no instance whatever in the LXX of our Book to indicate avoidance of the obvious anthropopathisms inherent in the idea of the Lord's having an אף. It bothers the translator so little that he elucidates the reference to the Lord in 77.10 (הֲשָׁכַח חַנּוֹת אֵל) אִם־קָפַץ בְּאַף רַחֲמָיו / (ἢ ἐπι-λήσεται τοῦ οἰκτιρῆσαι ὁ θεὸς) ἢ συνέξει ἐν τῇ ὀργῇ αὐτοῦ τοὺς οἰκτιρμοὺς αὐτοῦ.

The term אף, which originally denoted "nostril," came to mean "anger" by the association of heavy breathing in connection with that emotion. This was true in all cases, those involving man as well as those in which God was involved. This development took place long before the composition of the LXX; it was part of the development of the Hebrew language. No trace of the meaning "nostril" remains in such verses as 2.5 אָז יְדַבֵּר אֵלֵימוֹ בְאַפּוֹ; 2.12 כִּי־יִבְעַר כִּמְעַט אַפּוֹ; 6.2 יְהוָה אַל־בְּאַפְּךָ תוֹכִיחֵנִי; 7.7 קוּמָה יְהוָה בְּאַפֶּךָ; etc. Of the 29 times that אף is used in connection with the Lord, 26 are instances where אף clearly means "anger" rather than "nostril"; and the translator has correctly used ὀργή or θυμός. The 3 other instances are: 18.9, 16; and 74.1. In the last case, to have translated the phrase יֶעְשַׁן אַפְּךָ with ῥὶς καπνίζειν would not have conveyed the meaning as well as does the usage which our translator did employ, viz., 74.1: (לָמָה אֱלֹהִים זָנַחְתָּ לָנֶצַח) יֶעְשַׁן אַפְּךָ בְּצֹאן מַרְעִיתֶךָ: / (ἵνα τί ἀπώσω, ὁ θεός, εἰς τέλος,) ὠργίσθη ὁ θυμός σου ἐπὶ πρόβατα νομῆς σου. Although the anthropomorphism ("nostril") is not present here in the Greek, there is ample reason to doubt that this is due to anti-anthropomorphism on the part of the translator. First, the absence of any evidence for anti-anthropomorphism in his handling of the anthropomorphic figures of speech we reviewed in the previous chapter, e. g. "hand," "eyes," "ears," etc., and including פְּעָמֶיךָ = χεῖρας in 74.3. Second, the expression יֶעְשַׁן אַפְּךָ is used by the Psalmist as a parallel to זָנַחְתָּ; the idea of "anger" is much more important to the parallelism than the literal figure of speech. Third, we are not dealing with the word אף alone, but with an idiom consisting of 2 words, יֶעְשַׁן אַפְּךָ; and what is a perfectly understandable idiom in Hebrew might be far from clear in Greek or any other language. Not only the LXX translator, but many other translators not concerned at all with the problem of anthropomorphism have quite naturally, and correctly, associated אף with the idea of "anger" rather than literally "nostril", e. g., AV and JPS "why doth

p. 313. Cf. Schleusner, s. ὀργή / רֶגַע, for another explanation; also Mozley, *ad loc.*; Baethgen, *ad loc.* (p. 620), believes that the translator "identified" רגע with נערה.

Thine anger smoke"; Luther, "warum . . . bist so grimmig zornig"; Oesterley, "Thine anger burns lurid"; Kissane, "Why does Thy anger rage." In short, the use of ὀργή for אַף in 74.1 was motivated by stylistic rather than theological considerations.

With regard to 18.9 and 16, we cannot say that other translators have used periphrasis. AV, JPS, Luther, etc., translate אַף literally in these 2 cases; the LXX translator chose "anger". But that does not mean (as Flashar believes it does, *ZAW*, 21, p. 260) that anti-anthropomorphism is involved. The contrary can be shown to be the case: in 18.7 בְּאָזְנָיו was spelled out more literally than usual, εἰς τὰ ὦτα αὐτου; in 18.10 רַגְלָיו was reproduced literally τοὺς πόδας αὐτου; קוֹלוֹ in 18.14 was also rendered without any attempt to avoid the anthropomorphism. Consequently, we can rule out anti-anthropomorphism as a factor in our translator's use of ὀργή for אַף in 18.9, 16. But we cannot rule out style simply because modern translators have found no difficulty with a literal rendering. It is not unlikely that our translator used ὀργή in 18.9 to parallel כִּי־חָרָה לוֹ / ὅτι ὠργίσθη αὐτοῖς ὁ θεός in the preceding verse; similarly in 18.16 ὀργή may well have been used as a parallel to מִגַּעֲרָתְךָ / ἀπὸ ἐπιτιμήσεώς σου. The above suggestions are no more than tentative, and are made only in an attempt to find a reason for our translator's use of ὀργή in the very few cases where אַף seems to bear the meaning "nostrils" in MT, a problem which is not really within the scope of this paper inasmuch as we have already ruled out the hypothesis of anti-anthropomorphism. In view of the entire discussion of this problem, Fritsch's observations on this problem in the Pentateuch seem colored by the need to find evidence for anti-anthropomorphism even in places where it doesn't exist: (*op. cit.*, p. 12): "The Seventy accepted and translated the secondary meaning of this word, using the words ὀργή and θυμός, thus obscuring the physical association." One might wonder why the LXX translator should find it necessary to "obscure" (deliberately, one would suppose) the physical meaning of אַף when, as Fritsch readily admits (*idem*, p. 15), "in most cases the translators literally rendered the anthropomorphisms of the Hebrew text." His other hypothesis, the "LXX's consistent adherence to a definite pattern of translation," is not valid for Psalms; where our translator felt that "nostril" was the meaning, he did not hesitate to use ῥίς rather than ὀργή: 115.6 :אַף לָהֶם וְלֹא יְרִיחוּן / ῥῖνας ἔχουσιν καὶ οὐκ ὀσφρανθήσονται. To have followed a "consistent adherence to a definite pattern of translation" would have meant to use ὀργή here. But since this would not have provided the proper contrast with וְלֹא יְרִיחוּן / καὶ οὐκ ὀσφρανθήσονται, our translator quite naturally and correctly employed ῥίς.

21. Our Book has 4 instances of the verb אָנַף with the Lord as subject; it is consistently translated ὀργίζειν: 2.12 (נַשְּׁקוּ־בַר) פֶּן־יֶאֱנַף (וְתֹאבְדוּ דֶרֶךְ כִּי־יִבְעַר כִּמְעַט אַפּוֹ) / (δράξασθε παιδείας) μήποτε ὀργισθῇ κύριος (καὶ ἀπολεῖσθε ἐξ ὁδοῦ δικαίας. ὅταν ἐκκαυθῇ ἐν τάχει ὁ θυμὸς αὐτοῦ) — note that the translator clearly identifies the subject, κύριος; 60.3 (אֱלֹהִים זְנַחְתָּנוּ פְרַצְתָּנוּ) אָנַפְתָּ / (ο θεός ἀπώσω ἡμᾶς καὶ καθεῖλες ἡμᾶς,) ὠργίσθης; 79.5 עַד־מָה יְהוָה תֶּאֱנַף לָנֶצַח / ἕως πότε, κύριε, ὀργισθήσῃ εἰς τέλος; 85.6 הַלְעוֹלָם תֶּאֱנַף־בָּנוּ (תִּמְשֹׁךְ אַפְּךָ לְדֹר וָדֹר:) / μὴ εἰς τὸν αἰῶνα ὀργισθήσῃ ἡμιν (ἢ διατενεῖς τὴν ὀργήν σου ἀπὸ γενεᾶς εἰς γενεάν).

'Ὀργίζειν is used also to translate the verbs עָשַׁן and רִיב with the Lord as subject.[10] 80.5 יְהוָה אֱלֹהִים צְבָאוֹת עַד־מָתַי עָשַׁנְתָּ (בִּתְפִלַּת עַמֶּךָ:) / κύριε ὁ θεὸς τῶν δυνάμεων, ἕως πότε ὀργίζῃ (ἐπὶ τὴν προσευχὴν τοῦ δούλου σου); 103.9 לֹא לָנֶצַח יָרִיב (וְלֹא לְעוֹלָם יִטּוֹר:) / οὐκ εἰς τέλος ὀργισθήσεται (οὐδὲ εἰς τὸν αἰῶνα μηνιεῖ.).[11]

22. חָרָה appears with the Lord as subject twice in our Book. As with אָנַף the translator has used ὀργίζειν: 18.8 (וַיִּתְגָּעֲשׁוּ) כִּי־חָרָה לוֹ: / (καὶ ἐσαλεύθησαν) ὅτι ὠργίσθη αὐτοῖς ὁ θεός; 106.40 וַיִּחַר־אַף יְהוָה בְּעַמּוֹ / καὶ ὠργίσθη θυμῷ κύριος ἐπὶ τὸν λαὸν αὐτοῦ.

Note that in 18.8 the translator added **αὐτοῖς ὁ θεός** for reasons of style, so providing the verb with a subject and an object. Clearly, the stylistic consideration was more important to him than the anthropopathism of the verb; otherwise he would hardly have gratuitously stressed that its subject was **ὁ θεός**.[12] A similar consideration underlies his treatment of וַיִּחַר־אַף יְהוָה in 106.40, where he takes יְהוָה to be the subject rather than His אַף, which he renders as θυμῷ[13] (instead of θυμὸς κυρίου). The Targum, which usually avoids anthropopathisms, renders this verse וּתְקֵיף רוּגְזָה דַיְיָ. We might add that the LXX translation of וַיִּחַר־אַף as ὠργίσθη θυμῷ is not to be accounted for by the presence of the *maqqef* connecting the two words; a similar transla-

[10] In 104.32 and 144.5, where the subject is "mountains," עשן appears as καπνίζειν. עשן never appears with man as subject. ריב = δικάζειν in 35.1; 43.1; and 74.22. But ריב = κρίνειν in 119.154. There are no other instances of ריב in our Book.

[11] It may be observed here that μηνιεῖν is also used for נטר in Lev. 19.18, where God is not involved, and in Jer. 3.12, where God is involved.

[12] Cf. II Sam. 22.8, where the same Hebrew is reproduced by ἐθυμώθη κύριος αὐτοῖς.

[13] Cf. Ex. 22.23; 32.19 (Moses is the subject); Num. 22.22; 25.3; 32.10, 13; Deut. 7.4; 29.26; 31.17. But in Ps. 124.3: בַּחֲרוֹת אַפָּם בָּנוּ = ἐν τῷ ὀργισθῆναι τὸν θυμὸν αὐτῶν ἐφ' ἡμᾶς, because there was no better way to render the (possessive) suffixed אַפָּם.

tion is given for Ex. 22.23 and Deut. 31.17 where there is no *maqqef*.

23. There are 5 instances of the חָרוֹן of the Lord in our Book. It is always reproduced literally, either by *ὀργή* or by *θυμός*: 2.5 (אָז יְדַבֵּר אֵלֵימוֹ בְאַפּוֹ) וּבַחֲרוֹנוֹ יְבַהֲלֵמוֹ: / (*τότε λαλήσει πρὸς αὐτοὺς ἐν ὀργῇ αὐτοῦ*,) *καὶ ἐν τῷ θυμῷ αὐτοῦ ταράξει αὐτούς*; 69.25 וַחֲרוֹן אַפְּךָ יַשִּׂיגֵם: / *καὶ ὁ θυμὸς τῆς ὀργῆς σου καταλάβοι αὐτούς*; 78.49 יְשַׁלַּח־בָּם חֲרוֹן אַפּוֹ / *ἐξαπεστείλεν εἰς αὐτοὺς ὀργὴν θυμοῦ αὐτοῦ*; 85.4 הֱשִׁיבוֹתָ מֵחֲרוֹן אַפֶּךָ: / *ἀπέστρεψας ἀπὸ ὀργῆς θυμοῦ σου*; 88.17 עָלַי עָבְרוּ חֲרוֹנֶיךָ / *ἐπ' ἐμε διῆλθον αἱ ὀργαί σου*.[14]

24. The חֵמָה of the Lord appears in 10 instances in Psalms: 6.2; 38.2; 59.14; 76.11; 78.38; 79.6; 88.8; 89.47; 90.7; and 106.23. It is rendered *ὀργή* 7 times, *θυμός* twice (88.8; 90.7), and *ἐνθύμιον* once (76.11). The usual translation, with חֵמָה=*ὀργή*, may be illustrated by 6.2: יְהוָה אַל־בְּאַפְּךָ תוֹכִיחֵנִי וְאַל־בַּחֲמָתְךָ תְיַסְּרֵנִי: / *κύριε, μὴ τῷ θυμῷ σου ἐλέγξῃς με, μηδὲ τῇ ὀργῇ σου παιδεύσῃς με*. The same translation is given for 38.2: יְהוָה אַל־בְּקֶצְפְּךָ תוֹכִיחֵנִי וּבַחֲמָתְךָ תְיַסְּרֵנִי; the translator used *μηδὲ* to express the second negation which the Hebrew Psalmist simply left implied.

In the following example, the translator's understanding of the syntax is different from that of MT; but the anthropopathism remains: 59.13, 14 וּמֵאָלָה וּמִכַּחַשׁ יְסַפֵּרוּ: כַּלֵּה בְחֵמָה כַּלֵּה וְאֵינֵמוֹ / *καὶ ἐξ ἀρᾶς καὶ ψεύδους διαγγελήσονται συντέλειαι ἐν οργῇ συντελείας, καὶ οὐ μὴ ὑπάρξωσιν*.

The translator uses *θυμός* for חֵמָה in the following two instances: 90.7 (כִּי־כָלִינוּ בְאַפֶּךָ) וּבַחֲמָתְךָ נִבְהָלְנוּ: / (*ὅτι ἐξελίπομεν ἐν τῇ ὀργῇ σου*,) *καὶ ἐν τῷ θυμῷ σου ἐταράχθημεν*; 88.8 עָלַי סָמְכָה חֲמָתֶךָ / *ἐπ' ἐμὲ ἐπεστερίχθη ὁ θυμός σου*.

ἐνθύμιον is used for חֵמָה twice in 76.11 (incidentally the sole instances of *ἐνθύμιον* in the entire LXX): כִּי־חֲמַת אָדָם תּוֹדֶךָּ שְׁאֵרִית חֵמֹת תַּחְגֹּר: / *ὅτι ἐνθύμιον ἀνθρώπου ἐξομολογήσεταί σοι, καὶ ἐγκατάλειμμα ἐνθυμίου ἑορτάσει σοι*. The meaning of this verse is obscure in the Hebrew; the translation also presents problems. However, that anti-anthropopathism is no factor here can be seen in the fact that

[14] In the following verse we find an anthropopathism in the LXX for which there is no correspondent in the Hebrew: 58.10 כְּמוֹ־חַי כְּמוֹ־חָרוֹן יִשְׂעָרֶנּוּ: / *ὡσεὶ ζῶντας ὡσεὶ ἐν ὀργῇ καταπίεται ὑμᾶς*. The translator fails to understand חָרוֹן as contrasting with חַי, and gives us instead an adverbial use of בְּחָרוֹן. The fact that the subject of *καταπίεται* is the Lord makes *ἐν ὀργῇ* refer to Him, (though there is some possibility that it refers to the objects of the verb).

there is no distinction in the translations of חֲמַת אָדָם and the חמת with which the Lord will be girt; both are translated *ἐνθύμιον*.

25. The עֶבְרָה of the Lord occurs 4 times in our Book: 78.49; 85.4; 90.9 and 11. It appears as *ὀργή* in the first two of these instances, and as *θυμός* in the last two, e. g., 78.49 (יְשַׁלַּח־בָּם חֲרוֹן אַפּוֹ) עֶבְרָה וָזַעַם וְצָרָה / (*ἐξαπέστειλεν εἰς αὐτοὺς ὀργὴν θυμοῦ αὐτοῦ,*) *θυμὸν καὶ ὀργὴν καὶ θλῖψιν*; 90.11 (מִי־יוֹדֵעַ עֹז אַפֶּךָ) וּכְיִרְאָתְךָ עֶבְרָתֶךָ: / (*τίς γινώσκει τὸ κράτος τῆς ὀργῆς σου*) *καὶ ἀπὸ τοῦ φόβου σου τὸν θυμόν σου*.

26. There are 4 instances of the זַעַם of the Lord in our Book (38.4; 69.25; 78.49; and 102.11); it is consistently translated *ὀργή*, e. g., 38.4 (אֵין מְתֹם בִּבְשָׂרִי) מִפְּנֵי זַעְמֶךָ / (*οὐκ ἔστιν ἴασις ἐν τῇ σαρκί μου*) *ἀπὸ προσώπου τῆς ὀργῆς σου*; 69.25 שְׁפָךְ עֲלֵיהֶם זַעְמֶךָ / *ἔκχεον ἐπ' αὐτοὺς τὴν ὀργήν σου*.

The present participle occurs once in Psalms: 7.12 (אֱלֹהִים שׁוֹפֵט צַדִּיק) וְאֵל זֹעֵם בְּכָל יוֹם: / (*ὁ θεὸς κριτὴς δίκαιος,*) *καὶ ἰσχυρὸς καὶ μακρόθυμος μὴ ὀργὴν ἐπάγων καθ' ἑκάστην ἡμέραν*. While it may be true that this translation does not present the anthropopathism present in MT (i. e., וְאֵל זֹעֵם) the difference can hardly be attributed to a deliberate change on the part of the translator (as Baethgen, p. 597; M. Flashar, pp. 264–5). For, if he meant to avoid or soften anthropopathisms, why should he do so only here, with the verb, but not with the nouns in the four instances of זַעַם cited above? A more plausible explanation may be found in his having read וְאַל for MT וְאֵל, a phenomenon which also occurs in 90.2, 3: וּמֵעוֹלָם עַד־עוֹלָם אַתָּה אֵל: תָּשֵׁב אֱנוֹשׁ עַד־דַּכָּא / *καὶ ἀπὸ τοῦ αἰῶνος ἕως τοῦ αἰῶνος σὺ εἶ. μὴ ἀποστρέψῃς ἄνθρωπον εἰς ταπείνωσιν*.

27. קֶצֶף is attributed to the Lord 3 times in our Book; in every instance it is reproduced literally. It appears twice as a noun, and is translated by *θυμός*: 38.2 יְהוָה אַל־בְּקֶצְפְּךָ תוֹכִיחֵנִי / *κύριε μὴ τῷ θυμῷ σου ἐλέγξῃς με*; 102.11 מִפְּנֵי זַעַמְךָ וְקִצְפֶּךָ / *ἀπὸ προσώπου τῆς ὀργῆς σου καὶ τοῦ θυμοῦ σου*.

In 106.32 קֶצֶף is attributed to the Lord inasmuch as He is the object of the verb: 106.32 וַיַּקְצִיפוּ עַל־מֵי מְרִיבָה / *καὶ παρώργισαν αὐτὸν ἐφ' ὕδατος ἀντιλογίας*.

28. The כַּעַס of the Lord occurs once in Psalms; it is reproduced literally as *θυμός*: 85.5 וְהָפֵר כַּעַסְךָ עִמָּנוּ: / *καὶ ἀπόστρεψον τὸν θυμόν σου ἀφ' ἡμῶν*. In 2 instances, כַּעַס is attributed to God inasmuch as He is the object of the verb: 78.58 וַיַּכְעִיסוּהוּ בְּבָמוֹתָם / *καὶ παρώργισαν αὐτὸν ἐν τοῖς βουνοῖς αὐτῶν*; 106.29 וַיַּכְעִיסוּהוּ בְּמַעַלְלֵיהֶם (וַתִּפְרָץ בָּם

(מַגֵּפָה: / *καὶ παρώξυναν αὐτὸν ἐν τοῖς ἐπιτηδεύμασιν αὐτῶν*, (*καὶ ἐπληθύνθη ἐν αὐτοῖς ἡ πτῶσις*).

29. קִנְאָה is attributed to the Lord twice in our Book and reproduced literally: 78.58 וּבִפְסִילֵיהֶם יַקְנִיאוּהוּ: / *καὶ ἐν τοῖς γλυπτοῖς αὐτῶν παρεζήλωσαν αὐτόν*; 79.5 תִּבְעַר כְּמוֹ־אֵשׁ קִנְאָתֶךָ: / *ἐκκαυθήσεται ὡς πῦρ ὁ ζῆλός σου*.

30. God's שִׂנְאָה is mentioned, and literally translated, twice in Psalms: 5.6 שָׂנֵאתָ כָּל־פֹּעֲלֵי אָוֶן: / *ἐμίσησας* (B, A, *κύριε*) *πάντας τοὺς ἐργαζομένους τὴν ἀνομίαν*; ; 11.5 יְהוָה צַדִּיק יִבְחָן וְרָשָׁע וְאֹהֵב חָמָס שָׂנְאָה נַפְשׁוֹ: / *κύριος ἐξετάζει τὸν δίκαιον καὶ τὸν ἀσεβῆ, ὁ δὲ ἀγαπῶν ἀδικίαν μισεῖ τὴν ἑαυτοῦ ψυχήν*. The translator considered the pronominal reference of נַפְשׁוֹ to be אֹהֵב חָמָס rather than יְהוָה; and he took אֹהֵב חָמָס to be the subject of the verb. MT שָׂנְאָה requires a feminine subject, which is supplied by נַפְשׁוֹ. However, if the translator read שָׂנֵא, נַפְשׁוֹ would then have to be taken as the object of the verb, and its pronominal reference would have to be אֹהֵב חָמָס. In any case, we may rule out the possibility of a deliberate anti-anthropopathism here in view of 5.6 above, and in view of the following instance, in which the translator takes the subject of the verb to be the Lord, as against the Psalmist who is certainly the subject in MT: 31.7 שָׂנֵאתִי הַשֹּׁמְרִים הַבְלֵי שָׁוְא / *ἐμίσησας τοὺς διαφυλάσσοντας ματαιότητας διὰ κενῆς*. Buhl, in BH[3], would emend as שָׂנֵאתָ on the basis of 1 Ms. and Versions. So, too, Baethgen (*JPT*, 8, p. 62). As he also points out in his *Handkommentar, die Psalmen* (Göttingen 1904) p. 86, the second person gives more meaning to the following וַאֲנִי. Whether the *Vorlage* was second person or first person, the fact remains that the LXX translator did not shrink from attributing the emotion of hatred to God.

Conclusions

A. Although there may be an exegetical pattern in the LXX translation of Psalms, it would seem that anti-anthropomorphism and anti-anthropopathism played no part in that pattern. Indeed, the translator usually rendered the anthropomorphisms and anthropopathisms literally, and occasionally rendered some (such as בְּאָזְנֵי, בְּעֵינֵי, מִפְּנֵי, and מִלִּפְנֵי) even more literally than was necessary.

B. It would also appear that the LXX of Psalms is the work of a single translator; we found no significant differences in vocabulary or style within the 150 Psalms. In spite of occasional lapses, the translator seems to have had a very good knowledge of the Hebrew language.

C. The differences between MT and LXX are not always the result either of deliberate mistranslation or mistaken interpretation; in some instances they are due to differences between MT and the translator's *Vorlage*. Although great caution ought to be taken before emending MT on the basis of a conjectural reconstruction of the LXX *Vorlage*, it is not always unwarranted to do so (e. g., 42.6, 7 discussed in section **1**a).

Septuaginta, Vetus Testamentum Graecum, Auctoritate Societatis Litterarum Gottingensis editum. — Band IX. 1 Maccabaeorum liber I, herausgegeben von **Werner Kappler,** 1936. 8°. 146 S.; IX. 2 Maccabaeorum liber II, herausgegeben von **Robert Hanhart,** 1959. 8°. 116 S.; IX. 3 Maccabaeorum liber III, herausgegeben von **Robert Hanhart,** 1960. 8°. 70 S. Sämtlich bei Vandenhoeck & Ruprecht, Göttingen[1]). **Robert Hanhart,** Zum Text des 2. und 3. Makkabäerbuches. Probleme der Überlieferung, der Auslegung und der Ausgabe. Nachrichten der Akademie der Wissenschaften in Göttingen. I. Phil.-hist. Klasse. Jahrgang 1961, Nr. 13. 8°. 64 S. Vandenhoeck & Ruprecht, Göttingen.

These books have now been edited in a form that enables us to study their textual and other problems with confidence that we have an adequate picture of the textual tradition. Dr. Kappler was entirely responsible for 1M. With some exceptions the text of 2M and the Greek evidence of the apparatus are his work, but Dr. Hanhart contributed that of the versions and the quotations and gave the apparatus its final form. Dr. Hanhart is entirely responsible for 3M.

We can add very few witnesses to those which are used by Kappler and Hanhart. For the Latin there is the Durham fragment (Cathedral Library, B. IV. 6 fol. 169) containing 1M vi. 59–62, 63–vii. 2 of the sixth century. The significance of this fragment, not mentioned by de Bruyne in his edition, lies in its date. It is the earliest manuscript witness we have to the Vulgate of 1–2M, but its text is not otherwise important.

In Pérez de Urbel and González y Ruiz-Zorilla, *Liber Commicus* II, there is one relevant lesson, 2M iv. 36–58. It too is a Vulgate text, most resembling de Bruyne's Vulgate manuscript L, and next KB, all Spanish manuscripts.

We are still without the text of the León palimpsest, but one new Latin witness has come to light. At Oxford Ms. Laud. Lat. 22 of about A. D. 800 from Würzburg, which contains only 1–2M, has the same kind of text as B, the Bologna manuscript whose text de Bruyne edited. Though the Oxford manuscript is some 300 years older than B its text is no better

[1]) References to chapter and verse are given as follows: 1M ix. 13; to pages as follows: 1M 46, H 28.

Reprinted from *Göttingische Gelehrte Anzeigen.* 215 Jahrgang, 1963.

and no worse. Each corrects and supplements the other and of course they have errors in common (cf. H 22f.).

We have in the Göttingen editions of 1–2M a much fuller presentation of the Latin evidence for these books than was previously available, a feature for which we must be grateful to the editors who have drawn largely on the edition of the Latin of 1–2M by de Bruynę and Sodar. If opportunity allows, we would beg for an even fuller presentation of the Latin evidence. H refers to some Latin readings which are not in the apparatus of 1–2M and a few other Latin readings likewise not mentioned in these apparatuses will be cited in this paper. Hanhart and Kappler have done this work so well that in proportion the additional Latin readings to be cited would be few.

In Coptic Dr. Hanhart had akhmimic fragments of the *Passio Maccabaeorum*. A few years ago Professor W. H. Willis reported a complete Sahidic text of the *Passio* (2M v. 27–vii. 41) from the Crosby Codex of perhaps the latter part of the third century in the Library of the University of Mississippi. The text is not yet published, but Professor Willis is engaged on the preparation of an edition.

Each fascicle has an introduction which gives details of the manuscripts, versions and other evidence used, and an analysis of these witnesses. For 3M, unlike the other two books, Sinaiticus and the Latin are not available, but otherwise the same sources exist for the text of all three books. They can be classified as follows: (1) the uncials A, S (= א), V, (2) the *q* group of minuscles, (3) the Lucianic groups and the Syriac (4) the *codices mixti*, a small number of minuscles. Josephus and the Latin as far as they are available cannot be associated with any one group. This analysis, in which Kappler and Hanhart agree, seems well established and can be assumed as a starting point in any attempt to reconstruct the text of the three books.

In their treatment of the text the two editors seem to share the same opinions. Kappler tended to rely on the three uncials for guidance in 1M. The group *q* seemed to him to contribute very little and he obviously set out with a suspicion of the Lucianic witnesses which has been traditional in Göttingen Septuagint studies at any rate from the time of Rahlfs. De Bruyne's evidence from the Latin made it clear that this suspicion had to be tempered by the recognition that the Lucianic had a number of readings older than A. D. 300, some of which seemed right[2]). In the end Kappler decided in favour of eclecticism as the best procedure by which to arrive at the original text, though some of the suspicion of the Lucianic remained (1M 34).

Dr. Hanhart's views seem to be similar as far as 2M is concerned. In 3M he implies that the true text is usually found in the agreement of two or more of the classes of manuscripts mentioned above and that rarely

[2]) Now see Metzger, "Lucian and the Lucianic Recension of the Greek Bible", *New Testament Studies*, viii. 189—203 (April 1962).

does any manuscript or group give us the right reading when it stands alone. In particular the Lucianic is still regarded with suspicion. The valuable discussions in H contain further arguments in favour of Dr. Hanhart's views.

H has the following contents: a general statement of the principles of the edition; Chapter I which treats of the details of the formation of the text, contractions, orthography, and grammatical features; Chapter II on form or style is concerned with additions and omissions in the Greek tradition, in the Latin, the style of the letters in 2M i. 1–ii. 18 and the style of the narrative portions; Chapter III on the words and content has sections on synonyms, changes in expression, proper names, and on 2M vi. 18ff.; finally the conclusion draws together the preceding argument and illustrates it with further examples. The discussion is maintained throughout in a clear, well informed, well arranged and thoughtful presentation.

In Chapter I the treatment of contractions is interesting and suggestive and the discussion of orthography is learned and convincing. In particular we must welcome the instructive notes on *πρεσβυτέρ(ε)ιον* (H 11f.), *τεῖχος* (H 12, 14f.) and *ἑώρακα*. It is quite clear from these pages how much students of the Greek Bible owe to Dr. P. Katz[3]), but we have to distinguish between what our authors wrote and what is philologically correct. For example, *ἑόρακα* is the original form and meets the philological requirements, but *ἑώρακα* is the form used by Hellenistic writers including those of the Greek Bible, though *ἑόρακα* had been used by Attic writers down to and including Menander, and came back with the new Atticism of the second century A. D. P. Chester Beatty VI (963, Numbers-Deuteronomy, before A.D. 150) is the earliest manuscript evidence for the revival of this form.

Chapter II introduces some important modifications of the maxim *lectio brevior potior*. This principle is only applicable when other things are equal and this condition is fulfilled much less frequently than scholars have imagined. Even where other things are apparently equal the maxim may mislead us. H 18f. justifies the retention of *εἰς οὐρανόν* 2M iii. 15, *τοῖς ὅπλοις* iii. 28 and rightly rejects the conjectural excision of *κατὰ στιγμήν* 2M ix. 11, *εἰς ὄνομα* 3M ii. 9, *δημοσίᾳ* iv. 7.

The Latin evidence for omissions must not be too lightly accepted and H 22ff. rightly gives reasons for caution in regard to the shorter text sometimes to be found in Latin manuscripts. Thus H 22f. rightly prefers the longer text at 2M vi. 31, vii. 11, 18.

One small point may here be intruded into the discussion. At 2M vi. 31 La^{B} has the shorter text with La^{LXMT} against La^{OPVV}. It is noteworthy that La^{B} and La^{O} part company and the difference between these manu-

[3]) Dr. Peter Katz (Walters) died on 26 March 1962. He had made many valuable contributions to Septuagint studies and his death will be regretted by all students of the Greek Bible. It is hoped to publish several of his works.

scripts which usually are so close together may be explained as due to contamination. The passage in La[O] which is not in La[B] agrees verbally with the Vulgate. A study of the differences between La[B] and La[O] reveals that in some of them one reading agrees with the Vulgate and the other differs from it. We may suppose therefore that at 2M vi. 31 La[O] has been supplemented from the Vulgate and that the archetype of La[BO] had the shorter text with La[LXM*T*]. The shorter text of course is still erroneous.

The comment on the shorter text at 2M viii. 12 in H 23 is sound. The omission is probably due to *ὀμ.*, *ΕΦΟΔΟΥ και ..... στρατοπ ΕΔΟΥΟΙ* and Dr. Hanhart is quite right in arguing for the longer text. Likewise his defence of the longer text at 2M iii. 25 (H 27) is justified.

Dr. Hanhart's defence of 2M viii. 30 (H 34) is to be commended in principle. One small point which may be reconsidered is the spelling *αὑτούς*.

The discussion on synonyms in Chapter III contains much instructive detail. Dr. Hanhart presents a convincing argument for two occurences of *γένεσις* in 2M vii. 23 (H 40). The tendency to avoid the recurrence of the same word in the same context is present throughout the Greek Bible. It is possible that at 1M xi. 22 *τῇ ἄκρᾳ* S[ca] *L'* 58 311 340 La[B] SyI et II was omitted by the other witnesses because of *τὴν ἄκραν* at the end of the previous verse.

These views introduce important questions, and we must be grateful to the two scholars not merely for their careful treatment of these questions but also for the full collection of readings in the apparatus which alone makes possible any discussion of their treatment and the resulting text.

One point Kappler and Hanhart make repeatedly: most of the variants are stylistic. There are of course sheer mistakes which occur in all texts transmitted in manuscripts. There are also variations of substance. For example at 1M x. 49 the manuscripts vary in saying who did what. None the less most variations are in matters of grammar and lexicography.

This means that at many places we shall decide about the text on considerations of language. To do this adequately we must be able to decide first which reading is right and for this knowledge of the author's style is necessary, and secondly how the rejected readings came into being, for which we shall need some knowledge of the stylistic standards and fashions of the Hellenistic and Roman Periods.

These considerations apply equally to 1–3M, but, to begin with, we shall treat principally 1M. Here we can be more precise. The book was written in Hebrew about B.C. 100 and was translated into Greek perhaps by B.C. 50. Basically the Greek is ordinary *Koine* without literary features, but strongly influenced by Hebrew idiom. The author has over and above this his distinctive style. In detail this often enables us to decide which readings conform to the linguistic character of the book and which do not.

How did the readings which were out of character come into being? First barbarism, Semitism for example, was roundly condemned and, where we have two or more readings of which one reflects Hebrew idiom, we may, other things being equal, regard the more Hebraic reading as original and the other variants as attempts to substitute normal Greek. We may maintain this view with particular confidence in dealing with 1 M. It is true that the Hebrew Old Testament down to the third century A. D. influenced the text of the LXX, but for 1 M the Hebrew is lost and does not seem to have modified the Greek translation in its transmission. To this extent the conditions are simpler than where the Hebrew is extant. If this is so, readings in 1 M which reflect Hebrew idiom cannot fail to be original to the translation.

Secondly, where we have two forms of the text one of which is in more literary *Koine* than the other, the less literary text is to be preferred. For at least a hundred years after its production the Greek translation was open to this influence.

Thirdly, Atticism made its appearance as the prevailing literary fashion toward the end of the first century, and affected not merely the writing of authors from that time on but also the text of earlier works such as those of Herodotus and Xenophon. It has also left its mark on the LXX. Where we have two readings one of which conforms to Attic canons and the other does not we shall, again other things being equal, accept the non-Attic reading.

One factor of linguistic change cannot be shown to have operated. It is several times alleged that scribes have corrected the text at one point to make it correspond to other passages of our author. There is little or no evidence that scribes had this aim. 1 M was not a literary classic in Antiquity. Had we been examining the text of Plato or Demosthenes, we might have found in scribes a concern to maintain the integrity and consistency of the author's style, because they were standards of language in their own right. Where 1 M was concerned, the standards of style were external, and it was to these external standards that correction of style was normally made. Where we have to choose between readings which maintain the consistency of the style and language of 1 M and readings which do not, unless other considerations point to a different decision, we ought to prefer the reading which gives consistency.

Let us take up some concrete issues, now that these principles of criticism have been established. Greeks did not like barbarian proper names in the unmitigated uncouthness of the original language. Thus in Herodotus the many barbarian proper names are made to end in a vowel or in one of the few suitable consonants and are conformed to Greek declension. We shall expect that in 1 M the uncouth forms will go back to the original translation and the adapted forms will be scribal modifications.

Let us take Jerusalem for an example. It appears in the Greek Bible in two forms: the unmitigated transliteration *Ιερουσαλημ* and the adjusted form *Ἱεροσόλυμα*. As we expect *Ιερουσαλημ* is by far the commoner form in the manuscripts of 1M. Further, at xiii. 2 Dr. Kappler is right, on our argument, in rejecting *Ἱεροσόλυμα* of *L* and reading *Ιερουσαλημ* from the other manuscripts. But, if *L* is wrong when it reads *Ἱεροσόλυμα*, why is it wrong four times when it reads *Ιερουσαλημ*? The evidence is as follows: i. 14 *L*–19–93 46 55; i. 20 S V *L*–19–93 46 311; x. 43 *L*; xi. 34 *L'* 55. (There is no undisputed example of *Ἱεροσόλυμα* in 1M.) If we read *Ιερουσαλημ* in these four places, we shall be choosing the more barbaric form and one which conforms to the author's practice elsewhere. It would however require us to accept Lucianic evidence three times where it stands alone.

Similar considerations apply to *Ιωναθαν*. For a Greek this form would be unparalleled as a dative or genitive and normal only as an accusative. Consequently we find inflected nominatives, genitives and datives as variants at a number of passages; but nowhere is the inflected form attested by the entire manuscript tradition, though the manuscripts agree in giving the uninflected form eight times. This suggests that the uninflected form is original. In accepting this view we would depend in three or four passages mainly on Lucianic evidence. Dr. Kappler's theory leads him to read at xiii. 25 a form which has no evidence at all (1M 41). We will be forced to the conclusion that emendation is necessary from time to time but there is no call to indulge in it where we can arrive at an acceptable text from the manuscripts. Other things being equal, I would rather follow a Lucianic reading than a conjecture.

The authors of 1–4M have their rules for the presence and absence of the article with geographical proper names. Thus *Ἀσία* with one possible exception (1M xi. 13) always has the article in these books as it regularly does in the New Testament. On the other hand *Αἴγυπτος* usually does not. We have at least 21 examples of *Αἴγυπτος* without the article, nine of them in 1M. In 1M we also have three examples of *γῆ Αἰγύπτου*. *ἡ Αἴγυπτος* occurs at 1M xi. 13 and 3M ii. 25 as a variant and without variant at 3M iii. 20. We notice that at 1M xi. 13 the variants affect both *Ἀσία* and *Αἴγυπτος*. Here Kappler's text reads *τὸ τῆς Αἰγύπτου καὶ Ἀσίας*. *Αἴγυπτος* with the article and *Ἀσία* without it are both irregular. Better is the reading *τὸ τῆς Ἀσίας καὶ Αἰγύπτου* A *q l* 46 55 58 106 311 340 La^{B} which avoids the irregularities. Better still is the reading *ἀπὸ τῆς Ἀσίας καὶ ἀπ' Αἰγύπτου L* when the use of the article is regular and the repeated preposition will reflect Hebrew idiom.

At 1M i. 6 the order *τοὺς παῖδας αὐτοῦ τοὺς ἐνδόξους* reflects Hebrew practice where we normally have the noun with suffixed pronoun followed by the adjective with or without the article as sense and idiom require. This arrangement seems however to be unknown in uncontaminated Greek. It occurs elsewhere in the LXX, and at 1M iii. 15, iv. 7, 53, vii. 48, viii. 31, ix. 2 etc., and up and down the New Testament. Scribes did not like it as it was not normal Greek and sometimes altered the text. Thus Dr. Kappler gives us at iii. 3 *τὰ σκεύη τὰ πολεμικὰ αὐτοῦ*, but the Hebrew order *τὰ σκεύη αὐτοῦ τὰ πολεμικά* is read by *L*-19-93 311. If we follow the argument, this ought to be the right reading.

Normally in the LXX attributive *πᾶς* precedes its noun in dependence on the Hebrew practice where כל comes before the noun. Places where attributive *πᾶς* follows its noun are suspect. Let us see how far Hebrew idiom has influenced the Greek of 1M. There are about 165 instances of attributive *πᾶς* in the book. In most of these *πᾶς* precedes its noun without a variant order. This suggests that at ix. 11 we should interpret *οἱ πρωταγωνισταί, πάντες οἱ δυνατοί*. At iii. 27, iv. 15, 37, v. 63, vi. 59, vii. 7, viii. 4, xi. 70, xiii. 4, 53 (ten instances) in Kappler's text *πᾶς* follows its noun but there are the following variants: iii. 27 *πάσας τὰς δυνάμεις* *L*-19-93 La[G]; vi. 59 *πάντα ταῦτα* V 64-728-93-542 55 La; vii. 7 *πᾶσαν τὴν ἐξολέθρευσιν* S 58 311; xiii. 4 *πάντες οἱ ἀδελφοί μου* SV La[BW]; xiii. 53 *πασῶν τῶν δυνάμεων* 107 La[BW]. We may also notice iv. 37 *πᾶσα ἡ παρεμβολή* La; v. 63 *πάντων τῶν ἐθνῶν* La[G]; viii. 4 *παντός τοῦ τόπου* La. The two instances that remain iv. 15, xi. 70 may be termed abnormal as *πάντες* strictly speaking is followed not by a noun or pronoun but by a nominal phrase. Thus 1M is regular in its placing of *πᾶς*, but in achieving this expected regularity we have had to resort to Lucianic and Latin evidence.

Other traces of Hebrew idiom may be found in the apparatus as well as in the text. For example Hebrew had a dominant word order: verb, subject, rest of predicate, which while it was possible in Greek was not anything like as common. In fact a dominant word order was unknown in Greek and its presence in a Greek text would be an irritant which scribes would be tempted to mitigate. An examination of the variations of order in the apparatus will reveal examples of this. In general we may urge that the variant which reproduces a Hebrew word order is to be preferred to the variant that eliminates it, again other things being equal.

In some features *Koine* and Hebrew idiom are closer to each other than Attic Greek and Hebrew would be. *Koine* was more explicit than the older language. Thus is used *αὐτόν κτλ.* more generously than earlier Greek and here it was nearer to Hebrew with its frequent use of suffixed pronouns. Likewise prepositions were employed more freely and in particular the use of *ἐν* was greatly expanded. The reading that eliminates *αὐτόν κτλ.* and *ἐν* is to be regarded as an attempt to bring the Greek nearer to Attic standards.

At this point we may consider *ἅπας*. Frequently in Attic Greek *ἅπας* was used when the previous word ended in a consonant and *πᾶς* when it ended in a vowel. *πᾶς* remained the normal word in Hellenistic Greek but some books like Luke-Acts used *ἅπας* from time to time without strict attention to the Attic practice. Its presence probably suggested literary pretensions. As we have seen *πᾶς* is very common in 1M. Kappler prints *ἅπας* four times: v. 25 *ἅπαντα*] *πάντα* S *L'* 311 314; x. 30 *τὸν ἅπαντα χρόνον*] *τὸν αἰῶνα χρόνον* *q*; xi. 36 *τὸν ἅπαντα χρόνον*; xv. 8 *τὸν ἅπαντα χρόνον*] *τὸν αἰῶνα χρόνον* La[BW], *τὸν αἰῶνα τὸν ἅπαντα χρόνον* 58, *ἅπαντα χρόνον* V 46 55. While *εἰς τὸν αἰῶνα χρόνον* is a LXX expression (e.g. Ex.

xiv. 13), it is a very unGreek one and we may suspect that it is original at x. 30, xi. 36, xv. 8 and that *ἅπαντα* is substituted to restore grammar. Likewise *ἅπαντα* at v. 25 is a literary correction in keeping with the Attic rule. If this argument is correct, *ἅπας* is foreign to the text of 1M.

Other instances of literary correction may be detected. Particles which cannot stand first in a sentence were going out of use. *δὲ* has still a long life, but *ἄρα, γε, δή* are already uncommon. *ἄρα* occurs at 1M. ix. 8, but it is here represented by B O only among the Latin manuscripts. It is absent from 2,3M but occurs at 4M i. 3. 1–3M do not use *γε* but it occurs 13 times in 4M. *δή* occurs as follows: 1M ix. 44] om 107 534 340 La^{LXGV}, *νυν* AVq^{-107} 542 46^{5} (52) 55 56 58 106 311; 2M ix. 2] *δέ* La^{XV}, om La^{BOMP}; ix. 4] *ἤδη* V La^{L}, *ἀεί* 106, *δέ* La$^{B?O?M}$, om *L'* 55 311 La^{VP}; xiv. 7] *δέ* A' *l* 771 La^{LXVP}, om. La^{BOM}; 3M i. 9] om. 71–107; i. 29; ii. 11; 4M some 18 times. We may doubt whether any of these particles were in the original text of 1–3M.

τε also was passing out of use. It is not common in the LXX where many of the examples are textually uncertain. Acts is the only book to use it freely in the New Testament and there are no certain examples in the works which seem to display the lowest stratum of New Testament Greek, Mark, John, Pastoral Epistles, Revelation. The examples in 1M, viii. 7 not in La, xi. 34 om A La, xii. 11 om AV*L*–62 46 55 La^{LXV}; xii. 21 not in La, are all questionable and probably none of them should be in the text. *τε* is commoner in 2–4M, but even in these books many of its occurences are uncertain and should be eliminated.

ὡσεί is a rare word and restricted to a few books in the Greek Bible. Thus in the New Testament it is almost confined to Luke-Acts. While *ὡς* is common in the text of 1–3M *ὡσεί* occurs as follows: 1M vii. 32] *ὡς* A 62 46 106, om. 71 *L*–19–93 311, 2M xi. 5] *ὡς* 55 311, om La^{LXV}.

ἐκεῖνος as distinct from *κἀκεῖνος* was becoming exclusively an adjective. Thus, apart from one variant reading, *ἐκεῖνος* is used only adjectivally in Mark and is normally an adjective in Matthew and Luke-Acts. In 1–2M we have only two instances of *ἐκεῖνος* as a pronoun: 1M iv. 54 *ἐκείνῃ*] + *τῇ ἡμέρᾳ* SV*L*–19–93 55 58 311 (La^{B}) SyI; 2M xiv. 40 *ἐκεῖνον*] hos La^{XBWP}, eos La^{M}. On the other hand in 3M *ἐκεῖνος* is normally pronominal and only at vii. 15 an adjective. Certainly in 1M and probably in 2M the instance of pronominal *ἐκεῖνος* should be eliminated.

In the Greek Bible most writers prefer either *ἀπαγγέλλειν* or *ἀναγγέλλειν* which are used with the same meaning. Rarely can we be sure that the same writer uses both words. 1M uses *ἀπαγγέλλειν* (14 times) as do the Minor Prophets and Matthew and Mark, but we have at 1M ii. 31 *ἀνηγγέλη*. We may feel that despite all the Greek evidence we ought here to write *ἀπηγγέλη*.

ἔνθεν καὶ ἔνθεν is the established phrase (3 times) in those books. We probably ought to read it instead of *ἔνθα καὶ ἔνθα* at 1M vi. 45 with *L*–19–93 Sy II.

Outside the Pentateuch there are no certain examples of the adverb *αὐτοῦ* in the Greek Bible. *ἐνταῦθα*, *ἐκεῖ* and the like have taken its place. Whatever therefore we do at 1M v. 67 we ought not to read adverbial *αὐτοῦ* as Kappler does. The only objection to reading *βουλομένου* seems to be that this imputes vainglory and rashness to Judas.

ὅδε is going out of use in Hellenistic Greek as can be seen from the New Testament and the Apostolic Fathers. It occurs only once in 1M at xv. 15 *τάδε* with the variant *ταῦτα* SV 55 to introduce a letter. *οὗτος* is used elsewhere in 1M to introduce a document at viii. 22, x. 17,25,51, xi. 29, xii. 5,19, xiii. 35, xiv. 20,27, xv. 2. This suggests that we should read *ταῦτα* at xv. 15. *τάδε* will be introduced in keeping with the Classical use of this pronoun. On the other hand *ὅδε* is firmly fixed in the text of 2–3M.

The Lucianic variant is wrong at 1M xii. 40 *εὐλαβήθη*] *ἐφοβήθη* *L'* 46 106 311. As we are told by Moeris, *εὐλαβεῖσθαι* in the sense of *φοβεῖσθαι* is not Attic Greek but *Koine*. Here *ἐφοβήθη* is an Atticising correction. We must recognise however that, even if *εὐλαβήθη* were the Lucianic reading, it would still be right.

We have already noticed some passages from 2M. The influence of Semitic idiom is not easily discerned in most of the book. For 2M i. 1–ii. 18 however there may have been a Hebrew original (cf. H 28–31). Certainly we can detect traces of Hebrew idiom. In view of this the following readings in the apparatus among others are probably right: i. 4 *εἰρήνην ποιῆσαι*] *ποιῆσαι ὑμῖν εἰρήνην* *L'*; 5 *ὑμᾶς ἐγκαταλίποι*] tr. *L'*; 11 *ὑπὸ τοῦ θεοῦ* / *σεσωσμένοι*] tr. *L'*-62; 17 *ἡμῶν* / *ὁ θεός*] tr. *L'* 55; 20 *ἔπεμψεν*] + *αὐτούς* *L'*-62 311 Sy; ii. 4 *τοῦ θεοῦ* / *κληρονομίαν*] tr. 46–52; 7 *ὁ Ἰερεμίας* / *ἔγνω*] tr. *L'*-62.

At 2M i. 36 is one example of *καλεῖν* in the sense "name". It is not used in the sense of *ἐπικαλεῖν* "give an additional name, surname". Instead 2M has in the passive *λέγεσθαι*, ix. 2, x. 32, xii. 17,21,32, xiv. 6, xv. 36. *ἐπικαλεῖν* means only "invoke, call upon". We should therefore at x. 12 *καλούμενος*] *λεγόμενος* V*L'* 46–52 106 311 347 read *λεγόμενος*, as the meaning is "surname".

ὑπεράγαν 2M x. 34, xiii. 25 is peculiar to this book in the Greek Bible. It does not differ in meaning from the simple *ἄγαν* of the older language which the Atticists would prefer. At viii. 35 *ὑπὲρ ἅπαν*] *ὑπεράγαν* *L'* 46–52 55 311 we should restore this characteristic but unusual adverb despite H 39.

Nor should we neglect the suggestions of palaeography. *L'* 58 La^p Sy give at xv. 33 *ΝικανοροCΕΚΤησκεφαλη CΕΚΤεμνων*. It was easy for the eye of the scribe to pass from the first *CEKT* to the second so that other witnesses give us the text *ΝικανοροCΕΚΤεμνων*.

The same kind of error may have reduced 1M x. 64 *καθωσεΚΗΡΥΞενεμπροσθενautouΚΗΡΥΞ* *L*–19–93 58 311 Sy1 to *καθὼς ἐκήρυξεν* given by other manuscripts. *ἔμπροσθεν* belongs to the vocabulary of 1M, cf. iii. 30 (2), xiii. 27.

ἐᾶν can be an awkward verb to use and some writers in the LXX preferred *ἀφιέναι*. 1M has *ἐᾶν* at xii. 40, xv. 14, but 20 examples of *ἀφιέναι*. 2M has six examples of *ἐᾶν*, but in 1–3M there are no certain examples of the middle or passive. Thus at 2M vi. 13 *ἐᾶσθαι*] *ἔσεσθαι* 19 55 58 771 the future indicative is likely to be right. *ἔσεσθαι* recurs at vii. 19, ix. 17, xiv. 14. Likewise, at 3M v. 18 *εἰάθησαν*] *ἦσαν* L^{-728}–311, *εἴησαν* 728–*l*, *ἦσαν* introduces a compound tense, *ἦσαν* . . . . . . *περιβεβιωκότες*, that would not be acceptable to the Atticists. Further *ἐᾶν* does not recur in 3M.

It is doubtful if *ἅπας* is original in 2M. As we have seen *ὑπεράγαν* is to be preferred to *ὑπὲρ ἅπαν* at viii. 35. Elsewhere we have the following variants: iv. 16 *καθ' ἅπαν*] *κατὰ πᾶν* V*L'*; xiv. 9 *ἅπαντας*] *πάντας* *L*; xv. 30 *καθ' ἅπαν*] *καθ' ἅπαντα* *L*(64*)–93, *κατὰ πάντα* 64^{c}–l^{-93} 311. Only xiii. 6 *ἅπαντες* (H 44f.), which conforms to the Attic practice, has no variant. On the other hand *πᾶς* is abundant.

We may have doubts though perhaps not quite such strong doubts about *ἅπας* in 3M. We may note ii. 9 *ἁπάντων*] *πάντων* 728–l^{-347}; iii. 18 *ἅπαντας*] *πάντας* V 534–542 58; iv. 5 *ἁπάσης*] *πάσης* 64*–93, *ἀπειλῆς* 68; v. 51 *ἁπάσης*] *πάσης* V cf. *πάντων* *L'*–311; vi. 12 *ἅπασαν*] *πᾶσαν* L'^{-19}, om. 19 46 311; vi. 23 *ἅπαντας*] *πάντας* *L'*–311 46; vii. 6 *ἅπαντας*] *πάντας* V 534 58 610. On the other hand there is no manuscript evidence against *ἅπας* at ii. 7, iii. 5,21, v. 2,43. *πᾶς* is again frequent.

Let us now take up the long passage in *L*–311 at 3M V. 29. Dr. Hanhart though he relegates it to the apparatus points out that it is written in the style of 3M. He argues against the possibility of homoeoteleuton that the intervening text between the two examples of *πρόθεσιν* is too long for this factor to operate. This view of the conditions in which *ὁμ.* operates is to be met with from time to time, but a perusal of A. C. Clark, *The Descent of Manuscripts*, will show that it is not borne out by the facts. The fresh introduction of Hermon is a problem, but it is a problem on either view. Why for example should an interpolator introduce such an inconsistency into the passage he was adding? It is more probable that the author himself was responsible for the conflict in presentation.

It will not have escaped notice that many of the readings recommended in these comments are found, exclusively or not, in Lucianic witnesses. At first it may seem both foolish and ungracious to argue in favour of so many Lucianic readings after Rahlfs and his successors have accumulated much material in order to show that where the Lucianic witnesses diverge from other manuscripts they provide a text that is nearly always secondary.

On this remark there are two comments. The first is that there is an element of truth in the view that regards the characteristic readings of the Lucianic manuscripts as unoriginal. On any showing many of them are. For example, there are lists of readings at 2M p. 21 and 3M p. 19 which affect particles. Now we can take the view about these readings as about all other such that when they are alone, whatever the Lucianic witnesses read, they are wrong. They are wrong when they have *καί*, they

2*

are wrong when they lack καί. But, even if they are wrong only when they lack καί, they are wrong a certain number of times. This will be true of other such variants and in this way we can see that among Lucianic readings is a considerable secondary element. This will be true of the text of most manuscripts and need not surprise us.

The second comment is that the careful analyses of the Lucianic readings do not prove what they may be thought to prove. If we know already that Lucianic manuscripts are usually wrong, the lists of variants do not prove this, they merely provide material on which we may exercise this important knowledge that we already have. If we lack this knowledge, the lists do not supply it because, careful as they are, they do not of themselves prove which readings are right and which are wrong.

If these comments are apposite, we must examine the variants again. We must take for example the lists mentioned above at 2M p. 21, 3M p. 19 and consider them on their merits and when we have done this then make our conclusion the starting point for a new assessment of our manuscripts if this seems possible and desirable.

Let us take the variants in the two lists above mentioned that involve τε and καί. If the contention is right that τε is obsolescent at this period, then the Lucianic manuscripts will be right when they avoid it and Atticising when they have it. καί on the other hand was an overworked particle in Hellenistic Greek and doubly overworked in translations from the Hebrew. One way of improving style would be to reduce the occurences of καί. On this view the Lucianic manuscripts will be right when they have καί, wrong when they do not. In this way we can frequently decide on the rightness or wrongness of whole classes of variants. What is required is a knowledge of the nature and development of Greek in the Hellenistic and Roman periods, of the various literary fashions which operated, and of the particular nature of our texts.

If as our few examples have suggested the Lucianic manuscripts are sometimes right and sometimes wrong, how do we reconcile this with the fact that these manuscripts have doublets or complete readings, the mark since Westcott and Hort's day of a secondary text?

In considering this argument let us turn to the text of the New Testament from which it is drawn. Since Westcott and Hort it has been shown that not all apparent doublets are really such and that for their own purposes scribes have sometimes abbreviated what seemed to them tautologous expression. Again, it has been noticed that doublets have been found in texts other than the Syrian of which Westcott and Hort judged them to be characteristic. Even B (Vaticanus) has some examples.

This argument can be applied to 1-3M. As Dr. Hanhart has reminded us, 2M 35, the Latin has several doublets. But the Latin is also right at a number of places. Therefore the presence of doublets cannot be held to prove that the Latin is everywhere a secondary text. We can argue to the same conclusion for the Lucianic manuscripts. When they present an undoubted conflate reading, they are secondary, but this decision does not entail the conclusion that they are everywhere secondary. Elsewhere they will be right or wrong according to the nature of the readings involved.

We are in fact arguing for the rigorous and impartial application of the eclecticism in favour of which Dr. Kappler concluded, 1 M 37f. Each manuscript and group of manuscripts will contain original and secondary elements. We must choose the original and reject the secondary because they are original or secondary, not because they occur in these or those manuscripts.

Another reference to the text of the New Testament may be apposite here. More and more scholars are coming to realise that apart from sheer mistakes most of the variants to the New Testament text came into being before A.D. 200[4]). The different types of text known to us will be largely selections of existing variants. If this is true of the LXX also, it has a bearing on the status of the Lucianic manuscripts. The Lucianic text, if we may so describe it, is not a recension in the making of which a large number of new and worthless variants were created. It presents rather a distinct selection of already existing readings, some good and some bad. This will explain the fact that it has a large number of readings in common with other witnesses which are older than the historic Lucian or at least independent of his text.

If we may accept this opinion of the value of Lucianic readings, we may now recall a very significant feature of the text of 1 M. As we noted above 1M appears to have been written about B.C. 100 in Hebrew and the Greek translation was made perhaps by B.C. 50. The Hebrew original was later lost and does not seem to have had any subsequent influence on the Greek version. Scribes and correctors cannot be shown to have referred to it in copying or revising the Greek. Consequently where the text or variants reflect Hebrew idiom they must be reflecting a reading which is original to the translation. The alternative reading will represent an attempt to bring the version more into line with Greek idiom.

This argument is relevant outside 1 M both to the New Testament and the LXX. It is relevant to the New Testament because, though it cannot be shown that any part of the New Testament is a translation, we have to recognise in large parts of it the influence of Semitic idiom. Further, among variant readings in these parts there are some which reproduce Semitic idiom and some which avoid it. The parallel from 1 M strengthens the hand of those who argue that other things being equal the more Semitic reading is original and the reading which avoids Semitism is a stylistic correction.

The application to the LXX is different. Here it has been maintained that except where we are dealing with an obvious mistake the Greek text which differs from the Hebrew is preferable to the text which agrees with

---

[4]) See Vogels, *Handbuch der Textkritik des Neuen Testaments*², 162.

it. Now, however, if our diagnosis is right, we have in 1 M evidence of a tendency in scribes and revisers to eliminate Hebraic features from their text. We have to put this against a clearly demonstrable tendency to bring the Greek into line with the Hebrew. How can we choose our readings when we have to allow that both tendencies have been at work?

The answer to this question can only be produced in detail in course of long application to LXX studies. We do but make some suggestions for further consideration. First, where a difference of reading involves a difference in the Hebrew, we may assume that, other things being equal, the text that differs from the Massoretic Hebrew is more likely to be the original LXX. Secondly, where the variation is merely stylistic we may be inclined to decide in favour of the more Semitic reading. We must remember too that we have a criterion which can help us time and again to the right reading, the style of the book. Each book has its distinctive style, and as this is learned we can decide with increasing certainty between variants that otherwise would defeat us.

We may submit a further point. We hope that by this time it will be clear that the study of the text of the LXX and that of the New Testament are clearly related. Advances made in one branch of study usually profit the other as well.

This recognition enables us to acknowledge afresh a debt incurred by this review. All who study the Greek Bible are much indebted to the two editors. Thanks to them we have editions of these three books that aid us considerably in our studies. They contain much accurate, carefully presented information that we can get nowhere else. They have presented careful and instructive analyses of the tradition. Their orthographical and grammatical digests are invaluable to all editors of texts of this period whether in the Greek Bible or not. In this review I have mentioned a few points which I would like to see reconsidered. Many of the places where the editors are manifestly right have not been mentioned. They are obvious to all who use the works of Dr. Kappler and Dr. Hanhart. These two scholars have in these publications maintained the high level of work that we associate with the Göttingen LXX.

Oxford, The Queen's College G. D. Kilpatrick

ADDENDUM

When I wrote (p. 21) "I M appears to have been written about B.C. 100 in Hebrew and the Greek translation was made perhaps by B.C. 50. The Hebrew original was later lost and does not seem to have had any subsequent influence on the Greek version," I was perhaps too dogmatic. Hanhart reminded me of Jerome's statement in the *Prologus Galeatus* to the Vulgate of Samuel-Kings: Macchabaeorum primum librum hebraicum repperi. This statement occurs at the end of a long passage surveying the books of the Hebrew Bible, often growing in transliteration from Hebrew names as well as those used in the Christian Church. This survey seems to owe something to a similar list quoted from Origen's exposition of Psalms Eus.HE.V.25: *εἰσὶν δὲ αἱ εἴκοσι δύο βίβλοι καθ' Ἑβραίους οἵδε· . . ἔξω δὲ τούτων ἐστὶ τὰ Μακκα βαικά, ὅπερ ἐπιγέγραπται Σαρβηθσαβαναιελ.* Origen gives in this list transliterations of the Hebrew names of the Old Testament books and it is reasonable to infer that *Σαρβηθσαβαναιελ* represents another such transliteration from the Hebrew, corrupt as it may be. Origen does not say in so many words that he knew a Hebrew original of I Maccabees but it is a not unreasonable inference from his text.

If Jerome knew I Maccabees in Hebrew as he says, he seems to have made no use of it. This is in contrast to his dealing with Judith and Tobit where he professes to give us new translations from the Semitic texts. Why did he not give us a new translation of I Maccabees? Does his statement rest on an inference from Origen's words? We cannot exclude this possibility, though we may still think that it is more likely that Jerome's straight forward statement is the truth.

How did Origen come by his list? It is still a matter of debate how much Hebrew he knew and how far he was himself able to make transliterations into Greek script. P. Kahle, for example (*The Cairo Geniza,*[2] 157-164), suggested he used transliterations already made by Jews. Did he acquire the Hebrew names in his list of Old Testament books in the same way? If he did, then the presumably Hebrew title of I Maccabees in his statement becomes evidence not that Origen knew I Maccabees in Hebrew, but that some Jews at an earlier period so knew it.

Such considerations as these had led me not to take the remarks of Origen and Jerome too seriously as indicating the survival of the Hebrew original of I Maccabees at any rate until the end of the fourth century A.D. I could discover no clear traces of the influence of such a text on our Greek translation. Indeed the tradition of the Greek text appeared to me uniform. Its variation seemed explicable by way of mistake and deliberate change from an original usually discernible.

Recently the examination of I Macc.VII.19 has made me less certain about this. The text runs καὶ ἔθυσεν αὐτοὺς εἰς τὸ φρέαρ ,τὸ μέγα ἔθυσεν] ἔσφαξεν 58311. First, W. Bauer's suggestion that ἔθυσεν means merely "kill" is mistaken (*Wörterbuch,*[5] 726, cf. *The Bible Translator,* xii.120-132). It means "sacrifice, kill sacrificially," a meaning that is unexpected in the context. The variant reading ἔσφαξεν gives the sense we would find suitable. It is undoubtedly the easier reading with which we may compare Jer. xlviii (xli) 7 ἔσφαξεν αὐτοὺς εἰς τὸ φρέαρ.

In the Jeremiah passage σφάζειν renders the Hebrew root שחט , but שחט sometimes is rendered by θύειν. Other roots of which this is true are זבח and טבח, as follows:

שחט = θύειν , Ex.xii.21, Jud. xii.6 G[A+]σφάζουσιν , 2 Chr. XXIX.22 (3), 24, XX.15 (17), XXXV.1,6,11, is xxii.13, lxvi.3
= σφάζειν Gn. xxii.10, xxxvii.31, Ex. xii. 6, xxix.11,16,20, Lev.i.5,11, iii.2, 8,13, iv.4,15,24, etc., Jer. xlviii (xli).7
זבח = θύειν , normal
= σφάζειν , Lev.xvii.5, Ezk.xxxiv.3
= θύειν IK.xxv.11, Jer.xi.19
= ἔσφαξεν , Gn.xliii.16, Ex.xxii.1, Dt.xxviii.31, Ps.xxxvi.14, Pr.ix.2, Is.xiv.21, Ezk.xxi.10(15).

Presumably the Hebrew original of I Macc.vii.19 used one of these three verbs in the sense of "slaughter." The original translator rendered this mistakenly as ἔθυσεν meaning "he sacrificed." A corrector substituted the right rendering ἔσφαξεν . How did he come to do this?

There are three possibilities. First, he could simply have conjectured that ἔσφαξεν was what the passage required. Our difficulty is to find evidence for the existence of someone able to make such conjectures in the tradition of I Maccabees.

Secondly, he could have derived the verb from Jer.xlviii (xli).7. Again, we may ask whether there is evidence in the tradition for someone working on the text in this way.

Thirdly, there may have been independent recourse to the Hebrew original. This would explain the correction and also put us on the way to understand how the mistaken translation was made. If this suggestion seems reasonable, then it remains for us to scrutinize the variants of I Maccabees again to see if we can find other instances where alternative readings may be translations of a common underlying Hebrew. Until then this explanation remains only a possibility, but a possibility which cannot be disproved.

We may have a similar mistranslation at Ecclus. xxxi (xxxiv).24: θύων υἱὸν ἔναντι τοῦ πατρὸς αὐτοῦ To this Chrysostom has an alternative (vii. 526) ὡς ὁ ἀποκτείνων τὸν υἱὸν ἔμπροσθεν τοῦ πατρὸς αὐτοῦ.
The meaning "sacrifice" would be quite in keeping with the context which requires the mention of a monstrous crime. Either the slaughter of a son or the sacrifice of a son would be in keeping. The context is concerned with sacrifice, but the Hebrew is not extant. We may infer that the Hebrew had an ambiguous term, but that the first translator rendered this by θύειν meaning "sacrifice." It remains open to debate whether he translated correctly or not. We may suppose that Chrysostom gives us the version of a second translator who took the Hebrew term in the sense of slaughter.

SPECIMEN OF A NEW EDITION OF THE GREEK JOSHUA

MAX L. MARGOLIS (PHILADELPHIA)

1. The Specimen requires an introductory description of the scope and arrangement of the new Edition. As I have devisedly chosen for the Specimen page 429 of SWETE's edition, the same that the editors of the Larger Cambridge Septuagint, following the selection by Drs. HORT and SWETE of ten specimen pages in the Octateuch, had collated in all the extant MSS. known to them, a word is in place on this preliminary collation. I am indebted to Mr. MCLEAN for the collation of the Joshua page, and it is pleasing to record that I was introduced to the Cambridge scholar and his colleague, Professor BROOKE, by the late Dr. ISRAEL ABRAHAMS, in whose memory this Volume is published.

2. It is only recently that I was able to study the specimen collation. The page selected does on the whole serve its purpose; perhaps the following page 430 would have been more serviceable, since in v. 13f. the textual types are sharply marked in my apparatus; perhaps also an additional page with place-names (chapt. 15 or 19) would have been welcome. The textual type sometimes varies at given points in the book in one and the same MS., as I shall have occasion to show. The specimen collation contains the evidence of two uncials, MV (that of BAF was given in SWETE), and 78 minuscules. The edition in the Larger Cambridge Septuagint by BROOKE-MCLEAN (B.-M.), published in 1917, adds the evidence of the uncials Θ, G, K, Δ_8 and (in the preface) the small fragment Oxyrhynchus 1168; but of the minuscules only 28 were selected, with the addition, however, of b_2, somehow absent from the specimen collation, and the Lectionary d_2. To the apparatus thus available for page 429 SWETE, I have been able to add cod. Μετέωρα 216 (Rahlfs 461), the Haverford MS. of the Ethiopic—of both of which I have photographs—and (in transcript) the Syriac Lectionary Brit. Mus. Add. 12,133 (see FIELD, i, 334). I possess likewise photographs of F and the

Reprinted from *Jewish Studies in Memory of Israel Abrahams*. New York. 1927.

minuscules 15. 18. 29. 44. 54. 55. 56. 58. 64. 68. 71. 74. 75. 76. 82. 84. 106. 108. 118. 121. 122. 127. 128. 134. 343. 407. 426. 509. 610. 730 and of the Brit. Mus. MS. of the Syrohexaplar. Naturally I had before me the facsimile editions of BAGΘ and TISCHENDORF's edition of K (see my "K Text of Joshua," AJSL xxviii, 1–55), the Onomasticon in the editions of LAGARDE and KLOSTERMANN, the editions of patristic writers and of the secondary versions (Sahidic, Bohairic, Ethiopic, Latin, Syriac). My own work on the Greek Joshua was begun in 1910.

3. The preliminary notice then published on the grouping of the codices in the Greek Joshua (see JQR N. S. i, 259–263) was based practically on HOLMES-PARSONS and lacks, of course, the precision which I have now arrived at after sixteen years of labor. The sum of the witnesses yields four principal recensions, **PCSE**, and in addition a number of MSS. variously mixed which I name **M**. At the outset it must be remarked that all of our witnesses are more or less mixed; the classification has in mind the basic character of a text, which alone is the determinant.

4. **P** is the Palestinian recension spoken of by Jerome, that is the Eusebian edition of the Septuagint column in Origen's Hexapla-Tetrapla. In a (relatively) pure form this class numbers but few representatives, and these constitute two sub-groups: $\mathbf{P}_1$ = Gγ (= c B.-M.) c_1 (= *b*) c_2 (= b′) and $\mathbf{P}_2$ = b (= x) $\mathfrak{S}$ (the Syriac version of the Greek: $\mathfrak{S}^L$ = the Brit. Mus. MS. edited by LAGARDE, $\mathfrak{S}^M$ = the Syrus Masii, $\mathfrak{S}^F$ = the Syriac Lectionary referred to above) On(omasticon). On the relation of the three forms of $\mathfrak{S}$ to one another I have written at length in a monograph which is to appear in the Harvard Theological Series; much also pertaining to the character of the **P** recension and its two divisions will be found there. For our present purposes it will suffice to say that for the proper names $\mathfrak{S}$ steps out, since but with exceptions the version took them over from the Peshitta; but the loss is more than offset by On. As between Hexapla and Tetrapla, $\mathbf{P}_2$ on the whole represents the latter and $\mathbf{P}_1$ the former. But such is the eclecticism of the texts that $\mathfrak{S}$, contrary to the general rule, occasionally reverses its habit to place the tetraplaric reading in the text and the hexaplaric in the margin; then, again, some of the marginal readings go back to the Syrian recension (**S**); nay, **S** readings have also entered the text of $\mathfrak{S}$. b, the sole Greek MS. closely resembling the Greek underlying $\mathfrak{S}$, in a few instances stands alone in expressing the Hebrew in a manner at odds with the unanimous reading of all

the other group members. Thus 15. 25 the MS. reads και ασωρ και αδαθα in the place of και ασωρ την καινην of the others including On. On the other hand, b is invaluable because it alone, in a consistent manner, brings out adjustments to the Hebrew in the matter of word sequence or the use of the article which the Syriac translator was not able to express, or where he employed certain devices to express these matters it is only with the aid of b that we are in a position to become aware of them. As FIELD, not to say Masius, had no access to this MS., it is not be wondered at that their retroversion of the Syriac remained imperfect.

G is available only for the middle part of the book (end of chapt. 9 to 19. 23 αυτη η κληρονομια). **γ**, a close congener of G where it remains true to type, cannot take its place in the parts missing, since the cursive is a mixed text. My impression is that the underlying copy of **γ** was a text of a different type into which **P** readings were worked. c_1 and c_2 are twin codices; c_2, which LAGARDE followed largely in his so-called "Lucian," is the inferior of the two. On c_1 as the basic text of the Complutensian edition (𝔠) and on the corrector of the MS. see my monograph on Masius, § 9. The common ancestor of $c_{1.\,2}$, c, ascends to an uncial which resembled G not only in the form of the text, but also, as may be proved from omissions which are due to the skipping of one or more lines, externally in the number of letters to a line in a column. An important observation, which has escaped LAGARDE and HAUTSCH (*Der Lukiantext des Oktateuch*, 1909), but of which the editor of 𝔠 had an imperfect intuition (see my monograph, *ibid.*, especially section g), is that the opening of our book, to 2. 18 middle, formed part of the MS. which c used in the Pentateuch and then took up again Ruth 4. 11 (see RAHLFS, *Studie über den griechischen Text des Buches Ruth*, 1922, 77, 94); the gap was supplied from another MS. which, so far as the major part of our book goes, had a text belonging to $\mathbf{P}_1$. Nevertheless, its text is eclectic, now going with Hexapla now with Tetrapla.

5. **C** is a recension which was at home in Constantinople and Asia Minor. We are helped in localizing the recension by the aid of the Armenian version (see CONYBEARE, SCRIVENER-MÜLLER, ii, 151). Whether the recension had any relationship to the fifty copies ordered by Constantine from Eusebius, as CONYBEARE suspects, must remain a matter of conjecture. Jerome says nothing of a fourth recension; but then he is by no means exact, or the recension was at his

time just in the process of formation. The class **C** is made up of AMV (= N B.-M.) W (=Θ), the cursives **α** (=y) **ε** (=o, see presently) g (=l) r (=71) u (see presently) v (=b_2) ν_1 (=122) ν_2 (=68), and (basically) **𝕬**, also, to judge from the specimen collation, the cursives 318. 488. 527. 669. The test case, unfortunately impossible of verification for the last four MSS., is 19. 26 the omission of και αλιμελεχ (or however the name read in the archetypal copy) which goes through the entire membership (M, of course, is unavailable here) and is nowhere else to be met with. Hence all of these are shown to be the descendants of a common ancestor. A characteristic point of this recension is that, in accordance with the well-known prescription of Jerome, it passes over asterized elements in a manner to make it obvious that the editor had **P** before him. One example will suffice. 15. 9 the common text read και διεκβαλλει εις το ορος εφρων. Origen missed עיי. He took recourse to Aquila; in taking over the missing word he copied from the same source the preposition as he found it there; naturally he placed ορος in the genitive (as Aquila must have done likewise): και διεκβαλλει ※ επι κωμας: ορους εφρων. **C** mechanically passes over the complex sub asterisco and leaves και διεκβαλλει ορους εφρων with the genitive hanging in the air! However, if the recension had come to pass merely by way of subtraction, it would not deserve a place by the side of the other three principal recensions, **ESP**. In the first place, the recension shows elsewhere thought and skill. Here again we shall be content to cite one example. 15. 34–6 read in **P** και ζανω και ηνγαννιμ (**P**$_1$ ηνγοννιμ) ※ θαφφουα: και ※ την: ηναιμ και ιερμουθ και οδολλαμ (**P**$_1$ αδαλαμ) και σωχω και αζηκα και σαραειμ (**P**$_1$ σαγαρειμ) και αδιθαιμ και γαδηρα κ.τ.λ.. **C** reads: και ραμεν και ζανω και αδι[α]θαιμ και ηναειμ και ιεριμουθ και οδολλαμ και νεμρα και σωχω και αζηκα και σα[ρ]γαρειμ και γαδηρα. We recognize the influence of the common text in the insertion of the two items tacitly passed over by Origen; in the form σα[ρ]γαρειμ **C** is linked to **P**$_1$, but in οδολλαμ to **P**$_2$; naturally the asterized elements θαφφουα and την are passed over. But αδιθαιμ is transposed from 36 into verse 34, exactly where the common text has ιδουθωθ. Accordingly the author of the recension recognized in ιδουθωθ a pendant to αδιθαιμ; while giving preference to the form as he found it in **P**, he nevertheless kept to the sequence of the common text. At the same time he dispensed with ηνγαννιμ—not that he realized that this item is covered by ραμεν (corrupted from γανεμ, γαννειμ), for in that case he would have substituted the correct reading. But in writing νεμρα for μεμβρα(ν), the author shows that he commanded still other resources beyond common text and Hexapla-Tetrapla. Herein consists the second point, and a more important one at that, which gives the recension rank beside the three principal recensions. In a number of instances the place-names appear in a form which must have been the original antecedent to the corruptions in the common text such as lay before Origen Thus e.g. 15. 40 χαββα **C** explains χαβρα **ES**, from χαββαν (so instinctively restored in the Aldina) = כַּבַּן, an Aramaizing form in the place of χαββων **P** = כַּבּוֹן; in the same verse χαθλως **C** is the original of μααχως (from καδλως) E כתלויש contrast χαθλεις ($\mathbf{P}_1$ καθαλεις) = כִּתְלִישׁ; 50 ανωβ **C** the original of ανωχ **S**. ανων **E** = עֲנֹב for αναβ **P** = עֲנָב and so on. Perhaps we may suppose that **C** made use of the common text prevalent in Palestine, which naturally remained freer from corruptions in the geographical names. This Palestinian *koine* was only slightly touched up by Theodotion—*Urtheodotion* would accordingly be nothing but this Palestinian *koine*.

In view of the mixture of types to which almost all of our MSS. have been exposed, no complete unanimity among the constituent members of the class is to be expected. I reserve for the fuller Introduction to my edition to deal with the subdivisions and the defaulting members. But here already we may note the closer affinity between A and **α**, as evidenced by some 50 singular readings. Interesting is 19. 6: A has the singular reading αλβαθ for λαβαθ **C**; **α** reads αβλαβαθ, which I explain as $\overset{\beta\alpha}{\underset{\alpha\lambda}{}}$βαθ, where the superscribed letters indicated transposition, the scribe, however, mistook them for a correction.

6. Mixture may be the result either of conflation or of compositeness: "In the composite text, alternating stretches follow a given copy faithfully exactly as it presents itself; the cause being that in an ancestral codex missing portions had been filled up from another MS. with the least concern for diversity of type" (see my monograph on Masius, § 7b). One example we had in the case of c (see above). Another example is codex **ε** which, as I have shown in Masius (*ibid.*, d, Note), goes with **C** 1–10. 4 (as far as εκπολεμησαμεν) 14. 15 (beginning with του πολεμου)—20. 7 and 24. 30 to the end of the book; while in the intervening parts—10. 4 14. 15. 20. 8–24. 29—it comports

with e (see below), as it does again in the beginning of Judges. As for u, the codex belongs to **C** from 15. 5 middle to the end of the book.

7. **S** is the Syrian (Antiochian) recension. The class consists of two divisions: $\mathbf{S}_a$ = Kk_1 (= g B.-M.) k_2 (= n) *k* (= 127) w (= w_1 = 118, w_2 = w B.-M., w_3 = 537, the last on the basis of the specimen collation) 𝔏, and $\mathbf{S}_b$ = T, with the sub-groups: t = t_1 (= 84) t_2 (= t B.-M.) and *t* = t_1 (= 74) t_2 (= 76), and F = f (= p B.-M.) f_1 (= 610) f_2 (= d B.-M.) f_3 (= 125, on the basis of the specimen collation). The sub-group F indulges in textual omissions and contractions; f_2 frequently departs from type. The whole of the division $\mathbf{S}_b$ presents a mixed text, frequently adjusted to **C**; but its basic part belongs to **S**. Relatively purer is $\mathbf{S}_a$; but even there the texts sometimes fall apart. w belongs here basically, but it conflates its texts with superadded elements from **C** (comp. 12. 19b–22a ... και τιναχ και αξφ και θαναχ και μαγεδδων και κεδες και τον βασιλεα καδης, the elements from **C** are overlined), or it is found on the side of $\mathbf{S}_b$ (thus 6. 9 in the singular reading εμπροσθεν for οπισω), or it consorts with 𝔏 (e.g. 6. 24 in the singular reading εδωκε for εδωκαν); interesting is the singular coincidence with Theodoret 23. 13 εκ for απο. The text of w, moreover, is vitiated by omissions and wilful condensations; for an extreme case note the sacrifice of the geographical notices in chapters 13–21 (see my "K Text," 28–30). It is much to be regretted that K is extant only in fragments; at least 11. 13 it is free from the incorporation in textu of parallel renderings from α′σ′ sub nomine in k_1 (see "K Text," p. 24); as this mannerism recurs in k_1, we learn to look with suspicion upon insertions of this kind, even when they are reproduced in k_2 (minus the ascription) or when the ascription is wanting in both. Accordingly k has undergone amplification by the inclusion in the body of the text of glosses from the common ancestor; but this process must have begun early, for in the adduced passage the plus και εστωσας επι των θινων αυτων (from an unknown source) is common to K with all the Greek members of **S**. The supposition that Lucian indulged in doublets will, I believe, not be substantiated as a general practice. k_2, it must be said, has a propensity to abbreviating the text. In *k* the whole middle part from 4. 20 beginning to 21. 5 καταλελειμμενοις is wanting. 𝔏 is a mixed text, with leanings to **E** (specifically to ℭ); it has also undergone conflation by the introduction of glosses (see my paper in

JAOS xxxiii, 254–258). Still its text is unmistakably linked to **S**. A telling example is 19. 34 εις γην (so 𝕷 with k for την; thanks to the corruption it becomes at all possible to identify the underlying Greek behind the Latin, which would have become unrecognizable had the translator found the correct την) αθθοβωρ, a stylistic correction of εν αθθαβωρ **E** (see further below). An outstanding characteristic of the **S** recension is the correction of the Greek style, as shown by the substitution of Attic grammatical forms for Hellenistic. Otherwise Jerome's description of Lucian as but a form of the common text holds good. But it is a distinct form, as the proper names show with all the desired evidence.

8. The Egyptian recension, **E**, is preserved with relative purity in B and **β** (= B.-M. r). The close filiation between these two texts reduces the weight of their conjoint evidence. Where B stands alone, the question arises whether we are dealing with original elements of the recension, considering the mixture to which the congeners, even the nearest, are exposed, or with singularities of B. Still, often B, standing alone among its own class, receives support from extraneous texts. Hexaplaric plusses have entered the Coptic version (𝕮, extant nearly complete in the edition of THOMPSON, $𝕮^{T}$; larger and smaller fragments are available in the editions of CIASCA, $𝕮^{C}$, of MASPERO, $𝕮^{M}$, and SCHLEIFER, $𝕮^{S}$) and also the Ethiopic 𝕰 (= $𝕰^{D}$ in the edition of DILLMANN from codex F and $𝕰^{H}$ = Haverford MS.). The Bohairic 𝕭 fragments, edited by LAGARDE, show fundamentally an **E** text; the translator, however, is quite prone to textual contraction. The basic text of 𝕰 is akin to that of e (= B.-M. q, this text embodies all sorts of glosses, see my monograph on Masius, § 7), and this MS. is closely followed by **ε** (see above) in the alternate portions not derived from **C**. The fragment O (= Oxyrhynchus 1168) likewise belongs to **E**. h is (though not in the earlier part of the book) basically an **E** text, though it defaults occasionally and is contaminated with matter found in $\mathbf{S}_b$ and other textual types. Codex 707 (Sinai I) would seem, according to the specimen collation, to go basically with **E**; the hexaplaric additions it shares with e; note also verse 11 the reading ηυλισθη found in e (and besides in *a*). Here especially one would wish a page with proper names. The Coptic and Ethiopic versions unmistakeably point to the Egyptian provenance of their text. Hence the designation of the recension.

9. There remain a number of MSS. which may be classed together as **M**, i. e. mixed texts. Mixture is the general characteristic, the elements coming from the four principal recensions in diverse processes of contamination. Perhaps it may be said that the ground work is the **C** type, but not quite wholly so. Certain groups emerge. Thus the group A, which is largely contaminated with **P** (in both its forms). It divides into two sub-groups: a$=$a$_1$ ($=$ B.-M. a) and a$_2$$=$64; *a*$=$*a*$_1$ ($=$18) and *a*$_2$ ($=$128). The former sub-group is particularly given to tetraplaric readings, while the latter is more in contact with the class **M** as a whole.

10. A large group is the catenae group, N. Some 32 MSS. go to form it, i. e. above 52 (=e B.-M.). 53 (=f). 57 (=j). 85 (=z). 130 (=s). 344 (=v). cod. 343 which I have long had in photograph before me and 730 of which I secured a photograph just a year ago, then 16. 30. 73 (=H.-P. 237). 131, 236—all previously known from Holmes-Parsons—and, on the basis of the specimen collation, 46. 313. 320. 328. 346. 414. 417. 422. 489. 528. 529. 530. 550. 551. 552. 616. 716. 739. 761. The entire group is held together in 6. 10 by the reading και τω λαω / τω δε λαω, which is found outside the group solely in the mixed cod. d$_1$ (see below). By an oversight the variant is not entered for 343; but the MS. has it, as is shown on my photograph. Accordingly, in this instance B.-M.'s "efjsvz" represent the entire group. But the reading ιερουργουντες / ουραγουντες a verse above is confined, according to B.-M., to efjv^{a}z^m and u (it is also found in my r and *a*$_1$^{a}), hence within the group, prima manu, to efj. sv*z^t, as do also 343. 344*. 346, step out, all the others falling in line. Obviously, only a minority steps out. The principle of selection on the part of B.-M. is plain; they wished to include a small number, among which fsz are marked by divergent readings, z and still more so v by important marginal glosses. But then it may be questioned why it was necessary to duplicate e by j, since these two are so closely related, often enough standing off against the other four. Moreover, the reader does not know where any one of the six stands for itself or for a number of congeners not listed. It seems that, in order to get at adequate knowledge concerning the catenae group, we must after all possess a complete collation of the entire membership. As it is, I have been able to signalize two sub-groups; N$_a$="ejsz" and N$_b$="fv." 343. The division is quite palpable e.g. in 6. 13 f.—see my Masius, § 17, List A, textual form 5. But in order to appraise

the full process of the genesis of the sub-groups and the whole group, we must await the fuller information when all the members will have been collated. There are also outstanding questions as to the relation of the group to cognate texts in **M**. One thing has become certain to me; the group rests upon a common ancestor. I have the evidence that back of this common ancestor there was a copy in which there was a gap, due to a missing inner double leaf between 15. 7 and 17. 1. The character of the text before and after the gap is mixed, with leanings to the textual form of **S**; that form changes in the interval, becoming virtually a **C** text, hence the scribe of the ancestor must have supplied the missing part from a **C** text, thus rendering his MS. composite, whereas the underlying copy was uniform in its conflate character.

11. The other MSS. falling within the **M** class are: F and *φ* (= Rahlfs 461)—the minuscule made use of F, which stops at 12. 12 and has several gaps, in its present form, somewhat eclectically, but in general favoring the corrector (F^a or F^b against F*, in the gaps filled in by F^b the minuscule goes generally with F^c); naturally, in the gaps not filled out and from 12. 12 on some other MS. must have lain before the scribe. The codd. d_1 (= B.-M. k) and d_2 (= m) —these two share a number of singular readings, but often enough go apart; the latter cod. frequently condenses the text. Cod. i (the corrector often coincides with **β**). Cod. p (= 509). Lastly, u up to 15. 5 middle (see above). An example in which the codd. named share a singular reading is found 18. 22 σαμρειμ comp. σαμαρειμ P_1 and contrast σεμρειμ P_2C σαμειρ **S** σαρα (σαμβα N) from σαμρα = σαμραν, σαμραιν = צְמָרַיִם (Aramaizing pronunciation).

R (= B.-M. Δ_8) likewise belongs to the mixed class; so also, it would seem on the basis of the specimen collation, 126. 246. 319. 381. 392. 619.

12. The road to the original text of 𝔊 leads across the common, unrevised text. In order to get at the latter, we must abstract from the recensional manipulations. The operation is easy enough when we deal with additions. See my monograph on Masius, § 17. Variations in obelized elements point to divergences in the common text. But a large number of Origen's modifications consist in substitutions (especially in proper names) whereby the basic form is obviously covered up. But since Hexapla and Tetrapla differed, P_1 has frequently preserved the unrevised form which reveals itself as substantially in

agreement with **E**. Then, by the very nature of Origen's purpose, which was to save of the common text all that could be saved, readings have remained in **P** even when they do not square with the Hebrew. Often enough Origen failed to realize disagreements, exactly as they have escaped the attention of modern students. Comp. e.g. 4. 18 where 𝔊 read נצקן for נתקן. The example 19. 34 cited above for **S** shows how that recension likewise operated with a text akin to **E**.

13. Ultimately we must operate with **E**, but not without taking into account the residue of the common text imbedded elsewhere. The scant representatives of **E** in a relatively pure form, virtually the ancestor of B **β**, will have had singularities of their own which must be brushed aside. A study of the translator's mannerism of rendition becomes imperative. The proper names are, of course, vitiated by all sorts of scribal errors, but on the whole the rectification is possible. An example out of many is 13. 27; for και εναδωμ και οδαργαει read και ἐν αεμκ βαιθαρραν, hence 𝔊 read בית הרן as the Hebrew does Nu 32. 36. Nor are all omissions, though present already in the text underlying Origen's work, to be laid at the door of the translator. One example I have signalized in JQR N. S. iii, 319–336. Another example is found 8. 25. παντας τους κατοικουντας γαι, as the accusative shows (the nominative in $\mathbf{S}_a$ and **P** is recensional correction), belongs to v. 27 end = את כל יושבי העי, hence the omission of 25 end and 26 is due to a scribe's aberration from παντες ανδρες γαι to παντας τους κατοικουντας γαι.

14. The scope of my edition is to restore critically the original form of the version. I print the critically restored text at the top of the page. Below follow the forms assumed in the four classes, **E, S, P, CM**. Omissions and contractions of the text, by which certain witnesses or groups of witnesses step out as silent on the textual form, receive a rubric of their own. Then follow individual variations of class members, such as leave the characteristic class reading undisturbed in its main features. Lastly marginal readings in so far as they have not been embodied above. The subjoined Specimen illustrates the arrangement.

15. Without going into a full textual commentary, a few observations on the evidence assembled in the following pages may prove helpful. h clearly steps out of **E** in this section of the text. The MS has points of contact with $\mathbf{S}_b$, but basically it belongs to **C**. e 𝔏,

while basically of the **E** class, admit hexaplaric additions. So does also 707. B β 𝕰 are apparently the constant members. When disagreements occur among these three, we must reckon with individual idiosyncrasies. Then it becomes necessary to look about for other criteria. Thus the varying position of σοι verse 2 among members of the other classes shows that B (the evidence of 𝕰 is not clear) rightly omits the pronoun. The translator apparently forbore to express the pronoun. Its omission in n_{22} is isolated in the N group; probably also in 619 the omission is secondary. While in the Tetrapla the pronoun was placed after the adjective so as to accord with the order of the Hebrew, its place in the Hexapla was in front of the adj. The corrector of c_1 started to rectify the sequence by introducing the pronoun after the adj., but forgot to delete it before the adj.—hence the duplication reproduced by 𝔠. Elsewhere I have proved that the corrector was none other than the Complutensian editor. Both Hexapla and Tetrapla follow the Hebrew order in transposing the adj. in front of the object (υποχειριον την ιεριχω = בידך את יריחו). The Hexaplaric order, that is with reference to the position of the pronoun, is followed solely by A 𝔞. 381. Accordingly 381 is akin to A, specifically to a, as is shown in examples below; but of course there are also divergences. The omission of παντας in v. 3 is peculiar of B β (for the omission in k_2 is proved as secondary against the evidence of k_1; it is probably also spontaneous in 319); Origen certainly found it; I therefore restore it in the original of 𝕲. In v. 9, though β admits πορευομενοι και, the omission in B 𝕰 is supported further by 𝕷 u. 619; apparently no part of the original Greek text. But in v. 11 την πολιν is omitted solely in B and should therefore be restored.

In S, the naming of 125 as f_3 is justified by the singular reading right at the beginning: ιεριχω δε / και ιεριχω—a mannerism indulged in at the beginning of chapters (3, 4, 8, 12, 13, 18, 19, 21, 23) by f_2. Naturally the new MS shares with the entire sub-group f the omission per homoioteleuton in v. 3f., but not the similar omission in v. 8 peculiar to f. Thus the nearest congeners are $f_{1\cdot 2}$. w is clearly mixed; not only does it desert the smaller sub-group (**S**$_a$) in favor of the larger (**S**$_b$), but even the whole of **S** in favor of **PC**. Nevertheless, basically it belongs to **S**$_a$. As w is given to contraction, much cannot be made of omissions of hexaplaric matter. Still, where the element is introduced in k_1 sub οι λ_c or where the increment is found only in k, we are dealing with subsequent enlargements of which the original of **S** was free. Characteristic readings of **S**: οταν σαλπισωσιν v. 5, εναντι v. 7, κατεπαυσεν v. 11.

In **P**, γ steps out in many instances.

In **C**, hexaplaric additions are introduced specifically by M[m] 𝕬. Impure are r. 527 (the two seem to be akin), also *a* g. 318. 669. Once A stands out against all the others.

In **M**, A (specifically a). 381. 619 have a tendency to approximate **P**. Reversions to the unrevised text are found with particular frequency in u. 319. 619, likewise in N, but also in A Fφd_1. *a*ip go now with the unrevised text, now with **S**, d_2p also with C. Hexaplaric additions are found most frequently in Fφd_1. The archetype of N was on the whole free from these increments.

16. A few comments on the translator's manner of operation. He was apparently given to curtailments. He may or may not have read מפני בני ישראל in v. 1. But v. 3f. are certainly contracted. The translator certainly had before him v. 3 as far as הקיף את העיר. He may be trusted to have known that סבב means "surround"; but he chose to frame the phrasing as an order to the commander to "place about" the city all the warriors. The details he omitted from the translation, since they are embodied in the execution of the order. Similarly he omitted in v. 5 בשמעכם את קול השופר. In v. 6 he seems to have read ויבא for ויקרא; he omitted the direction to the priests, and instead combined ויאמר אלהם with אמרו (comp. ויאמרו ketib), so as to introduce immediately the directions to the people; naturally he omitted in v. 8 ויהי כאמר יהושע אל העם and construed the rest as part of the order; he read עבור ותקוע for עברו ותקעו and omitted in v. 9 תקעו השופרות and בשופרות and then in v. 10 ולא יצא מפיכם דבר and v. 11 הקף. As to the translator's additions, τη ημερα τη δευτερα v. 12 was taken by anticipation from v. 14 where he omitted it; other plusses, like τον εν αυτη v. 2, may have been found in his Hebrew text; but usually the increments are for clarifying the sense, as for example οντας in the same verse to express the concessive force (comp. Kimhi). The manner in which Origen adjusted the Greek to the Hebrew is sufficiently clear that comments may be spared. He kept as much of the received Greek, sometimes even when it did not quite square with the Hebrew, mainly bent upon incorporating all the elements omitted as well upon the sequence of the Hebrew words.

VI

Καὶ Ιερειχω συνκεκλεισμένη καὶ ὠχυρωμένη καὶ οὐθεὶς ἐξεπορεύετο ἐξ αὐτῆς οὐδὲ εἰσεπορεύετο. ²καὶ εἶπεν κύριος πρὸς Ἰησοῦν Ἰδοὺ ἐγὼ παραδίδωμι τὴν Ιερειχω ὑποχειρίαν καὶ τὸν βασιλέα αὐτῆς τὸν ἐν αὐτῇ δυνατοὺς ὄντας ἐν ἰσχύι.

---

1 ωχυρωμενη] + ※ απο προσωπου υιων ιηλ: P ουθεις E] ουδεις 2 εξ αυτης εξεπορευετο S ÷ εξ αυτης: P 3 εγω] > P την ιερ. υποχειριαν E] prm σοι S : υποχειριον σοι την ιερ. P_2 (σοι sub ※) C 4 ÷ τον εν αυτη: P οντας ES (= Just)] > PC εν] > P

E 1 ωχυρωμενη] + απο — ιηλ e 3 την ιερ. υποχειριαν B. 707. 𝕮 (uid) 𝕷 (uid)] σοι την ιερ. υπο χειρα β : την ιερ. υπο χειρα σην e 4 εν] > β

S 1 ωχυρωμενη] + απο — ιηλ k_1 (sub οι λ) k_2 𝕷 S_b 2 εξ αυτης εξεπορευετο S_a Just 3 εγω] > w Just σοι την ιερ. υποχειριαν (-ιαν k_1] -ιον) k 𝕷 Just: w S_b = P_2C 4 εν] > Just

---

P 3 εγω γl σοι την ιερ. υποχειριαν γ : σοι υποχειριον (+ σοι $c_1^{a?}$𝔱) την ιερ. c 4 οντας γ εν] > $b^{a?}$c

---

CM 1 ωχυρωμενη] + απο — ιηλ M^m (sub οι λ) 𝕬 Fφd_1 $n_8^m$$n_{16}^m$ (sub οι λ) n_5 ουθεις N (n_{16}†)·$n_{15\cdot21\cdot22}$u 3 εγω] > 318 aa_2 F*in_{21}p. 392. 619 την ιερ. υποχειριαν 619] την ιερ. υπο χειρα n_{22} : prm σοι u : σοι την ιερ. υποχειριον N^{rell} : σοι υποχειριον την ιερ. 𝔄 a. 381 υποχειριαν n_{17}^m : υποχειρον 319 7 σοι suprascr φ 4 οντας M^m (sub θ') r. 527 Fφd_1i$n^{-n_2\cdot13}$pu. 246. 319. 392 (θ' ο' χω n_{16}^m : ου χω n_{17}^m) εν] > vh

---

1 και ωχυρωμενη] > a_1 5 υιων] > 𝕷 2 εξεπορευετο] > b* εξ αυτης] w_2 d_1. 302 ουδε εισεπορευετο] > k Just 4 αυτης] > e 𝕷 f_2 τον εν αυτη] > n_{22} τον] > d_1

---

1 και ιερ.] ιερ. δε f_3 ιερ.] prm η Just συνκεκλεισμενη] prm ην d_2. 126: συνκεκαθισμενη i*: + ην Just Mas ωχυρωμενη] + πολις οχυρα $n_{1.4.10.25.31}$ 5 απο] προ Mas υιων] prm των e k M^m Fφ$n_8^m$$n_{16}^m$$n_5$ 2 εισεπορευετο ουδε εξεπορευετο εξ αυτης Fφ : εξεπορευετο ουδε εισεπορευετο εξ αυτης ip αυτης] αυτου 527 ουδε] prm και c : και r. 527 619: και ουδεις 𝔱 : και ουδε[ις] 𝔩 εισπεπορευετο 488 3 διδωμι v 7 σοι] σου AMgv_2. 527 dp. 319. 392 18 σοι την ιερ. υποχειριον σου n_{15} 3 ιερ.] + πολιν $n_{2.30}$ 4 τον] τους β F*i. 392 : και τους r F^bφp. 246. 319 επ αυτη n_{31} : επ αυτης e δυνατους] prm τους 𝔱 Mas : δυνατον $d_2$$n_{22}$ οντα n_{22}

[3]σὺ δὲ περίστησον αὐτῇ πάντας τοὺς μαχίμους κύκλῳ. [5]καὶ ἔσται ὡς ἂν σαλπίσητε τῇ σάλπιγγι ἀνακραγέτω πᾶς ὁ λαὸς

---

1 — συ—κυκλω: ※ και κυκλωσατε την πολιν παντες ανδρες (+ του P_2) πολεμου κυκλω της πολεως απαξ ουτως ποιησετε εξ ημερας [4]και επτα ιερεις λημψονται επτα κερατινας του ιωβηλ ενωπιον της κιβωτου και τη ημερα τη εβδομη κυκλωσατε την πολιν επτακις και οι ιερεις σαλπιουσιν εν ταις κερατιναις: **P** παντας] > **E** μαχητας **C** 2 ως αν] οταν **S** σαλπισητε] σαλπισωσιν **S** σαλπιγγι] + ※ του ιωβηλ εν τω ακουσαι υμας την φωνην της κερατινης: **P** ανακραγετωσαν **PC**

E 1 παντας] > Bβ κυκλω] + και—κερατιναις e 𝕷. 707 2 σαλπισωσιν 𝕷 σαλπιγγι] + του—κερατινης e 𝕷. 707

S 1 παντας] > k_2 μαχιμους k κυκλω] + και—κερατιναις k_1 (sub οι ⅄) $k_2 S_b$ 2 οταν kS_b σαλπιγγι] + του—κερατινης k ανακραγετω k_1 w 𝕮

P 2 ανακραγετω γ′

CM 1 παντας] > M 319 μαχιμους **M** (F*^{at} n_{16}†)$^{\cdot d_2}$ p κυκλω] + και—κερατιναις M^m (p. κιβωτου κ̅υ̅ in comm. b) 𝕬 Fφ d_1 n_8^m n_{10}^m (sub οι ⅄ ※) h 2 σαλπιγγι] + του—κερατινης M^m 𝕬 Fφ d_1 n_8^m n_{16}^m (sub ※) n_{17}^m p ανακραγετω A n_{28}. 126. 319

---

1 συ—κυκλω] > 𝔱 3–6 παντες—την πολιν] > F 5 και] > e 6 οι] > k_2 f_{13} 2 τη] > n$^{\cdot n_{2\cdot5\cdot8\cdot9\cdot11\cdot17\cdot21\cdot28\cdot30}}$: int lin n_3 7/8 του ιωβηλ] > k_2 8 υμας] > F*φ την—κερατινης] > k_2 την φωνην] > Fφp 2 ανακραγετω—αμα] > p

---

1 παραστησον a_1 d_2 αυτη] prm εν w : αυτην c ε. 488. 669 u παντας p. κυκλω F*^{i} p. 392 κυκλω a. παντας d_1 3–6 και—κερατιναις p. σαλπιγγι in comm. 5 et in hunc locum του ιωβηλ—κερατινης transfert 𝕬 3 πολιν] γην e Fφ 4 κυκλω] prm και k ουτως—ημερας p. κιβωτου (5) S_b h ποιησατε 𝕷 (uid) k_2γn_8^m : + ενωπιον της κιβωτου h εξ] prm επι S_b h επτα ιερεις] τη εβδομη οι ιερεις 𝕷 k M^m Fφ [[τη εβδομη] > F^{am}φ]] 5 κερατινας] σαλπιγγας S_b h : + σαλπιγγας e. 707 n_8^m n_{16}^m του ιωβηλ] ιερας S_b h του] τω 707 n_8^m n_{16}^m ιωβηδ e. 707 n_8^m n_{16}^m ενωπιον] prm και σαλπιουσιν S_b h γ F^{am}φ [[και] + οι ιερεις γ σαλπιουσιν] σαλπισουσιν *t* γ : σαλπισωσου t_2]] τη εβδομη ημερα e κυκλωσετε M^m 6 σαλπισουσιν k γ′ εν] > e. 707 S_b h c d_1 ταις κερατιναις] ταις σαλπιγξιν (τας σαλπιγγας f_2) S_b h 2 εσται—σαλπιγγι] σαλπισαντες τας σαλπιγγας 126 εσται] εσεσεσθαι 246 σαλπισητε] σαλπιειτε u : σαλπιζητε i 7 σαλπισωσιν] + οι ιερεις w 2 τη σαλπιγγι] ταις σαλπιγξιν 𝕷S_b 8 ιωβηδ e. 707 n_8^m n_{16}^m ημας 707 της φωνης γd_1 2 ανακεκραγετωσαν 392 2 αμα πας ο λαος 𝕬d_1

---

3 και κυκλωσατε] α′ [illegible] 𝕾^L 4 απαξ] *una via* 𝕾^M 4/5 ουτως—εβδομη] και ουτος πυησης εξ υμερας και επτα υερης αρουσιν τας επτα σαλπιγγας εμπροσθεν της κυβοτος και εν τη εβδομη ημερα f^b 5 κερατινας του ιωβηλ] α′ *tubas remissionis* σ′ *buccinas arietinas* 𝕾^M του ιωβηλ] του αγιου· της αφεσεως d_1 1 (+ 8) και—ιωβηλ] (α′ 𝕾^M) [illegible] σ′ [illegible] 𝕾 2 τη σαλπιγγι] τη κερατινη . . . ηχη F^b 2 ανακραγετω—αυτων] α′ σ′ [illegible] 𝕾

ἅμα· καὶ ἀνακραγόντων αὐτῶν πεσεῖται αὐτόματα τὰ τείχη
τῆς πόλεως, καὶ εἰσελεύσεται πᾶς ὁ λαὸς ὁρμήσας ἕκαστος
κατὰ πρόσωπον εἰς τὴν πόλιν.
[6]καὶ εἰσῆλθεν Ἰησοῦς ὁ τοῦ Ναυη πρὸς τοὺς ἱερεῖς [7]καὶ
εἶπεν αὐτοῖς λέγων Παραγγείλατε τῷ λαῷ περιελθεῖν καὶ
κυκλῶσαι τὴν πόλιν, καὶ οἱ μάχιμοι παραπορευέσθωσαν
ἐνωπλισμένοι ἐναντίον κυρίου. [8]καὶ ἑπτὰ ἱερεῖς ἔχοντες

---

1 αμα] > **PC** 1/2 αυτοματα—πολεως] παν το τειχος της πολεως αυτοματον **S** ÷ αυτοματα: **P** 2 πολεως] + ※ υποκατω αυτων: **P** ÷ πας: **P** ÷ ορμησας: **P** 3 ÷ εις την πολιν: **P** 4 ο του **E**] υιος ναυν coni.] ναυη ιερεις] + ※ και ειπεν προς αυτους λαβετε την κιβωτον της διαθηκης και επτα ιερεις λημψονται επτα κερατινας του ιωβηλ κατα προσωπον της (> **P**$_2$) κιβωτου κυ: **P** 5 ÷ αυτοις λεγων παραγγειλατε: **P** 7 ÷ ενωπλισμενοι: **P** εναντιον **E**] εναντι (= Cry) κυ] prm ※ κιβωτου: **P** και] prm ※ και εγενετο ως ειπεν ις προς τον λαον: **P**

E 1 αμα] > 𝔏^H 2 πολεως] + υποκατω αυτων e 𝔏. 707 4 ο του Β*β* ιερεις] + και—κυ e 𝔏. 707 7 εναντιον Β*β* κυ] prm κιβωτου 𝔏 και] prm και—λαον e 𝔏. 707

S 1/2 αυτοματα—πολεως w 𝔏*f*$_3$] παν το τειχος της πολεως αυτοματον k: αυτοματα παντα τα τειχη της πολεως 2 πολεως] + υποκατω αυτων k$_1$ (+ οι λ) k$_2$ 4 ιερεις] + και—κυ k 5 ειπεν αυτοις λεγων] > k

---

P 1 αμα *γ* τα] prm παντα *γ* 7 εναντιον *γ* και *γ*] prm και—λαον

CM 1 αμα 𝔄 *a*ιΝ. 319 2 πολεως] + υποκατω αυτων M^m (sub οι λ) 𝔄 F(uid)d$_1$ n$_8$^{m}n$_{16}$^{m} (sub οι λ ο′ ※) 4 ο του M^m Ν(n$_{16}$^{t})u. 619 : ο υιος i ιερεις] + και—κυ M^m (sub οι λ) 𝔄 F*φ*d$_1$n$_8$^{m}n$_{16}$^{m} (sub οι λ ου ※) 7 εναντιον M^{m}g Ν^{m18}u. 619 κυ] prm κιβωτου 𝔄 d$_1$ και] prm και—λαον M^m (sub οι λ) 𝔄 F*φ*d$_1$n$_{16}$^{m} (sub οι λ ※)

1/2 (αμα)—λαος] > 527 1 αυτοματα] > 𝔏^H 488. 669 d$_1$. 126 9 υποκρατω] > d$_1$ 2 εκαστος] > k$_2$ 3 κατα προσωπον] > 𝔏*φ*. 126. 246 4 ο του (sive υς) ναυη] ναυη f: > 𝔏*f*$_2$ 126 11 και] > n$_8$^{m}n$_{16}$^{m} 12 κιβωτου] > 𝔏 5 λεγων] > 707 *f*$_3$ d$_2$. 126 και] > e 669. 𝔄 n$_1$. 126. 392 7 ενωπλισμενοι] > d$_1$ 14 ις] > 𝔄 7—2 και—κυ] > *f*$_1$

---

1 αμα] ανω n$_{15}$ ανακραγεντων Α*α ν* 𝔞 Mas r F*φ* : ανακεκραγοτων t$_1$t$_2$^{a}F M *a*$_1$n$_{19}$: ανακεκραγοντων *f*$_3$ (in mg?) *γ* : ανακραγοτων *β* t$_2$**t* b VWg. 488. 669 p. 126. 319. 381. 619 h* αυτοματως *β* k$_2$* 2 εισελευσονται *φ*in$_5$ 3 προσωπον] + αυτου Mas 4 ηλθεν c$_1$*c$_2$𝔩 τους ιερεις] sup ras 669 : την πολιν 488 : + των υιων ιηλ *α ν* 𝔞 11 αυτους] + λεγων F^b*φ* διαθηκης] + κυ k*γ* 𝔄-codd F*φ* n$_8$^{m}n$_{16}$^{m} 12 του] τω 707 ιωβηδ e. 707 κυ] prm του 707 Mas: θυ k$_2$ 5 αυτοις] προς αυτους n$_{15\cdot 21}$ λαω] + λεγοντες p. 319 περιελθειν] παρελθειν *v* 𝔄 : εισελθειν 𝔈(?) : ελθειν 126 : + κυκλω e 6 κυκλωσαι] prm του e : κυκλωσατε k$_1$ c𝔩 F* πορευεσθωσαν 126. Cyr-cod : παραπορευομενοι εστωσαν n$_{14}$: παραπορευσεσθωσαν n$_{31}$ (ex corr εσ uid) 7 ενωπλισμενοι] sub ο′ n$_{16}$^{m} : ενοπλισαμενοι n$_{8\cdot 9\cdot 16\cdot 17}$: καθωπλισμενοι *β* : p. κυ n$_{7\cdot 13}$ 14 κιβωτου] prm της c$_2$𝔩 𝔞 Mas 7 κυ] prm του 𝔱 Mas εχοντας n$_5$n$_{31}$* (ε suprascr). 126. 246

ἑπτὰ σάλπιγγας ἱερὰς παρελθέτωσαν ὡσαύτως ἐναντίον τοῦ
κυρίου καὶ σημαινέτωσαν εὐτόνως· καὶ ἡ κιβωτὸς τῆς διαθήκης κυρίου ἐπακολουθείτω. [9]οἱ δὲ μάχιμοι ἔμπροσθεν
παραπορευέσθωσαν, καὶ οἱ ἱερεῖς οἱ οὐραγοῦντες ὀπίσω τῆς
κιβωτοῦ τῆς διαθήκης κυρίου σαλπίζοντες. [10]τῷ δὲ λαῷ

1 ÷ παρελθ$^{ε}_{α}$τωσαν ωσαυτως: P παρελθατωσαν P_2C εναντι S του] > S 2 και 1°] prm ※ παραπορευεσθωσαν: P 3 επακολουθειτω] + ※ αυτοις: P 3/4 εμπροσθεν παραπορευεσθωσαν E] ∼ 4 ÷ και: P ιερεις] + ※ σαλπιζοντες ταις κερατιναις και: P 5 ÷ της διαθηκης $\overline{κυ}$: P σαλπιζοντες E] prm πορευομενοι και SC (= Or_g) : πορευομενοι και σαλπιζοντες ※ ταις κερατιναις: P

E 1 παρελθετωσαν Be του] > β 2 και 1°] prm παραπορευεσθωσαν e 𝔏. 707 3 επακολουθειτω] + αυτοις e 𝔏. 707 4 ιερεις] + σαλπιζοντες—και e 𝔏. 707 5 σαλπιζοντες Bℭ] prm πορευομενοι και β : πορευομενοι—κερατιναις e 𝔏. 707

S 3 επακολουθειτω] + αυτοις k 3/4 εμπροσθεν παραπορευεσθωσαν w 5 σαλπιζοντες] prm πορευομενοι και S_g : + ταις κερατιναις 𝔏(?)

P 1 παρελθετωσαν c του] > γ 3/4 εμπροσθεν παραπορευεσθωσαν γ 5 σαλπιζοντες] prm πορευομενοι και γ

CM 1 παρελθετωσαν Wgrvνε. 318. 527 669 (ε sup ras) A*a* $F^{a?}$**φ** d_1N. 619 εναντι *α*. 318 $a_1$$a_2$ F*d$n_{25\cdot27}$ του] > *α*g. 319. 669 A F^bd$N^{-n_3\cdot12}$u. 126. 246. 381. 392. 619 2 και 1°] prm παραπορευεσθωσαν ν𝔞 3 επακολουθειτω] + αυτοις M^m (sub οι λ) 𝔄 (uid) F**φ**$n_5$$n_{16}$^{m} (sub οι λ ※) n_{17}^{m} 3/4 εμπροσθεν παραπορευεσθωσαν F**φ**ipu. 319. 392 4 ιερεις] + σαλπιζοντες—και ν𝔞. 318 F**φ**$d_1$$n_8$^{m} (indice ad και adposito) n_{16}^{m} (sub οι λ) n_{17}^{m} (do.) 5 σαλπιζοντες u. 619] πορευομενοι—κερατιναις M^m (sub οι λ) 𝔄 F**φ**d_1 $n_8^{m}n_{16}$^{m} (sub οι λ) n_{17}^{m} (do.)

1 επτα] > 126 ιερας] > 𝔏 παρελθετωσαν ωσαυτως] > γ 1/2 ωσαυτως—σημαινετωσαν] > φ 2/3 και 1°—$\overline{κυ}$] > n_{28} 2 και 1°] > 619 ευτονως] sup lin 619 της] > e 3 $\overline{κυ}$] > p 3–5 επακολουθειτω—$\overline{κυ}$] > n_{15} 3 οι δε μαχιμοι] > 619 μαχιμοι] > n_8 εμπροσθεν] > 𝔏(uid)f 4 παραπορευεσθωσαν] > 619 8 ταις > e_2𝔩 9 και] > F**φ**$n_8^{m}n_{16}^{m}n_{17}$^{m} 4 οι ουραγουντες] > k_2w𝔖$_l$ c (c_1 + ras 11 litt) 𝔩 5 της διαθηκης $\overline{κυ}$] > $k_2$$f_3$ d_2 της] > w_2 A F**φ**, 381. 619 h $\overline{κυ}$] > 𝔏 10 και] > e 5 λαω] > n_{22}

1 επτα] prm τας **φ** σαλπιγγας] πτερυγας n_{26} ιερας] του ιωβηλ F^b παρελθετωσαν] prm και c a_1 : και ελθετωσαν 126 : περιελθετωσαν n_{21} 2 και] του n_2 ευτονως σημαινετωσαν 381 σημανετωσαν t_2 g. 488 a_3 h : σημανατωσαν β 669 d_2u. 126. 246. 392 : + ωσαυτως r 3 $\overline{κυ}$] + παραπορευθησαν 707 επακολουθειτω] prm και $n_{11\cdot24}$: επακολουθουσα g : επανακ. n_{26} : παρακ. 392 : ακολουθειτω 126 οι δε] και οι g εμπροσθεν] ετοιμοι n_{11}^{t} : + ετοιμοι n_{24} : + εσωθεν 381^t 4 παραπορευεσθωσαν] προ- ℭ𝔏(uid) S_b : πορευεσθωσαν 126 ιερεις] + εμπροσθεν της κιβωτου της διαθηκης $\overline{κυ}$ F^{bm}**φ** 8 σαλπιζοντες] prm οι Mas 4 οι ουραγουντες] ο λοιπος οχλος απας 𝔱 ουραγουντες] θυραγουντες 318 : ιερουργουντες r. 527 a_1^{cor}N(n_{16}*)$^{-n_8t\, n_{9\cdot15}n_{17}t\, n_{21}}$u : λειτουργουντες d_2 : ακολουθουντες M^m F^{bm}**φ** : ουντες 319 : ουτως i^m οπισω] εμπροσθεν w S_b 9/10 πορευομενοι και] πορευεσθωσαν d_2 9 πορευομενοι] προπορευομενοι t_1 10 κερατιναις] + σαλπιγξιν e 5 τω δε] και τω d_1N($n_{16}^{t}n_{17}$^{t})

ἐνετείλατο Ἰησοῦς λέγων Μὴ βοᾶτε, μηδὲ ἀκουσάτω μηθεὶς ὑμῶν τὴν φωνήν, ἕως ἂν ἡμέραν αὐτὸς διαγγείλῃ ἀναβοῆσαι, καὶ τότε ἀναβοήσετε. [11]καὶ περιελθοῦσα ἡ κιβωτὸς τῆς διαθήκης τοῦ θεοῦ τὴν πόλιν εὐθέως ἀπῆλθεν εἰς τὴν παρεμβολήν, καὶ ἐκοιμήθη ἐκεῖ.

[12]καὶ τῇ ἡμέρᾳ τῇ δευτέρᾳ ἀνέστη Ἰησοῦς τὸ πρωί, καὶ ἦραν

---

2 υμων την φωνην **E**] ~ της φωνης **S** εως] prm ※ ουδε διελευσεται εκ στοματος υμων λογος: **P** αν ημεραν] της ημερας εν η **S** αυτος διαγγειλη **E**] αναγγελω υμιν **S**: ~ P_1 **C** : διαγγειλη αυτοις P_2 2/3 βοησαι **S** 3 και τοτε ανακραξετε **S** : και αναβοησετε ÷ τοτε: **P** 4 ÷ της διαθηκης: **P** του θυ] κυ **S** πολιν] + ※ κυκλω: **P** ευθεως] παλιν **S** 5 εκοιμηθη] κατεπαυσεν **S** 6 τη ημερα τη δευτερα **EC**] τη δευτερα ημερα **S** : ÷ ημερα τη δευτερα: **P**

E 2 υμων την φωνην Bβ της φωνης e εως] prm ουδε λογος e𝕷.707 αυτος διαγγειλη] αναγγειλη και αυτος e : + *uobis* 𝕮 4 του θυ] κυ 𝕷(?) πολιν] + κυκλω e𝕷.707

S 2 εως αν ημεραν διαγγειλη αυτοις w : εως της ημερας εν η αναγγελω υμιν kS_b : *usquedum dies uobis nuntietur* 𝕷 2/3 βοησαι k 3 αναβοησετε] ανακραξατε (-ξετε k_2^a) k 4 του θυ] κυ S_a την πολιν] prm κυκλω k : + κυκλω S_b ευθεως] παλιν S_{ag} : + παλιν S_b 5 εκοιμηθη] κατεπαυσεν S_a(𝕷 [uid]) 6 τη δευτερα ημερα k

P 2 αυτος διαγγελει γ : διαγγειλη αυτος c : διαγγειλη αυτοις b : διαγγειλη υμιν 𝕾 3 τοτε αναβοησετε γ 4 του θυ] κυ γ 6 τη 1°] > bc_1𝖙

CM 2 υμων την φωνην u. 319 της φωνης t^a *a*ip. 392 εως] prm ουδε—λογος M^m(sub οι λ) 𝕬 *a*d_1 n_8^m (sub οι λ) n_{16}^m (sub οι λ α′ ※) n_{17}^m (sub οι λ) αν ημεραν] της ημερας $F^{a\,m}$ (del $F^{b?}$) αυτος διαγγειλη *a*Nu. 319] αυτος (δι)αγγειλω $n_{4\cdot14\cdot21\cdot22}$ n_{28} (ω sup ras) : διαγγειλη αυτοις VW^a*a*vg F^bφ h 3 τοτε p. αναβοησετε a. 381. 619 4 του θυ] prm κυ $a_1 N^{n_{14}}$ h : κυ v𝕬. 527 Fφd_2n_{14}p. 381. 619 την πολιν] prm κυκλω M^m n_8^m (contra BM!) $n_{15\cdot21}$: + κυκλω va *a*$F^{a\,m}$$d_2N^{rell \cdot n_5 \cdot 8t \cdot 9 \cdot 15t}$ $n^t n_{16}^m$ (secundum BM!) n_{17}^m(!) h ευθεως] παλιν a_2

1 ενετειλατο—μηδε] > c ις] > 𝕷. 707 λεγων] > 𝕷 (uid) n_5 h 2 υμων] > d_1 ημεραν] > 318 8 εν] > k_1 3 και 1°—αναβοησετε] > 𝕷 (per homoioteleuton Aethiopicum) και 1°] > rv 4 της διαθηκης] > $𝕷^H$ του θυ] > n_{11} την πολιν] > B την] > 619 ευθεως] > 𝕷 n_2 6 το πρωι] > $n_{2\cdot30}$ το] > f_3 και 2°] > 126

1 βοατω 𝕷A a_1 μηδε] και μη A*a* μηθεις] τις i 7 ουδε 707 𝕾 n_{17}^m] ου ελευσεται 707 n_{17}^m 7/8 στοματος] prm του e *a* n_8^m 2 (19) ημεραν p. αυτος c ημεραν] η ημερα i : ημερα c 𝕷 (uid) A*a*ra φ$n_{2\cdot30}$p. 392 h διαγγειλη] διαγγελη r_2a Mas n_5 (secundum BM!) h : διαγγελαι $n_{1\cdot6\cdot7\cdot10\cdot13\cdot18\cdot20\cdot23\cdot25\cdot27\cdot31(ras)\cdot32}$ 8 αναγγελω] αναγγελη k_2 : αναγγειλω S_b 2/3 αναβοησαι] εκβοησαι e 3 αναβοησατε e c A. 318 a a d_2N(n_5^t) $^{n_{2\cdot7\cdot10\cdot15\cdot16\cdot17\cdot21\cdot31}}$: αναβοησητε d_1 : βοησετε 126 : + και ανεβοησαν *a*v περιελθουσα] παρ- d_1 4 την] prm εις g απηλθεν] παρηλθεν (sic) n_{22} : απελθετω n_{15} : απελθατω n_8^m (secundum BM) : απελθατω· απαρθητω n_{16}^m (secundum BM) n_{17}^m (απελθετω) : *feratur* 𝕷 4/5 εν τη παρεμβολη f_2 5 εκοιμηθη] ηυλισθη e. 707 va Mas *a* : κοιμηθητω n_8^m (secundum BM) n_{16}^m (do.) n_{17}^m n_{15} 6 τη 1°] prm εν $n_{0\cdot6\cdot22\cdot25\cdot27\cdot29\cdot32}$ δευτερα] ημερα n_5 εστη 319 το πρωι ις k_2 ις] prm ο k_1 n_{10}

4/5 ευθεως—εκει] σ′ [illegible] $𝕾^L$

21*

Alter und Heimat der vaticanischen Bibelhandschrift.

Von

Alfred Rahlfs.

Vorgelegt von R. Pietschmann in der Sitzung am 25. Februar 1899.

Der Bibelkanon, welchen Athanasius in seinem 39. Festbriefe [1]) aufstellt, hat im Alten Testamente zwei auffallende Eigentümlichkeiten: das Buch Esther fehlt, wie freilich auch bei Melito von Sardes u. a. [2]), unter den 22 Büchern, welche nach Angabe des Athanasius den Kanon der Juden ausmachen, und erscheint dafür unter den „Vorlesebüchern", und die Bücher der Makkabäer fehlen ganz, während alle anderen Kanonsverzeichnisse, so weit sie sich nicht auf den bloßen Kanon der Juden beschränken, wenigstens zwei Makkabäerbücher einschließen [3]). Beide Eigentümlichkeiten teilt der codex Vaticanus (B): er hat Esther, wie Athanasius, zwischen Sirach und Judith, während der Sinaiticus (S) Esther an Esra-Nehemia anschließt, und der Alexandrinus (A) Esther, Tobit, Judith und die beiden Esrabücher in dieser Anordnung auf Daniel folgen läßt, und er hat im Gegensatz zu S und A kein Makkabäerbuch, hat auch nie eins gehabt, wie Nestle in der Theol. Literaturzeitung 1895, Col. 148 f. aus der Lagenbildung der Hand-

1) Th. Zahn, Geschichte des Neutestamentlichen Kanons, 2. Bd. (im Folgenden stets unter dem bloßen Namen des Verfassers citiert) S. 203—212, woselbst auch die älteren Ausgaben aufgeführt sind. Zu dem griechischen und dem syrischen Texte, welche Zahn benutzen konnte, ist neuerdings der sahidische hinzugekommen, herausgegeben von C. Schmidt in den Nachrichten von der Königl. Gesellschaft der Wissenschaften zu Göttingen, Philolog.-histor. Klasse, 1898, S. 167 ff.

2) Zahn S. 328 Anm.

3) Das Fehlen der Makkabäerbücher in dem alten Texte des Kanons von Hippo (vom J. 393) wird von Zahn S. 252 Anm. 2 gewiß richtig als Schreibfehler beurteilt; Augustins Zeugnis für die Bücher scheint mir ausschlaggebend.

Reprinted from *Nachrichten der Königlichen Gesellschaft der Wissenschaften zu Göttingen.* Philologischhistorische Klasse, 1899. Heft. 1.

schrift nachweist. Ueberhaupt umfaßt das A. T. in B genau diejenigen kanonischen und Vorlesebücher, welche Athanasius in seinem 39. Festbriefe aufzählt.

Und nicht nur dies, sondern B hat die Bücher des A. T. auch in genau derselben Reihenfolge, wie Athanasius, während sonst die alten Handschriften und Kanonsverzeichnisse gerade in diesem Punkte die größten Verschiedenheiten zeigen[1]). Hier nur zwei Beispiele: bei Athanasius und B steht Hiob nicht am Anfang, sondern am Ende der poetischen Bücher des jüdischen Kanons, also hinter den Psalmen und den drei salomonischen Schriften, und Judith steht nicht nach der chronologischen Reihenfolge hinter, sondern vor Tobit[2]). Sehen wir ab von einigen späteren Kanonsverzeichnissen, welche sämtlich von Athanasius abhängig sind, nämlich dem unechten 60. Kanon der um 360 zu Laodicea in Phrygien abgehaltenen Synode[3]), dem Verzeichnis der 60 kanonischen Bücher[4]), der Stichometrie des Nicephorus[5]) und der s. g. Synopsis

1) Für die Handschriften genügt es, auf Swete's Vorbemerkungen zu seinem Old Testament in Greek, für die Kanonsverzeichnisse, auf Zahn zu verweisen.

2) Diese Anordnung wird sich daraus erklären, daß Esther und Judith als „libri mulierum" (Zahn S. 285; auch bei den Syrern, s. Nestle in Herzogs Realencykl.[3] III 170 24 f) zusammengestellt sind. Wenigstens faßt es so der Verfasser der Stichometrie des Nicephorus auf, wenn er Susanna als dritte im Bunde hinzufügt (vgl. unten Anm. 5).

3) Zahn S. 193—202. Der alttestamentliche Kanon ist genau der jüdische Kanon des Athanasius mit derselben Ordnung und Zählung der 22 Bücher, nur ist das bei Athanasius fehlende Buch Esther hinzugefügt. Aber hier verrät sich der Ueberarbeiter zu deutlich: um für Esther ohne Ueberschreitung der Zahl 22 Raum zu schaffen, hat er nach dem in der späten Synopsis des Athanasius (Zahn S. 316 6—10) gegebenen, übrigens schon sehr alten Recepte das bei Athanasius besonders gezählte Buch Ruth mit dem Buche der Richter zusammengefaßt (jedoch ohne „*Κριταί, Ρουθ*" durch *καὶ* zu verbinden, wie sonst in der Liste durchweg bei Zusammenfassung zweier Bücher geschieht) und nun an der frei gewordenen 8. Stelle das Buch Esther eingeschaltet, während Ruth und Esther sonst nur in einem ganz anders geordneten lateinischen Kanon (Zahn S. 285) mit Judith als „Weiberbücher" zusammenstehn; die Stellung, welche Esther dadurch erhalten hat, ist so abnorm, daß einige Textzeugen sich gedrungen fühlen, sie zu corrigieren und „Esther mit Ruth", resp. „mit Judith" an den Schluß des A. T. oder auch „Esther" allein hinter die historischen und poetischen Bücher zu stellen (vgl. Zahns textkritischen Apparat zu S. 202 6). Ueber den neutestamentlichen Teil des Kanons, welcher ebenfalls mit Athanasius übereinstimmt, jedoch die Apokalypse ausläßt, überlasse ich die Entscheidung den Neutestamentlern. (Die Vorlesebücher des Athanasius läßt der Kanon von Laodicea ganz weg, sowohl die alt-, wie die neutestamentlichen.)

4) Zahn S. 289—293.

5) Zahn S. 295—301. Daß diese beiden Verzeichnisse unter anderem auch

des Athanasius[1]), so findet sich jene Stellung des Hiob, so viel ich sehe, nur noch bei dem alten Melito von Sardes[2]), mit dem Athanasius auch die Ausschließung des Buches Esther gemein hatte, und ähnlich in S, wo aber auch noch die Weisheit Salomos und Sirach vor Hiob stehn, die Voranstellung Judiths vor Tobit nur noch bei Hieronymus[3]), der aber in diesem Punkte ebenfalls von Athanasius abhängig sein wird[4]), und in der verschollenen syro-hexaplarischen Handschrift des Masius[5]), denn den altlateinischen Catalogus Claromontanus[6]) kann man nicht wohl heranziehen, da Judith hier von Tobit durch drei andere Bücher getrennt ist.

Neben der sonst völligen Uebereinstimmung B's mit Athanasius ist nur eine Abweichung zu notieren: während Athanasius die Vorlesebücher als Bücher zweiter Ordnung erst nach Erledigung des ganzen alt- und neutestamentlichen Kanons in einem besonderen, für sich stehenden Anhange beibringt, stellt B sie, so weit sie dem A. T. angehören, zu den kanonischen Büchern des A. T. und zwar nicht hinter dieselben, wie man wohl erwarten könnte, sondern mitten unter sie, zwischen Hiob und die Propheten.

---

von Athanasius abhängig sind, zeigt sich klar in der Mittelgruppe, welche sie, wie jener, zwischen den kanonischen und den apokryphen Schriften haben:

Athan.:	Verz. der 60 Bb.:	Stich. des Nic.:
		Makk. 1—3
Weish. Sal.	Weish. Sal.	Weish. Sal.
Sirach	Sirach	Sirach
	Makk. 1—4	Psalm. Sal.
Esther	Esther	Esther
Judith	Judith	Judith
		Susanna
Tobit	Tobit	Tobit.

1) Zahn S. 302—318, bes. 307 f., wo die Abhängigkeit dieses späten Produktes von dem Athanasius, dessen Namen es trägt, nachgewiesen wird.

2) Euseb. h. e. IV 26.

3) Zahn S. 242 Anm.

4) Nur so vermag ich es mir zu erklären, daß Hieronymus im Prologus galeatus zuerst Weish. Sal., Sir., Jud., Tob. *und den Hirten* (also die Vorlesebücher des Athanasius in derselben Reihenfolge, nur mit Auslassung des nach Hieronymus kanonischen Buches Esther und der für das Abendland nicht in Frage kommenden Didache) aufzählt und von ihnen sagt: „non sunt in canone", und erst dann auch noch eine Bemerkung über die Makkabäerbücher macht, welche ja bei Athanasius überhaupt nicht genannt sind. — Von Hieronymus hängen wiederum die lateinischen Bibeln ab, welche dieselbe Reihenfolge haben (Sam. Berger, Histoire de la Vulgate, p. 331 ff.).

5) Bibliotheca syriaca ed. Lagarde 32g.

6) Zahn S. 159. Vgl. auch das lateinische Verzeichnis bei Zahn S. 285.

Aber diese Abweichung von dem Schema des Athanasius ist, glaube ich, doch leicht begreiflich. Das athanasianische Princip der Einteilung in kanonische und Vorlesebücher kreuzte sich hier mit dem andern Princip der Einteilung in Altes und Neues Testament, und es ist kein Wunder, daß die von jeher üblich gewesene und in der Natur der Sache selbst liegende Einteilung in A. und N. T. den Sieg über die neuere, mehr künstlich gemachte Einteilung in kanonische und Vorlesebücher davon trug. Wurde aber das strenge athanasianische Schema einmal durchbrochen, so war es im Grunde ganz einerlei, wo es durchbrochen wurde; auch am Schluß der kanonischen Bücher des A. T., wo die s. g. Synopsis des Athanasius die alttestamentlichen Vorlesebücher wirklich einreiht [1]), unterbrechen sie, da ja das N. T. noch folgt, die Reihe der kanonischen Bücher ebenso gut, wie da, wo sie in B stehn. Aber wie kam B dazu, sie gerade hierher zu stellen? Auch dies erklärt sich meines Erachtens wohl. Das A. T. zerfällt nach der Anordnung des athanasianischen Festbriefes in 3 Gruppen, welche Athanasius zwar nicht ausdrücklich so scheidet — denn die Formeln *μετὰ δὲ ταῦτα* und *καὶ λοιπόν*, mit denen er sie einführt, braucht er auch sonst —, welche sich aber ganz von selbst ergeben, nämlich 1) historische, 2) poetische, 3) prophetische Bücher [2]); und auch B hat, wie ich nachträglich sah, diese Gruppen ebenso geschieden, denn während er sonst am Schluß eines Buches nur den Rest der angefangenen Columne frei läßt, läßt er beim Uebergang zu den poetischen und zu den prophetischen Büchern, wie auch zum N. T., den ganzen Rest der Seite — außer der angefangenen noch eine oder zwei volle Columnen — frei und beginnt den neuen Abschnitt erst auf der folgenden Seite, die zugleich immer, gewiß nicht zufällig, einem neuen Blatte angehört [3]). Nun bringen die Vorlesebücher Nachträge zur zweiten (Weish. Sal., Sirach) und ersten (Esther, Judith, Tobit), aber nicht zur dritten Gruppe.

---

1) Zahn S. 307.

2) Ausdrücklich giebt diese Teilung Cyrill von Jerusalem, Athanasius' jüngerer Zeitgenosse, in dem Kanon, welchen er schon zwei Jahrzehnte vor Athanasius aufstellte, indem er die kanonischen Schriften des A. T. in 1) *τὰ ἱστορικά*, 2) *τὰ στιχηρά*, 3) *τὰ προφητικά* zerlegt (Zahn S. 179). Ebenso Gregor von Nazianz bei Zahn S. 216.

3) Die einzige Stelle, an der B sonst noch eine ganze Columne frei läßt, ist der Schluß des Markusevangeliums, bei welchem diese Maßregel aber ihren besonderen Grund hat (Westcott-Hort, New Testament II, Appendix, p. 29². Zahn S. 912); auch fängt hier die Fortsetzung nicht auf einem neuen Blatte, sondern auf der Rückseite desselben Blattes an.

Was war also natürlicher, als sie hinter die beiden ersten Gruppen, zu denen sie ihrem Inhalte nach gehören, und vor die dritte, mit der sie keinerlei Verwandtschaft zeigen, zu stellen? Hierfür sprach aber auch noch ein anderer, mehr äußerlicher Grund. Die poetischen Bücher oder, wie man damals sagte, *τὰ στιχηρά* [1]) oder *αἱ στιχηραὶ* [2]), resp. *στιχήρεις* [3]) *βίβλοι* sind in B stichisch in 2 Columnen geschrieben, während sonst 3 Columnen auf der Seite stehn; diese stichische Schreibung ist der Tradition entsprechend [4]) außerdem noch in den beiden ersten Vorlesebüchern (Weish. Sal., Sirach) durchgeführt; folglich schlossen sich die Vorlesebücher auch formell am besten an die zweite Gruppe an. Verliert somit diese Einreihung der Vorlesebücher das Auffällige, was sie vielleicht beim ersten Blick gehabt hatte, so muß man es nun umgekehrt fast auffällig finden, daß der Schreiber B's nicht noch etwas weiter gieng und die historischen Vorlesebücher von den stichischen trennte und mit der ersten Gruppe verband; denn wo sie jetzt in B stehen, hinken sie doch gar zu arg nach. Hier zeigt sich eben seine Abhängigkeit von Athanasius am deutlichsten: bei Athanasius ist die Anordnung Weish. Sal., Sirach, Esther, Judith, Tobit ganz natürlich, weil er diese Bücher in einem für sich stehenden Nachtrage außer Zusammenhang mit dem eigentlichen Kanon aufführt; sobald man sie aber so in die Reihe der kanonischen Bücher einzugliedern unternimmt, muß jene, im Vergleich mit der des eigentlichen Kanons chiastische Anordnung unnatürlich werden und die Disposition des Ganzen sprengen.

Wie im Alten, so stimmt auch im Neuen Testament, so weit es erhalten ist, B ganz mit Athanasius überein; leider bricht jedoch die Handschrift im Hebräerbrief ab, sodaß man nur noch vermuten kann, daß B auch dieselben neutestamentlichen Vorlesebücher, wie Athanasius, also die Didache und den Hirten, enthalten hat. Daß auch hier die Uebereinstimmung in der Reihenfolge der Schriften sich keineswegs ganz von selbst versteht, lehrt Zahns Abschnitt über „die Ordnung der neutestamentlichen Bücher" (S. 343—383). Besondere Hervorhebung verdient die Stellung des Hebräerbriefes. Nach dem griechischen und syrischen Texte des Festbriefes soll er zwischen den Gemeinde- und den Pastoralbriefen

1) Cyrill von Jerusalem, s. S. 75 Anm. 2.

2) Gregor von Nazianz und Amphilochius von Iconium bei Zahn S. 216. 218.

3) Epiphanius „über Maße und Gewichte" 4 10 (Lagarde, Symmicta II 156 27).

4) Vgl. Epiphanius a. a. O. 4 15 (Lag. S. 157 39 ff.), wo im Anhang zum Kanonsverzeichnisse Weish. Sal. und Sirach als noch zwei *στιχήρεις βίβλοι* aufgeführt werden.

des Paulus stehn, nach dem sahidischen Texte, für dessen Ursprünglichkeit C. Schmidt[1]) plaidiert, dagegen vor dem Galaterbrief. B stimmt mit dem Griechen und Syrer überein, ja er hat gerade in diesem Punkte die Anordnung seiner Vorlage corrigiert, um der Anweisung des Athanasius zu genügen, welcher gerade bei den paulinischen Briefen die Stellung ausdrücklich zu betonen für nötig erachtet[2]); denn die in B beibehaltenen Sectionszahlen der paulinischen Briefe beweisen noch, daß der Hebräerbrief in B's Vorlage hinter (nicht vor) dem Galaterbrief gestanden hat[3]). Somit wird B zugleich für die Textkritik des athanasianischen Festbriefes wichtig: der Grieche und Syrer haben uns hier den ursprünglichen Text bewahrt, der Kopte dagegen hat eine vorathanasianische Anordnung, welche sich in der sahidischen Bibelübersetzung weit über Athanasius hinaus erhalten hat[4]), aus seinem Bibeltexte in den Text des Athanasius hineincorrigiert.

Die Uebereinstimmung zwischen B und Athanasius kann nicht zufällig sein, sie beweist ein Abhängigkeitsverhältnis. Die Abhängigkeit kann aber nur auf Seite B's liegen, wie von vorn herein einzig wahrscheinlich, und wie die Anordnung der alttestamentlichen Vorlesebücher auch direkt beweist.

Somit können wir jetzt die Zeit B's so genau, wie nur wünschenswert, bestimmen. B muß jünger sein, als das Jahr 367, in welchem Athanasius seinen 39. Festbrief erließ, womit zugleich die noch neuerdings von O. von Gebhardt[5]) wahrscheinlich gefundene Vermutung Tischendorfs, daß B und S zu den von Eusebius im Auftrage Constantins für Constantinopel hergestellten 50 Bibelhandschriften gehören, endgültig erledigt ist. Da andrerseits auch Thompson, welcher S schon dem Anfange des 5. Jahrh. zuweist, doch von B sagt: „The Vaticanus is to all appearance the most ancient and may be ascribed to the 4th century“[6]), so bleibt für B nur das letzte Drittel des 4. oder höchstens noch der Anfang des 5. Jahrh. übrig.

Von nicht minderer Bedeutung ist unser Resultat für die wichtige Frage nach der Heimat B's. Die für das Richterbuch

1) In seinem zu Anfang citierten Aufsatze S. 184 f.

2) *Παύλου ἀποστόλου εἰσὶν ἐπιστολαὶ δεκατέσσαρες, τῇ τάξει γραφόμεναι οὕτως* (Zahn S. 211 44).

3) Zahn S. 361 Anm. 1.

4) Zahn S. 359. Die jüngere bohairische Uebersetzung hat dagegen die Anordnung des Athanasius (Zahn S. 361).

5) Herzogs Realencyklopädie[3] II 740 29 ff. 742 44 f.

6) Handbook of Greek and Latin Palaeography[2] S. 149.

von Grabe [1]), für das Neue Testament besonders von Griesbach, Hug [2]) und neuerdings wieder von Bousset [3]) aus der Beschaffenheit des Textes erschlossene und auch mir auf Grund analoger Beobachtungen an den Königsbüchern schon länger feststehende Herkunft B's aus Aegypten hat damit eine glänzende äußere Bestätigung erfahren. Denn wie die Festbriefe der alexandrinischen Bischöfe überhaupt officiell nur für Aegypten bestimmt waren, so hat auch der Kanon, welchen Athanasius in seinem 39. Festbriefe aufstellte, nur für Aegypten, wo er sofort großen Eindruck machte und mit Freuden begrüßt wurde [4]), officielle Geltung gehabt [5]), während sich ein Gleiches von anderen Ländern nicht behaupten läßt [6]), und auch nach Athanasius kein Kanonsverzeichnis des Morgen- oder Abendlandes bekannt ist, das mit dem seinigen genau übereinstimmte. Damit dürfen auch die Bemühungen neuerer Forscher, die Heimatsberechtigung unserer Handschrift in Asien oder Europa nachzuweisen, als erledigt gelten [7]).

Ist B aber ägyptisch, so wird man schwerlich um die schon von Grabe und Hug vertretene Annahme herumkommen, daß uns in B ein Repräsentant der Recension Hesychs erhalten ist. Denn bei einer Handschrift, welche sich in Umfang und Ordnung der heiligen Schriften so strikt an die officielle Kundgebung des ägyptischen Oberhirten bindet, ist auch anzunehmen, daß sie den

1) Vgl. Lagarde, Septuaginta-Studien I, S. 4; Grabe schloß aus der Uebereinstimmung B's mit den Citaten bei Athanasius und Cyrill. Vgl. auch G. F. Moore's Commentar zum Richterbuche in „The International Critical Commentary" (Edinb. 1895), p. XLVI.

2) Griesbach und Hug schlossen ebenfalls aus der Uebereinstimmung B's mit Athanasius und anderen sicher ägyptischen Zeugen.

3) Textkritische Studien zum Neuen Testament (Texte und Untersuchungen XI, 4) S. 74 ff.

4) Dies läßt sich noch verfolgen in der bohairischen Vita des Theodor von Latopolis, wie Pietschmann demnächst in einem Aufsatze „über den Osterfestbrief des Athanasius vom J. 367" zeigen wird.

5) Wie lange er diese Geltung behielt, bleibt die Frage. Vgl. S. 79 Anm. 2.

6) Ueber die recht späte Aufnahme des athanasianischen Kanons in die kanonistischen Sammlungen der griechischen Kirche s. Zahn S. 208. Größere praktische Bedeutung konnte diese Aufnahme schon deshalb nicht mehr haben, weil auch andere, recht abweichende Vätercanones ebenso sanctioniert worden sind (Zahn S. 186 f.).

7) Wer es liebt, sich auf den grundlosen Boden der reinen Hypothese zu begeben, könnte sich nunmehr, da das Land dafür, die Zeit nicht dagegen spricht, sogar vorstellen, daß der heilige Athanasius noch persönlich den Anstoß zur Herstellung unserer, offenbar für eine der Hauptkirchen Aegyptens geschriebenen Prachthandschrift gegeben hätte.

officiellen ägyptischen Text wiedergiebt. Als solcher ist uns aber durch die bekannten Aussagen des Hieronymus [1]) gerade für die Zeit, welcher unsere Handschrift angehören muß [2]), die Recension Hesychs bezeugt.

Hiermit wäre die von Alters her mit Recht berühmte, wenn auch oft überschätzte, vaticanische Bibelhandschrift zeitlich und örtlich festgelegt. Weiteres über sie muß ich meinen seit lange vorbereiteten Septuaginta-Studien vorbehalten, mit deren Veröffentlichung ich hoffentlich in nicht zu ferner Zeit werde beginnen können.

---

1) Librorum V. T[i] canonicorum pars prior graece ed. Lagarde, p. XIII.

2) Hierauf lege ich Gewicht, denn die Aussagen des Hieronymus gelten zunächst nur für seine eigene Zeit und dürfen nur mit der nötigen Vorsicht verallgemeinert werden. Gerade in ihrem Heimatlande Aegypten hat die Septuaginta eine besonders reiche Geschichte gehabt. Schon zwei Jahrhunderte nach Hieronymus findet Paul von Tella die Handschriften der Recension des Eusebius und Pamphilus, aus welchen er die Septuaginta ins Syrische überträgt, nicht in Palästina, sondern in Alexandria.

THE BISECTION OF BOOKS IN PRIMITIVE SEPTUAGINT MSS.

H. St. J. THACKERAY

(Ἑκάστῃ ζυγῇ βίβλος μία EPIPHANIUS.)

SOME years ago the present writer attempted to prove in the pages of this JOURNAL[1] that the Greek versions of two of the Prophetical books (Jeremiah and Ezekiel) contained indications that each book was divided into two parts for purposes of translation. In both cases a change of style was found to take place about half-way through the book.

In the present paper some evidence will be given of a rather similar kind with regard to three other books of the Septuagint. The facts here to be stated differ from those in the case of Jeremiah and Ezekiel, in that they appear to indicate a division of books not for purposes of translation, but merely for purposes of *transcription*. The differences found to exist in the earlier and later portions of the books are purely orthographical, not differences of rendering. Their importance consists in their witnessing to a practice of copyists, at a date far earlier than that of our oldest MSS, of dividing the several books of the Bible into two nearly equal portions: the two portions may, it is suggested, have been written on separate rolls. The uncials have, in a few orthographical details, faithfully transmitted to us the spellings of an earlier age, and give us some insight into the *format* of the archetypal MS or MSS of which they are descendants. The clues, so far detected, are few, but so striking as to demand explanation. The recurrence of the change in orthography at nearly the same point in three books (Exodus, Leviticus, Psalms) representing two of the divisions of the Hebrew Scriptures, taken together with the fact that a change of translators occurs at about the same point in two other books representing the third (prophetical) group, seems to establish the existence of the practice beyond a doubt. The evidence as regards the first three books will now be considered.

Exodus. The clue here is found in the use or disuse of the form ἐάν for ἄν with the relative pronoun ὅς (ὅστις, ὅσος) or with a conjunction (ἡνίκα). Dr J. H. Moulton has already called attention[2] to the fact that the papyri enable us 'to determine the time-limits of the peculiarity [the use of ὃς ἐάν, &c.] with fair certainty'. To the papyri evidence we will revert later. A casual glance at the opening chapters of Exodus

[1] Vol. iv pp. 245 ff, 398 ff.
[2] *Grammar of N.T. Greek*, Prolegomena 42 f.

Reprinted from *Journal of Theological Studies*. Vol. 9, 1907-8.

would not suggest that the use of ὃς ἐάν (ὃς ἄν) had any secrets to reveal. In the first half of the book both forms are used, apparently indiscriminately. But, if the investigation be carried on to the end of the book, it will be found that the forms with ἐάν are entirely absent from Codex B in the second half, while there is only a single instance of ἐάν in this part of the book in the two other uncials used in the Manual Cambridge edition (ἡνίκα ἐάν 34^{24} AF). The break comes between 23^{16}, where BAF read ὃν ἐὰν σπείρῃς and 23^{22}, where BF read ὅσα ἂν ἐντείλωμαι (A and 'Lucian' have the relative without particle), and BAF ὅσα ἂν εἴπω. We need have little hesitation in fixing on 23^{20}, the section beginning Καὶ ἰδοὺ ἐγὼ ἀποστέλλω τὸν ἄγγελόν μου, the concluding section of the 'Book of the Covenant', as marking the point where the second scribe in the archetype began his work. Excluding ὡς ἄν, ἕως ἄν, ὅπως ἄν, which are always so written throughout the book, the occurrences of the forms with ἄν and with ἐάν in the two parts in the three main uncials are as follows :—

	ὃς ἄν, etc.	ὃς ἐάν, etc.	Total.
Part I (Ex. 1^1—23^{19})			
B	7	14	21
A	11	10	21
F	7	8	15
Part II (Ex. 23^{20}—end)			
B	19	0	19
A	17	1	18
F	16	1	17

In Part I ἐάν is in most cases supported by at least one of the three MSS, in six instances by all three of them.[1] The evidence strongly suggests that in the parent archetype of all three MSS two scribes were employed, the second of whom used only the forms with ἄν : the first either wrote ἐάν only (the examples of ἄν in the uncials being due to later scribes), or he used both forms interchangeably. It should be added that the common ancestor of MSS containing such different types of text as are found in B on the one hand and in AF on the other must be very much older than those MSS : we are carried back to a MS which cannot well be later than the first century A.D. and may be even earlier.

Leviticus. Turning to Leviticus, we find almost exactly the same condition of things with regard to these forms. Both ὃς ἄν and ὃς ἐάν appear in the first half, ὃς ἐάν having preponderant authority in B and A : in the second half ὃς ἐάν almost entirely disappears. The break seems to come at the end of chapter 15 : it might be placed a few

[1] The evidence of the uncials is borne out by the fuller evidence available in Holmes and Parsons. Only one of the cursives, 32, sometimes supported by a few others, shews a tendency to write ὃς ἐάν in Part II.

verses earlier. The occurrences of the two forms in the MSS are as follows[1]:—

Part I (Lev. 1^1—15^{33})	ὃς ἄν, etc.	ὃς ἐάν, etc.	Total.
B	21	32	53
A	24	27	51
F	39	14	53
Part II (Lev. 16^1—end)			
B	48	7	55
A	44	8	52
F	45	9	54

The examples of ἐάν in Part II of Leviticus are rather more numerous than in the corresponding part of Exodus. It is noticeable, however, that three out of the seven examples in B and four of the instances in AF fall within the last nine verses of the book. The passages where ἐάν occurs with the relative in Part II are as follows:—18^{29}F, 20^6BA, ^{14}B, ^{17}B, 21^{18}AF, ^{20}F, 22^4F, 23^{12}A, 24^{15}BA (in this passage the reading ανος ὃς ἐὰν καταράσηται is undoubtedly a corruption, through loss of the letters AN, of ανος ανος ἐὰν κατ., which is read by FGM and most of the cursives), 25^{44}F, 27^{26}AF, ^{28}BAF, ^{29}BAF, ^{32}BAF. It will be seen that in Part II BAF unite in reading ἐάν only in the concluding verses: the form might owe its existence there to the hand of a διορθωτής who made a cursory perusal of the last page of the MS.

The test applied to Exodus and Leviticus does not appear to yield similar results in other LXX books, with the possible exception of the book immediately following, viz. Numbers. Up to the end of the Balaam episode (24^{25}) ὃς ἐάν and ὃς ἄν alternate in the MSS: after that point AF have twelve instances of ἄν and none of ἐάν. B, however, continues to write both forms up to the end of the book. If the evidence of AF proves anything here, the division comes at rather a later point than is usual elsewhere.

Psalms. The evidence in the case of the Psalter is a little more complex. On the one hand, we are fortunately in possession of more than one clue, suggesting a primitive division of the Greek book into two parts. On the other hand, the distinction between Parts I and II is not attested by all the uncials, and in the case of two Psalms in Part I (20 and 76 according to the LXX numeration) the orthography is not uniform with that which elsewhere characterizes that Part. The change in the orthography is attested by B in all the three criteria to be mentioned, while there are not wanting indications that ℵ and A are also descended from an archetype containing the two modes of spelling, though the distinction between the two parts has become,

[1] Ὡς ἄν, ἕως ἄν are excluded as before: ὅπως ἄν does not occur.

in the course of transmission, somewhat obliterated. The orthography of the seventh-century MS T remains unaltered throughout.[1] The combined evidence seems to indicate that a break was made in the parent MS at the end of Psalm 77 (78 Heb.). The clues which have been detected (there may of course be others) are three in number and are as follows:—

(i) Nouns in *-ία* (Part I) or *-εία*, *-εια* (Part II).

	Psalm				
Part I,	Psalm 19^{7}	δυναστεία	אA	δυναστία	B*
	[20^{14}	”	B*אAU]		
	64^{7}	”	א	”	B*T
	65^{7}			”	B*א
	70^{16}	”	א	”	B*
	18			”	B*א
	73^{13}	”	א*		
	77^{4}	”	א	”	B*T
	26			”	B*א
Part II,	79^{3}	”	B	”	אT
	88^{14}	”	BA	”	אT
	89^{10}	”	BאA	”	T
	102^{22}	”	B	”	א*
	105^{2}	”	BA	”	אT
	8	”	BA	”	אT
	144^{6}	”	BT	”	א*A
	11	”	BA	”	אT
	12	”	B	”	אT
	146^{10}	”	BA	”	אT
	150^{2}	”	B	”	אAT

Part I,	25^{8}	εὐπρέπεια	AU	εὐπρεπία	B*א
	49^{2}	”	א	”	B*AT
Part II,	92^{1}	”	B	”	אAT
	103^{1}	”	B	”	א*

Part I,	8^{2}	μεγαλοπρέπεια	—	μεγαλοπρεπία	B*אA
	[20^{6}	”	B	”	אA
	28^{4}	”	אU	”	B*AT
	67^{35}			”	B*א
	70^{8}			”	B*א
Part II,	95^{6}	”	Bא	”	AT
	103^{1}			”	AT
	110^{3}	”	אA	”	T
	144^{5}	”	B	”	אAT
	12	”	B	”	אAT

[1] The evidence of R, the Greek text of which is written in Latin letters, is ambiguous or valueless in orthographical matters (see Dr. Swete's text, vol. ii p. x). It is not clear whether it distinguishes between *-εια* and *-ια*.

(ii) The examples given in Dr Swete's Appendix where B writes αι for ε are limited to Part I, the last occurring at 77^{12}: from 29^{5} onwards to the point where A fails (49^{19}) B is in every case supported by A.[1] The last instance in B of the converse change (ε for αι) occurs at 74^{6}. The instances are as follows:—

(*a*) αι for ε: $23^{7.9}$ ἐπάρθηται, 29^{5} ἐξομολογεῖσθαι BA, 30^{25} ἀνδρίζεσθαι BAU, 31^{11} ἀγαλλιᾶσθαι BA, ib. καυχᾶσθαι BA, 32^{1} ἀγαλλιᾶσθαι BA, 32^{2} ἐξομολογ(ε)ῖσθαι BA, 33^{9} γεύσασθαι BA, 42^{2} μαι BA, 47^{13} διηγήσασθαι BA, ^{14} θέσθαι BA, ib. καταδιέλεσθαι BA, 48^{2} ἐνωτίσασθαι BA, 57^{3} ἐργάζεσθαι, 58^{2} μαι Bא, 61^{4} ἐπιτίθεσθαι, ^{11} προστίθεσθαι, 64^{12} παιδία, 67^{5} ἀγαλλιᾶσθαι, 75^{12} εὔξασθαι, 77^{12} παιδίῳ:

(*b*) ε for αι: the examples occur in 9^{22} (with A), ^{23}, ^{24}, 13^{3}, 14^{4} (with A), 44^{8}, 54^{22}, 71^{7} (with T), 74^{6} (with T).

(iii) The insertion or omission of the syllabic augment in εὐφραίνειν affords a third clue: in ψ 76, as already stated, the orthography attested by the principal MSS is that which is elsewhere limited in these MSS to Part II.

Part I,	15^{9}	ηὐφρ.	BAU	εὐφρ.	א
	29^{2}	,,	B*ATU	,,	א
	34^{15}	,,	BA	,,	א
	44^{9}	,,	BאAT		
	72^{21}	,,	Bא*		
	[76^{4}	,,	T	,,	Bא]
Part II,	88^{43}	,,	T	,,	BאA
	89^{14}	,,	T	,,	BאA*
	^{14}	,,	T		
	91^{5}	,,	T	,,	BאA
	93^{19}	,,	A	,,	T
	96^{8}	,,	AT	,,	Bא
	104^{38}			,,	BאAT
	106^{30}	,,	AT	,,	א
	121^{1}			,,	אAT

Two results so far have been obtained. (1) The slight but significant differences in orthography between Part I and Part II of the three books under consideration seem to indicate a division of the clerical labour of transcription, not a change of translators. This is quite clear in the Greek Psalter which has a somewhat peculiar vocabulary running right through the book. In Exodus and Leviticus no indications have been noted of a new style beginning at the points where the change in orthography takes place. In Exodus, however, it should be stated that the last six chapters have been held by some critics to be the work of a

[1] It should be added that A has other instances of the interchange of αι and ε in both parts of the Book.

second translator.[1] (2) The division of the Greek books into two parts, made or found already in existence by the scribes of the lost archetype, is based in each case on the same principle. Bulk, rather than subject-matter, is the determining factor. Each book is divided into two portions of nearly equal volume: the break is in each case placed *a little after* the middle point.

The Masoretes, we know, among other laborious calculations, ascertained which were the middle words in each book of Scripture: the points of bisection are indicated in our printed Hebrew Bibles. We may, thus, compare the Masoretic division of the books with that of the early scribes of the LXX. In each case it will be seen that the Greek scribes make their division a little later than the Masoretes. In Exodus the MT division comes at 22^{27}, that of the Greek copyists at 23^{19}. Leviticus[2] is divided by the Masoretes at 15^{7}, by the LXX scribes at 15^{33}. In the Psalter the Greek division is made irrespectively of the early partition into five books: on the other hand, it should be noted that the Masoretes place the middle of the book in the very same Psalm which closes Part I in the LXX, at the thirty-sixth verse of ψ 78 Heb. (77 LXX).[3]

Let us now consider the form and appearance which the parent archetype or archetypes of our uncial MSS must have presented. The common ancestor of BAF carries us back, as was said, to a period much earlier than the fourth century A.D. That century witnessed the transition from papyrus to vellum as the material used for literary writings.[4] Before that change took place there is reason to suppose that the MSS of Biblical (and secular) writings were 'usually small, containing only single books or groups of books', 'small portable MSS of limited contents'.[5] If we find, then, that the scribes of a primitive ancestor of BAF, in fixing the limits of their clerical labours, have taken the single book (not any larger collection such as the Law) for the unit, this is only what we should expect. The papyrus roll did not, as a rule, contain more than a single book. We may contrast with this division

[1] Robertson Smith ap. Swete *Introduction* p. 236.

[2] It may be noted, though the coincidence is no doubt accidental, that the LXX division of Leviticus (1–15 : 16–27) corresponds with a division of the book into an equal number of Synagogue lessons according to the arrangement of the Babylonian lectionary (five lessons in each part). See Ryle *Canon of O. T.* 236.

[3] According to another calculation, attributed in the Talmud to 'the ancients', the middle point was placed two verses later: *Kiddushin* 30 a cited by Strack in Hastings BD iv 729 b.

[4] Kenyon *Palaeography of Greek Papyri* 121.

[5] Westcott and Hort *Introduction to N. T.* 10, 268. Cf. 223.

of labour the large portions of Scripture transcribed *en bloc* by the three[1] scribes who produced Codex Vaticanus or the two[2] hands of the Codex Alexandrinus. But may we not go further and say that the employment of two scribes for each book suggests that the unit was not the single book, but the half-book, in other words that at least Exodus, Leviticus, and the Psalter occupied two rolls apiece? As Dr Kenyon says,[3] 'no papyrus roll of Homer hitherto discovered contains more than two books of the Iliad', i.e. on an average about 1,500 hexameter lines. Now, the shortest of the three LXX books under consideration, Leviticus, contains (according to the Stichometry of Nicephorus)[4] 2,700 στίχοι, i.e. nearly twice the ordinary complement of a papyrus roll, the στίχος being the length of a hexameter. A subdivision of even so short a book as Leviticus is therefore perfectly natural.

The MS of Aristotle's Ἀθηναίων Πολιτεία affords an illustration of the division of a literary work and the employment of several scribes. There we find at the end of the first century A.D. a division into four rolls, upon which four scribes have been employed. Three of the scribes are responsible for a roll apiece: the remaining roll is partly the work of the fourth scribe, partly of two of the others.[5]

Now, it has been shewn elsewhere that the Greek books of Jeremiah and Ezekiel are divided in just the same way into two parts, the break occurring in each case, as in Exodus, Leviticus, and Psalms, a little after the middle point: but with this distinction, that the break in the Prophetical books introduces a change of style and a second translator, not merely a change in orthography and a fresh scribe. It appears probable, therefore, that the practice of writing each of these two Prophetical books on two rolls goes back to the date of their translation, the second century B.C. It seems a natural inference that a division of Exodus, Leviticus, and the Psalter, made on the same principle, which must in any case go back some centuries earlier than the date of Cod. B, should also be referred to the time when the translations were first made, i.e. to the third and second centuries B.C.

It is, of course, not necessary to ascribe the same antiquity to the

[1] Swete *O.T. in Greek* vol. i p. xix.

[2] Dr Kenyon tells me that one hand wrote the Octateuch, the Prophetical books, Maccabees, and Job-Sirach: a second hand wrote the remaining books.

[3] *Op. cit.* 122.

[4] The number is supported by several cursive MSS. Swete *Introduction to O.T.* 346, 349.

[5] Kenyon's edition, pp. x ff. The rolls, it may be noticed, decrease in size, the first two being longer than the last two.

actual orthography which we have traced to the parent of our uncial MSS. If the practice of copying the several books on two rolls apiece continued for some centuries, the spellings which characterize the two parts of Exodus, for instance, may be the spellings of scribes of some intermediate date, say between 100 B.C. and 100 A.D. It will be worth while to examine two of the orthographical distinctions in the light of the large range of evidence obtainable from the papyri, namely, the writing of ὃς ἐάν for ὃς ἄν and the interchange of ε and αι.

(i) ὃς ἐάν—ὃς ἄν.[1] An investigation of the papyri, made independently of Dr Moulton's, and with the advantage of some recent publications (the Hibeh Papyri and the Leipzig collection of 1906) which were not available when he wrote, gives the following results.[2] The addition of + to a number indicates that, where a form is repeatedly found in one and the same document, the number of occurrences in that document have not been counted: + + indicates that there are several such documents. Moulton's abbreviation for centuries, viz. iii/B.C.=3rd century B.C., is adopted.

	ὃς ἄν, etc.	ὃς ἐάν, etc.
iii/B.C.	43 + +	(?) 4[3]
ii/B.C.	32 +	6[4]
i/B.C.	3	6 +
i/A.D.	5 +	39
ii/A.D.	13	79 + +
iii/A.D.	5	13 +
iv/A.D.	7	12 + +

It appears from these statistics that in iii/ii/B.C. down to 133 B.C. ὃς ἄν was practically universal: at that date ὃς ἐάν begins to come to the front, and from i/B.C. onwards is always the predominant form. The figures in both columns decrease in iii/iv/A.D., when the use of the indefinite relative in any form appears to have been going out. Papyri of i/B.C. are unfortunately very scanty. Until the appearance of Grenfell and Hunt's latest volume, the Hibeh Papyri, ὃς ἐάν might almost have been called non-existent before 133 B.C. We now know that it was a possible, but very unfashionable form, in the third century B.C.

[1] Cf. J. H. Moulton *op. cit.* 42 f; Mayser *Gramm. der Griech. Papyri aus der Ptolemäerzeit* 152 f.

[2] The Berlin Papyri have not been completely examined for the period from i/A.D. onwards. But such a large number of documents have been investigated for this period that this omission could not affect the relative proportion in the use of the two forms.

[3] Hibeh Papyri 96. 10 and 28 ὧι ἐὰν ἐπέλθηι, 259–258 B.C. (NB. ἐὰν ἐπέλθηι, where ἐάν is hypothetical, occurs in the same context, line 9): *ib.* 51. 3 ἃς [ἐ]άν, 245–244 B.C.: Petrie Pap. Part II 39 (g) ? iii/B.C.

[4] None earlier than 133 B.C., the earliest being Brit. Mus. Pap. vol. ii 220 col. 2, lines 6 and 8.

The last third of ii/B.C. (133–100 B.C.) was a period of transition when both forms appear in one and the same document. To that period or to the following century might very well be ascribed an archetype of our LXX uncials written by two scribes, one of whom wrote ὃς ἐάν and the other ὃς ἄν.

(ii) The interchange of ε and αι appears in some dozen instances in papyri dated B.C., beginning about 165 B.C.,[1] but does not become common till towards the end of i/A.D. The examples of this interchange in Part I of the Psalter might therefore conceivably go back to the autographs, though we should perhaps be safer in referring them to scribes of a slightly later date.

A further question remains. Did the bisection of the books, which in two cases at least goes back to the time of the Greek translators, originate with them, or did they find it already in the Hebrew originals? We cannot of course answer this question with certainty, but it seems to the present writer that there are some grounds for believing the practice to have been taken over from the Hebrew MSS. Two considerations in favour of this theory may be mentioned. (1) The Masoretes, at a much later date, calculated the middle points of the separate books. The motive for counting the number of words or of letters in a complete book is obvious, namely, to preserve the text from interpolations or omissions. The motive for bisecting the books is not so clear. May not this practice, which they appear to have inherited from an earlier age,[2] have arisen out of a primitive custom of transcribing each book on two separate rolls? (2) It may be accidental, but if we calculate the lengths of Parts I and II of the five books, which have been considered, *in the Masoretic text*, we find that the division is made on a definite principle. Part I bears practically the same proportion to Part II in each case. Part I, it appears, exceeds Part II by an amount equal to a fraction varying between one-fourteenth and one-sixteenth of the whole book. If, on the other hand, we make the same calculation *from the Greek text* in the Codex Vaticanus, this proportion is lost; in the longest of the books in the B text the excess of Part I over Part II is less than in the case of the shorter books. Of course this argument is open to objections, in particular to the objection that the MT does not exactly represent the Hebrew which the translators had before them. But the fact remains that we *can* trace a certain principle in the division of the books if we take the Hebrew text as our criterion. The following table, shewing the number of pages in an ordinary Hebrew printed Bible

[1] See Mayser *op. cit.* 107.

[2] See note 3 on p. 93.

occupied by Parts I and II of the five books, will indicate what is meant. The books are arranged in order of length.

	Pages.	Total.	Excess of Pt. I over Pt. II.
Psalms			
Part I (1–78 Heb.)	50½	93⅚	7⅙
Part II (79–end)	43⅓		
Jeremiah			
Part I	49	92½	5½
Part II[1]	43½		
Ezekiel			
Part I (1–27)	44⅓	83⅓	5⅓
Part II (28–end)	39		
Exodus			
Part I ($1–23^{19}$)	38½	72¼	4¾
Part II (23^{20}–end)	33¾		
Leviticus			
Part I (1–15)	27	50⅓	3⅔
Part II (16–end)	23⅓		

In conclusion, it is suggested that we may find in this primitive practice of allotting two rolls to a book a clue to the origin of the tradition (ὡς ᾄδεται λόγος), which first appears in Epiphanius, that the translators were divided into pairs, and that *to each pair was allotted a single book.* This appears to describe fairly accurately what happened in the case of two books: in the case of others the Greek text seems to warrant merely the existence of a pair of scribes. Epiphanius's words[2] will bear repeating here: ἑκάστῃ δὲ ζυγῇ βίβλος μία ἐπεδίδοτο, ὡς εἰπεῖν, ἡ βίβλος τῆς τοῦ κόσμου Γενέσεως μιᾷ ζυγῇ, ἡ Ἔξοδος τῶν υἱῶν Ἰσραὴλ τῇ ἄλλῃ ζυγῇ, (τὸ) Λευιτικὸν τῇ ἄλλῃ καὶ καθεξῆς ἄλλῃ βίβλος τῇ ἄλλῃ.

H. St. J. Thackeray.

PS. In Exodus a further distinction between Part I and Part II is afforded by the appearance in the latter of the unclassical ἔναντι (for ἐναντίον). The statistics for the two forms are as follows:—

	ἔναντι		ἐναντίον	
	Part I	Part II	Part I	Part II
B	1	16	36	14
A	0	20	37	8
F	1	21	21	7

Ἔναντι in Part I is confined to 6^{12} B, 6^{30} F: elsewhere BAF or BA (where F is wanting) consistently write ἐναντίον. In Part II, on the

[1] Omitting chap. 52, which appears to be a later addition (see *J.T.S.* iv 260). Parts I and II are the portions in the Heb. corresponding respectively to chaps. 1–28 and 29–51 in the Greek version.

[2] *De mens. et pond.* 3. The passage is quoted in Wendland's edition of Aristeas, p. 140.

other hand, there are only four passages where the three MSS combine in reading ἐναντίον (25^{29} $33^{13.\ 19}$ 40^{32}): ἔναντι occurs in 24^{17} A, 27^{21} AF, 28^{12} BAF, &c.

The distribution of the two forms in the remaining books of the Pentateuch is noteworthy. Genesis consistently has ἐναντίον. Ἔναντι is the predominant form throughout Leviticus and Numbers: in Deuteronomy it is written almost invariably by AF, while B usually has ἐναντίον.

In the historical books later than the Pentateuch both forms give place to ἐνώπιον.

JOSEPH ZIEGLER

URSPRÜNGLICHE LESARTEN IM GRIECHISCHEN SIRACH

Unter allen Büchern der Septuaginta gibt Sirach (Ecclesiasticus) dem Textkritiker die meisten und schwierigsten Rätsel auf. Immer wieder haben sich seit dem 16. Jahrhundert verschiedene Gelehrte um den griech. Text, der nach der Entdeckung grosser hebräischer Stücke besser beurteilt werden konnte, mit mehr oder weniger Erfolg bemüht; folgende Namen sind zu nennen (in zeitlicher Folge): Camerarius, Drusius, Grotius, Grabe, Bendtsen, Bretschneider, Schleusner, Böttcher, Fritzsche, Hatch, Schlatter, Ryssel, Nestle, Herkenne, Smend, Hart, Peters Box und Oesterley, de Bruyne, Kuhn, Rahlfs, Katz. Die Krone gebührt Rudolf S m e n d; 1906 gab er die Weisheit des Jesus hebräisch und deutsch mit einem hebräischen Glossar, ferner einen ausführlichen Kommentar, dem umfangreiche (159 S.) Prolegomena einleiteten, heraus; in seiner Selbstanzeige in den Götting. Gelehrten Anzeigen 10 (1906) 755-771 sind wichtige Nachträge verzeichnet; ein Jahr später (1907) erschien als wertwolles Arbeitsinstrument der Griechisch-Syrisch-Hebräische Index zur Weisheit des Jesus Sirach. Viele unklare und umstrittene Stellen hat Smend erfolgreich erklärt und so die beste Vorarbeit für den Sirach der Stuttgarter Handausgabe von Rahlfs (1935) geliefert. Aber auch der von R a h l f s hergestellte Text ist noch weit vom Ziel entfernt; den grossen Abstand zeigt K a t z in seiner ausführlichen und wirklich weiterführenden Besprechung der Stuttgarter Septuaginta in der Theol. Literaturzeitung 61 (1936) 278f., wo er in 134 Zeilen zu 270 Stellen eine « vorläufige Liste » seiner (meist auf Smend zurückgehenden) Textlesarten und Emendationen veröffentlichte. Allerdings schoss Katz in seinem Konjekturen- und Emendationeneifer weit über das Ziel hinaus; nach wiederholter, sorgfältiger Prüfung konnten von den 270

Reprinted from *Mélanges Eugène Tisserant,* I (Studi e Testi, 231). Vatican City. 1964.

vorgeschlagenen Textlesarten nur 70 in die neue Göttinger Ausgabe übernommen werden ([1]).

([1]) *Sigel und Abkürzungen*

H	= Hebräischer Text	La	= Lateinische Übersetzung (Vetus Latina)
G	= Griechischer Text (Übersetzung des Enkels)	Syh	= Syrohexaplarische Übersetzung
GrII	= Zweite griechische Übersetzung	Syr	= Syrische Übersetzung (Peschitta)
O	= 253–Syh	*a*	= 149–260–606
L	= 248–493–637	*b*	= 249–254–603–754
l	= 106–130–545–705	*c*	= 296–311–548–706

Benützte Literatur

Bendtsen = *Specimen exercitationum criticarum in Veteris Testamenti Libros Apocryphos e scriptis patrum et antiquis versionibus... quod... publice defendet* BENEDICTUS *Bendtsen*, Gottingae 1789

Böttcher = F. BÖTTCHER, *Exegetisch-kritische Aehrenlese zum AT*, Leipzig 1849

Box = G. H. BOX, *The Book of Sirach: The Apocrypha and Pseudepigrapha of the OT in English ed.* R. H. CHARLES I (Oxford 1913) 268-517

de Br. = D. DE BRUYNE, *Étude sur le texte latin de l'Ecclésiastique; Rev. Bén.* 40 (1928) 5-48

Bret. = *Liber Iesu Siracidae graece... illustratus a* C. G. BRETSCHNEIDER, Ratisbonae 1806

Camerarius = *Sententiae Iesu Siracidae...* IOACHIMO CAMERARIO *Pabepergen. autore*, Basileae 1551

Drusius = *ΣΟΦΙΑ ΣΕΙΡΑΧ sive Ecclesiasticus ... ex interpretatione* I. DRUSII, Franekerae 1596

Fr. = *Libri apocryphi Veteris Testamenti graece. Recensuit et cum commentario critico ed.* O. F. FRITZSCHE, Lipsiae 1871

Grabe = *Septuaginta Interpretum tomus III, ed.* J. E. GRABE, Oxonii 1720

Grotius = HUGONIS GROTII, *Annotationes in VT curavit* G. I. L. VOGEL, *tomus III*, Halae 1776

Hart = *Ecclesiasticus. The Greek Text of Codex 248 ed.* ... by J. H. A. HART, Cambridge 1909

Hatch = E. HATCH, *On the Text of Ecclesiasticus*, in *Essays in Biblical Greek* (Oxford 1889) 246-282

Herk. = H. HERKENNE, *De Veteris Latinae Ecclesiastici capitibus I-XLIII*, Lipsiae 1899

Houbigant = C. F. HOUBIGANT, *Notae criticae in universos Veteris Testamenti libros cum hebraice, tum graece scriptos*, Frankfurt 1777

Katz = P. KATZ, *Besprechung der Septuaginta-Ausgabe von Rahlfs*, in der *ThLZ* 61 (1936) 265-287 (Zu Sirach Sp. 278f.)

I. – Konjekturen

Bei der Textgestaltung wurde die Stuttgarter Septuaginta zugrunde gelegt; alle Konjekturen und Emendationen von Rahlfs wurden genau nachgeprüft. Die bessere Einsicht in die vorhandene Variantenmasse des griech. Textes und der verschiedenen Übersetzungen, namentlich der Vetus Latina (La), stärkte die Position mancher Textlesarten von Rahlfs, brachte aber andere zu Fall. Zu den zwei Vorgängen sei je ein Beispiel genannt.

27,18(20) *ἀπώλεσεν ἄνθρωπος τὸν ἐχθρὸν* (*νεκρον* 157) *αὐτοῦ*
homo qui perdit amicum (leg. *inimicum*?) *suum* La
homo qui (> ^{x}) *extulit mortuum suum* (> ^{x}) La^{sx}

Kuhn I II = G. Kuhn, *Beiträge zur Erklärung des Buches Jesus Sira I und II*, *ZAW* 47 (1929) 289-296 und 48 (1930) 100-121

Nestle = E. Nestle, *Marginalien und Materialien*, Tübingen 1893 (Zu Sirach S. 48-59. 94)

Oest. = W. O. E. Oesterley, *The Book of Sirach*: *The Apocrypha and Pseudepigrapha of the OT in English ed.* R. H. Charles I (Oxford 1913) 268-517

Pe. = *Das Buch Jesus Sirach oder Ecclesiasticus übersetzt und erklärt von* N. Peters (= Exeget. Handbuch z. AT 25), Münster i. W. 1913

Ra. = *Septuaginta id est Vetus Testamentum graece iuxta LXX interpretes ed.* Alfred Rahlfs, Stuttgart 1935

Ry. = V. Ryssel, *Die neuen hebräischen Fragmente des Buches Jesus Sirach und ihre Herkunft*, *Theol. Studien u. Kritiken* 73 (1900) 363-403. 505-541; 74 (1901) 75-109. 269-294. 547-592; 75 (1902) 205-261. 347-420.

Schla. = A. Schlatter, *Das neu gefundene Hebräische Stück des Sirach. Der Glossator des griechischen Sirach und seine Stellung in der Geschichte der jüdischen Theologie*, *Beiträge zur Förderung christl. Theologie* I 5-6 (Gütersloh 1897).

Schleusner = *Novus Thesaurus philologico-criticus sive Lexicon in LXX... ed.* J. Fr. Schleusner, vol. I-III, Londini 1829

Sm. = *Die Weisheit des Jesus Sirach erklärt von* R. Smend, Berlin 1906.

Ferner wurde gelegentlich zitiert:

R. Smend, *Griechisch-Syrisch-Hebräischer Index zur Weisheit des Jesus Sirach*, Berlin 1907.

J. Ziegler, *Zum Wortschatz des griechischen Sirach*: *Eissfeldt-Festschrift* Von Ugarit nach Qumran, *ZAW* Beihefte 77 (Berlin 1958) 274-287.

J. Ziegler, *Beiträge zur Ieremias-Septuaginta*, *Nachrichten der Akademie der Wissenschaften in Göttingen*, Philol.-hist. Kl. (Göttingen 1958) 45-235.

Ra. nimmt *νεκρόν*, das nur « unus cod. » (= 157) bezeugt, statt *ἐχθρόν* in seinen Text auf. Aber auch die lat. Hss. SX *mortuum* haben in ihrer griech. Vorlage *νεκρόν* gelesen. Auch sonst kann diese Verschreibung aufgezeigt werden: Sap. 15,14 *οἱ ἐχθροί*] *mortui* (= *οἱ νεκροί*) Arab und Num. 10,9 *ἀπὸ τῶν ἐχθρῶν ὑμῶν* = M] *a mortuis vestris* (= *ἀπὸ τῶν νεκρῶν ὑμῶν*) La. Die Vorschläge von Bret. *τὴν θήραν* und Kuhn II 107 *τὸν τρίχα* (bereits von Nestle S. 54 vorgeschlagen, aber sofort wieder verworfen) erledigen sich von selbst. Am meisten Chance hatte *κλῆρον*, das schon Böttcher auf Grund des syr. *mnthh* vorschlug; Sm. Pe. Oest. Katz stimmen Böttcher zu. Jedoch ist *κλῆρον* abzulehnen; wenn man das syr. *mnthh* (= *portionem*) in das naheliegende *mithh* (= *mortuum*) verbessert, dann erhält *νεκρόν* eine feste Grundlage.

Bei der Lesart der lat. Hss. SX *extulit mortuum* denkt man unwillkürlich an den Bericht im NT, dass der einzige Sohn der Witwe aus dem Städtchen Naim « als Toter hinausgetragen wurde »; allerdings lautet die griech. (und lat.) Fassung anders: *ἐξεκομίζετο τεθνηκώς* (*defunctus efferebatur*) Luc. 7,12. Das Verbum *ἐκφέρειν* (*efferre*) hat die oft in der profanen Literatur vorkommende spezielle Bedeutung zum Begräbnis hinaustragen, bestatten. Es ist nicht erlaubt, eine andere griech. Vorlage, etwa *ἀπεφόρησεν* (aus *ἀπώλεσεν*), das als *ἐξεφόρησεν* gedeutet wurde, anzunehmen. Wahrscheinlich ist nur frei *extulit* gewählt, weil das wörtliche *perdit* (*perdidit*) nicht recht passte.

38,28 (*φωνὴ σφύρης*) *καινιεῖ* (*τὸ οὖς αὐτοῦ*) B-S alii Fr.] *κενιει* A alii; *κινει* 542 543; *κναίει* Grabe Bret.; (*φωνῇ σφ.*) *κλινεῖ* Sm. Box Ra.

Ra. hat zu Unrecht die alte Konjektur *κλινεῖ* übernommen. Richtig haben Herk. und Ry. als hebr. Äquivalent *jḥrš* (= er macht taub, so Aeth) erkannt, das der griech. Übersetzer in *jḥdš* (= er macht neu) verlas, vgl. Pe. S. 320.

Im folgenden sind 15 Vokabeln verzeichnet, die den Anspruch erheben können als Konjekturen in den Text aufgenommen zu werden. Die Aufspürung der Konjekturen ist gewöhnlich dadurch erleichtert dass die Vokabel häufig ist und die Verlesung auch sonst festgestellt werden kann.

1. ἄνθρωπος (ex ανος) — αὐτός

10,17a *ἐξ αὐτῶν* Ra.] *ἐξ ανων* = *ἐξ ἀνθρώπων* Hatch p. 262 Sm. Zi. = Syr (V. 17b).

46,12c *αὐτῶν* Ra.] *ανων* = *ἀνθρώπων* Sm. Zi.

4,5 *ἀνθρώπῳ* Ra.] *αὐτῷ* Hart Zi. = H.

10,17 und 46,12 ist *ἀνθρώπων*, dagegen 4,5 *αὐτῷ* ursprünglich.

Die Verschreibung *ανος* - *αὐτός* lässt sich oft beobachten. Beispiele:

5,13 *ἀνθρώπου*] *αυτου* C | 10,11 *ἄνθρωπον*] *αυτον* C | 15,19 *ἀνθρώπου*] *αυτου* A 336 | 18,9 *ἀνθρώπου*] *αυτου* C 543 Aeth | 38,6 *ἀνθρώποις*] *αυτοις* 249-754 | 9,13 *ἀπὸ ἀνθρώπου*] *ab eo* (= *απ αυτου*) Arm.
Sap. 13,13 *ἀνθρώπου*] *αυτου* 339 755 | Zach. 12,1 *ἀνθρώπου*] *αυτου* A
Sir. 17,19b *αὐτῶν*] *των ανθρωπων* S*
Sap. 14,12 *αὐτῶν*] *ανθρωπων* 613 | Mac. II 7,21 *αὐτῶν*] *των ανθρωπων* A.

2. *βολίς* (*βέλος*) - *βασιλεύς* (*διαβολή*)

51,6 *βασιλεῖ διαβολή* Ra.] *καὶ βολίδος* Zi. = H

Sm. weiss nicht, wie die Textverderbnis zu heilen sei. Aber Pe. und Hart sind auf der richtigen Spur, wenn sie in *βασιλεῖ* ein verstecktes *βέλος* sehen. Hart verweist auf Jer. 9,8(7) *βολὶς τιτρώσκουσα ἡ γλῶσσα αὐτῶν* und auf Job 39,22. Die Job-Stelle ist besonders lehrreich, weil die gleiche Verderbnis vorliegt: *βέλει*] *βασιλει* B-S* Syh^{txt}. *Βέλος* ist die gewöhnliche Wiedergabe für *ḥeṣ* und kommt auch 2mal in Sir. vor (H fehlt an beiden Stellen). *Βολίς* wird seltener verwendet (fehlt in Sir.); Jer. 9,8(7) 27(50),9 Ez. 5,16 ersetzen Aquila und Symmachus *βολίς* durch *βέλος*. Vielleicht leben in *βασιλεῖ διαβολή* die beiden Lesarten *βέλος*-*βολίς* verborgen weiter. Die Verschreibung zu *διαβολή* (vor *γλώσσης*) ist durch die gleiche Wendung in V. 2c (*διαβολῆς γλώσσης*) gefördert worden. Die Entscheidung zwischen *βέλος* und *βολίς* ist nicht leicht; ich gebe *βολίς* als der selteneren Vokabel in Anschluss an Taylor und Ry. den Vorzug.

3. *ἐλεγμός* - *ἐμός*

3,1 *ἐμοῦ τοῦ πατρὸς ἀκούσατε, τέκνα* (+ *κρισιν* *L*)
ἀκούσατε τέκνα κρίσιν πατρός *O* Houbigant Nestle Ry. Sm. Katz: cf. Syr.
κρίμα τοῦ πατρὸς ἀκούσατε τέκνα 768 ed. Wechel
iudicium patris audite filii La (3,2)

Nestle S. 48f. hat auf die (bereits von Houbigant vorgeschlagene) Lesart *κρίσιν* hingewiesen und hält sie für « die einzig richtige Lesart », die auch durch die Peschitta (= Syr) verbürgt werde; alle Textkritiker schliessen sich Nestle an. Aber die Stellung von *κρίσιν* ist nicht ursprünglich; es gehört vielmehr an den Anfang, wo es La richtig hat. Sm. verweist auf die gleiche Stellung 23,7 (*παιδείαν στόματος ἀκούσατε, τέκνα*) und 41,14 (*παιδείαν... συντηρήσατε, τέκνα*). Dies zeigt deutlich, dass im ersten Wort (*ἐμοῦ*) das ursprüngliche Nomen stecken muss, und dieses ist *ἐλεγμόν*.

Die Vokabel *ἐλεγμός* (gewöhnlich für *thokaḥath*) steht 5mal bei Sirach; zweimal findet sich *ἔλεγχος*. Als Parallelworte treten *κρίμα, σύγκριμα, κρίνειν* auf:

35 (32 Ra.),17 *ἐλεγμόν* (*correptionem*) parallel *σύγκριμα* (*comparationem*)
48,7 *ἐλεγμόν* (*iudicium*) parallel *κρίματα* (*iudicia*)
16,12(13) *ὁ ἔλεγχος* (*correptio*) parallel *κρινεῖ* (*iudicat*).

Die in Klammern beigegebenen lat. Wiedergaben sind lehrreich: *correptio* steht auch 20,31 21,7 19,28a (Dublette), *iudicium* 19,28b (Dublette) 48,10. An *correptio* ist nichts auszusetzen, wohl aber an *iudicium*; dieses ist nämlich innerlateinisch aus *indicium* verderbt.

Bereits Herk. (und ihm folgend de Br.) hat zu 19,28b *indicium* statt *iudicium* gefordert.

In der Vulgata steht überall *iudicium*. Wenn wir die neue Textausgabe von San Girolamo aufschlagen, so steht 19,28 richtig *indicium*, dagegen unrichtig 48,7a *iudicium* (statt *indicium*) und 48,10 *iudiciis* (statt *indiciis*).

So wird auch an unserer Stelle *indicium* in La ursprünglich sein.

Somit ist 3,1 zu lesen: *ἐλεγμὸν πατρὸς ἀκούσατε, τέκνα*. Der *ἐλεγμὸς πατρός* 3,1b entspricht ausgezeichnet der *κρίσις μητρός* 3,2b.

4. *ἐπιδέχεσθαι – ἐπιλέγεσθαι – ἐπιδείκνυσθαι*

Drei Stellen (36,26 41,1 51,26) zu *ἐπιδέχεσθαι* verzeichnen Hatch-Redpath in ihrer Konkordanz, zwei weitere (6,18 50,21) führt Sm. in seinem Index auf:

36,26 (21 Ra.) *ἐπιδέξεται*] *επιλεξ*. 339; *επιδειξ*. 795 | 41,1 *ἐπιδέξασθαι*] *επιδειξ*. 578 | 51,26 *ἐπιδεξάσθω*] *επιδειξ*. 706.
6,18 *ἐπίλεξαι* Ra.] *δεξαι* 694; *excipe* La Syr = *ἐπίδεξαι* Böttcher Nestle Herk. Sm. Oest. Katz Zi.
50,21 *ἐπιδείξασθαι*] *επιδεξ*. *OL* alii Ra. Sm. Zi.

Für diesen Wechsel (*Δ-Λ, E-EI*) lassen sich noch weitere Stellen aufführen:

Sir. 6,23 ἔκδεξαι] εκλεξαι *L* alii; εκλεξον 755 | 35 (32 Ra.), 14 ἐκδέξεται] εκλεξ. B^c alii = Ald. | 51,16 ἐδεξάμην] εξελεξαμην 547.
Prov. 24,47 (32 Ra.) ἐκλέξασθαι] εκδεξ. 339 534-613 = H | Job 34,33 ἐκλέξῃ] εκδεξη S | Is. 66,4 ἐκλέξομαι] εκδεξ. B alii | Regn. II 19,38 (39 Ra.) ἐκλέξῃ] εκδεξηται A | Mac I 1,63 ἐπεδέξαντο (ἀποθανεῖν)] επελεξ. *L* alii; επεδειξ. 542 | Mac. II 7,29 ἐπίδεξαι (τὸν θάνατον)] επιλεξαι 19 alii; επιδειξαι 370 | 2,26 ἐπιδεδεγμένοις *q* La Arm] επιδεδειγμ. rel. | Mac. III 6,26 ἐπιδεδεγμένους *q*-58 311^c] επιδεδειγμ. rel. | Est. 2,3 ἐπιλεξάτωσαν] επιδειξ. A.

Ein Überblick zeigt, dass 6,18 ἐπίδεξαι (statt ἐπίλεξαι) παιδείαν zu lesen ist; vgl. zur Wendung ἐπιδέχεσθαι (oder ἐκδ.) παιδείαν 51,26 (ἐπιδεξάσθω... παιδείαν) | 18,14 (τοὺς ἐκδεχομένους παιδείαν) | 35 (32 Ra.),14 (ἐκδέξεται παιδείαν).

Diese Wendung gebraucht auch Symmachus Prov. 19,20 (bereits Böttcher hat auf diese Stelle verwiesen) ἐπιδέξεται παιδείαν (LXX anders), ein weiterer Beleg für die Verwandtschaft seines Wortschatzes mit Sirach, siehe Ziegler, Zum Wortschatz des griech. Sirach S. 284-286.

Zugleich sichert der Überblick die Konjektur Prov. 24,47 (32 Ra.) ἐκδέξασθαι (statt ἐκλέξασθαι) παιδείαν.

Weiterhin zeigt die Zusammenstellung, dass 51,21 ἐπιδέξασθαι (statt ἐπιδείξασθαι) in den Text gehört, wie es bereits richtig Ra. getan hat.

Die beiden Verba ἐπιλέγεσθαι (6,18) und ἐπιδείκνυσθαι (50,21), die in Sir. nur je einmal an den genannten Stellen vorkommen, sind somit aus dem Wortschatz des Sirach zu streichen; richtig ist dies bereits von Sm. in seinem Index geschehen.

5. εὐδοκία – εὐλογία

An zwei Stellen ist εὐδοκία statt des überlieferten εὐλογία zu lesen:

36,22 (16 Ra.) εὐλογίαν Ra.] ευδοκιαν 307 534 Ry. Sm. Box Katz Zi. = H.

Die Verschreibung in εὐλογίαν hat die Beifügung Ααρων (κατὰ τὴν εὐλογίαν Ααρων περὶ τοῦ λαοῦ σου) veranlasst; somit ist Ααρων als «schlechte Glosse» (Sm. S. 322) auszuscheiden. Die Grundstelle ist Ps. 105,4 ἐν τῇ εὐδοκίᾳ τοῦ λαοῦ σου = H.

42,15d καὶ γέγονεν ἐν εὐλογίᾳ αὐτοῦ κρίμα

Diese Verszeile steht nur in S^c 339 679 Sa Arm = H. Die Textkritiker Bret. Herk. Schla. Hart Sm. Box lesen richtig nach H ἐν εὐδοκίᾳ.

Auch 35(32 Ra.),14 hat La (32,18) in der griech. Vorlage *εὐλογίαν* gelesen: *εὐδοκίαν*] *benedictionem* = *ευλογιαν* La (32,18).

Aus den Psalmen lassen sich zwei Beispiele für den Wechsel *εὐλογία*-*εὐδοκία* anführen:

Ps. 3,9 *εὐλογία*] *ευδοκια* Sa | 18,15 *εὐδοκίαν*] *ευλογιαν* Sa 2035.

Für die Vertauschung *εὐδοκεῖν*-*εὐλογεῖν* liegen in Sirach keine Beispiele vor. Dagegen können drei Stellen aus den Psalmen genannt werden:

Ps. 48,14 *εὐδοκήσουσιν*] *ευλογησουσιν* B-S La alii | 118,108 *εὐδόκησον*] *ευλογησον* S Bo | 84,2 *εὐδόκησας*] *benedixisti* La = *ευλογησας*.

Der Sirach-Übersetzer verwendet gern (16mal) *εὐδοκία*; sonst steht es nur noch 10mal in der LXX: 8mal in den Psalmen und je 1mal in Par. I 16,10 und Cant. 6,3(4 Ra.).

6a. *εὐοδία* – *εὐδοκία*

Die Vokabel *εὐοδία* ist selten; Hatch-Redpath zählen zu den vier Stellen bei Sir. noch vier in späten Schriften auf. Nur einmal (10,5) ist *εὐοδία* (neben dem naheliegenden *εὐωδία*) einheitlich überliefert, aber sonst ist immer *εὐδοκία* als Variante bezeugt:

20,9 *εὐοδία*] *ευδοκια* 248 679 Dam. | 38,13 *εὐοδία*] *ευδοκια* V alii | 43,26 *εὐοδία*] *ευδοκια* A.
9,12 *εὐδοκίᾳ* B A Ra. (-*κιαις* S rel.)] *prosperitatibus* Syh = *ευοδιαις* Hart.

Mit Nestle Sm. Box ist anstelle des ungebräuchlichen Plural der Singular *εὐοδίᾳ* im Anschluss an *εὐδοκίᾳ* B A, « das durch *εὐδοκήσῃς* veranlasst ist » (Pe. S. 86), als Textlesart aufzunehmen.

Hart bemerkt zu 9,12: « *εὐδοκία* is a common corruption of *εὐοδία* = *ṣlḥ* cf 2 Chr. XXIX.23, Is. LIV(LV) 17, Je. II.37 » (S. 116). Die genaue Aufzeichnung der Stellen zeigt, dass diese Notiz nicht korrekt ist:

Par. I 29,23 (nicht « 2 Chr. ») *εὐδοκήθη*] *ευλογηθη* c_2; *ευοδωθη* *b* e_2 | Is. 54,17 *εὐοδώσω*] *ευδοκησω* A | Ier. 2,37 *εὐοδωθήσῃ*] *ευδοκηση* S* 410 (-*κηθηση*).

Es kann noch Ier. 14,10 genannt werden: *εὐδόκησεν*] *ευοδωσεν* B* (*ευωδ.*[c]).

Die Beispiele zeigen, dass Par. I 29,23 *εὐοδώθη* in den Text gehört.

Auch Sir. 11,17 hat die griech. Vorlage von La (*profectus*) εὐοδία statt des allgemein bezeugten εὐδοκία gehabt. Jedoch steht hier εὐδοκία fest, wie andererseits 20,9 εὐοδία nicht anzutasten ist. Nestle S. 94 möchte εὐδοκία lesen, ebenso J. Goettsberger, Einleitung in das AT (Freiburg i. Br. 1928) 276 Anm. 5; hier liegt ein Versehen vor, da H zu 20,9 fehlt und somit kein hebr. *ḥpṣ* die Vorlage bilden kann.

6b. εὐοδία – εὐλογία

11,22b εὐλογίαν (-για 46 alii) Ra.] *processus* La (11,24b) = εὐοδία Herk. Sm. Hart Pe. Zi.

Sm. hält εὐλογίαν für « schwerlich richtig » (S. 109) und meint, dass εὐοδία Übersetzung von *thqwh* sein könnte. Ich halte εὐλογίαν für sekundär, das von V. 22a (εὐλογία κυρίου) her beeinflusst ist.

7a. κατασπεύδειν – καταπαύειν

45,3 κατέπαυσεν Ra.] κατεσπευσεν Ry. Sm. Pe. Box = H.

H (*mhr*) verlangt κατέσπευσεν als ursprüngliche Lesart. Die gleiche Verschreibung lässt sich an fast allen Stellen beobachten:

43,5 κατέσπευσεν] κατεπαυσε(ν) *O*-S^{c}–V *L* alii | 43,13 κατεπαυσε(ν) S *L* alii | 50,17 κατεπαυσαν (-σεν) V alii

Ex. 10,16 κατεπαυσε q | Deut. 33,2 κατεπαυσεν f alii | Par. I 21,30 κατεπαυσεν af Tht.

7b. κατασπεύδειν – κατὰ σπουδήν

43,22 (ἴασις πάντων) κατὰ σπουδὴν ὁμίχλη Ra.] κατασπουδη ομιχλης *b*; κατασπένδει (giesst herab) Kuhn II 115; ἴασιν πάντων κατασπεύδει ὁμίχλη Zi.

Die Wiedergabe κατὰ σπουδήν (*mʿrph* H) ist auffallend. Man erwartet ein Substantiv mit dem Gen. ὁμίχλης, wie es die Minuskelgruppe *b* überliefert (noch besser würde κατασπονδή passen), oder ein Verbum, wie es Kuhn vorschlägt. Aber κατασπουδή, κατασπονδή, κατασπένδειν fehlen im Wortschatz des Sirach-Übersetzers (und auch in der LXX).

So möchte ich κατασπεύδειν vorschlagen, das in der LXX selten ist, aber gern in Sirach (8mal) verwendet wird. Dieser Vorschlag ist durch dås gleiche Vorkommen der Varianten Regn. I 21,9 (κατὰ σπουδήν] *κατασπευδον* A, *επισπευδων* O-A) und durch die ähnliche Wendung der Symmachus-Wiedergabe Prov. 19,13 (*σταγόνες κατασπεύδουσαι*) ausgezeichnet begründet. Am liebsten möchte man auch an unserer Stelle das Partizip (*κατασπεύδουσα ὁμίχλη*) herstellen; dagegen sprechen jedoch die zu weit wegführende Femininendung und die Stellung (das Partizip müsste nach dem Nomen stehen).

8. *λογισμός* – *λόγος*

27,6 *λόγος*] *λογισμός* O-V *L* 543 Pe. Zi. = H
42,3 *λόγου*] *λογισμοῦ* Zi. = H.

Sm. glaubt, dass an beiden Stellen *λόγος* « der Abwechslung halber » (S. 243) für *λογισμός* stehe. Aber da sonst in der LXX immer *λογισμός* *mahašaba* oder *ḥæšbon* entspricht, ist auch hier *λογισμός* als ursprünglich anzunehmen. Der Wechsel findet sich öfter:

5,10 *λόγος*] *λογισμος* 753 | 12,12 *λόγους*] *λογισμους* 672 743 | 23,13 *λόγος*] *λογισμος* V 744-768 = Ald. | 48,1 *λόγος*] *λογισμος* 254
43,23 *λογισμῷ* = *cogitatione* La (25b)] *sermone* La (25a) = *λογω* Herk. Sap. 1,16 *λόγοις*] *λογισμοις* 248 | Mac. IV 3,1 *λογισμός* 1°] *λογος* V (nach Swete, fehlt bei Ra.).

9. *λόγος* – *νόμος*

36 (33 Ra.), 3a (*ἐμπιστεύσει*) *νόμῳ* Ra.] *λόγῳ* Kuhn II 109 Katz Zi. = H.

Sm. verweist auf Ps. 118(119), 57.105, wo *νόμος* für *dbr* stehe (siehe unten), und rührt deshalb *νόμῳ* nicht an. Aber der Wechsel *λόγος-νόμος* ist innergriechisch, der oft beobachtet werden kann:

31 (34 Ra.), 8 *νόμος*] *verbum* (+ *legis* V) La (34,8) = *λογος* Zi. | 32 (35 Ra.),1 *νόμον* = *legem* La V (35,1)] *verbum* La Apc (35,1) = *λογον* Herk.
Ps. 118,57 *νόμον*] *λογον* Sa; *verbum* ... *legem* La G: lectio duplex | 118,105 *λόγος*] *νομος* S R A *L* alii | 118,142 *νόμος*] *λογος* S alii | 129,5b *λόγον*] *νομον* S 55 Bo | Ier. 8,9 *λόγον*] *νομον* B | 34,15 *λόγος*] *νομος* S* | Is. 1,10 *νόμον*] *λογον* S* alii | Mac. I 2,22 *τῶν λόγων*] *τον λογον* S alii; *τον νομον* A 56.

Hatch-Redpath führen zu Unrecht in ihrer Konkordanz für den Wechsel *νόμος* - *λόγος* Deut. 32,45 auf: A *τοὺς νόμους τούτους*; A liest jedoch *λόγους* = M.

Somit ist 36 (33 Ra.), 3a mit H λόγῳ (statt νόμῳ) zu lesen; νόμῳ V. 3a ist durch ὁ νόμος V. 3b (= H) und νόμον V. 2a (= H) beeinflusst.

10. ναός – λαός

36,19 (13 Ra.) λαόν Ra.] ναον Ry. Sm. Box Katz Zi. = H
49,12 λαόν B-S V 336 Syh Sa Aeth] ναον rel. Ra. Zi. = H
50,5 λαοῦ Ra.] ναου 603 Bret. Ry. Sm. Katz Zi. = H.

Auch sonst findet sich oft der Wechsel λαός - ναός:

45,9 ναῷ = H] λαω 358 | 50,1 ναόν = H] λαον 248 alii | 51,14 ναοῦ] λαου 542 613
Ion. 2,5 ναόν] λαον B* | Mac. I 10,80 λαόν] ναον S*.

Weitere Beispiele siehe Ziegler, Beiträge zur Ieremias-Septuaginta S. 48.

Es ist somit 36,19 49,12 50,5 nicht λαός, sondern ναός zu lesen. Dagegen ist 45,24 λαοῦ (λαω) beizubehalten (gegen Hart, der ναοῦ fordert).

11. οἰκέτης – ἱκέτης
οἰκετεία – ἱκετεία

Für *'ebed* hat der Übersetzer nicht das gebräuchliche δοῦλος oder παῖς (siehe unten Regn. III 8,30 und Dan. 9,17), sondern οἰκέτης (13mal), das zu seinen Lieblingswörtern gehört, siehe Ziegler, Zum Wortschatz des griech. Sirach S. 284.

Gewöhnlich (8mal) ist einheitlich οἰκέτης überliefert. An vier Stellen hat nur eine Minuskel ἱκέτης:

6,11 ικετας 578 | 7,20 ικετην 743 | 7,21 ειкετην 253 | 30,39a (33,31a Ra.) ικετης 157*.

Umgekehrt steht manchmal οἰκέτης statt des ursprünglichen ἱκέτης z.B. Sir. 4,4 ἱκέτην] οικ. V 493 alii und Ps. 73,23 ἱκετῶν] οικ. Sa *L*p Tht.p

Der Wechsel οι–ι liegt ganz nahe, da οι als ι gesprochen wurde (wie im Neugriechischen). Beispiele aus dem Pentateuch:

Gen. 44,16 οἰκέται] ικ. f | 50,18 ικεται ka? | Ex. 5,15 ικεταις fs | 12,44 ικετην s | 21,26 ικετου cs | Num. 32,5 ικεταις ci (παισιν A M alii) | Deut. 5,15 ικετης is | 15,15 ικετης c.
36,22 (16 Ra.) gehen die Zeugen stark auseinander:

οικετων S A V-253 L^{-637} alii (= 13 min.) La (*servorum*) Sa Aeth Mal. = H
ικετων B 637 alii (= 22 min.) Syh.

Ra. hat zu Unrecht *ἱκετῶν* im Text stehen; H erfordert deutlich *οἰκετῶν* (so bereits richtig Bret. Ry.).

Auch ohne Kenntnis der hebr. Vorlage müsste wegen der Parallelen Regn. III 8,30 (*τῆς δεήσεως τοῦ δούλου σου*) und Dan. 9,17 (*ο' τῆς προσευχῆς τοῦ παιδός σου, θ' τῆς προσ. τοῦ δούλου σου*) *οἰκετῶν* als ursprünglich erkannt werden. Die Vokabel *οἰκέτης* gehört zu den Lieblingswörtern (13mal) des Übersetzers, der immer *ʿebed* so übersetzt; deshalb ist auch 30,34(33,26 Ra.) *ἐν οἰκέτῃ* (statt *ἐν παιδί*) als ursprüngliche Lesart in den Text aufzunehmen, siehe Ziegler, Zum Wortschatz des griech. Sirach S. 284.

Nur einmal (4,4 *ἱκέτην θλιβόμενον*) steht bei Sir. das nur noch Ps. 73,23 und Mal. 3,14 vorkommende *ἱκέτης*. Sm. möchte auf Grund des lat. *rogationem contribulati* (= H) *ἱκετείαν θλιβομένου* lesen. Jedoch ist dies eine jüngere Lesart von GrII, die nicht die ursprüngliche Wiedergabe *ἱκέτην θλιβόμενον* verdrängen darf.

Die Vokabel *ἱκετεία* kommt zweimal in Sir. vor und hat ebenfalls die Varianten *οἰκετεία*:

32,17 (35,14 Ra.) *ἱκετείαν*] *οικετειαν* 106 548 Sa; *οικετηριαν* 543 (die verwandte Minuskel 578 hat *ικετηριαν*)
51,9 *ἱκετείαν*] *οικετιαν* 545[mg] = *habitationem* La (51,13) Sa.

La setzt deutlich *οἰκετείαν* voraus, das in keiner griech. Handschrift erhalten ist, so richtig J. Mader, Bibl. Zeitschrift 11 (1913) 25 und A. Vaccari, Verbum Domini 2 (1922) 72. Die Lesart *οἰκετίαν* 51,9 ist eine der in 545 zahlreichen aus La zurückübersetzten griech. Randnoten.

12. *ὀλίγος – λόγος*

20,13 (*ὁ σοφὸς ἐν*) *λόγοις* (*λογω* B alii)] *ὀλίγοις* 253 Katz Zi.; *ὀλίγοις λόγοις* Sm. = H
20,27 (*ὁ σοφὸς ἐν*) *λόγοις*] *ὀλίγοις* Nestle S. 94 Zi. = Syr (vid.)

Zum Wechsel *ὀλίγος* - *λόγος*:

19,1 *τὰ ὀλίγα*] *verba* Sa = *τὰ λόγια* | 35 (32 Ra.),8 *ἐν ὀλίγοις*] *εν λογοις* 542; *εν ολογοις* 545* (*εν ολ̣ηγοις* [c])
Sap. 2,2 *ὁ λόγος*] *ολιγος* 443 alii | 4,13 *ὀλίγῳ*] *λογω* 157 | 12,2 *κατ' ὀλίγον*] *κατα λογον* 336 | Ecl. 6,11 *λόγοι*] *ολιγοι* S | 10,1 *ὀλίγον*] *ο λογος* B*.

An beiden Sir.-Stellen ist *ὀλίγοις* ursprünglich. Das Ideal des Weisen, vor allem des Redners, ist *ὀλίγα*, nicht *πολλά*; sein Motto lautet: *ἐν ὀλίγοις πολλά* (35,8).

20,13 liegt in H eine Dublette (ebenso 37,20) *dbr* = *bmʿt* vor: *bmʿt* = *ἐν ὀλίγοις* ist primär, *dbr* = *λόγῳ* ist sekundär.

Sm. hat die Dublette in H (hier und 37,20) völlig verkannt und möchte sie sogar in G übernehmen: « Danach ist wohl *ἐν ὀλίγοις λόγοις* anzunehmen » (S. 183). Dies ist unzulässig; *λόγοις* ist eine nähere Bestimmung von *ὀλίγοις*. Ähnlich ist 34(31 Ra.),19 « das Wenig » (*τὸ ὀλίγον*) in La als *vinum exiguum* (31,22) verdeutlicht worden. Clem. hat hier *οἶνος* statt *τὸ ὀλίγον*; es ist der gleiche Fall wie an unserer Stelle, nur dass in La, nicht in H eine Dublette vorliegt.

Wie ist die Dublette in H entstanden? Wahrscheinlich aus einer Randglosse *dbr* zu *bmʿt*, die dann in den Text geraten ist. B alii haben *dbr* mit *λόγῳ* wiedergegeben, das im Anschluss an das ursprüngliche *ὀλίγοις* in den Plural *λόγοις* gesetzt wurde. Oder ist *dbr* eine Rückübersetzung von *λόγῳ*? Siehe unten zu 37,20 (*τρυφή* - *τροφή*).

13. *συνέχειν* – *συνάγειν*

14,4 *ὁ συνάγων* (*ἀπὸ τῆς ψυχῆς αὐτοῦ συνάγει ἄλλοις*).

In H stehen im Gegensatz zu G zwei verschiedene Verba: *mnʿ* und *qbṣ*. Sm. (S. 131) nennt die Wiedergabe mit *ὁ συνάγων* « gleichmacherisch » und hält die von Pe. vorgeschlagene Konjektur *ὁ συνέχων* für « unratsam ». Katz dagegen stimmt Pe. zu; er verweist auf Prov. 11,26, wo *συνέχειν* richtig für *mnʿ* steht, und auf Job 20,13, wo wie an unserer Sirach-Stelle *συνάγειν* bezeugt wird. Jedoch zeigt die Aufzählung der Zeugen, dass die *beiden* Verba *συνέχειν* und *συνάγειν* vertreten sind, und dass *συνέχειν* den Vorzug geniesst:

Prov. 11,26 *ὁ συνέχων* B-S A V rel.] *ο συναγων* 253 254-754 534-613 766
Iob 20,13 *καὶ συνέξει* 46 106 130 137 139 und 20 weitere Minuskeln] *και συναξει* B-S A V und 19 Minuskeln.

Weitere Beispiele des Wechsels:

Is. 52,15 *συνέξουσι*] *συναξουσιν* A alii | Ier. 2,13 *ὕδωρ συνέχειν*] *υδωρ συναγαγειν* PsAth. IV 509 | Esdr. I 9,17 *ἐπισυνέχοντας*] *επισυναχθεντας* B

So ist auch Sir. 14,4 mit Pe. Katz *ὁ συνέχων* als ursprünglich in den Text aufzunehmen.

14. σῶμα – στόμα

37,22 *στόματος* Ra.] *σώματος* Sm. Zi. = H.

Der Wechsel kann oft festgestellt werden:

20,29 *στόματι*] *σωματι a* | Tob. 13,7 *στόματι*] *σωματι* B
23,16e *σώματι*] *ore* La (V. 23) = *στοματι* Herk. | 38,16 *σῶμα*] *στωμα* 315* | 51,2 *σωμα*] *στομα* 603
Sap. 1,4 *σώματι*] *στοματι* 311 | Iob 6,4 *σώματι*] *στοματι* S 296.

Somit ist Sir. 37,22 *σώματος* statt *στόματος* zu lesen.

15. τρυφή – τροφή

37,20 *τροφῆς* B A 964 S^c alii Ra.] *σοφιας* S* *O-V L'* alii; *τρυφης* Sa Sm. Hart Pe. Katz Zi.
41,1 *τροφήν* Ra.] *τρυφην* Schla. Sm. Hart Pe. Katz Zi. = H.

Das ursprüngliche *τρυφή* ist fast überall in *τροφή* verschrieben worden:

11,27 *τρυφῆς*] *τροφης* 155 alii | 14,16 *τρυφήν*] *τροφην* 248 alii La (*cibum* V. 17) | 18,32 *τρυφῇ*] *τροφη* 493 | 37,29 *τρυφῇ*] *τροφη* 46 755.

Im Hebr. steht an allen Stellen *tḥ'nwg*, 37,20 sogar die Dublette *tḥ'nwg m'kl*. Die hebr. Vorlage verlangt, dass 37,20 und 41,1 *τρυφή* als ursprünglich in den Text aufzunehmen ist; die Vokabel *τροφή*, die Ra. an beiden Stellen hat, gehört nicht zum Wortschatz des griech. Sirach-Übersetzers.

Auch diese Dublette (37,20) in H hat Sm. wie die oben zu 20,13 erwähnte nicht richtig erkannt; er hält sie für eine « schlechte Dittographie » (S. 334) des vorausgehenden *mkl* (ebenso Pe.) und meint, dass bereits G der Fehler vorgelegen sei, « so dass *τροφῆς τρυφῆς* bei ihm zu lesen wäre » (S. 335). Eine solche griech. Dublette ist als ursprüngliche Wiedergabe dem Enkel nicht zuzutrauen. Richtig notiert Box: « *m'kl* in H is an addition (a conflate reading) ». Auch hier kann man (wie bei 20,13) fragen: Stammt *τροφή* von einer Randnote *m'kl* in einer hebr. Vorlage, oder stammt gar das hebr. *m'kl* von der griech. Variante *τροφή*? Es ist noch darauf hinzuweisen, dass Syr 37,29 die gleiche Dublette hat.

Die Bevorzugung von *τρυφή* ist auch deshalb begründet, weil der Wechsel *υ-ο* an fast allen Stellen bezeugt ist:

Gen. 49,20 *τρυφήν* B] *τροφην* rel.: ex 27 | Ier. 28,34 *τρυφῆς*] *τροφης* 62 Cyr. | Thr. 4,5 *τρυφάς*] *τροφας* B A-106 verss. | Prov. 19,10 *τρυφή*] *τροφη* 46 | Cant. 7,7 *τρυφαῖς*] *τροφαις* V (-*φες*)

Sap. 19,11 *ἐδέσματα τρυφῆς*] *εδ. τροφης* 766 verss.[p] Cant.[lem] | 19,21 *ἀμβροσίας τροφῆς*] *αμ. τρυφης* S* (vielleicht ursprünglich).

Idt. 12,9 *τροφήν*] *τρυφην* A.

An all den genannten Stellen muss die von Ra. in den Text aufgenommene Lesart in den Apparat verwiesen werden. Ebenso ist dies an folgenden von Sm. empfohlenen Stellen zu tun; sie können ohne nähere Erklärung hier aufgeführt werden, weil die hebr. (und syr.) Vorlage sie ohne weiteres fordert.

3,17 *ὑπὸ ἀνθρώπου δεκτοῦ* Ra.] *ὑπὲρ ἄνθρωπον δότην* Sm. Zi. = H

10,22 *πλούσιος καὶ ἔνδοξος*] *προσήλυτος καὶ ἄδοξος* (melius *ξένος* Zi.) = H

16,26 *ἐν κρίσει*] *ἐν κτίσει* = H

21,4 *ἐρημωθήσεται*] *ἐκριζωθήσεται* = La Syr

22,17 *ψαμμωτός*] *γλύμματος* = Syh Syr

25,15 *ἐχθροῦ*] *γυναικός* = La Syr

29,28 *οἰκίας*] *παροικίας* = La[Z*] (*hospitalitatis*)

30,15 *σῶμα*] *πνεῦμα* = H

34(31 Ra.),27d *ἀνθρώποις*] *ἀπ' ἀρχῆς* = H

35(32 Ra.),9 *ἑτέρου λέγοντος*] *ὅπου γέροντες* = H

37,26 *πίστιν*] *τιμήν* = H

39,14 *διάδοτε ὀσμήν*] *δ. φωνήν* = Syr

39,14 *αἰνέσατε ᾆσμα*] *αἰν. ἅμα* = Syr

40,6 *ἐν ὕπνοις*] *ἐν ἐνυπνίοις* = Sa Arm

40,6 *σκοπιᾶς*] *κοπιᾷ* = Arm

41,16 *ῥήματι*] *κρίματι* = H

42,21 *ὡς ἔστιν*] *εἷς ἐστιν* = H: cf. 1,8

44,19 *ὅμοιος*] *μῶμος* = H

45,8 *ἐστερέωσεν*] *ἐστεφάνωσεν* = H

48,10 *ἐν ἐλεγμοῖς* (*ελεγμος* A...)] *ἕτοιμος* = H

51,3 *ἐκ βρυγμῶν*] *ἐκ βρόχων* = H.

II. – Umstrittene Text-Lesarten

Bei vielen Lesarten, besonders bei solchen, die auch von den alten Unzialen (B-SA) bezeugt werden, kann man darüber streiten, ob man sie in den Text aufnehmen soll oder nicht. Hier muss vor allem der hebr.

Text, falls er vorliegt, genau eingesehen werden, dann ist der Zusammenhang zu beachten und schliesslich ist zu fragen, ob die Vokabel, die als ursprünglich in den Text aufzunehmen ist, zum Wortschatz des griech. Übersetzers gehört. Auch auf diesem Gebiet hat Sm. vielfach ausgezeichnete Vorarbeit geleistet. Die einzelnen Stellen brauchen hier nicht weiter erörtert zu werden.

Folgende bereits von den alten Unzialen (B-SA) bezeugten Vokabel-Varianten, die Ra. in den Apparat verwiesen hat, habe ich (meistens im Anschluss an Sm.) in den Text aufgenommen:

22,18 *χάλικες* A Sm. Zi. (*χάρακες* B-S Ra.)
26,18 *ἐπὶ πτέρνοις εὐστάθμοις* S* (*ἐπὶ στέρνοις εὐσταθοῦς* B A S^c rel.)
35(32 Ra.),9 *ἐξουσιάζον* S (*ἐξισάζον* B A rel.)
33,10 (36,7 Ra.) *ὁρισμοῦ* S (*ὁρκισμοῦ* B A)
42,1 (41,26 Ra.) *ἀπὸ ἀποκαλύψεως* B(-*ψεων*) A (*ἀπὸ καλύψεως* S)
43,17 *ὠδίνησεν* A (*ὠνείδισεν* B-S)
50,11 *ἀναβάλλειν* S* (*ἀναλαμβάνειν* BA S^c rel.)

Sm. hat die von mir bevorzugten Lesarten 22,18 26,18 33,10 für « richtig » erklärt. 35,9 und 50,11 entspricht die Sonderlesart von S der hebr. Vorlage; ebenso ist 43,17 *ὠδίνησεν* durch H gesichert. 42,1 ist *ἀπό* (= H) infolge Haplographie ausgefallen. Es wäre allerdings möglich, dass keine Haplographie vorläge; dann müsste *καὶ ἀποκαλύψεως* geschrieben werden. Jedenfalls passt nur *ἀποκάλυψις* in den Zusammenhang, zumal die LXX das auch in der griech. Literatur seltene *κάλυψις* nicht kennt.

An der letzten Stelle (50,11) hält Sm. die Lesart von S* für « möglich », d. h. vielleicht ursprünglich, da die LXX *'ṭh* gewöhnlich mit *ἀναβάλλειν* wiedergibt. Der Wechsel zwischen beiden Verben ist auch sonst bezeugt; Beispiele sind aufgeführt in meinen Beiträgen zur Ier.-Septuaginta S. 45. Aus Sap. ist hinzuzufügen 19,4 *ἐνέβαλεν*] *ανελαβον* 547; *ελαμβανον* 46 443.

Ra. hat viele von nur wenigen (« pau. ») Zeugen überlieferte Lesarten, die Sm. als ursprünglich erwiesen hat, in seinen Text aufgenommen. Aber dies hätte auch an folgenden Stellen geschehen sollen:

8,15 *κατὰ σοῦ* Ra.] *κακά σου* *O*-V 694 La (*mala tua*) Sm. Zi.
17,8 *τὸν ὀφθαλμὸν*] *τὸν φόβον* *b* alii
21,8 *εἰς χειμῶνα*] *εἰς χῶμα* *L* = Syr
24,6 *ἐκτησάμην*] *ἡγησάμην* S^c La (*primatum habui*)
28,10b *ἐκκαυθήσεται* (= 10a)] *αὐξηθήσεται* *L* 768

36(33 Ra.),13 *πᾶσαι αἱ ὁδοὶ αὐτοῦ*] *πλάσαι αὐτό L* La (*plasmare illud* 33,14)
38,19 *κατὰ καρδίας*] *κατάρα καρδίας L* alii = Syr
42,8 *πρὸς νέους*] *περὶ πορνείας O*-V *L* = H
50,29 *φῶς*] *φόβος l* 311 = H
51,8 *ἐχθρῶν* (*εθνων* B)] *πονηρῶν* V = H
51,19 *ἐπένθησα*] *ἐπενόησα* V-253 248 alii: cf. Sap. 14,2 *ἐπενόησεν*] *επενθησεν* V (Unzialfehler: *O*-*Θ*)

III. - Dubletten

Die Dubletten bereiten jedem Herausgeber grosse Sorgen. Oftmals ist es zunächst nicht leicht, die Dubletten als solche zu erkennen, weil es auch vermeintliche Dubletten gibt, und dann ist es manchmal sehr schwierig, die ursprüngliche Hälfte der Dublette festzustellen, weil diese kein sichtbares Zeichen ihres Alters hat. Wenn ein Teil der Dublette deutlich als sekundär angesprochen werden kann (dies ist leicht bei den späten aus dem Hebräischen stammenden Dubletten der *O*- und *L*-Rezensionen), dann muss dieser in den Apparat verwiesen werden.

Besonders zahlreich sind die Dubletten in La; sogar Tripletten sind festzustellen. D. de Bruyne hat sie in seinem Aufsatz in der Rev. Bén. 40 (1928) 15-41 (Le texte latin primitive) mit scharfem Auge erkannt und mit klarem Sinn richtig bewertet.

Bei stichometrisch geschriebenen Texten kann man manchmal schon äusserlich an den überlangen Verszeilen erkennen, dass eine Dublette vorliegt. Zugleich verrät gelegentlich die stilistische Form, dass ein Fremdkörper eingebaut ist. Beide Kennzeichen trägt 38,1: *Τίμα ἰατρὸν πρὸς τὰς χρείας αὐτοῦ τιμαῖς αὐτοῦ.*

Zur Bezeugung: B C 248 La om. *αὐτοῦ* 1°; S[c] 493-637 alii Clem. La om. *τιμαῖς αὐτοῦ.*

Herk. hält im Anschluss an Syr und die rabbinischen Zitate *πρὸ τῆς χρείας* für die « lectio vera » (S. 248) und scheidet *τιμαῖς αὐτοῦ* als « glossema » (S. 249) aus. Sm. und Pe. äussern sich nicht näher über die Dublette, die Ra. zu Unrecht in den Text aufnimmt.

Zwei Stellen sollen hier näher besprochen werden; die eine (27,3), wo eine vermeintliche Dublette vorliegt, und die andere (51,24), wo eine echte Dublette überliefert wird.

27,3 *ἐὰν μὴ ἐν φόβῳ κυρίου κρατήσῃ κατὰ σπουδήν,*
ἐν τάχει καταστραφήσεται αὐτοῦ ὁ οἶκος.

Zunächst möchte man hier eine Dublette sehen; Bret. will *ἐν τάχει* tilgen, dagegen halten Kuhn II 106 (« Doppelübersetzung ») und Katz (« Dublette ») *κατὰ σπουδήν* für sekundär. Dann müsste *κατὰ σπουδήν* zur zweiten Vershälfte (3b init.) gezogen werden. Wenn man es bei 3a fin. belässt, dann muss man es mit dem Verbum *κρατήσῃ* verbinden und mit « eifrig » (so Pe.) oder « diligently » (so Box) übersetzen. Dies ist aber unzulässig, denn *κατὰ σπουδήν* heisst nicht « eifrig » oder « diligently », sondern « schnell », « plötzlich » und müsste *vor* dem Verbum stehen (wie 20,18 *κατὰ σπουδὴν ἥξει* und 21,5 *κατὰ σπουδὴν ἔρχεται*). Jedoch ist es hier nicht als Dublette anzusprechen, sondern als Doppel-Wendung wie *ql mhrh*, auf das Sm. ohne nähere Angaben verweist. Es steht Joel 3(4),4 (*ὀξέως καὶ ταχέως*) und Is. 5,26 in der umgekehrten Folge (*mhrh ql ταχὺ κούφως*). Sm. hätte auch auf eine Sirach-Stelle verweisen können, und zwar auf 11,21 *διὰ τάχους ἐξάπινα bpthʿ pthʾm*; der gleiche hebr. Ausdruck findet sich Num 6,9 (*ἐξάπινα παραχρῆμα*), ferner (mit der Partikel *l* statt *b*) Is. 29,5 (*ὡς στιγμὴ παραχρῆμα*) und umgekehrt Is. 30,13 (*pthʾm lpthʿ* nur *παραχρῆμα*). Aus dem NT kann Marc. 6,25 *εὐθὺς μετὰ σπουδῆς* genannt werden. Somit ist *κατὰ σπουδὴν ἐν τάχει* keineswegs eine Dublette, sondern wie *διὰ τάχους ἐξάπινα* 11,21 ein Doppel-Adverb, das die grösste Eile, das plötzliche Eintreffen bezeichnet.

Wenn 27,3a-3b keine Dublette vorliegt, dann muss *κατὰ σπουδήν* zu 3b gestellt werden:

κατὰ σπουδὴν ἐν τάχει καταστραφήσεται αὐτοῦ ὁ οἶκος.

In der gleichen Weise ist auch an der oben genannten Joel-Stelle 3(4),4 die doppelte adverbiale Wendung in den Ausgaben (auch in der Göttinger Septuaginta) unrichtig auseinandergerissen: *ἢ μνησικακεῖτε ὑμεῖς ἐπ᾽ ἐμοὶ ὀξέως; καὶ ταχέως ἀνταποδώσω κτλ.* Es muss im Anschluss an die hebr. Vorlage interpunktiert werden: *ἢ μν. ὑμεῖς ἐπ ἐμοί; ὀξέως καὶ ταχέως ἀνταποδώσω κτλ.*

Trotzdem ist die Erklärung nicht voll befriedigend. Vielleicht hat Fr. richtig vermutet, dass hinter *κατὰ σπουδήν* ein Begriff « Reichtum, Schätze » als Objekt, das man vermisst, zu *κρατήσῃ* versteckt ist (Komm. S. 150).

51,24 *τί ὅτι ὑστερεῖσθαι λέγετε ἐν τούτοις.*

Pe. schreibt: « Die Erklärung von *λέγετε* ist noch nicht gelungen » (S. 451) und weist mit Recht die Lösung von Sm. zurück, der in *λέγετε* eine Dittographie des vorausgehenden *-τερειτε* sieht. Aber auch der Lösungsversuch von Pe. befriedigt nicht. Die Erklärung war dadurch von Anfang an verbaut, dass weder Holmes-Parsons noch Klostermann, der in seinen Analecta den cod. 253 « wegen seiner ungebührlich schlechten Vergleichung » bei Holmes-Parsons (S. 19) nachkollationierte, dessen Lesart richtig notiert haben: 253 hat nämlich *ἐλήγετε* statt *λέγετε*. Allerdings ist *ἐλήγετε* aus *λήγετε* entstanden (*ε* dittogr. des vorhergehenden-*ε*), das auch LaZ* (*degitis*) in der griech. Vorlage gelesen hat. Dieses *λήγετε* ist Dublette zu *ὑστερεῖτε* (oder *ὑστερεῖσθε*); *ὑστερεῖν* ist ein Lieblingswort des ersten Sirachübersetzers, das er 7mal verwendet. Die Vokabel *λήγειν*, die nur 6mal in Mac. II und III vorkommt, stammt aus GrII. Die Verschreibung des seltenen *λήγειν* in das häufige *λέγειν* liegt sehr nahe; sie ist auch an zwei Stellen in Mac. bezeugt: Mac. II 9,11 *λήγειν*] *λεγειν* A-106 62 und Mac. III 6,16 *λήγοντος*] *λεγοντος* 771. Die verderbte Schreibweise *λέγετε* zog dann in verschiedenen Minuskeln den Infinitiv *ὑστερεῖσθαι* nach sich, den Sw. und Ra. zu Unrecht in ihren Text aufnehmen; andere Handschriften haben die beiden asyndetisch nebeneinander stehenden Verba durch *ἤ* (S^c alii) oder *καί* (V 336 La) verbunden.

Alle Handschriften und alle Versionen haben die beiden Verba. Nur die Sixtina hat *λέγετε* getilgt; sie liest *ὑστερεῖτε ἐν τούτοις*, das richtig Fr. übernommen hat und auch die neue Göttinger Ausgabe bieten wird.

Zwanzig Stellen können aufgeführt werden, wo man Dubletten erkennen möchte; es ist aber schwer, sie eindeutig als solche anzusprechen und ihre sekundäre Hälfte sicher festzustellen. Es ist deshalb auch nicht ratsam, sie durch eckige Klammern [ ] (wie dies unten geschehen ist) im Text der Ausgabe kenntlich zu machen, weil die Gefahr besteht, die Klammern unrichtig zu setzen.

1. 1,8 *εἷς ἐστιν* [*σοφός*], *φοβερὸς σφόδρα*
2. 5,2 *μὴ ἐξακολούθει τῇ ψυχῇ σου* [*καὶ τῇ ἰσχύι σου*]
3. 6,21 *ὡς λίθος δοκιμασίας* [*ἰσχυρὸς*] *ἔσται*
4. 11,18 *ἀπὸ* [*προσοχῆς καὶ*] *σφιγγίας αὐτοῦ*
5. 13,2 *καὶ ἰσχυροτέρῳ σου* [*καὶ πλουσιωτέρῳ* (+ *σου* S A alii)]
6. 16,23 *καὶ ἀνὴρ* [*ἄφρων καὶ*] *πλανώμενος*
7. 19,1 *τὰ ὀλίγα·* [*κατὰ μικρὸν*] *πεσεῖται*
8. 20,7 *ὁ δὲ λαπιστὴς* [*καὶ ἄφρων*] *ὑπερβήσεται*
9. 22,12 *μωροῦ* [*καὶ ἀσεβοῦς*] *πᾶσαι αἱ ἡμέραι*
10. 23,10 *ὁ ὀμνύων* [*καὶ ὀνομάζων*] *διὰ παντός*
11. 25,18-19 *ἀνεστέναξεν* [*πικρά.*] [19] *μικρὰ πᾶσα κακία*
12. 30,14 *πτωχὸς ὑγιὴς* [*καὶ ἰσχύων*] *τῇ ἕξει*
13. 35(32 Ra.),18 *ἀλλότριος* [*καὶ ὑπερήφανος*] *οὐ καταπτήξει*

14. 37,14 *σκοποὶ ἐπὶ μετεώρου καθήμενοι* [*ἐπὶ σκοπῆς*]
15. 39,35 *ἐν πάσῃ καρδίᾳ* [*καὶ στόματι*]
16. 40,16 *ἄχι* [*ἐπὶ παντὸς ὕδατος*] *καὶ χείλους ποταμοῦ*
17. 41,11 *ὄνομα δὲ ἁμαρτωλῶν* [*οὐκ ἀγαθὸν*] *ἐξαλειφθήσεται*
18. 41,16 *πάντα πᾶσιν* [*ἐν πίστει*] *εὐδοκιμεῖται*
19. 48,18b-18c [*καὶ ἀπῆρεν·*] 18c *καὶ ἐπῆρεν χεῖρα*
20. 49,14 [*τοιοῦτος*] *οἷος Ενωχ.*

Manche der Dubletten mögen aus einer anderen hebr. Vorlage (auf dem Umweg von GrII) in unseren Text gelangt sein; so geht 39,35 *καὶ στόματι* auf die Randnote *wph* in H zurück.

IV. – Grammatisch-stilistische Varianten

Wenn bei grammatisch-stilistischen Varianten die Bezeugung durch die alten Unzialen (B-SA) bereits geteilt ist, dann ist die Entscheidung für die Textlesarten sehr schwierig. In den meisten Fällen bin ich Ra. gefolgt, damit sein sorgfältig erarbeiteter Text gefestigt bleibt. An folgenden Stellen habe ich mich nach wiederholter Prüfung gegen Ra. entschieden:

3,3 *ἐξιλάσεται* B—S* Zi. (*ἐξιλάσκεται* A S^c Ra.)
3,13 *καὶ ἐάν* S A (*κἄν* B; Variante von Ra. nicht verzeichnet)
8,19 *καρδίαν σου* S A (*σὴν καρδίαν* B)
11,12 *περισσεύων* S (*περισσεύει* B A)
12,3 *οὐκ ἔστιν* B (*οὐκ ἔσται* S A)
15,3 *ποτιεῖ* S A (*ποτίσει* B)
18,4 *ἐξιχνιάσει* B (*ἐξιχνεύσει* S A)
22,6 *σοφία* S* (*σοφίας* B A S^c rel.)
24,21 *οἱ ἔσθοντες* S A (*οἱ ἐσθίοντες* B)
29,19 *ἐμπεσεῖται* A S^c (*ἐμπεσών* B-S*)
31 (34 Ra.),7 *ἐξέπεσαν* S (*ἐξέπεσον* B A; Variante von Ra. nicht verzeichnet)
37,17 *καρδία* B*-S* (*καρδίας* A B^c S^c)
42,16 *πλήρης* B-S (*πλῆρες* A)
43,7 *ἐπὶ συντελείᾳ* S* A (*ἐπὶ -λείας* B; *ἐπὶ -λείαις* S^c)
43,16 *σαλευθήσονται ὄρη* S A (*σαλευθήσεται ὄρη* B)
44,15 *ἐξαγγελεῖ* A (*ἐξαγγέλλει* B-S)
47,22 *ἐγκαταλίπῃ* A (*καταλίπῃ* B-S)
48,4 *καυχήσεται* S A (*καυχᾶσθαι* B)
49,13 *ἡμῶν τείχη* S (*ἡμῖν τ.* B A)
50,8 *ἐπ' ἐξόδων* B (*ἐπ' ἐξόδῳ* S A rel.)

Der Artikel

In meinen *Beiträgen zur Ieremias-Septuaginta* habe ich ausführlich über den Artikel geschrieben und festgestellt, dass er oft erst später eingefügt wurde. Dies gilt besonders für die Verwendung des Artikels beim Gottesnamen (*κύριος*); aber auch in anderen Fällen ist er häufig sekundär. Die Ursprünglichkeit des Artikels wird erst recht fraglich, wenn bereits die alten Unzialen ihn nicht einheitlich bezeugen. So musste an einer Reihe von Stellen der bei Ra. im Text stehende Artikel in den Apparat verwiesen werden.

Zwei Fälle seien ausführlich genannt, nämlich der Gottesname *Kyrios* als Subjekt und als Objekt, hier jedoch nur in der Wendung *οἱ φοβούμενοι (τὸν) κύριον.*

κύριος – ὁ κύριος

Kyrios kommt als Subjekt 50mal vor. Davon sind 10 Stellen vorwegzunehmen, wo Kyrios nicht allein, sondern mit einem Adjektiv bzw. einem Attribut oder als sekundäre Variante (als Nominativ) des primären Genitiv vorkommt:

4,28 *Κύριος ὁ θεός*
36,22 (17 Ra.) *ὅτι σὺ εἶ κύριος ὁ θεός* (*ὅτι κύριος εἶ ὁ θεός* Ra.)
39,6 *ἐὰν* (+ *ὁ* A S alii) *κύριος ὁ μέγας θελήσῃ*
46,5c *ἐπήκουσεν αὐτοῦ* (+ *ὁ l* alii) *μέγας* (+ *ὁ* 795) *κύριος*
42,17 *ἐστερέωσεν* (+ *ὁ* 543) *κύριος ὁ* (> 248) *παντοκράτωρ*
32,21 (35,18 Ra.) *ὁ ὕψιστος* (*κυριος* A; *ο κυριος* 336)
42,18 *ὁ ὕψιστος* (*ο κυριος* B alii; *κυριος b* 443)
42,17a *τοῖς ἁγίοις κυρίου* S Ra. (*κυριος* B A alii; *ο κυριος* pauci)
43,9 *ἐν ὑψίστοις κυρίου* A S[c] Ra. (*κυριος* B-S* 130)
46,3 *τοὺς γὰρ πολέμους κυρίου* A S[c] Ra. (*κυριος* B-S* alii).

Ohne Artikel steht Kyrios (ursprünglich) 16mal; an 11 Stellen (1,9 1,30c 10,13 17,1 18,2 36,11 43,29 38,4 45,19 47,11 51,22) ist die Bezeugung geschlossen, an 5 Stellen (4,13 16,29 32,13 32,15 38,12) haben verschiedene Minuskeln (38,12 auch *L*) den Artikel eingefügt.

Mit Artikel steht Kyrios (wohl ursprünglich) 14mal; an 9 Stellen (2,11 3,2 5,3 5,4 27,24 32,22 43,33 44,2 47,22) ist die Bezeugung einheitlich, an 5 Stellen (10,14 10,16 15,10 26,28 46,9) haben verschiedene Minuskeln (10,16 auch V *L*; 46,9 auch V) den Artikel *nicht*.

An 10 Stellen sind die alten Unzialen (B-SA) nicht einig: 1,26 *κύριος* B A Ra., *ὁ κύριος* S, ebenso 18,11 38,1 46,17 (Ra. aber hier *ὁ κ.*) | 2,14 *κ.* S*, *ὁ κ.* B A S[c] Ra. | 4,14 *κ.* S, *ὁ κ.* B A Ra., ebenso 10,15 | 15,13 *κ.* B, *ὁ κ.* S A Ra. | 39,6 *κ.* B-S* Ra., *ὁ κ.* A S[c] | 43,5 *κ.* B-S Ra., *ὁ κ.* A.

Das Bild ist sehr bunt; es lässt jedoch erkennen, dass der griech. Übersetzer selbst nicht konsequent war. Aber ebenso kann man annehmen, dass oftmals der Artikel erst *später* eingefügt worden ist; dies bezeugen vor allem die Unzialen. Deshalb ist der Artikel im Text von Ra. 2,14 4,14 10,15 15,13 46,17 (hier ist Ra. inkonsequent; siehe oben) gestrichen worden, ebenso 10,14.16 und 46,9 wegen der Nachbarschaft (10,15 und 46,17), zumal *ὁ* 10,16 und 46,9 in V und vielen Minuskeln fehlt.

οἱ φοβούμενοι (τὸν) κύριον

Diese Wendung kommt in Sirach sehr oft vor: im Plural 12mal und im Singular 11mal. Bei der pluralischen Wendung ist der Artikel oftmals nur schwach bezeugt, so dass er als sekundär angesprochen werden kann. Ebenso steht der singularische Nominativ (*ὁ φοβούμενος κύριον*) immer o h n e Artikel (3,7; 6,17; 15,1; 21,6; 31,16; 35,14). Bei den anderen Fällen ist der Artikel an 3 Stellen allgemein bezeugt: 1,13 *τῷ φοβ. τὸν κ.* | 10,24 *τοῦ φοβ. τὸν κ.* | 25,10 *ὑπὲρ τὸν φοβ. τὸν κ.* Dagegen schwanken die Handschriften 31,17 *φοβουμένου τὸν* (> *b* 542 547) *κύριον* und 36,1 *τῷ φοβ. τὸν* (> B A alii) *κύριον*.

Ebenso uneinheitlich ist die Überlieferung in den Psalmen: 7mal ist der Artikel einheitlich überliefert; an zwei weiteren Stellen fehlt er nur in A 55 (113,19) und in 55 (127,1); schliesslich ist an zwei Stellen (14,4 und 21,24) die Überlieferung gespalten, aber es ist bedeutsam, dass die alten Unzialen B S A ihn nicht kennen. Deshalb hat Ra. nur Ps. 14,4 und 21,24 keinen Artikel, während er an den übrigen neun Stellen steht.

Richtig hält Baudissin das artikellose *φοβούμ. κύριον* in Sirach für ursprünglich, siehe Kyrios als Gottesname... I (Giessen 1929) 412 Anm. 1. Deshalb ist Sir. 2,7 10,19 31,17 der Artikel, den Ra. in seinem Text hat, zu streichen.

Lehrreich ist in dieser Hinsicht die bei Sirach 8mal vorkommende Wendung *ἀνοίγειν (τὸ) στόμα*.

15,5 *ἀνοίξει τὸ* (> B alii Zi.) *στόμα αὐτοῦ*
20,15 *ἀνοίξει τὸ* (> 543 603) *στόμα αὐτοῦ*

24,2 *τὸ* (> B A alii Ra. Zi.) *στόμα αὐτῆς ἀνοίξει*
39,5 *ἀνοίξει τὸ* (> B A alii Ra. Zi.) *στόμα αὐτοῦ*
51,25 *ἤνοιξα τὸ* (> 336) *στόμα μου*
22,22 *ἐὰν ἀνοίξῃς* (+ *το* *l* alii) *στόμα*
29,24 *οὐκ ἀνοίξεις* (+ *το* 307 443) *στόμα*
26,12 *τὸ* (> A S^{c} alii Zi.) *στόμα ἀνοίξει.*

Der Artikel ist an keiner Stelle einheitlich bezeugt. Ra. ist nicht konsequent verfahren, wenn er 24,2 und 39,6 den Artikel fallen lässt, ihn aber 15,5 und 26,12 behält. Am liebsten möchte man den Artikel überall streichen. Aber wahrscheinlich war der Übersetzer selbst nicht konsequent; er hat ihn im Anschluss an die hebr. Vorlage teils ausgelassen, oder dem griech. Syrachgefühl folgend teils gesetzt. Im NT, wo die Wendung ebenfalls öfter vorkommt, steht immer der Artikel.

So ist man berechtigt, den Artikel 15,5 und 26,12 als sekundär zu streichen. Dies ist auch an folgenden Stellen geschehen:

Präposition:

5,12 *ἐπὶ τῷ* (> B A alii Zi.) *στόματί σου*
14,1 *ἐν τῷ* (> B S alii Zi.) *στόματι αὐτοῦ*
47,2 *ἀπὸ τῶν* (> S A alii Zi.) *υἱῶν Ισραηλ*
29,2 *εἰς τὸν* (> S A alii Zi.) *καιρόν*
47,9 *κατέναντι τοῦ* (> S^{c} A alii Zi.) *θυσιαστηρίου*
7,8 *ἐν γὰρ τῇ* (> S A alii Zi.) *μιᾷ.*

Objekt:

7,20 *τὴν* (> B alii Zi.) *ψυχὴν αὐτοῦ*
37,8 *τὴν* (> S* alii Zi.) *ψυχήν σου*
26,13 *τὸν* (> S A alii Zi.) *ἄνδρα αὐτῆς*
43,24 *τὸν* (> A alii Zi.) *κίνδυνον αὐτῆς.*

Subjekt:

30,27 (33,19 Ra.) *καὶ οἱ* (> S alii Zi.) *ἡγούμενοι ἐκκλησίας*
44,12 *ἔστη τὸ* (> B alii Zi.) *σπέρμα αὐτῶν*: cf. 44,13 *μενεῖ* (+ *το* *L* alii) *σπέρμα αὐτῶν*
50,13 *πάντες οἱ* (> S alii Zi.) *υἱοὶ Ααρων*
50,16 *ἀνέκραγον οἱ* (> B-S alii Zi.) *υἱοὶ Ααρων.*

Oftmals fehlt der Artikel nur in einer der alten Unzialen, in B und namentlich in S. Auch hier möchte man am liebsten den Artikel als sekundär in den Apparat verweisen, aber die überwältigende Bezeugung lässt dies nicht zu.

Das Possessiv-Pronomen

Es lässt sich in allen Büchern der LXX beobachten, dass der griech. Übersetzer oftmals das Possessiv-Pronomen der hebr. Vorlage nicht berücksichtigt; erst recht lässt er es gern weg, wenn das hebr. Nomen kein Suffix hat. Oftmals ist das Poss.-Pron. erst später eingefügt worden, namentlich von den nach dem hebr. Text ausgerichteten Rezensionen des Origenes und Lukian. An vielen Stellen ist daher *μου, σου, αὐτοῦ-αὐτῆς-αὐτῶν* sekundär. Als Beispiel sei die bei Sirach 8mal vorkommende Wendung *ἐν καιρῷ* (oder *ἡμέρᾳ*) *θλίψεως* genannt. Sie steht wie im Hebr. ohne Poss.-Pron. 4mal (2,11 22,23 40,24 51,10) und gegen das Hebr. 4mal mit Poss.-Pron. (3,15 6,8b 6,10 32,26 = 35,24 Ra.). Aber an diesen 4 Stellen ist die Bezeugung nicht einheitlich; ich habe deshalb im Gegensatz zu Ra. hier das Poss.-Pron. in den Apparat verwiesen. Ebenso ist dies an den folgenden 9 Stellen geschehen:

3,31 *ἐν καιρῷ πτώσεως αὐτοῦ* Ra. (> B alii Zi.)
7,27 *ἐν ὅλῃ καρδίᾳ σου* (> B alii Zi.)
45,16 *περὶ τοῦ λαοῦ σου* (*αυτου* V L^{-248} alii; > S* 248 alii Zi.)
47,23 *μετὰ τῶν πατέρων αὐτοῦ* (= Regn. III 11,43; om. *αὐτοῦ* B alii Zi.)
7,36 *τὰ ἔσχατα σου* (> 307 315 603 753 Katz Zi. = H): cf. 28,6 *τὰ ἔσχατα* (+ *σου* 493-705 verss.) et 38,20 *τὰ ἔσχατα* (+ *σου* 493-637 alii)
12,5 *τοὺς ἄρτους αὐτοῦ* (> S* 694 La Zi. = H)
19,17 *τὸν πλησίον σου* (= Lev. 19,17; om. *σου* S alii Zi.)
30,38 (33,29 Ra.) *τὰς πέδας αὐτοῦ* (> S* A B^c alii Zi.)
39,7 *βουλὴν αὐτοῦ* (> S alii Zi.).

Die Präposition *ἐν*

Gewöhnlich entspricht *ἐν* dem hebr. *b*, wie es in der LXX üblich ist, manchmal ist jedoch nur der blosse Ablativ verwendet. Wenn aber gewichtige Zeugen *ἐν* für *b* überliefern, dann ist es gegen Rahlfs in den Text an folgenden Stellen aufzunehmen:

11,4d ἐν (= *b* pro *m*; > S A alii Ra.) ἀνθρώποις
45,8 ἐν (> B A alii Ra.) σκεύεσιν
48,17 ὤρυξεν ἐν (> B S A alii Ra.) σιδήρῳ.

Das zuletzt genannte Beispiel zeigt, dass ἐν nach -εν leicht ausfallen konnte. Gleich im nächsten Vers (ἐμεγαλαύχησεν ἐν ὑπερηφανίᾳ 48,18) fehlt ἐν in B-SA alii; hier hat es Rahlfs mit V alii richtig in den Text aufgenommen, siehe die unten genannten Stellen 45,19 ἐποίησεν ἐν und 47,10 ἔδωκεν ἐν. Deshalb ist auch 45,20 mit S A alii zu schreiben ἡτοίμασεν ἐν πλησμονῇ (statt ἡτοίμασεν πλησμονήν B alii Ra.).

Der Sirach-Übersetzer verwendet weiterhin ἐν für das hebr. *l*, das sonst häufig mit dem Dativ-Artikel wiedergegeben wird. Deshalb ist ἐν (= *l*) nach dem Rat von Sm. zu 10,18 (S. 96f.) ἐν γεννήμασιν in den Text aufzunehmen, auch wenn es nicht allgemein bezeugt ist. Ra. hat es ferner 45,15 (ἐν τῷ σπέρματι αὐτοῦ) und 45,19 (ἐποίησεν ἐν αὐτοῖς) zu Unrecht in den Apparat verwiesen.

Richtig steht ἐν (= *l*) im Text von Ra.:

35(32 Ra.),1 ἐν (> S alii) αὐτοῖς | 47,10 ἔδωκεν ἐν (> S alii) ἑορταῖς | 48,15 ἄρχων ἐν (> B C) τῷ οἴκῳ | 50,21 ἐδευτέρωσαν (vel -σεν) ἐν (> V) προσκυνήσει.

Wenn der Übersetzer so streng wie Aquila gewesen wäre, dann müsste ἐν (= *l*) auch an folgenden Stellen als ursprünglich angenommen werden:

4,7a συναγωγῇ] pr. εν C | 4,7b μεγιστᾶνι] εν μεγισταισι 404 | 8,11 τῷ στόματί σου] pr. εν *a*-534-613 694 | 12,1 τοῖς ἀγαθοῖς σου] pr. εν *O* La Sa.

Ferner müsste ἐν auch an den Stellen stehen, wo die hebr. Partikel *b* (= *in*) vorhanden ist. Jedoch besteht zwischen Aquila und dem Sirach-Übersetzer ein grosser Unterschied; deshalb ist Katz nicht zu folgen, wenn er 7,9 mit *O* 575 La Aeth Syr ἐν vor τῷ πλήθει als ursprünglich einfügen will.

Die Partikel *καί*

Gewöhnlich ist der Sinnspruch bei Sirach in zwei Vershälften oder 2 mal 2 Verszeilen (a b, c d) geteilt, deren zweite (b, d) mit καί beginnt. Abweichend von dieser Regel ist manchmal καί in a überliefert, fehlt aber in b. Die handschriftliche Bezeugung ist in solchen Fällen oftmals sehr schwach. Trotzdem ist im Text von Ra. *καί* 4,27a | 6,24a | 12,16a | 19,22a | 39,14a | 48,14a zu streichen, dagegen 19,1b | 37,5b | 39,14d | 42,20b | 48,3b (vor *κατ-* leicht zu übersehen) | 48,9b einzufügen.

Ferner ist *καί* 11,12 (vor *προσδεόμενος* = H) und 23,1c (vor *μὴ ἀφῇς*) gegen Ra. aus stilistischen Gründen eingefügt worden.

Der Sirach-Text der Göttinger Septuaginta wird somit gegenüber der Stuttgarter Ausgabe einen grossen Fortschritt bedeuten. Aber auch die neue Edition ist noch lange nicht am Ziel, sondern mitten unterwegs. Eine « editio perfecta atque omnibus numeris absoluta » wird niemals möglich sein, da Sirach unter allen Büchern der griechischen Bibel die höchsten Anforderungen an jeden Herausgeber stellt. Namentlich für das weite Feld der Konjekturen, die gerade in Sirach noch an zahlreichen, sich hartnäckig verschliessenden Stellen fällig sind, gilt der Satz, den Katz in der ThLZ 61 (1936) 274 für die ganze Septuaginta geschrieben hat: « Es bleibt noch unendlich viel zu tun ».

Griechisches Wörterverzeichnis

Nur die ausführlich besprochenen Wörter und Wendungen sind verzeichnet. In Klammern steht die Sirach-Lesart der Stuttgarter Septuaginta-Ausgabe von Alfred Rahlfs (= Ra.).

Würzburg.

V. THE SEPTUAGINT IN THE NEW TESTAMENT AND THE FATHERS

THE SEMITISMS OF ST. LUKE'S GOSPEL[1]

H. F. D. SPARKS

EVEN the most casual reader of St. Luke's Gospel is faced at the outset with a problem. After an author's preface of four verses, written in good idiomatic Greek, he is presented with a narrative of twenty-four chapters, of which the background, the ideas, and much of the phraseology, are unquestionably Semitic. The Semitic background, many of the Semitic ideas, and some of the Semitic phraseology, are, of course, easily explicable in the light of the subject-matter. But if we compare St. Luke with the other Synoptists, we are forced to admit that 'subject-matter' is very far from being a complete explanation; for not only do certain of the characteristic Semitic expressions, which all three share, occur with greater frequency in St. Luke, but there are in addition a whole host of peculiarly Lukan Semitisms, that is, constructions and phrases, sometimes complete sentences, which, awkward in Greek, are normal and idiomatic in Semitic. And they are to be found in all parts of the Gospel. Thus, Zacharias and Elisabeth 'were both righteous before God, walking in all the commandments and ordinances of the Lord blameless';[2] the Pharisees 'lie in ambush' for Jesus 'to hunt something out of his mouth';[3] the Day is to come 'as a snare, upon all those who are sitting upon the face of all the earth';[4] and the disciples, after the Resurrection, are enjoined to 'sit' in Jerusalem 'until clothed from on high with power'.[5] How came it, then, that an Evangelist, who to judge from his preface could write as good Greek as any of his contemporaries, nevertheless wrote the body of his Gospel in this curious Semitizing style? That is the problem.

A priori there are three possible solutions: (1) that the Gospel as it stands, apart from the Preface, is a translation into Greek of a Semitic original; (2) that the Semitisms are due to the Evangelist's use of Semitic sources, which either he or someone else translated; (3) that he himself was consciously Semitizing.

The first solution may easily be disposed of. St. Luke, it is agreed to-day, used at least two sources, St. Mark and Q; and both, when he used them, were in Greek. Consequently, any theory of a Semitic original for the Gospel as it stands is ruled out of court. The debate is accordingly between solutions 2 and 3, though neither of them is of necessity exclusive of the other.

[1] A paper read to the Oxford Society of Historical Theology on 25 February 1943.

[2] Luke i. 6. [3] Luke xi. 54. [4] Luke xxi. 34, 35. [5] Luke xxiv. 49.

Reprinted from *Journal of Theological Studies*. Vol. 44, 1943.

To begin with, our preference will probably be for 2. Jesus, we may argue, was a Palestinian Jew: so were His disciples. Therefore the primitive records of His words and deeds will inevitably have been handed down, not in Greek, but in Semitic. When and where the first Greek translations were made is relatively unimportant. What is important is recognition of the fact that any Greek tradition that has any claims to historicity at all must be built ultimately on a Semitic foundation: and we shall expect to see traces of the influence of that foundation, even in a quite advanced stage of the building. Since St. Luke's Gospel represents such a stage, his Semitisms, we may conclude, fall naturally into place.

Nor is this merely speculation. It is established that St. Luke knew St. Mark and Q in Greek. Whether either or both were initially composed in Greek is disputable; but, whatever their original language, their Greek shows very evident traces of the Semitic influences described above. And many of the traces persist in St. Luke. For example, St. Mark represents Jesus as assuring the disciples that they should 'in no wise *taste of death*, till they should *see the kingdom of God*';[1] or again, in Q, in the injunction 'Fear not them that kill the body', φοβοῦμαι is followed by the preposition ἀπό and the object in the genitive.[2] Both these characteristically Semitic expressions (and many more) are reproduced *verbatim* by St. Luke. Thus in order to account for a fair proportion of the Lukan Semitisms we need look no further than St. Mark and Q. And this explanation may be extended to cover whatever other sources St. Luke may have used; although what those sources were we can do no more than guess.

Yet however many of the Semitisms are attributable to sources there is clearly a substantial residuum which can only be due to the Evangelist himself. His continual re-phrasing of St. Mark is decisive on this point. As an illustration may be compared the Markan and Lukan versions of the Parable of the Wicked Husbandmen.[3] According to St. Mark, after the maltreatment of the first servant, the Lord of the Vineyard 'sent unto them again another servant'; and then 'he sent another'. St. Luke has re-phrased twice—'and he *added to send* another servant'; and then 'he *added to send* a third'. The expression 'to add to do something' in the sense of 'doing it again' is not Greek, but Semitic; so St. Luke has deliberately 'improved' on his source by importing a Semitic idiom. But this instance is in no way unique.[4] And as St. Luke treated St. Mark, so, it may be presumed, he also treated Q and his other sources.

[1] Mark ix. 1 || Luke ix. 27.
[2] Matt. x. 28 || Luke xii. 4.
[3] Mark xii. 1–12 || Luke xx. 9–19.
[4] Cp. e.g. St. Luke's predilection when rewriting the Markan narrative for

Of the possible solutions, therefore, it seems that both 2 and 3 are partially correct though neither is completely so. Some Semitisms St. Luke found in his sources and retained: others he added himself; for the evidence shows him to have been an habitual and deliberate Semitizer.

This inevitably calls for further elucidation, particularly when the Evangelist so described was a Gentile by birth and education, and, moreover, was writing for Gentiles. So far from having solved anything we are in reality only presented with the original problem in a fresh and acuter form. St. Luke, it is acknowledged, could write good Greek, and on occasion did so. Whence, then, his deliberate Semitisms?

When St. Luke wrote his Gospel he must have been a Christian of several years' standing. He had spent much time in the company of St. Paul, who spoke both Greek and Semitic; he had mixed freely with Semitic speaking Christians in Palestine; and he had read at least two accounts of Jesus' life and work written in a semitizing style. In consequence, it is not inconceivable that his native Greek had become so infected that he not only spoke, but also wrote, quite naturally, in the Semitic-Greek *patois* current among so many of his co-religionists. Indeed, in the light of the fact that he was a deliberate Semitizer, he will have done so consciously in order to 'stick to tradition'; that is, because he thought that such a style was the established medium for the writing of a Christian Gospel.

Confirmation, or otherwise, of this hypothesis has to be sought in any distinctive Aramaisms the Gospel may exhibit; since not only was Aramaic the particular Semitic language that St. Luke would come across among his Semitic-speaking friends, but it was also the foundation of the Gospel tradition. If we are to maintain that St. Luke's Semitisms are due to the *patois*, we are bound to ask what evidence there is for distinctive Aramaic influence on his style.

An investigation yields a disappointingly meagre return. Only two characteristically Aramaic expressions are at all common: the collocation of the verb 'to be' with the participle in place of the finite verb, as in ἦσαν δὲ αὐτῷ ἐγγίζοντες;[1] and the phrase 'to begin to do something', as in the constantly recurring 'he began to say'.[2] This is indeed very little; especially when one remembers that neither of these expressions is confined to Aramaic. And in view of St. Luke's studied omission, or translation, of the Aramaic words and names

the graphic 'And behold' at v. 12, 18, &c.; his re-phrasing of St. Mark's 'and they were all amazed' as 'and amazement came upon them all' at iv. 36; and his expansion of St. Mark's αὐτὸν κρατῆσαι into ἐπιβαλεῖν ἐπ' αὐτὸν τὰς χεῖρας at xx. 19.

[1] Luke xv. 1. [2] e.g. Luke iv. 21, vii. 24.

that St. Mark has preserved,[1] we are forced to conclude that the influence of the *patois*, if it was exerted at all, can only have been slight.

But although hardly any of St. Luke's Semitisms are demonstrably derivable from Aramaic, there are several which can be traced without question to Biblical Hebrew. Three of these may be conveniently illustrated from one verse: καὶ ἐγένετο ἐν τῷ εἶναι αὐτὸν ἐν μιᾷ τῶν πόλεων καὶ ἰδοὺ ἀνὴρ πλήρης λέπρας.[2] The opening phrase καὶ ἐγένετο, so frequent in St. Luke, is the familiar Old Testament 'and it came to pass'. Here, as often in the Old Testament, it is followed by 'in' with the infinitive and the personal pronoun. There is, furthermore, no main verb in the verse: instead, the graphic Hebraic 'and behold' leaves 'a man (in the nominative) full of leprosy' hanging in the air. The whole sentence just asks to be translated into Hebrew word for word. Yet common as are its idiosyncrasies in Hebrew, they are either unknown, or else very rare, in Aramaic. St. Luke has not Aramaized, but Hebraized, as he has very frequently elsewhere.

In a Gentile writing for Gentiles this is extraordinary. There is no reason to suppose that St. Luke made a special study of Hebrew. And even if he did, it is hardly likely that he became so soaked in its idiom as habitually to Hebraize his sources.

There remains but one other alternative: that the Hebrew idiom in which he wrote came to him from the LXX. As a Gentile Christian he will certainly have known the LXX; for it was the only means of access the non-Semitist had to those vital Scriptures which were the proof of the Christian preaching. What more natural than that an instructed Christian, such as St. Luke shows himself to be, should not only know his LXX, but know it well, and hold it in high esteem; so that when he came to write his Gospel he deliberately copied the LXX language and consciously wrote in what he would call 'Biblical' style? Viewed from this angle it is not the body of the Gospel with its Semitisms that requires explanation, so much as the preface with its cultivated Greek: but the preface can be explained without difficulty as another of St. Luke's essays in style, designed to commend to a critical public what they might otherwise have thought from its opening sentences a literary monstrosity.

So much for generalizations. It has now to be shown that this influence-of-the-LXX hypothesis is supported by the evidence of the Gospel itself; and the evidence is best summarized under five heads.

[1] Thus ταλιθὰ κοῦμι at Mark v. 41 and Ἀββᾶ at Mark xiv. 36 are both omitted by St. Luke; while St. Mark's ὁ Καναναῖος is translated by ὁ Ζηλωτής at Luke vi. 15.

[2] Luke v. 12.

1. *The Old Testament Quotations in St. Luke demonstrate that the author normally quoted from the LXX.* When he is dependent on St. Mark and Q he frequently leaves differences from the LXX unaltered;[1] but when not dependent on them,[2] or when expanding a quotation derived from them,[3] he approximates very closely indeed to the LXX.

2. *The forms of Old Testament proper names in St. Luke are almost always identical with the forms in the LXX.* The only exception of significance is the case of Elisha: whereas the LXX consistently has the indeclinable Ἐλεισαῖε, St. Luke declines Ἐλισσαῖος.[4] On the other hand should be noted: (*a*) St. Luke's preference for Ἰερουσαλήμ as against St. Mark's Ἰεροσόλυμα—Ἰερουσαλήμ is also the LXX's preference; (*b*) the appearance of Caïnam, son of Arphaxad, in the Genealogy—Caïnam appears in the LXX though not in the Hebrew text of Gen. xi. 12, 13; (*c*) the occurrence at Luke iv. 26 of the declinable form Σιδωνία for Sidon, which occurs nowhere else in the whole of Greek literature except in the LXX rendering of 1 Kings xvii. 9, which is precisely the passage to which St. Luke is referring.

3. *The characteristic vocabulary of St. Luke is very largely to be explained as drawn from the LXX.* As examples may be cited: (*a*) a characteristically Lukan word—the preposition ἐνώπιον, which though frequent in St. Luke and the LXX is never found outside the New Testament except occasionally in the papyri; (*b*) a technical term—ἀνατολή as applied to the Messiah at Luke i. 78 is the LXX translation of the 'Branch' at Jer. xxiii. 5 and Zech. iii. 8, vi. 12; (*c*) a word used in an abnormal sense—κοιλία is used by St. Luke in the sense of 'womb' seven times as it commonly is in the LXX,[5] but it is not so used elsewhere except in one passage in St. Matthew.[6] To these examples may be added St. Luke's use (five times) of ῥῆμα in the sense of 'thing', a usage which is otherwise confined to the LXX.[7]

4. *A high percentage of St. Luke's most striking phrases have either exact, or very close, parallels in the LXX.* Thus πορεύεσθαι ὀπίσω,[8] ἐπαίρειν τὴν φωνήν or τοὺς ὀφθαλμούς,[9] ποιεῖν ἔλεος μετά,[10] στηρίζειν

[1] e.g. Mark i. 3 || Luke iii. 4; Matt. xi. 10 || Luke vii. 27.

[2] e.g. Luke xxiii. 30.

[3] e.g. Luke iii. 5, 6.

[4] I regard as insignificant the case of Elijah, where St. Luke adopts the declinable Ἠλείας found in the Apocryphal Books, Josephus, and St. Mark, as against the indeclinable Ἠλειού of the LXX Historical Books; and also a few minor variations in the Genealogy.

[5] e.g. Gen. xxx. 2; Job ii. 9 b.

[6] Matt. xix. 12.

[7] Cp. e.g. Gen. xv. 1; 1 Kings i. 27.

[8] Luke xxi. 8: cp. e.g. Deut. vi. 14; 1 Sam. xxv. 42.

[9] Luke vi. 20, xi. 27, xvi. 23, xvii. 13: cp. e.g. Gen. xiii. 10; Ruth i. 9, 14.

[10] Luke i. 72, x. 37: cp. e.g. Gen. xxiv. 12; Judges i. 24.

τὸ πρόσωπον,[1] πίπτειν στόματι μαχαίρας,[2] are all good LXX. As a more lengthy parallel may be adduced the words of the angel to Mary οὐκ ἀδυνατήσει παρὰ τοῦ θεοῦ πᾶν ῥῆμα,[3] which may be compared with the question to Abraham μὴ ἀδυνατεῖ παρὰ τῷ θεῷ ῥῆμα[4] and also the similar phrase in Deut. xvii. 8.[5]

5. *In a number of instances St. Luke has re-phrased St. Mark either in accordance with LXX usage, or in characteristically LXX language.* Four instances must suffice. In the Parable of the Sower,[6] according to St. Mark, some seed fell εἰς τὰς ἀκάνθας: St. Luke says it fell ἐν μέσῳ τῶν ἀκανθῶν—a perfectly possible expression, but not nearly such idiomatic Greek as St. Mark's: the alteration is due to St. Luke's partiality for ἐν μέσῳ, which he has derived from the LXX.[7] At Mark ix. 31 Jesus 'was teaching his disciples and said to them': St. Luke has in the parallel passage 'put into your ears these words', a phrase which has several parallels in the LXX.[8] Again, St. Mark's Greek for 'respecting anyone's person' is βλέπειν εἰς πρόσωπον, for which St. Luke substitutes λαμβάνειν πρόσωπον,[9] a regular LXX translation of a common Hebrew idiom.[10] Finally, St. Luke has twice emended St. Mark's βλέπετε ἀπό, in the sense of 'beware of' to προσέχετε ἀπό:[11] the LXX has προσέχειν ἀπό six times, but Liddell and Scott quote no instances outside the Bible.

This evidence is, I submit, conclusive. Granted that St. Luke was dependent upon Semitizing sources; granted also that he may have been influenced to a slight degree by the Semitic-Greek *patois* of his Aramaic-speaking friends; the bulk of his Semitisms are to be ascribed to his reverence for, and imitation of, the LXX. They are, in fact, not 'Semitisms' at all, but 'Septuagintalisms'; and St. Luke himself was not a 'Semitizer', but an habitual, conscious, and deliberate 'Septuagintalizer'.

How does this conclusion affect our estimate of St. Luke's Gospel as a whole? In particular, what light has it to throw on the outstanding problem of the nature and value of the material peculiar to the Gospel?

[1] Luke ix. 51: cp. e.g. Jer. iii. 12; Ezek. vi. 2.

[2] Luke xxi. 24: cp. e.g. Isa. iii. 25; Jer. xxi. 7; Ecclus. xxviii. 18.

[3] Luke i. 37.

[4] Gen. xviii. 14.

[5] It may be that some of the longer parallels should be classed as quotations under § 1, but whether quotations or reminiscences they are equally evidence of LXX influence.

[6] Mark iv. 1–9 || Luke viii. 4–8.

[7] St. Luke has ἐν μέσῳ with the genitive eight times: St. Mark has it twice: in the LXX it is very common.

[8] e.g. Exod. xvii. 14; Jer. xxxiii. 15; Mal. ii. 2.

[9] Mark xii. 14 || Luke xx. 21.

[10] e.g. Lev. xix. 15; Ps. lxxxi. 2.

[11] Mark viii. 15 || Luke xii. 1; Mark xii. 38 || Luke xx. 46.

As is well known, it is argued by one side in the debate on this question, that in addition to St. Mark and Q, St. Luke used also another written source (L),[1] which he frequently preferred to St. Mark,[2] and which the modern historian can trust as a first-class authority;[3] by the other side it is argued that St. Luke had no other written sources besides St. Mark and Q,[4] and that his peculiar matter is sometimes his own writing up of fragments which he had gleaned from oral tradition, and sometimes his re-writing and re-interpretation for dogmatic reasons of material which he found in St. Mark.[5] The issue has still to be decided; but no one, it seems, has as yet considered the bearing on it of the Evangelist's Semitizing style.

It would be foolish to claim too much: to pretend, for example, either that the facts brought forward in the first part of this paper and the conclusion arrived at will settle the question outright, or that in reaching a settlement they are even of primary importance. Yet they are, I suggest, of some importance; and they should be taken into consideration along with other facts. For if, in the matter peculiar to St. Luke, we can detect any sections that are certainly not Septuagintalistic, i.e. if we can pick out either in dialogue or in narrative any definite Aramaisms, then the case for a written L is supported, at any rate to the extent that there is evidence for an historically reliable source or sources independent of the Evangelist. If, on the other hand, all the Semitisms in the peculiar matter can be accounted for as Septuagintalisms, then the evidence for an independent source or sources is weakened, and the case of those who maintain that L is no more than St. Luke's writing up of oral tradition and his re-writing of St. Mark, is proportionately strengthened.

By way of illustrating and expanding this contention, and indicating on which side the truth would appear to lie, we may briefly examine five specimen sections.

First, the Infancy Narratives (Luke i, ii). The whole of these narratives reads like a piece of one of the Historical Books of the Old Testament, particularly the opening of the First Book of Samuel. There are no traces of Aramaic whatsoever: the idiom is Biblical Hebrew. Even Torrey is forced to admit this; for, although he regards every other chapter in the Four Gospels as translated from Aramaic, he makes an exception here and conjectures for these two chapters only a Hebrew original. Yet in addition to their Hebraic

[1] e.g. Easton, *The Gospel according to St. Luke* (p. xxiii).

[2] e.g. Streeter, *The Four Gospels* (pp. 209 ff.).

[3] This would appear to be the logic of Streeter's statement that 'if the conclusions of this chapter are sound we must recognize in Proto-Luke the existence of another authority comparable to Mark' (*The Four Gospels*, p. 222).

[4] e.g. Creed, *The Gospel according to St. Luke* (p. lxvi).

[5] e.g. R. H. Lightfoot, *History and Interpretation in the Gospels* (pp. 164 ff.).

flavour, their vocabulary and phraseology are also very definitely Septuagintal: Zacharias, for instance, was ἐξ ἐφημερίας Ἀβιά, and he ministered at τὸ θυσιαστήριον τοῦ θυμιάματος—both LXX technical terms. If, therefore, there be a Semitic source behind Luke i, ii, that source must have been Hebrew; and it would further seem that the Greek translator, whoever he was, translated with one eye all the time on the LXX. It may be that the translator was St. Luke himself, if he knew any Hebrew: it may be, again, that he was some unknown Christian, whose version St. Luke drastically revised: or, it may even be that there was no Hebrew original, that St. Luke's source existed in Greek from the start, and that the LXX language is due either to the author, or to St. Luke, or to both. The number of these complicated possibilities is Legion. But it is far easier to suppose that St. Luke had no source at all; that when in Palestine with St. Paul he heard some traditions about Jesus' and John the Baptist's births: and that when he came to compose his Gospel he used them as an introduction to the Markan narrative, and cast them in a deliberately 'Biblical' mould.

Second, the Synagogue Story (Luke iv. 16–30). In this section there is but one possible indication of Aramaic influence, the periphrastic ἦν ἀνατεθραμμένος. As was seen above, this usage is common in St. Luke; it is found also both in classical Greek and the LXX; so that when we remember in addition that many of the Lukan occurrences are in introductions to sections (as here) which are plainly editorial, its assistance in proving an Aramaic background is hardly very great. Yet an unmistakably Semitic atmosphere pervades the story throughout. In the light of our general conclusion about the nature of St. Luke's Semitisms it is likely that the majority in this instance are Septuagintalisms: and such an analysis proves them to be. Thus, the phrase in verse 26, εἰς Σάρεπτα τῆς Σιδωνίας πρὸς γυναῖκα χήραν, is demonstrably an exact reminiscence of the LXX text of 1 Kings xvii. 9; while of the twenty-six words in the Isaiah quotation in verses 18 and 19, twenty-four are identical with the LXX. This evidence can be harmonized with the view that St. Luke was following a source, which here, as elsewhere, he preferred to St. Mark—provided we admit that he radically Septuagintalized it. But the alternative hypothesis is simpler, that he re-wrote, not some imaginary source, but the similar story in Mark vi. 1–6, and that he transferred its occasion from the middle of the Ministry to the beginning in order to draw out its symbolic significance.[1]

Third, the Parable of the Good Samaritan (Luke x. 29–37). This parable has far fewer Semitisms than either of the sections previously

[1] In this he anticipates John i. 11 ('He came unto his own, and they that were his own received him not').

considered, though four, at least, may be noted (the verb δικαιῶ used in the sense of 'vindicate'; the twice repeated 'fell among thieves'; the periphrasis 'he who did mercy with him'; and 'Go' introducing the final command); and all of them are most naturally accounted for as due to LXX influence. Concurrently with the decrease in the number of Semitisms there is a marked increase in the number of literary, or classical, words and phrases (e.g. ἡμιθανῆ, πανδοχεῖον, ὑπολαβών of 'answering',[1] or κατὰ συγκυρίαν). In fact, stylistically the parable reads very much like one of the chapters from the latter half of Acts,[2] where a similar combination of Septuagintal with more literary Greek is observable. And the reason is probably the same in both cases; that St. Luke is writing the story which he has to tell in his own words; and because he is recording a 'living' situation, and not merely 'what happened' in the past, he becomes in consequence less consciously 'Biblical'. At all events, this seems more plausible than the suggestion that he found in L a story already complete, which he then proceeded, not only to Septuagintalize, but also to classicize, into exact conformity with his literary style in Acts.

Fourth, the Healing of the Ten Lepers (Luke xvii, 11–19). The story opens with a first-class Hebraism—καὶ ἐγένετο with ἐν τῷ and the infinitive, followed by καί resumptive. Unless we conjecture a Hebrew source, this will be a Septuagintalism. And there are more to come—καὶ αὐτὸς διήρχετο διὰ μέσον; καὶ αὐτοὶ ἦραν φωνὴν λέγοντες; πορευθέντες ἐπιδείξατε; ὑπέστρεψεν μετὰ φωνῆς μεγάλης δοξάζων τὸν θεόν; καὶ αὐτὸς ἦν Σαμαρείτης. The section exhibits throughout the hall-mark of the Evangelist's Septuagintalizing style. It is conceivable, of course, that St. Luke Septuagintalized another source more thoroughly than he Septuagintalized St. Mark. It is more probable, however, that the Ten Lepers are an example of his own free composition, either based on what came to him from oral tradition, or a pro-Samaritan elaboration of the Single Leper in Mark i. 40–5.

Fifth, the Institution of the Eucharist (Luke xxii. 15–20). Assuming with the majority of scholars that St. Luke's text ends at verse 19b with 'This is my Body', we have to account both for the transposition of the order of the Cup and the Bread, and the peculiarly Lukan Words of Institution in verses 15 to 18. Some ascribe these verses to a special Passion source; others regard verses 17 and 18 as a re-writing of St. Mark, which St. Luke has prefaced in verses 15 and

[1] Although this is frequent in the LXX Job.

[2] e.g. πληγὰς ἐπιθέντες occurs again at Acts xvi. 23; and with ἐπιβιβάσας δὲ αὐτὸν ἐπὶ τὸ ἴδιον κτῆνος compare κτήνη τε παραστῆσαι ἵνα ἐπιβιβάσαντες τὸν Παῦλον (Acts xxiii. 24).

16 with 'a Paschal introduction to the scene as a whole'.[1] The language of verses 17 and 18 is consistent with either hypothesis. On the one side, we may argue that there would be almost certainly a very close similarity between any two sources at such a point in the story as this; on the other side, that the alterations which St. Luke has introduced into St. Mark are of precisely the kind we should have expected him to introduce. But verses 15 and 16 have no parallel in St. Mark: are they from another source or St. Luke's 'Paschal introduction'? Here a Semitism may help to a decision. *Ἐπιθυμίᾳ ἐπεθύμησα*, says Jesus, *τοῦτο τὸ πάσχα φαγεῖν*. This collocation of the cognate noun in the dative with the finite verb is a frequent LXX rendering of the common Hebrew idiom of the verb with its infinitive absolute, an idiom which, it is worth remembering, does not occur in Aramaic. If, then, verses 15 and 16 are a correct record of what Jesus actually said, He must on this occasion have spoken in Hebrew; and the Greek translator will have rendered faithfully in accordance with LXX practice. This is not impossible. But it is surely more likely that in *ἐπιθυμίᾳ ἐπεθύμησα* we should recognize another of St. Luke's Septuagintalisms; and, if this be so, the scales are weighted heavily in favour of the second hypothesis.

I am fully aware that in the discussion of these specimens we have done no more than balance probabilities. I am also aware, and I wish to stress, that the evidence of the Semitisms is only a fraction of the total available. Yet it is, none the less, worth considering. And for what it is worth, it points in one direction: namely, that St. Luke had no other sources besides St. Mark and Q; that he took St. Mark as a skeleton, and clothed that skeleton with flesh, from Q, from his own writing up of floating tradition, and from his frequent theological rewriting of material derived from St. Mark. Consequently, to contend in these circumstances that his peculiar matter is historically a first-class authority, 'comparable to St. Mark', is inadmissible. But I emphasize once again, in conclusion, there is no *proof* to be gained from the Semitisms: there is only *probability*.

H. F. D. SPARKS

[1] Creed, *The Gospel according to St. Luke* (p. 265).

New Test. Stud. II, pp. 303–25.

KENNETH J. THOMAS

THE OLD TESTAMENT CITATIONS IN HEBREWS

The textual origin of the O.T. citations in Hebrews has long been an enigma. From the time the texts of the two principal witnesses to the LXX, LXX^A and LXX^B, became available in the early part of the nineteenth century, it has been observed that the text of the citations in Hebrews does not exactly correspond to either. F. Bleek, who was evidently the first to make a systematic textual study of these citations, concluded that the author of Hebrews used a recension closely related to LXX^A.[1] Most commentators since have concluded that some text of the LXX was used, variously explaining variations from it as due to citation from memory, intentional adaptations by the author, and errors of transcription in his manuscript.[2] Others have suggested that the citations were taken from a lost version of the Greek O.T.[3] or from liturgical sources.[4]

However, in spite of the inconclusive results of past studies, comparison with the LXX text does seem to provide the key to the textual origin of the O.T. citations in Hebrews. These citations are closely related textually to the primary LXX texts, LXX^A and LXX^B. Six passages are cited *verbatim* according to these texts.[5] Only 56 variations of any kind from LXX^A/B are found in the 29 direct citations from the O.T.[6] Because of this obvious relationship to LXX^A and LXX^B, it is important to consider all the variations from LXX^A/B in order to establish the kind of relationship between the citations and LXX^A/B.[7]

[1] F. Bleek, *Der Brief an die Hebräer erlautert...* (Berlin, 1828–40), I, 374.

[2] All three of these explanations are propounded by H. B. Swete, *An Introduction to the Old Testament in Greek* (Cambridge, 1900), p. 402; F. H. Woods, 'Quotations', *A Dictionary of the Bible...*, ed. J. Hastings (Edinburgh, 1898–1904), IV, 187; and K. O. Stendahl, *The School of St Matthew* (Uppsala, 1954), pp. 160f.

[3] P. Padva, *Les Citations de l'Ancien Testament dans l'Épître aux Hébreux* (Paris, 1904), p. 101.

[4] H. V. Burch, *The Epistle to the Hebrews, Its Sources and Message* (London, 1936), pp. 58f.; C. Spicq, *L'épître aux Hébreux* (Études Bibliques, Paris, 1952–3), I, 336; S. Kistemaker, *The Psalm Citations in the Epistle to the Hebrews* (Amsterdam, 1961), p. 59. But see P. Katz, 'The Quotations from Deuteronomy in Hebrews', *Z.N.W.* XLIX (1958), 221. The only textual evidence for this theory is the citation of Deut. xxxii. 43 from the Odes in Heb. i. 6. The element of truth in this theory is that the author of Hebrews used passages familiar to his readers from worship and apologetic use. See C. H. Dodd, *According to the Scriptures: the sub-structure of New Testament Theology* (London, 1952); B. Lindars, *New Testament Apologetic* (London and Philadelphia, 1961); and C. F. D. Moule, *The Birth of the New Testament* (London, 1962).

[5] Ps. ii. 7 in i. 5*a*; II Sam. vii. 14 in i. 5*b*; Ps. cix. 1 in i. 13; Isa. viii. 18 in ii. 13*b*; Ps. cix. 4 in v. 6; and Gen. xxi. 12 in xi. 18.

[6] LXX^A/B is used to indicate all readings found in either LXX^A or LXX^B. Variations from LXX^A/B are all readings which differ from both LXX^A and LXX^B.

[7] The evidence of the N.T. witnesses makes it possible to establish with almost complete certainty the text of the citations in Hebrews, thus providing a sound basis for a critical study of the O.T. text

Reprinted from *New Testament Studies*. Vol. 11, 1964-5.

Analysis of variations from LXX$^{A/B}$

Hebrews i. 6 (Deut. xxxii. 43)

The author of Hebrews uses this quotation to demonstrate the superiority of the 'Son' over the angels. The text as found in LXX$^{A/B}$ does not suggest this interpretation as it has υἱοί as the subject of προσκυνησάτωσαν. However, the text found in the Odes has ἄγγελοι as the subject.[1] This text is immediately applicable as an indication of the worship of the 'Son' by the angels.[2] Since the Hymn of Moses (Deut. xxxii) was used liturgically in the Temple as a Psalm and in the Church as a part of the Easter vigil,[3] this form of the text was probably familiar at the time of the writing of Hebrews and used intentionally by the author to fit his purpose.[4]

Hebrews i. 7 (Ps. ciii. 4)

This citation has πυρὸς φλόγα[5] (flame(s) of fire) instead of πῦρ φλέγον (a flaming fire). There is a question as to whether the author of Hebrews considered φλόγα to be singular or plural. Technically, φλόγας is the accusative plural form of φλόξ, but it is very rarely used.[6] Rather, in the LXX the singular and plural forms are identical for both the dative and accusative forms.[7] The author of Hebrews, following LXX usage, has evidently considered φλόγα to be the plural form.[8] This perfects the parallelism with πνεύματα, with both φλόγα and πνεύματα being plural forms.[9] The revised reading indicates that each angel can be made into a flame of fire, reminiscent of Exod. iii. 2, in contrast to the 'Son', who remains the same forever. The

used by the author. The N.T. text has had sufficient authority to withstand correlation with the LXX with the result that in Hebrews only 15 of 56 variations from LXX$^{A/B}$ have been correlated with LXX$^{A/B}$ in any N.T. witnesses and in only 7 of 23 instances for which LXX^{A} and LXX^{B} differ is the alternate reading found in any N.T. witnesses. This result in Hebrews corresponds with that for the N.T. generally. Cf. Stendahl, *op. cit.* p. 164, and G. N. Zuntz, *The Text of the Epistles...* (London, 1953), p. 172.

[1] The Odes, or Canticles, follow the Psalter in most Greek MSS. since the fifth century. The text in Hebrews is exactly the same as Deut. xxxii. 43 in the Odes of LXX^{55}. The Odes in LXX^{A} has the same except for an additional οἱ before ἄγγελοι which may have been assimilated from the similar text in Ps. xcvi. 7 of the LXX. Witnesses to Deut. xxxii. 43 with the same text as LXX^{A} are LXX$^{FM^{mg}N\theta v}$ Bo Eth Sah^{mg} Just Or Eus Hil. These may be attempts to correlate the LXX text with the version in the Odes. Deut. xxxii. 43 in the LXX is known to have been translated from the Hebrew and not interpolated from another source, as the existence of a Hebrew antecedent has been established by the discovery of a Hebrew fragment in Cave 4 at Khirbet Qumran. See P. W. Skehan, 'A Fragment of the "Song of Moses" (Deut. 32) from Qumran', *B.A.S.O.R.* CXXXVI (1954), 12f. Cf. P. Katz, *op. cit.* p. 219.

[2] Lindars, *op. cit.* p. 211 n. 3.

[3] H. Schneider, 'Die biblischen Oden im christlichen Altertum', *Biblica*, XXX (1949), 28–65; F. Werner, *The Sacred Bridge* (London and N.Y., 1959), pp. 141f.

[4] Lindars, *op. cit.* pp. 244f.; Kistemaker, *op. cit.* p. 22.

[5] Parallels in Boh, Sah, and a few Lucian-type LXX minuscules.

[6] H. Stephanus, *Thesaurus Graecae Linguae* (Paris, 1831–65), VIII, 953.

[7] Cf. Ps. xxviii. 7 and Isa. lxvi. 15.

[8] Also translated as plural in Boh and Sah.

[9] Kistemaker, *op. cit.* p. 24, suggests the change was made to harmonize πυρὸς φλόγα with πνεύματα for proper balance and rhythm in liturgical use.

contrast is borne out in the following two quotations which indicate that the 'Son' has an eternal throne (i. 8), is from the beginning (i. 10), and never changes (i. 12). The author of Hebrews has used this change to strengthen the comparison between Jesus and the angels, emphasizing the stability of the 'Son's' nature in contrast to the ephemeral form of the angels.[1]

Hebrews i. 8–9 (Ps. xliv. 7–8)

As indicated above, this citation is part of the author's argument that the 'Son' is superior to the angels. The changes from the LXX^{A}/^{B} text indicate that the author of Hebrews is using it to show the 'Son's' association with God to the extent of sharing God's power and authority. This is not done by calling the 'Son' 'God', but by showing a close relationship between the 'Son' and 'God'.[2] The key to this interpretation is in understanding the first line to mean 'God is thy throne for ever and ever' instead of 'Thy throne, O God, is for ever and ever'. This is indicated by the use of βασιλείας αὐτοῦ[3] instead of βασιλείας σου and the change to καὶ ἡ ῥάβδος τῆς εὐθύτητος ῥάβδος[4] from ῥάβδος εὐθύτητος ἡ ῥάβδος. The use of αὐτοῦ forces ὁ θεός to be the subject so as to give an antecedent. The change of word order clearly establishes the parallelism of the two clauses, indicating that the Father's sceptre is also the 'Son's': 'Thy (the Son's) throne is God (the Father) for ever and ever *and* the sceptre of uprightness (the Son's) is the sceptre of his (the Father's) kingdom.' Thus, through the use of these changes the author of Hebrews has indicated that it is the 'Son' who is addressed and who is in closest association with God the Father, reigning with the power and authority of God over all, including the angels.

Hebrews i. 10–12 (Ps. ci. 26–8)

The contrast between the 'Son' and the angels is continued in this citation.[5] Σύ is moved to the beginning of the quotation for emphasis, immediately associating it with the σου of the preceding quotation which referred to the 'Son'. The addition of ὡς ἱμάτιον in i. 12 emphasizes the frequency and casualness with which creation (which includes the angels) is changed: the creation will be changed even 'as a garment'.[6] This is surely a

[1] Cf. contrast between God and the angels in IV Ezra viii. 20–3.

[2] Since the author of Hebrews is not concerned to address 'the Son' as God, the additional καί cannot be considered a separation of two quotations as suggested by Kistemaker, *op. cit.* p. 25.

[3] Αὐτοῦ is accepted as the original reading of Heb. i. 8 because of the strong witness of N.T.$^{P^{46}\aleph B}$ (which, in eleven other instances of minority readings in Hebrews, where they are together, are considered to have the original reading), the scribal tendency to use σου to avoid difficulties of interpretation, and the tendency to retain σου as found in the LXX.

[4] Parallel to change of word order found in LXX^{142}. Parallel to additional καί in LXX^{39,142}.

[5] This Psalm had already been given a Messianic interpretation in the LXX and in Matt. xxiv. 22 and Mark xiii. 20. Cf. B. W. Bacon, 'Heb. 1, 10–12 and the Septuagint Rendering of Ps. 102, 23', *Z.N.W.* III (1902), 280–5. Also Moule, *op. cit.* p. 79.

[6] Cf. similar idea in Isa. xxxiv. 4 which seems to be associated with Ps. ci. 27 because of the occurrence of ἑλ(ε)ίξεις.

special reference to the angels, of whom it has been said, 'They are new every morning (Ḥagigah 14*a*).'[1]

Hebrews ii. 6–8 (Ps. viii. 5–7)

The contrast between the 'Son' and the angels is continued by showing that God did not subject the world to come to angels but to man.[2] The author uses the Psalm with a dual application to both man and the 'Son',[3] as in verse 8 αὐτῷ is left unspecified so as to apply to both the 'Son' and man: everything is not yet in subjection to either man or the 'Son'. The author continues in the narrative to apply the themes of humiliation and exultation found in the quotation to both man and Jesus, who is now identified by name for the first time. Because of this dual application it was necessary for the author to omit καὶ κατέστησας αὐτὸν ἐπὶ τὰ ἔργα (τῶν) χειρῶν σου from the citation. Since he had already said that the 'Son' had participated in the act of creation (i. 10) he could not include a line which would ignore his part in the creation.

Hebrews ii. 12 (Ps. xxi. 23)

This citation substitutes ἀπαγγελῶ for διηγήσομαι. Although the words are synonyms, ἀπαγγελῶ is a more striking word having associations with both ἄγγελος and εὐαγγέλιον, associations important to the author's argument. The conclusive point of the argument that Jesus is superior to the angels is that Jesus has the highest qualifications as the 'messenger' (ἄγγελος) of the 'gospel' (εὐαγγέλιον) because he himself brings sanctification to his own brethren. Thus, both the messenger and the message are superior, attention to which is drawn by the use of ἀπαγγελῶ.

Hebrews ii. 13*a* (Isa. viii. 17)[4]

The citation begins with ἐγὼ ἔσομαι πεποιθώς instead of πεποιθὼς ἔσομαι. The addition of ἐγώ emphasizes that Jesus is speaking by forming a parallel with the next citation from Isa. viii. 18 which is used for the same purpose. This is important to the author as he wishes to stress the fact that Jesus identifies himself with man (cf. ii. 11). This identification is further emphasized by the exchange of ἔσομαι and πεποιθώς, connecting πεποιθώς with ἐπ' αὐτῷ, thus more directly showing God to be the object of Jesus' trust and laying stress upon Jesus' identification with man through their common dependence upon God.

[1] Interpretation of Lam. iii. 23 in Ḥagigah 14*a* (ed. I. Epstein, *The Babylonian Talmud* (London, 1935–48), Seder Mo'ed VIII, Ḥagigah, p. 83).

[2] This Psalm is used of Jesus in Matt. xxi. 16; I Cor. xv. 27; and Eph. i. 22.

[3] C. K. Barrett, 'The Eschatology of the Epistle to the Hebrews', in *The Background of the New Testament and its Eschatology*, eds. W. D. Davies and D. Daube in honour of C. H. Dodd (Cambridge, 1956), pp. 389f.

[4] These words are also found in II Sam. xxii. 2 but the citation is probably from Isa. viii. 17 since the next citation in Heb. ii. 13 is from Isa. viii. 18. Further, Isaiah has an ambiguous subject whereas in II Samuel the words are clearly ascribed to David. Cf. Lindars, *op. cit.* p. 176, for further discussion.

Hebrews iii. 7–11 (Ps. xciv. 8–11)

Two variations from LXX^A/B emphasize that the 'day of testing' was a period of 'forty years'. The insertion of διό[1] connects τεσσεράκοντα ἔτη to the preceding sentence rather than to the following one. This use is obviously intentional since the author later, in iii. 17, connects the phrase with προσώχθισεν as in the original text. Through this change τεσσεράκοντα ἔτη is related to τὴν ἡμέραν τοῦ πειρασμοῦ (iii. 8) to form a parallelism equating 'day' and 'forty years'.[2] This clarifies the author's argument in iii. 13, in which he maintains that σήμερον extends over an indefinite period of time.[3] Just as the 'day of testing' was not a single day but was forty years, so 'today' is not a single day. His use of the phrase 'every day' (ἑκάστην ἡμέραν) in connexion with 'today' in iii. 13 confirms this interpretation. The change to ἐν δοκιμασίᾳ from ἐδοκίμασαν further establishes the parallelism, altering the interpretation from a testing of God by man, as in the Psalm, to a testing of man by God, which is the normal use of δοκιμασία.[4] The clause, therefore, is made to read: '... where your fathers, during their testing, tried and saw my works for forty years', emphasizing that the Israelites themselves were being tested during their time in the wilderness. Thus, this clause is made parallel with the preceding clause: 'on the day of testing in the wilderness' (iii. 8), a time when the Israelites were being tested.

A third change in the citation is the substitution of ταύτῃ for ἐκείνῃ. This is not intended to designate some other than the wilderness generation. Rather, it serves as a reminder of Jesus' words with reference to 'this generation', as in Matt. xxiii. 36, in which he pronounced 'woes' upon the scribes and Pharisees. Such an echo of Jesus' words strengthens the O.T. quotation, used by the author as a warning against unbelief. It also serves to call to mind another, more contemporary example of unbelief in addition to that from Moses' time.

Hebrews iv. 4 (Gen. ii. 2)

The phrase ὁ θεὸς ἐν, from Gen. ii. 2*a*, is inserted after κατέπαυσεν.[5] In Gen. ii. 2 this single phrase supplies the subject and preposition for both parts of the sentence. By inserting the phrase in this position, it is possible to cite only the short section about God resting on the seventh day, it being

[1] Parallels in LXX^R,55,210 Boh Thdrt^pt.

[2] J. Moffatt, *A Critical and Exegetical Commentary on the Epistle to the Hebrews* (I.C.C., ed. A. Plummer, Edinburgh, 1924), p. 45.

[3] This understanding of Heb. iii. 7–11 was first expounded by Clement of Alexandria, *Cohortatio ad Gentes*, IX (J.-P. Migne, *P.G.* VIII, 196). He says that 'today' signifies 'eternity'.

[4] F. Rendall, *The Epistle to the Hebrews in Greek and English with Critical and Explanatory Notes* (London, 1883), p. 31; C. J. Vaughan, ΠΡΟΣ ΕΒΡΑΙΟΥΣ. *The Epistle to the Hebrews with Notes* (London, 1890), p. 66; W. Grundmann, 'δόκιμος, ἀδόκιμος, δοκιμή, δοκίμιον, δοκιμάζω, ἀποδοκιμάζω, δοκιμασία', in *Theologisches Wörterbuch zum Neuen Testament*, ed. G. Kittel (Stuttgart, 1933–), II, 258–64.

[5] Parallels in LXX^19,53,54,72,135,314,344 Orig^Lat Eus.

unnecessary to cite the first part about God finishing his work on the seventh day since there had already been an allusion to this fact (iv. 3). In spite of the fact that God has finished his work, he has excluded the faithless Israelites from his rest and set another day during which those with faith may enter into his rest (iv. 6–10). Therefore, the author uses the citation to emphasize the concept of God 'resting': God rested on the seventh day and there is still the opportunity for others to share this rest since the faithless Israelites have been denied this opportunity.

This interpretation is in sharp contrast to that of Philo, who has a text of Gen. ii. 2 in *De Post. Caini* 64 (18)[1] identical to that in Hebrews. Philo interprets Gen. ii. 2 as meaning that on the seventh day God began the creation of divine things, having finished the mortal creation on the sixth day.[2] He derives this interpretation by taking the active form κατέπαυσεν literally: 'God caused to rest.'[3] However, this does not imply that Philo thinks the physical and divine creations took place at separate times. Rather, he uses this means of expression to demonstrate their separate character. God's divine creation is conceived as being a continuing process, as it is 'the property of God to make'.[4] Thus, for Philo, the divine creation takes place on the 'seventh day', a day which comprehends all time. The author of Hebrews likewise develops the idea that a day can extend over an indefinite period of time (iii. 7–13) but emphatically rejects the idea that God labours on the seventh day (iv. 3*b*, 10). Even though God set 'another day' for those who believe to enter his rest, the author of Hebrews does not consider this to be a further work of God. It is possible that the author of Hebrews was aware of Philo's interpretation and was guarding against his view while using his text.[5]

Hebrews vi. 14 (Gen. xxii. 17)

This citation is used to indicate the promise given to Abraham by God. To emphasize the reference to Abraham, σε[6] is substituted for τὸ σπέρμα σου. The author is reassuring his readers that God will keep the promise made to them just as he kept the promise made to Abraham, as in both instances the promise was accompanied by an oath (vii. 20f.). The citation includes the promise made under oath to Abraham, and is followed by the assertion that Abraham himself 'obtained the promise' (vi. 15). The double use

[1] L. Cohn and P. Wendland, eds., *Philonis Alexandrini Opera quae supersunt* (Berlin, 1896–1926), II, 14.

[2] *Leg. All.* I, 16 (6) (Cohn and Wendland, *op. cit.* I, 64).

[3] Barrett, *op. cit.* p. 367 n. 1.

[4] *Leg. All.* I, 5 (3) (F. H. Colson and G. H. Whitaker, trans., *Philo with an English Translation* (Loeb Classical Library, London, 1929–41), I, 149); cf. J. Drummond, *Philo Judaeus: or, the Jewish-Alexandrian philosophy in its development and completion* (London, 1888), II, 16.

[5] This antithetic connexion between Philo and Hebrews is further developed in my unpublished Ph.D. thesis (1959) presented to the University of Manchester, *The Use of the Septuagint in the Epistle to the Hebrews*, pp. 248–316.

[6] Parallels in Boh and *Dialogues of Timothy and Aquila.*

of σε in the citation emphasizes that the promise was given specifically to Abraham.[1]

Hebrews viii. 5 (Exod. xxv. 40)

This quotation is used to document the fact that the tabernacle made by Moses was only a copy of the heavenly one. The addition of πάντα[2] and the use of δειχθέντα[3] instead of δεδειγμένον strengthen this documentation. The author depreciates the value and importance of the tabernacle built by Moses by showing that it was only a copy of a τύπος. The use of πάντα indicates that everything about the tabernacle of Moses is a copy and therefore inferior to the sanctuary of which Christ is the minister (viii. 2): 'all' was made according to the pattern (cf. Exod. xxv. 8 LXX). In addition, the author indicates that the heavenly sanctuary no longer serves as a τύπος for an earthly tabernacle by using the aorist form δειχθέντα instead of the perfect form δεδειγμένον. The distinction between the two forms, as expressed by W. W. Goodwin, is that the perfect tense indicates 'action finished in present time and so denoting an accomplished state' while the aorist tense indicates 'action simply taking place in past time'.[4] Thus, the heavenly sanctuary in the past did serve as a τύπος for the earthly tabernacle when it was shown to Moses, but it is no longer such a τύπος. The author is very particular not to refer to the heavenly sanctuary as a τύπος but always clearly designates it as *the* sanctuary. It is the 'true tabernacle' (viii. 2). There is no longer any need for the earthly tabernacle: it has been made obsolete by the new covenant (viii. 13).

Philo also cites Exod. xxv. 40 with an additional πάντα in *Leg. All.* III, 102 (33).[5] However, Philo's text is otherwise quite different and appears to be a combination of xxv. 8 and 40 (LXX): 'κατὰ τὸ παράδειγμα τὸ δεδειγμένον σοι ἐν τῷ ὄρει πάντα ποιήσεις.' Philo used the citation to demonstrate the superiority of Moses to Bezalel, whereas in Hebrews it is used to demonstrate the superiority of Christ to Moses. The use of this text to indicate superiority by both Philo and the author of Hebrews indicates that it is possible that the additional πάντα was suggested to the author of Hebrews from his knowledge of Philo's text and that he used it to fit his own interpretation of the quotation.

[1] J. H. Kurtz, *Der Brief an die Hebräer* (Mitau, 1869), p. 211, suggests the further possibility that the author may have thought Abraham did not live to see the birth of Jacob since the death of Abraham is recorded in Gen. xxv. 8, while the birth of Jacob follows in Gen. xxv. 26. This may have led him to limit the terms of the promise by omitting τὸ σπέρμα σου to include only that which he considered had been fulfilled in Abraham's lifetime. This seems unlikely since the chronology in Genesis clearly indicates that Abraham lived 15 years after the birth of Jacob. Cf. Gen. xxi. 5; xxv. 7, 26.

[2] Parallels in $LXX^{F,19,85,129,130,314,344,509}$ Boh Cyr Philo.

[3] Parallels in $LXX^{15,53,56,58,72,85,129,130,344,376}$.

[4] W. W. Goodwin, *Greek Grammar* (rev. C. B. Gulick, Boston, 1930), p. 267. H. P. V. Nunn, *A Short Syntax of New Testament Greek* (5th ed. Cambridge, 1938), p. 72, says, 'The Perfect is not used in Greek unless stress is laid on the fact that the action denoted by the verb has been brought to its appropriate conclusion, and that its results remain.'

[5] Cohn and Wendland, *op. cit.* I, 135f.

Hebrews viii. 8–12 *and Hebrews* x. 16–17 (Jer. xxxviii. 31–4)

These two quotations of the same passage offer the clearest example of the author's freedom with the text before him. Here is conclusive evidence that he knew the original text yet chose variant wordings to suit his purposes, as there are four instances in which he followed the $LXX^{A/B}$ text in viii. 8–12 but used different words in x. 16–17.[1] These four variations from the $LXX^{A/B}$ text in x. 16–17 are πρὸς αὐτούς for τῷ οἴκῳ Ἰσραήλ, ἐπὶ καρδίας αὐτῶν καὶ ἐπὶ τὴν διάνοιαν αὐτῶν for εἰς τὴν διάνοιαν αὐτῶν καὶ ἐπὶ καρδίας αὐτῶν, the addition of καὶ τῶν ἀνομιῶν αὐτῶν,[2] and μνησθήσομαι for μνησθῶ. This example confirms that the author deliberately chose to use variations from his LXX text.

The first part of Jer. xxxviii. 31–4 is cited only in Heb. viii. 8–12. Here the author uses συντελέσω[3] instead of διαθήσομαι, ἐποίησα[4] instead of διεθέμην, ἐπὶ τὸν οἶκον twice for τῷ οἴκῳ, and λέγει twice for φησίν. The key to understanding the author's use of συντελέσω and ἐποίησα seems to be in Jer. xli. 8, 15, 18, which contain the only occurrences of these words with διαθήκη in Jeremiah and are in a passage close to the one cited by the author. The striking fact is that συντελέω is used in Jer. xli. 8 and 15 in instances in which the covenant is kept or accomplished and ποιέω is used in Jer. xli. 18 in an instance in which the covenant is spoken of as broken. The only other occurrence of one of these words with διαθήκη in the LXX is the use of ποιέω in Isa. xxviii. 15, also in an instance in which the covenant is broken or annulled. These usages correspond with those in Heb. viii. 8f.: the Lord will establish (συντελέσω) a covenant with Israel and Judah; it will not be like the previous covenant he made (ἐποίησα), which was broken by their fathers. The covenant which is to be made will be kept, for it will be in the minds and hearts of God's people. It may be concluded that the author deliberately used these verbs as in Jer. xli in order to make clear the difference between the two covenants:[5] the new covenant will be kept, the old covenant was not kept. This is obviously the point of the quotation, as he refers in Heb. viii. 13 to the 'first' covenant as obsolete.

The author's use of ἐπὶ τὸν οἶκον... ἐπὶ τὸν οἶκον is apparently without intentional purpose. It seems to be the result of changing the preceding verb. Nowhere in the N.T. or the LXX is συντελέω followed by the dative, although there are examples of such in extra-biblical literature where it is

[1] Also Kistemaker, *op. cit.* p. 57.

[2] Parallels in $LXX^{38,49,90,613,764}$ Chrys Thdrt.

[3] Parallels in LXX^{41} Sym Syr-Hex. The use of συντελέσω in Symmachus is quite a coincidence, but was probably a translation independent of any earlier text or version, as suggested by Padva, *op. cit.* p. 77.

[4] Only LXX^{Q*} has this reading and there it is probably due to the influence of Hebrews as suggested by Moffatt, *op. cit.* p. 110.

[5] O. Michel, *Der Brief an die Hebräer* (7. Auflage, Krit. exeget. Komm. über das N.T., ed. Meyer, Göttingen, 1936), p. 100, considers this conclusion possible.

used to mean 'contribute'. The change may be the result of the author's personal preference for this form[1] or be from a text modified by liturgical use.[2]

As the passage reads in Jer. xxxviii. 31–4, λέγει is used the first time in most MSS. and φησίν the other two times according to all MSS. Such variation is characteristic of the LXX translation of Jeremiah.[3] There seems to be no interpretational difference between the two forms to the author of Hebrews as he uses φησίν in viii. 5 in the same way as λέγει is used in viii. 8, that is, to introduce direct narration. Therefore, he may have simply repeated the λέγει from the first line of the quotation in the subsequent phrases[4] in viii. 9 and 10 and x. 16 in place of the original φησίν,[5] or he may have taken them from a liturgical text.[6]

The author of Hebrews substitutes πρὸς αὐτούς in x. 16 in place of τῷ οἴκῳ 'Ισραήλ. The author is here directly applying the quotation to his readers and himself, for it is introduced as being the witness of the Holy Spirit 'to us' (ἡμῖν). By the use of πρὸς αὐτούς, the author is including his readers and himself under the designation 'the house of Israel'. The change may have been necessitated by the inclusion of Gentile Christians among those to whom the epistle was written. This would give a broader application to the phrase 'house of Israel'. At least it may be said, the change was made to make a direct connexion between ἡμῖν in verse 15 and the citation.

The exchange of phrases ἐπὶ καρδίας...ἐπὶ τὴν διάνοιαν from εἰς τὴν διάνοιαν...ἐπὶ καρδίας in x. 16 appears to have been for the purpose of bringing νόμους and καρδίας together. As suggested by S. Kistemaker, this exchange is due to the importance of the words 'law' and 'heart' in the earlier part of the discourse.[7] The preceding discussion in chapter x has referred to the failure of the 'law', while the discussion in chapters iii and iv referred to the failure of the 'heart' (cf. iii. 12 and iv. 12). With the putting of the laws on our hearts, we have a new confidence and a new hope, as indicated in the following discussion in x. 19–25.

The addition of καὶ τῶν ἀνομιῶν αὐτῶν in x. 17 is an intentional reference to the abolition of the sacrifices required by the first covenant. This is indicated by the use of ἀνομία, which has the basic meaning of 'not lawful'. The theme of lawlessness is first introduced by the author of Hebrews in i. 9 where the citation from Ps. xliv is interpreted to mean that the Son hated ἀνομία. In chapter viii the author speaks of the need for a new covenant because the first covenant had not been faultless and cites Jer. xxxviii. 31–4 in which it is stated that the Israelites 'did not continue in my covenant'

[1] Padva, *op. cit.* p. 77.
[2] Kistemaker, *op. cit.* p. 42.
[3] S. R. Driver, *The Book of the Prophet Jeremiah* (London, 1906), p. xlviii.
[4] Parallels in LXX[407,544] Thdrt and other Greek fathers.
[5] C. H. Toy, *Quotations in the New Testament* (New York, 1884), p. 225; B. Weiss, *Das Neue Testament Handausgabe* (Leipzig, 1902), p. 566.
[6] Kistemaker, *op. cit.* pp. 41 f.
[7] *Ibid.* p. 129.

(viii. 9). Since the first covenant is thought of in terms of laws given by God to man, the breaking of that covenant is an act of lawlessness. In speaking of the abolition of the first covenant in chapter x, the author indicates that this involves the end of the sacrifices and offerings which were part of that covenant because Jesus Christ has made the one sacrifice which takes away sins (x. 8–14). However, not only the violations of the first covenant have been dealt with through the sacrifice of Christ, but also the violations for all time (διηνεκές; x. 12). At this point in the argument, the author cites again portions of Jer. xxxviii. 33–4, repeating the part that states that the new covenant will consist of laws on the hearts and minds, adding the phrase under discussion. By this phrase he assures his readers that the violations of the new covenant are also forgiven, lest they think that these violations need further sacrifices. Further offering is unnecessary as further lawless acts are not remembered but forgiven (x. 18).

The author in x. 17 also substitutes μνησθήσομαι (a future indicative passive) for μνησθῶ (an aorist subjunctive passive). The future indicative passive is used by the author to emphasize further that the Lord will never remember their sins and lawless acts. According to 'Hermann's Canon', the distinction between the aorist subjunctive and the future indicative is that the latter refers to a particular time and to something lasting in contrast to the former's reference to an indefinite time and to something temporal.[1] C. J. Vaughan applies the distinction to this passage with '...the οὐ μὴ μνησθῶ giving the thought of the *single act* of forgetting, and the οὐ μὴ μνησθήσομαι carrying the forgetfulness into an endless futurity. *I will never in the furthest future remember their sins against them.*'[2] Thus his readers are assured that no further offering will be necessary because their sins and lawless acts have been completely forgotten forever.[3]

The author of Hebrews uses ἐπιγράψω[4] instead of γράψω in both viii. 10 and x. 16.[5] Both γράφω and ἐπιγράφω are used to translate כָּתַב, but there is a slight difference in meaning between the two. Γράφω is the general word for 'write', while ἐπιγράφω, particularly in the N.T., is used for the

[1] G. B. Winer, *A Treatise on the Grammar of New Testament Greek*..., trans. W. F. Moulton from 3rd ed. rev. (9th ed. Edinburgh, 1882), p. 636.

[2] Vaughan, *op. cit.* p. 196.

[3] F. E. Thompson, *A Syntax of Attic Greek* (London, 1904), p. 133, discovered in Homer's *Odyssey* that 'the Subjunctive differs from the Future Indicative in stating what is thought likely to occur, not positively what will occur'. This supports the suggestion made by W. F. Moulton, 'The Epistle to the Hebrews', in *A New Testament Commentary for English Readers*, ed. C. J. Ellicott (London, 1877–9), III, 326, that the author of Hebrews used the future indicative in x. 17 now that 'the firm basis of the promise has been shown'.

[4] This reading is supported in viii. 10 by all N.T. witnesses except N.T.$^{P^{46}B\psi}$, which are individually strong witnesses, but not as a group without additional support. Cf. Zuntz, *op. cit.* p. 62.

[5] LXX^{B} and the majority of LXX witnesses have γράψω. LXX^{A} and Arab have ἐπιγράψω but with a different word order than in Hebrews. Their word order emphasizes ἐπιγράψω which would have suited the purpose of the author of Hebrews had he known it. LXX^{Q,V,26,46,86,106,130,239,534,544,613,710} and some Greek and Latin fathers have ἐπιγράψω with the word order as in Hebrews and M.T. These do not appear to be a conflation of the LXX traditions since the LXX^{A} group is too weakly attested. Rather, they probably reflect the change made in Hebrews.

more permanent types of writing, such as inscribing or engraving (cf. Mark xv. 26; Acts xvii. 23; Rev. xxi. 21, the only other N.T. instances). Ἐπιγράψω is particularly appropriate here, as it emphasizes the permanent nature of the laws of the new covenant.[1]

Hebrews ix. 20 (Exod. xxiv. 8)

The author makes four alterations from LXX[A/B] to emphasize the difference between the two covenants while at the same time showing their similarity. The change of ἰδού to τοῦτο[2] appears to be a deliberate change to echo the words of Jesus at the Last Supper. According to Matt. xxvi. 28 and Mark xiv. 24, Jesus says, τοῦτό ἐστιν τὸ αἷμά μου τῆς διαθήκης.[3] A reference to these words of institution of the new covenant is appropriate here as the author has been comparing the two covenants with special reference to Christ as the mediator of the new covenant.[4] He correlates the institutions of the two covenants by the change of one word in the quotation by which all his readers immediately recognize that these are the words used by Christ, the mediator of the new covenant, while also realizing that they were spoken by Moses, who received the first covenant from God.[5]

The change of κύριος to ὁ θεός[6] and its placement at the end of the citation[7] are to avoid any possible ambiguity caused by the first change. The author has reminded his readers of the words of Jesus by the use of τοῦτο, but he does not want them to think it was Jesus who commanded the first covenant. Since his common tendency is to use κύριος for Jesus, ambiguity is avoided by the use of ὁ θεός which is placed at the end of the citation for emphasis, drawing attention to the fact that it was God who commanded.

The author uses ἐνετείλατο[8] instead of διέθετο to indicate that the first covenant was made by the command of God. The use of ἐντολή and ἐνετείλατο emphasizes the authoritative way in which the first covenant was made. This contrasts sharply with the way in which the second covenant was made

[1] Cf. Prov. vii. 3 in which ἐπιγράφω is also metaphorically connected with the heart to emphasize the permanence of such an inscription.

[2] Parallels in Sah and *Dialogues of Timothy and Aquila.*

[3] J. Jeremias, *The Eucharistic Words of Jesus*, trans. A. Ehrhardt from 2nd ed. (Oxford, 1955), pp. 134f., indicates the possibility that τῆς διαθήκης is an early exegetical gloss. However, διαθήκη is found in I Cor. xi. 25, which was written before Hebrews.

[4] H. T. Andrews, 'Hebrews', in *The Abingdon Bible Commentary*, eds. F. C. Eiselen, E. Lewis, D. G. Downey (New York, 1929), p. 1316, makes the curious statement: 'It is strange that the writer does not quote the words used by Jesus in the institution of the Lord's Supper, "This cup is the new covenant in my blood" (I Cor. 11[25]), but it is in keeping with the absence of any distinct reference to the Eucharist in the Epistle.' Although Andrews does not find in the quotation a reference to the words of institution, it is noteworthy that he considered such a reference to be appropriate here.

[5] Jeremias, *op. cit.* p. 84, maintains that the absence of the Eucharist from the list of subjects taught to beginners in Hebrews vi. 1f. is to be explained by the consideration that it was a subject to be taught to the more mature in order to keep it from profanation. If this is true then the veiled reference to the institution of the Lord's Supper in Heb. ix. 20 is meaningful to the instructed but safeguards the ritual words of institution from the uninitiated.

[6] Parallels in LXX[44,71].

[7] Parallels in LXX[71] Boh Eth.

[8] Parallels in LXX[71] and Philo.

as mediated by Jesus Christ (x. 1–10). The author emphasizes the voluntary nature of Christ's offering, which is in voluntary obedience to the will of God. The new covenant is not one of external laws, but a covenant made and followed by the desire of the heart. Thus, while the same words were used in their institution, the modes of inauguration were greatly different.

It is probable that Philo also cited Exod. xxiv. 8 with ἐνετείλατο in *Quaes. et Sol. in Ex.* II, 36,[1] which work is known only in the Armenian version. Unlike the author of Hebrews, who relates blood to purification and the forgiveness of sins, Philo relates the blood of sacrifice to a unity of mind and thought. Blood sacrifice overcomes the estrangement of mind and thought which exists by reason of their separate bodies. This is a denial of the meaning of sin and the significance of sacrifice as understood by the author of Hebrews. Since the author of Hebrews carefully indicates his understanding of blood in relation to the forgiveness of sins (ix. 22), it is possible that he is correcting Philo at this point. The common use of ἐνετείλατο seems to indicate a familiarity with Philo's text.

Hebrews x. 5–7 (Ps. xxxix. 7–9)

This citation has three changes from LXX$^{A/B}$ which emphasize the purpose of Christ's coming. The author uses εὐδόκησας[2] instead of ᾔτησας as in LXX^{B} or ἐζήτησας as in LXX^{ARTZ} and many others. A similar expression found in Ps. l. 18, ὁλοκαυτώματα οὐκ εὐδοκήσεις, may have provided the inspiration for the wording in this passage. The author could not say that God does not 'ask' or 'require' sacrifices and offerings, since he had just said that God had commanded them (ix. 19f.). However, it is no contradiction for him to say that God 'finds no pleasure' in them. He has already stated that the sacrifices of the old covenant were inadequate and only a shadow of the good things to come (x. 1). Accordingly, it is appropriate for Christ to say (the quotation is attributed to him in Hebrews) that God would have no pleasure in burnt and sin offerings from him. By the omission of ἐβουλήθην,[3] τοῦ ποιῆσαι is connected with ἥκω instead of with ἐβουλήθην so that ποιῆσαι indicates the purpose of ἥκω: Christ comes to do God's will. This emphasis is further indicated by placing τὸ θέλημά σου at the end of the quotation,[4] forming an antithetical parallelism with ἠθέλησας (x. 5).[5] These changes indicate that the main point of the citation is Christ's coming to do the will of God, which interpretation is confirmed by the repetition of the last phrase and the placing of θελήματι in the emphatic position in x. 10. Thus, the

[1] R. Marcus, ed., *Philo Supplement*, II (Loeb Classical Library, London, 1953), p. 77.

[2] Parallels in LXX^{2013} Boh Sah.

[3] Parallel in Sah.

[4] Parallels in LXX^{2013} and Sy.

[5] A. Nairne, *The Epistle to the Hebrews* (Cambridge Greek Testament for Schools, Cambridge, 1917), p. 98, says that this change gives the key to the fact that the emphasis is on the last phrase and not on σῶμα. Many commentators base their interpretation of this passage on σῶμα, for example Moffatt, *op. cit.* p. 138: 'Our author found σῶμα in his LXX text and seized upon it; Jesus came with his body to do God's will, i.e. to die for the sins of men.'

author has further demonstrated the difference between the two covenants: sacrifices and offerings were made under the old covenant because they were commanded by God while the new covenant is established by a sacrifice made to please God, the result of a desire to do God's will.

Hebrews x. 30*a* (Deut. xxxii. 35)

The text of this citation is like that found in *Targum Onkelos* and Rom. xii. 19 (ἐμοὶ ἐκδίκησις, ἐγὼ ἀνταποδώσω)[1] instead of that in the LXX[A/B] (ἐν ἡμέρᾳ ἐκδικήσεως ἀνταποδώσω...). The author of Hebrews possibly borrowed this form of the text from Romans[2] since it is more suitable than the LXX[A/B] text to contradict Philo's interpretation of this passage.[3] Philo interprets Deut. xxxii. 35 to mean that God will not judge men in the day of vengeance by connecting the phrase 'in the day of vengeance' with the preceding verse so as to read: 'Are not these laid up in store with Me, sealed up in My treasuries in the day of vengeance, when their foot shall have slipped?'[4] According to Philo, God has closed up the evils of men in his 'treasuries' so that they may not be held against them 'in the day of vengeance', which allows those who have slipped to repent, even in the day of vengeance. The author of Hebrews, however, uses this quotation to illustrate that God will punish his people. He uses this as a warning to those who may contemplate sinning deliberately after coming to know God through the Son. Therefore, he deliberately deviates from the LXX[A/B] text to avoid any interpretation, such as Philo's, which would indicate that God does not punish their sins. In the variant text, no connexion is possible between 'sealed up in My treasuries' and 'in the day of vengeance'.

Hebrews x. 30*b* (Deut. xxxii. 36)

The next verse from Deuteronomy is cited with the omission of the initial ὅτι. This causal particle in the original context showed the relationship of the two verses. Deut. xxxii. 35 referred to the vengeance God would have upon the enemies of his people with the following verse indicating that this punishment of their enemies was the vindication of God's people. The author of Hebrews, though, uses both citations to refer to God's punishment of those who reject the grace offered through his Son by interpreting κρινεῖ in the sense of 'judge', with the connotation of 'condemn' (cf. x. 27, 31).[5]

[1] The text of *Targum Onkelos* reads קֳדָמַי פּוּרְעָנוּתָא וַאֲנָא אֲשַׁלֵּים (A. Berliner, ed., *Targum Onkelos* (Berlin, 1884), I, 236).

[2] Cf. T. W. Manson, 'The Problem of the Epistle to the Hebrews', *Bull. J. Rylands Lib.* XXXII (1949–50), 16, for evidence that the author of Hebrews was familiar with Romans.

[3] Cf. Katz, *op. cit.* p. 220.

[4] *Leg. All.* III, 105 (34) (Colson and Whitaker, *op. cit.* I, 371).

[5] Bleek, *op. cit.* II (2), 696, tries to avoid this connotation by saying that God judges his people to determine who are really his. F. J. Delitzsch, *Commentary on the Epistle to the Hebrews* (Edinburgh, 1868–70), II, 191, claims that the author used κρινεῖ in its original sense by interpreting the citation to mean that the Lord executed judgement on behalf of his people. This is contrary to the plain sense of the context.

Since the author does not retain the causal relationship between the two citations, it is necessary for him to omit ὅτι.

Hebrews x. 37–8 (Hab. ii. 3*b*–4)

This citation, which follows a short phrase from Isa. xxvi. 20,[1] has several changes to assure his readers of the return of Christ. While Hab. ii. 3*b*–4 had already been given a messianic interpretation in rabbinic tradition[2] and the LXX$^{A/B}$ translation,[3] the citation is made even more specifically messianic in Hebrews by the addition of ὁ before ἐρχόμενος,[4] ὁ ἐρχόμενος being used of Jesus in Matt. xi. 3; Luke vii. 19; and John vi. 14 and xi. 27. Whereas these references in the Gospels refer to the first coming of Christ, Heb. x. 37 refers to the second 'coming' of Christ as an encouragement to the readers in their time of suffering.[5] The use of the future indicative χρονίσει[6] instead of the aorist subjunctive χρονίσῃ makes this encouragement even stronger by employing the subtle distinction between these two forms in order to indicate what positively will occur:[7] the Lord will positively not tarry. The μή between οὐ and χρονίσει is dropped without changing the meaning, as οὐ with the emphatic future indicative is equivalent to οὐ μή with the aorist subjunctive.[8] The position of the last two clauses of the citation is reversed to avoid connecting ὑποστείληται with ὁ ἐρχόμενος. Originally, the clause ἐὰν ὑποστείληται... referred to one who comes but who is not truly God's chosen one.[9] If the author of Hebrews had retained the original sequence, this clause would have referred to Christ himself, since the author had already made 'the coming one' definitely refer to Christ. In the new position this clause is connected with δίκαιός μου, which is now the subject of the last part of the quotation. The inversion places δέ at the beginning of the verse, which now indicates the change of subject, the new subject now being the Christian (cf. x. 39). It is necessary to connect the rearranged clauses, which is accomplished by the additional καί, drawing attention to the new position of the last clause.[10] The inversion strengthens the warning against apostasy which the author has been making in this passage, as now 'my righteous one' may be the one 'who shrinks back'.[11]

[1] Lindars, *op. cit.* p. 231, says that the use of the phrase from Isa. xxvi. 20 'fixes the interpretation of the Habakkuk passage in an eschatological sense'.

[2] Cf. *Sanhedrin* 97*b* (I. Epstein, ed., *The Babylonian Talmud* (London, 1935–48), Seder Nezikin VI, II, 658f.). The Qumran *Habakkuk Commentary* interprets this passage in terms of faith in the Teacher of Righteousness. Cf. W. H. Brownlee, *The Dead Sea Habakkuk Midrash and the Targum of Jonathan* (Durham, N.C., 1953), p. 5.

[3] Kurtz, *op. cit.* p. 342; Toy, *op. cit.* p. 127; and especially T. W. Manson, 'The Argument from Prophecy', *J.T.S.* XLVI (1945), 133f.

[4] Parallels in LXX^{46,95,130,185,311} Cyr Thdr Theophil.

[5] Cf. Acts i. 11; I Cor. xi. 26; I Thess. iv. 15–17; II Thess. ii. 1; Rev. i. 7; etc.

[6] Parallels in LXX^{26,62,86,147,410} Basil.

[7] See above under Heb. x. 16.

[8] W. W. Goodwin, *op. cit.* p. 288.

[9] Manson, *op. cit.* p. 134; Lindars, *op. cit.* p. 231.

[10] Nairne, *op. cit.* p. 106. D. R. Goodwin, 'On the Use of καί in Hebrews x. 38', *J.B.L.* v (1885), 85, argues that if ὁ δίκαιος were to be the subject of ὑποστείληται, the author would have used δέ instead of καί. Delitzsch, *op. cit.* II, 200, sufficiently answers this with the comment that it was necessary to insert καί because a δέ had already been retained, otherwise δέ would have been more natural.

[11] Also Lindars, *loc. cit.*

Hebrews xii. 5–6 (Prov. iii. 11–12)

The author in this passage is emphasizing that his readers are being treated as sons of God. Accordingly, they are to accept their hardships as discipline, such as a father would give to his son (xii. 7). The additional μου[1] after υἱέ makes it clearer that they personally are being addressed by God as sons. Again the motive for this addition is found by comparison with Philo, who interprets this passage to mean that discipline brings men into relationship with God: 'So we see that reproaching and admonition are counted so excellent a thing, that they turn our acknowledgement of God into kinship with Him, for what relation can be closer than that of a father to a son, or a son to a father?'[2] By contrast, the author of Hebrews emphasizes that they are disciplined *because* they *are* the sons of God (xii. 7f.), adding the personal pronoun to emphasize that they are already God's sons.

Hebrews xii. 20 (Exod. xix. 12–13)

The author has freely condensed this passage but retains enough of the original words to identify it. This citation is made in his description of the revelation at Sinai during which, in xii. 19, he refers to Exod. xx. 18f., in which the people begged Moses, 'You speak to us, and we will hear; but let not God speak to us, lest we die.' The author gives as the reason for their fear the command of God in Exod. xix. 12f. that neither man nor beast was to touch the mountain. Only the portion of the command most impressive to the people is cited, with a few changes incorporated to enhance its fearfulness. The citation indicates that even a brute beast would be held accountable if it should touch the mountain, thus exemplifying the fearfulness and unapproachableness of God. The author of Hebrews begins the citation with κἂν θηρίον, thus drawing attention to these words and emphasizing them. Κἂν immediately gives the idea that this was the most extreme aspect of the command. The reference to θηρίον, a wild animal which is beyond the control of the people, makes the command seem even more unreasonable. Finally, θίγῃ is used (suggested by its use in the preceding line of Exod. xix. 12) instead of ἁψάμενος, both meaning 'touch', but the former indicating a much lighter touch than the latter. The author uses θίγῃ to specify that the beast only has to touch the mountain lightly for the consequences to take effect, thereby emphasizing the severity of the warning.

Hebrews xii. 21 (Deut. ix. 19)

The author of Hebrews uses this quotation to show that Moses, as well as the people, was made afraid by the revelation of God in the giving of the first covenant. The first two words of the quotation express Moses' fear of God's anger against the children of Israel for making the golden calf. The last two

[1] Parallels in LXX[23] Cl Al Chrys Thdrt M.T. Targums.

[2] *Cong.* 177 (31) (Colson and Whitaker, *op. cit.* IV, 549 and 551).

words, καὶ ἔντρομος, are apparently added to make Moses' statement of fear even stronger, since ἔντρομος is generally used to express trembling or shaking in connexion with fear.[1]

Hebrews xii. 26 (Hag. ii. 6)

The quotation has been changed to emphasize οὐρανόν by the addition of οὐ μόνον and ἀλλά, the omission of καὶ τὴν θάλασσαν καὶ τὴν ξηράν, and the exchanged positions of τὴν γῆν and τὸν οὐρανόν. This is to show that those who are 'warned from heaven' will be at least as accountable as those who were 'warned on earth'. Since in Heb. xii. 18–29 the author has used γῆν and οὐρανόν, respectively, as symbols of the revelation at Sinai and the revelation to this generation, the reference to Hag. ii. 6, already understood as a prophecy of the messianic age,[2] indicates that those who reject the revelation through Jesus will receive the same judgement as those who rejected the revelation given at Sinai.

Hebrews xiii. 5

This saying is found in several different forms in a number of places in the LXX: Gen. xxviii. 15; Deut. xxxi. 6, 8; Jos. i. 5; and I Chron. xxviii. 20. None of the LXX forms is exactly the same as in Heb. xiii. 5, although LXX^{A} for Deut. xxxi. 6 differs only in that the verbs are in the third person. The identical text as in Heb. xiii. 5 is found in Philo's *De Conf. Ling.* 166 (32),[3] and Clement of Alexandria's *Stromata*, II, 20,[4] suggesting that this form had an Alexandrian source.[5] Philo[6] uses the saying as an assurance that God will help men to control their unbridled natures: God in his loving-kindness has given a message of hope to those who love discipline. The author of Hebrews appears consciously to avoid giving the citation this interpretation by not relating it to the situations mentioned in the first part of the chapter which give opportunity for the 'soul' to show its 'wild' nature: treatment of strangers, care of prisoners, and maintenance of marital fidelity. Rather, he relates it to his admonition, 'Keep your life free from love of money, and be content with what you have' (xiii. 5), indicating that God will provide for all physical needs. This is consistent with its use in its context in Genesis, Deuteronomy, and Joshua, in which God promised to give his people a land for their own.[7] The author of Hebrews does not change the form of the

[1] Cf. five occurrences of ἔντρομος in LXX: Ps. xvii. 8; Ps. lxxvi. 19; Dan. x. 11 (Θ); Wis. of Sol. xvii. 10; and I Macc. xiii. 2.

[2] Cf. *Sanhedrin* 97*b* (Epstein, *loc. cit.*).

[3] Colson and Whitaker, *op. cit.* IV, 101.

[4] Migne, *op. cit.* VIII, 1072.

[5] P. Katz, 'Οὐ μή σε ἀνῶ, οὐδ' οὐ μή σε ἐγκαταλίπω Hebr. XIII 5. The biblical source of the quotation', *Biblica*, XXXIII (1952), 524; Spicq, *op. cit.* I, 336.

[6] Philo may have originated this form of the text, starting with Gen. xxviii. 15 and enlarging it from Deut. xxxi. 6, 8, and used the combined form with reference to Jacob. Katz, *op. cit. Biblica*, XXXIII (1952), 523f., and *op. cit. Z.N.W.* XLIX (1958), 220ff.

[7] This is also the interpretation given in *Midrash Rabbah*, Gen. lxix. 6 (H. Freedman and M. Simon, eds., *Midrash Rabbah*... (2nd ed. London, 1951), II, 633) and Lev. xxxv. 2 (*ibid.* IV, 447).

citation used by Philo, but puts it in a new context. The form is very suitable for the author's purpose in Hebrews as it incorporates both the triple negative and the first person form of the verbs to make the quotation a strong promise by God to care for his sons.[1]

Hebrews xiii. 6 (Ps. cxvii. 6)

By the omission of καί after βοηθός[2] the citation is made more terse.[3] Since the author is citing this verse as a type of slogan which the Christian can repeat in times of persecution, it is appropriate that he make it as terse as possible. Ps. cxvii has always been associated with the Passover by the Jews and with Easter in the Church,[4] which is significant since the author in the following passage refers to the sacrifice of Christ and seems to allude to the sacrament of the Eucharist.[5] It is possible that this saying was used by Christians as a slogan to refer to the experience of the Eucharist (cf. Heb. xiii. 9).

RECONSTRUCTION OF TEXT

The above analysis indicates that possibly four of the citations (Heb. iv. 4; viii. 5; ix. 20; and xiii. 5) have readings borrowed from Philo, one citation (x. 30*a*) was borrowed from Romans, and one citation (i. 6) was borrowed from a liturgical form. The problem before us is which of the remaining variations from $LXX^{A/B}$ were originated by the author of Hebrews and which were borrowed from other sources. Of the remaining 48 variations, 26 have no known textual parallels while 22 are found elsewhere. It may be that those variations without parallels were drawn from unknown sources, while, on the other hand, it is also possible that the parallels to the variations in Hebrews were influenced by the text of Hebrews. The solution to the problem seems to be in determining the origin of the variations in Hebrews.

There are several possibilities to consider. (1) These variations may have originated to correlate the Greek more closely with the Hebrew. However, only two (Heb. xii. 5–6 and xiii. 6) more literally translate the Hebrew. (2) They may have originated during the transmission of the LXX to clarify the interpretation or to give a better style. Only a few of these variations, though, even fit into the original LXX context. For only a few of the variations (ὡς ἱμάτιον in Heb. i. 12,[6] ἀπαγγελῶ in ii. 12,[7] and the variations in x. 5–7[8]) has it been postulated that they originated in the context of the

[1] Spicq, *op. cit.* II, 419.

[2] Parallels in $LXX^{\aleph,R,55,156,286}$ it Gal. Ps. Aug Tert Cyp M.T. Targums. Textual evidence is split for both LXX and Hebrews. However, the evidence indicates that καί was originally in LXX and omitted in Hebrews. Cf. Zuntz, *op. cit.* p. 172.

[3] Moffatt, *op. cit.* p. 229.

[4] Werner, *op. cit.* p. 159: 'Ps. 118...is both the Easter and the Passover psalm *par excellence* and was always so understood.'

[5] Cf. n. 5, p. 313 above.

[6] C. Buchel, 'Der Hebräerbrief und das Alte Testament', *Theol. Stud. u. Krit.* LXXIX (1906), 522.

[7] Kistemaker, *op. cit.* p. 32.

[8] Bleek, *op. cit.* II (2), 634; Weiss, *op. cit.* II, 578.

LXX text itself. Most of the variations as found in the LXX MSS. are obviously the result of external influence. (3) The variations may have originated in liturgical usage.[1] However, even S. Kistemaker, who tries to apply this theory to all the Hebrews citations, is willing to conclude such for only six of the citations (Heb. i. 6; i. 7; iii. 7–11; iv. 4; viii. 8–12; xiii. 5).[2] (4) Hebrews itself may provide the most logical context in which these variations originated. Our research yields a pattern of significant changes which must be more than accidental. That interpretational significance was found for every variation from LXX^A/B except two (ἐπὶ τὸν οἶκον... ἐπὶ τὸν οἶκον and λέγει, both in Heb. viii. 8–12) indicates that they were intentionally chosen by the author. It is difficult to imagine that he could have found different O.T. texts with appropriate variations in every instance or that he would have had a single LXX text with all these readings differing from LXX^A/B to which he would attach interpretational significance in every instance. Since the variations were so appropriately used by the author, it is logical to conclude that they were originated by him.[3] Accordingly, we must conclude that the textual parallels to these variations (excepting those in Philo and Romans) were probably influenced by the text of Hebrews.

This result is in sharp contrast to that derived from an examination of the LXX^A/B readings in Hebrews for which LXX^A and LXX^B differ: no interpretational significance can be found for the 23 of these readings in Hebrews. Some commentators have suggested that the author of Hebrews chose one reading instead of another, but for grammatical or stylistic reasons: εἶπον (A) used instead of εἶπα (B) in Heb. iii. 7–11 to avoid the juxtaposition of two alphas in the phrase εἶπα ἀεί;[4] and the use of the anacoluthon διδούς (A) instead of διδοὺς δώσω (B) in Heb. viii. 8–12 to attain a simpler structure.[5] However, careful study indicates that these changes along with all the others for which LXX^A and LXX^B differ probably originated in the transmission of the LXX rather than in Hebrews. Certainly, no reason can be found in Hebrews for the author to have chosen the readings he has instead of the alternative readings. In fact, the author of Hebrews would probably have chosen the alternative reading as more appropriate in some instances if he had known it, for example ἀδικίαν (A) instead of ἀνομίαν (B) in Heb. i. 8–9.[6] Thus, there is no evidence that the author knew two different readings in these instances and chose between them. We conclude that the particular

[1] See n. 4, p. 303 above.

[2] Kistemaker, *op. cit.* pp. 13–60. He himself concludes that the author of Hebrews originated the variations in ten of the citations and implies that he did in two others: Heb. i. 8f., i. 10–12, ii. 6–8, vi. 13f., ix. 20, x. 5–7, x. 16f., x. 37f., xii. 5f., xii. 26; by implication ii. 13*a* and x. 30*b*. Heb. ii. 12 may have been changed by the author or in the liturgy, while four others he considers to have been borrowed from other sources: Heb. viii. 5, x. 30*a*, xii. 20, and xii. 21.

[3] Cf. conclusion with estimates of originality of the author of Hebrews in use of O.T. by Lindars, *op. cit.* p. 29; and Moule, *op. cit.* p. 80.

[4] Bleek, *op. cit.* II (1), 443.

[5] Winer, *op. cit.* p. 717.

[6] Bleek, *op. cit.* II (1), 162, even concludes that ἀδικίαν is the reading in Hebrews because it gives better sense with δικαιοσύνην.

LXX^A/B readings in Hebrews represent the text of the LXX used by the author of Hebrews in these instances.

The results of this investigation make it possible to reconstruct most of the LXX text used by the author of Hebrews for his quotations. Since it has been established that he intentionally used most of the variations from LXX^A/B found in his citations, it may be concluded that his LXX in these instances originally had readings as in LXX^A/B. Where the LXX^A and LXX^B readings differ from one another, his LXX had the readings as found in his citations. However, for two such instances it is not possible at this point to determine which was in his LXX text as he used variations differing from both LXX^A and LXX^B, that is ἐν δοκιμασίᾳ in Heb. iii. 9 instead of ἐδοκίμασαν (B) or ἐδοκίμασάν με (A) as in Ps. xciv. 9, and εὐδόκησας in Heb. x. 6 instead of ἐζήτησας (A) or ᾔτησας (B) as in Ps. xxxix. 7. Likewise, in the case of the two apparently non-intentional changes in Heb. viii. 8–12 (ἐπὶ τὸν οἶκον...ἐπὶ τὸν οἶκον and λέγει) it is impossible to conclude definitely whether these were in the author's LXX text or were changes made by the author. However, in the light of the pattern which we have discovered, it is likely that these two variations from LXX^A/B were made by the author and that the text of his LXX at these points was like LXX^A/B.

NATURE OF TEXT

Upon the basis of this reconstruction it is now possible to examine the nature of the text used by the author of Hebrews. P. Katz states that the proper question to be asked about the quotations in the N.T. is: 'Does a quotation follow the primitive text or an "edited" one?'[1] It is now possible to answer this question for the quotations in Hebrews.

In order to distinguish between primitive and edited readings, it is necessary to have two readings to compare. Edited readings can be identified as those with (1) more literal translations of the Hebrew text;[2] (2) grammatical and stylistic modifications to remedy grammatical problems, to avoid hiatus, and to substitute more modern word forms;[3] and (3) textual changes to correspond to particular interpretational views.[4] We can compare the readings used by the author of Hebrews for which there are existing variants, which include the differences between LXX^A and LXX^B and the significant variants from LXX^A/B. The comparison of these instances clearly indicates the nature of the text used by the author, since they include readings unavailable to the author.

Of the instances in which LXX^A and LXX^B differ, the text used by the author of Hebrews has primitive readings for all but two. The two edited

[1] Katz, *op. cit.* *Z.N.W.* XLIX (1958), 222.

[2] B. J. Roberts, *The Old Testament Text and Versions*... (Cardiff, 1951), pp. 29, 120; E. Hatch, *Essays in Biblical Greek* (Oxford, 1889), pp. 136f.; Lindars, *op. cit.* p. 27.

[3] Roberts, *op. cit.* p. 155.

[4] *Ibid.*

readings in Hebrews are both stylistic changes to avoid hiatus: εἶπον ἀεί (A) instead of εἶπα ἀεί (B) in iii. 10 and κἀγώ (A) instead of καὶ ἐγώ (B) in viii. 9.[1] This seems to indicate that such stylistic items were the first to be revised in the LXX. About half of the variants not found in Hebrews are more literal renderings of the Hebrew or correspond to the usual rendering of the Hebrew. Hebrews has τὸν αἰῶνα τοῦ αἰῶνος (A) instead of αἰῶνα αἰῶνος (B) in i. 8; αὐτοὶ δέ (A) instead of καὶ αὐτοί (B) (which also eliminates the grammatical problem created by δέ)[2] in iii. 10; λέγει (A) instead of φησίν (B) (which also provides a consistent translation of the same Hebrew word in the passage)[3] in viii. 8; διδούς (A) instead of διδοὺς δώσω (B) (also eliminating the anacoluthon)[4] in viii. 10; οὐ μὴ διδάξωσιν (A) instead of οὐ διδάξουσιν (B) in viii. 11; πολίτην...ἀδελφόν (B) instead of ἀδελφόν...πλησίον (A) or πλησίον...ἀδελφόν (Q) (a further editing of LXX^A to correspond to Hebrew word order) in viii. 11; μικροῦ (A) instead of μικροῦ αὐτῶν (B) in viii. 11; ὁλοκαυτώματα (A) instead of ὁλοκαύτωμα (B) in x. 6; δίκαιός μου (A)[5] instead of δίκαιος (B) in x. 38; and παιδεύει (A) instead of ἐλέγχει (B) in xii. 6. As indicated above, because of the nature of the changes in iii. 9, it is not possible to determine precisely the LXX text used by the author of Hebrews. However, LXX^B has the greatest divergence from the Hebrew in eliminating both με's. LXX^T has both με's corresponding literally to the Hebrew while LXX^A represents an intermediate stage with με only after ἐδοκίμασαν. As Heb. iii. 9 does not have either με, it probably is based on the primitive text as in LXX^B. Likewise for Heb. x. 6, which has εὐδόκησας instead of ἐζήτησας (A) or ᾔτησας (B), the more literal translation of the Hebrew, the author's LXX text possibly had the primitive reading as in LXX^A.

Another three variants not found in Hebrews are stylistic or grammatical refinements. Hebrews has ἀνομίαν (B) instead of ἀδικίαν (A) (which is a more literal antithesis to δικαιοσύνην)[6] in i. 9; σύ (B) instead of σοί (A) (a newer form occurring frequently in the first-century papyri)[7] in i. 12; and (ε)ἶδον (A) instead of (ε)ἴδοσαν (B) (a newer form increasingly used in the Hellenistic period and frequently used in the LXX)[8] in iii. 9. Two variants not found in Hebrews appear to be corruptions incurred in the transmission

[1] See F. Blass and A. Debrunner, *A Greek Grammar of the New Testament and Other Early Christian Literature*, trans. and rev. by R. W. Funk from 10th German ed. (Cambridge and Chicago, 1961), p. 11; W. W. Goodwin, *op. cit.* p. 12; and H. St J. Thackeray, *A Grammar of the Old Testament in Greek according to the Septuagint* (Cambridge, 1909), p. 137.

[2] Cf. Bleek, *op. cit.* II (1), 444, and Delitzsch, *op. cit.* I, 172.

[3] Cf. Driver, *op. cit.* p. xlviii.

[4] Kurtz, *op. cit.* p. 258; J. H. Moulton, *A Grammar of New Testament Greek* (Edinburgh, 1906–29), I, 222 ff.; Moffatt, *op. cit.* p. 110; C. F. D. Moule, *An Idiom Book of New Testament Greek* (Cambridge, 1953), pp. 179f.

[5] Considered to be the original LXX reading by Manson, *op. cit.* pp. 133f. However, it is thought to have originated in Hebrews by Moffatt, *op. cit.* p. 157; Zuntz, *op. cit.* p. 173; Lindars, *op. cit.* p. 231.

[6] Bleek, *op. cit.* II (1), 162.

[7] Thackeray, *op. cit.* pp. 93f.

[8] *Ibid.* pp. 212f.; Blass and Debrunner, *op. cit.* p. 44.

of the text. Heb. ii. 7 has δόξῃ καὶ τιμῇ (B) instead of δόξῃ καὶ τιμήν (A alone). LXX^R has δόξαν καὶ τιμήν, which is probably an attempt to correct the mistake in LXX^A by making two accusatives in place of the one dative and the one accusative form. The phrase as in LXX^B appears to be the original translation and was in the LXX used by the author of Hebrews. Heb. viii. 10 has διαθήκη (A) instead of διαθήκη μου (B). The additional μου appears to be an instance of haplography from the preceding sentence.

Two other variants not found in Hebrews seem to have originated for interpretational purposes. Heb. ii. 6 has τί (B) instead of τίς (A). Τίς was evidently originated by a Christian scribe to emphasize the messianic interpretation and application to Jesus.[1] Heb. viii. 10 has αὐτοὺς καὶ ἔσομαι (B) instead of αὐτοὺς καὶ ὄψομαι αὐτοὺς καὶ ἔσομαι (A). The additional phrase was probably suggested by its occurrence in Gen. ix. 16 and Exod. xii. 13, in both of which God sees a sign as a reminder of his covenant. The addition was made in certain witnesses to indicate that God promises to be the God of those on whose hearts he sees the sign written.

It is significant that where LXX^A and LXX^B are of mixed nature within a single citation, having both primitive and edited readings, Hebrews in at least two citations has only the primitive readings. In viii. 8–12, there are five primitive readings in agreement with LXX^A, and two with LXX^B. There is one each with LXX^A and LXX^B in i. 8–9. There are also four with LXX^A and possibly one with LXX^B in iii. 7–11. These facts give evidence as to the primitive nature of the LXX text used by the author of Hebrews.

The generally primitive nature of the readings in Hebrews is further confirmed by comparing the significant variants from LXX^A/^B which are not found in Hebrews with the LXX^A/^B readings in Hebrews. In all these instances Hebrews has the primitive readings. Hebrews has σὺ...κύριε in i. 10 which is omitted in LXX^ℵ; ἑλ(ε)ίξεις in i. 12 instead of ἀλλάξεις (LXX^ℵ* and others); μοι ἔδωκεν in ii. 13*b* instead of ἔδωκέν μοι (Syro-Hexapla and others); ἐπείρασαν in iii. 9 instead of ἐπείρασάν με (LXX^RT and others); and νόμους in viii. 10 instead of νόμον (LXX^ℵ*, Syro-Hexapla and others). All these variants are more literal renderings of the Hebrew. Another group of variants are grammatical and stylistic changes. Heb. v. 6 omits εἶ found in LXX^ℵR and other witnesses to supply the missing copula.[2] Heb. vi. 14 has εἰ μήν instead of ἦ μήν as in Philo, 13 minuscules, and other witnesses, to introduce the usual classical form.[3] Heb. viii. 9 omits ὥστε before ἐξαγαγεῖν as found in 13 minuscules and Theodoret to provide the usual conjunction to introduce a consecutive clause.[4] Heb. viii. 10 and x. 16 have καρδίας instead of

[1] Cf. Bleek, *op. cit.* II (1), 246, and Zuntz, *op. cit.* p. 48, who maintain τίς is the original reading in Hebrews because it is given this interpretation by the author. Τίς is supported only by N.T.^P46CP.

[2] The omission of copula forms, other than third person forms, is rare in Greek. Cf. W. W. Goodwin, *op. cit.* p. 195.

[3] Cf. Thackeray, *op. cit.* pp. 83f., and J. H. Moulton, *op. cit.* I, 46.

[4] Cf. W. W. Goodwin, *op. cit.* p. 308, and Moule, *op. cit.* p. 141.

καρδίαν as in LXX$^{\aleph}$, Clement of Alexandria and Chrysostom, to correlate with διάνοιαν, its parallel in the preceding line.[1] Heb. i. 5*b* omits the καί before ἐγώ as in five minuscules and other witnesses. The additional καί appears to be a reflexion of the citation by Paul of II Sam. vii. 14 in II Cor. vi. 18, where it is used to connect the citation with the preceding one. Evidently, certain scribes mistook the καί as being part of the citation, and it found its way back into certain LXX texts and witnesses. Two variants not found in Heb. viii. 8–12 appear to have interpretational significance. Heb. viii. 9 has πατράσιν αὐτῶν instead of πατράσιν ὑμῶν as in LXX$^{\aleph}$, Clement of Alexandria and six other Church fathers. The variant ὑμῶν appears to have been particularly used by the Church fathers to emphasize that the contemporary Jews were like their disobedient ancestors. Heb. viii. 10 omits the phrase καὶ τῷ οἴκῳ 'Ιούδα found in 14 minuscules and other witnesses. The additional phrase is repeated from Jer. xxxviii. 31 in xxxviii. 33 to eliminate the discrepancy between the two references.[2] Thus, there is overwhelming evidence that the author of Hebrews used a LXX text of a generally primitive nature.[3]

ORIGIN OF LXX

These results may now be considered in relation to the two theories as to the relationship of the LXX^{A} and LXX^{B} texts: (1) they represent separate translations of the Hebrew text, variously edited over a period of time to result in their present forms;[4] (2) they are related to one translation of the Hebrew but now have various differences as the result of two separate histories of editing.[5] Of course, the relationship of LXX^{A} and LXX^{B} must be considered separately for each section of the O.T., as the LXX is not a uniform piece of translation.[6] However, most of the quotations in Hebrews are from the Prophets and the Writings (19 of the 29), which were translated later than the Law and have a separate tradition.[7] Also, all but two of the

[1] Moffatt, *op. cit.* p. 110.

[2] Cf. B. F. Westcott, *The Epistle to the Hebrews* (2nd ed. 1892, Grand Rapids, Mich., reprinted 1952), p. 223, and Bleek, *op. cit.* II (2), 454.

[3] The O.T. readings in Hebrews remain comparatively free from editing through the second century as is evident in their use by the Church fathers. In 12 instances for which LXX^{A} and LXX^{B} differ, the Church fathers follow the text as in Hebrews in all but one instance, that is the different word order of Ps. ci. 26 (Heb. i. 10). Where we now have significant variants from the LXX$^{A/B}$ text, the Church fathers have the variants in six instances while following the LXX$^{A/B}$ text in nine instances. Thus we have a total of 20 primitive readings as against seven edited readings, a slightly higher percent of edited readings than in Hebrews.

[4] A. Sperber, 'New Testament and Septuagint', *J.B.L.* LIX (1940), 248, proposes that LXX^{A} and LXX^{B} represent two translations, with LXX^{A} having a close affinity with the asterisk readings of Origen's *Hexapla*, and LXX^{B} with the obelus readings.

[5] This view was held almost universally up to this century. Recently, M. L. Margolis proposed that LXX^{A} and LXX^{B} represent two recensions in Joshua: LXX^{A} as a witness for the Constantinopolitan Recension and LXX^{B} as a witness for an Egyptian Recension. See H. M. Orlinsky, 'On the Present State of Proto-Septuagint Studies', *J.A.O.S.* LXI (1941), 81 ff.

[6] Roberts, *op. cit.* p. 181.

[7] *Ibid.* p. 116; Thackeray, *op. cit.* pp. 12–16, and *The Septuagint and Jewish Worship: a study in origins* (London, 1921), pp. 12f.

instances used for determining the nature of the text in Hebrews were from the Prophets and the Writings. Thus, certain generalizations about the relationship of LXX^{A} and LXX^{B} in the Prophets and the Writings may be made from the evidence in Hebrews.

The results of this study indicate the improbability of LXX^{A} and LXX^{B}'s representing two translations. The evidence indicates that the author used a single text, a text which does not correspond with either LXX^{A} or LXX^{B} in their present forms. The LXX^{A} and LXX^{B} texts are mixed in nature, while the author used primitive readings almost entirely. Since it is impossible to think that the author would have selected only the primitive readings from a text of a mixed character, his text must have had a generally primitive character. If LXX^{A} and LXX^{B} represent two separate translations, it is difficult to account for the overwhelming agreement between the present forms of LXX^{A} and LXX^{B}, both of which are of mixed character.[1] Rather, the evidence in Hebrews supports the theory that LXX^{A} and LXX^{B} represent two traditions from a single translation, which may be called the Septuagint. According to this theory, the terms 'primitive' and 'edited' may be taken at their face value. The author of Hebrews had a text of this translation still in its comparatively pure, 'primitive' form. It appears that this text was used by the author of Hebrews before it had been subjected to any very extensive editing.[2] The two edited readings indicate the beginning of such a process. It is significant that both of these were edited in order to avoid hiatus. Through the process of editing, the texts of LXX^{A} and LXX^{B} eventually became a mixture of primitive and edited readings, as they are in their present forms. The differences between them are the result of two traditions, probably due to their existence in two separate localities. Thus, LXX^{A} and LXX^{B} for the Prophets and the Writings appear to be two descendants of one translation, an early form of which was used by the author of Hebrews.

[1] Sperber, *op. cit.* p. 266, says LXX^{A} and LXX^{B} were brought into agreement at the expense of LXX^{A} because LXX^{B} had become more or less the established text.

[2] Roberts, *op. cit.* p. 120, implies that the editing process did not begin until the second century A.D.

Justin's Old Testament quotations and the Greek Dodekapropheton Scroll

P. KATZ, Cambridge

The Editor of the Greek Bible, both O. and N. T., while welcoming patristic quotations as valuable additions to the manuscript evidence, is aware of delicate critical questions. Patristic texts suffer in transmission, and revision is nowhere more frequent than in Biblical quotations. The Vienna edition of Cyprian's *Testimonia* is the renowned example for a mistaken decision[1] which, in neglect of Hans von Soden's careful monograph[2], is still reflected in Legg's edition of St. Mark[3]. Among Greek texts the outstanding example is Philo the MSS of whose text fall into two groups. One quotes the LXX text of our best MSS and at times is even superior to them. The other which exists only in a minority of treatises, but in a few as the only text surviving, is different. As late as 1950 it was necessary to demonstrate that the latter is confined to the lemmata unconfirmed by Philo's own exposition and characteristic of a textual stage of LXX text centuries later than Philo[4]. However early any Father may be we must never take his quotations at their face value. Late text forms may obliterate the original quotations. Lagarde[5] was right in speaking of *patres rescripti* in comparing such texts to palimpsests.

The first author after Philo to quote the LXX frequently is Justin Martyr. The only evidence for his text is a carelessly copied 14th century MS[6]. Except for some marginal readings there are no variants. This text cries out for emendation[7]. A

[1] This was first seen by Lagarde, Sanday, and Turner.

[2] Das lateinische N. T. in Afrika zur Zeit Cyprians, Leipzig 1910.

[3] Hans von Soden, Gnomon 13 (1937) 53.

[4] Peter Katz, Philo's Bible, Cambridge 1950.

[5] P. de Lagarde, Mitteilungen II, pp. 53ff.

[6] Harnack, TU 1, 1/2, p. 79.

[7] Wolfgang Schmid, Die Textüberlieferung der Apologie des Justin, ZNW 40 (1941) 87—138.

Reprinted from *Studia Patristica,* Vol. 1, Part 1. Berlin, 1957.

number of the quotations are proved by the context to have been doctored. There are numerous passages in which Justin takes a stand against "Jewish falsifications of the Bible" and passionately defends as genuine, readings which in fact are early Christian interpolations. As was seen repeatedly[1] but ignored by Swete[2], these interpolations have disappeared from the long quotations heading Justin's exposition and have been replaced by the text of the LXX as we read it now. As a result the peculiar points on which Justin's arguments depend are no longer found in the lemmata to which he refers[3]. The same applies to those quotations of which our single MS gives only the first and last verses connected by *καὶ τὰ ἑξῆς* or *καὶ τὰ λοιπὰ μέχρι* (*ἄχρι*) *τοῦ*... Here also we miss the very words and verses to which Justin appeals as proof and for the sake of which he premises a whole psalm or chapter[4]. While this latter feature is due to sheer negligence, the former reflects the course of textual history. The peculiar readings, mostly in the Psalms, were primitive Christian interpolations[5], creatures of a day, and accordingly survive only in remote backwaters, such as the Greek and Sahidic of Upper Egypt, and in Fathers down to Clemens Alexandrinus Origen with his emphasis on the Hebrew was the first to eliminate them.

---

[1] A. Hilgenfeld, Theol. Jahrbb. 9 (1850) 394f. 398ff.; E. Hatch, Essays in Biblical Greek, Oxford 1889, pp. 188ff.; W. Bousset, Die Evangelienzitate Justins des Märtyrers, Göttingen 1891, pp. 19ff.; A. Rahlfs, Septuaginta-Studien II, 1908, pp. 203ff.

[2] Introduction to the O. T. in Greek, Cambridge 1900, pp. 417ff. Nothing in B. J. Roberts, The Old Testament Text and Versions, Cardiff 1951.

[3] Ps. XCV.5 *ἐκεῖνα γὰρ* εἴδωλά *ἐστι δαιμονίων* Dial. 41. 55; Ps. XCV. 10 *ἐβασίλευσεν* ἀπὸ τοῦ ξύλου Dial. 41 (neither enlargement in Dial. 73); Ps. XVIII. 6 ἰσχυρὸς *ὡς γίγας δραμεῖν ὁδόν* Dial. 69 (cf. Dial. 76). *ἰσχυρός* is omitted in the full quotations Apol. I 40, Dial. 64.

[4] ZNW 46 (1955) 137, n. 11; E. Hatch, op. cit., p. 188.

[5] I. L. Seeligmann, The Septuagint Version of Isaiah. A Discussion of its Problems, Leiden 1948, traces similar "actualizations", as he calls them, in the Isaiah Septuagint, and still more in the Mishna, for which I refer to his paper: Voraussetzungen der Midraschexegese, Congress Volume Copenhagen, 1953, Supplement to V. T., vol. I.

A second group of quotations in Justin presents a completely different aspect. Far from being either naïve or Christian, they are learned and Jewish, isolated patches of post-septuagintal interpretation grafted upon an otherwise unmistakable LXX text. They therefore are closely similar to, or identical with, Aquila and Symmachus who cannot have been Justin's sources. It was therefore plausible to consider these quotations as due to late sporadic revision similar to that observed in the inferior Philonic evidence[1]. A fresh discovery, however, seems to open up a different vista. Fragments of a Greek scroll, containing the Minor Prophets, written late in the first century A. D. and hidden during the revolt of Barkochba, still await final publication. After their discovery in August 1952, D. Barthélemy gave a preliminary account of them[2] which, based on the fragments so far studied, is a masterpiece of circumspection and condensation. The new text is true LXX, yet approximated to the Hebrew in places when the LXX translation proved mistaken or loose. Its literalness verges on clumsiness; at times a Hebrew different from that underlying the LXX is followed. The changes mostly concern single words in a context easy to identify owing to its very imperfection[3].

Barthélemy begins with calling to mind the setting of Justin's Dialogue with the Jew Tryphon. During the suppression of Barkochba's insurrection Justin complains to Tryphon about the attitude of contemporary rabbis towards the LXX. Its exactitude is doubted in places and a "Jewish" interpretation is offered instead. Messianic passages are emasculated and prophecies pointing to Jesus Christ disappear. Justin discusses some passages according to both the traditional and the "Jewish"

[1] Theol. Zeitschrift 5 (1949) 16f.; Actes du Premier Congrès de la Fédération Internationale des Associations d'Études Classiques, Paris 1951, pp. 176ff.

[2] D. Barthélemy, Redécouverte d'un chaînon manquant de l'Histoire de la Septante, Revue Biblique 60 (1953) 18—29.

[3] According to H. S. Nyberg, Studien zum Hoseabuche, Uppsala Univ. Årsskrift 1935 no. 6, the translation was made from a careless copy and betrays unfamiliarity with the exegetical tradition, an inadequate knowledge of Hebrew, and, in consequence, irresponsible conjecture.

texts and sometimes bases his exposition on the latter in order to meet his opponents half-way.[1] B. then enumerates the reasons which had hitherto shaken confidence in the view that the MS version of Justin's quotation is reliable. This scepticism he says is disproved by the new scroll. A fragmentary quotation of Micah IV. 3—7, compared with Dial. 119, not only indicates numerous agreements against the LXX, but even the gaps are much more easily filled in from Justin than from the LXX. A second text, Zech. II. 12, at least has *ἐκλέξεται* = Dial. 115 against *αἱρετιεῖ* LXX. No more parallels to Justin's quotations are found but the new text, in being more literal and in rendering a Hebrew text different from ours, is seen to be the work of early Jewish revisors. To characterize its peculiarities B. compares the later Jewish translations. Aquila agrees in 18 out of 28 instances with the scroll and the relation to Symmachus is still closer, Theodotion yields little.

These statements are impressive in themselves, but only preliminary. The climax is his demonstration that the only four known remnants of the Quinta, the Jewish translation found by Origen in Nicopolis near Actium in Greece, have their exact parallel in the new text. He combines this fact with Grossouw's observation[2] that the Upper-Egyptian translations, of which at least the Achmimic is complete, have twelve agreements with the Quinta and never disagree with it, while Theodotion disagrees four times, Aquila and Symmachus eleven times each. Thus he identifies the new text with the Quinta, as a first attempt out of which the more consistent texts of Aquila and Symmachus developed. Being fresh translations following throughout principles which the Quinta only sporadically applied to the LXX, they are the culmination of a development and not its beginnings. Thus far Barthélemy.

Among the texts compared the Upper-Egyptian have been proved to be undoubtedly pre-hexaplaric approximations to the

---

[1] None of the few quotations which Justin professes to borrow from the Jews' own version are taken form the Minor Prophets.

[2] W. Grossouw, The Coptic Versions of the Minor Prophets. Monumenta Biblica et Ecclesiastica 3, Rome 1938, p. 112.

Hebrew and the same can be said even about a Greek source neglected by Barthélemy, Pap. Washington W[1]. All these texts are third century. They, and still more so the Greek source of the Egyptian texts, cannot have been influenced by the hexaplaric LXX column; for the Hexapla, though completed about 250, was hidden for half a century in Caesarea before Pamphilus and Eusebius published its LXX column, early in the fourth century. There are more examples of pre-Origenic revision, some of them recently discovered texts, such as the Chester Beatty and the Antinoopolis Ezechiel[2], and Daniel 967[3], and in the Pentateuch not only Pap. 963 (Num. Deut., ca 200 A.D.) shows similar revisory influences but, as has been recently demonstrated, in Exod.-Deut. the majority group of MSS led by A represents a pre-hexaplaric approximation to the Hebrew[4]. The same has long been suggested for Job by Burkitt[5] and is now proved by an early third century Berlin fragment containing a stichus from Theodotion[6]. For Judges W. G. Lambert has pointed to insertions (XII. 11f.) from the Hebrew, yet prior to Origen[7].

In this context Barthélemy's discovery is welcome because for the first time the provenance of an early Hebraizing revision is traced, so that in the Minor Prophets this form of text almost ceases being anonymous[8]. He has not made this point; but it clearly

---

[1] H. A. Sanders, The Minor Prophets in the Freer Collection. Univ. of Michigan Studies, Human. Series vol. XXI, New York 1927, pp. 25—29. Among the agreements of W with Justin is the wrong breathing *ἀνθάρῃ* Mic. IV. 3.

[2] J. Ziegler, ZAW 61 (1945/8) 76—94; Ezechiel, Göttingen 1952, p. 28; Nachtrag zu Ezechiel in his Daniel, Göttingen 1954, pp. 77f.

[3] J. Ziegler, Daniel, pp. 19ff.

[4] D. W. Gooding, Recensions of the Septuagint Pentateuch, London 1955. Reviews in ThLZ 80 (1955) 596f. and WdO II, p. 294.

[5] The Old Latin and the Itala, Cambridge 1896, pp. 8f. 32—34. According to him Cyprian quotes the original Greek Job, Ambrose the text of our Greek uncials which was supplied from Theodotion previous to Origen, and the Origenic text is quoted by later Latin Fathers.

[6] Theol. Zeitschr. 5 (1949) 22; Actes (cf. p. 345 n. 1 above), p. 181.

[7] In a review of I. Soisalon-Soininen, Die Textformen der Septuagintaübersetzung des Richterbuches, V. T. II (1952) 185.

[8] Some of the variants shared by Justin and the new text are due to the parallel text Is. II. This applies to four of the five coincidences of Mic. IV. 3 = Is. II. 4; the fifth, *οὐ μή*[1], agrees with the Isaiah text

emerges from his material and the parallels given above. We cannot yet tell how much more we shall learn from B.s full edition. We may, however, never know whether Justin's strongly Aquilanic readings *ἐπηρμένον αὐτό* = נִשָּׂאהוּא Mic. IV. 1 (LXX *μετεωρισθήσεται*); *φωτιοῦσιν ἡμᾶς* for יוֹרֵנוּ IV. 2 (LXX *δείξουσιν ἡμῖν*), and his odd *ποταμωθήσονται* = נָהֲרוּ IV. 1 (LXX *σπεύσουσιν*) were taken from this new source and may therefore be primary, or interpolated from Aquila at a later date and therefore secondary. In addition there are some similar readings in the Apology and the question whether a "Jewish" text like B.s "Quinta" and its reflection in the Dialogue plays a part in the Apology too becomes legitimate, though we may never know the answer. The two readings which I am going to adduce are each found in one of Justin's quotations, while in the others we read the LXX text. The first is Apol. I 52 *εἰς ὄνειδος* = לְחֶרְפָּה Is. LXIV. 11 (10), where 𝔐 has לְחָרְבָּה and 𝔊 *συνέπεσεν*. Justin's text is identical with that of Symmachus but the full quotations Apol. I 47 and Dial. 25 have the LXX wording. Here 𝔐 (and 𝔊) are certainly correct. If, however, Justin followed a revised text throughout, the "correct" version found in the long quotations may nevertheless be secondary. The second example is found in Apol. I 50 where we first read Is. LIII. 12, followed by a full quotation of Is. LII. 13 — LIII. 8. In LIII. 12. 𝔐 has יַפְגִּיעַ which the LXX did not understand and therefore rendered by *παρεδόθη*, one of its guess words applied wherever there was a blank in this translator's very imperfect Hebrew. Instead Aquila says *occurret*, Symmachus *ἀντέστη*, and Theodotion *torquebit*. Justin's translation *ἐξιλάσεται* differs from all of them, and is excellent. B. would doubtless trace it to the "Quinta". Elsewhere, however, Justin has the LXX text (Apol. I 31, Dial. 13). In neither passage does Ziegler's edition refer to Justin.

It is worth while considering the date of origin of all these pre-Origenic Hebraizing texts. It cannot be later than any of

---

as read by S* and a few others. Similar influences from parallel texts are frequent; they disclose an unguarded attitude which, however, does not exclude an early date.

its witnesses. How much earlier it may be can only be inferred from more general considerations. Philo, about 40 A. D., quotes and expounds the unadulterated LXX as an inspired text from which an equally inspired exposition draws the most profound mysteries. In this he represents a Judaism still unshaken by the cumulative experience of Christianity in its midst, which in its rise both usurped the LXX and turned it against the Israel in the flesh, and of the destruction of the temple which brought to an end the second commonwealth. Before the Jewish war the Jewish Christians in Jerusalem had done nothing to sever the ties connecting them with temple worship. After the collapse, however, the final break occurred. The task of consolidation required fresh methods, and one of the chief means was work on both Hebrew and Greek Scriptures. Any looseness, hitherto tolerated, became intolerable. As to the Hebrew, attention was given first to fixing an authoritative text and, much later, to determining the Canon of Scripture. In the Greek also there were two stages. The first was that of adjusting the traditional LXX by emending what was worst. This stage is represented by our new text and by all the pre-hexaplaric Hebraizing revisions mentioned above. As B. has well seen, it cannot be understood otherwise than as the work of Jewish scholars working after, perhaps very soon after, 70 A. D. The second stage, beginning half a century later with Aquila, goes farther. It was then no longer a question of emending the LXX in places. The LXX had been baptized into Christianity, as it were, and, apart from this, no longer tallied with the reconstituted Hebrew Bible, either quantitatively or qualitatively. Thus its place was taken by completely fresh translations. After less than a century the Church caught up with this development through Origen's Hexapla. Yet St. Augustine's struggle before accepting the Vulgate shows how much the Church resented this break with its past which was a transition from Hellenism to Rabbinism. Meeting these qualms the Vulgate was in fact a compromise both in the way in which Jerome was either accommodating or else took over untouched the apocryphal books of the LXX.

Seen from the Jewish angle things moved alarmingly quickly. The Quinta, however little we may know about it, had been one of their great texts[1]. Not only was it deemed worthy of filling the last column in the hexaplaric Psalter found by Cardinal Mercati in the Ambrosiana in 1896, but this column had marginal variants which, according to the clear testimony of Origen and Eusebius, refer to its second edition. In this it compares with the translations of Aquila and Symmachus of which too there existed second editions. In consequence, within a century there were three great Jewish Bibles in Greek: the Quinta, an emended LXX from the last quarter of the first century, and two entirely new translations, Aquila's and Symmachus', each roughly fifty years later than its predecessor. If B. is right the last Jewish LXX introduced the methods which came to prove useful for wholly fresh translations, after they had been used sporadically only in the Quinta. It may be too early to trace this development in detail, but a succinct note may be useful in presenting some additional material for a comparison of these very methods common to the Quinta, Aquila, and Symmachus[2].

Certainly any final assessment must wait for the full edition. It has still to be seen whether other finds in the same cave might turn the scale in favour of a later date. However, as was said before, B.s own assessment rests on two strong points. The first is the close relationship to the Upper-Egyptian versions (and Wash. W), which are doubtless pre-hexaplaric and early, since time must be reserved between the versions and its Greek archetype. The second is the historical development with its three stages of initial deference to the LXX, the revisions, and finally their replacement[3].

[1] After more than fifty years reference must still be made to the brilliant paper of Eduard Schwartz, Zur Geschichte der Hexapla, Nachr. d. Gött. Ges. d. Wiss., Phil.-hist. Klasse, 1903.

[2] (See below p. 351, appendix 1).

[3] (See below p. 352, appendix 2).

Appendices

No. **1** (see above p. 350): Even after the publication of the full text the basis for comparing the new text with the remnants of the "Three" is likely to be narrow. To widen the range I have gone through the Psalms in Field's Hexapla. The following is confined to a few observations about the relation between Aquila and the Quinta. If we may trust our evidence they have much in common. (1) They share the translations *ἰσχυρός* for אֵל Ps. IX. 32 (X.11); XXVIII. 3, and *στερεέ μου* for צוּרִי XXVII.1, *εἰς νῖκος* for לָנֶצַח XLVIII.10 etc, and *νικοποιῷ* for לַמְנַצֵּחַ LV. 1, *ἑκουσιασμοί* for נְדָבוֹת CIX. 3 (cf. ThLZ 77 (1952) 157). (2) Their relationship remains obvious even though there are small differences: חֻקֵּי־ is *ἀκριβασμοί* in *A'*, *ἀκριβάσματα* in *E'*, the causative יַרְקִידֵם XXVIII. 6 *σκιρτώσει* in *A'*, *σκιρτοποιήσει* in *E'*, and for יְנוּבוּן *bring forth fruit A'* has *γεννηματίζοντες*, *E' γεννηματίσουσι* which recalls the great number of Aquila's both wilful and dreadful coinages. (3) Aquila selected a single Greek equivalent for any Hebrew word without regard for its connotations, even if these were not covered by the Greek word chosen, so that his translation frequently cannot be explained without recourse to the Hebrew. In this he is joined by the Quinta, for both use *γεῦμα taste* for טַעַם XXXIII. 1 (superscription), *ἀγαθὸν γεῦμα* for טוּב טַעַם *good insight* CXVIII. 66 where the LXX has the good paraphrase *χρηστότητα καὶ παιδείαν*, expressing the connotation of טַעַם, *prudence, intelligence.* (4) In other instances the Quinta shares another of Aquila's peculiarities, that of rendering homonyms or near-homonyms "homonymously", although the words have only a common sound, not an identical sense. Thus e. g. when both translate עָתָק *insolent* LXXIV. 6 by *παλαιός old* = עָתֵק, this need not be a confusion due to lack of exegetical tradition of which Aquila had only too much; it may, on the contrary, be deliberate preference for identical renderings of all derivatives of the same root, though the tradition underlying the pointing (which we may suppose they knew well) indicates that the two words stand for different meanings[1]. (5) We might even be justified in maintaining the same explanation in instances when the same had happened already in the LXX, in which one would think rather of confusion. I give two examples. The Bible has the homonyms צִי I *ship* and צִי* II pl. *desert animals*. Among the four instances of צִי I Ez. XXX.9 is corrupt and can be emended from 𝔊𝔖, Is. XXXIII. 21 has a correct *πλοῖον*, but the remaining two passages, of which the latter alludes to the former, both think of יצא Qal, Num. XXIV. 24 𝔊 *ἐξελεύσεται* cf. 𝔖𝔗o; Dan. *Θ* XI.30 *οἱ ἐκπορευόμενοι*, or Hiphil, Num. XXIV.24 Sam. יוֹצִיאֵם and Dan. 𝔊 XI.30 *ἐξώσουσιν αὐτόν*. For צִיִּים II the confusion is confined to Aquila and the Quinta: Is. XXIII. 13 *A' ἐξερχομέ-*

---

[1] Elsewhere *A'* renders עתק by *μεταίρειν* Gen. XII. 8; Prov. XXV. 1; Ps. VI. 8; he has *μέταρσις* for עָתָק in I. Rg. II. 3; Ps. XXXI. 19, and for עָתִיק in Is. XXIII. 18.

νοις and Ps. LXXIII. 14 *A' ἐξελευσομένοις, E' ἐξεληλυθότι*. Not only is here צִי II traced back to the better known root יצא and treated as its derivative, but by taking recourse to יצא the two homonyms are rendered alike, and in doing so Aquila and the Quinta dealt with צִי II as the LXX had occasionally done with צִי I. This is an intricate procedure worth elucidation. Also in a second instance the precedence of the LXX seems to have been followed to some extent. Whereas חיל III = יחל *wait, put one's trust in God* was generally well understood, the rare חיל II *continue in vigour* was not. In Ps. IX. 26 (X. 5) *βεβηλοῦνται* 𝕲 read יָחִילוּ as יֵחַלּוּ Niphal of חלל *to profane* cf. *inquinatae sunt* Vulg., *polluuntur* Ps. Rom.; *A' E' ὠδινήσουσιν* use the meaning of חיל I cf. Ps. Hebr. *parturiunt*. (6) Among Aquila's oddities his *ποταμωθήσονται* = נָהֲרוּ Mic. IV.1 is one of the oddest. He may be right in considering נהר as a denominative, for in Hebrew it is rare and confined to the metaphorical use of peoples convening, *streaming*. Greek, however, allows of nothing comparable. It would be strange to find the same device in the Quinta. When in Ps. XLIII. 20 Symmachus and the Quinta render תְּכַס from כסה *to cover* by *ἐπεπώμασας* from *ἐπιπωμάζω cover with a lid or cover*, it would be hazardous to surmise that the Quinta chose this word instead of *ἐπικαλύπτω* (𝕲 *A'*), because it wanted to point to כּוֹס *cup* = *πῶμα* (*drink, draught*), *drinking cup* (Hesych.). In fact Symmachus uses *ἐπιπωμάζω* in Ps. LXVIII. 11 for the *hapax legomenon* אטר, the simple verb in Ps. CXXXIX. 10 for כסה. Moreover *πῶμα lid* and its derivatives are frequent in non-Attic Greek from Homer onwards. (7) Beside similarities a development could be traced from the Quinta to Aquila and Symmachus, but such speculations are better postponed.

No. 2 (see above p. 350): There is an earlier very full discussion of the problems posed by Barthélemy's find by P. Kahle, ThLZ 79 (1954) 81—94. He concurs with Ziegler and others in considering this text and other Hebraizing papyri as pre-Christian and Jewish, but would date them before the break in the history of Judaism to which, in fact, they owe their origin. These texts he parallels with that from which, as he still insists, Philo took those quotations which do not tally with our best LXX evidence. For the Upper-Egyptian versions of the Minor Prophets, on the other hand, he assumes dependence on the Hexapla, because they have many doublets which remind him of the existence side by side of the obelized old text and Origen's asterized insertions. Nothing in the nature of the texts concerned justifies this artificial division nor do the doublets prove his point. In the mistranslation of Amos VI. 6 *τὸν διϋλισμένον οἶνον* for בְּמִזְרְקֵי יַיִן the Achmimic certainly adds the correction *ἐν φιάλαις* after *οἶνον* as a doublet; but how is Kahle to explain Justin's reading *ἐν φιάλαις οἶνον* Dial. 22, since he is convinced that non-septuagintal readings in Justin are genuine? If Justin's reading was current in 150 A. D., Achm. is most unlikely to have drawn on the Hexapla for its doublet. There was no access to the hexaplaric LXX column either in the second or third centuries and, besides, none of the hexaplaric MSS has this reading.

There is a wealth of supporting arguments in Kahle's comprehensive paper, among them some which have long been shown to be gravely mistaken (Theol. Zeitschrift 5 (1949); Actes . . ., 1951). Although there is little hope to convince Kahle I would conclude by putting right one of his fresh mistakes. On col. 89 Kahle characterizes the Oxyrrhynchus fragment 1007 (Brooke-McLean, Numbers and Deuteronomy, p. VI) = 907 (Rahlfs) as one of many varieties of a Greek Targum which strove after ever closer approximation to the Hebrew. His sole reason is the reading *τῇ γυναικί* Gen. II. 24 which he says is "closer to the text used in the N. T. (Mt. 19, 5, Eph. 5, 4 *sic*) and in Philo (leg. alleg. 11, 14 *sic*) than the Christian Septuagint". Certainly A and its satellite *y* (121) — and the margin of the Catenae MS *v* —, and, after A the Cambridge editions, have it. However, as early as 1907 Nestle (Sept.-Stud. V, p. 24), who also gave a long list of untrustworthy singular readings of A in Gen., warned against Swete's text and tersely stated: "Nach diesem Tatbestand kann gar kein Zweifel sein, daß der Dativ im A. T einfach Eintrag aus dem Neuen ist (Mt. 19, 5; Mc. 10, 7; Eph. 5, 31)." The majority reading *πρὸς τὴν γυναῖκα* = Eph. V. 31 (against 𝔓[46] and other witnesses) adopted by Rahlfs is the true LXX, and *τῇ γυναικί* a backreading from the N. T. Philo alleg. II § 49 and Eph. reflect the original LXX, and Pap. 1007 too joins the overwhelming majority of our evidence. Pap. 1007 does nothing to support the theory of a variety of Greek Targums.

VI. THE SIGNIFICANCE OF THE SEPTUAGINT

The Phenomenon of Biblical Translation in Antiquity

Sebastian Brock

To-day one takes for granted that the Bible should be translated, yet the translation of the Hebrew Old Testament into Greek was a phenomenon quite without parallel in antiquity. We are nowadays familiar with the practice of translating great works of literature, both religious and secular, but this tradition of literary translation originated in the Western world only with the Romans, and they of course confined their attention to Greek.

Reprinted from *Alta: The University of Birmingham Review*. Vol. 2, No. 8, 1969.

Translation, in the Greco-Roman world, from other languages into Greek or Latin will be found to be concerned exclusively with either works of an eminently practical nature, such as agricultural treatises, or official documents of one sort or another ranging from international treaties to marriage contracts.

The Jewish scriptures were the only oriental religious writings to achieve the distinction of translation into Greek. This is all the more surprising when once consideres the great interest taken by Greeks and Greek speakers in, for example, Zoroaster: a vast pseudepigraphical literature was composed in Greek in Zoroaster's name, yet no one ever considered going back to the original and translating the *Gathas*.

If one looks beyond the Greco-Roman world there are at least some precedents for the translation of religious texts. For example, among the multitude of works collected in the library of that Assyrian bibliophile, Asshurbanipal (7th century BC), is a bilingual (Akkadian/Sumerian) hymn to the moon god Sin. There are indeed quite a number of Akkadian translations of Sumerian works of religious character—hardly a surprising situation, considering the large debt of the Babylonians and Assyrians to the Sumerians in the sphere of religion. But the translators who produced the Septuagint, the Greek version of the Old Testament, can hardly have been aware of all this; and in the Greek world there is no precedent at all.

The fact that the Jewish scriptures did get translated was due, as I shall try to show, to the peculiar position of Judaism in the Greek world, with a very large proportion of its practicers actually Greek speaking, and without any knowledge of the original language of their own sacred scriptures.

How then did the Septuagint actually come into existence? I will begin by giving the picture as hellenised Jews liked to see it. According to a legend, already current in the 2nd century BC, the Pentateuch was rendered into Greek at the command of the Macedonian king of Egypt, Ptolemy II Philadelphus, who lived in the early part of the 3rd century BC. The actual translators were 72 specially selected Jews, six from each of the twelve tribes; and their work took them exactly 72 days, 'as though this co-incidence had been intended' (*Ep. Aristeas* 307). In a later and more developed form of the legend the translators were said to have worked paired off in separate cells, and the divine character of their translation was assured when it was found that the resulting thirty six versions agreed word for word with one another.

The earliest formulation of this legend about the origin of the Greek Pentateuch (nothing is said of the rest of the Old Testament) is to be found in a letter which purports to be written by a certain Aristeas, a courtier of this king, Ptolemy II, to Philocrates his brother. Neither men are Jews, and the implication throughout is that the whole project was undertaken primarily to enable Greeks to read the Jewish scriptures. The letter, however, is manifestly the work of a Jew, and one writing in the second half of the second century B.C. Furthermore it is evident that the letter was not even destined for Greek readers, but simply for fellow Jewish ones—Jews, that is, of the Greek speaking diaspora in Egypt. The whole aim of the letter was in fact to authenticate the Greek version of the Pentateuch in the face of criticisms that were evidently circulating at about this time, criticisms that the Greek translation did not accurately reflect the current Palestinian Hebrew text. Only this interpretation of the letter's purpose can explain the great stress laid on the origin of the Hebrew text from which the translators worked: it had been brought especially for the purpose from Jerusalem,—and selected by the High Priest himself, the copies of the Hebrew Bible in Alexandria not being sufficiently accurate for such an important undertaking.

The Letter of Aristeas thus lays the initiative for the translation with Ptolemy II, and not, as one might naturally have expected, and as I shall argue, with the inner need of the Jewish community in Egypt, to whom Hebrew had become a foreign language. A number of modern scholars concur with the author of the Letter on this point. It would be thoroughly in keeping, they argue, with Ptolemy II's character and interests to have commissioned such a translation; indeed it may even have been part of a general programme by the Ptolemaic government of translating oriental law codes.

On the surface this seems plausible enough, but when looked at closely the parallels adduced of other translations are not close. While it is true that the Egyptian law code was probably rendered into Greek at the orders of the Ptolemaic administration, this differs in two important respects from the case of the Greek Pentateuch. First, the Jewish community in Egypt was vastly smaller in size than the native Egyptian one, and in comparison to the latter, quite insignificant in the eyes of the government. And secondly: while the Pentateuch was known to the Greek world as *Nomos*, or Law (a very inadequate rendering of the Hebrew word *Thora*), actual laws play only a small part in it, and even these laws, being primarily of a religious character, are of quite a different type from those of the Egyptian law code. In point of fact there is clear evidence from contemporary papyrus documents that the Jews in Egypt did not pay much attention to their own (Biblical) law codes. For example, they lent money among themselves at interest, something condemned not only in the Bible, but later too in the Talmud.

Again, the few instances of large scale official translation in the Greco-Roman world, like that of the Carthaginian Magon's work on agriculture—commissioned by the Roman Senate in 146 BC—were all of a definately practical nature; and the Pentateuch does not conform to this requirement either.

This leaves pure curiosity as the only possible motivation for Ptolemy II, if in fact he really did commission the work of translation. But this too comes up against a difficulty. While Ptolemy II's cultural interests were certainly far-reaching, to commission a translation of the whole Pentateuch seems to be totally atypical of the Greek attitude to orientals: their interest, where there was interest at all, was selective. They were not interested in oriental cultures *per se*.

Wholesale translation of oriental texts was in fact totally alien to the Greek outlook, and nothing of the sort was done by the Ptolemies from Egyptian, as one might more obviously have expected, supposing for the moment that the Greek Pentateuch really was commissioned by Ptolemy II. The kind of works they were interested in were historical compilations, written in Greek, such as the History of Egypt by the Egyptian priest Manetho, which covered the period down to the conquest of Alexander the Great. But even Manetho's work, which was dedicated to Ptolemy II, had not been commissioned by the king, as the Letter of Aristeas claims for the Greek Pentateuch.

The conclusion must be that the picture given in the Letter of Aristeas of the circumstances accompanying the translation of the Pentateuch are completely misleading. There is, however, one feature in the account that does ring true: when Ptolemy commissions the work, it is not Greeks who set out to learn Hebrew in order to undertake the translation, but bilingual orientals (in this case of course Jews) are sought out for the purpose. This is a very significant point, and conforms with the general practice of the Greco-Roman world, where the few oriental works that (at a later date) did find their way into Greek or Latin were almost invariably undertaken by native speakers who also knew Greek (and, incidentally, usually on their own initiative). This state of affairs continues to apply in the patristic period, when a certain amount of oriental hagiographic material was translated into Greek, and likewise in Byzantine times, with the Greek rendering of such things as the collection of Indian tales, later known as *Kalilah and Dimnah*, which was to have an enormous vogue all over Europe, especially in the 17th and 18th centuries.

This means that the Christian scholars, Origen in the 3rd century and Jerome in the 4th, who undertook to study Hebrew for the purposes of improving Biblical translations from that language, were doing something virtually without precedent. And on the negative side it is clear that the Greek found his own literature completely self-sufficient, and was never moved by curiosity or interest to learn any oriental language. This was largely a manifestation of cultural snobbery: the Romans did not hesitate to learn Greek and translate from Greek, since Greek had a long literary history whereas they had none. *Graecia capta ferum victorem cepit*—Greece enslaved, in turn enslaved her uncultured conqueror. The important point in Horace's neat lines is that the conqueror was uncultured. The Greeks themselves had been victorious over the East under Alexander and his successors, and the East had just as glorious a cultural history behind it as did Greece, conquered by Rome. But it was precisely because the Greeks already had a cultural tradition of their own that they did not fall under the spell of their new subjects.

To return to the Septuagint. Once it is admitted that the picture given by the author of the Letter of Aristeas—namely that the translation was commissioned by Ptolemy II so that Greeks might have access to Jewish scriptures—is a false one, we are left with the alternative: that the work was done *by* Hellenised Jews, and *for* Hellenised Jews, something that one would have expected all along, and which would never have been questioned, but for the fantasy presented by the Letter of Aristeas. On Sabbath there would be regular reading of the Law and the Prophets, and the written Greek translation may well have taken its origin in such a milieu: at first the practice would have been to make use of an oral translation only, but eventually it would have appeared more practical to have a written one, especially when bi-lingual speakers grew more and more scarce. Such, anyway, was the manner in which the Aramaic translations of the Old Testament, the Targums, came into being, but in their case at a much later date, Hebrew still being, in the 3rd century B.C., a living language in Palestine, even though in rather a limited way.

But liturgical requirements were hardly the only incentive for undertaking the translation of the Pentateuch (and, later, the rest of the Old Testament) into Greek. St. Paul calls the Pentateuch a schoolmaster, and this, for a Jew, was true in a much wider application than Paul makes of it. A schoolmaster who speaks a language which his pupils do not understand is naturally not going to have much success. Hellenistic Jews must have been brought up on the Old Testament (and the Pentateuch in particular) in the same way that Greeks were educated on the classics of Greek literature. It has often been said that Homer was the Bible of the Greeks, but it would be just as accurate, if not more so, to say that the Bible was the Homer of the Jews.

The combination of these two needs, then, the liturgical and the educational, were the real incentive behind the Greek translation of the Pentateuch. Once this momentous first step had been taken, it was only natural that the other religious writings of the Jews should follow suit—that is to say, the Prophets (which in Jewish terminology also include most of the 'historical books'), and the Writings (Psalms, Job, Proverbs, etc.), not to mention books later excluded from the canon, such as Enoch.

Once the decision to undertake such a task of translation had been made, how were the translators to go about it, since they had no real precedent to work on? The Septuagint (the name is extended from the Pentateuch only, after the LXX(II) translators, to the whole of the Greek Old Testament) contains a wide variety of styles of translation, ranging from the very free and often paraphrastic renderings of Job and Proverbs, with a delight in Homeric vocabulary, through the undistinguished but generally acceptable Greek of the Pentateuch (itself not a unity), to the painfully literal style of books like Samuel, or, worse still, Ecclesiastes. This variety of styles in fact follows a more or less chronological development, beginning with the more free type, and gradually moving towards the excessively literal one; and side by side with this, is the continual desire to 'correct' existing translations, bringing them into closer line with their Hebrew originals. (It is generally supposed by modern scholars that the Pentateuch was the first to be translated. Job and Proverbs, despite their greater freedom, are probably later. They stand apart because of their subject matter, belonging to the category of wisdom literature, which was particularly liable to transformation in the process of translation).

The lack of any precedent on which the translators could work helps to explain some of the more surprising features of the translations, such as the complete lack of consistency in the rendering of technical terms instanced in the description of the temple fittings at the end of Exodus. It was only with time that any attempt was made to normalise technical terms. A similar situation is found in the early church of the Western Roman Empire when it became necessary to transfer Christian technical terms like 'Saviour', 'Baptist' etc. from Greek into Latin. At first there was great variety of usage, but gradually it became regularised, with each Greek term allowed only one Latin equivalent.

In the case of the Septuagint standardisation had in fact already begun in a small way in the course of the practice of oral translation in synagogue, before a written translation had been undertaken. The name of God, which in the Authorised Version appears as 'Jehovah' or 'the Lord', and in modern writers as 'Yahweh', is a case in question. By the third century B.C. the Tetragrammaton, or divine name, was considered too sacred to pronounce, and instead of observing a holy silence whenever it appeared in the course of reading the scriptures, the practice was to substitute *Adonai* ('my Lord') for 'Yahweh'. Now throughout the Septuagint Yahweh is regularly rendered by the Greek *Kyrios* ('Lord', whence, *via* the Vulgate, 'the Lord' of English translations). What is striking, however, is that *Kyrios* is treated as a proper name. Nevertheless this process had not gone very far, and did not include such things as the attribute of Yahweh, 'Sabaoth', where the various renderings in modern versions go back to the plurality of terms to be found in the Septuagint—'of Hosts', 'Almighty', and the simple transliteration, 'Sabaoth'.

Because of this lack of a satisfactory technique of translating, the Greek Bible contained many inadequacies, and critics were soon to be found who pointed out that there were often considerable differences between Hebrew and the Greek. These criticisms certainly came from Palestine (where Hebrew was still a live language), rather than Egypt, and they posed a serious problem for hellenistic Jewry, who naturally wished to read the word of God in an authentic form.

One reaction to this dilemma is to be found in the Letter of Aristeas, whose real purpose, as has been seen, was to reassure Alexandrian Jewry that the translators of the Septuagint (*i.e.*, in this case, the Pentateuch only) employed the best Hebrew manuscript possible as a basis for their work, and that the whole undertaking had the blessing of the Jerusalem High Priest himself. This process of idealisation soon developed into a full scale claim for the inspiration of the Greek Pentateuch (and, by extension, the whole Greek Old Testament). Philo of Alexandria, writing in the first half of the 1st century A.D., goes so far as to say that the authors of the version should be called, not so much translators, as 'prophets and priests of mysteries, whose sincerity and singleness of thought has enabled them to concur with the purest of spirits, the spirit of Moses' (*Life of Moses*, II.vii.40). To Philo a prophet was essentially a person who transmitted to mankind a message that he had received from God. The prophet is thus an interpreter, and so the translators, as interpreters of the word of God in Hebrew for the benefit of Greek speaking Jewry, could with some justice be called prophets. And if the translation itself was inspired, then there was no need to worry if it in fact differed a little from the Hebrew original—revelation could, after all, take on different forms.

But Philo's high regard for the Septuagint was not universal. Over a century earlier than Philo, roughly contemporary with the Letter of Aristeas, a Palestinian Jew in the preface to his Greek translation of his grandfather Jesus ben Sira's work, known now under the title Ecclesiasticus, excuses the inadequate nature of his own work, and points out that even in the Law and the Prophets the original and the translation will often be found to differ when compared.

The translator's quandary is of course a universal one: should one be faithful primarily to the individual words, or to the general sense, of the original? Basically there are the two alternatives—first, free translation aiming at conveying the general sense, and second, literal translation, whose aim it is to produce an exact replica of the original, even down to such details as word order, though at the expense, as a result, of the sense. Obviously there is no exact dividing point between these two, and to-day the general practice is to adopt varying degrees of freedom, with literal translations confinded to schoolboy 'cribs' and so on. In antiquity, however, the literal style of translation played a much greater part, and the distinction between free and literal is usually clear, especially once certain theories of translation had developed, for then the character of a translation definitely denoted a *parti pris.*

In the case of the free translation, it could be said that the original is brought to the reader, but with the literal type the reader is forced to go to the original; or, to put it another way, in the first it is the reader who is stationary, but in the second it is the original. Looked at like this, in a case where the original is regarded as particularly sacrosanct, the tendency will be to make the reader approach it, and not it the reader. The original become as it were Aristotle's unmoved mover. And the same with pedagogical cribs, where the whole point is to bring the reader to the original work.

Within the Christian Church the implications of all this were first formulated by Jerome, in the fourth century, though the ideas behind the formulation went back, as will be seen, a long way. Jerome's rule, by which he himself abided, was to adopt a literal style of translation where sacred texts were concerned, but a free one for all others. As he explains in one of his letters (no. 72): 'in scripture, even the order of the words is a mystery'. The semi-apologetic note to be discerned here is designed for Jerome's more cultured critics, for whom the free style was the rule for rendering all literary works—exemplified above all in Cicero's translations from the Greek. Cicero, who himself had not a little to say on translation methods, actually condemns literalism as a feature of *interpretes indiserti*, boorish translators. And indeed, if one looks at actual practice in Roman times, literal translation will be found only in official and legal documents, where the purpose is to avoid any possible ambiguity, while the free style is reserved for literary translations only—indeed it would scarcely be an exaggeration to say that all early Latin renderings from Greek literature were paraphrases rather than translations. Actually, to men like Cicero and Quintilian, translation was primarily an intellectual exercise, and not aimed at any more practical end. The emphasis is thus on the very act of translating and not on the original or the reader. This particular aspect is no longer to be found in the case of Patristic translations, where the emphasis is focussed on the readers' needs.

Returning once again to the Septuagint: No such theories as those just outlined were available to the original translators of the Greek Bible, precisely because their work was totally without precedent. Consequently their work did not fit exactly into either of the two categories of the later theorists, although in general it belongs to the literal camp. However, since, as Jerome put it, 'the very word order of scripture is a mystery', the Septuagint posed a problem, for it was not quite literal enough to convey to its readers these particular mysteries of the Hebrew original. As it has been seen, one solution to this difficulty was to consider the translation itself as inspired. A second solution was to take the more drastic step of actually correcting the translation, in order to bring it into closer line with the Hebrew original. The main Jewish advocate of the first view (already adumbrated in the Letter of Aristeas) was Philo of Alexandria, who significantly did not know Hebrew; in Christian circles this view was supported notably by Jerome's correspondent, Augustine.

The second attitude, which considered the Septuagint to be an inadequate rendering and one requiring correction was found first in Palestinian Jewish circles, and later adopted by Origen, and, more especially, Jerome. The work of these early Jewish correctors in Palestine is only known to us fragmentarily, but recent finds of manuscripts in Israel have thrown a lot more light on their methods, and the gradual improvement of their technique can now be traced to a certain extent, with the whole process culminating in the work of the proselyte Aquila of Pontus, in the early second century A.D.

In 1952 some Bedouin brought a number of parchment fragments containing a Greek text to the Ecole Biblique in Jerusalem (then Jordan). These fragments turned out to be from the XII Minor Prophets in

Greek, but with a text differing in a large number of points of detail from our current Septuagint text. Further finds, announced ten years later in 1962, of fragments of the same manuscript were made, discovered by Israeli archaeologists in the Wilderness of Judaea. The writing of these fragments can be dated with a pretty fair degree of certainty to the first century A.D.

As soon as the text of these fragments was studied, it became clear that they revealed a systematic correction of the original Septuagint version of the Minor Prophets, bringing it into closer alignment with the Hebrew original. The aim of the correctors was to have every detail of the original reflected in the Greek, regardless of the inevitable nonsense—at least for a Greek reader without a knowledge of Hebrew—that often resulted. Their interest was extended to *minutiae*: in Hebrew there is a particle *gam*, meaning 'also, too': in the majority of the translations of the books of the Old Testament this particle is either neglected, or simply rendered by Greek *kai*, 'and'. The revisers, to whom every single word of the original was significant, regularly inserted the Greek particle *ge* wherever the Hebrew had *gam*. Another typical instance resulted in a soloecism in Greek:

Hebrew has two forms of the first person singular personal pronoun, *ani* and *anoki*. The earlier translators of course simply rendered both indiscriminately by the single Greek equivalent, *ego*. The revisers, however, regarded the choice of one or the other of these Hebrew forms as significant and so had to find some means of bringing out the distinction in Greek. Their solution was to render the shorter form, *ani*, by Greek *ego*, but the longer one, *anoki*, by the Greek *ego eimi*, 'I am', regardless of the fact that a finite verb often followed the personal pronoun, thus producing sentences like 'I am (=*anoki*) will purify you', and so on.

This elaborate revision was evidently part of a long process which only reached its climax many years later in the work of Aquila of Pontus. Previous to the publication of these finds of a first century revision, it had generally been assumed by modern scholars that Aquila's second century work consisted of a completely new translation into Greek, but now it is clear that ancient writers were quite correct when they called Aquila's work simply an 'edition', *ie* of the Septuagint, and that this edition merely perfected the technique of bringing the old translations into as exact conformity as possible with the Hebrew. Despite its mechanical character one cannot but admire the ingenuity of Aquila and his anonymous predecessors in their attempt to make the Greek reflect every possible feature of the Hebrew—even the length of individual words. Of course all this makes Aquila's work invaluable for the modern textual critic who wishes to discover whether the Hebrew text he was using differed from the present Masoretic text; but one wonders what, if anything, his readers made of it, unless they already had a knowledge of Hebrew, in order to interpret the version. And possibly it was with a sly malignity that Justinian ordered the Greek speaking Jews in the Byzantine Empire to use Aquila's edition rather than the Septuagint proper. Aquila, who incidentally had an exceptionally good knowledge of Greek, was continually prepared to sacrifice Greek syntax, but he never extended this to altering the gender of nouns, a step which was actually taken in a thirteenth century interlinear version of Jonah into Greek.

Although it is thanks to a Christian scholar, Origen, that most of the fragments of Aquila that we possess survive at all, this extremity of literalism was impracticable to the Church, and even Jerome, to whom the literal style was the proper one for biblical translation, condemns Aquila as being 'enslaved to the Hebrew'. The fact was that the extreme taken by Aquila and his predecessors was only viable so long as some knowledge of the original language survived generally, but as the Christian Church moved away from its Jewish roots very soon this requirement no longer obtained. Aquila is virtually unintelligible without some knowledge at least of Hebrew.

Nevertheless, Christians too are found correcting the text of the Septuagint—but with a very different end in mind, in the case of the most famous of them, Origen. In the third century, conscious of Jewish charges that Christians had in places altered the text of the Septuagint (incidentally quite true), Origen determined to produce an edition of the Septuagint, bringing it into complete agreement with the Hebrew, in order to meet the Jews on their own ground. This he did by comparing the Septuagint with its later editions, in particular that of Aquila, and correcting it from them. The resulting massive work—alas lost except for fragments and a Syriac translation of the Septuagint column—is called the Hexapla, so named because it contained six columns: the Hebrew, a

Greek transliteration of the Hebrew, Aquila's edition, two other Jewish editions of the Septuagint, and the corrected text of the Septuagint.

Origen stresses on several occasions that his edition was meant primarily as a tool in Christian apologetics against the Jews (and the very arrangement of the Hexapla was aimed at helping the Christian controversialist to learn a little Hebrew); and he emphasizes that it is not meant for ecclesiastical use by ordinary Christians. In this, respect for the received text outweighs any scholarly desire that Christians should read as accurate a translation as possible. Implicitly, if not explicitly, Origen seems to have regarded the Septuagint as an inspired work, or at least one hallowed by time and its continued use by the church during the course of two centuries.

Jerome on the other hand is emphatic in denying this, and he states that 'an interpreter and a prophet are two very different things'—referring to Philo's claim that the translators were in a true sense also prophets. Thus, in his Latin version of the Bible, known as the Vulgate, Jerome worked direct from the Hebrew in the Old Testament, and not *via* the mediary of the Septuagint—as Augustine, in his correspondence with Jerome, says he would have preferred. But Jerome was no imitator of Aquila: he intended that his version should be comprehensible to his readers, who had no knowledge of Hebrew, and accordingly some compromise with the 'sense' at the expense of the 'word' had to be made, although in general Jerome considered his work to be of the 'word for word' rather than the 'sense for sense' type of translation.

The basic question that tacitly underlies the various Patristic views of translation never, however, seems to have been properly formulated. It was generally admitted that the scriptures were inspired, but the exact nature of the inspiration is never discussed—did it apply to just the sense, or to the very words as well? If inspiration were verbal, then translations should of necessity be as close as possible to the original Hebrew; and this was certainly the attitude of Aquila and his forerunners, and of the rabbis in general. To them, the Torah or Law was dictated to Moses by God himself, while in the Prophets, it is the Shechinah, or divine presence, which talks to the human mediaries. And in fact the work of Aquila was closely connected with that rabbinic school of the first and second century A.D. which succeeded in stabilising the Hebrew consonantal text, as well as formulating extremely elaborate rules for the exegesis of scripture, taking into account all the *minutiae* of the text. Rabbi Aqiba, the most famous representative of the school, was fond of quoting Deuteronomy xxxii 47: 'for there is no word too insignificant for you', which nicely typifies the attitude of the whole school to Holy Writ.

Such a view of the plenary inspiration of the Hebrew Old Testament placed hellenised Jews and Christians in a difficult position, for they did not know Hebrew, and an Aquila style translation was just about as unintelligible as the original itself. As we have seen, many, like Philo, cut the Gordian knot and claimed that the Septuagint itself was inspired (a claim, incidentally, that has recently been reiterated by the French biblical scholar, Père Benoit). In Christian circles inspiration, and implicitly verbal inspiration, of the Bible seems to have been widely held. Gregory of Nazianzus, for example, states that every accent is significant. But few seem to have considered the full implications of this—just as many fundamentalists to-day, who believe in plenary inspiration, tacitly assume that this applies to the version in which they themselves read the Bible, forgetting the existence of the original, not infrequently at variance with that version.

The first person who actually raised the point seems to have been a certain Agobard Bishop of Lyons, in the 9th century. Agobard pointed out to a correspondent that a belief in the verbal inspiration of the Bible (i.e. the original texts) would logically compel the translator to convey even details such as the gender of Hebrew nouns. The example he gives is the Hebrew *ruah* 'spirit', which is feminine in gender, while Latin *spiritus* is masculine: a translator who believed in verbal inspiration of the original should accordingly treat *spiritus* as a feminine, because even the gender is significant. Since, however, no translator of the Bible has ever done this, it is clear, Agobard says, that inspiration is merely confined to the sense.

Actually this extreme step which Agobard describes was eventually taken, in a thirteenth century interlinear Hebrew-Greek version of Jonah, where the Greek *anemos* 'wind', which is masculine in gender, is construed as a feminine, to conform with the corresponding Hebrew *ruah* (meaning 'wind', as well as 'spirit').

The *modus vivendi* achieved by Jerome, theoretically a literal translation, but in fact making concessions to the sense, was the only satisfactory way out, once a knowledge of the original language had been lost in Christian circles. It was imperative that the version should be intelligible to the mass of the people who heard it read in church. In such a context the Aquila type of translation was an impracticable ideal, though it could have its uses for the preacher who was fond of comparing versions: for such a man Origen's Hexapla, or, in the Latin Middle Ages, Jerome's commentaries, provided an inexhaustible store of information.

From the second century A.D. onwards Greek itself came to be regarded as a foreign language by many converts to the Christian church. The case of the hellenised Jews to whom Hebrew had become incomprehensible repeated itself: as Christianity spread further and further afield, there came to be more and more Christians who knew no Greek. And just as Egyptian Jews had translated the Hebrew Old Testament into Greek, so non-Greek speaking Christians rendered, first the Greek New Testament, and then the Old Testament, into their vernaculars.

Earlier, I mentioned the curious fact that no Greek ever learnt a foreign language in order to translate from it. Nor did he learn one in order to translate into it, although this might have been expected in the case of the missionaries of the early Church, judging from the practice of their modern counterparts. But no, the unwritten rule still applies—the early versions of the Bible are all the work of bi-lingual orientals. Irenaeus, bishop of Lyons in the second century, while interested in converting the Celts in his diocese, never thought of using any other language than Latin or Greek in his missionary activities. But perhaps this example is a little unfair, for in the west, where Latin developed into the various Romance languages, translation of the Bible is always a very late phenomenon, not occurring before the Middle Ages, simply because Latin had a much greater hold on the countryside than did Greek in the east. Thus in the east, where Greek was very much the language of the towns only, the need for vernacular translations came very much earlier. And these translations, wherever their authors are known, are always the work of native bi-linguals, such as Mesrop for Armenian, and Ulfilas for Gothic.

Once again the precise circumstances surrounding the origin of these translations are unfortunately quite unknown or very obscure. But one thing is clear: a written vernacular version was not normally regarded as being an instrument of evangelisation, as it often is to-day. The version was only made at a later stage, some times very considerably later, after Christianity had become well established. This is particularly evident in the case of the Armenian version. For a very long time Armenian speaking Christians had only a Syriac liturgy and Bible, and no written Armenian translation. Here the long delay was partly due to the absence of any written literature at all in Armenian, until Mesrop's creation of an alphabet, (it was in fact, missionary requirements that finally led Mesrop to this step). In the meantime oral translation must have been the practice—there would be a running commentary or translation of the liturgy in the vernacular. In fourth century Palestine, a pilgrim from France, Etheria, found the same situation: the liturgy was celebrated in Greek, but for the benefit of those who could not understand Greek, there were oral translations into Syriac and Latin.

The Akkadian translations of Sumerian texts had originated in interlinear glosses, which with time were extended to a full scale interlinear version. Some at least of the Christian versions of the Bible may have come into existence in a similar way. This certainly seems to have been the case with certain vernacular versions of the Bible in the Latin Middle Ages, and perhaps also with the Coptic versions in Egypt: here we possess, among other things, a Greek manuscript of Isaiah with interlinear Coptic glosses. With some other languages, however, this sort of thing would never have been really feasible, simply because the direction of writing in the original and translation differed, as with Hebrew and Greek, Syriac and Greek, Armenian and Syriac.

The conflict of loyalties between 'word' and 'sense' in translation was recurrent: the controversy was taken up again, for example, by the Arabic translators of Greek philosophical and medical literature in the 9th century. The greatest of these translators, the Nestorian Christian Hunain ibn Ishaq, opted for the 'sense', and that too was the choice of two great great western scholars, whom I should like to quote in conclusion. The first of these is the medieval Jewish philosopher, Maimonides, who counselled a potential translator as follows:

'Let me premise one canon. Whoever

wishes to translate and purposes to render each word literally, and at the same time to adhere slavishly to the order of the words and sentences in the original, will meet with much difficulty. This is not the right method. The translator should first try to grasp the sense of the subject thoroughly, and then state the theme with perfect clarity in the other language. This, however, cannot be done without changing the order of the words, putting many words for one word, or vice versa, so that the subject be perfectly intelligible in the language into which he translates'.

The second is the Renaissance humanist Erasmus of Rotterdam, who writes:

Language consists of two parts, namely words and meaning, which are like body and soul. If both of them can be rendered I do not object to word for word translation. If they cannot, it would be preposterous for a translator to keep the words and deviate from the meaning.

NOTE CONJOINTE SUR L'INSPIRATION DE LA SEPTANTE

A. M. DUBARLE

LA VALEUR DE CERTAINS ARGUMENTS PROPOSÉS EN SA FAVEUR

L'exposé précédent de F. Dreyfus (1) me permet de ne pas rappeler l'état de la question. Je me bornerai à l'énoncé d'un certain nombre de difficultés qui m'empêchent de considérer comme démonstratifs les arguments avancés par les tenants de l'inspiration de la Septante.

I. — Les citations de la Septante dans le Nouveau Testament

L'argument a été présenté par P. Benoit (2) et il a reçu l'assentiment de P. Auvray (3) et P. Grelot (4). Les auteurs du Nouveau Testament ont cité des textes d'après la forme particulière qu'ils avaient reçue dans la Septante et la modification en jeu est essentielle à la force probante de la preuve scripturaire que les apôtres mettent en œuvre. Ils attestent par là que ce texte de la LXX est parole de Dieu et donc inspiré.

Un passage rencontré dans S. François de Sales peut cependant amener à se demander ce que représente une citation d'une version de l'Écriture. « Certes, l'infâme et exécrable action qu'Onan faisait en son mariage était détestable devant Dieu, ainsi que dit le sacré texte du trente huitième chapitre de Genèse ; et bien que quelques hérétiques de notre âge, ...aient voulu dire que c'était la perverse intention de ce méchant qui déplaisait à Dieu, l'Écriture toutefois parle autrement, et assure en particulier que la *chose* même qu'il faisait était *détestable* et abominable

(1) F. Dreyfus, *L'inspiration de la Septante. Quelques difficultés à surmonter.* Voir plus haut, pp. 210-220.

(2) P. Benoit, *La Septante est-elle inspirée ?* dans *Vom Wort des Lebens, Festschrift Meinertz,* 1951, pp. 41-49, repris dans *Exégèse et théologie,* 1961, I, pp. 3-12.

(3) P. Auvray, *Comment se pose le problème de l'inspiration des Septante,* dans *Rev. Bib.,* 59 (1952) pp. 321-336 ; voir pp. 331-332.

(4) P. Grelot, *Sur l'inspiration et la canonicité de la Septante,* dans *Sc. Eccl.* (Montréal), 16 (1964) pp. 387-418 ; voir p. 409.

Reprinted from *Revue des Sciences Philosophiques et Théologiques.* Vol. 49, 1965.

devant Dieu » (5). S. François invoque ici le texte de la Vulgate, très différente dans le mot à mot du texte hébreu original, qui lit : « et ce qu'il avait fait fut mauvais aux yeux de Iahweh ». Mais cette insistance sur les termes propres à la Vulgate ne signifie pas que pour S. François elle soit inspirée.

On répondra que les apôtres n'ont pu faire un raisonnement boiteux dans le moment où ils établissent un point de doctrine capital, qu'ils utilisent un passage de la LXX comme parole de Dieu et qu'ils attestent par là qu'il l'était. La différence entre l'original et la LXX jouait un rôle essentiel dans le raisonnement, ce qui n'est pas le cas dans le texte invoqué par S. François. Tout ceci est parfaitement juste. Mais ce passage peut montrer aussi qu'en citant une version de l'Écriture, en insistant sur des particularités verbales qui la distinguent de l'original, on ne réfléchit pas nécessairement sur ces différences. Une confiance générale dans la valeur de la version suffit à expliquer une utilisation où, sans y prendre garde expressément, ce sont des passages quelque peu modifiés par le traducteur qui sont exploités. S. François savait que la Vulgate était l'œuvre de S. Jérôme, « tant savant homme », mais, à l'exemple du Concile de Trente il vénérait cette « ancienne traduction, laquelle, comme dit le Concile, l'Église a si longuement, si continûment, si unanimement approuvée » (6). Cela suffisait pour qu'il ne se mette pas en peine de comparer minutieusement la teneur du texte dans l'original et la Vulgate à propos d'une citation faite à l'adresse d'un public qui n'était pas spécialement érudit.

Il n'y a pas lieu de supposer plus d'acribie chez les apôtres.

Les auteurs du N. T. ne sont nullement soucieux de distinguer soigneusement l'Écriture de ce qui n'est pas elle. L'époque apostolique s'est préoccupée de transmettre efficacement un dépôt, non d'en faire un inventaire rigoureux, de distinguer ce qui devait être conservé inviolablement à jamais comme parole de Dieu et ce qui n'était qu'enveloppe plus ou moins provisoire. L'Écriture est citée à côté des livres non canoniques : *Hénoch* 1, 9 dans *Jud.* 14-15 ; l'*Assomption de Moïse* dans *Jud.* 9 ; *Ahicar* 88 (ou 114) faisant suite au « vrai proverbe » (*Prov.* 26, 11) dans *2 Pi.* 2, 22 ; un livre apocryphe dans *Mat.* 23, 34 et *Luc* 11, 49, d'après l'avis de nombreux exégètes (7). Certaines citations difficiles à

(5) S. François de Sales, *Introduction à la vie dévote ;* l. III, c. 39. L'orthographe a été modernisée ; les italiques sont dans l'original.

(6) S. François de Sales, *Les controverses;* P. II, c. 1, art. 6 ; p. 176 et 179 dans l'édition d'Annecy, 1892.

(7) Ainsi tout dernièrement S. Légasse, *Scribes et disciples de Jésus,* dans *Rev. Bib.* 68 (1961) ; voir pp. 323-333. Ce texte évangélique est très proche de *Jubilés* 1, 12 (en version éthiopienne) : « et je leur enverrai des témoins afin de leur rendre témoignage, mais ils ne les écouteront pas. Ils tueront les témoins et ils chasseront ceux qui cherchent la loi ». Le rapprochement n'est signalé par aucun des commentaires évangéliques que j'ai consultés. Il est fait par R. H. Charles, *The Apocrypha and Pseudepigrapha of the Old Testament,* 1913.

identifier se rapportent peut-être aussi à des apocryphes. Paul fait allusion à des traditions juives : le rocher dans le désert (*1 Cor.* 10, 4), Jannès et Jambrès (*2 Tim.* 3, 8) tout comme à des données scripturaires. On est persuadé qu'il y a des écritures sacrées ; les citations qui en sont faites nous permettent de reconnaître un noyau indubitable : la Loi, les Prophètes, les Psaumes, d'autres livres encore. Mais nul ne se soucie de donner une liste complète et exclusive. Même l'Apocalypse, qui défend de rien ajouter et de rien retrancher (*Apoc.* 22, 18-19) ne nous a pas rendu le service de donner une énumération définitive et autorisée de ces livres saints, auxquels elle s'est référée tacitement tout au long de ses visions.

Dans ces conditions il apparaît bien incertain de tirer des conclusions précises de la citation des termes de la LXX.

Sans discuter tous les cas qui ont été ou pourraient être allégués, il peut être utile d'en considérer un de plus près : celui du discours de Pierre dans *Act.* 2. Luc rapporte en grec les paroles de l'apôtre. Veut-il dire que Pierre a parlé en grec? Non, assurément. Veut-il même dire que le texte grec qu'il offre est l'équivalent fidèle de l'araméen utilisé par Pierre? Si l'on répond oui, on aboutira à reconnaître que Pierre a reproduit le *Ps.* 16 d'après un targum araméen, oral ou écrit, où se trouvait déjà le sens de « corruption », ce qui est plausible, puisque l'hébreu de Qumrân admettait déjà une telle signification. Mais dans ce cas il n'y a plus de témoignage implicite rendu à la LXX, qui la privilégierait par rapport aux autres versions.

Mais on peut répondre non à la question ci-dessus et dire avec raison que l'attribution à un personnage d'un discours composé ou remanié par le narrateur est un procédé habituel des historiens bibliques ou profanes de l'antiquité. Luc n'a fait que se servir d'un genre admis communément. On peut donc prendre avec souplesse le témoignage qu'il nous donne sur les termes de la prédication de Pierre. Il reste cependant assez difficile de préciser dans quelle mesure l'auteur inspiré engage son jugement sur le détail des affirmations contenues dans un discours plus ou moins fictif qu'il rapporte. A coup sûr il donne implicitement ce discours comme un exemple efficace et salutaire de la prédication apostolique. Mais garantit-il également chaque étape du raisonnement, si bien que nous devrions considérer qu'il fait sienne l'estime de la LXX comme parole authentique de Dieu, qui s'y exprime tacitement? Il ne faut pas se hâter de l'affirmer. Le texte d'*Act.* 2, 25 attribue le *Ps.* 16 à David, et le contexte, en insistant sur la sépulture royale encore visible à Jérusalem, sur la connaissance prophétique chez David des promesses messianiques dont sa descendance était favorisée, montre bien que cette attribution n'est pas une simple manière de parler (8). Il faudrait donc tenir l'origine davidique du *Ps.* 16 comme également couverte par

(8) Dans le texte parallèle d'*Act.* 13, 35-36, l'insistance sur David comme auteur du *Ps.* 16 est bien moindre.

l'inerrance scripturaire. Les partisans de l'inspiration de la LXX sont-ils prêts à faire leur cette conclusion? Quant à soutenir que chaque assertion orale des apôtres, même à se limiter à l'exercice effectif de leur mission religieuse, jouissait d'une inerrance égale à l'inerrance scripturaire, il n'y a probablement pas beaucoup de théologiens qui s'y risqueraient.

Ainsi, jusqu'à plus ample justification, l'argument tiré des citations de la LXX dans le N. T. souffre de plusieurs incertitudes qui empêchent la conclusion d'apparaître comme nécessaire.

II. — La conservation du texte inspiré

P. Grelot trouve un argument en faveur de l'inspiration de la LXX dans le fait que certains livres dits « deutérocanoniques » ne nous ont été conservés que dans cette version : Tobie, Judith, 1 Maccabées, Ben-Sirah (du moins jusqu'à la fin du XIXe s., où les trois cinquièmes environ du texte hébreu ont été récupérés), peut-être Baruch. Si la LXX n'est pas inspirée, « l'Église n'aurait plus en mains que des versions *juridiquement* authentiques, dotées à ce titre d'une canonicité 'équipollente', mais dont la fidélité demeurerait pratiquement invérifiable? La vigilance de la Providence divine aurait-elle été mise en échec à ce point par quelques accidents historiques? » Il serait donc préférable de penser que le texte grec lui-même est inspiré (9).

Il n'est pas tellement clair, en fait, que la perte d'un original inspiré supposerait une négligence ou une inefficacité de la Providence divine, inacceptables en principe, puisque P. Grelot lui-même admet qu'il y eut sûrement des livres inspirés qui se sont perdus au cours des âges, par exemple les documents iahwiste et élohiste, incorporés partiellement dans le Pentateuque, ou des épîtres de S. Paul. Il reconnaît d'ailleurs, que le principe d'une perte possible est d'application difficile (10). Ainsi, d'un côté, il admet qu'un livre inspiré considéré dans sa totalité peut se perdre, quitte peut-être à subsister partiellement dans un livre qui se conservera, et d'un autre côté il ne l'admet qu'à la condition que l'original perdu soit remplacé par une version couverte par l'inspiration. Le principe invoqué aurait besoin, on le voit, d'être établi plus sûrement et précisé.

Un croyant admet sans peine qu'une Providence veille sur la transmission fidèle des livres inspirés dans l'Église. Mais il sait aussi que cette Providence est compatible avec de menus accidents, qui ne com-

(9) P. Grelot, *art. cit.*, p. 410.

(10) P. Grelot, *L'inspiration scripturaire*, dans *Rec. Sc. Rel.* 51 (1963) 337-382 ; voir pp. 378-379. D'ailleurs, ce principe que des écrits inspirés au plein sens du mot aient pu se perdre n'est pas admis par tous les théologiens, ni celui que tous les écrits d'un apôtre ou d'un prophète inspiré étaient couverts par l'inspiration ; voir A. Barucq et H. Cazelles, *Les livres inspirés*, pp. 26 et 32, dans *Introduction à la Bible sous la direction d'A. Robert et A. Feuillet*, 2e éd., 1959, t. I.

promettent pas gravement la fonction religieuse que les livres saints ont à remplir. En dehors de la LXX, le N. T. ne nous a pas été conservé avec une exactitude mathématique ; des mots ont été omis, ajoutés, changés. Le rôle de la critique textuelle est de tendre vers une édition aussi parfaite que possible, mais qui restera toujours une approximation déficiente d'un original inaccessible (par exemple, l'épître dictée par S. Paul). On pourrait dire, il est vrai, que l'Église apostolique, du moins, a possédé un certain temps l'original inspiré lui-même dans toute sa pureté. Sans doute. Mais alors même elle ne possédait pas un texte sans faute de l'A. T. ; elle n'en avait qu'un équivalent quelque peu déformé, suffisant pour le but religieux de la révélation à transmettre.

En certains cas la LXX, par un heureux hasard, nous a conservé des fragments du texte inspiré accidentellement perdus dans le texte hébreu actuellement à notre disposition. Ainsi dans *Ps.* 144 (145), 13 le distique commençant par la lettre *nun* dans cet acrostiche alphabétique manque en hébreu et la traduction s'en trouve dans le grec.

En tout cela il y a une part de hasard imprévisible et dont on ne peut d'avance fixer les dimensions. Tout certain qu'il est d'une Providence veillant à la conservation des livres inspirés, un croyant devra se garder de tracer des limites précises à cette Providence et de décider ce qu'elle peut permettre ou non.

L'application de ce principe si vague serait sujette à des difficultés supplémentaires. Les livres de Tobie et de Judith, par exemple, sont-ils dans leur texte grec une traduction fidèle d'un modèle sémitique, ou un remaniement très libre, comme le suggèrent leurs larges différences d'avec la Vulgate, que S. Jérôme dit avoir exécutée d'après un texte chaldéen (c'est-à-dire araméen) ? Et ce remaniement ultime n'est-il pas seul inspiré, à proprement parler ? L'Église est-elle à son printemps ou à son automne ? Les dix-neuf siècles pendant lesquels lui ont manqué les originaux sémitiques d'un certain nombre de livres saints sont-ils à peu près la totalité de sa durée ou une quantité négligeable par rapport à ce qui lui reste à vivre, durée pendant laquelle une heureuse découverte peut lui restituer le trésor actuellement égaré (11) ? Nous raisonnons au milieu de trop d'incertitudes pour pouvoir conclure avec assurance à partir de ce principe d'une Providence entourant le dépôt des Écritures.

(11) Ceci n'est pas une supposition purement gratuite. A la fin du XIXe s. on a retrouvé des manuscrits couvrant les trois cinquièmes environ du texte hébreu de Ben-Sirah et de minuscules fragments assez détériorés, récupérés à Qumrân, ont permis d'assurer que ces manuscrits médiévaux précédemment découverts n'étaient pas des retraductions tardives. De même on a retrouvé à Qumrân les restes de trois ou quatre manuscrits de Tobie, sur lesquels on n'a encore que peu de renseignements. P. Grelot envisage comme très possibles de nouvelles découvertes de ce genre (*Sur l'inspiration et la canonicité de la Septante*, p. 413).

III. — La création linguistique de la Septante

Les traducteurs grecs de l'A. T. ont dû, estime P. Grelot, « dans une certaine mesure, refondre le langage qu'ils employaient pour que le message de la révélation ne fût point trahi » (p. 406). Une telle entreprise, aboutissant à un texte fixé, qui a transmis l'A. T. à l'Église apostolique et fourni un langage déjà constitué aux écrivains du N. T., aurait, à la différence des targums araméens, constitué « un travail véritablement créateur » (p. 407) et ceci demandait l'inspiration (12).

Le fait même qui est à la base de l'argument ne semble pas avoir l'ampleur qui lui est attribuée. Les traducteurs grecs n'ont pas toujours créé un langage technique, chargé de significations nouvelles. Ceci a été réalisé par la théologie chrétienne pour des mots, comme « personne, nature, consubstantiel, sacrement », etc. Il n'y a guère dans l'A. T. de ces notions techniques, recourant à un vocabulaire spécialisé. La pensée s'y exprime le plus souvent par des comparaisons et un langage non élaboré conceptuellement. Comme terme comportant un contenu vraiment original on pourrait citer « alliance », mais ici au *berith* hébreu correspond presque adéquatement διαθήκη du grec. S'il y a eu création, c'est au niveau de l'hébreu qu'elle s'est réalisée. Mais là où l'importance d'une notion se traduit par le foisonnement du vocabulaire, par exemple pour la « pauvreté », on constate que les équivalences se font au petit bonheur, chaque mot hébreu ayant plusieurs traductions grecques et chaque mot grec correspondant à plusieurs originaux hébreux.

Récemment J. Barr, dans un ouvrage qui bousculait allègrement certaines tendances de la philologie biblique, a contesté qu'il y ait une correspondance régulière de la pensée avec les particularités linguistiques d'une grammaire ou d'un lexique. Ce que le message biblique a d'original s'exprime par des structures complexes : des phrases ou des ensembles littéraires (13). A ce niveau l'œuvre des traducteurs a suivi en gros son modèle hébraïque, sans que les changements d'ordre dans les livres des Rois, les Proverbes ou Jérémie affectent sérieusement la signification de ces écrits.

Ceci soit dit sans vouloir déprécier l'étude de l'usage linguistique de la LXX. Même s'il comporte une très large part de contingence humaine, il reste qu'il a conditionné en fait l'usage du N. T. et des Pères de l'Église : à ce titre il mérite l'attention (14).

(12) P. Grelot, *art. cit.*, pp. 406-407. C'est un aspect particulier de l'argument n° 3 formulé brièvement par F. Dreyfus, plus haut, p. 211.

(13) J. Barr, *The Semantics of Biblical Language*, 1961. Sur cet ouvrage on peut voir *Rev. Sc. ph. th.* 48 (1964) pp. 49-51.

(14) Comme l'a rappelé D. V. Hadidian, *The Septuaginta and its Place in Theological Education*, dans *Exp. Time*, 76, (1964-65) pp. 102-103.

IV. — Le cas du III Esdras

Les paragraphes précédents n'ont fait que polémiquer contre les considérants invoqués en faveur de l'inspiration de la LXX. Toutefois les publications dont ils ont discuté les arguments et les conclusions ont écarté certaines difficultés. Elles ont montré, par exemple, qu'il y a dans l'A. T. hébreu des doublets, tous deux inspirés malgré leurs divergences : les deux recensions du décalogue, les récits que le livre des Rois possède en parallèle avec les Chroniques, Isaïe ou Jérémie. De ce point de vue rien ne s'oppose à ce qu'il y ait un doublet encore plus ample, celui de l'original hébreu et de sa traduction grecque (15).

Cette remarque pourrait aider à formuler quelques réflexions favorables à *III Esdras*, (Esdras A), ou du moins tendant à laisser la question ouverte. Le Concile de Trente, en promulguant une liste des livres canoniques, entendait bien que cette liste était exhaustive et que les livres qui n'y figuraient pas étaient non canoniques. C'est ce que n'a pas reconnu T. Denter, d'après lequel le jugement du concile est « un jugement positif, qui ne veut rien exprimer sur les livres non nommés » (16). Toutefois le Concile n'a pas jugé nécessaire de nommer ces livres non canoniques. Par là il a laissé la possibilité de considérer *III Esdras* comme un doublet de *I Esdras* et de quelques parties de *II Chr.* et *Neh.* (17). Le Concile a affirmé l'inspiration de *I Esd.* Il n'a pas dit que *III Esd.* était un livre substantiellement différent et non inspiré ; il laisse donc la liberté de penser que *III Esd.* présente avec *I Esd.* du texte hébreu le même rapport que les Proverbes ou le livre des Rois dans la LXX avec leur original hébreu : substantiellement le même contenu, mais quelques additions dans le grec et un ordre largement différent. On sait que les définitions d'un concile doivent être interprétées de manière restrictive : « Declarata seu definita dogmatice res nulla intelligitur, nisi id manifeste constiterit » (18). *III Esd.* n'a pas été rangé dans la liste des livres canoniques par le Concile, mais il y a un biais par lequel on peut néanmoins continuer

(15) P. Grelot, *art. cit.*, p. 410 ; P. Auvray, *art. cit.* p. 334 ; de même J. D. Barthélemy, dans sa conférence des Journées bibliques de Louvain, le 26 août 1963.

(16) T. Denter, *Die Stellung der Bücher Esdras im Kanon des Alten Testamentes. Eine kanonsgeschichtliche Untersuchung*, 1962, p. 124. Cet ouvrage a traité de manière trop sommaire et peu exacte le décret du Concile de Trente sur le canon des Écritures ; voir sur ce point les remarques de F. Dreyfus, plus haut, pp. 216-219.

(17) C'est ce que dit T. Denter, p. 129, à cette nuance près qu'il y voit une conclusion nécessaire : « unter dem 'ersten Buche Esdras' des vom Konzil aufgestellten Kanons müssen wir auch Esdras A verstehen ». Il s'appuie sur la prémisse très contestable que le terme « vulgata editio » désignait la Vetus Itala dans la pensée des Pères du Concile. Sur ce point voir les autorités citées en sens contraire dans la note de F. Dreyfus, n. 26.

(18) Ce sont les expressions du Code de droit canonique, can. 1323, 3.

à le tenir pour canonique, c'est de le considérer comme une partie de la LXX, elle-même tenue pour inspirée et canonique.

Ceci soit dit non pour adhérer à cette opinion, mais pour éviter d'invoquer contre elle l'autorité du Concile de Trente.

Conclusion

Des objections ne constituent pas une prise de position personnelle. Pour éviter une attitude purement négative et favoriser un échange de vues dans la clarté, il n'est pas inutile de faire ici quelques brèves considérations.

L'Église nous présente des livres comme canoniques, c'est-à-dire régulateurs de la foi, et inspirés de Dieu, croyance dont ces livres témoignent également. D'autre part, aussi bien ces livres que l'Église demandent qu'on n'ajoute rien, qu'on ne retranche rien à ce dépôt de la parole divine consigné dans les livres saints (*Deut.* 4, 2 ; 13, 1 ; *Apoc.* 22, 18-19). L'application de cette règle double aux exigences antithétiques peut se faire de deux manières complémentaires : en partant d'un maximum ou d'un minimum.

On peut partir d'une position de sécurité, la possession d'un maximum, tout ce qui dans l'Église a pu être considéré comme Écriture sainte, et ne le réduire que sur des arguments démonstratifs. Il s'agit de ne rien perdre d'un dépôt très précieux. Mieux vaut courir le risque de porter un fardeau trop lourd que celui d'être privé d'un capital nécessaire. Dans cet état d'esprit on peut plaider la cause de la LXX.

On peut, au contraire, vouloir s'en tenir initialement à un noyau indubitable et n'y ajouter que sur des arguments démonstratifs. Dans le cas présent, pour ne pas remonter aux origines en négligeant tout un travail accompli dans l'Église pendant des siècles, on considérera le canon scripturaire qui s'est peu à peu dégagé dans une masse plus large et qui a été promulgué définitivement au concile de Trente. Ce canon concerne au moins une forme des livres énumérés, normalement l'original hébreu, araméen ou grec, suivant les cas, pour les livres de l'A. T. Rien n'est dit explicitement sur l'inspiration d'une version comme la LXX. L'Église a conscience de ne posséder concrètement ces livres saints que d'une manière imparfaite, puisque le même Concile demandait que l'on en prépare des éditions plus correctes. Même dans leur langue originale les écrits bibliques ont souffert au cours de leur transmission et leur texte est toujours un peu altéré. Le fait que l'original sémitique soit perdu complètement pour quelques livres de l'A. T. et ne soit connu qu'imparfaitement à travers une traduction est simplement un cas plus caractérisé d'une déficience générale dans la possession effective des écrits canoniques. Il n'apparaît pas nécessaire de postuler l'inspiration de la version qui nous a conservé tous les ouvrages de la liste canonique.

L'Écriture ne nous parvient jamais à l'état pur. Pour être efficace et intelligible il faut qu'elle soit convoyée par la tradition de l'Église, qui la propose de manière vivante. Même si la LXX n'est pas inspirée, elle est un élément particulièrement précieux de l'ancienne tradition du peuple de Dieu aux abords de l'ère chrétienne. Elle a joué un rôle important pour recueillir et fixer un certain nombre de développements doctrinaux qui n'étaient pas totalement absents des textes originaux, mais y recevaient une attestation moins ample. Elle a contribué à modeler le langage du N. T. et des Pères. A tous ces titres elle mérite le respect.

Les deux tendances sommairement décrites ci-dessus iront-elles à la rencontre l'une de l'autre dans une opposition constructive et parviendront-elles à déterminer un point d'équilibre, où se ferait l'unanimité? Ou, au contraire, leur contestation mutuelle ne s'apaisera-t-elle que par lassitude d'une controverse impuissante à persuader l'interlocuteur? Quoi qu'il en soit, il était bon de poser clairement le problème théologique en jeu.

A.-M. Dubarle, O. P.

The Septuagint and its Place in Theological Education

DIKRAN Y. HADIDIAN

F. W. DANKER[1] in his article on 'Aids to Bible Study; The Septuagint—its History', refers to the remark by the eminent Biblical critic and Hebraist, Ferdinand Hitzig, to his students: 'Gentlemen, have you a Septuagint? If not, sell all you have, and buy a Septuagint'. E. Stauffer[2] gives the answer as to why a man ought to sell all his possessions and buy a Septuagint: '. . . *The OT was the Bible of primitive Christianity.* What the writers of the NT read in the OT became the normal starting point for their own formulation of ideas. What the OT has to say about God and Man and history is presupposed in the NT as something already known and acknowledged. From this fact we have to draw the appropriate methodological consequences: wherever in the NT the presuppositions of Christian Theology are not sufficiently self-evident, we must turn in the first place to the OT to find their antecedents. . . . The writers of the NT were deeply versed in the LXX, its language, its text, and its textual tradition. This is adequate ground for us to take the LXX as our constant aid in understanding the NT, and in the main to use the Greek Text for OT references.'

Persuading New Testament scholars that the LXX is essential in their studies and teaching is not difficult, even though the tendency is to refer to the Hebrew Old Testament thought as the normative milieu in which New Testament thought germinated. It is permissible for an Old Testament scholar such as D. M. Freedman[3] to

[1] *Concordia Theological Monthly*, XXX. iv. [April, 1959], 27.

[2] *Paul: The Theology of the Apostle in the Light of Jewish Religious Piety* [1961], 28.

[3] *Journal of Biblical Literature*, lxxviii. [1959] 331.

Reprinted from *The Expository Times*, Vol. 76, 1964-5.

state: 'The thought-pattern of Biblical religion was firmly fixed in the Hebrew language by long centuries of usage; and Aramaic, not less than Greek, is essentially a translation tongue for theological communication even if it was the native language of the speaker or writer. The language of Biblical religion is Hebrew, as the Dead Sea Scrolls have shown, not only for sectarian Judaism of the first century B.C., but also for NT Christianity of the first century A.D.' But it is not acceptable on any grounds. No language has the monopoly on revelation. A translation tongue is more important than the original tongue. In the controversy related to the Aramaic vs. Greek version of the Gospels the advocates of 'Aramaic originals' sought solutions to many riddles by re-translating Greek into Aramaic. The fact is that the Gospels in translation became the Scripture of the Farly Church and it is *in translation* that various people of the world read and interpret the Scriptures. For the layman in the Church in any age the gospel comes in his vernacular. There is no 'dogmatic necessity', if I may borrow a phrase from James Barr, in adopting Hebrew or Greek as *the* Biblical language or the language of revelation.

The problem is slightly different for Biblical Scholars. When the text of the New Testament is to be read and interpreted and understood, which of the two languages or of the two Bibles should one 'buy' by selling all his possessions? The present writer would like to make a strong plea on behalf of the Septuagint. The present situation in the Seminary curriculums 'old' and 'new' or 'revised' may be described as one that is contrary to the methodological consequences that E. Stauffer speaks about. In all the Seminaries and Divinity Schools the Old Testament departments offer several courses in Hebrew (on three different levels). Exegesis is based on Hebrew Text; courses are offered in Aramaic, Arabic, Coptic, Akkadian, Ugaritic, Ethiopic and Syriac. How well is the scholar and his student prepared for a better interpretation of the New Testament where the use of the LXX is the common rule? H. J. Schoeps points out that 'far more important is the problem of a special mode of thought in the LXX and of a characteristic piety'. This piety is the immediate background and milieu of New Testament thought rather than the piety of Hebrew Old Testament. Furthermore, the hermeneutical method in the New Testament of the Old Testament text may be described as that of the *midrash pesher*. Full acquaintance with this method is essential in understanding and interpretation of the New Testament use of the Old Testament.

James Barr[1] concludes his article on 'The Position of Hebrew Language in Theological Education' with these words: '. . . One other point should be added—the paramount importance of the Septuagint in the discussion of the Hebrew-Greek contrast in thought and language. In discussions of the background of Hebrew thought behind the New Testament vocabulary, and in the approach made more familiar by the Kittel dictionary and the various wordbooks, there is more and more reference to the Septuagint, and entirely in principle. But it must be doubted if the theological scene today shows sufficient basic competence in the handling of the Septuagint. . . . The permanent importance of the relation between the Old Testament and the New, and the present prominence of the Greek-Hebrew contrast, probably alike demand a greater attention to the Septuagint.'

The French proverb states, '*Ce n'est que le premier pas qui coûte*'. But who among our theological educators will take the first step and present the methodological consequences of emphasizing the LXX in Biblical and theological studies?

Dikran Y. Hadidian

Hartford Seminary Foundation,
Hartford, Conn.

[1] *The Princeton Seminary Bulletin*, lv. [1962] 23.

III

DIE BEDEUTUNG DER SEPTUAGINTA-FORSCHUNG FÜR DIE THEOLOGIE

R. HANHART

I

1. Septuaginta-Forschung ist eine Hilfswissenschaft der biblischen Exegese. Dieser Satz ist richtig, sofern wir die Lxx lediglich in ihrer Bedeutung als jenes Mittelglied in der Geschichte des biblischen Textes betrachten, das sowohl für die Judenschaft der griechisch-hellenistischen, als auch für die erste Christenheit der römisch-hellenistischen Zeit auf Grund einer äußeren Notwendigkeit rein profan geistesgeschichtlicher Art, auf Grund der allgemeinen Verbreitung der griechischen Sprache der Koine als Reichssprache der hellenistischen Welt, das einzige Mittel der Erfahrung, der Mitteilung und Bewahrung des an Israel ergangenen Offenbarungswortes war. Von diesem Ort der Betrachtung her kommt diesem griechischen Übersetzungstext keine eigenständige Bedeutung zu. Er wird als Bibeltext der jüdischen Diaspora in der hellenistischen Welt lediglich das getrübte Abbild eines durch den Zwang geschichtlicher Verhältnisse verlorenen oder doch weithin unzugänglich gewordenen Urbildes sein, ein Abbild, dem nur in dem Maße theologische Bedeutung zukommen kann, als es etwas von dem ursprünglichen Glanz des Urbildes widerzuspiegeln vermag. Er wird aber auch als Bibeltext der ersten Christenheit in der hellenistischen Welt, als die an Israel geschehene alttestamentliche Verheißung, deren Erfülltsein und Vollendetsein der Glaubensgegenstand des neutestamentlichen Zeugnisses war, obwohl die frühe Christenheit weithin nicht mehr unmittelbar vor das Problem der Übersetzung des ursprünglichen Offenbarungswortes gestellt war, sondern von Anfang das Wort in dieser übertragenen Gestalt vorfand, und damit der Erkenntnis seiner wesentlichen Andersheit gegenüber dem ursprünglichen Wort der Ursprache mehr und tiefer entfremdet sein mußte als die hellenistische Judenschaft, von dem ihm anhaftenden Zeichen der Trübung einer ursprünglich reiner fließenden Quelle kaum gänzlich befreit worden sein. Das späte Israel und die erste Christenheit der hellenistischen Welt waren sich des Übersetzungscharakters des von beiden als Offenbarungswort, aber in restlos verschiedener Weise, aufgenommenen und interpretierten griechischen AT in seiner n e g a t i v e n Bedeutung fraglos bewußt.

Reprinted from *Theologische Existenz Heute*. N. F. 140. 1967.

2. Und so könnte denn von diesem Ort der Betrachtung aus die Bedeutung der Lxx, auch wenn wir sie in die gegenwärtige theologische Diskussion einordnen und die Frage nach der Bedeutung ihrer Erforschung für das Anliegen der verschiedenen Disziplinen der Theologie stellen, lediglich darin bestehen, daß sie ein Mittel für die Erkenntnis jenes Schriftwortes ist, das sie selber nicht darstellt, auf das sie nur undeutlich, in fremder Sprachgestalt, hinweist: des AT in seiner ursprünglichen, hebräisch-aramäischen Gestalt. Wie die Lxx — unter dieser Voraussetzung — im hellenistischen Judentum lediglich die Bedeutung hatte, in dem Maße, in welchem es für den der Sprache der Väter entfremdeten Juden der Diaspora überhaupt noch möglich war, das Wort der Ursprache in Erinnerung zu rufen, so wird sie dann in der christlichen Theologie der Gegenwart lediglich die Bedeutung haben, für die im Unterschied zur Hauptmasse der Diasporajuden in ihrer größeren Zahl neben der griechischen auch der hebräischen Sprache mächtigen Theologen der Gegenwart den Weg zu dem den Übersetzern vorliegenden Text der Ursprache freizulegen. Die Bedeutung der Lxx wird dann zuerst in der geschichtlichen Tatsache gesehen werden, daß ihre Überlieferung — sehen wir einmal von den Bruchstücken des AT von Qumran ab — in ihren ältesten Ausläufern nahezu ein Jahrtausend älter ist als die ältesten Zeugen des AT in der Ursprache in der uns überlieferten Textform der Masoreten. Und die Bedeutung dieser geschichtlichen Tatsache wird dann lediglich in der Hoffnung des Alttestamentlers bestehen, daß diese im Verhältnis zur Masorah so viel älteren Übersetzungstexte auch einen viel älteren, besseren, ursprünglicheren Text der Ursprache als Vorlage voraussetzen und lediglich in der Hoffnung des Neutestamentlers, von dem auf diesem Wege gewonnenen ursprünglichen Text des AT in der Ursprache her die im neutestamentlichen Kanon überlieferte Auslegung des alttestamentlichen Wortes besser zu verstehen.

3. Die Frage ist nun für uns diese: Ist dieser Ort der Betrachtung der einzig mögliche? Hat die Lxx-Forschung lediglich diese Bedeutung einer Hilfswissenschaft für die alt- und neutestamentliche Exegese, oder kommt ihr die Bedeutung einer selbständigen Disziplin zu?

Die Lxx-Forschung hat eine bestimmte Textform des biblischen Textes zum Gegenstand. Fest steht daher: Sie gehört der Disziplin der Exegese an. Wenn ihr selbständige Bedeutung zukommt, dann nur innerhalb der Exegese als selbständiger Disziplin neben der alt- und der neutestamentlichen Wissenschaft. Die Frage nach einer selbständigen Funktion innerhalb der theologischen Disziplinen wie sie für die Kirchengeschichte in ihrem Verhältnis zu den Disziplinen der exegetischen, der dogmatischen und der praktischen Theologie besteht[1], und zu Recht besteht, d. h. die Frage, „ob sie auf eine selbständig zu stellende Frage hinsichtlich der christlichen Rede von Gott“ antworte oder aber „die unentbehrliche Hilfswissenschaft“[2] dieser Disziplinen sei, besteht für die Lxx-Forschung nicht. Die Frage aber, ob der Lxx-Forschung innerhalb der exegetischen Theologie neben der alt- und der neutestamentlichen Exegese eine selbständige und gleichwertige Bedeutung zukomme, besteht für die Lxx-Forschung gleicherweise zu Recht, wie die Frage nach einer selbständigen Bedeutung der Kirchengeschichte als theologischer Disziplin neben Exegese, Dogmatik und praktischer Theologie.

Die Unsicherheit in der Beantwortung dieser Frage scheint sich widerzuspiegeln in der Geschichte der Lxx-Forschung. Eine Disziplin, der diese Bezeichnung mit Recht zukäme, hat in der Periode der Kirchenväter, der Scholastik und auch der Reformation nicht bestanden. Wenn die griechischen Kirchenväter nicht das hebräisch-aramäische AT, sondern das griechische AT in der Form der Lxx auslegten, dann war damit zwar die Lxx als Schriftwort und Gegenstand der Auslegung an die Stelle des hebräisch-aramäischen AT getreten, aber nicht in einer bewußten Gegenüberstellung dieser beiden Texte, sondern einfach weil der Text der Lxx der eine alttestamentliche Text der griechischen Kirche war und den meisten der Ausleger nur in dieser Form zugänglich war. Auch das Werk des Origenes war kein Vergleich der beiden Texte mit der Absicht wissenschaftlicher Erforschung. Durch alle drei Perioden beschränkt sich die vergleichende Erforschung beider Texte auf die Gegenüberstellung einzelner Verse, wo sie sachliche Differenzen bieten, seit der reformatorischen Exegese zuweilen unter Diskussion der Echtheitsfrage. Lxx-Forschung, die das Problem selbst in Angriff nimmt, setzt erst mit dem Späthumanismus ein, bei Scaliger und Hody auf der einen, Lightfoot auf der anderen Seite.

4. Es sind, so viel ich sehe, drei Fragen, die gegenüber der vorhin gezeichneten Beschränkung der Lxx-Forschung auf eine Funktion als Hilfswissenschaft für die alt- und neutestamentliche Exegese erhoben werden müßten, eine geistesgeschichtliche, eine geschichtliche und eine theologische Frage.

A. Die geistesgeschichtliche Frage lautet: Ist das Faktum der Übersetzung allgemein als Offenbarung geehrten Wortes in eine fremde Sprache nicht ein Phänomen von solcher geistesgeschichtlicher Tragweite, daß der Ertrag dieses Vorgangs, das Offenbarungswort in der Gestalt der fremden Sprache, wenn es lediglich als kontinuierliche Fortsetzung in der Überlieferungsgeschichte schriftlich niedergelegten Offenbarungswortes gewertet wird, in seinem eigentlichen Wesen nicht erkannt werden kann?

[1] K. Barth, Kirchliche Dogmatik I 1, S. 3.
[2] K. Barth, a. a. O.

B. Die geschichtliche Frage lautet: Muß unter der Voraussetzung, daß diesem Übersetzungswerk eine solche eigentümliche, aus dem Wesen des Originals der Ursprache nicht ableitbare Bedeutung zukommt, nicht auch der geschichtlichen Epoche, in der das übertragene Wort an die Stelle des ursprünglichen Offenbarungswortes getreten ist, eine Bedeutung zugemessen werden, die sich ihrem Wesen nach weder von der alttestamentlichen, noch von der neutestamentlichen Zeit her verstehen läßt?

C. Die theologische Frage lautet: Kommt unter der Voraussetzung einer solchen geistesgeschichtlichen und geschichtlichen Eigenbedeutung des griechischen AT in der Gestalt der Lxx nicht auch ihrem Zeugnisgehalt eine Eigenbedeutung zu, die nicht in ihrem rechten Lichte erscheinen kann, wenn die Lxx lediglich als unselbständiger Ausläufer des hebräisch-aramäischen AT oder aber als unbedeutende Vorstufe des neutestamentlichen Schrifttums betrachtet wird[3]?

Die geistesgeschichtliche und die geschichtliche Frage sollen hier nicht entfaltet werden. Es soll hier lediglich das Ergebnis ihrer Untersuchung in den Punkten, die für die theologische Frage, um die es uns hier geht, von Bedeutung sind, zusammengefaßt und in einigen für diesen Zusammenhang erhellenden neuen Erkenntnissen ausgezeichnet werden.

Die Untersuchung der geistesgeschichtlichen Frage hat ergeben, daß nach Ausweis aller Zeugnisse des vorchristlichen Judentums, der griechischen Übersetzung des AT selbst wie auch der direkten Aussagen im pseudepigraphischen Aristeasbrief, im Prolog zur griechischen Übersetzung des Jesus Sirach und im Kolophon zum Buche Esther, die Übersetzung des AT in die griechische Sprache aus inneren, glaubensmäßig bedingten Bedürfnissen der der Sprache der Väter mehr und mehr verlustig gehenden Judenschaft in der Zerstreuung entstanden ist, daß die in diesen Voraussetzungen begründete Bedeutung dieses Übersetzungswerkes als Offenbarungswort des israelitischen Gottes aber nicht das Verständnis des Übersetzungsaktes selbst als Offenbarungsgeschehen, als zweite Offenbarung nach dem ursprünglichen Ergehen des Wortes an den ersten Zeugen, mit sich bringt, sondern daß es lediglich in dem Maß als es getreues Abbild des Originales der Ursprache war und lediglich in seiner relativen Bedeutung als Abbild des Urbildes den Anspruch erheben durfte, göttliches Offenbarungswort zu sein[4]. Das bedeutet für unseren Zusammenhang: Die glaubensmäßig bedingte Begrün-

[3] J. Ziegler, Die Septuaginta, Erbe und Auftrag, Würzburger Universitätsreden, Heft 33, 1962, S. 28, ersehnt eine „Theologie der Septuaginta".

[4] Vgl. VT 12 (1962) 139—161.

dung der Übersetzung des Offenbarungswortes in die griechische Sprache bedeutet zwar, als Preisgabe der Sprache der Väter, einen geistesgeschichtlichen Einschnitt in die Kontinuität der Überlieferungsgeschichte von solcher Tragweite, daß ihm keine Analogieerscheinung der vorangehenden Epochen an die Seite gestellt werden kann, sie bedeutet aber als bewußte Rückversicherung mit dem Offenbarungswort der Ursprache gerade nicht einen Bruch, sondern eine neue Besinnung auf die vorangehenden Epochen der Offenbarung in der Sprache der Väter.

Die Untersuchung der geschichtlichen Frage hat auf dem Hintergrund dieser geistesgeschichtlichen Entscheidung ergeben, daß die Zeit, in der das Übersetzungswerk des griechischen AT entstand, die wir hier roh umreißend als die Zeit der makedonisch-hellenistischen Weltherrschaft, des nationalen Niederganges in Israel und der erloschenen Prophetie bezeichnen wollen, trotz des einmaligen Phänomens der Übersetzung offenbarten Wortes in die fremde Sprache, keine Zeit von eigenständiger epochaler Bedeutung ist, sondern sowohl nach jüdischer wie nach christlicher Geschichtskonzeption nur als eine Zeit des Überganges und der Vorbereitung verstanden werden kann[5]. Das bedeutet für unseren Zusammenhang, daß das Übersetzungswerk der Lxx als ein diese Zeit des Niedergangs und des Übergangs charakterisierendes Phänomen theologiegeschichtlich ebenfalls nur die Bedeutung eines Niederganges, als das Offenbarungswort der aus dem Zwang der Verhältnisse griechisch-sprechenden Judenschaft, und eines Überganges, als das den ersten christlichen Zeugen gegebene Verheißungswort, haben kann, dessen Erfüllung die Offenbarung des neutestamentlichen Zeugnisses ist.

Die Frage nach der Möglichkeit eines andern theologiegeschichtlichen Verständnisses dieser Epoche und damit der sie charakterisierenden Übertragung des AT in die griechische Sprache, nach welchem an diesem Punkte gerade die Höhe und Vollendung der alttestamentlichen Verheißung erreicht und damit erst die Grundlage und Voraussetzung für das geschaffen worden wäre, was der Gegenstand des neutestamentlichen Zeugnisses ist, kann uns hier nicht weiter beschäftigen, auch die Frage nach der Möglichkeit eines rein profangeschichtlichen Verständnisses dieses Phänomens nicht. Die getroffene geistesgeschichtliche und geschichtliche Entscheidung aber bildet für die Frage nach der theologischen Bedeutung der Lxx und damit für die Frage nach der Einordnung ihrer Erforschung im Ganzen der theologischen Disziplinen die unumgängliche Voraussetzung. Sie macht den Schluß notwendig, daß die Übersetzung der Lxx als das Offenbarungswort der griechisch sprechenden Judenschaft in ihrem Wesen bestimmt werden muß in ihrem Verhältnis zur vorhelleni-

[5] Vgl. den vorausgegangenen Aufsatz „Zur geistesgeschichtlichen Bestimmung des Judentums".

stischen Überlieferung Israels und in ihrer Andersheit gegenüber der zeitgenössischen Geisteswelt des Hellenismus, und daß erst von hier aus — denn in diesem ihrem Wesen bleibt sie unverändert — ihre Bedeutung für die Überlieferung der neutestamentlichen Zeugen ermessen werden kann.

Diese gleichsam negative Wesensbestimmung der Lxx auf dem Hintergrund eines Urbildes, des alttestamentlichen Zeugnisses in der Ursprache, eines wesenhaft anderen Bereiches, der zeitgenössischen hellenistisch-synkretistischen Geisteswelt und eines ihr zwar wesentlich zugeordneten Bereiches, in dessen Licht sie aber eine restlose Neuinterpretation erfährt, des neutestamentlichen Zeugnisses, kann nun aber nicht bedeuten, daß dieses Werk eines jeden eigentümlichen Wesens und Charakters entbehre. Der Wille zur bekenntnishaften Treue gegenüber dem alttestamentlichen Zeugnis in der Ursprache, der sich eine Ehre darein legt, lediglich das Abbild des Urbildes zu erreichen und die bewußte Abgrenzung gegenüber Glaubensvorstellungen des außerisraelitischen Bereiches kann durch die dadurch notwendige neue Besinnung auf den Grundgehalt alttestamentlicher Zeugnisaussage, auf die „Mitte des Alten Testamentes" hin, bewirken, daß dem Übersetzungswerk die Dimension einer neuen, bis dahin nicht gekannten Tiefe der Einsicht in das zu eigen wird, was das Wesen des alttestamentlichen Zeugnisses ausmacht, einer Dimension, die dann auch in der Übernahme des griechischen AT durch die ersten neutestamentlichen Zeugen, obwohl theologiegeschichtlich auch hier der Lxx lediglich die Bedeutung eines Abbildes des ursprünglichen alttestamentlichen Zeugnisses zukommt, nicht verloren geht oder wieder verdrängt wird, sondern zum mitbestimmenden Element in der Formulierung der neutestamentlichen Zeugnisaussage wird.

II

Die Antwort auf die theologische Frage kann uns nur von einem Bild des der Lxx eigentümlichen Charakters her gegeben werden. Wenn wir dieses in rohen Umrissen hinsichtlich seines Wesens, seines Inhaltes und seiner Form zu zeichnen versuchen, dann fassen wir die griechische Übersetzung des AT in der Gestalt des alexandrinischen Kanons als Einheit, absehend von der Frage nach einer möglichen Scheidung der Übersetzungstraditionen, absehend auch von der Scheidung der Übersetzungstexte von den ursprünglich in griechischer Sprache verfaßten. Denn diese beiden Erscheinungen liegen innerhalb der umfassenden Frage, um die es hier geht, ob und in welchem Maße das alttestamentliche Zeugniswort in der Gestalt der fremden Sprache seines eigentlichen Wesens verlustig gehe.

Erste Frage:

Ist das, was uns als das Wesen des alttestamentlichen Zeugnisses in seiner ursprünglichen Gestalt entgegentritt, die Glaubenserkenntnis eines Unvollendetseins, das ängstliche Harren auf ein verheißenes Kommendes, die Erfüllung des Gesetzes hin, auch das Wesen des alttestamentlichen Zeugnisses in der übertragenen Gestalt der Lxx? Ist es als solches bewahrt, verdeutlicht, verdunkelt oder aufgehoben?

Antwort:

Es ist nicht nur jene allgemein geistesgeschichtliche Erscheinung einer jenseitsbestimmten Religion, die mit der Entstehung und Geschichte der hellenistischen Welt seit der Reichsgründung Alexanders des Großen in allen Kulturbereichen hervortritt[6]. Es ist in Israel-Judäa nicht nur jenes Zukunftsbild einer Vollendung, nach welchem auf Grund einer Neuinterpretation des prophetischen vorexilischen Glaubenserbes Israel als Mittelpunkt der Versammlung der Völkerwelt unter der Königsherrschaft des israelitischen Gottes erscheint. Es ist eine Zukunftshoffnung und ein Vollendungsglaube in der in dieser Zeit entstehenden Übertragung des AT in die griechische Sprache, die diesem Werk in besonderer Weise eignet, und die jene allgemein israelitische Erscheinung als besonderes Glaubensanliegen der Übersetzer ausweist.

[6] Man vergleiche hinsichtlich des allgemein religionsgeschichtlichen Phänomens und besonders im Licht des frühhellenistischen Griechentums die großartige Schilderung dieser universalen Stimmung bei Kurt Latte, Religiöse Strömungen in der Frühzeit des Hellenismus (Die Antike 1 [1925] 146—157) für eine Zeit, in der das Jenseitsbestimmte auf Grund der allgemeinen Resignation gegenüber den irdischen Wechseln noch nicht in Erscheinung getreten war (S. 151 f.) — sie dürfte im israelitischen Bereich etwa der Zeit des Predigers entsprechen — S. 157: „In der Religiosität des Frühhellenismus liegen die schroffsten Gegensätze unvermittelt nebeneinander. Die Kluft zwischen der Verstandeskühle der Gebildeten und dem Wunderglauben der Masse, zwischen den Anhängern des Alten und den Bekennern der orientalischen Religionen ist unüberbrückbar. Während die hellenische Kultur eine letzte schöpferische Periode durchlebt, kündet sich bereits gärend eine neue Zeit an, in der das Griechentum nur ein Baustein neben anderen sein sollte. Und doch sind einheitliche Linien für die geschichtliche Betrachtung unverkennbar: die Entwicklung vom Intellektualismus zu einer rein gefühlsmäßigen Frömmigkeit, von der nationalen Religion zu einem die Welt umspannenden Glauben. Früher als andere Völker hatten die Hellenen an ihrer Götter universale Geltung geglaubt, aber sie hatten auch in einer langen Epoche des überwiegenden Rationalismus rein verstandesmäßige Gottesvorstellungen ausgebildet, die keine Gefühlswerte mehr boten. Deshalb mußte ihre Religion im Kampfe mit dem Orient unterliegen, und die Griechen bezahlten den Ruhm, der Welt eine übernationale Gottesidee geschenkt zu haben, mit ihrem Zerfall als Volk."

Die Hoffnung auf Vollendung und Erfüllung ist das allgemeine Wesen des Glaubens im nachexilischen Israel, das zuerst bei Ezechiel und Deuterojesaja unverhüllt ausgesprochen ist[7], und das im Buche Daniel seine tiefste Gestalt gewonnen hat. Sie ist aber das eigentümliche Wesen der griechischen Übersetzung des AT in der Gestalt der Lxx, in der sie erst ihre endgültige begriffliche Prägung erhält.

Es ist dieses Werk der Neugestaltung des alttestamentlichen Zeugnisses in der griechischen Sprache, in dem diese Zeit des Wartens auf ein Kommendes in ihrem Wesen offenbar wird: In ihm erst wird jene im AT nur verborgen anklingende Aussage, daß Israel mit der Vollendung der Schriftprophetie in der Zeit der erloschenen Prophetie lebte[8], deren Wesen im Warten auf das Kommen eines letzten Propheten besteht, zum Glaubenszeugnis erhoben. In ihm wird das gesamte frühere Zeugnis, der vorexilischen, der exilischen Zeit und der Zeit der Heimkehr, von dieser Erwartung her neu gesehen und dementsprechend übertragen. In ihm bricht zuerst unverhüllt der Glaube an die Auferstehung der Toten auf.

Das griechische AT in der Gestalt der Lxx ist die Schau des alttestamentlichen Glaubenszeugnisses im Lichte der kommenden Erlösung.

Es ist ein behutsames Wachstum in dieser Richtung. Aber es ist dem geübten Auge sichtbar und läßt sich nicht leugnen. Bedeutsam ist aber, daß es zuerst ein kontinuierliches Wachstum aus dem vorgegebenen alttestamentlichen Zeugnis in der Ursprache ist und seine Kräfte nicht aus anderen Bereichen bezieht. Sein Ursprung liegt in jenen Zeugnisaussagen, die in sich die Kraft jener endzeitlichen Neuinterpretation bargen, deren geistesgeschichtliche Vorstufe die Prophetie nach 587 in ihrem Verhältnis zur vorexilischen ist[9], das Zeugnis Deuterojesaias und Ezechiels, hinsichtlich der Auferstehung Aussagen wie Is. 26, 14. 19; Iob. 19, 25; Dan. 12, 2. Von hier geht das Wachstum aus. Es mag zuerst in wörtlicher Übertragung ein kaum erkennbarer endzeitlicher Klang mit hineinkommen — eine richtige Beobachtung ist von hier her dem etwas gewagten Satz G. Bertrams „Die Begriffe Leben, Glück und Frieden, an sich wört-

[7] Vgl. W. Zimmerli, Das Alte Testament als Anrede, München 1956 S. 74 f. „In der Prophetie nach 587 brechen darin Aussagen, die schon bei einigen vorexilischen Propheten in Heilsverheißungen, die dort noch seltsam am Rande blieben, gemacht waren (neuer Wüstenzug bei Hosea, Verherrlichung Jerusalems bei Jesaia), voll auf. Sie erwarten das kommende, volle Bekenntnis Jahwes zu seinem Volke, seiner erwählten Stadt und seinem Tempel. Wieder sind es äußere geschichtliche Geschehnisse, auf die die Propheten warten, aber wieder ist es ganz deutlich, daß in diesem Geschehen als seine eigentliche Mitte das volle Kommen Jahwes zu seinem Volke erwartet wird." Vgl. K. Barth, Kirchliche Dogmatik, IV, 1 (1953) S. 520 f.

[8] Ps. 74, 9 Dan. 3, 38 Mac. I 4, 46; 9, 27; 14, 41; vgl. oben S. 25.

[9] Vgl. oben Anm. 7.

lich wiedergegeben, beginnen zu transzendieren“[10] nicht ganz abzusprechen —; es kann dann weitergehen mit endzeitlicher Umdeutung zeitlich begrenzter Ankündigungen, der Unheilsankündigung in eine Vorstufe noch angedeuteten endzeitlichen Heils, so in Is. 6, 12. 13 wo die groß werdende Verödung (עזובה) in das Wachsen des (endzeitlichen) Restes (οἱ καταλειφθέντες πληθυνθήσονται) umgedeutet wird, in der älteren (ο'-)-Übersetzung von Dan. 8, 10, wo der endzeitliche Feind, der die Sterne zur Erde niederwirft, selbst zum Gerichteten wird, der vom Himmel zur Erde niedergeworfen wird. Es können dann die andeutenden Aussagen des kanonischen Zeugnisses ihre theologische Ausgestaltung und Vertiefung finden, so der Auferstehungsglaube im Mac. II 7, 9 ff; 12, 43 f.; 14, 46 Ps. Sal. 3, 10—12 — schriftgebundener allerdings als das etwa gleichzeitig im apokalyptischen Schrifttum geschieht (Äth. Hen. 22, Apok. Bar. (syr.) 30, 1—5; 50, 2—51, 3, Esdr. IV 7, 29 ff.). Es können zuletzt Aussagen und Begriffe des kanonischen Zeugnisses als Schriftbeweis der endzeitlichen Glaubensvorstellung herangezogen werden, so das Bildwort vom Holz des Lebens in Gen. 3, 22 Is. 65, 22 (Lxx hat gegen 𝔐 ξύλον τῆς ζωῆς) als „Typus der Rettung im eschatologischen Sinn“ in Sap. 14, 7; so Deut. 32, 39 (ich löse und mache lebendig) Is. 43, 2 (Feuer wird dich nicht verbrennen), Ez. 37 (die Wiederbelebung der Gebeine), Prov. 3, 18 (das Holz des Lebens) als Beweis für die Auferstehung[11] in Mac. IV 18, 14—18. Man wird im Zusammenhang einer endzeitlichen Ausrichtung des alttestamentlichen Zeugnisses durch die Übertragung in die griechische Sprache auch jene zwar falsche aber großartige Etymologie von צלמות als σκιὰ θανάτου bei der Lxx sehen dürfen, auf die J. Ziegler wieder den Finger gelegt hat. Beides zeigt sie in gleicher Deutlichkeit, sowohl die Bindung an das Wort in der Ursprache, ohne dessen Legitimation sich der Übersetzer verloren weiß — daß die Etymologie falsch ist, wird man ihm, wenn man daran denkt, daß auch Theodor Nöldeke noch für sie eingetreten ist, kaum anrechnen wollen —, als auch die bewußte Vertiefung des ursprünglichen Wortgehaltes, die J. Ziegler in der Weise charakterisiert hat: „Ein Schauder überrinnt uns, wenn wir dieses Wort ‚Todesschatten‘ lesen oder sprechen; wir sind dahin versetzt, wo kein winziger Lichtstrahl mehr leuchtet, wir befinden uns bereits im jenseitigen Ort, wo ewige Finsternis ausgebreitet ist, wo der gewaltige alles beherrschende Tod seinen Schatten wirft.“[12]

Zweite Frage:

Ist das, was uns als der Inhalt des alttestamentlichen Zeugnisses entgegentritt, Jahwes Offenbarung als der eine Gott Israels, der sein Volk richtend und begnadigend erwählt und erlöst, und Israels Bekenntnis zu ihm als diesem einen, in der Übertragung des AT in die griechische Sprache als diese eine Mitte wiederholt und bewahrt? Drängt diese Übertragung selbst, ihrem inneren Wesen nach,

[10] RGG III, 5. Bd. (1961) 1708.

[11] Vgl. Bertram a. a. O.

[12] A. a. O. S. 13.

auf die Bewahrung dieser einen Mitte hin, läßt sie sie lediglich bestehen, oder hebt sie sie auf?

Antwort:

Es gibt keinen Ort in der griechischen Übersetzung des AT, in welchem das Bekenntnis Israels, wie es sich im ursprünglichen Wort kundtut, aufgehoben wäre. Es zeigt sich aber sichtbar eine Bemühung um Wahrheit und Treue seiner Wiedergabe, deren innere Ursache allein das Anliegen bewußter Herausarbeitung und Bewahrung des Bekenntnisses sein kann. Jahwe, Kyrios, der richtende, begnadende, verwerfende, erwählende, erlösende Gott Israels, ist die Mitte auch des AT in seiner griechischen Gestalt.

Das Offenbarungswort Jahwes, das Bekenntnis Israels, bleibt das eine und gleiche in und mit der in der Übertragung des AT mitbegründeten Wandlung im Wesen des israelitischen Glaubens zur Erwartung auf das letzte Ende, die Erfüllung des Gesetzes hin. Nicht der erst in diesem Zeitpunkt in die Mitte tretende Glaube an die Erlösung des Alls, Israels *und* der Völker, nicht der erst jetzt erwachende Glaube an die Auferstehung der Toten erscheint je — und das ist nicht selbstverständlich — losgelöst von seiner immer gleichen Mitte, dem um seines Volkes Israel willen handelnden Gott Jahwe.

Aber auch hier ist diese Wiedergabe der alttestamentlichen Mitte in ihrer griechischen Übertragung nicht lediglich eine Wiederholung. Sie ist eine bewußte Auszeichnung auf diese Mitte hin. Sie ist bestimmt durch den Willen zur Bewahrung des Glaubens an die unlösbare Verbindung Jahwes mit Israel durch alle Wandlungen im Glauben Israels hindurch.

Und diese Wandlung wäre einer Preisgabe der alttestamentlichen Mitte durchaus offen gewesen. Das immer deutlichere Hervortreten der drei Züge, die das Wesen des nachexilischen Glaubens ausmachen, seine jenseitsbestimmte Vertiefung, seine Vollendung in der Erwartung der Erlösung aller Völker, der leiblichen Auferstehung des Einzelnen, barg die Möglichkeit zur Aufhebung des dem Glauben zugrunde liegenden Bekenntnisses zu Jahwe als dem Gott Israels, Israels als dem Volke Jahwes in sich.

Und hier *mußte* das Phänomen der Übersetzung in die fremde Sprache zuerst eine Kraft *für* diese Aufhebung sein. Der Bruch, der durch das Ereignis der Übersetzung in der Geschichte des israelitischen Glaubens eintrat, die Preisgabe der Sprache der Väter als unveräußerlicher Teil der Offenbarung, hätte seine *natürliche* Fortsetzung in der Preisgabe weiterer der Offenbarung Israels eigentümlicher Wesenszüge, in der Öffnung für die dem Gehalt der fremden Sprache eigentümlichen gehabt.

Die innere Notwendigkeit, aus der heraus der Glaube an die Heimkehr des Fremden[13] sich mit der ursprünglich in anderen Wurzeln gründenden Hereinnahme der fremden Sprache in den innersten Bereich der Offenbarung vereinigen mußte, hier barg sie nicht nur die Möglichkeit, sondern die Wahrscheinlichkeit einer solchen allgemeinen Öffnung für das Fremde in sich.

Wenn es nicht geschehen ist, muß hier eine Kraft gegen die natürliche Fortsetzung wirksam gewesen sein.

Und diese Kraft ist wirksam gewesen. Diese Fortsetzung war keine natürliche Fortsetzung. Dieser Bruch in der Geschichte des israelitischen Glaubens ist kein aus den Gesetzen der Geschichte erklärbarer.

Der Bruch mit dem Glauben an die Sprache der Väter als Sprache der Offenbarung war geschehen. Das Wort der Offenbarung war in die fremde Sprache übertragen worden. Der Fremde war als miterlöstes Glied in den Glauben Israels einbeschlossen worden. Aber der Glaube des Fremden war am Glauben Israels zerbrochen.

Dritte Frage:

Ist das, was uns als die ursprüngliche Form des alttestamentlichen Zeugnisses entgegentritt, das Zeugnis von Jahwe, dem Gott Israels, in Geschichte, Prophetie und Lehre, in der Sprachgestalt der Sprache der Väter, in den eigentümlichen Denkformen des israelitischen Glaubens, auch die Form des alttestamentlichen Zeugnisses in der übertragenen Gestalt der Lxx?

Wenn durch ihre Neugestaltung in der Sprache des Fremden Wesen und Inhalt einer Glaubenswelt in ihrer Ursprünglichkeit bewahrt werden können, so ist eine Bewahrung der Form nur noch in bestimmten Grenzen möglich. Denn die Sprache des Fremden selbst ist im Verhältnis zur Ursprache eine neue Form. Die Sprache ist Gefäß des Gedankens. Darum kann hier die Frage nicht wie hinsichtlich des Wesens und des Inhaltes absolut gestellt werden. Sie kann lediglich lauten: Läßt sich in der Form der Übersetzung des AT in die griechische Sprache die Bemühung der Übersetzer erkennen, die eigentümliche Aussage-, Sprach- und Denkform der Ursprache nur in dem Maße auf Kosten der fremden Sprache preiszugeben als es um der fremden Sprachgesetze willen notwendig ist, oder besteht ihr Anliegen darin, in der übertragenen Darstellung von Wesen und Inhalt des alttestamentlichen Zeugnisses die eigentümliche Form der fremden Sprache in Erscheinung treten zu lassen?

[13] Vgl. W. Zimmerli, a. a. O. S. 74 f.

Antwort:

1. Die Form des alttestamentlichen Zeugnisses in griechischer Sprache bleibt in ihren wesentlichen Bestimmungen die gleiche wie in der Ursprache: Die drei Grundformen der Zeugnisaussage, Geschichte, Prophetie und Lehre, bleiben in der griechischen Gestalt des Zeugnisses gewahrt, und keine neue Grundform kommt hinzu, auch in jenen späten, aus dem Geist der griechischen Sprache entstandenen Zeugnissen israelitischen Glaubens nicht.

Es ist wahr, daß die beiden Formen literarischer Aussage, die Israel mit Griechenland gemeinsam sind, die Geschichte und die Lehre, durch die Neugestaltung des israelitischen Zeugnisses in der griechischen Sprache in ihrem äußeren Charakter eine tiefgreifende Änderung erfahren haben — der Weg vom Zweiten zum Dritten Makkabäerbuch in seinem Verhältnis zur israelitischen Chronistik bis zum Ersten Makkabäerbuch und der Weg von der Weisheit Salomons bis zum Vierten Makkabäerbuch in seinem Verhältnis zur israelitischen Spruchweisheit bis zum Buche des Jesus Sirach gibt davon lebhaftes Zeugnis — aber diese Änderung bleibt durchgehend innerhalb der Grenze, in der die griechische Aussageform das israelitische Zeugnis in seinem Wesen und Gehalt nicht anzutasten vermag.

Der Israelite des ausgehenden Judentums hat das eigentümliche Wesen seines Bekenntnisses — laut Ulrich von Wilamowitz in „abscheulichem Septuagintagriechisch“[14] — auch dort bewahrt, wo er sich die letzten Feinheiten des spätantiken historiographischen Stils in seiner „asianischen“ Ausprägung angeeignet hat.

Es ist ein Zeichen für die tiefe Bedeutung dieser Grenze, daß das griechisch sprechende Israel die dem Griechentum eigentümlichen, Israel ursprünglich fremden Formen literarischer Aussage — die spärlichen Ausnahmen bestätigen nur die Regel — nicht in sein Eigenes aufgenommen hat.

2. Die Form des alttestamentlichen Zeugnisses wird in der Übertragung in die griechische Sprache nur in dem Maße dem fremden Sprachcharakter angeglichen als es um der Eigengesetzlichkeit der fremden Sprache willen notwendig ist. Die Übersetzung der Lxx gehört in ihrer Ganzheit, mit allen in ihr enthaltenen Möglichkeiten der Differenzierung, jener Form der Übersetzung an, in welcher der Hörer dem ursprünglichen Wort der Ursprache entgegen bewegt wird[15]. Das ursprüngliche Wort der Ursprache bleibt die Mitte. Die

[14] Hermes 34 (1899) 635 Anm. 1.

[15] F. Schleiermacher, Über die verschiedenen Methoden des Übersetzens, 1813 (Sämtliche Werke III 2, Berlin 1838, S. 218); vgl. Franz Rosenzweig, Die Schrift und Luther, 1926 (Kleinere Schriften, Berlin 1937, S. 142).

Übertragung geschieht um seiner willen und weist auf es zurück. Sie soll in dem Maße als es für den der Sprache der Väter entfremdeten Israeliten noch möglich ist, das ursprüngliche Wort der Offenbarung in die Erinnerung zurückrufen.

Diesem einen Ziel sind alle anderen Absichten der Übersetzer untergeordnet. Auch das im allgemeinen aufrecht erhaltene Bestreben, der Eigengesetzlichkeit der fremden Sprache gerecht zu werden, kann um dieses Zieles willen preisgegeben werden. Was später, von anderen geschichtlichen Voraussetzungen her, zum Prinzip werden sollte, im Übersetzungswerk des Aquila, ist als Anlage schon in der ursprünglichen Lxx vorhanden und tritt als Übersetzungsgrundsatz in der fortgesetzten Arbeit, die seit seiner Entstehung an diesem Werk geschieht, immer deutlicher in den Vordergrund: Die von der Übertragung her geforderte neue Form bleibt an dem Punkte unberücksichtigt, wo sie Wesen und Inhalt des ursprünglichen Zeugnisses beeinträchtigte.

Es ist ein Zeichen dieser bewußten Unterordnung der formalen Belange des Offenbarungswortes unter die reine Bewahrung seines Wesens und seines Inhaltes, daß der überlieferungsgeschichtliche Weg des griechischen AT nicht in der Richtung einer Neugestaltung des alttestamentlichen Wortes aus dem griechischen Geiste geht, sondern in der Richtung einer griechischen Wiederholung des ursprünglichen Wortes auf Kosten des griechischen Geistes.

3. Die Israel eigentümlichen Grundformen des Denkens sind durch die Übertragung des alttestamentlichen Zeugnisses in die griechische Sprache nicht zugunsten der dem fremden Sprachgeist eigentümlichen Denkformen preisgegeben worden. Das griechische Wort als Aussage des alttestamentlichen Zeugnisses wird Träger des israelitischen, nicht des griechischen Geistes.

Wenn überhaupt innerhalb der allgemeinen Anthropologie für bestimmte Glaubensbereiche besondere Grundformen des Denkens in Anspruch genommen werden dürfen, dann muß es an dieser Stelle, der Offenbarung Israels, geschehen. Und wenn an einer Stelle Form und Inhalt in unlösbarer Einheit verbunden sind, dann ist es hier, wo der Gegenstand des Glaubens in den dem Glaubensbereich eigentümlichen Denkformen Gestalt gewinnt.

Dies ist aber der Ort, wo sich die Frage nach der Möglichkeit einer Scheidung zwischen der Form der Sprache und dem Inhalt des Glaubens- und Erkenntnisgegenstandes in einer Schärfe und Unbedingtheit stellt, wie es hinsichtlich der Literaturform und des Sprachcharakters nicht erfordert war. Wenn es feststeht, daß der Zeugnisgegenstand in seiner übertragenen Gestalt in dem Maß als es nach der Eigengesetzlichkeit der fremden Sprache möglich war, literarische Form und sprachlichen Charakter der Ursprache bewahrt hatte, so stellt sich hinsichtlich der in der Ursprache manifestierten Grundformen des Denkens die Frage, ob sie überhaupt der Übertragung in die Begrifflichkeit der fremden Sprache, des fremden Glaubensbereiches, fähig sind, ob nicht aus innerer Notwendigkeit mit der fremden Sprache auch die Denkformen des fremden Glaubensbereiches übernommen werden müssen. Lassen sich die Grundformen des Denkens, die das Wesen einer Sprache ausmachen, auf die fremde Sprache übertragen? Ist nicht die in der Verschiedenheit der Sprache ausgeprägte Verschiedenheit der Denkformen die innere Ursache dafür, daß mit der Übertragung des Wortes notwendig Wesen und Inhalt des fremden Glaubens in den Glaubensbereich des ursprünglichen Wortes einbrechen?

Die Antwort wird hier gewagt werden dürfen, daß, was noch nie geschehen war, hier geschehen, was von geistesgeschichtlichen Voraussetzungen her unmöglich schien, hier Wirklichkeit geworden ist. Die erste Berührung zwischen Israel und Griechenland war eine Umprägung der Sprache Griechenlands durch die Denkformen Israels. Israel hat das Wort Griechenlands nicht in sein Eigenes aufgenommen: Aber Griechenland hat sich dem Wort Israels geöffnet. Die Denkformen blieben das Eigentum Israels. Die Begriffe der fremden Sprache standen gleichsam als Chiffre für sie. Es war das verborgene und kaum bemerkte Eindringen eines Fremdkörpers in den Bereich des griechischen Geistes. Es war eine Gegenbewegung gegen den griechischen Geist, die auf diese Weise, im Anfang kaum wahrnehmbar, eindrang. Es war von Anfang und blieb das Wort Israels in der Gestalt der griechischen Sprache. Es war nie das Wort Griechenlands in der Gestalt der israelitischen Denkformen. Die griechische Sprache wurde ihrer eigenen Denkformen entäußert, sie nahm die Denkformen des israelitischen Wortes, aber ohne zunächst ihres inneren Wesens ansichtig zu werden, in sich auf. Das alttestamentliche Zeugnis in der griechischen Gestalt blieb dem griechischen Geiste fern und fremd.

An diesem Punkt scheint es mir notwendig, eine Anfrage an das in vielem klärende und auch heilsame Buch von James Barr, The Semantics of Biblical Language, Oxford 1961, zu richten. Es geht uns nicht zuerst um die Frage, ob überhaupt ein Zusammenhang zwischen Denkform und Sprachstruktur, Denkweise und Etymologie festgestellt werden kann[16] — die Schwierigkeit eines solchen Versuches erkannt und den hier so oft angewendeten Dilettantismus verurteilt zu haben, dürfte zu den Verdiensten dieses Buches gehören —, es geht uns aber um die Frage, ob die ursprünglich mit dem Inhalt eines fremden Kultur- und Glaubensbereiches

[16] Vgl. W. Baumgartner, Bibliotheca Orientalis 19 (1962) 265 f. H. Conzelmann in Ev. Th. 24 (1964) 171.

gefüllte Denkform und Sprachstruktur, wenn sie zum Gefäß eines neuen Glaubensinhaltes wird — mag dessen Denkform und Sprachstruktur anthropologisch mit dem des fremden Bereiches auch weitgehend identisch sein —, durch den Akt der Übertragung, die Füllung mit dem neuen Glaubensinhalt, nicht notwendig einer Besinnung unterworfen werden mußte, durch die das Unterschiedliche der beiden Denk- und Sprachformen — daß es ein solches gibt, streitet auch Barr nicht ab — erst eigentlich bewußt und absichtlich herausgestellt werden mußte, einerseits durch Ausscheidung der Denkformen und des Sprachgutes, die dem fremden Glaubensbereich zu tief und zu gefahrvoll verpflichtet waren, andererseits durch Neufüllung und Neuprägung des fremden Gutes auf Grund einer immer neu bedachten Orientierung am neuen Inhalt in seiner ursprünglichen Form. Zwei Phänomene scheinen mir dadurch, daß Barr diese Möglichkeit zu wenig beachtet, nicht in das ihnen gebührende Licht zu kommen:

1. Der bewußt gegen heidnische Vorstellungen der Umwelt sich abgrenzende („apologetische") Charakter dieses Übersetzungswerkes, der sich bei einigen Begriffen — *θεράπων, θεὸς τοῦ οὐρανοῦ . . ., ἄγγελος* als Bezeichnung fremder Götter[17] — einfach nicht abstreiten läßt;
2. Sein dadurch — aber nicht nur dadurch — bedingter eigentümlicher, einmaliger, im Verhältnis zur zeitgenössischen Profanliteratur heterogener Charakter.

R. Bultmann hat einen Hauptfehler der Abhandlung Thorleif Bomans über Das hebräische Denken im Vergleich mit dem Griechischen, Göttingen 1952[18], die neben dem Theologischen Wörterbuch zum NT Barrs wichtigster Angriffsgegenstand ist, darin gesehen, daß Boman für seine Untersuchung die Sprache der Lxx zu wenig berücksichtigt. Es ist bezeichnend, daß dies ein Hauptpunkt ist, an welchem sich Bultmann und Boman, denen von Barr die eine und gleiche Konzeption zugeschrieben wird, voneinander scheiden.

III

1. Diese Wesensbestimmung der Lxx, als einer in Wesen, Inhalt und Form gegenüber der zeitgenössischen Glaubensaussage des hellenistischen Geistes völlig heterogenen, weil das Offenbarungswort Israels gegen den Widerstand der hellenistischen Glaubens- und Denkmöglichkeiten, aber im Sprachgefäß des griechisch-hellenistischen Wortes, vertretenden und bewahrenden Aussage, ist das, was ich die oft nicht genügend berücksichtigte Bedeutung der Lxx für die Theologie — wir dürfen in dieser Hinsicht sagen des Christentums und des Judentums — nennen möchte: sie liegt nicht

[17] Vgl. VT 12 (1962) 159 f.

[18] Gnomon 27 (1955) 551—558; 2. Aufl. des Buches von Boman 1954, 3. Aufl. 1959.

in einer Öffnung dieses Glaubensbereiches für die durch die Aufnahme der griechischen Sprache erschlossene hellenistische Geisteswelt in ihrer hellenistisch-synkretistischen Spätform: was ist an solchen Berührungen überhaupt erkennbar?: im Übersetzungswerk der Lxx eine Reminiszenz an eine geprägte Form griechischer Literatur zu finden, sei es in ihrer vorhellenistisch-klassischen, sei es in ihrer hellenistisch-synkretistischen Gestalt, dürfte sehr schwierig wenn nicht unmöglich sein.

Fast ebenso schwierig wird es aber auch bleiben, in der hellenistischen Literatur der beiden letzten vorchristlichen Jahrhunderte, Aussage und Aussageform des griechischen AT wieder zu erkennen, es sei denn in jenen überlieferungsgeschichtlich schwer faßbaren, auch chronologisch schwer einzuordnenden gnostischen oder praegnostischen Gebilden etwa des Töpferorakels[19], des Poimandres, oder des *ἱερὸς λόγος*[20], für deren Aussagegehalt aber die kaum bestreitbare Kenntnis des AT in der Gestalt der Lxx zum mindesten in ihren Frühformen gerade nicht wesensbestimmend gewesen zu sein scheint; abgesehen von der gnostischen Überlieferung und hinsichtlich eines früheren, von religionsgeschichtlichen Elementen der verschiedensten Bereiche noch nicht in solchem Maße überlasteten Bereich wüßte ich nur das schöne 55. Epigramm des Kallimachos zu nennen, in welchem ein von einer Frau, Kallistion, dem Gott von Kanope, Serapis, für ihr krankes Kind geweihter Leuchter also redend gedacht ist: *ἐς δ'ἐμὰ φέγγη ἀθρήσας φήσεις. „Ἕσπερε, πῶς ἔπεσες"*, wo ich mir den greisen Bibliothekar von Alexandria gerne in der griechischen Übersetzung des Buches Jesaia — denn damals mußte sie schon bestehen — blätternd und dabei auf Is. 14, 12 *πῶς ἐξέπεσεν ἐκ τοῦ οὐρανοῦ ὁ ἑωσφόρος* stoßend denke.

IV

Dieses ist die Wesensbestimmung der Lxx, die in ihrer Bedeutung für die Theologie auch hinsichtlich des Problems „das AT in der Gestalt der Lxx im Zeugnis des NT" oft stärker berücksichtigt werden müßte. Die Bedeutung der Lxx für dieses Problem liegt nicht in dem Faktum, daß die neutestamentlichen Zeugen das alttestamentliche Zeugnis nicht in der vorhellenistischen Gestalt des Urbildes, sondern in der hellenistischen des Abbildes übernehmen; denn auch den Christen galt es wie den Juden in dieser ihnen allein zu-

[19] Vgl. R. Reitzenstein, Vom Töpferorakel zu Hesiod (Reitzenstein-Schaeder, Studien zum antiken Synkretismus, Berlin 1926, S. 38—68).
[20] Vgl. C. H. Dodd, The Bible and the Greeks, London 1935, S. 99 ff.

gänglichen Gestalt als das eine Offenbarungswort Israels. Ihre Bedeutung liegt auch nicht in dem besonderen Charakter, der der griechischen Übersetzung — oder den griechischen Übersetzungen — des AT, soweit sie als Ganzes aus dem Schrifttum des NT überhaupt erkennbar ist, im Unterschied zur vorchristlichen Lxx in ihrer überlieferten Gestalt eigen wäre. Ihre Bedeutung für das neutestamentliche Zeugnis liegt zuerst darin, daß das AT den neutestamentlichen Zeugen in dieser eben bewußt und gewollt nach dem alttestamentlichen Offenbarungswort in der Ursprache ausgerichteten, es durch die hellenistische Geisteswelt hindurchbewahrenden, es gegen den Strom ihres eigenen Weges vertretenden griechischen Gestalt vorgegeben war, und daß das AT in dieser Gestalt durch seine Aufnahme in das neutestamentliche Zeugnis wohl einer restlos anderen Interpretation, aber einer Interpretation, die in dieser Hinsicht mit dem Anliegen des ausgehenden Judentums einig ging, geöffnet worden ist.

Dieser Sachverhalt hat — wie mir scheint — durch die Auffindung jener alten, vorhexaplarischen Papyrustexte, die in einem bis dahin nicht gekannten Maß rezensionelle Eingriffe überliefern, deren wichtigstes und oft einziges Kriterium die Übereinstimmung mit dem hebräischen Grundtext ist, eine bedeutsame Aufhellung erfahren — es sind die Texte, deren wertvollster Exponent die nach weitgehend übereinstimmendem Urteil in die Zeit vor 50 n. Chr. datierte[21], 1952 in einer Höhle des Naḥal Ḥever südlich des Wadi Murabbaʿât gefundene Zwölfprophetenrolle ist —, und in der Aufhellung dieses Sachverhaltes scheint mir ihre einzige theologische Bedeutung zu liegen. Ihre theologische Bedeutung liegt nicht darin, daß durch sie die alte Streitfrage zwischen der Einheitshypothese der Schule Lagarde-Rahlfs-Katz und der Vielheits- oder Targumhypothese P. Kahles und seiner Schüler in eine neue Phase getreten wäre — hier ist sie oft m. E. zu Unrecht gesucht worden —, die theologische Bedeutung dieser Funde liegt darin, daß hier zum ersten Mal eindeutig sichtbar wird: die innerjüdischen Bemühungen um die Wesensgleichheit des griechischen Übersetzungstextes mit dem hebräisch-aramäischen Urtext, die auch vor Eingriffen in die überlieferte Gestalt des Lxx-Textes nicht halt machten, haben ihre erste Ursache nicht in der durch seine Aufnahme in der Urkirche veranlaßten Verwerfung des Lxx-Textes — wer wollte eine solche Ursache um 50 n. Chr. annehmen, und wollte man das, dann wäre es merkwürdig, wenn der älteste gefundene Text dieser Art der älteste überhaupt wäre —, die erste Ursache kann nur in

21 Vgl. die Urteile in P. Kahle, The Cairo Geniza, Oxford 1959, S. 226 f. und D. Barthélemy, Les devanciers d'Aquila, Leiden 1963, S. 163—168; die (vorläufige) Textausgabe, S. 169—178.

dem wiederholt hervorgehobenen Theologumenon liegen, daß der Offenbarungscharakter der griechischen Übersetzung einzig und allein in seiner Wesensgleichheit mit dem Wort der Ursprache bestand; und weil die gleiche Bemühung um eine Annäherung des Übersetzungstextes an den Urtext auch im frühchristlichen (vorhexaplarischen) Schrifttum erkennbar ist — NT, Justin —, kann es sich nur um ein Juden und Christen ursprünglich gemeinsames Theologumenon handeln. Hinsichtlich der traditionellen Erklärung der späteren Übersetzungen im Judentum der christlichen Zeit seit Aquila als Gegenbewegung gegen die Aufnahme des AT in der Form der Lxx bei den ersten christlichen Zeugen wird man aber heute vorsichtiger sagen müssen, daß wohl die konsequente Durchführung nicht aber die Entstehung dieser neuen Übersetzungsbemühungen ihre Ursache in der Übernahme der Lxx durch die Christen gehabt haben dürfte.

Die Interpretationsgrundlage des griechischen AT in dieser auch von der Einheitshypothese her zugegebenen Vielgestalt war den neutestamentlichen Zeugen durch das vorchristliche Judentum gegeben, auch und gerade in jenen Phänomenen, in denen die durch die Übertragung verursachte Neubesinnung auf das Wesen des alttestamentlichen Zeugnisses zu einer deutlicheren Auszeichnung seines Grundgehaltes geführt hatte, und auch in jenen Phänomenen, die der religionsgeschichtliche Weg des Judentums — denn dieser ist natürlich auch weitergegangen — nicht in bewußter Abgrenzung gegen die hellenistische Umwelt und nicht in bewußter Rückversicherung an das legitimierte Zeugnis der vorhellenistischen Zeit gezeitigt hat.

Was man auch als ursprüngliche Lxx-Textform von V. 4 des zweiten Gottesknechtliedes Is. 42 ולתורתו איים ייחלו befürworten mag, ob mit der gesamten Lxx-Überlieferung καὶ τῷ ὀνόματι αὐτοῦ ἔθνη ἐλπιοῦσιν oder auf Grund der hebräischen Vorlage καὶ τῷ νόμῳ αὐτοῦ ἔ. ἐ. — die paläographische Nähe läßt das Zweite als wahrscheinlicher erscheinen —, sicher ist, daß die Textform τῷ ὀνόματι αὐτοῦ dem neutestamentlichen Zeugen Matth. 12, 18—21 vorgegeben war, vom Judentum her vorgegeben war und darum nicht als christliche Umdeutung der Hoffnung auf das Gesetz auf den das Gesetz im Evangelium aufhebenden Gott interpretiert werden darf.

Nur auf vorchristliche Tradition zurückführbar und darum nicht als christologische Interpretation erklärbar ist aber auch die in Hebr. 10, 5 aufgenommene Lxx-Fassung von Ps. 39 (40), 7 σῶμα δὲ κατηρτίσω μοι als Übersetzung von אזנים כריתה לי und auch die auf Rahlfs zurückgehende Rekonstruktion einer ursprünglichen Lxx-Fassung ὠτία δὲ κατηρτίσω μοι auf Grund einer altlateinischen Handschrift (La^G) und des Psalterium Gallicanum unterliegt Bedenken.

Und in dieser Funktion der Vorbereitung für das neutestamentliche Zeugnis darf das Judentum durchaus als Einheit gesehen werden. Gerade die angedeutete Wegbewegung vom ursprünglichen Wortlaut des alttestamentlichen Wortes in der Ursprache hinweg geht quer durch den hebräischen Text des palästinensischen und den griechischen des „hellenistischen“ Judentums hindurch. Was früher als hellenisierende Umwandlung im Übersetzungstext erklärt war, erscheint heute mehrfach im hebräischen Urtext der Funde von Qumran, wie ja schon früher im Übersetzungstext Elemente festgestellt waren, die gegen den überlieferten Urtext Vorstellungen vertraten, die, wollte man den Schnitt zwischen hellenistischem und palästinensischem Judentum zwischen dem hebräisch-aramäischen und dem griechischen AT ansetzen, jeder Erklärung entbehrten. Es ist im Grunde die weitblickende und in seiner Zeit durchaus nicht in der Luft liegende Theorie J. Wellhausens, daß die beiden heiligen Texte des vorchristlichen Judentums, der Urtext und der griechische Übersetzungstext des AT, unter wesensgleichen theologie- und geistesgeschichtlichen Einflüssen gestanden hätten[22], die, durch seither fließende Quellen im wesentlichen bestätigt, in einer neueren Forschungsrichtung, deren Initiator Max Leopold Margolis und deren letzter Exponent H. M. Orlinsky ist, zu jener tiefgreifenden Revision des Bildes von den geistesgeschichtlichen Grundlagen der Übersetzung der Lxx geführt haben, auf Grund derer früher allgemein behauptete Grundkonzeptionen für die Wesensbestimmung der Lxx in ihrem Verhältnis zum Urtext und damit des hellenistischen Judentums in seinem Verhältnis zum palästinensischen, wie die Vermeidung des Anthropomorphismus, erneut in Frage gestellt werden.

Es soll mit dieser Charakterisierung der Lxx und mit dieser Bestimmung ihrer Bedeutung für die Theologie nicht bestritten werden, daß die Übertragung des AT in die griechische Sprache sowohl für das späte Judentum als für das frühe Christentum auch die Ermöglichung jener geistesgeschichtlichen Berührung mit der griechischen Antike in ihrer Spätform bedeutete, die für die Geschichte beider Bereiche von allergrößter Tragweite war — und nichts gibt uns das Recht, diese Berührung nur negativ zu bestimmen —, wohl aber sollen damit Bedenken gegen den Versuch angemeldet sein, diese Berührung hier an ihrem Ansatzpunkt gleichsam linear als natürliche Kontinuität statt vielmehr dialektisch als das erste sich Abstoßen zweier ursprünglich heterogener Elemente zu erklären[23].

22 J. Wellhausen, Der Text der Bücher Samuelis, Göttingen 1871; vgl. P. Katz, Septuagintal Studies in the mid-century, Festschrift für Dodd, S. 198 f., 200; vgl. II S. 36.

23 Schön sagt P. Katz: „Man darf sagen, daß die der Antike fremde und anstößige Eigenständigkeit der Kirche neben Staat und Gesellschaft ihre ursächliche Parallele in der die Sonderexistenz der Synagoge zum

Das bedeutet auch, daß ein Schatten der Trauer über jener geschichtsphilosophischen Konzeption liegt, die sich von Clemens Alexandrinus über Euseb, Augustin bis in die Gegenwart verfolgen läßt, nach welcher die Vorsehung des göttlichen Heilshandelns sich darin manifestiert hätte, daß sich die Öffnung der alttestamentlichen Offenbarung für den griechisch sprechenden Weltkreis gerade noch im richtigen Augenblick verwirklicht hätte, um auch ihre neutestamentliche Erfüllung der ganzen Welt zugänglich zu machen. In den Worten Augustins: „Quamobrem, etiamsi aliquid aliter in hebraeis exemplaribus invenitur quam isti posuerunt, cedendum esse arbitror divinae dispensationi quae per eos facta est, ut libri quos gens Iudaea caeteris populis vel religione vel invidia prodere nolebat, credituris per Dominum gentibus ministra regis Ptolemaei potestate tanto ante proderentur."[23a] Das heilsgeschichtliche Schema in all seiner Tiefe und Schönheit vermag angesichts dessen, was dieses erste Zusammenstoßen zwischen alttestamentlicher Botschaft und Griechentum — in positiver und in negativer Hinsicht — in Wahrheit bedeutete, eben nur das Daß der Berührung anzudeuten, von seinem Wie aber nichts auszusagen, nichts etwa von jenem innerjüdischen Ringen um die Gerechtigkeit und Wohlgefälligkeit dieser Berührung mit dem Fremden, das sich tief ins 2. nachchristliche Jahrhundert hinein erstreckt, und das bis zur Verfluchung des Tages führen konnte, an welchem das Gesetz in die griechische Sprache übersetzt wurde[24], nichts aber auch von jener neutestamentlichen Neubestimmung griechischen Wortes, wie sie etwa im Anruf des Apostels offenbar wird, nach dem zu trachten, „was wahr, ehrenhaft, gerecht, heilig, wohlgefällig, wohllautend ist, was Tugend und Lob bedeutet (Phil. 4, 8. 9)", über dessen Wesen wir, wenn wir sagen, daß er ohne die Übersetzung des AT in die griechische Sprache und ohne die Berührung mit der griechischen Geisteswelt, nicht möglich gewesen wäre, noch gar nichts ausgesagt haben.

V

Dieses Anliegen soll abschließend und zusammenfassend als Frage am Beispiel des Kyrios-Namens als Gottesbezeichnung erläutert werden; denn in diesem Einzelproblem geht es um eine Entscheidung, die, weil ihr Gegenstand den Zentralbegriff des alttestament-

Ausdruck bringenden Sprachgestalt der Lxx als Übersetzung hat." (RGG III, 5. Bd. [1961] 1706).

23a De doctrina Christiana II, 15, 22; vgl. VT 12 (1962) 149.

24 Vgl. VT 12 (1962) 144.

lichen Zeugnisses bildet, als allgemein verpflichtend für den gesamten Wortbereich des griechischen AT gelten darf.

Es geht zuerst um die Frage, ob die Wahl des Kyrios-Namens als Übersetzungsformel für יהוה in der Lxx — wie man sich auch zur Frage stelle, ob die Bezeichnung Jahwes als אדני den Lxx-Übersetzern auch schon vorgegeben war oder aber auf Grund ihrer Wahl des Kyrios-Namens erst in den hebräischen Text eingeführt worden ist — phänomenologisch, relgionsgeschichtlich und psychologisch richtig erklärt ist, wenn man sie aus dem religiösen Anliegen der Übersetzer erklärt, den Gott Israels, um mit A. Deißmann zu sprechen „(vom) Erdengewand des Nationalismus und des Semitismus, das ihn noch oft in seinen majestätischen Bewegungen hemmte" zu befreien und ihm die „internationale und intertemporale Weite" eines universalen Gottes zu verleihen, „derer man jetzt für die Welt und die Zukunft der Religion" bedurfte, und für deren Verwirklichung der Kyrios-Name „wie geschaffen"[25] war, und wenn man auf diese Weise das griechische AT in der Gestalt der Lxx zum entscheidenden Faktor im Übergang von israelitisch-nationalem Partikularismus zu spätjüdischem und dann christlichem Universalismus macht. Es ist nicht in erster Linie der lexikographische Befund, der es notwendig macht, hier Bedenken anzumelden — nichts ist in solchem Maße auf Grund neuer Funde immer neuer Revisionsbedürftigkeit unterworfen wie die Lexikographie —; immerhin müßte gesagt werden, daß nach dem heutigen Stand der Forschung der Name Kyrios als monotheistische Bezeichnung des einen Gottes in der Zeit, in die die Übersetzung des AT in ihrem Hauptbestand zu setzen ist, noch kaum belegt ist, zum mindesten also nicht vorherrschen konnte[26]; noch Bousset konnte in seinem Buche[27] sagen: „Ja in diesen (sc. hellenistischen) Zusammenhang rückt jetzt auch die griechische Übersetzung des AT mit ihrer Wiedergabe des Jahvenamens durch *κύριος* ein. Die Übersetzung ist eben auf einem Boden entstanden, auf dem diese allerallgemeinste Gottesbezeichnung (neben *ϑεός*) üblich war und verstanden wurde. So bekannte sich das Judentum mit seiner Bibel zu dem Kyrios, dem es allein Verehrung zollte[28]". Aber schon bei ihm mußte dieser Satz unvermittelt wirken, nachdem er zuvor für die drei Enklaven, in denen der Gebrauch des Terminus in diesem Sinn überhaupt nachweisbar war,

[25] A. Deißmann, Die Hellenisierung des semitischen Monotheismus, 8. Sept. 1902 (Internationaler Orientalistenkongreß in Hamburg) S. 173 f.

[26] W. Foerster in ThWB III (1938) 1048 ff. 1081; vgl. F. Hahn, Christologische Hoheitstitel, FRLANT 38 (1963) 68 ff.; Dodd, The Bible and the Greeks 1935 (²1954) S. 11.

[27] Kyrios Christos², 1921, (1. Aufl. 1913).

[28] S. 98.

Kleinasien, Ägypten und Syrien[29], keine Belege beizubringen vermocht hatte, die mit Sicherheit älter sind als das 1. Jh. v. Chr.

Es ist aber in erster Linie das gezeichnete Bild vom Wesen der Lxx als Ganzes — hier im Besonderen die Tatsache, daß die Wiedergabe anderer Gottesbezeichnungen im griechischen AT eher als eine Neigung eine scheue Abneigung davor zeigen, den Gott Israels mit den der umliegenden Heidenwelt vertrauten Epitheta zu versehen —, in deren Licht es notwendig scheint, zu fragen, ob die universalistische Erklärung der Wahl des Kyrios-Namens von den Glaubensvoraussetzungen der Übersetzer aus nicht wie eine Metabasis eis allo genos erschiene — auch dann wenn sich der lexikographische Befund wieder verschieben sollte —, ob das Verhältnis zwischen Partikularismus und Universalismus in Israel überhaupt zusammengesehen werden dürfe mit der Erschließung des alttestamentlichen Zeugnisses für die griechisch sprechende Heidenwelt und ob dieses Problem überhaupt in seinem eigentümlichen Charakter erkannt werden kann, wenn es mit geschichtlichen und kulturgeschichtlichen Phänomenen dieser Art in Zusammenhang gebracht wird — zu den gleichen Zweifeln gelangt hinsichtlich der alttestamentlichen Forschung im Anfang des 19. Jh. R. Smend[30] —; bei Deißmann war der Versuch sichtbar zeitgeschichtlich-politisch motiviert, und gerade dieser Umstand weckt die stärksten Zweifel an seiner Gangbarkeit.

Es geht im Lichte dieses Bedenkens nun aber auch um die Frage, ob auf Grund der überlieferungsgeschichtlichen Tatsache, daß in allen bis heute aufgefundenen jüdischen Lxx-Texten der Jahwename nicht mit κύριος, sondern mit dem Tetragramm wiedergegeben wird, die übersetzungstechnische Korrelation zwischen dem hebräischen Jahwe und dem griechischen Kyrios überhaupt geleugnet und darum die theologische Überlegung über die Ursachen dieser Wahl bei der Lxx als Rückprojektion christlicher Verhältnisse in das vorchristliche Judentum abgetan werden dürfe.

Ph. Vielhauer ist auf das Problem in seiner Auseinandersetzung mit F. Hahn[31] eingegangen. Er sieht auf Grund der neueren Funde, unter Berufung auf P. Kahle, die noch zu Boussets Zeiten ungeklärte Sachlage nunmehr in dem Sinne geklärt, daß erst die Christen es waren, welche das Tetragramm durch κύριος ersetzten, nachdem, um mit Kahle zu sprechen, „der göttliche Name, in

[29] S. 95 ff.

[30] R. Smend, Universalismus und Partikularismus in der Alttestamentlichen Theologie des 19. Jh., Ev. Th. 22 (1962) 169—179, vor allem 177 f.; K. Barth, Kirchliche Dogmatik IV 1 (1953) 525 f.

[31] Ev. Th. 25 (1965) 28—30 (jetzt in: Aufsätze zum NT, München 1965, S. 141 ff.).

hebräischen Buchstaben geschrieben, nicht mehr verstanden wurde". Und deshalb stellt sich für ihn die überlieferungsgeschichtliche Frage hinsichtlich des Kyrios-Namens im NT nur noch in dieser Weise: „Wie kamen die Christen dazu, *κύριος* für Jahwe zu setzen?"[32]

Sehen wir einmal ganz von der Bruchstückhaftigkeit der Überlieferung ab und geben wir zu — solange kein Fund da ist, der das Gegenteil bewiese, dürfen wir das —, daß im rechtgläubigen Judentum der vorchristlichen[33] und der christlichen Zeit[34] der Gottesname im kanonischen Schrifttum der Lxx durchgehend mit dem Tetragramm wiedergegeben sei, und daß dieser Gebrauch im kanonischen Schrifttum — dafür dürfte die althebräische Schreibung des Jahwe-Namens im Habakuk-Kommentar der Höhle 1 sprechen — sich nicht nur auf die gottesdienstlich verwendeten Handschriften einschränkte —; was sagt denn dieser Befund hinsichtlich der Frage aus, ob und in welchem Maße im griechisch sprechenden Judentum der Kyrios-Name als Bezeichnung des israelitischen Gottes, als Bezeichnung Jahwes, gebraucht werden durfte und gebraucht wurde? Doch allerhöchstens dies, daß das Anliegen der griechisch sprechenden Juden, daß die griechische Übersetzung seines Offenbarungswortes lediglich in seiner Bedeutung als Abbild des Urbildes Offenbarungscharakter besitze, zuerst in der Nennung des Gottesnamens Ausdruck finden mußte und hier in einer Weise wie es im übrigen Wortgebrauch der fremden Sprache nicht erfordert war.

Doch allerhöchstens dies, daß die Furcht vor der Aussprache des Gottesnamens, wie sie sich im Hebräischen in der Ersetzung von יהוה durch אדני manifestiert, schon im vorchristlichen Judentum der hellenistischen Zeit existierte.

Nichts vermag dieser Befund auszusagen hinsichtlich der Frage, ob das Qere Adonai des masoretischen Textes bereits die Voraussetzung für die Wiedergabe des Jahwenamens mit *κύριος* in der Lxx (E. Stauffer, K. G. Kuhn, L. Cerfaux, F. Hahn), ob das Qere Adonai eine Rückwirkung der Lxx-Übersetzung des Jahwenamens sei (Baudissin, G. Quell, J. Ziegler), oder ob der Kyrios-Name als Bezeichnung für Jahwe in der Lxx primär überhaupt nichts mit dem hebräischen אדני zu tun habe. Diese Frage bleibt vorderhand offen.

Nichts vermag er auszusagen über ein kategorisches Verbot der Aussprache des Kyrios-Namens als Gottesbezeichnung im vorchristlichen Judentum, nichts über die Frage, in welchem Maße bereits in dieser Zeit der Kyrios-Begriff von seiner alttestamentlichen Neu-

[32] S. 30.

[33] Papyrus Fouad 266; Leviticus-Fragment von Höhle 4.

[34] Zwölfprophetenrolle, Aquila-Fragmente der Geniza, Mercatische Fragmente.

bestimmung her im griechisch sprechenden Judentum verwurzelt war, und darum nichts hinsichtlich der Frage, in welchem Maße die Wahl des Kyrios-Namens bei den neutestamentlichen Zeugen im alttestamentlichen Wortgebrauch begründet war.

Wenn die vorchristliche hellenistische Judenschaft — und das deutet auch Vielhauer an[35] — den Kyrios-Namen für Jahwe, wenn auch nicht in der synagogalen Schriftlesung, so doch im außergottesdienstlichen Sprachgebrauch, im Verkehr mit der heidnischen Umwelt, und in der Interpretation des kanonisierten Offenbarungswortes in Apokalyptik, Lehre und Geschichtsschreibung, kannte und brauchte, dann wäre doch die Behauptung, die Übertragung von alttestamentlichen Jahweaussagen auf den Kyrios Jesus müßte jetzt nicht mehr primär von der Tatsache her erklärt werden, daß in der Lxx für Jahwe Kyrios eintrat, ebenso unhaltbar wie etwa die Behauptung, durch die Vermeidung der Aussprache des Gottesnamens Jahwe und ihre Ersetzung durch das Qere Adonai wäre in der Judenschaft die ursprüngliche Bedeutung des Tetragramms in Vergessenheit geraten. Die theologische Verbindung zwischen Kyrios und Jahwe bestand im vorchristlichen Judentum mindestens im gleichen Maße wie die zwischen Adonai und Jahwe, und diese Tradition konnte den ersten christlichen Zeugen nicht verborgen sein. Was sie vom Judentum nicht übernahmen, das war nicht der Kyrios-Name als Bezeichnung für Jahwe, sondern seine in religiöser Furcht begründete rein chiffrehafte Ersetzung durch das Tetragramm.

Man darf hier weiter gehen: Wenn wir heute auf Grund der zwar spärlichen aber durch keine Ausnahme relativierten Aussagen der Überlieferung sagen dürfen, daß in den griechischen Übersetzungstexten — mit Sicherheit in der gottesdienstlichen Lesung — an Stelle des Jahwe-Namens auch im griechischen Text das Tetragramm stand, wenn es andererseits aber auch feststeht, daß der Kyrios-Name als Bezeichnung für Jahwe im vorchristlichen Judentum bekannt und anerkannt war, dann ist von hier aus nicht die Tatsache ein Problem, daß auch die ersten christlichen Zeugen den einen Gott des Alten und des Neuen Bundes und den, von dem sie erkannt und geglaubt hatten, daß er Christus der Sohn des lebendigen Gottes und Gott war, Kyrios nannten, sondern die — auch den ersten christlichen Zeugen bei der Nennung dieses Namens fraglos nicht unbekannte — Tatsache, daß die vorchristliche Judenschaft offenbar den Kyrios-Namen dann, wenn sie mit ihm Jahwe, den Gott Israels bezeichnete, von der gleichen Heiligkeit umgeben wußte, wie wenn sie den Adonai-Namen aussprach, daß also der

[35] S. 30.

griechische Kyrios-Name im vorchristlichen Judentum nichts anderes war und nichts anderes bedeuten durfte als der hebräische Adonai-Name und daß er in dieser Bedeutung von den Christen übernommen wurde. Beide Tatsachen, die erst im Licht dieser neuen Zeugnisse als gesichert gelten dürfen, sind in gleicher Weise bedeutsam: sowohl die Tatsache, daß die Furcht vor dem Aussprechen des hebräischen Jahwenamens schon in vorchristlicher Zeit bestand, daß also die Nachricht des babylonischen Talmud, der Gebrauch des Tetragramms, d. h. die Nennung des Jahwenamens, wäre schon nach dem Tod Simons des Gerechten (270 v. Chr.) aufgegeben worden, der geschichtlichen Wahrheit durchaus nicht fernzuliegen braucht — Andeutungen davon sind ja auch in der Lxx, Philo und Josephus überliefert[36] —, als auch die Tatsache, daß sich diese Furcht auch auf das Äquivalent im griechischen Übersetzungstext übertragen hatte. Denn diese beiden Tatsachen bestätigen unsere auf Grund anderer Argumente gewonnenen Erkenntnisse:

1. daß die Übersetzung der Lxx im vorchristlichen Judentum die eine und alleinige Bedeutung hatte, den griechisch sprechenden Juden das zu sein, was den hebräisch sprechenden das AT in der Sprache der Väter war,

2. daß das, was dieser Übersetzungstext dem hebräisch-aramäischen Urtext gegenüber an Neuem bot, nicht in einem dem alttestamentlichen Zeugnis fernen und fremden Bereich gründet, sondern nichts anderes ist, als die Bewahrung und Unterstreichung des genuinen vorhellenistischen alttestamentlichen Zeugnisses.

Baudissin, der in der religionsgeschichtlichen Ableitung des Kýrios-Namens als der allgemeinen monotheistischen Gottesbezeichnung in der hellenistisch-synkretistischen Welt mit Deißmann und Bousset übereinstimmt, wehrt sich denn auch mit aller Macht — nach seinem Verständnis mit Bousset — gegen Deißmanns universalistische Interpretation[37]. Man wird soweit mit Deißmann, Bousset und Baudissin zusammengehen dürfen, daß man der Wahl des Kyrios-Namens als Bezeichnung für Jahwe einen nicht rein negativ abgrenzend apologetischen, sondern auch positiv missionierenden Aspekt zugibt. Nur würde sich von unserem überlieferungsgeschichtlichen und theologischen Befund her, dieses Anliegen darin verwirklicht haben — und darin, müßten wir uns nicht nur von Deißmann, sondern auch von Bousset und Baudissin abgrenzen —, daß man sich für einen Begriff entschied, der rein begrifflich die Vorstellung des Herrseins Gottes über das All auch im Nichtisraeliten wecken mußte, ohne ihn aber gleichzeitig an die genuin hellenistisch-synkretistische religiöse Entwicklung

[36] Die Äquiavalenz von יהוה und אִדני als Gottesbezeichnung ist für die vorchrl. Zeit durch Damaskusschrift Kap. 19, 1 gesichert: „Man schwöre nicht bei Aleph-Lamed und nicht bei Aleph-Daleth."

[37] Kyrios II, Giessen 1929, S. 311 f.; vgl. MSU 7 (1961) 10, Anm. 3.

zum Monotheismus hin zu erinnern — ein geistesgeschichtliches Analogon dürfte das Verständnis des ἄγνωστος θεός in Act. 17 sein. Auch wenn wir — was mir wahrscheinlicher bleibt — die Priorität im hebräischen Bereich, im Übergang von יהוה zu אדני sehen, kann das Zugeständnis dieses missionierenden Aspektes in der Wahl des Kyrios-Namens im griechischen Bereich durchaus aufrecht erhalten werden. Nur würde unter dieser Voraussetzung noch deutlicher, daß der innere Grund für die Vermeidung des Jahwe-Namens und seine Ersetzung durch κύριος — אדני — im hebräischen und im griechischen Bereich — nicht die Eröffnung seines Verständnisses für außerisraelitische Gottesvorstellungen war, sondern umgekehrt die in seiner Heiligkeit und Einzigkeit begründete Verhüllung seines Namens.

Ich glaube nicht, daß neue Funde je einmal noch solch tiefgreifende religionsgeschichtliche, geistesgeschichtliche oder theologische Verschiebungen verursachen können, wie sie hier angenommen werden müßten, auf der einen Seite unter der Voraussetzung, daß der Kyrios-Name im vorchristlichen Judentum als Gottesbezeichnung überhaupt nicht existierte, auf der anderen Seite unter der Voraussetzung, daß sich der vom vorchristlichen Judentum angeeignete Kyrios-Name in der Zeit der Entstehung der Lxx als der Terminus für die spätantike Vorstellung des einen universalen Gottes erwiese. Es sind innere Gründe, die in solchen Fragen allein noch zu einer Entscheidung führen können. Neue Funde — und unter diesen dürfte dem der Mercatischen Fragmente im Ende des vergangenen und dem der Zwölfprophetenrolle in der Mitte dieses Jh.s im biblischen Bereich in dem der gleichzeitigen Profangräzität an Bedeutung keiner gleichzustellen sein — bringen überlieferungs- und theologiegeschichtlich nur noch leise und sanfte Korrekturen mit sich; aber gerade über diese gilt es, sich zu verwundern.

VI

Die Frage nach der Bedeutung der Lxx-Forschung für die Theologie konnte hier nur im Versuch einer Klärung ihres Grundproblems einer Beantwortung näher gebracht, die Bedeutung dieser Gestalt des AT für das neutestamentliche Zeugnis nur angedeutet, ihre Bedeutung als das alttestamentliche Offenbarungswort, das die Voraussetzung für die Entstehung eigentlich christlicher Literatur bildet, nicht mehr erörtert werden. Aber auch für diese beiden Probleme bildet die Entscheidung in der hier gestellten Frage die erste Voraussetzung, dergegenüber alle weiteren Entscheidungen sekundärer Natur sind:

Ich fasse den Ertrag der Untersuchung in fünf Thesen zusammen:

1. Die geistesgeschichtliche Fragestellung hat ergeben, daß die Übersetzung des AT in die griechische Sprache in vorchristlicher Zeit restlos und einzig am ursprünglichen alttestamentlichen Offenbarungswort in der Sprache der Väter orientiert war und nur in dem Maß den Anspruch, Offenbarungswort zu sein, erheben durfte, als sie der Forderung, getreues Abbild dieses Urbildes zu sein, gerecht wurde.

2. Daraus folgt für die geschichtliche Fragestellung, daß die Zeit der alttestamentlichen Überlieferungsgeschichte, die durch die Notwendigkeit und die Zulassung griechischer Übertragung des alttestamentlichen Offenbarungswortes charakterisiert ist, lediglich als die Zeit eines rückwärts oder vorwärts gewandten Übergangs, nicht als Epoche von eigenständiger Bedeutung bestimmt werden kann.

3. Die Untersuchung seines besonderen Charakters erweist dieses Übersetzungswerk als ein in Wesen, Inhalt und Form das Erbe des vorhellenistischen Israel vertretendes und dieses gegen den Widerstand der zeitgenössischen hellenistischen Vorstellungswelt hindurchbewahrendes Unternehmen, dessen eigentümliche Bedeutung zuerst in der durch die Neubesinnung auf dieses Erbe verursachten tieferen Erfassung und Ausprägung des alttestamentlichen Zeugnisgehaltes besteht.

4. Aus These 1 und 2 folgt, daß Lxx-Forschung auch innerhalb der exegetischen Disziplin kein Bereich von eigenständiger Bedeutung ist, sondern lediglich ein Mittelglied, zwischen alttestamentlicher Exegese, mit der sie den Auslegungsgegenstand, und neutestamentlicher Exegese, mit der sie die Sprache und die Gestalt des im neutestamentlichen Zeugnis offenbaren alttestamentlichen Wortes gemeinsam hat.

5. Aus These 3 folgt im Licht der Thesen 1 und 2, daß Lxx-Forschung innerhalb dieser Einordnung im Ganzen der exegetischen Disziplinen die besondere Funktion hat, den Charakter des alttestamentlichen Zeugnisses in einem Stadium herauszustellen, das trotz und in seiner negativen Bestimmung als Abbild eines reineren Urbildes ein Stadium der letzten Reife ist. Um es auf eine kurze Formel zu bringen: Es wäre m. E. nicht gut, eine „Theologie der Lxx" zu schreiben, die nicht in das Ganze einer „Theologie des AT" eingeordnet wäre; innerhalb einer Theologie des AT aber gebührte ihr ein bis dahin nicht gewährter Ehrenplatz.